LIBRARY OF SECOND TEMPLE STUDIES

71

formerly the Journal for the Study of the Pseudepigrapha Supplement Series

Gleanings from the Caves

Gleanings from the Caves

Dead Sea Scrolls and Artefacts from The Schøyen Collection

Edited by
Torleif Elgvin

With Associate Editors
Kipp Davis and Michael Langlois

t&t clark
LONDON · NEW YORK · OXFORD · NEW DELHI · SYDNEY

T&T CLARK
Bloomsbury Publishing Plc
50 Bedford Square, London, WC1B 3DP, UK
1385 Broadway, New York, NY 10018, USA

BLOOMSBURY, T&T CLARK and the T&T Clark logo are
trademarks of Bloomsbury Publishing Plc

First published 2016
Paperback edition first published in 2018

A catalogue record for this book is available from the British Library.

ISBN: HB: 978-0-5671-1300-9
PB: 987-0-5676-8587-2
ePDF: 978-0-5672-8571-3

A catalog record for this book is available from the Library of Congress.

Series: Library of Second Temple Studies, volume 71

Typeset by Newgen Knowledge Works (P) Ltd, Chennai, India

To find out more about our authors and books visit
www.bloomsbury.com and sign up for our newsletters.

This book is a product of the project 'Biblical Texts Older than the Bible' at University of Agder. The project has received generous support from the University of Agder, the Research Council of Norway, and NLA University College. Torleif Elgvin has received further support from the Norwegian Non-Fiction Literature Fund for writing his contributions.

For Hanan Eshel (ז״ל) and Martin Schøyen

Table of Contents

List of Figures

List of Tables

Contributors

Marta Balla, Nuclear Reactor, University of Technology and Economics, Budapest. balla@reak.bme.hu
Matthew Boulanger, Southern Methodist University. mboulanger@mail.smu.edu
George J. Brooke, University of Manchester. george.brooke@manchester.ac.uk
Kipp Davis, University of Agder. davis.cjp@gmail.com
Jan Dušek, Protestant Theological Faculty, Charles University, Praha. dusek@etf.cuni.cz
Torleif Elgvin, NLA University College, Oslo. torleif.elgvin@nla.no
Esther Eshel, Bar Ilan University. eshelesti10@gmail.com
Hanan Eshel, Bar Ilan University
Michael D. Glascock, University of Missouri
Jan Gunneweg, The Hebrew University of Jerusalem. jan.Gunneweg@huji.ac.il
Årstein Justnes, University of Agder. arstein.justnes@uia.no
Michael Langlois, University of Strasbourg. dida@mlanglois.com
Johannes van der Plicht, University of Groningen. j.van.der.plicht@rug.nl
Ira Rabin, Bundesanstalt für Materialforschung und –prüfung, Berlin. ira.rabin@bam.de
Martin Schøyen, The Schøyen Collection. www.schoyencollection.com
Roman Schütz, Bundesanstalt für Materialforschung und –prüfung, Berlin. Roman.Schuetz@mpikg.mpg.de
Naʿama Sukenik. naamasuk@gmail.com
Joan Taylor, King's College London. joan.taylor@kcl.ac.uk
Bruce Zuckerman, USC Dornsife College of Letters, Arts and Sciences. bzuckerm@college.usc.edu

Foreword

Torleif Elgvin

The main purpose of this volume is to provide the scholarly world with precise descriptions and editions of the Judaean Desert fragments in The Schøyen Collection. Also presented are artefacts found in the Judaean Desert. This book is a unique combination of text and artefact editions and material analyses of the parchments that supplement the traditional philological analysis of the texts.

The texts published here represent gleanings from many caves: they supplement the evidence of previously published texts from Qumran, the Bar Kokhba caves of the second century AD, and Wadi ed-Daliyeh from the fourth century BC.

I have studied these texts and artefacts for a number of years, from 2008 in close collaboration with Esther and Hanan Eshel. The research process was augmented through the project 'Biblical Texts Older than the Bible' at the University of Agder from 2012 onwards, with support from the Norwegian Research Council. This volume is to a large extent the product of teamwork, with the undersigned, Kipp Davis, and Årstein Justnes as the main actors. We have enjoyed a close collaboration with a much larger scholarly team, of which many have studied the texts and artefacts on site in The Schøyen Collection. Jan Gunneweg sampled the scroll jar in 2008, Naʿama Sukenik conducted an on-site study of the *Temple Scroll* wrapper in 2011. Michael Langlois inspected the fragments in 2014, and twice came to the University of Agder as a guest scholar. Joan Taylor visited the collection in 2014 to study the cylindrical jar.

Some of the physical tests performed on fragments and artefacts from the Judaean Desert represent pioneering research that will show the way for the next generation of scholarship. Ira Rabin's 2012 on-site testing of the fragments has given new insight into the techniques of parchment production in antiquity, and demonstrate extensive differences in parchment preparation and quality between scrolls such as 1QIsaᵃ, 1QS/1QSb on the one hand, and texts written on parchment of a poorer quality on the other.

This volume is the 22nd publication of manuscripts in The Schøyen Collection. For a list of previous volumes, see p. 507.

My thanks are extended to my many collaborators in this project.[1] In particular I thank Martin Schøyen for his dedication to Qumran scholarship, his persistent search over the years for fragments and artefacts from the Judaean Desert, and his willingness to give scholars open access to the texts and artefacts in his collection. For electronic images we are indebted first to Bjørn Rørslett and then to Bruce Zuckerman and his team. I am also indebted to Pnina Shor and the conservators at the IAA scrollery for generously allowing me access to the IAA collection, to compare Schøyen fragments with

---

[1] Many of the editions are the fruit of teamwork, although the authors of the separate chapters bear the final responsibility for their editions. We are indebted to Eibert Tigchelaar and Gunnar Magnus Eidsvåg for their valuable feedback. Prior to Michael Langlois' detailed palaeographical study conducted in 2014, Ada Yardeni provided a useful preliminary report regarding the palaeography of most of the fragments. Kipp Davis is responsible for the graphical reconstruction of the fragments between the column margins.

fragments of 4QRP[b], 11QtgJob, and scrolls from Murabbaʿat. Thanks should also be extended to our patient linguistic editor, John Connolly, and to Emanuel Tov for his critical reading of the text editions. This volume is dedicated to Martin Schøyen and to Hanan Eshel (ז״ל), who passed away in the midst of our labours 7 April, 2010.

Oslo, June 2015, Torleif Elgvin

Abbreviations and Sigla

The title abbreviations for all journals, series, and texts follow Patrick H. Alexander et al., eds, *The SBL Handbook of Style: for Ancient Near Eastern, Biblical, and Early Christian Studies* (Peabody, Mass.: Hendrickson, 1999).

א א֯ א֯	certain letter, probable letter, possible letter, respectively
○	ink traces that likely correspond to a letter that cannot be confidently identified
[ ]	space between fragments or where the surface of the manuscript is missing
vacat	interval indicating that the writing space was intentionally left blank
>	word(s) lacking
=	is equivalent to
≈	is similar to
pr	preceded by
*	original Hebrew or Greek text
corr	corrected Hebrew or Greek text
< >	original text (in English translation)
{}	corrected text (in English translation)
II 5-7	the second column of the manuscript, lines 5-7
frg. 12 iii 4-5	fragment 12, column 3, lines 4-5
𝔐	the consonantal Masoretic text (as in *Biblia Hebraica Stuttgartensia*)
𝔐^A	The Aleppo Codex
𝔐^L	Codex Leningradensis, vocalized form
𝔐^Q	*qerê* for the Masoretic Text
𝔐^K	*ketib* for the Masoretic Text
ms	single manuscript
mss	a few manuscripts
Mss	many manuscripts
C	Cairo Genizah
𐤔𐤔	Samaritan Pentateuch, MS 6 (C) of the Shekhem Synagogue (Abraham Tal)
𝕲	Greek version of the Old Testament
𝕲^S	Codex Sinaiticus
𝕲^A	Codex Alexandrinus
𝕲^B	Codex Vaticanus
𝕲^V	Codex Vetenus
𝕲^O	Origen, hexaplaric recension
𝕲^L	the Lucianic text
𝕲^C	Complutensis
𝔏	witness to the Old Latin version
𝔖	the Peshitta, ed. the Peshitta Institute, Leiden
𝔖^A	Codex Ambrosianus, editus ab A.M. Ceriani 1876
𝔗	the Targum, ed. A. Sperber
𝔗^O	Targum Onkelos
𝔗^N	Targum Neofiti
𝔗^J	Targum Pseudo-Jonathan
𝔙	the Vulgate, ed. Monachi Sancti Benedicti
α′ σ′ θ′ ο′	Aquila, Symmachus, Theodotion, and the Seventy
Vrs	All or most ancient translations

Part One

—

Overview

I

Acquisition and Ownership History: A Personal Reflection

Martin Schøyen

By the time I had begun collecting manuscripts in 1955 and biblical manuscripts in 1986, the ultimate challenge had become to acquire a fragment of the Dead Sea Scrolls with a biblical text. Everyone I consulted said it would be impossible, since it was then believed that all known fragments were in public institutions, mainly in Israel, Jordan, and France. None of the great manuscript collectors of the time, such as Martin Bodmer and Chester Beatty, had succeeded in acquiring any fragments from the Judaean Desert.

On visiting Kando's shop in Jerusalem in March 1993, I found Kando (Khalil Iskander Shahin) sitting on a chair in the middle of the room facing the window, wearing his red Turkish fez, as he used to do. I had come to know him and his sons in 1978 when I bought Syrian tetradrachms of Vespasian from them. When I asked whether there was any chance of acquiring Dead Sea Scroll fragments from him or anyone else, his answer was short and gruff: 'Those days are gone!' That was his final word on the matter; he passed away a month later at the age of 83.

In those years I joined the scholars chasing numerous 'ghost scrolls': fragments that were rumoured to exist, but that no one had ever actually seen, and which never surfaced even in photographs. They were just ghosts, invented to get attention or to be incorporated into the Dead Sea Scrolls legacy. The most famous of these ghosts was a *1 Enoch* scroll in two or three parts. Its existence was reported by John Strugnell, who also claimed to have seen it himself. It was first said to be in Jordan, then in Kuwait, but it has never surfaced.

Another famous example is the 'Angel Scroll' claimed to have been found east of the Dead Sea, and now said to be in a Benedictine monastery on the German-Swiss border. This scroll has never been seen by anybody—not even in photographs—the intriguing Enoch-like text is known only from a transcription. The purported text has been studied by scholars such as Stephen Pfann, Émile Puech, and Adolfo Roitman (Gross 1999). Strugnell believed this could actually be the same Enochic scroll he had seen.

Despite the disappointment that followed these 'ghost scrolls', Strugnell warmly encouraged me to continue in my quest to locate unknown Dead Sea Scroll fragments. In a letter of 24 November, 1999, he said: 'A manuscript collector should be insatiable, as Phillipps your model was.'[1] My ultimate challenge was to achieve what neither the great manuscript collectors nor major libraries and museums had managed (apart from those in Israel, Jordan, and France); it was for me a 'Mission: Impossible'.

I returned to Jerusalem in 1993. One afternoon while I was speaking with Sadi and Taher Barakat they got a telephone call from their brother Fayez Barakat in Beverly Hills, asking if they had any customer for his Dead Sea Scrolls jar. This was one of the jars claimed to have been found in Cave 1 during the winter of 1946–47, and which once belonged to John Allegro. I could not believe my ears. I bought

---

[1] At his death in 1872 Sir Thomas Phillipps had amassed some 60,000 manuscript items, the largest private manuscript collection ever. 1,100 of his manuscripts are now in The Schøyen Collection.

it there and then; unseen, over the telephone (MS 1655/1).[2] At the same time I bought a bronze inkwell and incense altar (MS 1655/2, MS 1655/4), claimed to be surface finds from Khirbet Qumran, and also from Allegro's collection.

This surprising and promising start of the quest for the impossible sparked new energy, and made me realize I had to think along entirely new lines to have any chance of success.

What about the two American junior scholars, William H. Brownlee and John C. Trever, who were left alone without their professors at the American School of Oriental Research in East Jerusalem in February 1948? Professor Millar Burrows was in Iraq and the others had left Jerusalem due to the impending war, which broke out on 15 May 1948. The students were the first Westerners to handle and photograph the scrolls belonging to St. Mark's Monastery in 1948. Maybe the Metropolitan Athanasius Samuel had given them a fragment or two in recognition of their assistance to him?

I contacted Professor James M. Robinson at the Institute for Antiquity and Christianity (IAC) at Claremont, California, who knew Brownlee and Trever. In 1990 Robinson had been instrumental in publishing the Crosby-Schøyen Codex (MS 193): a third-century papyrus codex.[3]

During my visit to the IAC at Claremont in March 1994, Robinson took me to the nearby Ancient Biblical Manuscript Center. There we were admitted into the climate controlled vault that housed the safe of Trever with his important negatives of Dead Sea Scrolls. The safe also contained a tiny fragment from the *Rule of Benedictions*, one of two appendices to the *Rule of the Community*. The following story was first published in 'A further fragment of 1QSb' (Brooke and Robinson 1994): 'Trever made clear that Brownlee had entrusted it to him for safe-keeping before his death, but the fragment remained Brownlee's property, and since his death in 1983 had belonged to his widow Sarah Louise Brownlee. Discussions with her and her children led to the acquisition of the fragment by The Schøyen Collection just before her untimely death on 5 August 1994.' When I first held this Dead Sea Scroll fragment in my hands, I did not even dare to ask whether it was for sale; thinking it inappropriate. It was Robinson who took the initiative and approached Sarah Louise Brownlee. The bulk of the purchase price was donated by the Brownlee family to the William H. and Sarah Louise Brownlee Memorial Endowment of the Institute for Antiquity and Christianity of the Claremont Graduate School.

Together with this fragment (MS 1909) I received a file of correspondence between Archbishop Athanasius Samuel and Brownlee. In a letter dated 8 December, 1973 the Archbishop says: 'Concerning the scroll fragment that I sent you earlier, I wish to present this to you as a token of my friendship and respect for your labours on the behalf of the Dead Sea Scrolls. Please, do accept this small gift and feel free to display and use it as you feel will be most beneficial.' Later I also received four of the eight pottery sherds found by Brownlee at Khirbet Qumran prior to the excavations (MS 1655/3; no. 33 in Brownlee's collection).

Even if the *Rule of the Community* remains one of the most important sectarian scrolls, it was not a copy of a biblical text; so my quest continued. After this, Robinson and I approached Trever, asking whether he had any fragments from the time he photographed the first scrolls discovered in Cave 1. He said he actually had, but that they were of no interest as they contained no writing. Therefore he was reluctant to sell them. I nevertheless took the opportunity and acquired them. There were some 24 fragments from the edge of the great Isaiah Scroll, 1QIsa[a], with parts of its parchment cover sheet as well as some repair material (MS 1926/1). As this is the only complete scroll, and one of the most important of the biblical scrolls, I was delighted to acquire these pieces. There was also a fragment from the *Genesis Apocryphon* (MS 1926/2), pieces of the protective sheet of the *Genesis Apocryphon*, a fragment

[2] The manuscripts and artefacts in The Schøyen Collection are designated with their inventory numbers (MS = manuscript, but also used for artefacts). The collection runs at present from MS 1 to MS 5555, comprising about 20,450 items.

[3] This is the oldest Christian liturgical manuscript and the earliest source containing the complete books of Jonah and 1 Peter.

from the edge of the *Rule of the Community* scroll (MS 1926/3), as well as some unidentified darkened fragments. Trever wrote to me in a letter dated 11 February, 1995: 'Most of the fragments I possessed were from the bottom of the bag in which the Syrians had put the three large manuscripts (1QIsaᵃ, 1QS, and 1QpHab) and the Metropolitan told me to keep them as a reward for my work on his Scrolls at that time. The fragments had fallen off prior to my photographing the Scrolls.' A label that accompanied the fragments when I acquired them says: 'Dead Sea Scroll fragments from Qumran Cave I. Received by John C. Trever in Jerusalem, February 21, 1948.'

I sent the fragments to Bruce Zuckerman at West Semitic Research for infrared photography with the faint hope there could be writing on the darkened fragments after all. There was. Besides writing on the fragment of the *Genesis Apocryphon*, one batch of four dark fragments sticking together showed remains of texts from two Daniel scrolls (1QDanᵃ and 1QDanᵇ, Dan 2.4–5; 3.26–27), with letters not present on any other Dead Sea Scroll (MS 1926/4a+b). One of these biblical texts was copied in the mid-first century AD and the other in the second half of the first century BC, less than 150 years after the finalizing of the Book of Daniel between 167 and 164 BC. Mission accomplished!

During a later visit in 1993 I had a long conversation with William and Edmond Kando, two of Kando's sons. Kando had brokered transactions between the Bedouin discoverers and archaeologists for most of the fragments found in caves 1, 2, 4, 6, and 11, as well as Murabbaʿat and Naḥal Ḥever. Since Kando had sold fragments to several tourists and collectors from Europe and the USA who visited his shop in the 1950s and later, I suggested that they should check their father's files and contact some of the customers mentioned there, or those they still remembered. Since these customers now would be old, they or their descendants might perhaps not be interested in keeping their fragments any longer. Four fragments were found; two of them were passed on to Professor James H. Charlesworth for research and subsequent sale to me.

In a signed statement William Kando says the following about the provenance of these fragments: 'We hereby confirm that the Joshua (MS 2713) and Judges (MS 2861) fragments, from Qumran acquired through James H. Charlesworth and the Joel (MS 4612/1) and Leviticus (MS 4611) fragments, were acquired by my father from members of the Bedouins in 1952–53. At that time the caves in Qumran were not numbered and many of the locations not known, but we believe that all these fragments (except Judges) came from the cave near Khirbet Qumran later known as Cave 4. We sold these fragments to our old customer of the Kando family in Zurich in 1956.' William Kando later added that they did not know from which cave the Judges fragment came.[4] The name of the collector is not revealed here, as the heirs of this collector still had more fragments. Later they actually offered me another fragment of this Judges scroll, which I did not acquire.

The same statement continues: 'We can also confirm that the fragments from the *Temple Scroll* (MS 5095/1 and MS 5095/4) with its linen wrapper (MS 5095/2) and a date palm leaf pen (MS 5095/3) you acquired, actually were found together with the *Temple Scroll* itself in 1956, in the jar with a lid we still have in our shop, in the cave now known as Cave 11. In 1961 we presented the fragments, wrapper and pen as a gift to our customer in Zurich.'

As for the small fragments of 2 Samuel (MS 5233/1), Psalms (MS 5233/2), and Deuteronomy (MS 5214/1) that I later acquired, they were bought from the Bedouin in 1952–56, and William Kando states that he was reasonably sure they came from Cave 4. His father sold them to an American priest in 1972, who later served in Switzerland. His heirs in Zurich offered them for sale, with the provision that his name to be kept confidential.

---

[4] Palaeographical and mineral analysis presented in this volume now suggest that these four fragments were found in Bar Kokhba caves, probably Wadi Murabbaʿat or Naḥal Ḥever, find-sites discovered by the Taamire Bedouin in 1951 and 1952, close in time to their finding Cave 4. Furthermore, mineral analysis may suggest that one fragment was found in a natural cave in the cliffs, most probably Cave 11.

The remaining fragments published in this volume came from a distinguished family collection, which was based in Lebanon c. 1965–69. It was moved to Europe in 1969 and kept in Zurich from 1993. Nearly all these fragments were purchased from the Bedouin between 1952 and 1956 and were also believed to come from Cave 4. I know the identity of the owners of this family collection, but the family asked me to be so kind as not to reveal it, which I hereby honour.

There were also cases where the names of the vendors could be revealed; when the seller had no more fragments, or they were previously published, like the Georges Roux Collection. Roux's Genesis fragment, probably from Murabbaʿat, was published in 1980 (Puech 1980), and his palaeo-Hebrew Leviticus fragment 'L' in 1985 (Freedman and Matthew 1985, Appendix A, Plate 5). Since they were already published and extraordinarily expensive I did not acquire them. I suggested to the vendor that he should offer the palaeo-Hebrew Leviticus to the Israel Museum,[5] since the other fragments of this important scroll are housed in the collection of the Israel Antiquities Authority.

After some Dead Sea Scrolls fragments were published on the website of The Schøyen Collection (www.schoyencollection.com), several fragments have been offered to the collection from various sources, but not acquired. Usually they were offered at exorbitant prices. Others did not have proper documentation of their provenance, or belonged to collections in Israel. These last ones, like a *Temple Scroll* fragment in the collection of Arnold Shaer in Jerusalem, were not acquired. I thought it more prudent that they remain in Israel. In any event, it is most likely that an export licence would not have been granted. As for fragments with a reliable provenance that I did not acquire, I suggested to the vendors that they offer them to Israeli institutions.

The quest that started as a 'Mission: Impossible' in 1986, gradually proceeded to become a collection of c. 115 fragments from around 27 different scrolls. Of these, 20 are biblical (one or two of these appear to contain 'reworked' biblical texts). Of the at least eight other Qumranic texts, two are clearly authored within the Qumran community while two small fragments contain parts of hitherto unknown texts. The fragments originate from the three major Qumran caves (Caves 1, 4, and 11), from at least two Bar Kokhba caves, and from the Abu Shinjeh Cave in Wadi ed-Daliyeh north of Jericho. From this last cave came not Dead Sea Scrolls, but slave contracts from Samaria, dated as early as 358–337 BC. In addition the collection holds ten artefacts from Qumran or the wider Dead Sea region.

Fifteen of the 24 books of the Hebrew Bible are represented in the collection. No less than 13 of these books have fragments that represent the earliest textual witnesses to the passages they contain. The fragment MS 5439/1 from 4QRP[b] is palaeographically dated to the second century BC, placing it among the older known biblical manuscripts.

After these acquisitions there were no more fragments left in the market that could add substantially to The Schøyen Collection, and no further acquisitions were made. At the beginning of the quest it was believed that no fragments were in private hands, but the acquisitions of The Schøyen Collection opened the market and brought long-forgotten treasures to light. Afterwards more fragments could be bought both by institutions and private collectors, fragments that hopefully will be published by scholars and that will increase our knowledge of these ancient texts.

At this stage there should be room for a short reflection on what these biblical fragments do represent. Sacred biblical objects, such as the original tablets of the Ten Commandments or autographs of biblical books have been sought in vain. They are the cause of legends, wars, and a huge body of literature. They are perhaps of too sacred a nature to be owned by any institution or person. The early witnesses to the Holy Scriptures published in this volume are as close as one can get to such sacred objects. They should be treated with due respect and veneration both by their keepers and the scholars who handle them. As their present custodian the undersigned is privileged and honoured not so much to

---

[5] This fragment was sold to Southwestern Baptist Theological Seminary in 2010 (Patterson 2012, 35).

own as to for a very limited time be their humble keeper, not based on my own collecting virtues, but *Soli Deo Gloria.*

By kind invitation of Emanuel Tov, editor-in-chief of the *Discoveries in the Judaean Desert* series, 29 fragments from five scrolls in The Schøyen Collection were published in vols 26, 28, 32, 37, and 38. Through the tireless efforts of Weston Fields, and as a member of the Dead Sea Scrolls Foundation Board of Advisors, I had the privilege of co-sponsoring the publication of vols 20 and 38, and to sponsor vols 26, 32, and 34. These three volumes were kindly dedicated to Martin Schøyen and The Schøyen Collection.

Even if some of the fragments have already been published in *DJD* and elsewhere, I am most grateful that the whole Judaean Desert material of The Schøyen Collection can now be made available in one volume, due to the efforts directed by Torleif Elgvin, with a number of co-workers: Esther Eshel, Hanan Eshel, Årstein Justnes, Kipp Davis, George Brooke, Jan Dušek, Michael Langlois, Ada Yardeni, Ira Rabin, Roman Schütz, Naʿama Sukenik, Jan Gunneweg, Matthew Boulanger, and Joan Taylor.

I offer my thanks to George Brooke, Magen Broshi, Sarah Louise Brownlee, James Charlesworth, Weston and Diane Fields, Marilyn Lundberg, Florentino García Martínez, James Robinson, John Strugnell, Emanuel Tov, and John Trever. Special thanks are also extended to Bruce Zuckerman and Bjørn Rørslett for their excellent infrared photographs.

I am grateful to William Kando whose enthusiasm, knowledge, and connections were instrumental in making most of this collection come into existence.

Magen Broshi showed special kindness when he in 1993 let me into the Dead Sea Scrolls vault at the Israel Museum and enabled me to handle several scrolls, including the great Isaiah Scroll and Bar Kokhba documents.

Thanks are also due to Weston Fields who in 1997 climbed with me and my wife to Caves 1, 2, 3, 4, and 11, and enabled a visit to the Dead Sea Scrolls vaults at the Rockefeller Museum, where the two conservators were kind enough to let me once again handle the great Isaiah Scroll—while it was there for conservation—as well as numerous fragments.

At last a very special thanks to the late Muhammad edh-Dhib (Muhammad the Wolf), who kindly invited me, my wife, and Weston Fields to his house in Bethlehem in 1997; and who told me his own version of the now famous account of how he found the first scrolls in Cave 1 in the winter of 1946–47.

Martin Schøyen with Muhammad edh-Dhib in 1997

II

The Fate of Scrolls and Fragments: A Survey from 1946 to the Present[1]

Hanan Eshel

During the eighteen years between 1947, when the first seven Dead Sea Scrolls were discovered at Qumran, and 1965, when the excavations at Masada that turned up fragments of fifteen scrolls were completed, there was an almost unbroken stream of major discoveries in the caves of the Judaean Desert. In the subsequent period, between 1965 and the mid-90s, no written documents appeared on the antiquities market, and archaeologists did not discover any further scrolls. Therefore scholars started to believe that no more scrolls were to be found in the Judaean Desert. Nevertheless, more fragments have turned up during the last decade, and information about others is floating around. This chapter surveys the information about fragmentary texts, economic documents, and other texts from the Judaean Desert that were discovered or whose existence has come to our knowledge in recent years, with the hope of encouraging collectors and museums to get the fragments still at large studied and published before they deteriorate even more. We will deal both with fragments from the Qumran caves and documents from the two Jewish Revolts.

This chapter is divided into four parts. First I survey the history of archaeological research during the Golden Age of discoveries in the Judaean Desert; the eighteen years during which most of the scrolls and documents were discovered. This description is important for an understanding of why some fragments discovered before 1965 were published only recently. Special attention is directed to those fragments that did not make their way to the collection at the Rockefeller Museum or to the Shrine of the Book.

In the second part I consider fragments from the Qumran caves that, although found before 1956, came to public notice only in recent years because they were kept by antiquities dealers and collectors. The first publication of a fragment owned by an anonymous collector dates back to 1980. This phenomenon intensified after the project of publishing the thousands of fragments held in the Rockefeller Museum was basically completed in 2002. In this section I also look at the inscriptions found at Khirbet Qumran, because those found by de Vaux were published only recently, and additional ostraca were found at Qumran during the last fifteen years.

In the third part we look at textual fragments, economic documents, and inscriptions from the time of the Bar Kokhba Revolt, some of which were kept for many years by collectors and antiquities dealers and were published only recently, while others were discovered in the Judaean Desert caves after 1984 (see H. Eshel 1997 on these refuge caves). The final section deals with some biblical texts that have only recently become known and may derive from an unknown Bar Kokhba cave.

---

[1] This chapter is adapted from a more annotated version (H. Eshel 2010b). Parts of it, including the last section, are rewritten for the present publication. By agreement with Eshel, Torleif Elgvin has conducted an editorial update.

A. The Golden Age of Discoveries in the Judaean Desert

In the winter of 1946/47 (probably as early as November 1946, cf. Kiraz 2005, 91; Trever 1977, 98–99) Muhammad edh-Dhib, a Bedouin of the Taamire tribe, entered a cave that had been sealed by a stone wall in the limestone cliffs on the northwest shore of the Dead Sea and found eight cylindrical jars with covers. He reported that three scrolls, the complete Isaiah scroll, the *Community Rule* (with the appendices *Rule of the Congregation* and *Rule of Blessings*—a fragment of the latter ended up in The Schøyen Collection), and *Pesher Habakkuk*, were in one of the jars. Four other scrolls were later found in the detritus on the floor of the cave (the second Isaiah scroll, the *War Scroll*, the *Thanksgiving Scroll*, and the *Genesis Apocryphon*). Today this is known as Qumran Cave 1. Muhammad edh-Dhib tried to sell the scrolls from the jar to an antiquities dealer in Bethlehem, but the latter refused, because he knew of no scrolls ever found in the country before. As a result, they were brought to a local shoemaker, Khalil Iskander Shahin (known as 'Kando'), in the hope that he could find use for the leather found in the cave. Shahin, a member of the Syrian Orthodox (Jacobite) church, purchased the scrolls from the Bedouin. He resold the three scrolls found in the jar, along with the *Genesis Apocryphon*, to Mar Athanasius Samuel, the metropolitan of the small Syrian Orthodox community of Bethlehem and the Old City of Jerusalem, for 24 Palestine pounds. Because of the British mandatory law then in force the government had to be given first refusal on archaeological finds. Mar Samuel claimed that the scrolls he had purchased had been found in St. Mark's Monastery in the Jewish Quarter of the Old City. Prof. Eliezer Sukenik purchased two jars and two of the scrolls that had not been acquired by Mar Samuel (the *War Scroll* and the *Thanksgiving Scroll*) on 29 November, 1947, for 35 Palestine pounds. Sukenik's two jars are exhibited at present in the Shrine of the Book. He acquired yet another scroll, the second Isaiah scroll, on 22 December, 1947.

In late February 1948 Mar Samuel's representatives brought the three scrolls found in the jar to the American School of Oriental Research (ASOR), where they were photographed by John C. Trever. In late March the four scrolls held by Mar Samuel were taken out of Jerusalem; they reached the United States in January 1949. In June 1954 these scrolls were bought by proxy for the State of Israel by Sukenik's son, Yigael Yadin.

After the War of Independence ended in January 1949, a Belgian UN observer, together with an officer of the Jordanian army, initiated a search that identified the cave in which the first seven scrolls had been discovered (*DJD* 1:6). In excavations by the Dominican priest Roland de Vaux and the British archaeologist G. Lankester Harding, fragments that had been missed by the Bedouin and broken jars that could be pieced together were discovered. Other fragments found in Cave 1 between 1947 and 1949 were acquired by the École biblique et archéologique in Jerusalem. The fragments from Cave 1 were parts of some 70 different scrolls published in *DJD* 1 in 1955. Small fragments of six Cave 1 scrolls are represented in The Schøyen Collection.

After Cave 1 had been located, and because the cylindrical jars were unique, not known in any other Second Temple archaeological sites, de Vaux decided to open excavations at Khirbet Qumran, about a kilometre south of the cave. As jars identical to those of Cave 1 were found there, de Vaux concluded that the jars were evidence of a link between the scrolls in the caves and Khirbet Qumran (de Vaux 1973, 49–50).

In late 1951, documents from caves in Wadi Murabbaʿat, *c.* 15 km south-west of Qumran, appeared on the antiquities market in Bethlehem and East Jerusalem. Some of these documents bore the name of Shimon son of Kosiba, the leader of the Second Jewish Revolt in AD 132–36. De Vaux and curators of the Rockefeller Museum purchased these fragments from the Bedouin and set out in January-February 1952 to excavate the four caves on the northern side of Wadi Murabbaʿat. The Murabbaʿat finds include six biblical scrolls, two parchment strips from an arm phylactery, an illegible parchment slip of a mezuzah, and approximately 100 economic documents and letters written on papyrus. The oldest document from

Wadi Murabbaʿat dates from the seventh century BC, while the most recent documents were from the Middle Ages. Most of the documents found in the Wadi Murabbaʿat caves date from the early Roman period and were brought to the caves during the Jewish Revolts against the Romans. Six documents were brought to the caves by refugees of the First Jewish Revolt (see H. Eshel 2002a), but most were brought there in AD 135, at the end of the Bar Kokhba Revolt. Special importance attaches to an economic document (Mur 24) that begins, 'on the twentieth of Shebat, year two of the redemption of Israel by Shimon son of Kosiba, prince of Israel, in the encampment situated at Herodium', and to a set of seven letters written during the Bar Kokhba Revolt. Two of them were sent from the headquarters of Shimon son of Kosiba to Yeshua son of Galgula, the commander of the Herodium garrison (Mur 43–44). A fifth cave, located in the southern slope of Wadi Murabbaʿat, was discovered in March 1955. It yielded large fragments of a Hebrew scroll of the Twelve Minor Prophets (DJD 2:50, 181–205).[2]

While Père de Vaux and his associates were digging in the Wadi Murabbaʿat caves, the Bedouin, looking for additional scrolls in the vicinity of Qumran, found another cave containing scrolls (Cave 2) south of the first one.[3] After its discovery, de Vaux and his associates conducted a survey of the caves near Qumran in March 1952. On 24 March they found the Copper Scroll, along with fragments of fourteen other scrolls, in Cave 3.[4] Thus de Vaux and his associates returned to East Jerusalem after their first discovery of a complete scroll, along with fragments, at Qumran. In August 1952 Bedouin discovered Cave 6, west of Khirbet Qumran. This is a natural crevice in the limestone, very close to the seam between the limestone and the marl terrace, which consists of softer lime material.[5] Because of the proximity of Cave 6 to the marl terrace and, because one of them said he had seen a dove fly into a cave in the marl terrace, the Bedouin decided to look for additional caves there. During the last week of August 1952 they discovered a manmade cave carved out during the Second Temple period, known today as Cave 4a, where they found thousands of parchment fragments. They began to sift the dirt on the floor of that cave and the adjacent Cave 4b looking for additional fragments. After about a month, during which they found more than 15.000 fragments, the Bedouin, who were pushed aside by other Bedouin who would not allow them to continue sifting the dirt in the cave, brought de Vaux to the cave on September 1952. In eight days of digging de Vaux found the last thousand fragments left in Cave 4a.[6] A grand total of more than 16,000 fragments, from some six hundred scrolls and three hundred literary works, were found in this cave. Because of the straight cuts in some Cave 4 fragments de Vaux conjectured that a Roman legionary entered Cave 4a in the winter of AD 68, when the Tenth Legion occupied Qumran, and cut up the scrolls with his sword, cf. Josephus' description in Jewish War 2.229 and Antiquities 20.115. During the excavation of the two caves designated Cave 4, de Vaux discovered yet another cave north of 4a (today known as Cave 5), with fragments of 25 scrolls (see DJD 3:167–97). It was only after de Vaux completed his work in Caves 4 and 5 that the Bedouin brought him to Cave 6, where they had found fragments of 31 scrolls, most of them written on papyrus (see DJD 3:105–41).

After so many fragments were found in Cave 4, an international committee of scholars was set up to raise money to purchase the scrolls, clean up and piece together the fragments, and publish the results.[7]

---

[2] On the discoveries in Wadi Murabbaʿat, see DJD 2, published in 1960.

[3] Fragments of 33 different scrolls were found in Cave 2, the most important being those of Sirach. See DJD 3:48–93.

[4] On the fragments found in Cave 3, which come from 14 parchment and papyrus scrolls, see DJD 3:94–104. For the official publication of the Copper Scroll, see DJD 3:201–317. For a recent contribution see Brizemeure et al. 2006.

[5] The caves were numbered, not according to when they were discovered by the Bedouin, but the order in which scholars learned of their existence. Because the Bedouin brought de Vaux to the cave they had found before they entered Cave 4 only after he completed the excavations in Cave 5, that cave received the designation Cave 6. Since it is a natural cave in the cliffs the sediments of Cave 6 are similar to those of Caves 1, 2, and 11.

[6] On the archaeological excavations in Caves 4a and 4b, see DJD 6:3–22, published 1977.

[7] On the history of the international committee, see the summary in Fields 2006, 59–75.

Because the Bedouin had more than 15,000 fragments from Cave 4 in their possession, a long and arduous process of buying them began.[8] The dealer who acted as middleman between the Bedouin and the Rockefeller Museum curators was the same Khalil Iskander Shahin ('Kando'), who, after the discovery of the first scrolls in 1947, had closed his shoemaking business and set himself up as an antiquities dealer. Over the years he opened two shops, one in Bethlehem and the other in East Jerusalem. The first fragments from Cave 4a were purchased by the Rockefeller Museum curators on 13 September, 1952, even before the start of the scientific excavation of the cave (Milik 1959, 17). Most of the fragments from Cave 4a were acquired by the museum during the first three years after the discovery of the cave, but the last such fragments did not come into its possession until July 1958 (Reed 1991, 46). In the present volume only one text from The Schøyen Collection is identified with a previously published scroll from Cave 4.

In July 1952, at Khirbet Mird, Bedouin discovered papyri from the library of the Kastellion monastery, which had been built on the ruins of the Second Temple period Hyrcania fortress. The monastery was active from the fifth to the fourteenth century. Subsequently a Belgian team from the University of Louvain set out in the spring of 1953 to look for additional fragments. In the end, Bedouin and archaeologists together turned up some 180 fragments of written papyri: around 100 written in Arabic (one of them a very old copy of the Quran), 68 fragments of Greek documents, and about ten texts in Palestinian Christian Aramaic. Most of these fragments are in the possession of the University of Louvain; a few have been transferred to the Rockefeller Museum.[9]

In August 1952 and July 1953, the curators of the Rockefeller Museum purchased from Khalil Iskander Shahin ('Kando') an important group of fragments and economic documents from the time of the Bar Kokhba Revolt. The Bedouin claimed to have discovered them in Wadi Seiyal; in other words, that they came from caves located in Israeli territory (which meant that they would not have violated the Jordanian antiquities law when they explored these caves).[10] The southern half of the Judaean Desert, the only section under Israeli control between 1948 and 1967, was shaped like a triangle, with its vertices at Sodom, Arad, and En Gedi. The international border crossed the wadis south of En Gedi, leaving their western stretches in Jordanian territory and their eastern sections in Israel. The border was demarcated in such a way that Wadi Seiyal, which runs from Arad to the area north of Masada, fell entirely in Israeli territory, whereas Naḥal Ḥever, which runs toward En Gedi, was almost entirely in Jordanian hands, except for its easternmost section. By stating that they had found the documents in a cave in Wadi Seiyal, the Bedouin claimed they were found in Israeli territory. Had they said 'Naḥal Ḥever' instead, they would have had to explain that they came from caves in the eastern stretches of that wadi, then controlled by Israel. Even though today it is clear that most of these documents came from the Naḥal Ḥever caves, they have been designated the 'Wadi Seiyal collection'. Along with the

---

[8] Most of the fragments from Cave 4 were acquired by the Jordanian government for 15,000 dinars ($42,000) in early 1953. Other fragments were purchased later with funds from McGill University in Montreal; University of Manchester, England; Heidelberg University, Germany; the Vatican Library; McCormick Theological Seminary, Chicago; École Biblique et Archéologique, Jerusalem; and the University of Oxford. A contribution was also received from All Souls' Church in New York City. When Cave 4 was discovered, the Jordanians promised that institutions that made cash contributions to defray the cost of acquiring the fragments would receive those purchased with their money after the publication project was completed. In July 1960 the Jordanian government reneged on this pledge, deciding not to allow the fragments to be removed from the Rockefeller Museum and to return the funds received from these institutions. According to Allegro, Bedouin who lived near the Mar Saba monastery in Naḥal Qidron still had scroll fragments in their possession in 1961, see Allegro 1964b, 109.

[9] On the texts from Khirbet Mird, see *DJD* 39:92–97. For a list of the papyri from Khirbet Mird now in Belgium and the Rockefeller Museum, see Reed 1994, 217–25. As far as I know, one unregistered papyrus was found in Khirbet Mird written in Christian Aramaic and describing the birth of Jesus.

[10] For the story of the acquisition and the full publication of most of the documents of the Wadi Seiyal collection, see *DJD* 27.

fragments that the Bedouin claimed to have found in Wadi Seiyal the museum acquired four fragments from Genesis and a document written on 6 Adar of the third year of Shimon son of Kosiba, which the Bedouin said they had found in Naḥal David.[11]

During the digging season of February–March 1955 at Khirbet Qumran, the archaeologists found four manmade caves, which seemed to have served as homes, in the marl terrace. The three caves south of the site yielded scroll fragments. Eighteen tiny fragments, written in Greek, were found in Cave 7; most scholars conjecture that the residents of this cave did not know Hebrew or Aramaic.[12] In a nearby cave (8Q) they found parchment fragments from a mezuzah, a head phylactery, and fragments of three scrolls in Hebrew (Genesis, Psalms, and a prayer to exorcise evil spirits). Cave 9 yielded a single fragment with six legible letters. Cave 10, west of the site and above Cave 4, did not produce any scroll fragments, but only an ostracon with the letters *yod* and *šin*.[13]

In March 1956, Michael Avi-Yonah and his colleagues conducted an archaeological survey of Masada. They confirmed that the royal palace described by Josephus in his *Jewish War* was that on the northern slope of the fortress. They also discovered a papyrus fragment written in Hebrew or Aramaic, an ostracon that mentioned 'Hanani son of Shimon', and a Greek inscription.

In January or February 1956, Bedouin spotted a bat flying out of a cave whose entrance was blocked by a large rock, south of Cave 3. They moved the rock aside and entered a large natural cave in the limestone. Evidently the rock had been placed in the entrance on purpose, to seal off the cave. In this cave (Cave 11) they found pieces of four scrolls in relatively good condition, that is, roughly on a par with the seven scrolls from Cave 1, along with fragments of 27 other scrolls. The Bedouin brought de Vaux to the cave in mid-February 1956. After the discovery of Cave 11 the Bedouin were again in possession of relatively intact scrolls and many fragments. This time the Jordanians decided that they would negotiate with Kando to acquire the scrolls, but that scholars who wanted to publish them would have to raise funds and reimburse the Jordanian government for the purchase price. The relatively complete scrolls from Cave 11 are (1) the Psalms Scroll (11QPsª), of which 28 columns survive. This scroll contains 35 psalms from the last section of the canonical book of Psalms, along with eight other psalms not found in the Masoretic text. This scroll, 3.89 metres long, was published by James Sanders (*DJD* 4; Sanders 1967).[14] (2) A scroll with an Aramaic targum of the Book of Job (11QtgJob). It has 38 surviving columns, but circular pieces from the middle of the column, which cannot be pieced together, are all that remain of 28 of them. The last eight columns in the scroll, with a total length of 1.10 metres, are attached. The *Targum of Job* was published in 1971, and republished in 1974 and 1998.[15] (3) The book of Leviticus in palaeo-Hebrew script (11QpalaeoLevª). Approximately one metre with fourteen columns of this scroll survive, containing parts of twelve chapters of the biblical book (Freedman and Mathews 1985).

The fourth well-preserved scroll from Cave 11 is the *Temple Scroll*. Starting in 1960, Yigael Yadin had been in contact with an American clergyman, Joe Uhrig. Uhrig served as middleman between Yadin in Israel and Kando in Bethlehem. Through this middleman Kando offered Yadin what is now known as

---

[11] It seems likely that these fragments were discovered in the Cave of the Pool in Naḥal David. On these fragments, see *DJD* 38:117–24; Baruchi and Eshel 2006.

[12] On the fragments from Cave 7, see *DJD* 3:142–46. The roof of Cave 7 collapsed when the marl from which it was carved out became soaked after heavy rains: two blocks of marl were found with mirror-image Greek letters on them, imprinted from papyri.

[13] On the fragments from Caves 8 and 9, see *DJD* 3:147–63.

[14] For the fascinating story about how Sanders opened this scroll in an unorthodox way, see Sanders 2002, 396–400.

[15] Van der Ploeg and van der Woude 1971; Sokoloff 1974; *DJD* 23. In 1961, all of the small fragments found in Cave 11, along with those of the *Targum of Job*, were purchased for 10,000 Jordanian dinars (at the time, each dinar was worth one pound sterling), contributed by the Royal Dutch Academy of Sciences.

the *Temple Scroll*. In December 1961 Yadin paid the American clergyman an advance of $10,000 for the scroll. But in the end Yadin received neither the scroll nor his advance back. On June 1967, during the Six-Day War, on Yadin's orders the scroll was taken from its hiding place under the floor of Kando's Bethlehem home and brought to Yadin, who had it photographed that same day. Unfortunately, during the eleven years the scroll was hidden in Bethlehem it suffered more damage than during the 1,900 years it had been buried in Cave 11; its upper part had rotted away.[16] After negotiations that lasted for nearly a year the scroll was purchased by the State of Israel. The present volume publishes some minor fragments of the *Temple Scroll*, and more importantly, the remnants of the linen cover wrapped around the scroll when it was stored in Cave 11 with the cord bound around it. A small fragment with an unknown Aramaic text published here may also derive from Cave 11 (MS 4612/3, see p. 296).

Six months after the Six-Day War, Yadin acquired for the Shrine of the Book the leather box of a head phylactery discovered at Qumran. Its importance lies in the fact that it still contained three original parchments. The fourth parchment inside this box was not original, it had been inserted by Kando after the original parchment disintegrated. Since the exact cave in which this phylactery was found is not known, it is labelled XQPhyl 1–4 (Yadin 1969).

No additional scrolls were found in caves near Khirbet Qumran after the discovery of Cave 11 in January 1956. Consequently the Bedouin began looking for scrolls and economic documents in caves in the southern part of the Judaean Desert, which was part of Israel before the Six-Day War. In 1959 Israeli scholars heard rumours that Bedouin had found additional documents in Wadi Seiyal. This led Yohanan Aharoni to conduct an archaeological survey of the area in the last week of January 1960. He found three caves that contained relics from the period of the Bar Kokhba Revolt (Aharoni 1961). Cave 32 is a large cave completely ransacked by the Bedouin. In this cave bones of seven individuals were found. In Cave 33 he found a large group of arrows. In Cave 34, one discovered by the archaeologists, he found two parchments from a head phylactery and a small fragment later identified as Num 18.21; 19.11 (*DJD* 38:209). These parchments were found close to the nest of a vulture, and were probably brought by the vulture from Cave 32 to Cave 34.

In the light of these findings it was decided to launch the Judaean Desert Campaign—a systematic survey of the caves in Israeli territory. The campaign was conducted during the last week of March and first week of April in 1960. It involved four separate teams, headed by Nahman Avigad, Yohanan Aharoni, Pesah Bar-Adon, and Yigael Yadin. A torn Greek papyrus was found in the Scouts' Cave (renamed, a year later, the 'Cave of Treasure') in Naḥal Mishmar (Lifshitz 1961; *DJD* 38:203–4). The most important finds of this campaign were made in the large cave on the northern slope of Naḥal Ḥever, where Yadin's team found a small fragment of the book of Psalms (*DJD* 36:141–66; another 12 fragments of the same scroll had been found by Bedouin and are part of the 'Wadi Seiyal collection'), along with fifteen letters (one on a wooden tablet, the rest on papyrus) dispatched from Shimon son of Kosiba's headquarters to the three commanders of En Gedi.[17] As a result, this cave was designated 'Cave of the Letters'.

The second stage of the Judaean Desert Campaign was conducted a year later, in March 1961. In a Naḥal Mishmar cave Bar-Adon turned up a hoard of 429 Chalcolithic vessels. The private archive of Babatha, daughter of Shimon, comprising 35 documents in Nabataean, Aramaic and Greek, written on

---

[16] Editor's note: According to Kando (personal communication with Martin Schøyen) most of the damage occurred in the pre-1956 period. The scroll was probably deposited upside-down in the jar, leading to damage on the end upon which it was standing.

[17] On the written artifacts found in Cave of Letters in 1960, see Yadin 1971, 124–31. For the official publication of the letters, see Yadin et al. 2002, 278–366.

papyrus and dating from between AD 93 and 132, was found in the Cave of the Letters,[18] along with the smaller archive of a farmer from En Gedi named Eleazar son of Shmuel, consisting of six Aramaic and Hebrew documents written during the Bar Kokhba Revolt.[19] Also found in this cave were the marriage contract of Salome Komaise, the daughter of Levi, whose other documents had been found by Bedouin and are part of the 'Wadi Seiyal collection'.[20] A small fragment of the book of Numbers was found near the entrance to the cave, along with further fragments of a Nabataean document published earlier by Father Jean Starcky, also part of the 'Wadi Seiyal collection' (Yardeni 2001). In the light of these findings, there is no doubt that most of the documents included in the 'Wadi Seiyal collection' actually came from the Cave of the Letters in Naḥal Ḥever.

During the second season of Operation Judaean Desert, Yohanan Aharoni's group dug in the Cave of Horror, on the southern bank of Naḥal Ḥever. The designation 'Cave of Horror' was given to this cave because it contained more than 40 skeletons of Jewish refugees who fled there at the end of the Bar Kokhba Revolt. The archaeologists found nine small fragments of a scroll bearing a Greek translation of the Twelve Minor Prophets, three fragments of a scroll of a Hebrew prayer, a Greek papyrus fragment, and four ostraca of names laid alongside people who were buried in the cave.[21] Many fragments of the Greek scroll of the Twelve Minor Prophets (see *DJD* 8) were already part of the Wadi Seiyal collection, another indication that some of those documents actually came from the Cave of Horror in Naḥal Ḥever.[22]

After the two seasons of the Judaean Desert Expedition, the Bedouin came to the conclusion that there was no point in continuing to look for scrolls and documents in the southern Judaean Desert and turned their attention to caves north of Jericho. In April 1962 the Rockefeller Museum, through Kando, received papyri from a cave in Wadi ed-Daliyeh, dating from the fourth century BC. After some of them had been acquired by ASOR, the Bedouin led Paul Lapp to the cave in December 1962. ASOR conducted two seasons of excavations there, directed by Lapp, in January 1963 and February 1964. The skeletons of some 300 refugees from the city of Samaria, who had fled from the armies of Alexander the Great, were discovered, along with fragments of eighteen economic documents of a size that makes it possible to decipher their content, along with fragments of another twenty economic documents. The cave also yielded 128 bullae used to seal the documents. All the Wadi ed-Daliyeh documents are economic documents written in Aramaic. Ten of them are deeds of slave sales (documents 1–9, 18); two describe transactions in which a slave was given as security for a loan (documents 10 and 12); one is a court decision concerning ownership of a slave (document 11). Another attests to the manumission of a slave or the fact that he no longer served as security (document 13). Three documents deal with the sale of real estate: one is a deed of consignment of a room in a sanctuary (document 14),[23] the second is a deed of sale of a house (document 15), and the third is a deed of pledge of a vineyard (document 16). Also found were a receipt of payment in relation to a pledge (document 17) and a small fragment with a sworn declaration (fragment 23). Fragment 22, the most ancient found in Wadi ed-Daliyeh, can be dated to

[18] For the publication of the Greek documents from Babatha's archive, see Lewis 1989. The Nabataean and Aramaic documents were published in Yadin et al. 2002, 73–141, 170–276.

[19] On Eleazar son of Shmuel's archive see, Yadin 1971, 172–83. The archive was published in full in Yadin et al. 2002, 37–70, 142–68.

[20] *DJD* 27:224–37. On the archive of Salome Komaise daughter of Levi, see Cotton 1995 and H. Eshel 2002b.

[21] For the publication of the hymn and the Greek papyrus, see *DJD* 36:167–72; Qimron 2006.

[22] We cannot accept the premise that all the documents in the Wadi Seiyal Collection come from the Cave of the Letters and the Cave of Horror. At least two documents seem to come from a cave in the upper stretch of Naḥal Ḥever; see Amit and Eshel 1995/96. Two other documents evidently originated in Wadi Hammamat, on the eastern side of the Dead Sea, see H. Eshel 1998.

[23] On the importance of this document, see H. Eshel 1996.

between the thirtieth and thirty-ninth year of Artaxerxes II (*i.e.*, 375–365 BC). Document 1, which is the most recent, was written in 335 BC.[24] All the Wadi ed-Daliyeh documents were written 'in the city of Samaria in the province of Samaria'. A number of small fragments from Wadi ed-Daliyeh, found by the Bedouin, are published for the first time in this volume. The documents of Wadi ed-Daliyeh are important for reconstructing the history of the city of Samaria. In particular, a comparison of the documents from Wadi ed-Daliyeh with later documents found in the Judaean Desert indicates a major change in the socio-economic conditions of the country (see H. Eshel 2007). Most of the Wadi ed-Daliyeh documents are about slaves, whereas the later ones never mention them.

The excavations at Masada, led by Yadin, ran from October 1963 through April 1965. Fifteen Hebrew scrolls were unearthed in the fortress (one on papyrus). There were also eighteen papyri in Latin, nine papyri in Greek, and two bilingual papyri (in Greek and Latin); 150 ostraca with inscriptions in Latin and Greek; and 701 ostraca with texts in Aramaic and Hebrew, most of them evidently vouchers for provisions.[25] The scrolls found at Masada can be divided into three groups: seven biblical scrolls, four scrolls with parts of apocryphal texts, and four other scrolls. The biblical scrolls include a fragment of Genesis; two Leviticus scrolls; three fragments of a Deuteronomy scroll; fifty fragments of an Ezekiel scroll; and two scrolls of Psalms. The apocryphal texts include the most important scroll found at Masada, seven columns from Sirach 39–44 (Yadin 1965).[26] This scroll was discovered in a room in the casemate wall, not far from the snake path gate. Another apocryphal text is based on Genesis, the third scroll being an apocryphon based on the Book of Joshua. The last scroll in this category contains a fragment related to the *Book of Jubilees*. The most important of the last group of four scrolls contains parts of the hymn collection *Songs of the Sabbath Sacrifice*, of which nine copies were found in the Qumran caves. Fragments of two other as-yet-unidentified scrolls were also found. The last work is written in Palaeo-Hebrew script on both sides of the papyrus. The word *lirnana* 'sing joyously' appears twice on one side, along with the place name 'Mt. Gerizim'.[27] Of special importance is the fact that the two biblical scrolls were found buried in the synagogue built by the Zealots on Masada (H. Eshel 2009b, 87).

After the excavations on Masada came to an end, no more documents were discovered in the Judaean Desert until 1986. During the 18 years of the Golden Age of archaeological research in the Judaean Desert most of the documents were discovered by the Bedouin. In most of these cases Kando was the middleman between the Bedouin and the archaeologists. The scrolls from Qumran Caves 1, 2, 4, 6, and 11 were found by the Bedouin and reached the Rockefeller Museum and the Shrine of the Book primarily through his hands. Similarly, the scrolls and documents found in Wadi Murabbaʿat, Khirbet Mird, Naḥal David, and Wadi ed-Daliyeh passed through him. The so-called Wadi Seiyal Collection, most of which actually derives from the Cave of Letters and the Cave of Horror in Naḥal Ḥever, also came to the Rockefeller Museum through Kando.

---

[24] For photographs of the documents and fragments found in Wadi ed-Daliyeh, along with readings and translations of the 11 most intact documents, see *DJD* 28:3–116. For the publication of the bullae from Wadi ed-Daliyeh, see *DJD* 24.

[25] For a popular summary of the Masada excavations, see Yadin 1966 (on the scrolls pp. 168–91). For the publication of the scrolls, see Talmon and Yadin 1999. The Latin papyri found at Masada include the salary slips of a Roman legionary and a document about the distribution of medical supplies, and most importantly, a papyrus with a quotation from the Aeneid of Virgil. For the publication of the Latin and Greek documents, see Cotton and Geiger 1989. For the publication of the Aramaic and Hebrew ostraca, see Yadin and Naveh 1989.

[26] This book was published to mark the opening of the Shrine of the Book on 20 April, 1965. Reprinted with notes on readings and bibliography in Talmon and Yadin 1999.

[27] Talmon believed that the fact that this papyrus was written in the Palaeo-Hebrew script later used by the Samaritans, and the reference in it to Mt. Gerizim, indicate that it was a Samaritan prayer (Talmon and Yadin 1999, 138–49). For the possibility that it is rather a Jewish prayer recited on 21 Kislev, the holiday instituted to mark the destruction of the Samaritan temple, see H. Eshel 1991.

The curators of the Rockefeller Museum made great efforts to acquire all the Judaean Desert scroll fragments and keep them together at the museum. Their efforts were amazingly successful; more than 95% of the fragments did end up at the museum, making it possible to piece many fragments together and identify them correctly. Nevertheless, a small number of fragments were scattered among various public and private collections. Those in public collections include the following: (1) 377 fragments in the possession of the Bibliothèque Nationale in Paris derive from 18 scrolls found in Qumran cave 1. (2) Fragments of 20 scrolls found at Qumran are held in the National Archaeological Museum on the Citadel in Amman (15 scrolls from Cave 1, four scrolls from Cave 4, and the Copper Scroll from Cave 3). (3) The University of Louvain, Belgium, holds 14 Greek Papyri of the New Testament from Khirbet Mird as well as a booklet written in Christian Palestinian Aramaic (Reed 1994, 223–25; Baillet 1963; Verhelst 2003). (4) Four phylactery parchments from Cave 4 are now at the University of Heidelberg in Germany (Reed 1994, 66–67). (5) The Franciscan Flagellation Museum on Via Dolorosa in the Old City of Jerusalem has two fragments from Cave 4: one from a Joshua apocryphon (4Q379); the other is the only surviving fragment of a composition called *Renewed Earth* (4Q475). They also have a Hebrew document from 'year two' of the Bar Kokhba Revolt from Wadi Murabba'at that escaped attention until recently.[28] (6) The Musée de la Terre Sainte (Holy Land Museum) of the Catholic Institute in Paris owns a fragment from a Psalms scroll found in Cave 4 (4Q98=4QPs^q, *DJD* 16:145–49), along with the deed of sale of a field from the time of the Bar Kokhba Revolt (see below and *DJD* 27:124–29). (7) The Oriental Institute at the University of Chicago has a fragment from *Wiles of the Wicked Woman* (4Q184).[29] (8) Several tiny fragments, evidently from Wadi Murabba'at, are at McGill University in Montreal.[30]

In addition to these fragments held in public collections, we also know of a number of fragments in private hands. Fragments of three scrolls from Qumran Cave 1, formerly in the possession of Mar Samuel, are now owned by the Syrian Orthodox Church in New Jersey (Reed 1994, 31–32). Two fragments from Cave 4 were purchased by Michel Testuz of France. One of them is a Hebrew fragment of the Book of the Hosea (4Q78=4QXII^c); the second, an Aramaic fragment from the work known as *Testament of Jacob* (4Q537). Both were published by the collector himself (Testuz 1955).[31] In 1980 another fragment from a Wadi Murabba'at Genesis scroll was published (Puech 1980). Its owner wished to remain anonymous.[32] We should also mention three biblical fragments stolen from the Rockefeller Museum in 1966, when the members of the diplomatic corps accredited to the Kingdom of Jordan had been invited to view the

[28] See *DJD* 22:262–65; *DJD* 36:464–73. These two fragments from Qumran are said to have been offered for sale in 1953 or 1954 by a Jordanian policeman stationed in the town of Salt (*DJD* 36:465 note 6). The document from Wadi Murabba'at was published by Eshel, Eshel, and Geiger 2008. I would like to thank Torleif Elgvin for drawing our attention to this document, thus leading to its 2008 publication.

[29] Eibert Tigchelaar is not certain that this fragment really belongs to 4Q184; see Reed 1994, 78.

[30] See Reed 1994, xviii. The John Rylands University Library in Manchester has several fragments with no writing from Qumran Cave 1, sent to be studied by H. J. Plenderleith; see the report he published in *DJD* 1:39–40 and Ira Rabin's discussion in the present volume, pp. 61ff.

[31] For the identification of these fragments as parts of scrolls from Cave 4, see *DJD* 15:237–42. On the Aramaic fragment, see *DJD* 31:171–75.

[32] This was the first instance of a phenomenon that increased after 2002, that private collectors allowed publication of fragments in their possession. Generally speaking, the scientific publication of an artefact in a private collection increases its value. The situation of the Dead Sea Scrolls is somewhat unique, however, because Kando and his heirs did not have direct connections with collectors who could pay the small fortune they were demanding for the scrolls. Consequently they relied on scholars to put them in contact with collectors. Scholars are more interested in unpublished scrolls than in those that have already been published, so in this case antiquities dealers may prefer that the scrolls in their hands remain unpublished.

scroll fragments. The three missing items are the largest fragment of 4QSam[b] and two fragments from the oldest Daniel scroll, 4QDan[c]. No one knows the whereabouts of these fragments today.[33]

B. Recently Published Texts from Qumran

After this survey of the eighteen glorious years of archaeological exploration of the Judaean desert, we turn to the fragments published after 1984. My presentation is chronological, beginning with those found in Qumran and proceeding to those from the time of the Bar Kokhba Revolt.

The Leviticus scroll from Cave 11, in palaeo-Hebrew script, was published in 1985 (Freedman and Mathews 1985). An appendix to this volume included a large two-column fragment (labelled fragment L) that had not been acquired by the Rockefeller Museum but was purchased by the French Prof. Georges Roux in January 1967. The authors wrote that they had not included the fragment in the body of their edition because they only learned of its existence at a late stage and because of the poor quality of the photographs of the fragment made available to them. In fact, two unclear photos of the fragment were included in the book. Nevertheless they did propose an initial deciphering of the fragment. The first column of this fragment contains text from Lev 21.7–12, and the second column Lev 22.21–27. Four years later, Émile Puech published an excellent photo of this fragment along with an improved reading (Puech 1989).[34]

After Yadin's death in 1984, three tiny fragments of Qumran scrolls were found in his desk drawer. They were transferred to the Shrine of the Book and later connected to three different scrolls from Cave 11.[35]

In January 1992, while Bruce Zuckerman and Stephen Reed were cataloguing photographs of scrolls held by the Shrine of the Book, they found a photograph of a circular fragment written in Aramaic, with parts of ten lines. Even at first glance it was clear that this fragment belonged to 11QtgJob; it contained Job 23.1–8, and is now labelled fragment 6a. Before the discovery of this photo, twenty-seven circular fragments were known; their shape indicates that they were adjacent to one another when the scroll was rolled. Moths had eaten most of the scroll except for this round 'plug' (called a 'wad' by scholars). The photographs found in the Shrine of the Book were taken on June 1967, while the Six-Day War was still in progress. Because this was also the day when the first photographs were taken of the *Temple Scroll*, it is likely that this fragment of the Job targum had been in Kando's home along with the *Temple Scroll*, and was brought together with it to Yadin on June 1967. By 1993 the original fragment had not been located yet (Zuckerman and Reed 1993). Five years later, with the official publication of the Job Targum in the *DJD* series, it was reported that the new fragment had been located and attached to the other fragments of this scroll (*DJD* 23:101).

A small fragment from the *Community Rule* (1QS), discovered in Cave 1 in 1947, was published in 1994 (Brooke and Robinson 1994; *DJD* 26:227–33). This fragment had been given by Mar Athanasius Samuel to

---

[33] On this incident, see the article by Felice Maranz (Maranz 1991). This Samuel scroll is among the oldest found at Qumran, and its textual variants are extremely important. Fortunately, all three fragments were photographed before they were stolen. For a photograph of the missing Samuel fragment, see *DJD* 17 plate XXIV. For photographs of the two missing fragments of Daniel, see *DJD* 16 plate XXXIV. On the fact that the two fragments were stolen, see *DJD* 16:269. On the importance of the missing Samuel fragment, see Cook 1984.

[34] According to Puech, this fragment was purchased in 1963. This fragment was part of the exhibits in the United States mentioned below, and is now in an advanced state of decomposition.

[35] The first fragment consisted of the upper margin and three lines with parts of verses from Ps 18.21–29. Tigchelaar identified it as part of 11QPs[d] (*DJD* 23:66–67). The second belongs to 11QJub (containing *Jub.* 7.4–5) and the third to 11QHymn[b], a hymn that resembles *Words of the Luminaries*, of which three copies were found in Cave 4 (see H. Eshel 2001b; *DJD* 36:485–89).

the Qumran scholar William Brownlee in 1973. After Brownlee died in 1983 his widow sold the fragment to Martin Schøyen. The fragment in question, which has parts of four lines, links up perfectly with the fifth column of the last part of 1QS, known as the *Rule of Benedictions* (1QSb). The article that accompanied the publication of the fragment included two photographs of it, the first taken in 1973 and the second in 1994. A comparison of the two is instructive: whereas one can make out nineteen letters in the earlier photograph, only fourteen are visible in the second one, as a small piece has fallen off in the meantime. In other cases, the surface of fragments owned by private owners deteriorate.[36] Tiny fragments from the first two columns of the *Genesis Apocryphon* from Cave 1, also in The Schøyen Collection, were published two years later (Lundberg and Zuckerman 1996).

That same year, Haggai Misgav published four fragments of scrolls owned by the Hecht Museum at the University of Haifa (see *DJD* 28:223–29). Two years later, André Lemaire published a small fragment with the right margin and the beginning of four lines from column XIV of the *Temple Scroll*. This fragment includes the laws of the sacrifices to be offered on the first day of the first month, which is the first day of the priestly days of ordination. A year later, Lemaire published another small fragment, with parts of five lines in Aramaic, XQOffering ar (Lemaire 1996; Lemaire 1997; *DJD* 36:490–91). This fragment, too, deals with the laws of sacrifice, but has not yet been associated with any identified scroll. The two fragments are part of a private collection in Jerusalem.

In 2000, Armin Lange published in *DJD* a fragment of a scroll that had been purchased in the 1960s by a Finnish clergyman who insisted on remaining anonymous but who bequeathed it to the State of Israel (the fragment is now in the Shrine of the Book). This fragment had parts of six lines, but Lange was unable to identify them. After it was published, it was identified as coming from one of the copies of *4QInstruction*, 4Q418 (*DJD* 36:492–93; Puech and Steudel 2000; Tigchelaar 2001, 125).

In 2003 I was asked to serve as the academic adviser to several American collectors who owned rare copies of the Bible when they organized exhibitions about the history of the Bible and its English translations. Over a period of two years, until February 2005, the exhibitions were mounted in several cities in the southern United States and the Midwest. They included several fragments of Qumran scrolls that had not been acquired by the Rockefeller Museum in the 1950s and had remained in Kando's possession. Because the exhibit dealt with the history of the Bible, the collectors preferred to include passages from biblical scrolls. In a first article we were allowed to publish six of the fragments included in the exhibit, four of them from biblical scrolls that we initially identified with 4QIsa[b] (two fragments), 4QGen[f], and 8QGen (E. Eshel and H. Eshel 2005). The two nonbiblical fragments were a small fragment from a scroll similar to the *Book of Jubilees* (4Q226 = 4QpseudoJubilees), which recounts either the banishment of Hagar or the binding of Isaac. Another fragment, written on papyrus, contains the end of chapter 8 and the beginning of chapter 9 of *1 Enoch*. Because we did not know from which cave this fragment derives, it was designated XQpapEnoch (E. Eshel and H. Eshel 2005). Based on this text we proposed corrections to restorations suggested by Josef Milik for two fragments of the book of *1 Enoch* found in Cave 4.

The items from the American travelling exhibitions were published in three catalogues (Biondi 2003; Biondi 2004; Noah 2005). Our second article (E. Eshel and H. Eshel 2007) dealt with six fragments whose

[36] This factor now causes antiquities dealers to do their utmost today to sell the fragments still in their possession before they crumble into dust. Three other factors have caused them to think that they should try to sell such fragments now, before it is too late: (1) the fact that in the 1990s collectors paid vast sums for Qumran fragments; (2) the announcement of some of those collectors that they are not interested in acquiring additional fragments; (3) the economic slowdown of recent years. For the first time since the scrolls were discovered, these factors have led antiquities dealers to the conclusion that they may have missed the boat; that is, that they could have received more for the fragments had they sold them in the 1990s. Given the precarious state of the fragments, any further delay is liable to reduce their value.

photographs were published in these catalogues (five biblical fragments and a small fragment of *4QInstruction*, 4Q416). The same article also discussed a fragment from 11QPs^c, now in the possession of Ashland Theological Seminary in Ohio, a photograph of which was in a pamphlet published by the seminary.[37] The Ashland fragment links up with one of the fragments shown in the exhibition; it seems likely then that the two were still connected when discovered in Cave 11 in 1956. Over time, however, it crumbled, so that one part is now in Ohio and the other was part of the exhibits. Except for these two fragments of the Psalms scroll from Cave 11, the other five fragments discussed in this article were all believed to have come from Cave 4 (E. Eshel and H. Eshel 2007).[38]

Since the early 1990s The Schøyen Collection has acquired a large number of fragments. Many of them have been displayed on the collection's website, usually with a photograph (www.schoyencollection.com/dsscrolls; www. schoyencollection.com/bible).

Sixty-three Hebrew, Aramaic, and Greek inscriptions found in Roland de Vaux' excavations at Khirbet Qumran were published in 2003 (Lemaire 2003).[39] These inscriptions were written on sherds and various stone objects (such as weights). Some of the inscriptions on potsherds were written on the intact vessels, indicating their volume or contents; others were ostraca, that is, inscriptions written in ink on broken pieces of pottery. In 1996, in an excavation at Khirbet Qumran directed by James Strange, two more ostraca were found, one in relatively good condition, and the other broken (Strange 2006). The intact ostracon is a deed of gift in Hebrew, whereby a certain Honi conveys his property to a man named Eleazar son of Nahmani. This ostracon was published by Frank Moore Cross and Esther Eshel (Cross and Eshel 1997). In line 8 they read *kemaloto la-Yaḥad* 'when he fulfils [his oath] to the Community'. Thus they suggested that this deed of gift was a draft of an account written for Honi, who wanted to join the *Yaḥad*, by Eleazar son of Nahmani, an overseer of the Community.[40] After the publication of the ostracon, various alternative readings were proposed, most of which proposed readings other than *kemaloto la-Yaḥad*.[41] Until the discovery of this ostracon at Qumran, only three deeds of gift from the Judaean Desert caves were known (two in Greek and one in Aramaic), and in all three the property is conveyed to female members of the family (wives or daughters), who needed the deeds so that the family property could pass to them, since according to Roman law they were not considered legal heirs (see Cotton 2002). The ostracon from Qumran is the first deed of gift found in the Land of Israel in which the recipient is a man.

An ostracon with the inscription 'Eleazar son of Yeshua *ha-borit*' (the soapmaker), found in the Khirbet Qumran excavations conducted by Yitzhak Magen and Yuval Peleg, was published in 2006.[42] In 2007 an inscription from the antiquities market was published. Although it is written in ink on stone and not on parchment, its content and date (late first century BC) indicate that it should be studied together

---

[37] See *ATS Koinonia* 37 (67) (January 2005) 4. According to this publication, this fragment had been recently donated to the Seminary by a private collector. Its ownership can be traced back to the Kando family. We are grateful to Dr. Gavriel Barkai of Bar-Ilan University for giving us a copy of this publication.

[38] This article deals with fragments of which photographs appeared in the catalogues; but some are colour photographs that are hard to decipher, while others lack a scale.

[39] On an important ostracon used for scribal exercises at Qumran, see also *DJD* 36:509–12. On another inscription found at Qumran that may have been carved into an Iron Age weight, see H. Eshel 2001a.

[40] This interpretation is based on the description found in the *Rule of the Community*: 'If fate decrees that he approach the company of the Community, following the decision of the priests and the majority of the members of their covenant, his property and also his wages shall be handed over to the overseer of the revenues of the Many; but it shall be inscribed to his credit, and shall not be spent to the profit of the Many' (1QS VI 18–20).

[41] See primarily Yardeni 1997; Nebe 1999; Qimron 2003, and Cross' reply to those proposals, *DJD* 36:505–7.

[42] Magen and Peleg 2006, 72. On the manufacture of borax in the caves near Khirbet Qumran, see Amar 1998a.

with the Qumran scrolls. The inscription is a religious text, written in 87 lines in two columns, presumably found east of the Dead Sea. The speaker in this text is the angel Gabriel, and the text is designated 'The Vision of Gabriel'.[43]

C. Bar Kokhba Period Texts Published Since 1984

In 1985, Joseph Patrich published inscriptions that had been found in a cistern in a cave in a rock shelf on the northern slope of Naḥal Michmas (Wadi Suweinit). The cistern is adjacent to a ritual bath carved into this rock shelf. The caves seem to have been carved out between 159 and 152 BC, when Jonathan the Hasmonaean made his headquarters there (1 Macc. 9.73). Inside the cistern there are inscriptions and drawings made with a carbonized stick. These include illustrations of seven-branched candelabra, a five-pointed star with smaller five-pointed stars inside it, and two lines with the Hebrew alphabet: the letters from ʾalep to mem are preserved in the first line, while the second line has the entire alphabet. Beneath the star there is an Aramaic inscription, translated 'Joezer was uprooted, the guards entered'. According to Patrich, Joezer wrote this graffito after he was hurt when Roman legionaries were about to enter his hiding place in the cistern, at the farthest edge of the cave complex. Even though Patrich found the spouts of four jars typical of the Bar Kokhba period in the cave complex, palaeographical reasons led him to date the inscription to the time of the First Jewish Revolt (Patrich 1985). In early 1998, coins and other relics of the Bar Kokhba era were found in a cave on the southern slope of Naḥal Michmas, opposite the cave complex with Patrich's cistern. After comparing the forms of the letters in the cistern inscriptions with other documents found in the Judaean Desert, we proposed dating the cistern inscriptions to the Bar Kokhba Revolt rather than to the First Revolt (Eshel, Zissu, and Frumkin 1998).

After Yadin's death in 1984 it came to light that he had acquired from Kando fragments of three documents from the Bar Kokhba period. One of these is a bilingual 'double' papyrus text. On the inside it was written in Aramaic, while the surviving portions of the text on the outside were written in Hebrew. The other two documents are in Greek. Yadin also had a photograph of a fourth document, a loan contract written in Hebrew on parchment. Yadin did not buy this document, which remained in Kando's possession.

Two years after Yadin's death, Magen Broshi and Elisha Qimron published the bilingual papyrus (Broshi and Qimron 1986; DJD 27:26–37). This document, which is a deed of sale of a house, begins, '... of [the month of] Adar in the third year of the freedom of Israel by Shimon son of Kosiba the prince of Isr[ael in the villa]ge of Baru...' The seller was named Yehonatan son of Eli, and the buyer was Shaul son of Harshah.[44] The property changed hands for thirty-six dinars, which seems to be a very low price, reflecting the grim economic conditions during the Second Revolt (see H. Eshel 2003c).

In the spring of 1986 the first season of excavations in a small cave west of Jericho was carried out. Fragments of five papyrus documents were found there (DJD 36:3–113). One of them should be dated to the fourth century BC (P.Jericho 1). The inner side of this Aramaic document contains a list of persons who had borrowed money. The owner of the document had lent money—a total of 21 shekels—to more than a dozen individuals. On the back of the papyrus are the sums paid by the borrowers (the total comes to not quite 13 shekels, leaving them with a debt of slightly more than 8 shekels). The cave was

[43] Yardeni and Elitzur 2007, Bar-Asher 2009; Henze 2011; Elgvin 2014.

[44] Another document dated to Adar of the third year of the Bar Kokhba Revolt, written by the same scribe, was published by Milik in 1954. In that document, too, the sale price was very low. Kefar Baru is evidently to be located east of the Dead Sea, at Minaat el-Hassan, above the hot springs of Wadi Hammamat, about five kilometres northwest of Machaerus. This makes it likely that both documents derive from a refuge cave east of the Dead Sea, not identified by archaeologists.

named 'Avior Cave', after one of the names mentioned in this document. The other four documents found in this cave are from the Bar Kokhba period—two in Aramaic (P.Jericho 2–3) and two in Greek (P.Jericho 4–5). The Aramaic documents seem to be a loan contract and a deed of sale. The two Greek documents are also deeds of sale, one for real estate and the other for seed.

One of the Greek documents purchased by Yadin is a declaration of assets by one Simonos, made in December AD 127 as part of the land census ordered by the procurator of the Province of Arabia, Titus Aninius Sextius Florentinus (*DJD* 27:181–94). This document is quite similar to the declaration filed by Babatha daughter of Shimon during the same land census (P.Yadin 16). Like Babatha, Simonos lived in Mehoza, near Zoara, at the southern shore of the Dead Sea. Also like Babatha, he filed his declaration in Rabbat-Moab (modern a-Rabba). It seems likely that the two documents were written on the same day (in December). The declaration indicates that Simonos and his brother Jonathan were partners in a date orchard. Later, Simonos was identified as the first husband of Salome Komaise, daughter of Levi, which means that this document had been part of her archive, found by the Bedouin in the Cave of the Letters.

In 1994, Magen Broshi and Elisha Qimron published the document of which only a photograph had been found in Yadin's files (XHev/Se 49, see Broshi and Qimron 1994; *DJD* 27:121–22). This document was written in Hebrew on parchment in 'Kislev, year two of the redemption of Israel by Shimon son of Kosiba'. In it, one Yehosef son of Hananiah acknowledges that he is borrowing four dinars, equivalent to one tetradrachma, from Judah son of Judah. At the bottom of the document are the signatures of the borrower and of three witnesses. The fact that they went to the extreme of writing this document on parchment (which was more expensive than papyrus) for a loan of only one tetradrachma, and that three witnesses affixed their names to it, is evidence of the harsh economic conditions prevailing in the time and place of the loan. This document, acquired from Kando, is currently on display at the Hecht Museum at the University of Haifa.

The second Greek document that Yadin purchased was first published by Hannah Cotton in 1991. This is a three-line papyrus fragment, it too contains a declaration of assets as part of the census decreed by Titus Aninius Sextius Florentinus. In 1993, Cotton noticed that another fragment of the same declaration was part of the Seiyal collection at the Rockefeller Museum. The latter is shaped like a capital L; the Yadin fragment fits into it perfectly. From the Rockefeller fragment it turned out that the declaration had been made by someone whose father's name ended in -*LWS* and that it was submitted in April of AD 127, not December. Two years later, Cotton realized that the declaration had been filed by Salome Komaise, the daughter of Levi's brother, and hence that it must have come from the Cave of the Letters along with the rest of her archive (XHev/Se 61, see *DJD* 27:174–80).

In 1993, the Israel Antiquities Authority launched Operation Scroll to survey caves in the northern portion of the Judaean Desert before the Jericho area was handed over to the Palestinian Authority. As part of the effort, the caves on the ridge west of Jericho ('Ketef Jericho') were scoured again. Because the documents found in the Avior Cave in 1986 had been buried in a terrace built in the entrance to the cave and in a crack in the cave floor, it was decided to investigate whether the monks who lived in these caves during the Mamluk era had removed most of the dirt from the Avior Cave, as documents had been found only in the terrace and the crack in the floor. In excavations conducted below the lower entrance of the Avior Cave, fragments of fourteen economic papyri were unearthed. Four small fragments can be dated to the fourth century BC (P.Jericho 6); the rest are from the time of the Bar Kokhba Revolt, including five in Aramaic (P.Jericho 7; 8; 12; 13; 15), four evidently in Hebrew (P.Jericho 9; 10; 11; 14), and four in Greek (P.Jericho 16–19).[45] In 1993, the right-hand part of the document found inside the cave in 1986 (P.Jericho 2) was found below the entrance to the cave. The newly found fragment clarified that the document was not a loan contract, but a deed of sale in which the purchaser pledged to pay the

[45] For the official publication of the documents from the Avior Cave, see *DJD* 38:3–113.

balance of his debt to the seller. The date formulas in four of the documents from the Avior Cave cite the name of the ruler. In P.Jericho 7 this is, 'on the twenty-fifth of Tevet [year] three [of] Domitian C[aesar]': the third year of Domitian's reign was AD 85. In P.Jericho 9 we find, '[in] the twenty-fourth of our lord [A]grippa': which means that this document, too, dates from AD 84/5. The date of the document is based on the fact that Nero awarded Agrippa II 'the town of Julias in Perea [Transjordan; *i.e.*, east of Jericho] with fourteen villages around it' (*Antiquities* 20.159). P.Jericho 13 seems to have been written in AD 116, in the 'eighteenth year of Trajan Caes[ar]'. P.Jericho 16, a Greek document dated May AD 128, refers to Hadrian. It deals with the supply of agricultural produce to a Roman military unit (on this document, see also Haensch 2001).

A year later, Haggai Misgav published a fragment of a bilingual (Aramaic and Greek) document owned by the Hecht Museum at the University of Haifa, evidently to be dated to the eighth year of the Province of Arabia, *i.e.* AD 114. It seems likely that this document was brought to one of the Judaean Desert caves at the end of the Bar Kokhba Revolt (*DJD* 28:223–24).

During the first half of the 1990s the Bedouin systematically robbed some 3,500 tombs in the cemetery at Khirbet Qazone, on the tongue of the Dead Sea. Here they found two Greek papyri, evidently from the second or third century AD, now belonging to the Moussaieff collection. One of them is a deed of sale that cites a Nabataean name (Politis 2006, esp. 216 note 6).

In a 1997 publication, Ada Yardeni connected a deed of sale for a plot of land, written in the late first or early second century AD, whose relatively intact upper part (now in the Musée de la Bible et Terre Sainte in Paris) had been published by Milik in 1957, with four other fragments from the lower half of the same document, kept with the documents from Wadi Murabbaʿat (designated Mur 26). This indicates that this deed was found in Wadi Murabbaʿat (*DJD* 27:124–29).

In November 2002, a cave at the En Gedi oasis (the Har Yishai Cave) was surveyed and excavated. The artifacts discovered included pottery, a stone vessel, a dozen arrowheads, and eleven bronze coins that had been restruck by the Bar Kokhba administration (see Porat, Eshel, and Frumkin 2006; idem 2007a). Fragments of two Greek documents were also found; one, a deed of sale for a plot of land, and the other evidently a letter (Cohen 2006).

In the summer of 2004, Bedouin of the Rashaidah tribe found four fragments of a scroll in a tiny cave in Naḥal Arugot, along with pottery from the time of the Bar Kokhba Revolt. The surviving fragments of this scroll contain verses from Leviticus 23–24 (Eshel, Baruchi, and Porat 2006). One of the fragments consists of the upper margin of the scroll, two others contained parts of two columns that can be joined together. Based on these remains, we could calculate the width of the two columns and ascertain that there were 36 lines per column. Before the discovery of these fragments, fourteen Bar Kokhba-era scrolls were known, including passages from the other four books of the Pentateuch. The fragments from Naḥal Arugot are the first representing Leviticus.[46] The text is identical to the Masoretic Text, except for the word *sukkot,* written in the long orthography (with a *waw* between the *kaf* and the *tav*), whereas in the Masoretic text it is written defectively (no *waw*).

In 2009 the Israeli authorities seized a deed written in Hebrew mixed with Aramaic on papyrus with a complete text of fifteen lines, dated to 'year four after the destruction of the House of Israel'. Since the script is typical of the second century, the deed is written four years after the crushing of the Bar Kokhba Revolt, *i.e.* AD 140 (Eshel, Eshel, and Yardeni 2009). The deed refers to locations south of Hebron (Bet Amar, Upper Anav, and Aristobuliah), and may have been found recently by the Bedouin in the Cave of the Tetradrachm south east of Hebron, where two other documents (XḤev/Se 9 and XḤev/Se 69) were found. The new document deals with properties that the widow Miriam daughter of

---

[46] For the hypothesis that the scrolls from the time of the Bar Kokhba Revolt found in the Judaean Desert caves indicate that they were read for the last time at Passover AD 135, see Baruchi 2005.

Ya'acov had inherited after succeeding her late husband Shaul bar Shimon as heir, and which could be sold by her brother-in-law Avshalom bar Shimon. The discovery of the texts mentioned here suggests that there is still a chance of finding additional scrolls and documents in the Judaean Desert caves.

D. Fragments of Five Scrolls of Unknown Provenance

In the period 2000–2009 fragments of three biblical scrolls in private ownership were published. Their provenance—Qumran or the Bar Kokhba-era refuge caves—is unknown.[47] All three are written in a script typical of the first century AD; the text of two of them is identical to the Masoretic Text. The first fragment, designated XJosh and belonging to The Schøyen Collection, was published in 2000 and is republished in the present volume as Mur/ḤevJosh. This fragment preserves parts of two columns from Joshua 1–2 (*DJD* 36:231–39). The second scroll is a copy of Judges (XJudg). Its state is more complicated, since at least seven surviving fragments, scattered in four different collections, are known. One fragment contains verses from Judg 1, another fragment verses from Judg 3, and the last five fragments belong to the same column with parts of Judg 4.[48] The fact that all seven fragments only surfaced after 1990 suggests that the remnants of this scroll may have been found by Bedouin in the 1980s. Of the third scroll three fragments that join together were published without authorization in 2003 (Puech 2003b). They are republished in the present volume. This text preserves parts of two columns from Lev 26. Puech argued that this text should be dated to after AD 70, and thus probably originated in a Bar Kokhba cave. Also MS 4612/1 (Joel), published in this volume, may derive from a Bar Kokhba cave. There are reasons to suggest that XJudg, and perhaps other scrolls as well, may have been found relatively recently in one or more Judaean Desert caves. Unfortunately, Israeli archeological institutions have been unable to locate this cave (or caves). In 2008 James Charlesworth published on the web an image of a scroll of Deut 27.4–6 that includes the Samaritan commandment to build an altar on Mt. Gerizim.[49] He dated the script to the mid-first century BC. The fragment, whose authenticity has been questioned, is claimed to come from Cave 4, which seems questionable to us. This fragment belongs to Azusa Pacific University.

E. Epilogue

This survey has shown that we owe a deep debt of gratitude to the curators of the Rockefeller Museum, who between 1947 and 1965 managed to acquire most of the fragments found in the Judaean Desert and

---

[47] Editor's note: recent palaeographical and mineral analyses suggest a Bar Kokhba provenance for these three scrolls as well as Ḥev(?)Joel (see the respective text editions and the chapter by Kipp Davis p. 129).

[48] Two fragments of this scroll are in the Hecht Museum at the University of Haifa, a third is in The Schøyen Collection, the fourth and fifth belong to two different private collectors who wish to remain anonymous. The fragments owned by the Hecht Museum were published in 1994; see *DJD* 28:227–29. They were still unidentified in 2003 and were identified as parts of the Judges scroll only after the fragment from The Schøyen Collection, which included parts of Judges 4, was published. For the publication of that fragment, see *DJD* 28:231–33. For the identification of the first Hecht Museum fragment, which also has a part of Judges 4, as part of the same scroll, see H. Eshel 2003b. The second Hecht Museum fragment, which contains portions of verses from Judges 3, was identified as belonging to the same scroll by Puech, see Puech 2003a. Puech believes that this scroll came from Qumran, but there is no proof of this hypothesis. Later, Puech published a fourth fragment from the same scroll, with portions of Judges 1, see Puech 2006. For the publication of the last fragment, see Eshel, Eshel, and Broshi 2007.

[49] http://www.foundationjudaismchristianorigins.org/ftp/pages/dead-sea-scrolls/unpub/deuteronomy27-4b-6-frag.html, accessed 10 June, 2014.

bring them together in one place. It is only too easy to imagine what would have happened to the study of the Qumran scrolls had they been discovered after the Six-Day War. There is little doubt that in that case they would have been scattered all across the globe, making it impossible to piece them together and photograph them to the same scale.[50] Here I have surveyed what is known about the fate of the few fragments that were not acquired by the Rockefeller Museum. These were damaged over the years, also in the period when they were still in Kando's possession.[51] It seems that the time during which we can still retrieve information about these fragments is running out. Hence it is crucial to make every effort to acquire them, or at least to have them photographed before it is too late.[52]

I tend to believe that there is still a chance of finding scroll fragments in the Judaean Desert, perhaps even in the caves near Khirbet Qumran, adding the use of ground-penetrating radar.[53] I hope that the present review will encourage other scholars to conduct surveys and digs in the Judaean Desert caves, so that such documents can be discovered in a scientific dig and not through the plunder expeditions that the Bedouin continue to conduct there.

---

[50] In 1985 looters found about 1600 Aramaic ostraca from the fourth century BC, at Khirbet el-Kôm in the southern Judaean Hills. These ostraca have been scattered all over the world, including private collections in London, Zurich, New York, Jerusalem, and Sydney. In some cases, fragments of a single document are in different collections. Sometimes inscriptions from two sides of the same sherd have been published as two separate documents, because the scholars worked on the basis of photographs and never saw the actual artefacts. It is easy to imagine the fate of the study of the Dead Sea Scrolls if the fragments found in Cave 4 had found their way onto the international antiquities market. For an article summarizing the importance of the Khirbet el-Kôm ostraca, including a list of most of the scholarly literature on this subject, see Lemaire 2006.

[51] I will note some egregious cases in which Kando damaged fragments that passed through his hands. The people of Athanasius Samuel searched Cave 1 in November 1948. According to Allegro, Kando at one stage was afraid of intervention by Jordanian authorities and buried large pieces of parchment on his Bethlehem property, pieces that were reduced to lumps of worthless glue (Allegro 1964, 21). Trever corrects the timing of this event to the aftermath of the November 1948 looting (Trever 1977, 123, 132, 150; 231–32, note 8). According to the editors of 4QInstruction, when Kando brought the largest surviving fragments of this work (4Q416 2) to the Rockefeller Museum, he stuck it to his body to conceal it from inspection at a police roadblock. When it reached the museum it was soaked in sweat that damaged it (*DJD* 34:73). A similar fate involved parts of column 18 of the Greek Translation of the Twelve Minor Prophets from the Cave of Horror (8ḤevXIIgr), which were kept by a Bedouin under the lining of his keffiyeh, a situation which did not increase the legibility of those fragments (see *DJD* 8:2). Kando divided one of the Greek texts from the Wadi Seiyal collection into two parts, evidently because the person who purchased the fragment, which ultimately reached Yigael Yadin, did not have enough money for the entire document. Small fragments of the *Temple Scroll* were glued together with postage stamps. As already mentioned, one of the original parchments of the head phylactery bought by Yadin fell apart before it was purchased.

[52] Based on the information available to us, as of 2009 there are still more than forty Qumran texts in private hands. This number includes the thirteen fragments we have published (see E. Eshel and H. Eshel 2005 and 2007) and those published in the present volume. In 2007 the Shrine of the Book was offered sixteen fragments, but the offer was turned down.

[53] When Magen Broshi and I dug at Qumran in 2001, ground-penetrating radar allowed us to find a collapsed cave in the marl terrace. See H. Eshel and M. Broshi 2003; Kislev and Marmorstein 2003. I hope that with appropriate equipment it will be possible to discover similar Qumran caves with scroll fragments in the future.

III

Texts and Artefacts from the Judaean Desert in The Schøyen Collection: An Overview

Torleif Elgvin

A. Overview

The Schøyen Collection of texts from the Judaean Desert comprises around thirty manuscripts, reaching back to the Second Temple period and the Bar Kokhba Revolt. Most of the texts published in this volume are small fragments of scrolls containing 'biblical' verses or passages,[1] while some seem to be excerpted or reworked versions of biblical traditions.

Three manuscripts belong to scrolls with large margins, which would fit Emanuel Tov's category of *de luxe* editions (Tov 2004, 125–29): MS 4611 (Lev), MS 2713 (Josh), and MS 4612/1 (Joel). These scrolls, written in an ornamental late Herodian script, have large margins and columns that were both high and narrow.[2] Three fragments derive from small-sized scrolls: MS 4612/4 (GenMiniature), MS 5441 (Ruth), and MS 5095/7 (Fragment with Text from 4QCommGen A).

There are fragments of two Aramaic scrolls: small fragments of the *Genesis Apocryphon* (MS 1926/2) and a small piece of a hitherto unknown text designated Eschatological Fragment (MS 4612/3).

Small fragments of the *Rule of Blessings* (1QSb, MS 1909), the *Temple Scroll* (11QT[a]), and a text from *Commentary on Genesis A* (MS 5095/7) represent compositions related to the *Yaḥad*.

The small papyrus fragments from Wadi ed-Daliyeh are from another time period. These are financial documents written in the city of Samaria in the mid-fourth century BC.[3]

Apart from the small Schøyen pieces of 1QDan[a,b], 1QS, 1QSb, 1QapGen, 1QIsa[a], and 11QT[a], only one fragment, MS 5439/1, has been identified with a scroll published in *DJD*, viz. 4QRP[b] (4Q364).

Two fragments are written on coarse and poorly prepared leather (MS 2713 [Josh], MS 4612/1 [Joel]), and this has accelerated the process of deterioration. Most of the fragments are written on the hair side of parchment.[4] On fragments from such scrolls sections of the tanned upper layer are prone to flaking off, leaving less ink and fewer letters for modern researchers to detect. The grain structure of the hide in these parchments can often be discerned, but to varying degrees depending on the different levels of scraping under tension they experienced in their preparation. The Wadi ed-Daliyeh documents are written on papyrus.

---

[1] For pragmatic reasons we will use the anachronistic term 'biblical' without quotation marks in the continuation. For the same reasons the text editions are sorted into the three traditional categories: Pentateuch, Prophets, Writings. Some of the Schøyen fragments are not included in this volume, but will appear in future publications.

[2] These conventions may point to specific scribal milieus in first and second century Judaea (see the chapter by Kipp Davis p. 129). These three scrolls and XJudg were more probably found in Murabbaʿat or Naḥal Ḥever than the Qumran caves.

[3] In this volume we use the designations BC and AD in line with the convention in other publications of texts from The Schøyen Collection.

[4] The preparation of ancient parchment involved application of de-hairing liquour or dough, scraping, drying under tension, and a light tanning of the upper surface. Neither the *DJD* series nor Tov 2004 distinguish between leather and parchment.

Among the artefacts we have the privilege to present fresh analyses of a 'scroll jar' with a surprising place of origin. Two independent physical tests of the clay suggest that the jar was made in the northern Negev and at a certain time was brought to the Dead Sea region. Its cylindrical shape is typical of Qumran, and its material characteristics suggest a long-time sojourn in a cave, perhaps Cave 1 or Cave 2.

Tests performed on the *Temple Scroll* wrapper and cord confirm the testimony of the Bedouin that this scroll was found inside a jar in Cave 11. A C-14 test of the wrapper may suggest that the deposit in Cave 11 happened after AD 70. A palm fibre tool (one of three of its kind from the Qumran caves) reported to have been found in Cave 11 contained remnants of ink and some other substances.

A miniature incense altar and inkwell, reported by Kando to be surface finds by a Bedouin at Khirbet Qumran, were more likely found in Naḥal Ḥever, and brought there by refugees from En Gedi or Mahoza under the Bar Kokhba Revolt. The inkwell, one of three extant inkwells from the same workshop in the first or early second century points to a remarkable quality of Nabataean workmanship.

B. Provenance and Designation of Fragments

A number of fragments from the Judaean Desert have surfaced in the last fifteen years. During this period The Schøyen Collection has acquired fragments from around 15 different scrolls.[5] Since 2009 Azusa Pacific University has acquired fragments from five scrolls,[6] Southwestern Baptist Theological Seminary nine,[7] a further twelve belong to the Green Collection of Oklahoma City,[8] and three fragments of Amos 7.17–8.1 to the Lanier Theological Library, Houston (Patterson 2012, 23–37; Tov 2014). While the Schøyen fragments have been acquired over a longer period of time than those in the other collections, all the recently surfaced fragments are asserted by the vendors to have passed through the hands of the renowned antiquities dealer Khalil Iskander Shahin, or 'Kando'. All, with the exception of XJudg and the minor ones from Wadi ed-Daliyeh, are claimed to have come from Qumran, most probably from Cave 4.[9]

There is some controversy concerning the provenance of the recently surfaced fragments. Eibert Tigchelaar notes that only one fragment has been identified with previously published Cave 4 manuscripts (MS 5439/1, 4Q364 8a), and that the proportion of non-biblical texts is remarkably different from Cave 4. He further notes that most of these fragments are written in crude scribal hands, different from most Cave 4 scrolls.[10] These features have led Tigchelaar to question the asserted Qumran provenance, and to ask if many of the new fragments could come from an unknown cave discovered by the Bedouin.

---

[5] Altogether around 105 fragments including 29 small ones from Wadi ed-Daliyeh.

[6] Azusa Pacific University holds fragments of Lev 10.4–7; Deut 8.2–4; 27.4–6; Hab 2.1–3(?); Dan 5.14–15.

[7] In 2010–11 the seminary acquired fragments containing Exod 23.8–10; Lev 20.24; 18.28–30; Deut 9.25–10.1; 12.11–14 (two scrolls); Ps 22.3–12; Dan 6.22–24; 7.18–19 (papyrus), an unidentified fragment with only few letters preserved, as well as a previously published fragment of 11QpalaeoLev[a]. See Patterson 2012, 28–37.

[8] The Green Collection includes fragments from Genesis through Numbers, as well as fragments of Jeremiah, Ezekiel, Jonah, Micah, Daniel, and Nehemiah; a Psalm and a fragment of 4QInstruction. At the Forth Worth exhibition in 2012 the Green Collection put on display fragments of Num 8.4–5; Jer 23.6–9; Ezek 28.22; Jonah 4.2–5; Dan 10.18–20; and Neh 2.13–16 (Loveless 2012, 105).

[9] Ira Rabin's mineral analysis (see below p. 61) and late palaeographical dates suggest that around eight Schøyen fragments have a provenance different from Cave 4.

[10] The appearance of the scripts in a number of Schøyen fragments exhibits a conspicuous nonuniformity in letter sizes, forms, and ductus, in line spacing and word spacing. This is true for MS 4612/5 (Num), MS 5214/1 (Deut 6), MS 5214/2 (Deut 32), MS 5480 (1 Sam 5), MS 5233/1 (2 Sam 20), MS 5233/2 (Ps), MS 5440 (1 Kgs), MS 5441 (Ruth). Cf. Ada Yardeni's remark on the recently published Lanier copy of Amos 7.17–8.1, 'The writing utensil was worn because of which the shapes of the letters are not flawless (unlike most scrolls written with carefully designed utensils)' (in Tov 2014, 5).

He cautions against labelling fragments prematurely with '4Q' or '11Q' designations (personal communication, cf. Tigchelaar 2012, 209–14).

It should be noted that unlike the other private collections The Schøyen Collection includes a number of non-biblical texts from the Judaean Desert. Among these are Eschatological Fragment ar (MS 4612/3), Fragment with Text from 4QCommGen A (MS 5095/7), and Ḥev(?)Unidentified Fragment (MS 5095/5). The fragment with text from *Commentary on Genesis A* and the fragment of 4QRP[b] represent links to Cave 4 or the *Yaḥad*. Furthermore a couple of biblical texts seem to contain features compatible with the so-called Qumran scribal practice. The biblical texts published here reflect a wide range of textual traditions. While the sample size is small, this textual variety is analogous to what is reflected in the biblical scrolls from the Qumran caves.

None of the fragments (or artefacts) published here were found by archaeologists, and remain unprovenanced. Nevertheless, there is no reason to doubt that the small fragments of 1QDan[a,b], 1QS, 1QSb, 1QapGen, 1QIsa[a], and 11QT[a] were indeed found by the Bedouin in Cave 1 and Cave 11. While Ira Rabin's analysis found no evidence that all the texts published here were not written on ancient skin from the Judaean Desert, we cannot at this stage rule out the possibility that some of the fragments contain modern ink.[11] We have noted the exceptional feature that even small fragments in The Schøyen Collection and the American collections[12] preserve textual variants suggested by the editors of *BHK* and *BHS*, and some of them follow line-for-line and word-for-word the layout in previously published text editions. In his palaeographical analysis Michael Langlois notes many 'hesitant hands', and some of them mix earlier and later scribal features. Some of these features may cast doubt on the authenticity of a fragment.[13]

The fragments in this volume are designated by their classification number in The Schøyen Collection (*e.g.* MS 1909). This is followed by a reference to the most probable place of discovery, as '4Q(?)', '11Q(?)', 'Ḥev(?)', or 'Mur/Ḥev',[14] and the name of the composition. Tigchelaar, editor of the forthcoming Brill series *The Dead Sea Scrolls Editions* (*DSSE*), has suggested numbering those fragments that do not appear in either the 1994 Reed catalogue or the main Israeli and Jordanian collections with designations such as DSS F.101=DSS F.Gen1, DSS F.102=DSS F.RP1, etc. In this series the Dead Sea Scrolls fragments from The Schøyen Collection are numbered DSS F.101–DSS F.136. These corresponding designations are included at the beginning of each text edition.

C. Mineral Analysis

In October 2012 Ira Rabin conducted XRF and FTIR analysis of the Schøyen fragments to analyze the mineral components present in the skin and papyri (see p. 61). The results show that a few fragments possibly survive from scrolls that may have been deposited in a natural cave in the cliffs, not a cave in the marl terrace such as Cave 4. One of them, MS 4612/3 (EschatFrg ar), has phosphate deposits that

[11] Christopher Rollston points out that the fact that the material is ancient in no way guarantees that the text written on it is authentic. See *i.e.* http://www.rollstonepigraphy.com/?p=685 (accessed 22 May, 2014).

[12] We find some of the same features in fragments in the Southwestern Baptist Theological Seminary, Azusa, and Lanier collections. Details of the fragments in the Green Collection are not available.

[13] Rollston considers palaeographical inconsistencies as a significant cause for doubt on the authenticity of texts (Rollston 2005).

[14] Two biblical texts are designated 'Mur/Ḥev'. While other Bar Kokhba locations cannot be excluded, a variety of factors suggest that these texts were removed from Murabbaʿat or Ḥever; these are sites discovered by the Bedouin in 1951–52, close in time to their discovery of Cave 4. Ḥev(?)Joel is another Bar Kokhba text, but the mineral analysis rules out Murabbaʿat as place of discovery.

might be attributed to the bat guano from Cave 11. As the characteristics of the majority of the fragments are compatible with a sojourn in a cave in the marl terrace, these are potentially texts deriving from Cave 4.[15] Two fragments that contain late Herodian scripts, MS 4612/1 (Joel) and MS 5439/2 (a small fragment with remnants of a stichometric text) lack the aragonite that characterizes the Qumran cave environments; an absence that points to the Bar Kokhba caves as the most likely places of discovery.

Rabin's analysis of the fragments gives valuable information about the process of scroll manufacture in antiquity. The results indicate that a number of fragments, including the blank protective sheet of the *Genesis Apocryphon*, were from scrolls that had been prepared in water containing lead. This is the case for MS 5480 (1 Sam 5), MS 5440 (1 Kgs), MS 5214/2 (Deut 32), MS 5233/2 (Ps), MS 4612/11 (Prov), and MS 4612/9 (Jer).[16] This feature might point to sites with water pipes containing lead as places where these skins and scrolls were prepared. In the fragment of 4QRP[b] substantial amounts of lead were identified in the ink, but not in the parchment. This could be explained by the use of water pipes containing lead already in the second century BC, or by the use of a lead vessel to prepare the ink.[17]

Most of the fragments in this volume do not exhibit mineral traces of water sources close to the Dead Sea (such as those at Ein Feshka). This strongly indicates that these fragments derive from scrolls manufactured outside the Dead Sea region. This is true for MS 4611 (Lev), XJudg, MS 5214/1 (Deut 6), MS 5214/2 (Deut 32), MS 5233/1 (2 Sam 22), MS 4612/9 (Jer), MS 4612/1 (Joel), MS 5233/2 (Ps), MS 5441 (Ruth), and MS 4612/3 (EschatFrg ar). Thus most of the scrolls represented in The Schøyen Collection were brought to Qumran from elsewhere, if they were indeed found there. According to Rabin none of the Schøyen fragments showed features matching them with fragments from Murabba'at in the Reed Collection that she had studied earlier. However, she emphasizes that the sampling was not exhaustive, and that the results from some fragments prevent forming any conclusions about their provenance.

D. Date of the Fragments

The Schøyen fragments from the Judaean Desert stem from different periods. Langlois has conducted a palaeographical analysis that appears as a separate chapter (p. 79). As for the dating of the fragments, his results are condensed in the following table together with previously dated scrolls:

Table 1. *Diachronic listing of palaeographical dates assigned to Judaean Desert fragments in The Schøyen Collection*

Date	Scrolls
Second century BC, second half	MS 5439/1 (4QRP[b])
First century BC, second quarter	MS 1909 (1QSb)
Mid-first century BC	MS 4612/11 (Prov)
	MS 5480 (1 Sam 5)
First century BC, third quarter	MS 4612/9 (Jer)

---

[15] MS 2713 (Josh) and MS 2861 (XJudg) may be exceptions. These scrolls were published under the designations XJosh and XJudg in *DJD*. William Kando had no information about the origin of the scroll of XJudg, present in eight fragments in four collections. Ira Rabin's analysis of these two scrolls did not provide results sufficient for any conclusion about mineral environment. The late date of these two scrolls as well as of MS 4611 (Lev) and MS 4612/1 (Joel) suggests a different place of discovery than Qumran.

[16] Rabin notes that (apart from the 1QapGen protective sheet) lead contamination in the post-discovery period cannot be excluded, but this would be highly unlikely.

[17] Lead is not found naturally in Israel. However, water pipes containing lead have been found in a few ancient sites. Langlois has redated the script of 4QRP[b] to the late second century BC (see p. 81).

	MS 5233/2 (Ps)
First century BC, second half	MS 4612/5 (Num)
	MS 4612/4 (GenMin)
First century BC, third quarter	MS 5233/1 (2 Sam 20)
First century BC, last quarter	MS 5095/7 (CommGen A)
End of first century BC	MS 4612/3 (EschatFrg ar)
	MS 5440 (1 Kgs)
	MS 1926/2 (1QapGen)
	MS 1926/4b (1QDan[b])
Turn of the era	First sheet of 11QT[a]
Early first century AD	MS 5214/1 (Deut 6)
Mid-first century AD	MS 5439/2 (Ḥev(?)Unidentified Fragment)
	MS 5441 (Ruth)
	MS 1926/4a (1QDan[a])[18]
First Century AD, third quarter	MS 5214/2 (Deut 32)
	MS 4612/1 (Joel)
First Century AD, second half or early second Century	MS 4611 (Lev)
	MS 2861 (XJudg)
End of first or early second Century AD	MS 2713 (Josh)

Fragments from about 15 scrolls derive from the period when there was without a doubt a sectarian settlement at Qumran.[19] Some of them may have been copied there.

E. Plan of Text Editions

Each edition follows the same basic structure:

1) *Physical description*: a short description of the extant features for each fragment, in conversation with Ira Rabin's mineral analyses.

2) *Palaeography*: dates for each fragment are provided, and readers are referred to the full palaeographical analysis conducted by Langlois for comprehensive descriptions. In a number of instances we provide additional information supplied by Yardeni, who examined photographs of most of the fragments in 2010.

3) *Transcription of the fragment with notes on readings*: each fragment is transcribed in isolation from any predetermined literary context. In an effort to present only what the editors see preserved of each text, we have prioritized a minimalistic approach at this stage. Uncertain letters are here indicated by open circles.

4) *Parallel texts from the Judaean Desert*: wherever we have been able to identify the text of a fragment we follow with a short survey of other copies of the same composition from the Judaean Desert and a short presentation of parallel texts.

[18] The date for 1QDan[a] is derived from Trever 1965, the date for 1QDan[b] is our own.

[19] In this book the term 'sectarian' is used to mean 'related to the *Yaḥad*'. We distinguish between the settlement (and scrolls) of Qumran and the *Yaḥad* as a wider sociological entity, represented in different geographical locations. See Elgvin 2005; Schofield 2009, 42–67, 266–81. Jodi Magness (2002, 64–65) dates the establishment of the sectarian settlement to the early first century BC, Jan Gunneweg pushes the date on to the late 40s BC (Gunneweg and Balla 2010, 58–59), while Joan Taylor (2012, 250–61) argues that the sectarians took over a Hasmonaean stronghold in the early years of Herod's reign, around 34 BC.

5) *Reconstruction of the text with translation, notes and comments*: at this stage we attempt to reconstruct the text in conversation with other textual witnesses. Ink traces from badly damaged letters that under point 3) appeared as open circles in the transcription, may here be identified as letters qualified by supralinear circlets. All texts have been digitally reconstructed in an effort to suggest the most plausible readings for the many *lacunae*. Our translation of biblical texts usually takes the JPS edition as point of departure. Differences between the text in question and the Masoretic version are indicated by italics in the translation. Alternative readings are provided in the apparatus, and orthographic variants are indicated within parentheses. Hebrew and Greek readings in the apparatus and in the notes and comments are presented unvocalized and unaccented in an attempt to avoid unnecessary anachronisms. Each edition includes plates, both of the isolated fragment and the graphical reconstructions represented in the transcriptions.

Following a complete presentation and discussion of the individual readings both extant and reconstructed for each fragment, there is some reflection on their textual character. At this stage the opportunity is taken to compare the fragment to the principal versions of the biblical text in 𝔐 (Masoretic text),[20] 𝔊 (Old Greek), 𝔪 (Samaritan Pentateuch),[21] as well as other early witnesses. The editors have remarked on the place of some of the fragments in the history of textual or literary development for the biblical book in question.

F. New Photographs and Methods for Reconstruction

The text editions presented here benefit from the availability of new, high quality infrared photographs, first made by Bjørn Rørslett in 2007, then by Bruce Zuckerman and his team in 2011.[22] We are greatly indebted to these coworkers. The editors have conducted microscopic examinations of the fragments, and some of the editions include images captured by a Dino-Lite digital microscope. All the images of the texts included in this volume were photographed at 1200 dpi, and then thoroughly examined in Photoshop CS6 v.13.0 x 64 using new techniques for determining their measurements, placement, and script. In addition, RTI captures of all the fragments were frequently consulted for providing more detailed information about their surfaces and structures. To secure the precision of our reconstructions, careful attention has been paid to line spacing, letter sizes, style of script and the arrangement of texts in several instances to include various types of section markers. We have depended upon the appearance of letters and words from the individual fragments, which better accounts for variation in letter- and word-spaces.

[20] Tov now designates only Judaean Desert scrolls from find-sites other than Qumran as 'proto-Masoretic' (text identical with 𝔐). Those texts from Qumran with slight differences from 𝔐 are called '𝔐-like texts' (Tov 2012, 108). Different textual and literary approaches are represented in the processes that led to the development of proto-Masoretic and 𝔐-like scrolls (cf. Ulrich 1998, 85). As I see it their common bond is that such a scroll was chosen as 'master scroll' for each biblical book in temple circles some time in the late second temple period (thus Tov 2008, 175–84).

[21] One should note Tov's qualification of the anachronistic principle of sorting early texts according to closeness to later textual witnesses (Tov 2002, 152): 'The principle behind this classification is the recognition that all texts can be grouped according to the degree of closeness to the 𝔐, 𝔊, or 𝔪 without accepting the claim that these three texts are the central pillars (recensions, texts, text-types, etc.) of the biblical text... It may be unusual to classify ancient texts according to the degree of their closeness to later textual witnesses, certainly if these are medieval (𝔐 and 𝔪), but this comparison is necessary, since the base forms of these texts already existed in the last centuries before the turn of the era' (the underlined words were added in Tov's later edited version, Tov 2008, 144).

[22] A new series of photographs of the Schøyen fragments was taken by Bruce Zuckerman and his team in January 2011. This project was sponsored by Mark and Becky Lanier and the Lanier Theological Library, and we are indebted to their kind support. This series of photographs will be accessible on InscriptiFact after the publication of the present volume.

Word spaces can vary considerably in size from one manuscript to the next—in some cases they appear very small, with practically no separation between words, such as in 4QBer[a] (4Q286) and 4QM[a] (4Q491) frgs 1–3, 11 i. Most scrolls preserve space between words close-to-equalling a letter space, as in 1QS and 4QInstruction[b] (4Q416). A handful of texts were inscribed with very large spaces between words, often wider than just a single letter; compare 4QS[b] (4Q256) and 4QapocrJer C[b] (4Q387). Similarly, letters themselves will differ dramatically in size from one hand to another. This is especially the case with very wide letters—such as ʿayin, šin, and occasionally *bet*, and letters that are generally considered 'narrow', such as zayin, waw / yod, and medial and final *nun*. These variances will in turn require that reconstructions from one text to the next should follow as precisely as possible the particular conventions and techniques employed by the scribe in question.

This can be illustrated further from texts in the present volume. A number of the small fragments from The Schøyen Collection appear to have been inscribed by unpractised hands. In several instances this has resulted in little or no separation between words, such as in MS 5214/1 (Deut 6), MS 5480 (1 Sam 5), and possibly MS 5440 (1 Kgs). However, in some of these poorly penned texts the word separations are clear, such as in MS 4612/5 (Num) or MS 4612/11 (Prov). Also notice the difference in space that is occupied by the narrow *lamed* in MS 4612/9 (Jer), compared to significantly larger examples from MS 5214/1 (Deut 6) and MS 5441 (Ruth). Simply put, factoring in the precise spacing that each individual scribe employed in his own work is an essential component for the enterprise of reconstruction. When this sort of procedure for reconstruction is implemented, it is relatively certain—barring the presence of scribal errors, corrections, or elsewhere unattested section markers and dividers—that a good sense of the dimensions, and in some cases even various reading alternatives can be achieved.

In the editions that follow, the editors have depended upon the formation of individual letter and word-spaces extant on each fragment wherever possible, and reproduced these directly on the photographic plates in our efforts to provide the most plausible alignment of the fragments between the column margins, and the best possible readings. For example, the preserved portions of MS 5440 (1 Kgs) appears to align with 𝔐, but several attempts to reproduce the words in the *lacunae* to reflect 𝔐 proved impossible, because of awkward gaps in the reconstruction. Similarly, for MS 4612/1 (Joel) we have suggested an otherwise unattested expanded text that more accurately accounts for the available space in the *lacunae*, using the actual script and word-separators in this fragment in our reconstruction.

The reader will notice that in light of the small size of many of the fragments, only a handful of letters are preserved on some of them. As an example, for MS 5480 (1 Sam 5) only seven or eight letters are clearly visible. For most of the fragments the editors have depended upon some speculation in their reconstructions. In these instances we have attempted to match the hands as closely as possible with other fragments, based on the appearance of the overlapping letters. The introduction of letters from other fragments into the reconstructions are not intended to provide a precise, visual reproduction of the manuscripts themselves, but rather to supply accurate measurements of space that in turn bolster the precision of our readings. In such cases, the variation in size that might occur with an individual letter is on the factor of less than a single millimetre, which is assumed by the editors to be an acceptable range from which to produce close estimates for line lengths and hypothetical readings. Very occasionally, we have also attempted to repair badly damaged letters based on their extant traces. An inventory of the fragments appears below, which provides necessary details about the sources of unattested letters or repaired letters for the reconstructions in each.[23]

---

[23] The techniques employed herein are inspired by the detailed epigraphic and reconstructive work in Langlois' monograph (Langlois 2011). Most of the sources for reconstruction were other fragments within The Schøyen Collection, not restricted to those that appear in this volume.

Table 2. *Inventory of letters used in photographic reconstructions*

Fragment	Designation		Source
MS 4612/4	GenMiniature	כ	MS 4612/2
		ם	
		ע	8QMez
		ק	
MS 5439/1	4QRP^b (4Q364)		* 4QRP^b
MS 4612/5	Num	ה	MS 4612/2
		כ	
		ם	repaired
		נ	MS 4612/8
		ן	MS 4612/2
		ע	
		פ	MS 4612/2
		ק	repaired
		ת	MS 4612/2
MS 5214/1	Deut	ד	MS 5233/2
		ז	MS 4612/4
		כ	MS 4612/11
		ד	MS 5233/2
		ל	MS 4612/10
		ן	
		ע	
		פ	
		ר	
MS 5214/2	Deut	ה	MS 4612/9
		ו	
		ז	MS 4612/6
		כ	MS 4612/9
		מ	
		ן	
		ע	
		ס	MS 4611
		פ	MS 4612/10
		ר	MS 4612/9
		ת	
MS 2713	Josh		* MS 4611
MS 5480	1 Sam	ב	MS 4612/10
		ח	
		מ	MS 4612/9
		ם	MS 4612/5
		ן	MS 4612/10
		ס	MS 5233
		פ	MS 4612/10
		ת	MS 4612/9
MS 5233	2 Sam	ד	MS 4612/5
		ח	MS 4612/10

Fragment	Designation		Source
		ט	repaired
		כ	MS 4612/2
		מ	repaired
		ם	MS 4612/2
		נ	MS 4612/10
		ז	MS 4612/2
		פ	MS 4612/10
		צ	repaired
		ר	MS 4612/2
		ש	MS 5214/2
MS 5440	1 Kgs	ד	MS 5233/2
		ט	MS 4612/12
		כ	MS 5426
		ך	MS 5233/2
		ל	MS 5426
		ם	MS 4612/2
		ס	MS 4612/10
		פ	MS 4612/9
		ף	MS 4612/4
MS 4612/9	Jer	ג	MS 4611
		ד	MS 5233/2
		ס	MS 4611
		ק	MS 5214/2
MS 4612/1	Joel		* MS 2713
			* MS 4611
MS 5233/2	Ps	א	MS 5214/2
		ה	repaired
		ז	MS 4612/10
		צ	repaired
		ר	MS 4612/9
		ת	
MS 4612/11	Prov	ג	repaired
		ד	MS 4612/9
		ח	MS 4612/10
		ט	repaired
		ם	MS 5214/2
		ז	MS 4612/10
		ס	repaired
		פ	MS 4612/10
		ש	MS 5214/2
MS 5441	Ruth	ה	MS 4612/2
		ח	MS 4612/12
		ט	
		ם	MS 4612/9
		פ	MS 4612/10
		צ	MS 4612/11

Fragment	Designation		Source
		ק	MS 4612/2
		ר	MS 1909
		ת	MS 4612/2

IV

Material Analysis of the Fragments

Ira Rabin

A. Introduction

The International Qumran project conducted at the BAM Federal Institute for Materials Research and Testing in 2007–10 aimed at establishing an optimal methodology for an accurate characterization of the Dead Sea Scrolls to address such questions as archaeological provenance, origin, and attribution of fragments to a specific sheet (Rabin 2013). Using equipment of various degrees of complexity we have shown that part of the historic information stored in the material can be revealed by proper characterization of the material. The on-site investigation of the Dead Sea Scrolls fragments from The Schøyen Collection in October 2012 offered the first chance to test this methodology in a field study. For the first time, we used mobile and non-invasive technology exclusively, since we could not transport all of our laboratory equipment to Norway for this project. Moreover, besides the technical limitations dictated by the available equipment, we had to cope with limited time: it was impossible to perform the number of scans required for optimal characterization of over 30 fragments within the fourteen days available. Nevertheless this study presents an important step in the material analysis of the Dead Sea Scrolls, since the devices we used are easily transportable, well known, and easily accessible throughout the world.

Our set-up included a mobile μ-XRF spectrometer, a handheld FTIR spectrometer and a multispectral USB-microscope. The μ-XRF spectrometer (ARTAX, Bruker)—a mobile laboratory instrument with an interaction spot of 70μm—allowed us to obtain the elemental composition of the fragments by collecting spectra from line scans that provided statistically relevant numbers of measurements. In contrast to the XRF device, the mobile FTIR spectrometer (Exoscan, Agilent) has an interaction spot of approximately 5mm. This allowed only the identification of contaminants present in sufficiently high quantities, a severe handicap compared with a high resolution laboratory FTIR microscope. Furthermore, the restriction to non-contact technology limits IR-spectroscopy to measurement in reflection mode, which is not well suited to analyzing uneven and extremely heterogeneous materials. Therefore, we could not use FTIR for a reliable identification of the binder in the inks. The multispectral microscope (Dino-Lite), on the other hand, gave us information about the morphology of the surface. We also used this microscope to determine the thickness of the fragments and the regions of interest on each fragment for X-ray spectrometry. In addition, we used UV induced fluorescence to test for the presence of vegetable tannins on the fragments' surfaces.

A Note on XRF

X-ray fluorescence (XRF) relies on the study of characteristic patterns of X-ray emissions from atoms irradiated with high-energy X-rays. However, only elements with atomic numbers higher than 11 (Na) can be reliably detected with this technique. XRF cannot assess carbon, the main element of the organic writing material (parchment, papyrus) and soot inks under investigation. Therefore, we base our studies on the characterization of impurities or various compounds introduced intentionally or unintentionally in the course of the history of the scroll. The recorded intensity of the emission signal is not directly proportional to the amount of the element present but depends on many factors, *i.e.* the initial data obtained from the XRF spectrum can only testify to the presence or absence of certain elements but not to their quantity. We calculate the quantities of the individual elements with the computer program developed by the BAM Qumran project (Wolff et al. 2012). Since the scrolls are extremely heterogeneous, we used the line scanning mode to characterize the material in order to avoid random results. Our distinction between the elements introduced during the production (intentional) and storage (unintentional) is mostly based on lateral homogeneity. Therefore, no reliable conclusions can be drawn when:
– heterogeneous distribution of an element indicates that it might stem from more than one source;
– there is an insufficient number of scans for a reliable characterization of the scroll.

It must be stressed that a proper characterization of the material is the crucial step for results based on the XRF analysis. Before the new high-speed XRF scanner (Jet Stream, Bruker) was available, the measurement protocol included pre-screening of the scrolls by imaging techniques to determine the areas of similarity for the line scanning. Jet Stream technology considerably reduced the time and increased our accuracy: we can now map large areas in real time, and, therefore, accurately address both of the cases stated above. Unfortunately, Jet Stream was not available for our field trip.

B. Results[1]

The scrolls in The Schøyen Collection are written on parchment-like material, leather, and papyrus.[2] The larger portion of the scrolls is written on the hair side of parchment-like material that in this study we will call parchment.[3]

---

[1] A detailed report on the individual fragments has been submitted to The Schøyen Collection and the editor of this volume (Rabin, unpublished report). The edition of some of the Schøyen fragments analyzed here has been postponed to a later publication (MS 4612/2abc, MS 4612/6, MS 4612/8, MS 4612/10, MS 4612/12, MS 5234, MS 5426). The connection of the MS inventory numbers with biblical and other texts in parentheses have, for the sake of the reader, been added by the general editor after the analysis.

[2] In the case of highly deteriorated small fragments the differentiation between leather and tanned parchment-like material is extremely difficult and requires bench equipment.

[3] The formal, currently accepted definition of parchment is based on the production process established in the early Middle Ages: parchment is an animal skin de-haired in a lime bath, dried under tension and never tanned. The transition from de-haired skin (where the three-dimensional fibre-work is still present) to flat writing material (with a two-dimensional fibre-work) takes place when the skins dry under tension. We consider this to be the crucial step in the distinction between skins and parchment. We hope that the incorporation of the results from the studies on various production processes in antiquity will lead to the adoption of a new, adequate definition.

1. Technology of Parchment Production in Antiquity

An important benefit of this field study lies in the investigation of the manufacture of ancient parchment. The production technology of the larger part of the skin-based material of the Dead Sea Scrolls, as reported in the first physical and chemical study, did not involve lime soaking but enzymatic depilation. In antiquity, this was customarily carried out by application of dung, flour, or vegetable baths. The production involved drying under tension, a stage that provided this material with properties similar to those of parchment. Unlike the medieval process, vegetable tannins were sometimes applied to the surface in the last stage of the treatment, which produced an interesting hybrid between leather and parchment (Poole and Reed 1962). This general description of the manufacture of the parchment of the Dead Sea Scrolls lacks detail with regard to skin treatment after flaying, the use of materials to assist drying, and finishing steps. From the detailed descriptions of parchment making in the Middle Ages we know that chalk and powdered pumice were applied on the flesh side to assist cleaning and drying of the de-haired skin.[4] Certainly, similar steps must also have existed in antiquity. Extremely thin parchments from times before the use of lime testify to production processes in which a skin could be separated into two usable parts: grain and flesh splits. In our opinion, the somewhat confused Talmudic discussion of the rules of inscribing grain and flesh splits indicates that this technique was either not common or not in use when the Talmudic description was written.[5] The art of manual splitting of skins disappeared with the introduction of lime. Furthermore, aluminum sulphate salts, known as alum $[MAl(SO_4)_2 \times 12H_2O, M=Na, K, NH_4^-]$ have been used from early times to produce soft, white leather of excellent quality. This leather, however, differed greatly from the usual tanned one, in that it was not resistant to water. In the Middle Ages, leather goods manufactured by alum thawing included parchment for writing (Reed 1972, 62) that would be more flexible than the common rigid medieval parchment better suited to codices.

Ronald Reed divided the fragments at his disposal into three groups: leather, parchment-like and gewil-like. According to Reed the last group, pale yellow in colour, differed from the parchment-like group in its suppleness and similarity to the modern gewil. He concluded that different preparation processes were probably responsible for this difference since all other properties tested appeared to be quite similar, including tanning on the surface. In his original interpretation of the results, Reed strongly relied upon rabbinic sources about the preparation of writing materials. Later, however, he revised his conclusions, acknowledging that the gewil-like parchments at his disposal were never tanned (Reed 1972, 262). Since the gewil described in the Talmud requires dressing with vegetable tannins, he tentatively concluded that this type of material, of pale colour and soft, velvety handle, cannot correspond to the gewil as described in the Talmud.

Similarly, our studies show that the Dead Sea Scrolls material can be divided roughly into three groups: leather,[6] parchments of a light tint, and those of various shades of brown. The latter ones are invariably tanned, whereas the middle group is characterized by the presence of various sulphate salts. Some of the pale parchments, among them the *Temple Scroll* (11Q19),[7] are remarkably similar to medieval European parchment. Therefore we have formulated the working theory that in the Judaea of the Hellenistic period two different parchment-making traditions existed side by side: an 'eastern' one (represented by the tanned parchments of Qumran, closely resembling Aramaic documents from the fifth century BC (Driver 1954), and a 'western' one (represented by the untanned/lightly tanned ones, similar to early Christian Greek parchments). Comparing Reed's classification with ours, we conclude

---

[4] http://indenwittenhasewint.blogspot.com/ (accessed 23.05.2014).
[5] See detailed discussion on the Talmud prescriptions in Haran 1990.
[6] Only two fragments can definitely be classified as leather: MS 2713 (Josh) and MS 4612/1 (Joel).
[7] See detailed description of the composition of this scroll on p. 327.

that his 'gewil-like' parchment coincides with our 'western' type. At this point we would also caution that our designation might turn out to be as misleading as his.

Unfortunately there is no textual evidence that indicate whether de-hairing liquors could contain vegetable tannins. Nevertheless this hypothesis seems quite plausible. Likewise, we do not know whether treatment with tannins could be a general finishing step in the manufacture of skin-based material, or whether tannins were only applied immediately before inscription by the scribes. In their independent studies, Reed and Wallert (Reed and Poole 1964; Wallert 1996b) found evidence that tannins were applied on the surface. Wallert detected tannins only on the grain (writing) surface and suggested that there could be a connection between tannins and 'flaking off' observed on the writing side of the fragments. Reed, however, mentions that he found no difference between the treatment of hair and flesh sides, and concludes that the de-hairing steps could also involve tannins. Thus, to reconstruct ancient technology we must rely on the analysis of the end products, *i.e.* ancient parchments. With rare exceptions, the end products reached us in a rather degraded state so that our analysis must take the effects of degradation into account. At the current stage of technology much more conclusive results could be achieved with destructive techniques. Still, non-destructive testing of a large number of scrolls supplies precious information by means of scrolls sorting based on their similarities. In addition, it considerably reduces the need for destructive analysis.

For the time being, we will use the terms 'eastern' and 'western' parchment to differentiate between two types, namely tanned ('eastern') and lightly tanned/untanned ('western'), respectively. Usually we see a striking difference in the elemental composition of the two types. Sulphur (S) appears as the most abundant element in the second group only, whereas potassium (K), present in plant extracts, is mostly evident on scrolls that have undergone vegetable tanning. It is noteworthy that in the lightly tanned parchments the levels of potassium are not necessarily very high. Unfortunately, potassium and sulphur may result from more than one source. Therefore, when only minute amounts are detected with a single non-destructive method such as XRF no precise attribution is possible. In such cases it is advisable to double-check the presence of tannin by FTIR or Raman spectroscopy.

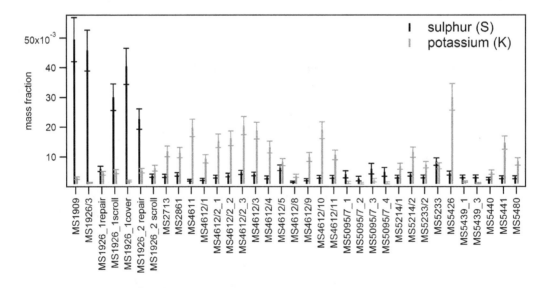

Figure 1. *Sulphur and potassium content of the parchment and leather fragments*

Figure 1 shows that we can roughly divide the results into four groups: (1) The larger one that includes brown parchments and leather displays a high amount of potassium consonant with vegetable tanning ('eastern'). (2) The concentration of sulphur far exceeds that of potassium in five fragments only, namely MS 1909 (fragment of 1QSb), MS 1926/1 (original fragments of 1QIsa[a] designated 'scroll' and 'cover', see pp. 309ff), MS 1926/3 (uninscribed fragment from 1QS) and MS 1926/2 (white 'repair parchment' from 1QapGen, see pp. 283ff). The last one is the only extant fragment from the white, uninscribed parchment that was covering a large portion of the ruined columns of the *Genesis Apocryphon*. John C. Trever called it 'backing to the leather, similar to that used on the Isaiah scroll for repairs' (Trever 1948a, 15). These five fragments seem to belong to what we call the 'western' type. (3) In two cases, *viz.* MS 5095/7 (4QCommGen A I 10) and MS 5439/1 (4QRP[b]), potassium is at the limit of quantification, though their colour suggests that the fragments have been tanned. (4) In the fourth group—the repair parchment of 1QIsa[a] (MS 1926/1 repair), 1QapGen (MS 1926/2, scroll), MS 4612/8 and MS 5440 (1 Kgs)—sulphur and potassium are present in equally moderate amounts. In these last cases, though, [K]>[S] is consonant with tanning so they could still be classified as an 'eastern' type. However, these are cases that should be assessed with laboratory equipment, such as μ-FTIR and μ-Raman spectroscopy, and scanning electron microscopy, to understand at what stage and how these elements were introduced.[8]

The large discrepancy affecting the measurement of sulphur and potassium in the group of small fragments (MS 5095/7) deserves an explanation. *Figure 2* shows one of the fragments during the measurement: it practically floats, so that the measurement spot moved out of focus during a single line scan, leading to a larger scatter of the recorded intensities. In the past, this group probably constituted a single fragment. When the measurement uncertainties are taken into account, the experimental result supports this hypothesis.

Figure 2*. Fragment from MS 5095/7 under X-ray beam[9]*

[8] The *Genesis Apocryphon* is in many ways exceptional. Its initial pale beige colour turned almost black as a consequence of deterioration.

[9] It is positioned on a card with a hole to ensure that the X-ray beam does not encounter another material under the fragment.

Let us now consider the 'western' group in more detail. In The Schøyen Collection, this group is limited to fragments from the first scrolls discovered by the Bedouin and kept at present in the Shrine of the Book. Since Reed's samples derived from the Rockefeller collection (IAA), we expect more scrolls of the 'gewil' or 'western' type to be still present in the IAA collection. An XRF screening of this collection would easily reveal them.

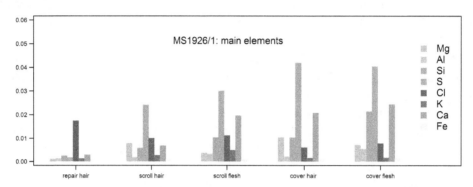

Figure 3. Comparison of the main elements in the fragments from MS 1926/1 (1QIsa[a])

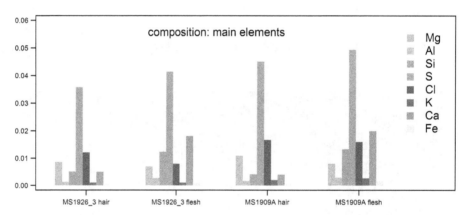

Figure 4. Comparison of the main elements in the fragments from MS 1926/3 (1QS) and MS 1909 (1QSb)

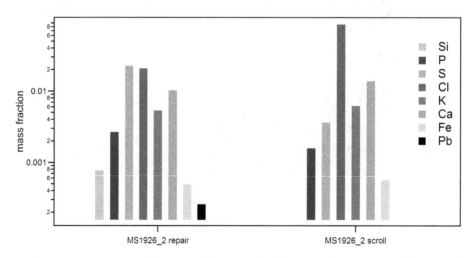

Figure 5. Comparison of the main elements in the fragments from MS 1926/2 (1QapGen)

Figures 3–5 present the average elemental composition of the fragments calculated from the line scans conducted on the grain and flesh sides. When significantly different amounts of light elements (≤ Ca) appear on the *recto* and the *verso*, we can investigate the difference between them. In the group shown in *Figure 3*, the element distribution confirms that the fragment 'repair' is quite different from both 'scroll' and 'cover'. The main element of the 'repair' is chlorine, followed by calcium and silicon. The fragments 'scroll' and 'cover' have a similar elemental composition, with sulphur as the main element. The large error bars show that it is heterogeneously distributed on the surface.[10] The presence of aluminium in conjunction with sulphur points strongly to the use of alum in the production process. The exact attribution is complicated by two factors. Firstly, aluminium has here more than one source; secondly, common alum [$KAl(SO_4)_2$ x 12 H_2O] usually contains potassium, *i.e.* we would expect high concentrations of potassium in these samples. Unfortunately, we cannot see other forms of alum [$NaAl(SO_4)_2$ x 12 H_2O and $NH_4Al(SO_4)_2$ x 12 H_2O] since neither Na nor NH_4^- can be detected with our μ-XRF.[11] Therefore, in these cases use of other types of alum cannot be experimentally established but rather suggested. Furthermore, we see that in the 'scroll' and 'cover' fragments of 1QIsa[a] the flesh side is richer in Si and Ca, pointing to an analogue from the Middle Ages; the hair side is richer in Mg. The last observation is important—no other parchments we have studied had this feature. Although the distributions are extremely similar, they cannot correspond to one and the same skin (in this case all the concentrations on each side should be within the error bars), but rather to skins prepared in the same batch.

In *Figure 4*, the similarity between the average composition of the fragments from 1QSb and 1QS (MS 1909, MS 1926/3) is such that they may derive from a single skin, or at least from the same preparation batch. Moreover, they are almost identical to those from the fragments of 1QIsa[a] (MS 1926/1) in *Figure 3*.

Summarizing, two fragments from 1QIsa[a], one from 1QSb, and one from 1QS are made in the same way and seem to originate from the same workshop, characterized by the use of expensive materials and a high degree of workmanship. Assuming that our assessment is correct and that the fragments studied indeed correspond to 1QIsa[a], 1QS, and 1QSb (as noted in Trever's description), we conclude that they come from the same workshop and that it is highly probable that 1QS and 1QSb belonged to one scroll. Certainly, this conclusion is based on the study of a small group of tiny fragments. One should study the original scrolls, since the present assessment did not allow a quantification of the variability across a skin.

In *Figure 5* (left) we encounter another parchment that we classified as 'western', the 'repair' parchment of 1QapGen. Despite a considerable amount of sulphur, its composition differs significantly from the pale parchments MS 1926/1 (1QIsa[a]), MS 1926/3 (1QS), and MS 1909 (1QSb), on the one hand, and from MS 1926/1 ('scroll' and 'repair') on the other. Here we find not magnesium, but phosphorus; the levels of chlorine are much higher than in other pale parchments; and finally, it contains a considerable amount of lead. Therefore, despite its colour, it seems to indicate the existence of yet another manufacturing process.

This review of the results shows that our optimistic division into two types, based on a relatively small number of fragments tested, was somewhat premature. The detection of calcium in antique parchments that have no sediments from cave floors is another important discovery. It probably testifies to the use of Ca compounds during the drying stage since the concentrations of Ca and Si are more abundant on the flesh side. In parchment produced by soaking in lime liquors, we detect no significant difference in the Ca content on either side.

---

[10] It should be noted that detection of chlorine depends on the amount of sulphur present, because sulphur may absorb the fluorescence of chlorine. To a certain extent our quantification routine takes this effect into account (Wolff et al. 2012).

[11] NH_4^- cannot be detected by XRF technique, while detection of Na requires a different setup.

2. Origin

The composition of mineral impurities in spring water from the coastal region of the Dead Sea (such as Ein Feshka) is similar to that of the Dead Sea itself, with its strikingly low ratio of chlorine to bromine (35–50) compared with normal seawater (> 300) (Bentor 1961; Nisselbaum 1975). Such a fingerprint value allows for distinguishing local springs from any other water source throughout the country. Therefore, we used the traces of mineral impurities from water used in the preparation of parchment as a way of recognizing the Dead Sea region as a parchment production site. One of the aims of the high resolution screening of the fragments is to obtain a reliable fingerprint of impurities from the production sites as opposed to those from storage in the caves, and from contamination after their modern discovery. The latter plays a minor role in connection with the fragments of The Schøyen Collection, since these fragments do not seem to have undergone the intensive conservation treatment common for scrolls in the main collections in Jerusalem. However, the issue of distinguishing between fingerprints of residues from the caves and those from manufacture cannot always be resolved. In the present study, given the short time available, it became a challenging task to properly evaluate each scan on site in order to decide whether additional scans were necessary.

To illustrate the issue of lateral homogeneity let us consider the profiles of the elements Cl, Br, and Ca in *Figure 6a* measured on the fragment MS 4612/1 (Joel). The individual intensities have been scaled for a more convenient graphic presentation. Ca, a representative of traces of storage in the caves, shows an uneven profile and does not reflect a solid and continuous layer on the fragment. Cl and Br stay largely unaffected by its presence and form a relatively even profile. According to our hypothesis the ratio of Cl/Br is attributable to one source and can be used to indicate the region of production. The situation is different in *Figure 6b* with the line scan profiles from MS 4612/8. Ca shows a similarly uneven profile; Br stays quite stable, whereas the intensity of Cl mostly follows that of Ca rather than that of Br. In this case it is clear that a portion of the amount of Cl does not share a common origin with Br. Had it been possible to produce an XRF image of the whole fragment, we might have found a surface bare of sediments and been able to separate the intensities of Cl due to the different sources.

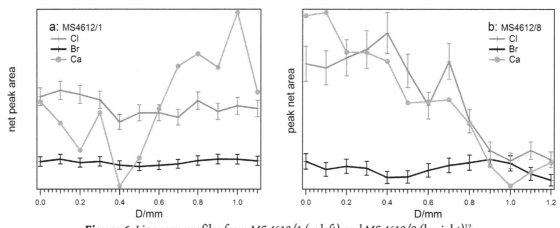

Figure 6. *Line scan profiles from MS 4612/1 (a: left) and MS 4612/8 (b: right)*[12]

Due to a lack of lateral homogeneity we could not determine a reliable Cl/Br ratio for a number of the fragments investigated—MS 2713 (Josh), MS 4612/2, MS 4612/8, MS 4612/10, MS 4612/11 (Prov), and

---

[12] The intensities are scaled vertically for a better graphic presentation.

the four fragments from the group MS 5095/7—because all the line scans were laterally heterogeneous and the distributions of Cl could not be clearly determined.

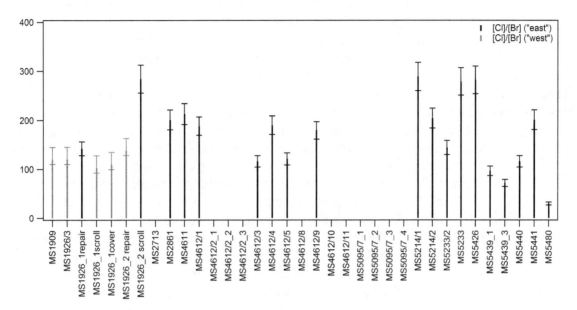

Figure 7. *[Cl]/[Br] ratios*

With the exception of MS 5480 (1 Sam 5) all the fragments displayed ratios exceeding the fingerprint from the Dead Sea region. We have already seen that Cl can be found in traces of storage in the caves, *i.e.* it can originate from different sources. In such a case, however, the issue can be tackled using full high-resolution characterization, since residues from storage in the caves rarely appear as a continuous layer. However, if the hides were cured with table salt before de-hairing, as was often done in the Middle Ages, and the salt were not completely washed out, we would be confronted with an excess of Cl evenly or unevenly distributed throughout the skin. Naturally, the addition of salt would increase the Cl/Br ratio in an unpredictable fashion. The *Genesis Apocryphon* seems to represent such a case. When we first investigated three fragments of this scroll we discovered that the Cl profile shows outliers that turned out to be due to halite islands. It was reported in the literature that extreme changes of temperatures in the post-discovery period resulted in re-crystallization of the salts in the scrolls (Wallert 1996a). The *Genesis Apocryphon* is known to have undergone freeze-thaw cycles during the unrolling. Therefore we attributed the presence of salt crystals on its fragments to the effects of conservation and excluded the salt islands when calculating the average amount of Cl. The fragment in The Schøyen Collection has a different post-discovery history. As a consequence no Cl islands are found, but a more or less evenly distributed high concentration of chlorine, resulting in a considerably higher Cl/Br value than previously reported (Wolff et al. 2012). Different from all the fragments studied previously, the present results indicate the possible existence of multiple sources of chlorine during the parchment production.

3. Archaeological Provenance

The ability to determine the find site of scrolls is important and was one of the first aims of the BAM Qumran project. Since many sites are located close to Qumran, the ability to identify specific caves would also be highly desirable. These two problems can be separated. The identification of the storage site should be based on recognizable residues preserved on the objects. In principle, it is possible to distinguish Qumran areas based on the geology of the site: ratios of Sr/Ca have a specific range of values (Lisker et al. 2010). Furthermore, the sediments of the caves contain calcium carbonate polymorphs—calcite and aragonite, the latter predominant in the natural caves. Our analysis of minerals from Cave 11 to represent natural caves and various samples of the marl to represent manmade caves of Qumran (such as Cave 4) has confirmed that aragonite and dolomite are more abundant than calcite in a natural cave, whereas calcite followed by aragonite is characteristic of the marl.

All this, however, is far from sufficient for an unequivocal attribution of an object to a specific cave. Strong winds can carry sediments from cave to cave, blurring a clear fingerprint. Moreover, we do not know exactly how the manmade caves were built. In the absence of sediments from the Qumran excavations we must seek another way of building data arrays to describe a particular find place. One possibility is offered by the objects themselves, provided that the objects preserve the original traces and that we can correctly attribute these (Rabin and Hahn 2013). We have used the fragments from the Reed collection—allegedly containing only fragments with known archaeological provenance—to build a database of characteristic features for Cave 4 and the Murabbaʿat caves. Unfortunately, we were able neither to test our data outside the primary set nor to investigate any fragments found on the floors of other caves. Therefore, we are still at the phase of collecting and comparing data. Hence, collecting data on the composition of the individual fragments is an important aspect of the work conducted on the fragments from The Schøyen Collection. For this reason we attribute great importance to this study, even though we would try to avoid providing insufficiently-grounded answers to the hotly debated question of archaeological provenance.

The chances of correctly assigning specific fragments to a certain cave would be greatly improved if each cave had very specific features. Cave 11, the so-called bat cave, seems to possess such a fingerprint. A stringent odour from objects in this cave was noticed by the scholars. The odour was caused by the presence of volatile nitrogen compounds such as ammonia that resulted from bat droppings. Unambiguous identification of the nitrates formed on the surface of the objects during their time in the cave requires an analytic procedure that was unavailable to us during our field study in Norway. However, one of the fragments studied (MS 4612/3, Eschatological frg. ar) displays spots that look like discolouration of the parchment. Surprisingly, XRF screening revealed a composition attributable to ammonium magnesium phosphate, another compound closely associated with bat droppings. The line scan across the spot shown in *Figure 8* depicts the growth of the intensities of magnesium and phosphorus in the area of the spot compared with decreased intensities of other elements indigenous to the parchment: S, K, and chlorine. The decrease is due to the partial absorption of their signal by the layer constituting the spot.

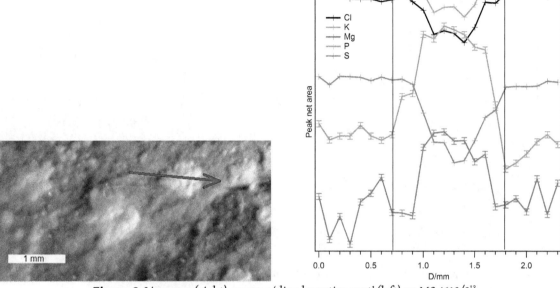

Figure 8. *Line scan (right) across a 'discolouration spot' (left) on MS 4612/3*[13]

Visually, the surface of this fragment including the spots closely resembles that of one fragment from the Job targum (11Q10) ascribed to Cave 11 (cf. *Figure 9*). We have not been able to find similar fingerprints on fragments from other caves. If the spots can indeed be attributed to deposits from Cave 11 we might have found another fingerprint for this cave. It is important to note, however, that no usual sediment residues could be found on MS 4612/3, a fragment written on thin and high quality parchment of a light brown colour.

We usually use FTIR and Raman spectroscopy to characterize sediments on the surface of the fragments. Unfortunately, the full FTIR spectra in reflection mode measured on the fragments in The Schøyen Collection cannot be easily interpreted. The spectra depend strongly on the roughness of the surface and hence cannot be directly translated into the tabulated absorption data. Therefore we limited our determination to the presence of such minerals as are characteristic of the Qumran caves (calcite, aragonite, and dolomite), and sorted the spectra according to their similarity. In *Figure 9* we present fragments from the storage caves with very similar FTIR spectra. They differ only in the absence (left) or presence of aragonite (right) accompanying calcite.

[13] The intensities are scaled for a better graphic presentation.

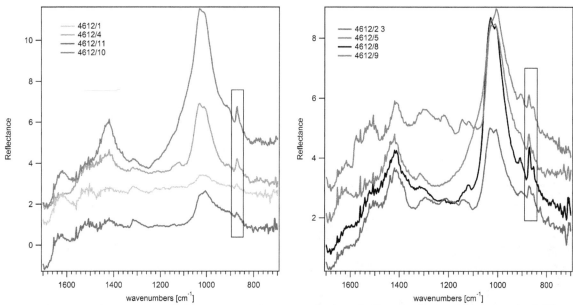

Figure 9. *FTIR spectra with characteristic absorption of calcite (left) and calcite and aragonite (right)*[14]

MS 2713 (Josh), MS 5233/1 (2 Sam 20), MS 5426, and MS 5439/1 (4QRP[b]) also displayed similar IR spectra, which are not shown here. The rest of the scrolls show individual spectra with or without traces of alumino-silicates.

Before conducting this study we had reasons to believe that tracing the region of Qumran according to Sr/Ca ratio would at least be straightforward for the 'eastern' parchments, since the production process of these scrolls did not seem to involve treatment with Ca-compounds. Use of the Sr/Ca parameter in addition to the typical minerals would increase the reliability of an attribution to the region of Qumran. The studies of The Schøyen Collection show, however, that our view was too simplistic, and that—at least in a number of cases—the presence of calcium could be attributed to the production process. As mentioned in the introduction, the use of powdered pumice and calcium carbonate in parchment production is attested in the Middle Ages. A similar practice might have already existed in antiquity. We have seen an enhanced presence of silicon and calcium in fragments MS 1926/1–3 (1QIsa[a], 1QS, 1QapGen) that did not have any trace of sediments from a cave floor (probably to be explained as a result of their storage in the jar). In some other fragments in the collection, *e.g.* MS 2713 (Josh), calcium can be attributed to more than one source. This complicates an unambiguous determination of the sediment traces needed for the correct determination of the Sr/Ca ratio. As in the case of chlorine discussed in the previous section, one might be able to separate different contributions by using high resolution XRF imaging or a combination of an XRF line scanner with high resolution surface morphology study.

4. Lead

A number of the fragments contain a relatively high amount of lead. Unlike the case of the *Genesis Apocryphon* repair parchment (MS 1926/2), contamination from the environment cannot be totally excluded. A homogeneous distribution of lead may indicate water contaminants in the production process

---

[14] The rectangle indicates the characteristic region for calcite/aragonite recognition in our spectra. The large peak at ~1000 cm⁻¹ corresponds to alumino-silicates.

rather than modern air pollution. We have set the threshold to a certain value corresponding to the amount of lead found on the surface of some samples of the *Temple Scroll* studied previously in Berlin. Since all other fragments of the *Temple Scroll* contained little lead, we attributed this greater presence of lead to contamination from the environment. As we see in *Figure 11* this threshold exceeds the lead concentration in most of the fragments.

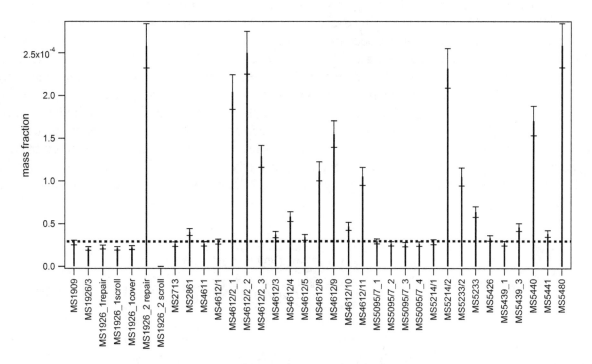

Figure 10. *Lead quantity measured in the fragments*

The actual amount of lead is quite low in most of the fragments and could have been the result of pollution. However, the lead found in the repair piece of the *Genesis Apocryphon* cannot be ascribed to the environment, since the fragment shared its history with its neighbour to its right in the figure. These two fragments were extracted or had fallen off during the first inspection of the scroll at the American School of Oriental Research in Jerusalem. Trever placed both fragments in a single box, which passed unopened to The Schøyen Collection. Hence the two fragments have been subjected to the same environment from the time the scroll was deposited in the cave. The lead must therefore have entered the white parchment at an earlier stage. We believe that it was most probably introduced during the preparation of the parchment through exposure to lead-contaminated water. The same is probably the case for other fragments where the amount of lead substantially exceeds that of the threshold established by the previous studies of the 11QTᵃ fragments. A number of lead water pipes contemporary with the settlement at Khirbet Qumran have been excavated in Israel. Unfortunately, no systematic study on such installations is available. In all other cases, lead could have been introduced unintentionally, *i.e.* through lead pollution during the post-discovery time.

In this respect three fragments from catalogue number MS 4612/2 are quite interesting. They were catalogued as belonging to the same scroll. However, the different amounts of the individual elements as well as their ratios exceeded the error of measurement. This allowed us to conclude that the fragments belonged neither to the same sheet nor to the same scroll, if all the sheets were prepared in one batch.

5. Papyrus

We have little experience with studies of papyrus since our work on Qumran has mostly concerned skin-based material. During the BAM Qumran project we only had access to a single papyrus fragment. Therefore we have never developed a quantification routine to calculate the composition from the XRF data. Recently we started to work on Egyptian papyri, so the observations and data collected on the papyri in Norway will be more thoroughly evaluated later. For the time being, we list some observations with respect to the four fragments inspected in Norway.

We found trace amounts of bromine and lead, but no lead in MS 4612/6. The presence of these elements in papyrus can be attributed to modern environmental influences. Finding Br contamination in the papyrus is important. On the one hand it shows that deposition of Br from the environment could occur, on the other, it also shows that this factor is negligibly small. Infrared spectra show presence of calcite in MS 4612/6, MS 4612/12, and MS 5234, but none in MS 4612/7 frg. 14—the only one inspected with FTIR in the group MS 4612/7 (Wadi ed-Daliyeh). Moreover, the IR spectrum collected from this fragment looks suspiciously similar to modern papyri. We have not found any literature on material analysis that includes infrared spectra of papyri. It seems that no extensive work has been done yet in this area.

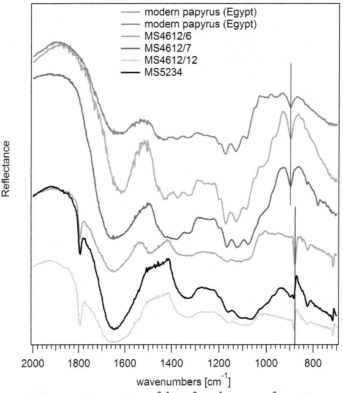

Figure 11. *Comparison of the infrared spectra of papyri*

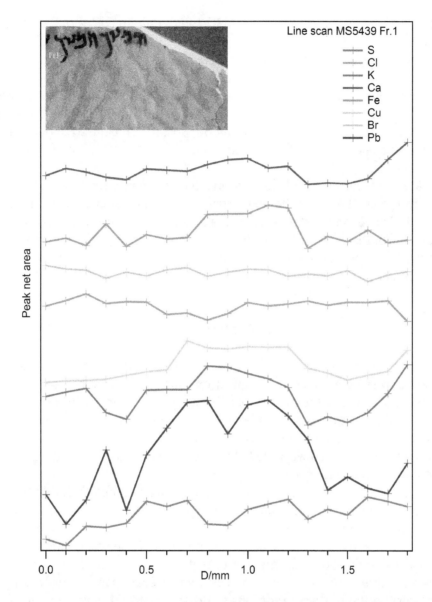

Figure 12. *Line scan over ink. Insert shows the scan position and direction*

6. Inks

All the inks inspected in this study are carbon inks. In the case of the *Genesis Apocryphon* (the scroll represented by MS 1926/2) the carbon ink contains an addition of copper. By contrast with the report by Nir-El and Broshi (1996), where elevated amounts of copper and lead were found and attributed to traces from a bronze inkwell, no lead could be identified in the ink of the Schøyen fragments of 1QapGen, nor in the fragments of the *Genesis Apocryphon* studied in Berlin. Therefore we believe that copper was introduced intentionally, since carbon inks containing copper appear to have been known at the time of the Qumran settlement (Zerdoun 1983, 80). Only four scrolls inscribed with ink containing copper have been tentatively identified in the IAA collection. Since that identification was done on the assumption of ink corrosion, the real number will not be established until this collection has been screened with XRF. The multispectral imaging (MSI) today employed by IAA to re-photograph the scrolls is not suited for such tests.

Most of the inks inspected until now could not have been 'seen' by the XRF method. Since carbon inks and parchment contain basically the same impurities, ink layers can only be identified if such impurities appear in an amount sufficiently greater than the parchment on which it is written. This, apparently, is rarely the case. Therefore, inks cannot be studied by non-invasive methods alone. Though carbon inks produce no spectrum in the infrared region, μ-FTIR can be used to determine ink binders. This has been shown in the chapter devoted to the micro-analysis of the ink from the larger bronze inkwell (MS 1655/2, p. 463).

In the study of MS 5439, consisting of three connected fragments (numbered 1, 2, and 3 counting from the left), we found that the ink of the text in frg. 1 (4QRP[b]) correlates with slightly enhanced intensities of Cu, Fe, K and Pb. Bromine stays constant; a small decrease in the intensity of chlorine is due to the partial absorption of its intensity by the ink layer. Thus, no increased intensity of these elements could be found in the ink. However, the enhanced intensity of lead might indicate different origins of parchment and ink in this case.

C. Conclusion

The Qumran project in Berlin has developed a methodology for the material study of the Dead Sea Scrolls that aims at addressing archaeometric questions such as sorting the scrolls, their origin and archaeological provenance. The database constructed within the Qumran project was limited to the fragments from the Reed collection and a number of fragments from the Shrine of the Book.

In the on-site study of the Dead Sea Scrolls collection in Norway we were able to test the reliability and feasibility of the results obtained with the help of non-invasive mobile techniques under the pressure of the limited time available for the analysis.

In spite of the limitations and the impossibility of achieving a complete mapping of the fragments in the collection, we were able to obtain a much clearer picture of parchment production in antiquity. Specifically, we determined that 1QIsa[a], 1QS, and 1QSb were produced in the same manner, in a way that differs greatly from the manufacture process behind most of the scrolls. Moreover, if MS 1909 indeed belongs to 1QSb we could show that the parchments of 1QS and 1QSb are indistinguishable. Our hypothesis on the contemporary coexistence of at least two different parchment-making traditions was confirmed. But the correlation of these traditions to broad cultural differences appears now to be an oversimplification.

The preservation of a fragment from the so-called 'repair' parchment belonging to the *Genesis Apocryphon* allowed us to determine its mode of production, and to show that it was manufactured differently from the main scroll. This study allows reconstructing, at least partially, the history of the *Genesis Apocryphon*.

Thanks to this study we were able to revise our simplistic view that Cl/Br ratio necessarily corresponds to the traces of the water used to produce the parchment. We have learned that the element chlorine can originate from such sources as skin curing and/or sediments in addition to the water. Moreover, we have learned that the element Ca does not originate exclusively from cave sediments, but can also result from the compounds used during skin manufacture in the times that preceded the use of lime for de-hairing the skins.

In conclusion, this on-site study confirmed that mapping of the elemental composition of the Dead Sea Scrolls and sorting of the fragments according to their material similarity will improve our understanding of their origin.[15]

[15] I would like to express my gratitude to Martin Schøyen, who has allowed such intensive examination of his Dead Sea Scroll fragments. The presence of a variety of fragments of different dates and materials in The Schøyen Collection enabled this pioneering study. I am also indebted to Torleif Elgvin, with whom I have enjoyed a close cooperation on these studies during the last years; and to Reinhard Franke, my assistant in the screening of the fragments. It is my hope that this study will inspire similar testing and analysis of fragments in other collections, so that we can build a larger database for a continuing material investigation of ancient texts.

V

Palaeographical Analysis of the Dead Sea Scrolls in The Schøyen Collection

Michael Langlois

A. Introduction

1. Purpose

The purpose of palaeographical analysis is to understand the way in which a particular scribe writes and shapes letters. Conducting such an analysis prior to the establishment of the text is essential when discussing the identification of ambiguous traces, as is often the case when fragments have deteriorated over the centuries: fractures, lacunae, evanescence are the lot of all epigraphers and do not spare Dead Sea Scrolls editors. Even when a manuscript is in good condition, scribes make mistakes, correct a letter by changing it into another, or simply write different letters of the alphabet in a very similar way.

Furthermore, palaeographical analysis makes it possible to compare two given scripts, so as to ascertain their affinities, differences, and perhaps conclude that they belong to the same hand. This is an important factor when identifying fragments of the same manuscript, although one should keep in mind that a scribe's career is not limited to a single scroll, nor is a single scroll necessarily copied in its entirety by the same scribe.

The idiosyncratic morphological features that enable the identification of a given hand often fall within broader morphological tendencies. These tendencies can be classified and traced throughout centuries; the resulting typology can then be used to propose a relative or absolute dating for a given script. This corollary benefit of palaeographical analysis is often overestimated:

1. Many typological markers within Judaean scripts are not well attested in explicitly (or even stratigraphically or chemically) dated inscriptions. As a result, they lack absolute dating, so that the palaeographer must settle for relative dating based on typological developments.

2. Typological evolutions are slow and not linear; a new ductus can be in existence for quite some time before suddenly gaining popularity, and can likewise remain in use after having lost popularity. Its chronological distribution could in fact be modelled by means of a Gaussian function; our present knowledge prevents us from ascertaining with precision the parameters of such a function, but additional research may prove successful.

3. In the meantime, I will propose palaeographical dates using mere ranges, *e.g.* 'second half' or 'third quarter' of a century, but the reader should bear in mind that these are not absolute dates. Such ranges indicate the most likely period in which (in my opinion) a manuscript was copied, but it is always possible that a manuscript was copied earlier or later. This is especially true for narrow ranges (*e.g.* a quarter of a century) that do not even cover the entire career of a scribe; I use such narrow ranges to indicate probability and typological developments.

2. Methodology

The palaeographical analysis presented here implements new methodological principles and takes advantage of technologies previously unavailable:

1. All manuscripts have been photographed using high resolution censors in both visible and infrared lights. Some of the resulting digital images exceed 200 pixels per mm, thus revealing the smallest morphological features.

2. Even the most sophisticated imaging technologies should not, however, replace a direct visual examination of the manuscripts. In some cases, a second visual examination was carried out several months after the first one; difficult letters were also examined using a digital microscope under both visible and infrared lights.

3. By contrast, my examination was deliberately blind to previous examination of these manuscripts. I did not try to identify the content of these fragments, nor did I look for possible matches among known scrolls. In fact, several manuscripts were already published elsewhere (with or without the consent of the owner) or previously examined by other palaeographers. My analysis may consequently differ from theirs.

4. For each manuscript, every occurrence of every letter of the alphabet has been studied. This was achieved by manually tagging the digital photographs, so that each occurrence could easily be found and studied in its material context. All occurrences were then grouped and aligned to serve as an illustration of the palaeographical description. The order in which they appear has been preserved (from right to left), so that the reader may quickly find a particular occurrence on the manuscript. Only a few instances of heavily damaged letters or exceedingly numerous occurrences of a single letter have been left out.

5. Instead of drawing a facsimile, which is customary in epigraphy but subjective and sometimes tendentious, I have used imaging algorithms to produce black-and-white pictures of the actual letters. The result is not as pleasing to the eye as a traditional facsimile, but it is more reliable and better reflects the reality and difficulties exhibited by some letters. For the same reason, I have not 'cleaned' nor 'repaired' any letter by image editing software. Moreover, when two letters overlap, I have refrained from reconstructing the hidden extremities of the letters; on the contrary, I have deliberately retained part of the adjacent letter. This method presents another advantage: the charts readily show a scribe's tendency to affix letters or create ligatured forms.

6. The traditional order of the Hebrew alphabet has been followed, but the reader may be surprised to be presented with final letter forms before their medial counterpart. As a matter of fact, medial forms are secondary in nature, resulting from semiligature; I have thus decided to present the original (final) form first, and then to indicate the changes undergone in the secondary (medial) form.

7. It is only *after* I analyzed a fragment that I considered possible matches. This is the reason why I decided to study separately fragments that were presented to me as belonging to the same manuscript (MS 4612/2). The palaeographical analysis revealed that such an ascription was not without problems, and other issues led us to postpone the publication of these fragments. When I was convinced that a fragment belongs to an existing manuscript, I appended to my analysis an addendum stating whether (and to what extent) the new identification would narrow down the initial palaeographical dating.

8. My initial study followed the order of the manuscripts' inventory numbers, starting with MS 1909 and ending with MS 5480. I have then ordered the manuscripts by date, so that the reader can observe the evolution of various Judaean hands throughout the two centuries covered by this collection. Likewise, manuscripts belonging to the same period have been ordered according to their palaeographical affinities.

9. On this basis, palaeographical charts have been prepared and can be consulted at the end of this chapter. They present the manuscripts in the same order (from right to left) and use the same black-and-white pictures that illustrate the individual descriptions, with the same advantages. Letters are reproduced in real size, which enables the reader to compare the absolute and relative sizes of various scripts. By contrast, the illustrations that accompany individual descriptions are reproduced on a 4:1 scale, which helps the reader to observe specific morphological features.

B. MS 5439/1 (4QRP[b])[1]

The parchment is smooth, the hand is confident and regular, with a standard letter height comprised between 2.5 mm and 3 mm. No ascender has been preserved, and descenders exceed 5 mm in height (cf. ך). Strokes are thick throughout.

ה has a narrow traverse and tall parallel legs; the protrusion is as wide as the traverse, and both are thicker than the legs.

ו is rather short, convex, with a short rounded hook at its head.

Final ך is large, with a wide slanted traverse slightly curved at its left end but without horn. It joins the vertical below its summit; the vertical is slanted and has a typical elbow at the bottom, followed by a large slanted base.

ל is narrow, with a discreet rounded hook.

Medial מ is of varying size, with a curved traverse, angular shoulder and straight or slightly concave vertical. After the elbow, the base is wide, sometimes protruding to the left of the traverse. The left arm is penned last and joins the traverse after the curl, in the same axis.

ע is narrow, with a short diagonal slightly curled at the top, joined at mid-height by a straight left arm.

---

[1] For the text edition, see p. 153. The attribution to specific books was made by the general editor after Langlois' analysis, to make it easier for the reader.

ת has two tall parallel slanted legs, the left slightly shorter than the right and curled at the bottom but without a developed foot. The traverse is narrow and the shoulder rounded.

Overall, the few letters preserved on this fragment are of regular height, following the process of normalization in the third and (beginning of) second centuries BC. No developed Hasmonaean feature has been observed, but this may be due to the fact that many letters of the alphabet have not been preserved. I carefully conclude that MS 5439/1 was copied sometime in the second century BC.

Addendum

Material and palaeographical features led the editors to identify the fragment as belonging to 4QRP[b] (4Q364). I am pleased to confirm this identification from a palaeographical standpoint; the thick traverse of ה is due to doubling, as can be seen at the end of 4Q364 8 i 2; the same elbow is visible at the bottom of the final ך in 4Q364 8 ii 1; ל is indeed narrow, with a sometimes slightly shaded head as in 4Q364 5a 2.

Once this identification is accepted, we can in turn look for more palaeographical features from these additional fragments in order to date this manuscript. In particular, some of the letters that were not attested in this fragment (especially א, י, ק and ש) appear to be slightly more developed. I conclude that MS 5439/1 was copied in the second half of the second century BC.

C. MS 1909 (1QSb)[2]

The hand is regular, with a standard letter height of *ca.* 2.5 mm. Descending letters measure up to 4 mm (cf. ק l. 2), which might also be the case for ascending letters (cf. ל l. 1).

ך (l. 2) features a two-horned head, but it is unclear if it is drawn following the two-stroke ductus that develops in the second half of the first century BC. The head is slanting backwards and is followed by a short, slightly concave descender.

The horizontal traverse of ה (l. 3) is not thicker than the legs, and features a long protrusion. The legs are parallel and quite straight, except for a

---

[2] For the text edition, see p. 273.

slightly concave right leg, which ascends as a small horn.

ו is likewise slightly concave and exhibits a small hook-shaped angular head. A case of curved ו with a very small head (l. 2) betrays the influence of a cursive script.

י rarely exhibits the wide chevron shape, with a slightly longer leg that develops through the Hasmonaean period. More often, the head is small, triangular, and the leg as long as that of ו. This can lead to a confusion common in latter Hasmonaean hands.

A partial ל (l. 1) ends with a long oblique stroke, but the ascender is missing, so that we can't use its height or the shape of its head as a typological marker.

ק (l. 2) features a straight, slightly slanted tail preceded by a wide belly with an angular head. The formal two-stroke shape is current in the Hasmonaean period and continues in some Herodian hands, but the short tail resists the tendency to lengthen in the Herodian period.

ר (l. 1) has a straight, slightly slanted leg that does not extend downwards. The shoulder, at the edge of the fragment, seems quite angular, but the head exhibits a nice curve unlike later Herodian scripts.

The size of the ת (l. 3) fits the standard frame: the two legs are parallel and of equal length, and the left leg ends with a horizontal foot. The right leg is preceded by a slanted traverse that joins the left leg below its head; note the two-stroke shape.

To sum up, the script exhibits features consistent with the middle of the first century BC, while resisting features that develop in later Herodian times. However, one should take into account the small number of letters preserved on this fragment; many letters are not attested at all, while others are attested once, so that other shapes may have occurred elsewhere (compare the ו). This prevents a more accurate dating; I therefore conclude that MS 1909 was copied sometime around the middle of the first century BC.

Addendum

The identification of this fragment with 1QSb allows for a more specific dating based on the palaeo-graphical analysis of other letters that are not attested here. א, for instance, occasionally uses the new ductus that develops in the middle of the first century, while other letters have more conservative features. This leads me to conclude that MS 1909 (as well as 1QSb) was copied sometime around the second quarter of the first century BC.

D. MS 4612/11 (Prov 4.23–5.1)[3]

The parchment is rough, and the hand only partially regular, with a standard letter height comprised between 2 mm and 2.5 mm. No descending letter is attested (ק l. 2 has no descender), while ascending letters measure about 4.5 mm in height, although what seems to be the top of a ל at the beginning of l. 3 may suggest a height reaching 5.5 mm.

א (l. 1) has a convex left leg curled at the bottom. The top has disappeared, so it is uncertain whether the ductus follows the chevron shape that develops in the second half of the first century BC. The diagonal is straight, and is joined at mid-height by a raised, slightly convex right arm.

ב (l. 1) is short, angular and large. The left horn slants backwards and is followed by a straight slanted traverse. The right arm is straight and seems drawn without lifting the pen by means of a raised shoulder. The base protrudes to the right, but is concave and seems penned by means of a looped elbow rather than from left to right, a ductus that develops in the first century BC.

ה is tall and narrow, with an inconsistent ductus: sometimes the left leg and traverse are drawn together by means of a looped protrusion, and sometimes they simply cross. In other instances, the protrusion is thickened without necessarily being looped. The left leg is slightly concave and curved at the bottom. The right leg is sometimes drawn together with the traverse by means of a raised shoulder, in which case it tends to be concave, while in other instances it seems to be an independent straight stroke.

ו (l. 1) is tall and narrow, with a slanted straight vertical topped by a short angular hook.

---

[3] For the text edition, see p. 240.

A partial ח (l. 2) reveals a slanted or convex left leg preceded by a slanted traverse that joins it below its summit. The right leg seems penned together with the traverse by means of a looped shoulder (more than a thick raised one), following a technique that develops in the first century BC.

י is a simple suspended triangle, sometimes prolonged by a thin and short vertical.

Medial כ is narrow and tall, with a small concave traverse followed by a raised elbow. The vertical is long, straight or slightly concave. The elbow exhibits a varying ductus: it is sometimes rounded, sometimes angular. The base is wide and straight, slightly slanted.

ל (l. 1) features a large traverse and long oblique, which become popular in the second half of the first century BC, but is not crammed as can be seen in later Herodian hands. The ascender exhibits thickening, but not the tick that becomes popular in the first century AD.

A partial final ם (l. 2) reveals a large protruding horn followed by a straight traverse, angular elbow and straight vertical. The base is missing, but the left vertical is intact; it is straight, slightly slanted, and crosses the traverse.

Medial מ exhibits a one-stroke ductus, with a looped left horn, narrow traverse, and a raised or looped right shoulder. The right arm is straight, followed by an angular elbow and large (but non-protruding) slanted base, so that the letter remains wide open.

Medial נ is tall, with a slightly concave vertical followed by a likewise concave base of varying width.

ע (l. 2) is relatively small, and has not reached the full size that develops in the Herodian period. The right arm is long and convex, almost vertical at the top, and is joined at mid-height by a short diagonal straight left arm.

Medial צ (l. 1) is large, with a tall, straight, slanted vertical followed by a wide straight slanted base. The right arm exhibits further development: it is not only convex, but curled at the top, which is more at home in later Hasmonaean hands.

ק (l. 2) features a large straight traverse curved upwards at its left end and prolonged to the right by a rounded hook. The left vertical crosses the head and does not seem to be prolonged by a tail.

A partial ר (l. 2) reveals a curved head, rounded shoulder and straight vertical.

ת (l. 1) is narrow, with parallel straight legs of equal length. The left leg has a short foot and ascends above the traverse. The traverse is very narrow and followed by a rounded shoulder.

Overall, this script belongs to a late Hasmonaean semiformal book hand. I conclude that MS 4612/11 was copied around the middle of the first century BC.

E. MS 5480 (1 Sam 5.10–11)[4]

The parchment is rough, the hand hesitant, quite small, with a standard letter height comprised between 1.5 mm and 2 mm. Descending letters do not exceed 2.5 mm in height (cf. ק l. 1), while ascending letters may have reached 4 mm (cf. ל l. 2).

ה (l. 1) is narrow but exhibits a wide and thick protrusion that develops in the Hasmonaean period. The traverse is straight, as are the legs. The right leg protrudes to the top; it may have been penned together with the traverse, but the loop is flat. The left leg is barely shorter.

ו is tall, straight, with an open hook at its head.

ז is even taller but slanted, with an upper tick pointing backwards, similar to later Herodian hands. The tick, however, slants upward at an angle that is closer to the curled ductus that develops in the first century BC and becomes popular at the turn of our era. It might thus be an early attempt at making the curled head angular.

י has a chevron shape with outspread legs; the right leg is longer than the left, so that י becomes closer to ו.

ל has a tall ascender, slightly curved in the upper part. The traverse is straight, with an angled hook at its right end. The oblique is straight and open, unlike that of later, Herodian hands.

ע is quite inconsistent, with a diagonal that is sometimes barely convex, and sometimes almost

---

[4] For the text edition, see p. 203.

horizontal at the bottom. The left arm is sometimes thin and convex, sometimes thick and straight.

ק has a wide traverse curved upwards at its left end, and rounded at is right end to produce a large hook. The diagonal is inconsistent, sometimes very short, sometimes long, but never closes the letter. The left vertical is short, drawn separately, and joins the traverse before its end so as to leave a protrusion.

ר (l. 1) is small, with a short convex vertical topped by a round shoulder. The traverse is as long as the vertical and curled upward at its left end to produce a slanted horn.

A partial שׁ (l. 2) reveals a V shape with symmetrical straight arms. The middle stroke is short, parallel to the right arm, and joins the left arm at mid-height.

In conclusion, the few letters attested on this small fragment belong to a formal but hesitant hand from the later Hasmonaean period. The limited number of letters warrants caution in dating this manuscript, but its features lead me to conclude that MS 5480 was copied around the middle of the first century BC.

F. MS 4612/9 (Jer 3.15–19)[5]

The hand is hesitant and the strokes uneven, penned on rough parchment. Letter height varies between 2 and 3 mm, while descending letters measure up to 4 mm in height (e.g. ק l. 5), and ascending up to 5 mm.

א is drawn in a simple three-step ductus. The right arm joins the diagonal almost at mid-height, and rarely exhibits curve or thickening at its top. The

---

[5] For the text edition, see p. 215.

left leg is shorter and tends to be concave; it joins the diagonal at its top, a technique that appears in the second half of the first century BC.

ב is square and features a two-horned head; the left horn tends to be taller and slanted backwards, while the right horn is in fact a raised shoulder or flat loop. The vertical stroke is straight or slightly concave, and quite short. The base is likewise straight or slightly concave, and not much longer than the traverse. It does not protrude to the right, as can be seen in later Herodian hands.

ד also features a two-horned head, but contrary to ב there is no raised or looped shoulder: the vertical is usually made after lifting the pen (except, perhaps, l. 5), a technique that appears in the second half of the first century BC. The vertical is straight or slightly concave, and of standard height.

ה is narrow, with two straight parallel legs of comparable height. The right leg is slightly taller, so that the traverse joins it below its top without being slanted. Sometimes the scribe does not lift the pen as he draws the traverse and right leg. The left leg, on the contrary, is drawn in a separate stroke and sometimes crosses the traverse. This ductus is more frequent in semicursive than formal scripts, and can be found in Hasmonaean and Herodian hands.

ו is tall and straight, sometimes slightly slanted. Its head features a simple hook of varying width.

ח is drawn without lifting the pen, a ductus that appears in the second half of the first century BC. The two legs are straight and parallel; the traverse is either straight and horizontal (l. 4) or slanted upwards to the left.

י has a chevron shape; it is short and suspended, and the left leg resists the tendency to lengthen observed in some formal hands. In fact, some occurrences of י exhibit thickening so as to look like triangles, a shape that tends to disappear in Herodian scripts.

Medial כ is narrower than ב, with a small curved traverse and more or less rounded elbow.

ל has a tall ascender thickened at the top, which becomes common in the second half of the first century BC, but it lacks the tick that appears in later Herodian hands. The traverse is of uneven width, which might suggest a transition from the Hasmonaean to the Herodian period.

Final ם is large but not square; it follows the old semicursive ductus, which has undergone slight changes throughout the Hasmonaean period. However, the angular aspect and reduced size suggest a late Hasmonaean or early Herodian semicursive script.

Medial מ features a curved traverse, larger than that of כ but more rounded than that of ב. It is drawn together with the vertical, the elbow and the base, without lifting the pen. The elbow is usually rounded but can be orthogonal (l. 5), which foreshadows later Herodian formal hands. The left arm is drawn last, unlike later Herodian scripts.

Final ן has a small straight descender and an angular head; its overall shape is reminiscent of semicursive scripts, and it bears no sign of later, Herodian developments.

ע is large, with a straight diagonal joined in the middle by a left arm. The simple ductus and large size are common in semicursive scripts from the late Hasmonaean and early Herodian periods.

Medial פ (l. 5) has a small hooked head followed by a straight vertical and an angular elbow. The base is straight and long.

Final ץ (l. 5) features a long vertical descender preceded by a curved right arm. The same ductus is observed in the medial צ (l. 5), where the vertical stroke is however followed by a rounded elbow and a long base.

ר has a tick at the left end of its traverse, while the right end is prolonged by a usually rounded elbow, although some angular elbows are sometimes observed (*e.g.* l. 2).

ש is of standard size and angular shape. The left and right arms are straight and symmetrical. The oblique is likewise straight, but thinner and smaller; it is parallel to the right arm and joins the left arm at mid-height. It does not exhibit developments observed in later Herodian hands.

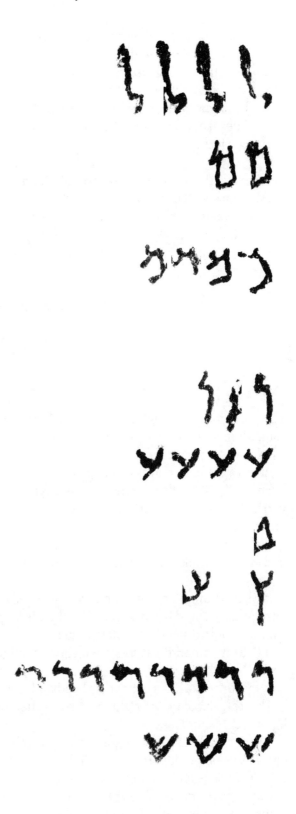

ת is narrow and tall, with equally long legs; the traverse is horizontal and the shoulder more or less rounded. The left leg rises above the traverse, and may have been drawn together, without lifting the pen, although no clear loop can be seen. The foot is sometimes rounded, sometimes angular, and of varying width.

To sum up, the script is quite irregular and, although formal in nature, exhibits influence from semi-cursive forms. Other times, it uses techniques that appear in the middle of the first century BC or hesitates between Hasmonaean and Herodian shapes. This could well be the period in which the manuscript was copied, especially since no typical later Herodian development has been detected. I conclude that MS 4612/9 was copied sometime in the second half (preferably third quarter) of the first century BC.

G. MS 5233/2 (Ps 9.10, 12–13)[6]

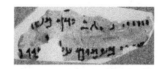

The parchment is rough and the hand hesitant, with some inconsistencies. The standard letter height is medium at about 2.5 mm. Descending letters exceed 3.5 mm (cf. ך l. 2), while ascending letters seem to exceed 4.5 mm (cf. ל l. 3).

ב has a concave traverse that produces two small horns of equal height; the shoulder is raised and the vertical slightly concave. The base is drawn without lifting the pen, from right to left.

ג (l. 2) is tall, with a left leg that reaches above mid-height, unlike later Hasmonaean hands.

ד (l. 2) is angular, with a tall backward-slanted horn and a slanted traverse. The shoulder is looped, which is indicative of a developed ductus.

ו (l. 3) is tall and features a wide, open, angular hooked head.

י, by contrast, has a triangular head and tends to be shorter, although the right leg can be taller when ligatured.

Final ך (l. 2) has a wide slanted traverse followed by a looped shoulder and a long slightly convex descender. The traverse exhibits a small curl at its left end so as to produce a short pointed horn, while the looped shoulder protrudes to the right.

[6] For the text edition, see p. 235.

The beginning of a medial כ (l. 3) reveals a narrower, concave traverse followed by an angular shoulder and vertical arm. The elbow seems thicker, but the base is lost.

ל exhibits limited development; its ascender is thickened at the top so as to produce a triangular head pointing forward, but this is apparently not the flag that becomes popular in late and post-Herodian hands.

Final ם (l. 3) is large, with a tall straight left horn and a slanted traverse followed—after lifting the pen, it seems—by a straight vertical and slanted base. The left vertical is slightly convex and crosses the traverse.

Medial מ has a concave traverse producing a short curved left horn. The right shoulder is either raised or angular. The vertical is straight, the base narrow and slightly slanted. The left arm is short and curved so as to broaden the opening of the letter.

ע has a more or less long diagonal with a round elbow and a short right arm slanted to the right or to the left, which might suggest a transition period. The left arm is straight, slanted, and of varying thickness.

A partial ש (l. 2) reveals an angular base with a slanted left arm and a long, convex right arm. The right arm is further curved at its top, or even angled after the new Herodian fashion. The middle stroke joins the left arm at mid-height.

The end of a ת (l. 3) reveals a protruding (perhaps looped) left shoulder and a wide foot.

To sum up, the hand attested by this manuscript is irregular, with a few and sometimes contradictory morphological features. Since the number of letters preserved on this fragment is limited, it is difficult to suggest an accurate date. The presence of a few techniques that develop in the Herodian period leads me to conclude that MS 5233/2 was copied in the second half (preferably third quarter) of the first century BC.

H. MS 4612/5 (Num 16.2–5)[7]

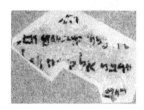

The parchment is rough and the hand hesitant and inconsistent, with a standard letter height comprised between 2 mm and 2.5 mm. No descending letter is attested (ק has no visible tail), while ascending letters seem to exceed 4.5 mm (cf. ל l. 3).

א (l. 3) is tall, with a long convex left leg further curved inward at the bottom. The diagonal is straight and supports a short right arm without ornamentation.

ב exhibits a somewhat inconsistent ductus; it is sometimes small, sometimes large, and its strokes can be concave or convex. The traverse is usually curled at its left end, but this is not always the case. The base may or may not protrude to the left, and seems to have been penned from left to right.

ד is angular, with a thin backward slanted horn at the left end of a straight thick traverse. The right vertical is penned in a second stroke, a tendency that develops in the second half of the first century BC.

ו (l. 2) is tall and narrow, with an open but small hooked head.

ח (l. 3) has a thin and narrow traverse joining thicker legs.

י is somewhat inconsistent, sometimes large and triangular, sometimes tall and narrow, sometimes hooked with a thinner and longer right leg.

A partially erased medial כ (l. 2) reveals a long descender followed by a wide slanted base curled upwards at the end. The traverse seems comparatively narrow, possibly curved or angular at its left end.

ל has a wide traverse and acute hook with a straight diagonal. The neck is sometimes acute, while the ascender can by straight or slanted.

Final ם features an impressive thick horn contrasted by a thinner traverse. The right shoulder is raised; the vertical is sometimes concave, sometimes convex. The base is sometimes slanted, sometimes horizontal and concave. The left vertical may have been drawn without lifting the pen, and crosses the traverse.

ק has a straight traverse, round hook, and straight diagonal. The left vertical crosses the traverse and closes the letter; it seems short, without descender.

ר has a curled left horn and more or less rounded shoulder followed by a straight vertical.

A partial ש (l. 2) reveals a wide base with a convex right arm and inner tick. The left arm is short, straight and slanted. The middle stroke joins the left arm at its base.

A partial ת (l. 2) seems quite narrow, with a concave right leg and a slanted foot at the bottom of the left leg.

To sum up, the hand attested by this manuscript is hesitant and inconsistent, which makes it difficult to date, especially given the limited size and degraded state of the fragment. Based on the presence of a few techniques that develop in the Herodian period, I conclude that MS 4612/5 was copied in the second half of the first century BC.

I. MS 4612/4 (Gen 36.7–16)[8]

The parchment is rough and the hand very small, with an average letter height ranging between 1 mm and 1.5 mm only. Descending letters reach 2.5 mm, with a maximum of 2.7 mm (cf. ך l. 6), while ascending letters can reach 3 mm in height (cf. ל l. 4). This unusually small script size accounts for the lack of drawing precision and complicates palaeographical analysis.

א is drawn in three strokes, lacking the later Herodian developments. The oblique axis is straight, while the left leg is convex and tends to produce an inner foot. The right arm joins the oblique axis at mid-height, sometimes slightly below.

---

[8] For the text edition, see p. 141.

ב has a concave traverse preceded by a vertical horn. The shoulder is raised, and reaches almost the same height as the left horn. The right arm is short and the elbow orthogonal. The base is drawn without lifting the pen, from right to left, unlike the new ductus that develops in the second half of the first century BC. The base is short, barely protruding to the left.

ג has a slanted linear right leg joined at mid-height by a short left leg that seems to be drawn after lifting the pen.

ד (l. 2) exhibits a two-horned head, with both horns slanting backwards. It is not clear whether the right horn is a raised shoulder or if the vertical is drawn after lifting the pen—the latter ductus appearing in the second half of the first century BC. In the latter case, the vertical is slightly concave, but exactly at the level of the traverse. It may be preferable to opt for the first ductus, in which case the vertical is simply straight.

ה is narrow, with slightly curved legs of comparable lengths. The right leg does ascend above the traverse and seems to be drawn without lifting the pen. The left leg is drawn afterwards, but the traverse is short and barely protrudes.

ו has a straight (sometimes slightly concave) vertical topped by a hooked head. The hook is angular and of varying width, which may be due to the small size of the script.

By contrast, ז has no hook but the concave ductus produces a backward bending head.

ח (l. 5) is narrow, with a linear traverse that joins the two legs below their summit, thus producing two small horns. No looped or raised elbow is observed, unlike later Hasmonaean and Herodian developments.

י is short and suspended. It has a triangular shape, with two equally long legs, with a sometimes thinner right leg.

Medial כ (l. 7) is tall with a wide, raised, oblique traverse followed by a raised shoulder, a vertical arm, an angular elbow, and a large base.

ל has a short ascender and narrow traverse. The long oblique is uncommon in formal hands before the Herodian period, but is found earlier in semi-cursive hands. The occasional thickening at the top might be due to the small size of the script, and not

to the analogous tendency that develops in the second half of the first century BC. The last ל (l. 8), however, seems to feature a long hook at its summit; such hooks are more at home in later Herodian formal book hands. Once again, the very small script size obscures typological markers.

Final ם (l. 2) is angular and closed. The right vertical is concave and the base is large. The traverse is curved upwards at its left end, to the point of creating a curl. This is not a loop, however, as the left vertical crosses it and may have been penned last.

By contrast, medial מ (l. 5) is narrow, open and rounded. The left arm is long and protruding, increasing the overall width of the letter.

Final ן exhibits a straight, slanted vertical that descends below the base line.

Medial נ has the same straight, slanted vertical, but it is here followed at an angle by a short base.

ע is quite developed, with a curved right stroke that tends to become a right arm followed by a round elbow and a slanted base, as can be seen in later Hasmonaean hands. But this new ductus is not used throughout, which may suggest a transition period or a mix of semiformal and semicursive shapes.

Final ף (l. 8) has a vertical descender topped by a thick triangular head, or more specifically by a looped head whose angular appearance is probably due to the small size of the script.

Medial פ (l. 7) has a small angular head and a slanted base; the angle is unusual, and if one takes into account the angle of the head (compare the head of final ף), it appears that this specific occurrence of פ exhibits rotation, so that we would expect other occurrences to have a slightly slanted base and likewise slightly slanted vertical, as can be seen throughout Hasmonaean and Herodian hands.

Medial צ (l. 6) has a straight raised right arm that joins the vertical at mid-height. The vertical is slightly slanted, followed by an elbow and a protruding horizontal base.

ר features a curved traverse producing a tall horn and rounded raised shoulder, unlike later forms found in the second half of the first century BC.

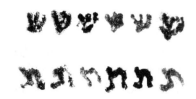

ש has a V shape, with a slanted left arm and convex right arm. The middle stroke is slightly slanted
and joins both arms at their base.

ת has a convex traverse followed by a rounded
shoulder and straight right leg. The left leg is as tall
as the right leg and followed by a foot of varying
length. The traverse joins the left leg below its top,
and sometimes almost crosses it; the two are not
drawn together as in later, Herodian hands.

To sum up, the very small size of this script blurs typological boundaries. On the one hand, it seems to
be a vulgar semicursive Hasmonaean hand. But the presence of seemingly later forms may point to a
semiformal Herodian hand. The limited number of letters does not help, of course, and warrants caution. I hesitantly conclude that MS 4612/4 may have been copied sometime in the second half of the
first century BC.

J.　MS 5233/1 (2 Sam 20.22–24)[9]

The parchment is rough and the hand quite small, with a standard letter height comprised between
1.5 mm and 2 mm. Descending letters measure less than 3 mm in height (cf. ך l. 2), while ascending letters reach 4 mm.

א has a long diagonal that tends to be curved at
the bottom and protruding to the right. The left leg
and right arm are slanted and reach the diagonal at
mid-height.

ב has a short concave traverse contrasted by a
long protruding base. The right shoulder is angular
or raised, and the vertical is straight or convex.

ה has short outspread legs upon which rest a
narrow traverse and a thickened protrusion.

ו is barely slanted and features a narrow hooked
head.

י, by contrast, tends to have a wider head and
thinner leg, but the difference is minimal.

A damaged final ך (l. 2) reveals a slightly slanted
traverse and a straight descender followed at an angle by a wide slanted base.

---

[9] For the text edition, see p. 208.

Medial כ (l. 2) has a narrower traverse and a much shorter vertical. The base is horizontal and slightly narrower.

ל has a broad horizontal traverse followed by an angular hook and a long straight diagonal, in accordance with developments through the first century BC. The letter is sometimes narrower, however, which may be indicative of a transition period. The ascender is usually not thickened, although traces may sometimes indicate otherwise.

A damaged medial מ (l. 3) reveals a square shape with a concave vertical.

ס (l. 3) has a straight slanted left vertical and a large slanted traverse. The shoulder is rounded, and the diagonal closes the letter, a phenomenon that appears in the middle of the first century BC.

ע (l. 1) has two vertical outspread arms resting on a wide base, following the new ductus that appears in the late first century BC. The elbow is rounded, and the arms exhibit no further development.

ק (l. 1) has a straight vertical with a short tail. The traverse is horizontal and wide, followed at an angle by a rounded diagonal that closes the letter.

The head of a ש (l. 3) reveals slanted arms and a short middle stroke connected to the left arm above mid-height.

ת (l. 1) has a convex right leg topped by a round shoulder and short traverse. The left leg protrudes to the top and is bent inward at the bottom, followed by a large horizontal foot.

Overall, the few letters preserved on this damaged fragment belong to a late Hasmonaean or preferably early Herodian semiformal hand, which leads me to conclude that MS 5233/1 was copied sometime in the second half (and preferably the last third) of the first century BC.

K. MS 5095/7 (CommGen A)[10]

The parchment is smooth, the hand is trained and regular, with a standard letter height comprised between 2.5 mm and 3 mm. No descender has been preserved, whereas ascending letters may have reached or exceeded 4.5 mm in height (cf. ל).

ה has a thick straight traverse slightly protruding to the left, sometimes also to the right. The legs are thinner, parallel, and of comparable height.

ו (l. 1) is tall, slanted, with a large hooked head.

By contrast, י has a triangular-shaped head and is noticeably shorter. It is not impossible, however, that additional occurrences of these two letters would have revealed more resembling shapes, as is common in formal hands from the second half of the first century BC.

ל (l. 2) is tall and narrow; the hook is rounded and open, but its length is unknown. Likewise, the head of the ascender is split over two fragments, so that its shape is uncertain; however, it does not seem to be ornamented.

Final ם is tall, broad and angular. The traverse is straight and slanted; it is preceded by a tall, backwards slanted horn and followed by an angular shoulder. The right vertical is slanted, sometimes slightly concave or convex, which impacts the shape of the elbow—rounded or angular. The base is straight, slanted and broad, but it does not reach as far as the left horn, so that the left vertical must be slanted in order to join the traverse after the horn. In one occurrence, it seems that the left vertical was drawn first, upwards, and looped into the traverse in a triangular fashion so that to produce a horn. In this way, the entire letter can be drawn without lifting the pen. The limited number of occurrences prevents us from ascertaining to what extent this new ductus is used by this scribe.

Medial מ (l. 1) is comparatively small, with a slanted narrow traverse preceded by a tall horn and followed by a raised shoulder. The right vertical is

[10] For the text edition, see p. 291.

slightly slanted, followed by an angular elbow. The base is barely concave; it is broad and protrudes to the left, but the protrusion is compensated by the addition of a long left arm beneath the horn.

ר (l. 2) features a large, straight, horizontal traverse preceded by a backwards slanted horn. The elbow is small, angular, and followed by a straight slanted leg.

To sum up, the few letters preserved on this fragment have been penned by a trained scribe using techniques common at the end of the Hasmonaean period and the beginning of the Herodian period. Developments observed in the ductus of some letters point to the latter part, but many letters of the alphabet are not attested, which prevents a more accurate dating. I conclude that MS 5095/7 was copied in the second half (preferably the last quarter) of the first century BC.

L. MS 4612/3 (Eschat. Frg. Ar)[11]

This small fragment is copied by a smooth and beautiful book hand of medium size. Standard letters measure about 2 mm in height, while descending letters can reach 4.5 mm (cf. ר l. 1). The trace of a ל (l. 3) suggests that ascending letters may have reached 4 mm in height.

ד (l. 2) is small and square, with a thick traverse and slightly thinner vertical. The left end of the traverse is thickened so as to produce a triangular horn. At the right end, the traverse joins the vertical below its summit and does not seem to be penned together with it.

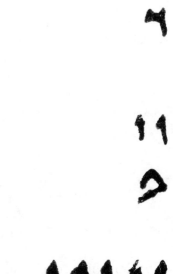

ו is tall, with a narrow solid hook as its head. The vertical is straight, sometimes slightly concave or convex at the bottom.

The beginning of a ט (l. 3) reveals a large angular hook drawn after lifting the pen so as to lengthen the right arm. The right arm is raised; it has not become a horizontal base as can be seen in later Herodian hands.

י has a triangular shape with a concave base and a longer right leg. It tends to become narrower and/or taller, to the point of approaching the general shape of ו, but the solid triangular head of י remains different from the hollow hooked head of ו.

---

[11] For the text edition, see p. 295.

Final ךּ (l. 1) is tall, with a long, thin, curved descender contrasted by a thick straight traverse. At its left end, it features a triangular horn similar to that of ד.

Medial כ (l. 2) does not only move the tail at an angle into a horizontal base, it also loses its triangular left horn; the traverse has become thin and very narrow, curved so as to produce a small horn.

Medial מ adopts the new two-stroke Herodian ductus, with a diagonal, a vertical and base drawn without lifting the pen. The left tick is added later on top of the diagonal. The base is long and slanted, almost parallel to the short diagonal so that the letter is wide open.

Final ן is curved and wide, with a thickened head that contrasts with a thin descender. Thickening is achieved by a two-way oblique stroke and not by the shading common in the Hasmonaean period.

ר (l. 1) features the triangular horn already observed in other letters; it also has a thick traverse and thinner vertical connected by a smooth shoulder.

A partial שׁ (l. 3) reveals an angular, V shape ductus with a slanted left arm and diagonal right arm. The middle stroke is long, parallel to the right arm, and joins the left arm at mid-height.

To sum up, this manuscript was penned by a highly skilled scribe in a formal but smooth hand that integrates some of the new Herodian techniques, at least in the few letters that are preserved. This leads me to conclude that MS 4612/3 was copied towards the end of the first century BC.

M. MS 5440 (1 Kgs 16.23–26)[12]

The parchment is rough and the hand quite small, with a standard letter height comprised between 1.5 mm and 2 mm. Descending letters do not even reach 3 mm in height (cf. ן l. 2), and no ascending letter is attested.

[12] For the text edition, see p. 211.

א adopts the new Herodian ductus; the left leg is convex, but not curled at the bottom. The diagonal is straight, sometimes almost convex. The right arm is likewise convex or straight, and without tick, except perhaps in one instance, although it may just be spread ink.

ב is somewhat inconsistent, with a concave traverse that usually—but not always—rises to produce a straight or curled left horn. The right shoulder is raised and followed by a straight or convex vertical. The elbow is sometimes rounded, sometimes looped, sometimes angular. The base is concave, although in one instance it seems to have been doubled by a left-to-right stroke.

ה is also somewhat inconsistent; the legs are parallel and usually straight, although the right leg tends to be concave, and can be slightly longer or shorter than the left leg. Sometimes, one leg is twice as thick as the other leg. The traverse is straight and connected to the right leg through a raised shoulder; on the left end, it protrudes and loops into the left leg, following the ductus that develops in the Hasmonaean period.

ו is rather short, with an angular hooked head, as are some occurrences of י, although י is usually shorter and less acute. Other instances of י have a triangular head but keep a longer right leg. These fluctuations may suggest a transition period, especially in the second half of the first century BC where some scripts barely distinguish ו and י.

Medial מ (l. 3) adopts the new Herodian ductus, with a long diagonal drawn together with the right vertical and the base. The shoulder is angular and the elbow rounded; the base is quite narrow, so that the diagonal protrudes and opens the letter. The left horn is penned last.

Final ן (l. 2) is doubly curved, concave in the upper part and convex in the lower part. Its tail is thin and its head thickened leftward.

Medial נ is less concave and angled so as to create a narrow horizontal base.

ע has a long slanted right arm followed by a round elbow and long slanted oblique. The left arm is perpendicular to the oblique and joins it at the elbow.

Medial צ (l. 1) features a doubly curved diagonal, concave at the top and convex at the bottom. It is

followed at an angle by a wide base slanted upwards, which is probably due to the ligature or a
semicursive influence. The right arm is tall, convex
and joins the diagonal above mid-height.

ק (l. 2) is wide but rather short, with a slanted
traverse, raised hook and round oblique that does
not reach the tail, so that the letter remains open.
The left vertical is slanted, slightly concave, and
topped by a hook that protrudes to the right, similar to the triangular loop that develops in some Herodian scripts.

ר has a tall, curled or angular, horn and a narrow,
slanted traverse. The shoulder is angular and the
vertical is straight but of varying height.

ש features a V shape with straight arms; the
right arm is slanted, while the left arm is almost
vertical. The middle stroke is parallel to the right
arm and joins the left arm at mid-height (or lower,
in one instance). The right arm is sometimes curved
at its top, as in late Hasmonaean scripts, or angled
after the new Herodian fashion.

ת has a tall, slanted left leg followed by a sometimes straight, sometimes rounded horizontal foot.
The right leg is parallel, as tall and slanted, and
topped by a slightly slanted traverse.

Overall, this small semiformal script exhibits hesitations and inconsistencies, but its characteristics
otherwise match the early Herodian period. I conclude that MS 5440 was copied at the end of the first
century BC.

N. MS 5214/1 (Deut 6.1–2)[13]

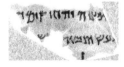

The parchment is rough and the hand hesitant, inconsistent. The strokes are uneven, the script of medium size, with a standard letter height of about 2 mm. No descending letter is attested (ק l. 1 has a
short tail), while the ascender of a broken ל (l. 3) may suggest a total height of about 3.5 mm to 4 mm
provided that line spacing is consistent.

א (l. 2) has a tall, slanted left leg that protrudes
above the diagonal, which is indicative of a late development. The bottom of the left leg features an
inner tick that developed from the curve found in

---

[13] For the text edition, see p. 173.

earlier hands. The right arm is long, straight, without tick, and parallel to the left leg.

ב (l. 2) has a broad concave traverse further curved at its left end but does not feature a tall horn. A raised right shoulder leads to a straight arm, followed by an angular elbow and wide concave base drawn from right to left, unlike the new Herodian ductus.

ה is quite inconsistent, with legs that are sometimes short, sometimes tall, the left leg being sometimes shorter and sometimes longer than the right leg. The traverse is thick and protrudes to the left, but the protrusion is sometimes rounded, sometimes triangular, almost hooked, as can be seen in the early Herodian period.

ו is tall and usually narrow, but in one instance thick and somewhat shorter. The vertical tends to be concave in the upper part and convex at the bottom. It is headed by an angular hook, sometimes short, sometimes long.

ח (l. 1) is very unusual, with a thin curved left leg and a thick parallel right leg. The traverse is very thin and slightly concave; it almost protrudes to the left.

י (l. 1) has a straight vertical headed by a hooked head. It is slightly shorter and wider than ו, but such a similar outlook is frequent at the turn of our era.

The ascender of an otherwise lost ל (l. 3) is thick, perhaps slightly thickened backward at the top as is common in Hasmonaean and early Herodian hands, but does not feature the flag that becomes popular among later Herodian scribes.

Final ם (l. 1) is tall, wide and angular. It follows a one-stroke ductus adapted from a semicursive script, starting with a tall slanted left horn, a wide straight slanted traverse, an angular shoulder, a tall arm rounded at the bottom followed by a wide concave base ending in a loop so as to draw the left vertical upward. The left vertical crosses the traverse and reaches as high as the left horn.

Medial מ (l. 1) adopts the new Herodian ductus, with a diagonal followed at an angle by the right vertical and a large base. The diagonal is concave and receives an orthogonal tick.

ע (l. 2) has two parallel vertical arms; both are developed, concave, and rest on a slightly slanted base.

Medial צ (l. 1) has a barely slanted but concave diagonal followed at an acute angle by a short base. The right arm does not touch the diagonal; it is vertical, short, with a rounded elbow, which is indicative of a developed form.

ק (l. 1) has an S-shaped hook and a vertical headed by an angular tick, which explains the unusual double-horned summit. The hook is otherwise angular and crammed, while the vertical is short, thick and without descender.

ר (l. 2) is angular, with a slanted traverse and straight vertical. The traverse is curved at its left end to produce a sharp, angular horn.

ש has a long left arm, convex at the top and concave at the bottom, protruding at the bottom—a ductus that remains popular in Herodian cursive (and semicursive) scripts. The right arm is broad and convex, sometimes slightly rounded at the top but without tick. The middle stroke is long, curved, and parallel to the right arm.

ת (l. 2) has a simple two-stroke ductus; the left leg is tall, slanted, and followed by a horizontal foot. The right leg is parallel, slanted, and topped by an angular hook producing a short slanted traverse.

To sum up, the few letters preserved on this small fragment exhibit hesitations and inconsistencies that prevent an accurate dating. They seem to belong to a Herodian semiformal hand with a few developments, which leads me to conclude that MS 5214/1 was probably copied sometime at the beginning of the first century AD.

O. MS 5439/2 (Unidentified Fragment)[14]

The hand is skilled and precise, with a standard letter height comprised between 2 mm and 2.5 mm. Descending letters might exceed 4.5 mm (cf. ק l. 3), while ascending letters reach 5 mm in height (cf. ל l. 2).

א (l. 3) has a thin left leg drawn in one stroke with the diagonal, according to the new Herodian ductus. The diagonal is delicately thickened by this skilled hand. The right arm is thin at its base but

---

[14] For the text edition, see p. 299.

thickened at the top so as to create a tick, indicative
of later Herodian calligraphy.

A partial ה (l. 3) reveals a short, straight, thick
left leg and a very slightly protruding traverse.

ו is tall and narrow, slightly slanted and sometimes concave, with a small hooked head.

י (l. 2), by contrast, tends to be convex, with a triangular head, but remains tall as opposed to the
usually shorter forms in the post-Herodian period.

ל is large, with a wide traverse and an angular
hook. The diagonal seems straight and oblique. The
ascender is rather short and features a forward
thickening at home in the Herodian period, although not as angular as the flag that becomes popular in late Herodian and post-Herodian times.

Final ץ (l. 3) has a slightly concave descender
thickened at the top. The right arm is straight,
oblique, and features a leftward tick at the top consistent with the calligraphy observed elsewhere.

To sum up, the few letters preserved on this fragment belong to a skilled formal hand from
the late Herodian period. A number of letters of the Hebrew alphabet are not attested and could reveal
post-Herodian features, but on the basis of the extant text I cautiously conclude that MS 5439/2 was
copied around the middle of the first century AD.

P. MS 5441 (Ruth 2.1–2)[15]

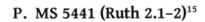

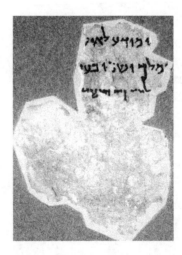

The parchment is rough and the hand hesitant, of medium size, with a standard letter height of about
2.5 mm. Descending letters measure up to 4.5 mm in height (cf. ך l. 2), while descending letters exceed
4 mm and may have reached 5 mm (cf. the partially erase ל l. 3).

א (l. 1) is angular and ornamented, with a straight thin left leg followed without lifting the pen by a straight thick diagonal. The right arm is short, joins the diagonal at mid-height and features an elbow followed by a vertical, slightly slanted tick. The left leg also has a tick pointing inward and slightly slanted. This ductus is indicative of a late or post-Herodian hand.

ב (l. 2) is rather small, square, with a concave traverse and slightly concave vertical. The traverse is thickened at its left end but produces no horn. The shoulder is raised so that both ends of the traverse reach the same height. The base protrudes to the left and may have been penned from left to right, but it does not protrude to the right.

ד (l. 1) is angular and drawn in one stroke. The traverse is straight and rather narrow; it features a backward slanting horn at its left end, and a looped shoulder at its right end so that the vertical is drawn without lifting the pen. The vertical is short, thin and straight so that the shoulder protrudes to the right in a fashion that becomes popular in late Herodian scripts.

An almost complete ה (l. 3) reveals a wide and thick protrusion left of the traverse, contrasted by thin (incomplete) legs. The left leg and the traverse may well have been penned together; as for the right leg, the absence of looped shoulder may indicate that it was penned separately, unlike later Herodian trends.

ו is tall, rather thick, with a short angular hook as its head. The vertical is not always straight, but can sometimes be slightly concave or convex.

The top of a ז (l. 2) reveals a small head thickened backwards, perhaps in an attempted triangular shape that would be at home in later Herodian times.

י is tall but has a solid head that distinguishes it from the hook-headed ו.

Final ך (l. 2) is large, tall and unusually thick. The traverse is straight and ends in a triangular horn that becomes popular among late Herodian hands. The vertical is straight, long and thick; it is slightly curved at the bottom.

ל features a wide linear traverse and an acute hook that develops in the first half of the first century AD. The head is thickened but without the characteristic tick of later Herodian ornamented scripts.

Medial מ is small, with a thin left arm that is drawn after the thick traverse, the vertical and the base. The ductus is not very consistent; the traverse is curved upwards at its left end, but the right shoulder is sometimes rounded, sometimes almost raised. The vertical is sometimes almost convex, sometimes almost concave. The elbow is either angular or rounded. The base is narrow, barely as large as the traverse, and slightly slanted so that the letter is wide open.

ע is rounded, with a convex right arm prolonged by a curved oblique. The left arm is likewise convex, almost vertical. It has no tick, while the right arm is barely thickened; none of the later Herodian developments can be observed.

ש is wide and quite angular, with an overall V shape. The left arm is straight, slanted, and thickened at the top, sometimes with a right-pointing tick. The right arm is more slanted, longer, and angled at the top so as to produce a left-pointing tick. The middle stroke is shorter and thinner, slightly curved, and also features a tick that becomes popular in later Herodian formal scripts. Its position is somewhat inconsistent, sometimes joining both arms at their base, sometimes attached to the left arm below mid-height.

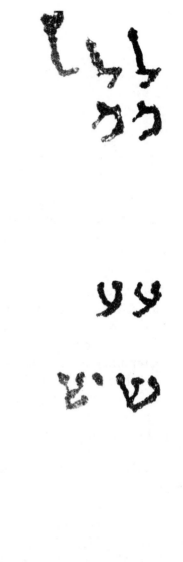

To sum up, this semiformal but hesitant script exhibits some but not all of the late Herodian features. I conclude that MS 5441 was copied around the middle of the first century AD.

Q. MS 5214/2 (Deut 32.5–9)[16]

The parchment is rough but the hand rather consistent, of medium size, with a standard letter height of about 2.5 mm. The height of descending letters is about 4 mm, while ascending letters reach 5 mm (cf. ל l. 5).

א is angular, with a straight slanted left leg drawn together with the diagonal in the new Herodian fashion. The right arm is short, straight, and joins the diagonal at mid-height. Both left leg and right arm have a backward tick, which is indicative of later and post-Herodian hands.

ב is likewise angular, with a short slanted traverse followed by a straight vertical arm. The base is large, straight, parallel to the traverse and protrudes in both directions.

ד (l. 4) is square, with a traverse as large as (or even larger than) the vertical. The two strokes are joined by a triangular shoulder popular in late and post Herodian scripts.

ו (l. 3) is straight and vertical, with an angular hooked head (albeit partially erased).

ח (l. 5) is penned in one stroke, with two looped protruding shoulders at home in late Herodian or post-Herodian times. The right leg is concave, the left leg is partially erased.

י is usually narrow and tall, though slightly suspended, and thus shorter than ו. It has a narrow and angular hooked head.

Final ך is angular, with a slanted horn, a straight and slightly slanted traverse, a looped shoulder and a straight vertical. The vertical is prolonged by a convex descender.

---

[16] For the text edition, see p. 177.

ל has a large traverse and an angular hook; the diagonal is long, straight or slightly convex. The ascender is tall and topped by a leftward tick that develops into a flag, which suggests a late or post-Herodian date.

Final ם (l. 4) is square, large and closed. The left horn is thick, slanted, but barely protrudes. The traverse is straight and slanted; the right vertical is straight, with angular shoulder and elbow. The base is horizontal and straight. The left vertical is slightly slanted so as to join the traverse before the horn.

Medial נ is tall and narrow, with a straight vertical thickened at the top or even ticked backwards. The base is straight and very narrow.

Medial צ (l. 4) has a straight, barely slanted vertical followed by a straight base. The right arm is almost horizontal, with an upward tick at its end, a tendency that develops in the late Herodian period.

ק (l. 2) has a short and thin descender connected to the traverse through a triangular loop. The traverse is straight, slanted, and leads to a partially rounded hook. The oblique is straight, thinner at the end and does not close the letter.

ש has a simple V shape, with a straight left arm and slightly convex right arm. The middle stroke is parallel to the right arm and joins the left arm at (or slightly below) mid-height. The right and left arms do not seem to feature the ticks that become popular in late and post-Herodian formal hands.

To sum up, this manuscript was penned by a skilled late Herodian or early post-Herodian formal book hand, which leads me to conclude that MS 5214/2 was copied sometime in the second half of the first century AD, perhaps in the third quarter.

R. MS 4612/1 (Joel 4.1–5)[17]

This skilled book hand is precise and regular, with standard large letters of *ca.* 3 mm in height. The only descending letter (ק l. 1) barely exceeds 4 mm, while ascending letters easily reach 6 mm (cf. ל l. 1 and 6).

א (l. 1) exhibits a thick left leg drawn upwards and progressively getting thinner as it reaches the top, which is quite unusual—perhaps even for this scribe, as it is the only occurrence of א on this fragment. The leg joins the diagonal at its top, which is indicative of a Herodian ductus. The diagonal is thin and partially erased; the right arm seems quite vertical and must have joined the diagonal below mid-height. The arm is thin and thickened at the top; in fact, a direct examination reveals a backward tick, which becomes popular among late and post-Herodian formal hands.

ב is wide and angular, with a triangular left horn and a straight horizontal traverse. The shoulder is angular; the vertical is straight, slanted, and followed by a thickened elbow, which indicates that the base is actually drawn from left to right, after lifting the pen, although in does not protrude to the right. The base is large, slanted, and protrudes to the left.

ד has a tall left horn slanted backwards, at least in one of the two occurrences (l. 5). The straight and wide traverse is followed by a crossed or triangular right shoulder, which becomes popular in the late Herodian period. The vertical is straight and barely longer than the traverse.

ה (l. 1) features a wide traverse protruding to the left in a triangular fashion. It covers two otherwise simple straight parallel legs of almost identical height.

ו is straight and slanted, with a triangular head of varying size.

ז (l. 3), by contrast, has a tick that protrudes to the right of the vertical stroke; the triangular shape of the head is consistent with the scribe's ductus and at home in late and post-Herodian times.

ט (l. 2) features a wide base, barely slanted, upon which rest two arms. The left arm is straight, almost vertical, and headed by a leftward tick, which appears in the latest Herodian hands and becomes popular in post-Herodian times. The right arm is in fact a curved hook, shorter than the left arm but broad enough to fill this large letter which seems to have been penned in one stroke, from left to right.

Medial כ (l. 1) has a very narrow traverse contrasted by a broad base. The left end of the traverse has a triangular shape consistent with the ductus observed earlier, and is followed at an angle by a straight and tall vertical arm. The elbow is slightly rounded, followed without lifting the pen by the traverse.

ל is tall, with a straight traverse of varying width followed by an angular hook. The diagonal is straight and open. The ascender is headed by a triangular flag consistent with the scribe's ductus and at home in late and post-Herodian book hands.

A partially preserved final ם (l. 1) is tall, wide and angular. The base is slightly slanted and followed by a straight vertical. The traverse protrudes to the left by means of a horn that seems triangular.

A partial medial מ (l. 3) reveals a long protruding left arm headed by a thick slanted horn. The base seems thinner and slightly slanted.

Medial נ (l. 2) is tall and relatively wide; the base is straight, horizontal, and thickened at the end. It follows a rounded elbow and straight vertical arm. At the top, a thickened head is consistent with the late morphological developments observed elsewhere.

Medial פ (l. 2) features a simple hooked head, without the additional tick that appears at the middle of the first century. The right vertical prolongs the symmetrical hook and is thus slanted. It is followed at an angle by a straight base drawn without lifting the pen.

Medial צ features a thick, barely slanted vertical followed at an angle—without lifting the pen—by an equally thick horizontal base. The right arm orthogonally joins the vertical above mid-height. In the first occurrence, it is thin at its base and thicker at its top; in the second, it is thick throughout, with a small tick at its top. The left vertical has a flag at home in the latest and post-Herodian book hands.

ק (l. 1) is broad, with a straight horizontal traverse followed by a rounded hook with a short diagonal that does not reach the descender. The latter is headed by a triangular horn consistent with the scribe's ductus.

ר is broad and short, with straight traverse and leg. The shape of the shoulder is blurred, but the left end clearly features a triangular horn, as expected in such a late or post-Herodian formal book hand.

ש is wide, due to a long, barely convex right arm. At its top, a leftward tick is consistent with the ductus observed above. The middle arm is parallel, shorter, and in one occurrence thickened at the top. The left arm is straight, slanted, and sometimes thickened at the top, almost flagged.

ת features a large traverse followed by an angular shoulder and straight right leg, although one occurrence (l. 2) has a more rounded shoulder and slightly convex right leg. The left leg is straight, vertical, and followed at an angle by a slanted foot; in one instance (l. 2), however, the left leg is slightly convex and the foot horizontal. At the top, a triangular horn is purely ornamental and indicative of a late, developed ductus.

To sum up, this manuscript was copied by a skilled formal book hand exhibiting developments that appear in the latest Herodian scripts. I conclude that MS 4612/1 was copied in the second half of the first century AD, perhaps in the third quarter.

S. MS 4611 (Lev 26.3–9, 33–39)[18]

The hand is consistent, of medium size, with a standard letter height of *ca.* 2.5 mm. This medium size is contrasted by the length of descending letters, which can reach 5.5 mm (cf. ק col. i l. 5), while ascending letters reach 5 mm in height (cf. ל col. i l. 8).

Since the manuscript has been distorted (as can be seen here on the infrared photograph), I have digitally straightened the two columns using an image processing algorithm (cf. pictures below) so that the letters presented below (as well as in the palaeographical chart at the end of this chapter) better reflect the scribe's original ductus.

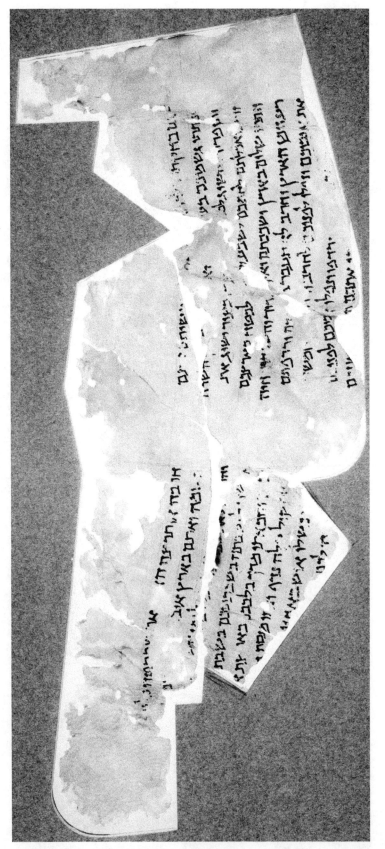

[18] For the text edition, see p. 159.

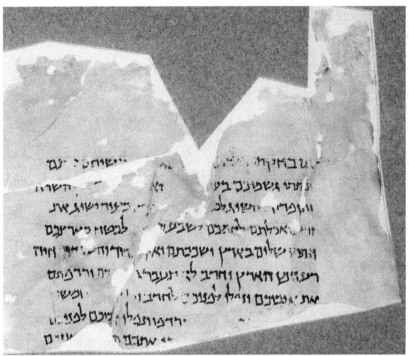

MS 4611 col. i, with lines digitally straightened

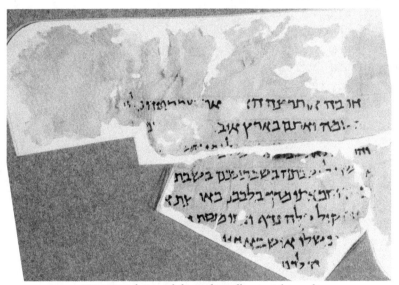

MS 4611 col. ii, with lines digitally straightened

א has a thick diagonal that connects to a usually thinner left leg below its top. The right arm is thicker at its top, sometimes to the point of creating a tick pointing to the right, which suggests a mid- to late Herodian book hand.

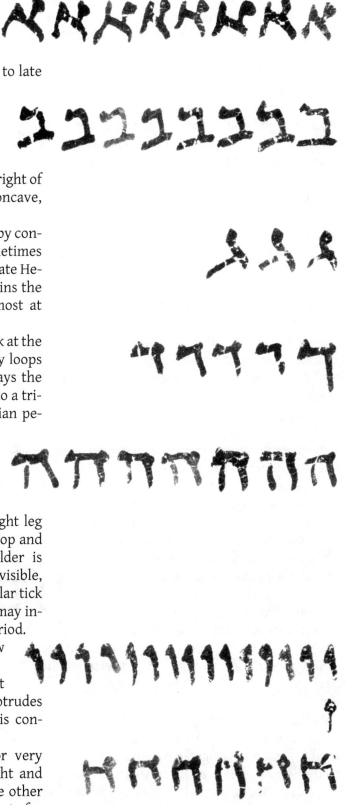

ב is wide and open, with an angular and almost square shape. The traverse features a tick at its left end and an orthogonal shoulder at its right end. The base starts to the left of the traverse and protrudes to the right of the vertical stroke. It is sometimes slightly concave, especially at its right end.

ג has a concave head, often compensated by convex bottom. The head is also thickened, sometimes producing a tick, which is consistent with a late Herodian ductus. The left leg is straight and joins the right stroke above its base, sometimes almost at mid-height.

ד is large and square, with a triangular tick at the left end of its traverse. The shoulder usually loops into the vertical stroke, but this is not always the case. The angular ductus shapes the loop into a triangle, which fits well a mid- to late Herodian period.

ה is of standard size, with a limited protrusion of the traverse beyond the left leg. The left leg is sometimes thinner than the right leg, especially at its top, so that its contact with the traverse is limited. The right leg tends to be curved, slightly concave at the top and slightly convex at the bottom. The shoulder is looped; the loop is sometimes flat, barely visible, but more often angular, producing a triangular tick at the top of the right leg. These variations may indicate a transition into the late Herodian period.

ו is tall and straight, with a small, narrow triangular head.

ז (col. i l. 4) is, like ו, tall and straight; but the head is shaped by means of a tick that protrudes to the right of the vertical stroke, which is consistent with a mid- to late Herodian period.

ח is wide and square, with straight or very slightly curved legs. The traverse is straight and connects to the left leg below its top; at the other end it loops into the right leg, which accounts for the occasional protrusion.

ט (col. i l. 4) is wide, with a very large hooked head at home in the late Herodian period. The formal, angular ductus displays further sophistication by means of a tick at the end of the hook and a thickening at the top of the left arm, which lacks (at least in this instance) a fully developed tick as can be seen in some post-Herodian scripts.

י has a larger head than ו; its vertical stroke is more or less shorter and tends to be thinner at the bottom. As a result, the two letters are usually easy to distinguish.

Final ך (col. ii l. 5) features a broader traverse with a tick at its left and right ends. The tail seems slightly curved and thinner at the bottom; the tick at its top may correspond to a looped ductus well attested in late Herodian and post-Herodian periods.

Medial כ tends to have a narrower traverse than ב, with an upper curve or tick at its left end. The shoulder is angular and tends to double but without any loop or tick. The vertical stroke is straight and the elbow orthogonal. The base is broader than the traverse, extending to the left.

ל has a tall, straight and almost vertical ascender. At its top, it features a triangular head of variable width, sometimes discreet but more often prominent, which is indicative of a transition to late Herodian and post-Herodian scripts. The traverse also exhibits variable width, from narrow (*ca.* 1 mm, *e.g.* col. i l. 5) to wide (*ca.* 2 mm, *e.g.* col. ii l. 6).

Final ם is big and square, with a protruding traverse and tick at the top. Shoulder and elbow are orthogonal, while the right arm and base are straight or slightly concave. The left vertical stroke is bent inward at the top and does not always reach the traverse. At the bottom, on the contrary, it tends to go below the base.

Medial מ has a narrow head followed by a sharp or curved shoulder. The vertical stroke is quite straight, sometimes slightly concave. The elbow, like the shoulder, is sometimes sharp or curved. The base is twice as long as the traverse and reaches as far as the long left arm.

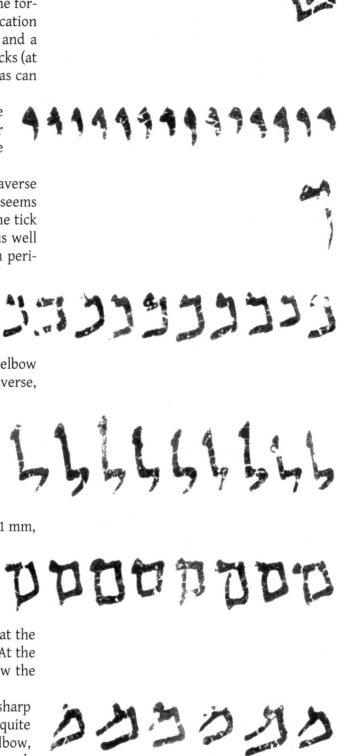

Final ן is short and curved, concave at the top and convex at the bottom. The head may be thickened, but not to the extent of medial נ as is often the case in post-Herodian scripts.

Medial נ features straight or slightly concave vertical and horizontal strokes of comparable length. The top is thickened and curved, sometimes—but not always—producing a right-pointing tick. These variations suggest a transition to late and post-Herodian scripts.

ס (col. ii l. 6) has a large traverse followed by an angular shoulder, a short arm and a slightly curved elbow. The left arm crosses both the traverse and the base.

ע is wide, with two parallel arms. The right arm is smaller than the left arm, and both tend to be concave at the top, which fits best the late Herodian period. The elbow is sharp, and the base is longer and slightly more inclined than that of other letters.

Final ף (col. ii l. 6) features a hooked head whose left arm tends to be thinner, with a tick at the bottom. The right arm is straight and extends into a short tail oriented backwards.

Medial פ has the same outlook, except for the right arm which is followed by an elbow and a large base that protrudes to the left. These characteristics are all consistent with a late Herodian script.

Medial צ features ticks on top of both arms, which favor a late Herodian or post-Herodian period. The elbow and base are consistent with shapes observed earlier, and are naturally absent from final ץ, whose tail is long and tends to become thinner and curved at the bottom.

ק, by contrast, has a shorter tail; its traverse is large and features a triangular tick at its left end looping into the tail, as can often be observed in late Herodian and post-Herodian formal scripts.

ר is square and has a tick at the left end of its traverse. The shoulder is usually curved, which makes it easy to distinguish it from ד, but a few occurrences exhibit a sharper (though never looped) shoulder.

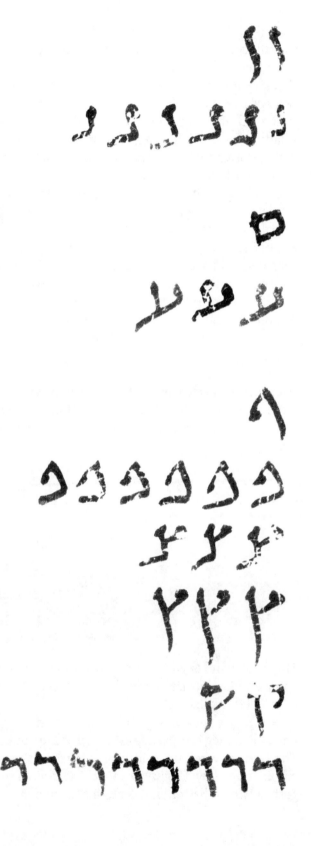

ש is wide, with a straight left arm and
slightly curved right arm. Both arms join at
their base, where the middle stroke sometimes joins them, although it usually
reaches the left arm above. The right arm is angled
to the left at its top, while the middle stroke has a
smaller tick. The left arm also features a left-pointing tick of varying size, which favours a late Herodian or post-Herodian date.

ת is large, with a traverse that reaches
the left leg below its top, or with an occasional triangular ornamentation. The right
end of the traverse is followed by a curved (or rarely
sharp) shoulder and a straight right leg. The right
leg tends to become thinner at the bottom, and
sometimes extends below the left leg. The left leg,
by contrast, has a large foot that remains straight,
unlike a growing tendency in post-Herodian
scripts.

Overall, the palaeographical analysis points to a late Herodian formal script; several letters exhibit variations that seem to reflect an evolution or transition from Herodian to post-Herodian scripts, which
leads me to conclude that MS 4611 was copied sometime during (or slightly after) the second half of the
first century AD.

T. MS 2861 (Judg 4.5–6)[19]

This book hand is skilled and assured, drawing large letters with a standard height comprised between
3 mm and 3.5 mm. Descending letters exceed 4 mm (cf. ז col. i l. 3), ascending letters seem to reach about
5.5 mm (cf. ל col. i l. 2).

א is large, with a long and thick straight diagonal. The left leg is thin and thickened at the bottom.
The right arm rests at mid-height on the diagonal
and is topped by a rightward tick. The ductus suggests a late or, better, post-Herodian period.

---

[19] For the text edition, see p. 193.

ב has a tall backward-slanted left horn on top of a straight slanted traverse. The shoulder is angular and the vertical straight and slanted. The base is wide, thick, and protrudes on both sides; it seems penned from left to right, following a ductus that develops through the Herodian period.

ד (l. 3) has a triangular left horn popular in the latest Herodian and post-Herodian hands. The traverse and vertical are straight, and there does not seem to be a triangular right shoulder.

ה has thin parallel legs covered by a thick traverse. The left leg seems slightly curved leftward at the bottom. The traverse protrudes to the left in a triangular fashion consistent with the scribe's ductus.

ו is tall and straight, slightly slanted, with a solid triangular head. The bottom is sometimes slightly curved forward.

A partially erased ח (l. 2) reveals a doubly curved left leg, convex at the top and concave at the bottom. The traverse is straight, slanted, and connected to the legs below their summit.

ט (l. 2) has a wide slanted base upon which rest two arms. The right arm is oblique, headed by a large hook, and drawn together with it so as to join the base at its right end. The left arm has a leftward tick that appears in the latest Herodian hands and becomes popular in post-Herodian times.

י is of varying width; its head is either triangular or hooked, and its left leg is barely shorter than that of standard letters.

ל has a wide traverse, usually horizontal but sometimes slightly slanted. The hook is angular, with a thin diagonal, quite long but open and ending before the neck. The ascender seems to feature a forward flag, as is common among late Herodian and post-Herodian formal hands.

Final ם is wide and square, with a long protrusion supporting a tall vertical triangular horn. The traverse is otherwise straight, followed at an angle by a straight slanted vertical. The base is broad but stops before the horn, so that the left vertical is barely slanted.

Two occurrences of medial מ are almost erased, so that its morphology is uncertain.

Final ן (l. 3) has a thick head and a convex descender whose reduced length follows a growing
tendency in the second half of the first century.

Medial נ has a concave vertical, sometimes bent
backward at the top. The base is wide and barely
slanted.

ע is wide, with a long diagonal curved at the top
but without an elbow or long tick. The left arm is
straight and thickened at the top, again without
tick.

Medial פ features a hooked head with an additional tick that appears at the middle of the first
century. The right vertical is slanted and followed
at an angle by a base of varying incline and length.

Medial צ (l. 4) is tall, with a long slightly slanted
vertical and a narrow base. The right arm is short,
oblique, and curved upward at its end. The vertical
is thickened at the head so as to produce a small flag
that appears in the latest Herodian hands.

ק has a broad traverse followed by an acute hook
and shorter diagonal, so that the letter remains
open. The descender is thin, of unknown length. It
stands beneath (and in one instance to the right of)
a triangular horn indicative of a late or post-Herodian ductus.

ר (l. 2) also has a triangular horn, which ends a
large and thinner traverse. The shoulder is
rounded, and the vertical slightly slanted.

ש has a straight, barely slanted left arm, while
the right arm is longer and convex. It bears at its
top a tick that develops in the middle of the first
century AD. The middle stroke seems shorter and
parallel, without tick. The left arm is thickened at
its top, but without tick.

ת is broad, with a wide traverse followed by a
rounded shoulder and straight right leg. The left leg
is likewise straight and connected to the traverse
through a triangular shoulder, which develops in
the second half of the first century AD. The foot is
large and slightly slanted.

To sum up, this elegant and consistent formal book hand exhibits numerous features that appear in the
latest Herodian scripts and become popular in post-Herodian hands. I conclude that MS 2861 was copied
during or slightly after the second half of the first century AD.

U. MS 2713 (Josh 1.9–12; 2.3–5)[20]

The hand is large and regular, with a standard letter height of *ca.* 3 mm. Descending letters measure up to 4 mm (cf. ו col. i l. 7) while ascending letters can exceed 5.5 mm in height (cf. ל col. i l. 9).

א exhibits a tick at the top of the right arm as well as the bottom of the left leg, which fits best the late Herodian period. The oblique traverse and the left leg are drawn in a single stroke, while the right arm joins the traverse above its bottom.

A partial ב (col. i l. 9) also exhibits a tick at the left end of its traverse. Its shoulder and elbow seem very angular, while its base is longer than its traverse.

ג (col. i l. 9) is traced in a single stroke; the right leg is straight, almost vertical, with a tick at its head. The left leg is horizontal, concave, and joins the right leg at its base, which is consistent with a late Herodian hand.

It is followed by a ד (col. i l. 9) that features a tick at both ends of its traverse. The right tick also serves as the head of the leg, which allows for a single-stroke tracing of the letter. The leg is straight and almost vertical.

---

[20] For the text edition, see p. 185.

ה features the same ductus, with a tick at the right end of the traverse connecting it to the right leg. The traverse protrudes to the left by means of a downward tick, which suggests a late or post-Herodian period. The left leg is parallel to the right leg; both are straight and of the same length.

ו is tall and straight, with a slight curve towards the left at the bottom, which becomes common in post-Herodian hands. Its head is narrow, shaped like a triangle with a small horizontal base.

What could be a partially erased ז (col. i l. 7) exhibits a tick that protrudes to the right at the top of the vertical stroke. The bottom end seems bevelled, perhaps even curved to the left, though this is unclear since the ink has faded.

י, like ו, is shaped with a triangular head on top of a vertical stroke, but the head is usually slightly larger and the vertical stroke quite smaller, which makes it easier to distinguish between the two letters.

Final ך (col. i l. 2) exhibits a wide traverse with a tick at its left end and a loop at its right end. Such a ductus appears in the late Herodian period and develops in post-Herodian hands as is the case here with a loop protruding both to the right and the top.

Medial כ (col. i l. 6) shares the same tick as the ב at the left end of its traverse, but the traverse itself is slightly narrower while the vertical stroke is, on the contrary, taller. The base is broader than the traverse and protrudes to the left.

ל is both tall and wide, with a sharp, angular shape. The oblique stroke is long and reaches down to a virtual baseline. The ascender slants forward and features a triangular head consistent with this scribal hand and indicative of a late or post-Herodian period.

Final ם is large, square, and angular, with a tick (rather than a loop) connecting the left arm and the traverse.

Medial מ (col. i l. 1) is drawn in three stages: the oblique stroke is not drawn together with the left vertical stroke, nor with the upper tick. The tick, common in the late Herodian period, exhibits further development and has now become an angular hook, which appears in the latest Herodian hands and develops in the post-Herodian period.

Medial נ features a wide base and a straight vertical stroke, except for a small tick at the top.

The tick is more visible on the final ן (col. i l. 7), whose tail is short and curved. Both the reduced length and the ticked head of the final ן are at home in post-Herodian times.

A final ץ and a partial medial צ share the overall formal and angular ductus observed elsewhere; they feature ticks on top of both arms, which is consistent with this developed hand and fits the latest or post-Herodian trends.

A partial ק (col. i l. 1) features a large traverse and a short tail; the two are connected by a triangular tick that protrudes both to the top and to the left.

ר is square, sometimes even broader than tall (*e.g.* col. i l. 8). Its shoulder is angular, and the left end of its traverse features a tall and narrow tick.

ש is wide, with an almost vertical or slightly slanted left arm connected to the right arm at their base. The middle stroke is parallel to the right arm and reaches the left arm almost at mid-height. Both right arm and middle stroke are curved to the left at their top; the curve sometimes becomes angular, especially at the top of the right arm, so as to look like a tick. The left arm also features a left-pointing tick, which is indicative of further development than what is usually observed in Herodian scripts.

ת also exhibits a fully developed shape, with a tick or hook at the top of its left leg; the traverse is not drawn at the same time, so that the tick is not an angular loop but pure ornamentation. The left leg is prolonged at its bottom by a foot that also features a tick, which formalizes a tendency, seen in some post-Herodian scripts, to curve the foot upward.

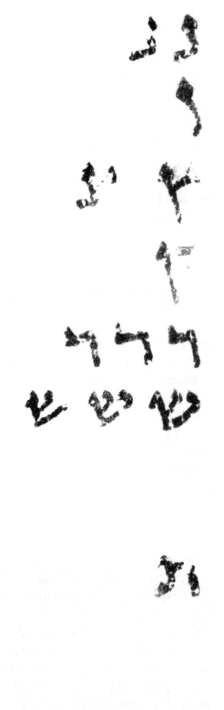

In conclusion, this manuscript features one of the most developed and ornamented formal scripts among the Dead Sea Scrolls. Even the latest Herodian hands (such as Mas 1k) barely match the level of sophistication observed here. Although a date in the third quarter of the first century AD cannot be excluded, this hand better fits the post-Herodian period. In fact, ornamented formal hands of the early second century AD do not exhibit clear typological developments, which prevents a more accurate dating; indeed, the script of this manuscript is more developed than that of many Murabba'at scrolls. I conclude that MS 2713 was probably copied between the end of the first century AD and the beginning of the second century.

V. Conclusion

The 20 manuscripts examined here were penned by scribal hands from different periods, of different types, sizes, and skills. The oldest scroll (MS 5439/1, 4QRP[b]) was copied in the second half of the second century BC, while the youngest manuscript (MS 2713, Josh) dates to the end of the first century AD or the beginning of the second century. Both hands are skilled and confident, as is the case for several other Dead Sea Scrolls in The Schøyen Collection; see also MS 1909 (1QSb); MS 5095/7 (CommGen A); MS 4612/3 (Eschat. Frg.); MS 5439/2 (Unid. Text); MS 5214/2 (Deut 32); MS 4611 (Lev); MS 2861 (Judg).

The standard letter height is usually comprised between 2 mm and 2.5 mm, although it reaches 3.5 mm with the largest hand, that of MS 2861 (Judg). As opposed to this large script, a very small hand can be observed on MS 4612/4 (GenMiniature), with a standard letter height ranging between 1 mm and 1.5 mm.

In two cases, the hand of a manuscript (as well as its textual and material features) has been identified with that of another: MS 5439/1 belongs to 4Q364, and MS 1909 belongs to 1QSb. Other cases of identifications can be examined:

1. MS 4612/11 (Prov) and MS 5480 (1 Sam 5) exhibit very similar scripts, with a small difference in letter height that might be due to skin contraction. There are noticeable differences in י (triangle vs. chevron shape), but the scribe is not always consistent, which may account for these variations. Unfortunately, many letters of the alphabet are not attested in both manuscripts; they might have confirmed or infirmed the ascription of these two fragments to the same hand.

2. MS 4612/4 (GenMiniature) and MS 5233/1 (2 Sam 20) have both been penned by a small semiformal hand and share numerous palaeographical features. Differences can be observed in א, ל and ע, especially, but some of them could perhaps be explained by the extremely small letter height of MS 4612/4—presuming it is not the scribe's usual letter size. This argument is too weak, however, to conclude that the same hand penned both manuscripts, and it must once again be emphasized many letters of the alphabet are not attested on both fragments.

As mentioned above, a number of hands exhibit inconsistencies that may raise concerns as to the authenticity of some manuscripts. In some cases, the degraded state of the fragments seems posterior to the copying of the actual scroll (*e.g.* MS 4612/9 [Jer]; MS 5214/1 [Deut 6]; MS 5440 [1 Kgs]), which would support their authenticity, although sophisticated forgeries cannot be ruled out.

The quality of the script is often correlated to that of the skin. While the skilled hands of MS 4612/3 (Eschat. Frg.) or MS 4611 (Lev), for instance, benefit from a smooth surface, the naive hands attested on many manuscripts are worsened by the use of parchment with a rough surface. This correlation might indicate that the latter manuscripts were not produced in the same environment. In fact, the lack of affinities with Qumran scrolls leads me to suggest that those fragments, if authentic, may well come from a previously unknown location. Additional research and the publication of new manuscripts will no doubt increase our knowledge on this matter.

Table 3.1. *Synoptic palaeographical charts of the Dead Sea Scrolls in The Schøyen Collection*
(MS 5439/1, MS 1909, MS 4612/11, MS 5480 and MS 4612/9)

MS 4612/9	MS 5480	MS 4612/11	MS 1909	MS 5439/1
3rd quart. of 1st c. BC	Mid-1st c. BC	Mid-1st c. BC	2nd quart. of 1st c. BC	2nd half of 2nd c. BC

Table 3.2. Synoptic palaeographical charts of the Dead Sea Scrolls in The Schøyen Collection (MS 5233/2, MS 4612/5, MS 4612/4, MS 5233/1 and MS 5095/7)

MS 5095/7 Last quart. of 1st c. BC	MS 5233/1 Last 3rd of 1st c. BC	MS 4612/4 2nd half of 1st c. BC	MS 4612/5 2nd half of 1st c. BC	MS 5233/2 3rd quart. of 1st c. BC

Table 3.3. *Synoptic palaeographical charts of the Dead Sea Scrolls in The Schøyen Collection* (MS 4612/3, MS 5440, MS 5214/1, MS 5439/2, and MS 5441)

MS 5441 Mid-1st c. AD	MS 5439/2 Mid-1st c. AD	MS 5214/1 Early 1st c. AD	MS 5440 End of 1st c. BC	MS 4612/3 End of 1st c. BC

Table 3.4. *Synoptic palaeographical charts of the Dead Sea Scrolls in The Schøyen Collection*
(MS 5214/2, MS 4612/1, MS 4611, MS 2861 and MS 2713)

MS 2713	MS 2861	MS 4611	MS 4612/1	MS 5214/2
End of 1st or 2nd c. AD	*2nd half of 1st or 2nd c. AD*	*2nd half of 1st or 2nd c. AD*	*3rd quart. of 1st c. AD*	*3rd quart. of 1st c. AD*

VI

High Quality Scrolls from the Post-Herodian Period

Kipp Davis

Four of the texts from The Schøyen Collection featured in this volume are somewhat distinct in that they exhibit a high quality, ornamental late or post-Herodian script: MS 4611 (Lev), MS 2713 (Josh), MS 2861 (Judg), and MS 4612/1 (Joel).[1] These scrolls are furthermore interesting as a group because they all appear also to have been similarly structured into especially narrow columns, measuring on average between 7–8 cm. The Judges text is preserved in eight fragments (housed in four collections), that contain portions of three different columns from the first part of a Judges scroll. These columns have been reconstructed to an approximate width of 7.5–7.8 cm, and the editors of this text suggest that columns contained more than 25 lines. The Leviticus scroll has been reconstructed to an estimated height of 31–32 cm, containing 46 lines per column. The two fully extant columns measure 7.5 cm and 7 cm respectively. The Joshua text is reconstructed to a height of *c.* 26 cm, and containing 28 lines. The first, fully extant column on the fragment measures 8 cm wide, and the second column has been reconstructed to the same width. The only column in the Joel fragment is reconstructed to a width of 7.5 cm, but since there is no surviving material from other columns, it is impossible to know the column height. Nevertheless, the very elegant script and the narrow column-width help to identify Schøyen Joel with the other three.

Three of the fragments, Leviticus, Joshua, and Joel, preserve large top or bottom margins. Moreover, fragments from three of the texts, Leviticus, Joshua, and Judges all appear very similar in colour, in both the preserved portions, and in those places where the surface has worn off. Schøyen Joel is much darker, but also appears similar to the other three in its patterns of deterioration, and in the consistency and condition of the leather.

There is in this group of four texts a pattern of similarities, not only in script, but also in their column structure and physical appearance. These similarities possibly point to a common scribal milieu, a common source of production, or perhaps a series of accepted scribal conventions for certain kinds of texts in the late and post-Herodian periods. Furthermore, this pattern may also help to establish probabilities for their provenance and origin. For the discussion that follows these four texts will be treated together and henceforth referred to as the 'Schøyen post-Herodian' texts.[2] This chapter will seek to address such

---

[1] Michael Langlois has dated all four of these texts to at least the second half of the first century AD. He further qualifies MS 4612/1 (Joel) as perhaps belonging to the third quarter of the first century AD, and MS 2713 (Josh) to the end of the first or beginning of the second century AD. See Langlois's full discussion on p. 79ff.

[2] The idea that these fragments might be late Herodian as opposed to post-Herodian—that is, dated to the third-quarter of the first century AD—is possibly influenced by their supposed provenance and possible connection to Qumran. The assignment of some of the Qumran scrolls to the late Herodian instead of the post-Herodian period occasionally seems to be a product of their provenance. Cf. *e.g.* Trever 1965, 334, when speaking of 1QDan[b] (1Q72): 'The even more marked regularity of the heights of the letters; the absence of the elongated *kaph*, *mem*, and final *mem*; the closed *qoph*, and the enlarged *'ayin* all tend to suggest the end of the Qumrân palaeographical development, or the end of the Herodian period. Were its provenance not known to be Cave I and its relation to 1QDan[a] and 1QPrayers not established by its original fusion with those clearly

possibilities by comparing this group of four to relevant examples from the Qumran caves, and to the literary texts discovered in Murabbaʿat, Masada, Wadi Sdeir, and Naḥal Ḥever. Texts under discussion here will be limited only to those that feature highly stylized, formal scripts similar to those in the Schøyen post-Herodian group, and which also appear to have been structured into high and narrow columns. In what follows, I will explore structural and scribal tendencies that appear in these texts, will identify any noteworthy patterns, and will then attempt to extrapolate from the data relevant information for helping to establish the provenance of the post-Herodian Schøyen texts, and their potential relationship to a wider group of structurally significant scrolls in the Judaean Desert.

A. Qumran

Late Herodian and post-Herodian texts are somewhat uncommon among the Qumran Scrolls. Furthermore, so are texts structured in high and narrow columns. Emanuel Tov characterised the relationship in the Qumran scrolls between column height and column width as 'a positive correlation', by which he seems to mean that line-lengths will tend to be longer in higher columns, and shorter in lower columns.[3] According to B. Webster, 'Chronological Index of the Texts from the Judaean Desert' (2002), a total of 47 manuscripts from the Qumran caves are designated 'late Herodian',[4] with another seven texts that qualify as 'late to post-Herodian'.[5] From this list, 25 texts have preserved portions of 'scriptural' books. From this group of 25, I have selected eight texts that both seem to closely resemble the elegant late formal script in the Schøyen post-Herodian group, and which appear in narrow columns. These are presented in *Table 4*. The primary specimen of a late Herodian formal hand from Qumran for comparison is the beautiful, baroque script that appears in 1QDanᵃ (1Q71), represented in *Figure 13* below.

Qumrân scrolls, one might even be inclined to date this document with the early second century AD examples now known.' Since the provenance of the Schøyen fragments is difficult to establish, I will tend to refer to the group of four featured in this article as 'post-Herodian' as opposed to 'late Herodian', in light of their closer resemblance to texts dated to the late first and early second centuries AD. It should be noted that this decision does not preclude a Herodian assignment, nor the possibility of a Qumran provenance for the group, but it is believed to reflect a more cautious appraisal of their scribal peculiarities.

[3] In my own independent survey from the information supplied in the *DJD* series, and supplemented by Tov 2004 and others, it appears that on average, literary compositions from Qumran reflect closer to between a 1:1–2:1 height-to-width ratio. While there is a considerable range in both scroll height as well as average column width, Tov's intuition would seem to be basically correct. From my calculations, the scrolls can be grouped into three groups that conform loosely to his arrangement of texts according to sizes of writing blocks: most 'small scrolls', under 10 cm in height, preserve columns ranging in width between 6–11 cm; most 'medium-sized scrolls', between 13–25 cm in height, preserve columns ranging between 8–13 cm; and most 'large scrolls', measuring over 30 cm in height, preserve columns ranging between 10–13 cm wide.

[4] Cf. Webster's 'Table 5: *Chronological Synopsis of Qumran texts*' (*DJD* 39:371–75). 'Late Herodian' is determined by Webster to mark the range between AD 30–68. (cf. 'Table 1: *Era and Dates Used in the Chronological Index*', 358–59).

[5] Webster (*DJD* 39:359), marks the 'post-Herodian' range between AD 75–131. For detailed discussions about the late Herodian and post-Herodian formal scripts that are featured in this essay, cf. Cross 1961b, 173–81, and Yardeni 2002, 174–77.

Table 4. *Qumran scrolls copied in late Herodian formal hands and in narrow columns*[6]

Text	Column width	Column height
2Q6 (2QNumᵃ)	± 29 letter spaces	N/A
2Q16 (2QRuthᵃ)	35–42 letter spaces, 7.7–8 cm	8 lines, 7.6 cm
3Q2 (3QPs)	28 letter spaces	N/A
4Q85 (4QPsᶜ)	8.5 cm	33 lines, 26 cm
4Q87 (4QPsᵉ)	35–37 letter spaces	25–26 lines
4Q89 (4QPsᵍ)	26–40 letter spaces, 6.4–9.5 cm	8 lines, 8.1 cm
4Q98ᶜ (4QPsᵗ)	*c.* 40 letter spaces	N/A
11QtgJob	30–42 letter spaces	15–18 lines

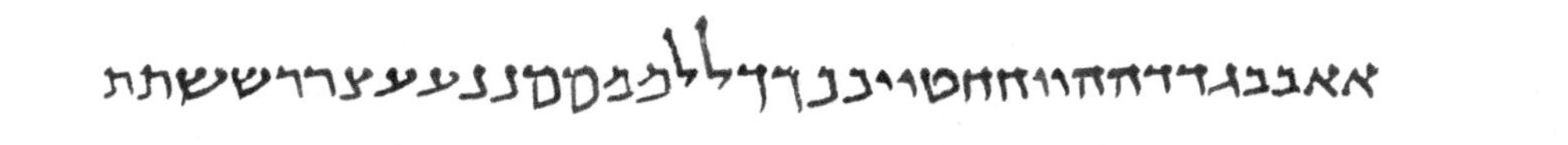

אאבבגגדדההחחחטטייככללמםנןנסעעפצצקרשתת

Figure 13. *A late Herodian formal hand, 1QDanᵃ (1Q71)*

Five of the eight scrolls in the table preserve portions from the book of Psalms, and this may suggest that these texts form their own distinct structural category, apart from what we observe in the Schøyen post-Herodian group. Thus, the Psalms scrolls are disqualified from this study by their conspicuous common 'hymnic' content. While only two of the Psalms scrolls in this list are structured stichometri-cally, all five of them share this poetic feature,[7] and this in turn appears to have factored into their production in narrow columns.[8] 2QRuthᵃ and 11QtgJob can also be removed from this inventory because of their low column height.

That leaves only 2QNumᵃ as a comparable example of a late Herodian text with a narrow and a po-tentially high writing block, although we have no way to know the height of the columns for this text. Nevertheless, a possible clue towards determining the height of this scroll may be the exceptionally high 6 cm bottom margin—the largest among all the Qumran scrolls. Tov has suggested that the com-bination of large top and bottom margins is the primary distinguishing feature of '*de luxe* editions', which very commonly contained high writing blocks of over 30 lines per column.[9] Tov admits that his compartmentalization of these texts is somewhat impressionistic, but this number, along with the av-erage measurement of +32 cm for the height of these scrolls will suffice to establish a control group for

---

[6] The presence of a handful of post-Herodian texts in the Qumran caves would seem to conflict with the archaeological interpretation of the connection between the caves and the occupation of the Qumran site which ended in the Jewish War. Webster, *DJD* 39:359, counts only six texts with post-Herodian sorting dates (4Q21, 4Q278, 4Q344, 4Q468k, 6Q30, 9Q1), but only three of these (4Q278, 4Q344, 6Q30) are 'entirely post-Herodian'.

[7] For the Cave 4 Psalms scrolls, cf. Skehan, Flint and Ulrich in *DJD* 16:7–167. The editors record the following content in order in each manuscript: the stichometrically structured 4QPsᶜ preserves Ps 16.7–10; 17.1(?); 18.1–14, 16–18, 32–36, 39–41; 27.12–28.3; 28.4–5; 35.27–28; 37.18–19; 42.5; 44.8–9(?); 45.8–11; 49.1–17; 50.13b–51.5a; 52.5b–53.1 (p. 49); 4QPsᵍ preserves Ps 119.37–43, 44–46, 49–50, 73–74, 81–83, 89–92 (p. 105). Of those scrolls appearing in prose format, 4QPsᵉ preserves Ps 76.10–12; 77.1; 78.6–7, 31–33; 81.2–3; 86.10–11; 88.1–5; 89.44–48, 50–53; 103.22(?)–109.1(?), 8(?), 13; 114.5; 115.15–116.4; 118.29; 104.1–3, 20–22; 105.1–3, 23–25, 36–45; 146.1(?); 120.6–7; 125.2–126.5; 129.8–130.6 (p. 73); 4QPsᵗ preserves portions of Ps 88.15–17 (p. 155). 3QPs is also likely structured in prosaic format, and preserves portions of Ps 2.6–7; Baillet, *DJD* 3:94.

[8] In addition to these four, 4QPsᵇˑᵈˑᶠˑʰˑˡˑⁿˑᵖˑʳˣ are reconstructed in columns measuring less than 9 cm on average. The narrow column measures may be a distinctive feature specifically belonging to the Cave 4 Psalms scrolls. 11QPsᵃ presents an average column-width of 9 cm, and 11QPsᶜ (11Q7) is reconstructed to an average column-width of 13 cm. Fragments from 11QPsᵃ and 11QPsᵇ⁻ᶜ were published by Florentino García Martínez, Eibert Tigchelaar, and Adam S. van der Woude (*DJD* 23:29–36, 49–61).

[9] Tov 2004, 118–20.

making comparisons between the Qumran scrolls as well as those from other sites to the Schøyen post-Herodian group.[10]

With only one similar example in the Qumran scrolls, it seems likely at the outset that the Schøyen post-Herodian texts were not among the scrolls discovered at Qumran. Nevertheless, the situation of the Schøyen texts should also be considered in terms of the numbers of late Herodian texts relative to the distribution of the Qumran scrolls in the caves.[11] The following list records the percentage and the ratio of late or post-Herodian texts assigned to each of the Qumran Caves:

    Cave 1: 5% (2/40)[12]
    Cave 2: 15% (4/26)
    Cave 3: 33% (3/9)
    Cave 4: 7% (39/±560)
    Cave 5: 40% (6/15)
    Cave 6: 45% (5/11)[13]
    Cave 8: 40% (2/5)
    Cave 11: 50% (11/22)

Statistically speaking, the Schøyen post-Herodian texts have little in common with the much earlier scrolls from Cave 1. Cave 8 also bears little resemblance to these scrolls based on the very limited number and quality of fragments discovered there, and Cave 6—for its high concentration of papyrus texts. If we are searching for a probable Qumran cave assignment for the Schøyen post-Herodian group from the relative dates of the texts that we know, then Cave 4 must also be considered doubtful, since considerably less than 10% of all texts unearthed from there were late. The best candidates based on this survey are Caves 3, 5, and 11—in which +30% of all texts are late Herodian. Cave 2 must also be considered a good possibility, since it contained the only other possibly comparable text from Qumran, 2QNum[a]: a non-poetic composition that was probably structured in high and narrow columns, as suggested above.

In summary, from the entire inventory of Qumran texts, there is only one possible (but uncertain) comparable example of a late or post-Herodian text written with a high and narrow column arrangement. 2QNum[a] survives as a developed Herodian, 'scriptural' text that may have been constructed in high and narrow columns. As the following table illustrates, the complete collection of Qumran texts from this period show a consistent difference in their more conventional column structures. Based on the accumulation of data according to this feature, the Schøyen post-Herodian texts appear as particularly out of place from among the whole collection of Qumran scrolls.

[10] The scroll height figure is an average calculation derived from all examples containing columns of at least 30 lines.

[11] All figures include only texts with designations, and have excluded all unclassified fragments.

[12] 1QDan[a] is the only text from Cave 1 which clearly post-dates the first quarter of the first century AD. But cf. Trever 1965, 334, and n. 2 above. 1QpHab is the closest Cave 1 contemporary to 1QDan[a], and is also dated to the first quarter of the first century AD, or perhaps earlier; cf. Baillet, *DJD* 3:72, and idem, *DJD* 7:53.

[13] Papyrus texts are excluded on the basis of their forming a separate category of manuscript production here, and throughout this study.

Table 5. *Complete inventory of Qumran scrolls palaeographically assigned to the late Herodian period*

Wider writing-block	Uncertain
4QIsa^c (47–56 letter spaces, 13 cm)	3QJub, 3Q9
4QIsa^d (62 letter spaces, 11 cm)	4Q288, 4Q289, 4Q290
4QPs^j (42–56 letter spaces)	
4QPs^s (52–63 letter spaces)	
4QDan^b (11.4–11.7 cm)	
4QtgJob (+ 32 letter spaces)	
4Q286 (47–56 letter spaces)	
4Q287 (63 letter spaces, 10.5–11 cm)	
4Q378 (±48 letter spaces)	
4Q421 (45–47 letter spaces, approx. 9–9.5 cm)	
11QDeut^b (13 cm)	11Q15, 11Q16
11QPs^a (9–13.9 cm)	
11Q11 (8.5–14 cm)	
11QJub (46–50 letter spaces)	
11QM (12.1 cm)	
11QT^b (67 letter spaces)	
11Q21 (58 letter spaces)	

This data indicates a high probability that the fragments in the Schøyen post-Herodian group do not belong with the Qumran scrolls. Furthermore, the near-total absence of literary texts similarly structured in high and narrow columns also suggests that this is probably a significant scribal feature; one that either post-dated the Qumran scrolls altogether, or one that the collectors of the Qumran scrolls chose not foster.

B. Masada

Table 6. *Masada scrolls copied in late or post-Herodian formal hands and in narrow columns*

Text	Column width	Column height
Mas 1c (MasDeut)	40–45 letter spaces, 8.5 cm	42 lines, 40 cm
Mas 1d (MasEzek)	32–43 letter spaces, 8.2–9.2 cm	42 lines
Mas 1f (MasPs^b)	21–24 letter spaces, 6.2 cm	44 lines

Parchment fragments from twelve literary texts were discovered at Masada.[14] From this group, seven preserve text from previously known 'scriptural' compositions, and four have been identified with other known 'Bible related' or 'extra-biblical' works: the *Genesis Apocryphon* (MasapocrGen), a 'Joshua Apocryphon' (MasapocrJosh), *Jubilees* (or possibly *pseudo-Jubilees*) (MasJub or MaspsJub), and the *Songs of the Sabbath Sacrifice* (MasShirShabb). No identification has yet been offered for the remaining two fragments.

---

[14] All the Masada texts were published in Talmon and Yadin 1999. Another papyrus fragment, 1039–320 also belongs to this collection. It is characterised as a 'text of Samaritan origin', and was inscribed in palaeo-Hebrew. Cf. Talmon and Yadin 1999, 138–47.

While Shemaryahu Talmon palaeographically dated all the Masada scrolls with the lone exception of MasShirShabb to before the mid-first century AD, he is almost certainly wrong about several of them, including the other three 'Bible related' texts mentioned above.[15] In actual fact, MasDeut, MasEzek, MasPs[b], along with MasLev[b] and MasPs[a] all belong comfortably in the mid-first century AD, and are properly designated late Herodian, or possibly even post-Herodian.[16] Much like the Qumran texts featured earlier, the Psalms scrolls should probably also be precluded from this discussion, since they are poetic texts that were structured stichometrically.[17] MasLev[b] can also be excluded from this investigation, since the columns contain only 25 lines.

The remaining two scriptural Masada texts (MasDeut, MasEzek) have in common with the Schøyen post-Herodian group these same distinguishing characteristics: all three were written in an elegant, developed Herodian script, and were structured in high and narrow columns. MasShirShabb shares with these examples a very similar elegant late script, and is also structured in narrow columns, *c.* 8.0 cm. However, this scroll with columns 16.5 cm high and containing 21 lines falls well outside the structural dimensions from the other examples that correspond to Schøyen post-Herodian group. The preserved columns in MasDeut and MasEzek were fairly uniform in width, between 8–9 cm, and in MasPs[b] 6.2 cm. The presence of another two scrolls that preserve close scribal and structural similarities provides a sampling of evidence for compatible structural features with the Schøyen post-Herodian group. Different from what we discovered for the Qumran scrolls, there is some evidence for these similarities as a scribally significant feature. It is possibly one that helps to confirm the presence of a sort of scribal convention in place for some texts in the late Herodian period. However, since all these manuscripts were discovered and properly provenanced by archaeologists, Masada can be excluded as a potential place of discovery for the Schøyen post-Herodian texts.

C. Murabbaʿat

Table 7. *Murabbaʿat scrolls copied in late or post-Herodian formal hands and in narrow columns*

Text	Column width	Column height
Mur 1 (MurGen)	27–29 letter spaces, 8–9 cm	50 lines
Mur 1 (MurExod)	28–30 letter spaces, 8.8–9 cm	50 lines

[15] Talmon in Yadin 1999, assigned MasEzek to the mid first century BC, MasPs[b] and MasapocrGen to the early–mid first century BC, MasLev[a], MasDeut, and MasPs[a] to the late first century BC, MasLev[b] and MasapocrJosh to the late first BC–early first century AD. Cf. corrections offered for the dating of MasDeut in García Martínez 1994, 78 to *c.* 50 AD (cited in Lange 2009, 104); MasEzek is dated by Eibert Tigchelaar (2005, 273–75) to the first century AD (cf. Lange 2009, 328). Tigchelaar also seems to posit later dates for all of the texts discovered outside of Qumran: 'The discussions about the archaeological as well as the historical provenance of scrolls found at other sites in the Judaean Desert, call for a palaeographic comparison of the scripts of the so-called late Herodian and post-Herodian manuscripts' (p. 274). On MasPs[a], cf. Nebe 1989, 93, who compares the script with that in MasShirShabb, but states that it is not as fully developed in this fragment. He dates the ms. between 25–50 AD (cf. Lange 2009, 403–4).

[16] Further and more detailed palaeographical studies of all of the Masada scrolls are necessary, but my challenge to Talmon's dates derive preliminarily from careful comparisons to the charts produced by both Cross (1968) and Yardeni (2002), and also in close conversation with Yardeni's observations about characteristic features for scripts. Most generally, the forward 'leaning' direction, the 'widening' of letters (cf. Cross, who characterises late-post-Herodian scripts by way of 'thick lines and squat configuration'). Also the style and shape of ornamentations that are produced by the cut of the calamus reed in the Masada texts sets them in very close company to virtually all other formal scripts that we know from the late-post Herodian period. By way of contrast, there is very little to no correspondence to early-mid-Herodian scripts like Talmon has suggested.

[17] Yadin 1999, 94.

Mur 1 (MurNum)	29 letter spaces, 8.4 cm	50 lines
Mur 2 (MurDeut)	35–40 letter spaces, 10.5–12 cm	30–31 lines
Mur 3 (MurIsa)	30 letter spaces, approx. 5.4 cm	29 lines

There were extensive textual finds in the Murabbaʿat caves, but fragments from only five literary Hebrew texts on leather or parchment.[18] Nevertheless, this yield far outstrips the sampling of comparable scrolls surveyed from Masada above in this search for common structural features shared with the Schøyen post-Herodian group. Four of the Murabbaʿat scrolls preserved portions of 'scriptural' texts, and three of these conform closely to the structural dimensions of the Schøyen post-Herodian group. In addition to these, Mur 88 (MurXII) is a special example, since it is a relatively intact scroll, written in an elegant, developed Herodian hand much like the other Murabbaʿat scrolls and the Schøyen post-Herodian group. However, the consistently wider columns measuring between 12–13.5 cm (43–60 letter spaces on average) precludes this fine specimen from further consideration as a parallel example for this study of texts structured in high and narrow columns.[19] Nevertheless, this text does exhibit some physical qualities that will be important for providing other material comparisons to some of the Schøyen post-Herodian texts.

The scrolls from Murabbaʿat are especially significant in this investigation primarily because of the pattern of similarities they share: they were all written in elegant post-Herodian scripts, but also they all contained columns ranging between 29 letter spaces and 8.4 cm to 40 letter spaces and 12 cm.[20] All of these texts were formatted in high columns, containing 50 lines in MurGen/MurExod, 30–31 lines for MurDeut, and 29 lines for MurIsa.[21] It is also interesting to note that the Murabbaʿat collection yielded only single copies of texts, with no additional copies. This group contained copies of every text from the Torah—except for Leviticus, as well as a fragment from Isaiah, and a fairly complete copy of the Twelve.

The presence of so many common structural features prompts us to consider that the Schøyen post-Herodian scrolls were discovered in Murabbaʿat, and that all of these scrolls together possibly originated from the same source. If so, then this would mean that the collection contained a complete Torah, copies of Joshua and Judges, a copy of Isaiah, a complete copy of the Twelve, and another scroll containing at least one of the other Minor Prophets. It is of interest to note that the condition and quality of MS 4611 (Lev) is comparable to all three of MurGen, MurExod, and MurNum, and that MS 2713 (Josh), XJudg, and MS 4612/1 (Joel) are all very similar in colour, quality, and in their manner of deterioration to MurXII.[22]

[18] All the Murabbaʿat artefacts and texts were published by Benoît, Milik, and de Vaux in *DJD* 2.

[19] These figures are drawn from MurXII cols VII–XXI. Columns XXII and XXIII appear as outliers, having preserved identical columns measuring 10 cm and 35 letter spaces wide. From our own inspection of MurXII in the IAA collection February 2014, Torleif Elgvin and Kipp Davis noted that the columns are between 11–12 cm on average, and consistently measure 26 cm high.

[20] Another fragment, XGenᵃ, possibly has a Murabbaʿat provenance (Puech 1980). It only preserves a few lines, but its column width can be reconstructed to *c.* 6 cm.

[21] MurIsa is very light in colour, almost white, and preserves part of an uninscribed, introductory column. The script is small compared to MurXII, which was written in columns measuring 39 lines high.

[22] Nevertheless, Elgvin and Davis have noted from their inspection that each text from the Schøyen post-Herodian group does show some slight differences in colour from the Murabbaʿat scrolls. MurGen-MurExod is lighter brown in colour. MurNum is medium to light brown in colour. MurDeut is dark brown, and neither manuscript appears with the same reddish hues as in the Schøyen post-Herodian group.

D. Naḥal Ḥever

Table 8. *Naḥal Ḥever and Wadi Seiyal scrolls copied in late or post-Herodian formal hand and in narrow columns*

Text	Column width	Column height
5/6Hev 1a (5/6HevNumᵃ)	38–41 letter spaces	N/A
XHev/Se 2 (XHev/SeNumᵇ)	27–35 letter spaces	44 lines, *c.* 39.5 cm
XHev/Se 3 (XHev/SeDeut)	33–38 letter spaces	39 lines, *c.* 28 cm

Six literary texts were discovered from Naḥal Ḥever and Wadi Seiyal, and three of these are comparable to the post-Herodian Schøyen fragments.[23] All three were 'scriptural' compositions: two copies of Numbers and one copy of Deuteronomy. The largest scroll discovered at Naḥal Ḥever was a fairly extensive copy of Psalms, 5/6Hev 1b (5/6HevPs). The Psalms scroll contained at least Ps 1–41, with the good possibility that this text represented the complete 𝔐 Psalter.[24] Line lengths in this scroll are on average 35 letter spaces, and measure approximately 8 cm. The columns were reconstructed to a height of 28 lines, and estimated to be 20.5 cm high. This text is also probably not to be included in this study with the comparison to the post-Herodian Schøyen group, owing to its stichometric arrangement. Furthermore, it also does not qualify because its column blocks are slightly lower than most of the other cited examples, all of which appear to have consisted of over 30 lines on average.

As with the other texts from Murabbaʿat and the noted specimens from Masada, 5/6HevNumᵃ, and XHev/Se 2–3 all bear similar features to the Schøyen post-Herodian texts, most prominently, their elegant post-Herodian formal scripts. Judging from the fairly well preserved portion of Num 27–28 in XHev/SeNumᵇ, and from the adjoining columns of XHev/SeDeut, these texts were also arranged in high and narrow columns, probably consisting of 44 and 39 lines respectively. These three texts from Naḥal Ḥever and Wadi Seiyal are included in the total inventory as evidence perhaps for a standard of accepted scribal conventions for certain kinds of texts in place in the late and post-Herodian periods.

E. Wadi Sdeir

Table 9. *Sdeir scrolls copied in late or post-Herodian formal hand and in narrow columns*

Text	Column width	Column height
Sdeir 1 (SdeirGen)	33–45 letter spaces, 10–10.8 cm	39 lines

Only one literary text from Wadi Sdeir survives, and this text similarly is comparable to the post-Herodian Schøyen texts in script and layout.[25] SdeirGen preserves an elegant post-Herodian hand, and was structured into high columns consisting of 39 lines. However, the extant column containing Gen 35.6–36.17 is slightly wider than those surviving from all of the post-Herodian Schøyen texts, and is closer to the average width of column blocks in the Qumran scrolls.[26] While this scroll is the only one known from Wadi Sdeir, it possibly reflects the situation at Qumran, where there were texts produced in the

---

[23] The literary texts from Naḥal Ḥever and Wadi Seiyal were published in *DJD* 38:133–200.

[24] *DJD* 38:145.

[25] The Wadi Sdeir texts were published by Catherine Murphy and Ada Yardeni in *DJD* 38:117–29.

[26] Column widths in the Qumran scrolls reflect a fairly dramatic deviation even within individual manuscripts, and this is largely a product of their conformity to the dimensions of individual sheets that are stitched together to form entire scrolls. Nevertheless, columns range on the low end between 4–17 cm, for an average of 10.4 cm, and on the high end between 4.6–18.4 cm, for an average of 11.15 cm.

late Herodian period included in the collection, but none structured according to a standard that seems to have been established for some texts like those in the post-Herodian Schøyen group.

F. Conclusions and Summary

The conclusions drawn from the above survey indicates two things: first, we can confirm that there is a detectable pattern in column structure and dimensions that conforms to palaeographical features observed for texts from three sites and for the Schøyen post-Herodian group. This pattern suggests that there were standard construction procedures in the post-Herodian period that were applied to some texts, which delimited these scrolls to layouts in columns that ranged between 30–50 lines, but within writing blocks under 10 cm wide.

Second, there is a notably higher concentration of texts that reflect this pattern from three sites, especially compared to the much larger and predominantly older cache of texts discovered at Qumran. From Murabbaʿat, these types of scrolls account for 3:5 of the total number of literary texts discovered; from Masada, the ratio is 3:12, but more significantly 3:5 of those fragments from which we either know or can estimate column heights; from Naḥal Ḥever, the ratio is 3:6 from the total of literary texts discovered. These sites may be loosely characterised as 'post-Qumran' environments, and this provides some added weight to posit that the post-Herodian Schøyen group were likewise not retrieved from the Qumran caves. The data suggests that these scrolls were not likely copied prior to the destruction of Herod's temple.

Based on the variety of factors, it seems reasonable to conclude that the Schøyen post-Herodian texts rather much more likely were found at one of the other Judaean Desert sites.[27] A Murabbaʿat provenance seems most probable for at least Leviticus, Joshua, and Judges in light of the very close similarities in script and in column dimensions between these fragments and the Murabbaʿat scrolls. The parchment of the Leviticus and Judges fragments is also very close in quality to several of the Murabbaʿat scrolls, and their patterns of deterioration appear similar.[28] Rabin has said that the absence of dolomite in the Schøyen copy of Joel eliminates Murabbaʿat as a possible place of discovery for this text.[29]

Perhaps more interestingly, these common features in structure now illustrated from texts discovered in several Judaean Desert sites also suggest the presence of a common scribal milieu which was prominently active in the second-half of the first century AD until the Bar Kokhba Revolt. In addition to those texts surveyed, the presence of another Genesis fragment possibly from Murabbaʿat mentioned above, and a fragment of Leviticus from Naḥal Arugot[30]—both of which would appear to also conform to the same structural and scribal patterns—would bolster this idea. If this is the case, then this group

---

[27] It should be noted here the possibility that some of the Qumran texts may also have been mis-assigned, and actually come from Naḥal Ḥever or Murabbaʿat. Both Naḥal Ḥever and Murabbaʿat were discovered by the Taamire Bedouin in 1951–52; close in time to their discovery of Cave 4. We may surmise that some of the fragments from all three sites were possibly mixed together both by Bedouin and Kando. For more cf. Roland de Vaux's personal account concerning the discovery and publication of texts from Murabbaʿat, 'Historique de découvertes', in *DJD* 2:1, 3–8. Also Fields 2010, 115–29 which includes de Vaux's account translated into English.

[28] Rabin is careful to point out that the Joshua and Joel fragments are leather, and not finely prepared parchments.

[29] Rabin has also noted that the Joel fragment lacks the aragonite that is typical of the sediments in Qumran caves; see p. 72.

[30] Eshel, Baruchi, and Porat (2006) published the Arugot fragment, which was discovered in a cave that functioned as a refuge during the Bar Kokhba Revolt. It was written in an elegant, post-Herodian hand similar to the other examples surveyed in this essay. Its writing block has been reconstructed to a width of 27–33 letter spaces and 36 lines high.

must have been a very well trained and highly skilled professional guild who enjoyed a range of distribution for their products up and down the Dead Sea region.

While it is attractive to imagine such a group working in the region, both the Leviticus and the Judges scroll have been determined by Rabin's scanning to have been produced outside of it; both quite possibly having come from the same location.[31] There were quite likely many caves in the Judaean Desert that served as hiding caches for Jewish families who stored their precious scrolls to protect them from the crisis in Jerusalem in AD 70, during the Kitos War in AD 115–17, or during the Bar Kokhba rebellion in AD 132–35. The presence of a fairly significant number of similarly structured scrolls in the sites surveyed above suggests that some of these texts were carried into the Judaean Desert, and possibly also attests to a scribal standard that extended beyond a single guild, perhaps reflecting an established set of criteria for some texts beginning in the mid- to late first century AD.

---

[31] These parchments seem to have been prepared in the same manner, with light tanning of the surface of the hair side—the side used for writing. The chlorine/bromide ratio indicates a place of production of these skins outside the Dead Sea region. See further the contribution by Rabin, p. 61.

Part Two

—

Pentateuch (Torah)

VII

MS 4612/4. 4Q(?)GenMiniature (Gen 36.7–16)

Torleif Elgvin, Kipp Davis

DSS F.101, DSS F.Gen1[1]

A. Physical Description

The fragment measures 3.4 × 2.2 cm, and preserves parts of eight lines with no margins. The parchment is very dark brown with an even distribution of brighter spots. Most of the letters are visible to the naked eye.

According to Ira Rabin's analysis the Cl/Br ratio is compatible with what we would expect for parchment prepared outside the Dead Sea region. The skin contained mineral components reflecting cave sediments with a strontium/calcium ratio compatible with the area of Qumran (Rabin, unpublished report). The ink layer is very thin.

The fragment displays a remarkably small miniature script, with a letter height of about 1.5 mm on average. The line spacing is 4–5 mm.

B. Palaeography

Michael Langlois characterizes the script as a vulgar semicursive Hasmonaean hand, with some semi-formal Herodian features. He hesitantly concludes a date somewhere in the second half of the first century BC (see p. 93).

***Figure 14.1.** MS 4612/4*

---

[1] Designations according to Eibert Tigchelaar's system for fragments not included in Stephen A. Reed's 1994 catalogue (Reed 1994).

C. MS 4612/4

]○[ ]◌[̇]○[	1
[עשו אבי אדום בהר]	2
[̊ת אשת עשו ויהיו בני]	3
[לגש לאלכז בן עשו]	4
[נחת וזרח] [מ○]	5
○	
[ת צבען אשת עש]	6
[○לפז בכור עשו אל○]	7
○	
[לוף געתם אל]	8

Notes on Readings

Line 1. Remnants of three letters of this line are preserved, but appear unusual. The second one is most likely a poorly written final *mem*, although the ink traces are strangely positioned and appear to form additional, unnecessary strokes. The situation and odd appearance of this letter at the top of the fragment is perplexing and difficult to explain. The last letter is perhaps *mem*, *ʿayin*, or *šin*.

Line 4. לאלכז. We might expect לאלפז from the appearance of ○לפז in line 7 below. Judged by its appearance the fourth letter looks like a *kap*, less probably *bet*, and certainly not *pe*, cp. *pe* in line 7.

Line 5.]○מ[. There is a hole in the leather before the last clearly preserved letter, *mem*. It is difficult to fit a letter into this lacuna without breaking the line. The easiest solution is to presuppose that a damaged spot on the leather caused the scribe to make a longer word space. In this case the scribe would have left a space of 2 mm between these two words, which is about 1–1.5 mm greater than the average word separator in this fragment. On the one hand, this would seem to be a relatively substantial difference, but on the other hand, the increase of a single millimetre is practically negligible.

Lines 6, 8 supra. ○. Above the *ʿayin* of the last word in line 6 there appears to be a supralinear, very small trace of ink that appears most like an *ʿayin* (see *Figure 14.2*). Another trace can be discerned above *gimel* and *ʿayin* of געתם in line 8. One must take into consideration the exceptionally minuscule size of these marks, and whether they might actually be letters, or merely something else on the leather. The small sized text of MS 4612/4 is difficult enough to read, to say nothing of these extremely tiny marks which are virtually invisible to the naked eye.[2] The height of each is only 1 mm, and it strains credulity to imagine that even the most careful scribe could make such fine insertions, or that they would even have been noticed by the reader. If there really were a scribal insertion above line 8, the pen-strokes would be practically microscopic. It seems more likely that the example in line 8 at least is simply a tiny mark on the leather, especially compared with other darkened spots on the leather.[3] The first mark may be a letter.

---

[2] Cp. with examples of supralinear *ʿayins* in 1QIsaᵃ I 1 and in 4Q541 24 ii 6, inserted as correction letters, illustrated in *Figure 14.2*. The supralinear *ʿayin* appears in 4QapocrLeviᵇ ar as correction letter for an erased *ṣade*; *cf. DJD* 31:252–53, plate XIV. A supralinear *ʿayin* is also found in a fragment of 11QTᵃ published here, see p. 304.

[3] Cf. *e.g.* above the *taw* on the right edge of line 3, in the space between lines 2-3 on the left edge, and in the gap between lines 3–4 above לאלכז.

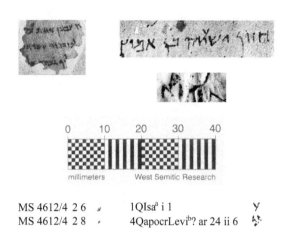

| MS 4612/4 2 6 | ℷ | 1QIsaᵃ i 1 | Y |
| MS 4612/4 2 8 | ⸴ | 4QapocrLeviᵇ? ar 24 ii 6 | 🗴 |

Figure 14.2. Supralinear insertions: 1QIsaᵃ and 4QapocrLeviᵇ? ar compared with MS 4612/4
Image of 1QIsaᵃ from Trever 1972, of 4QapocrLeviᵇ? ar courtesy IAA

D. Genesis Scrolls in the Judaean Desert and Identification

The text in MS 4612/4 is positively identified with Gen 36.7–16, which is not preserved in any other published copy of Genesis from the Judaean Desert. On the basis of its exceptionally small script and its mineral characterics compatible with Cave 4, this fragment has been designated 4Q(?)GenMiniature.

Eighteen copies of Genesis from Qumran have been published,[4] in addition to four copies from other Judaean Desert sites.[5] From among the other copies of Genesis, only 8QGen (*DJD* 3:146–47, plate XXXI) is written in a similarly small script, though not quite as small as that in MS 4612/4. 8QGen preserves four small fragments that cover Gen 17.12–19; 18.20–25. The average line spacing in these fragments is 6 mm, and in one case extends up to 9 mm (frg. 4 l. 4–5, but this case could represent an open section).

In 2005 Esther and Hanan Eshel published a tiny fragment with 15 letters of Gen 13.1–3, which had been exhibited in the US (Eshel and Eshel 2005, 144–46). The ownership and present location of this fragment are not known. Its line spacing was 4.5–5.5 mm, and the Eshels identified it with 8QGen and designated it 8QGen frg. 1a. While working on the present edition, Esther and Hanan Eshel suggested identifying MS 4612/4 with the same scroll. After a close inspection of their material features this identification does not seem acceptable to the present authors. Most notably, when all the fragments are compared together to scale in *Figure 14.3*, it is clear that the script and line spacing in both 8QGen and Eshels' 'frg. 1a' are considerably larger. While some of the letters in 'frg. 1a' do appear similar in size to those in MS 4612/4, they are generally less elegant. The letters in our fragment are all more uniform, more sharply inscribed, and there is a more even distribution in spacing between individual

---

[4] 1QGen (1Q1), 2QGen (2Q1), 4QGen-Exodᵃ (4Q1), 4QGenᵇ⁻ᵏ (4Q2–10), 4QpalaeoGen-Exodˡ (4Q11), 4QGenᵐ (4Q12), 6QGen (6Q1), and 8QGen (8Q1). 4QGenʰ has been redistributed among four copies, 4QGenʰ¹·ʰ²·ʰ⁻ᵖᵃʳᵃ·ʰ⁻ᵗⁱᵗˡᵉ (4Q8, 4Q8a, 4Q8b, 4Q8c). 4QGenʰ⁻ᵖᵃʳᵃ is a paraphrase of Gen 12.4–5, and 4QGenʰ⁻ᵗⁱᵗˡᵉ preserves only the word בראשית. Two further copies belonging to the collection of the Kando family were recently exhibited in the US. A large fragment that covers major parts of Gen 37.14–39.5 (22 × 40 cm), preserving one full column and parts of two more, is currently with the Kando family (Loveless 2012, 102–3). It was exhibited as part of *Dead Sea Scrolls & the Bible: Ancient Artifacts, Timeless Treasures* at Southwestern Baptist Theological Seminary, Forth Worth, Texas, from 2 July, 2012. A small fragment of Gen 33.19–34.2, property of the Kando family, was also exhibited at Forth Worth (Loveless 2012, 101). This fragment was published by Eshel and Eshel (2005) after its inclusion in an exhibition in the US. It probably derives from a separate scroll and should not be identified with 4QGenᶠ (4Q6), as asserted by the Eshels. The Green Collection also includes a fragment of Genesis.

[5] MurGen (Mur 1), MasGen (Mas 1), SdeirGen (Sdeir 1), and XGenᵃ (possibly deriving from Murabbaʿat).

letters and words. We conclude that differences in both script and line spacing indicate that MS 4612/4 and 'frg. 1a' are not identical, and that both derive from scrolls other than 8QGen.

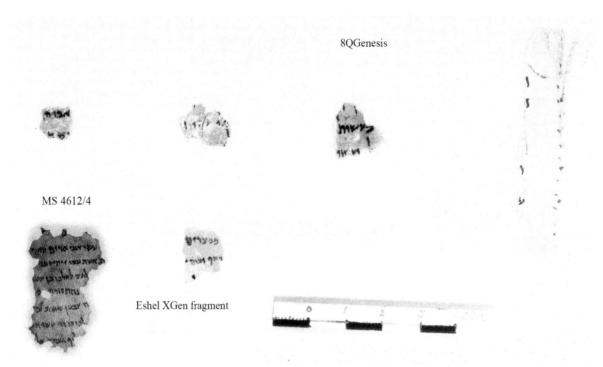

Figure 14.3. *8QGen (PAM 42.594), MS 4612/4, and 'frg. 1a' compared to scale*
PAM photograph courtesy IAA

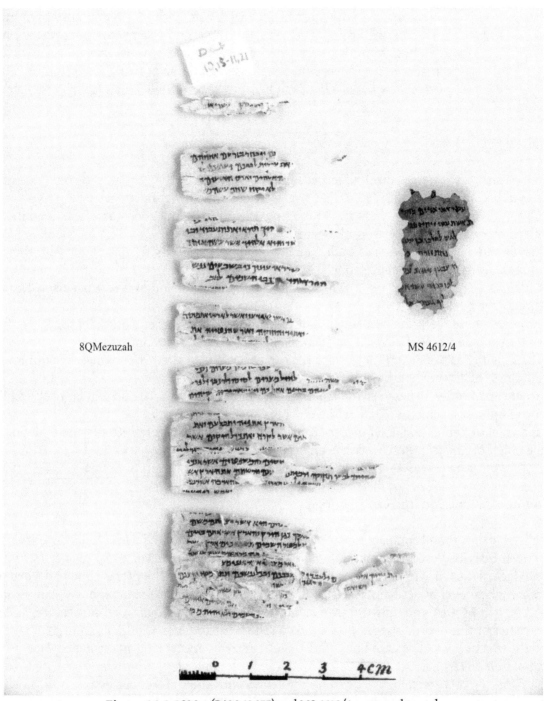

8QMezuzah

MS 4612/4

Figure 14.4. 8QMez (PAM 42.357) and MS 4612/4 compared to scale
PAM photograph courtesy IAA

E. MS 4612/4 (Gen 36.7–16)

[רב משבת יחדו ולא יכלה ארץ מגוריהם ל]שׁ[את את]ם֯[מפני]מ֯[קניהם ⁸וישב עשו בהר]   1

[שעיר עשו הוא רב אדום ⁹ואלה תלדות] עשו אבי אדום בהר [שעיר ¹⁰ואלה שמות]   2

[בני עשו אלפז בן עדה רעואל בן בשמ]ת אשת עשו[¹¹ויהיו בנ]י אלפז תימן אומר צפו]   3

4   ‏[וגעתם וקנז וקורח ו•••• ‏¹²‏ותמנע היתה פי]לגש לאלב̇ז בן עשו̇ ותלד לאלפז את]

5   ‏[עמלק אלה בני עדה אשת עשו ‏¹³‏ובני רעואל היו] נחת וזרח ‏[מז̇]ה ושמה אלה היו בני בשמת]

6   ‏[אשת עשו ‏¹⁴‏ואלה היו בני אהליבמה בת ענה ב]ת̇ צבען אשת עש̇ו̇] ותלד לעשו את יעיש]

7   ‏[ואת יעלם ואת קרח ‏¹⁵‏אלה אלופי בני עשו בני]א̇לפז בכור עשו אלו̇]ף̇ תימן אלוף אומר]

8   ‏[אלוף צפו אלוף קנז אלוף •••• ‏¹⁶‏אלוף קורח א]ל̇וף געתם אל]וף עמלק אלה אלופי]

Translation

1.   [... too many for them to dwell together, and the land where they sojourned could not su]pp[ort the]m[because of their]li[vestock. ⁸So Esau settled in the hill country of]

2.   [Seir — Esau was *the chief of* Edom. ⁹This is the line of] Esau, the ancestor of the Edomites, in the hill country of [Seir. ¹⁰These are the names of]

3.   [Esau's sons: Eliphaz, *the son of Adah*, Reuel, the son of] Esau's wife[Basma]t. ¹¹And the sons of[Eliphaz] were [Teman, Omar, Zepho,]

4.   [Gatam, Kenaz, *Korah and* •••• . ¹²Timna was a con]cubine belonging to Esau's son *Elikhaz*;[for Eliphaz she bore]

5.   [Amalek. Those were the descendants of Esau's wife Adah. ¹³And these *were* the sons of Reuel,] Nahath and Zerah, *Miz[zah and Shammah*. Those were the descendants of]

6.   [Esau's wife Basmat. ¹⁴And these were the sons of] Esa[u's]wife [Oholibamah, daughter of Anah, daug]hter of Zibeon: [she bore for Esau Jeush,]

7.   [Jalam, and Korah. ¹⁵These are the chiefs of the children of Esau. The descendants of]Esau's first-born Eliphaz: the chie[f of Teman, the chief of Omar,]

8.   [the chief of Zepho, the chief of Kenaz, *the chief of* •••• , ¹⁶the chief of Korah, the c]hief of Gatam, the chi[ef of Amalek; these were the chiefs of]

Notes on Reconstruction and Comments

The small-sized letters and compact format of this text may be compared with phylacteries that appear to have been inscribed on scraps of leather or whatever other materials were readily available. But unlike phylacteries from Qumran MS 4612/4 exhibits a careful hand. The precise line and word spacing suggests a higher level of scribal precision, more comparable with the small, but sharply ruled and inscribed text in 8QMez,[6] the only Qumran *mezuza* written with obvious word separators. The scribal characteristics of this text do suggest it should be reconstructed in a regular column. We have reconstructed the text of MS 4612/4 with lines of 61–73 letter spaces, measuring an estimated 7 cm. However, it is not possible to reconstruct a text based on 𝔐; cf. especially lines 2, 3, 4, 5, and 8.

This reworking of a genealogy list can be compared with the differences between 𝔐, 𝔰𝔲, and 𝔊 in the genealogies in Gen 5.3-32; 11.10-30. According to Tov (2015, 221-38), in these cases both 𝔰𝔲 and 𝔊 consciously reworked an earlier version such as was preserved in 𝔐.

Line 1 (36.7). ‏ל[ש̇]את את[ם̇] מפני]מ̇]קניהם‎. There are only small traces of three letters preserved on the line, but these seem to align fairly closely with 𝔐 𝔰𝔲.

Line 2 (36.8). ‏עשו הוא אדום‎ 𝔐 𝔰𝔲 = 𝔗ᴶ [‏עשו הוא רב אדום‎]. The space available leads us to reconstruct a longer text than 𝔐 in the beginning of line 2. We have opted to restore this line according to 𝔗ᴶ, which

---

[6] Cf. Baillet, *DJD* 3:158, and his description of 8QMez, 'le souci d'une belle présentation n'est pas absent de ce rouleau, qui n'est pourtant pas fait, en principe, pour être lu'.

renders עשו הוא רבה דאדומאי 'Esau was the chief of the Edomites'. The suggested phrase עשו הוא רב אדום would be parallel to עשו אבי אדום in the continuation. Another alternative could be to reconstruct עשו הוא אבי אדום.

Line 2 (36.10). [ואלה] = 𝔊 𝔰𝔪 𝔖 𝔙 𝔐ᴹˢˢ | אלה 𝔐.

Line 3 (36.10). [בני עשו]. *filiorum eius* 𝔙.

Line 3 (36.10). [אלפז] = 𝔐 𝔰𝔪 (אליפז).

Line 3 (36.10). [אלפז בן עדה] + אשת עשו 𝔐 𝔰𝔪 𝔊 (γυναικος Ησαυ) 𝔖 𝔙. The text of verse 10 in the Hebrew witnesses would be too long if used to reconstruct this line. We suggest that MS 4612/4 read אלפז בן עדה. Since אשת עשו recurs at the end of the verse, it would be easy for a scribe to omit the phrase to avoid repetition.

Line 3 (36.10). [רעואל בן בשמ]ת = 𝔐 𝔊 𝔖 | רעואל בן מחלת 𝔰𝔪. The single remaining letter could also accommodate the reading from 𝔰𝔪, which consistently calls this wife of Esau (Reuel's mother and daughter of Ishmael) Mahlat and not Basmat (vv. 3, 4, 10, 13). Cf. also our reconstruction in line 5 below. According to Gen 26.40, Esau married Judith and Basmat (the latter with a father different from the one in Gen 36.3 𝔐), and in Gen 28.9 Mahlat daughter of Ishmael. 𝔰𝔪 smoothens out the tension in 𝔐 between 28.9 (Basmat, daughter of Elon the Hittite) and 36.3 (Basmat, daughter of Ishmael).

Line 3 (36.10). אשת עשו = 𝔐 𝔰𝔪 𝔊 𝔖 | *uxoris eius* 𝔙.

Line 4 (36.11). [••••ו]. > 𝔐 𝔰𝔪 Vrs. Considerations of space could suggest a *vacat* most plausibly following וקנז. This would introduce a sense division separating the list of the descendants of Eliphaz from the offspring of his wives and his concubine Timna. 𝔐ᴸ and 𝔐ᴬ have no section division in vv. 7–16. A section marker in the midst of a geneaology would not be expected, so a longer and different text should be presupposed, which includes an additional name or two. In the genealogy of vv. 9–14 Eliphaz has six sons, while the list of tribal chiefs in vv. 15–19 (𝔐, 𝔰𝔪) adds another son, Korah, in v. 16. The inclusion of the name Korah together with another name in line 4 would accommodate the problem of line length here.

Line 4 (36.12). לאלבֿז. אליפז 𝔐 𝔰𝔪 𝔊 (Ελιφας). We suggest the scribe either wrote לאלבֿז due to the phonetic similarity between *bet* and *pe*, or more probably לאלבֿז, which would represent a scribal error.

Line 5 (36.13). [ובני רעואל היו]. ואלה בני רעואל 𝔐 𝔰𝔪 𝔊 (ουτοι δε υιοι Ραγουηλ) 𝔖. The reconstruction of this line is difficult. No head of the *lamed* of רעואל, expected from the other witnesses, is visible before נחת. This could be explained through a damaged spot on the skin that may have caused a larger than usual word separation. Rather, we suggest a slightly different text in MS 4612/4 with the words ובני רעואל היו where 𝔐 and 𝔰𝔪 have ואלה בני רעואל.

Line 5 (36.13). [מז]ה ושמה [וזרח] נחת. נחת וזרח שמה ומזה 𝔐 𝔰𝔪 𝔊 (Ναχοθ Ζαρε Σομε καὶ Μοζε) 𝔖 (ܘ...ܙܪܚ ܘܡܘܙܐ). The text probably mentioned the names of Reuel's sons in a sequence different from 𝔐 and 𝔰𝔪. There is trace of the letter following *mem* that could be construed as a *he*. It is probably best interpreted as the head of a *zayin* that slopes down to the left (compare *zayin* in the preceding word), resulting in [מז]ה. It seems that this text followed the same pairing of names as in 𝔐/𝔰𝔪 (Nahat and Zerah, Shammah and Mizzah), but reflected a different internal sequence in the last pair.

Line 5 (36.13). [בשמת] = 𝔐 𝔊 (Βασεμμαθ) 𝔖 | מחלת 𝔰𝔪. Cf. discussion of [בשמ]ת in line 3 above. While we have made the decision to follow 𝔐 and 𝔊 in both instances, an alignment with the 𝔰𝔪 reading of this name remains equally possible.

Line 6 (36.14). צבען = 𝔐 (צִבְעוֹן) 𝔰𝔪 (צבעון).

Line 7 (36.15). אֳלפז = 𝔐 𝔰𝔪 (both: אליפז).

Line 8 (36.16). [אלוף קרח] = 𝔐 𝔊 | > 𝔰𝔪 | ܘܒܐ ܩܪܚ 𝔖 (transposed). 𝔰𝔪 omits these two words of 𝔐 and 𝔊, thus making the list of chiefs conform with vv. 8–14, which do not mention Korah. 𝔖 has a different sequence, 'chief Gatam, chief Korah, chief Amalek'.

Line 8. [••••]. > 𝔐 𝔴 Vrs. Considerations of space suggest two possibilities: either MS 4612/4 had a text that was around 13 letter spaces longer than 𝔐 in lines 7–8, or there was a *vacat* measuring *c.*15 mm at some point in the space of line 8. There is no section division in 𝔐^L or 𝔐^A here, and a section marker at this point of the text would hardly make sense. The space here is very close in size to the gap in the Eliphaz genealogy in line 4 above, where we suggest inserting קורח together with an unknown name. If Korah is added in the reconstruction of line 4, the name of another chief should be inserted here, perhaps one of the chiefs mentioned in vv. 41–42, Yetet, Pinon, or Iram.

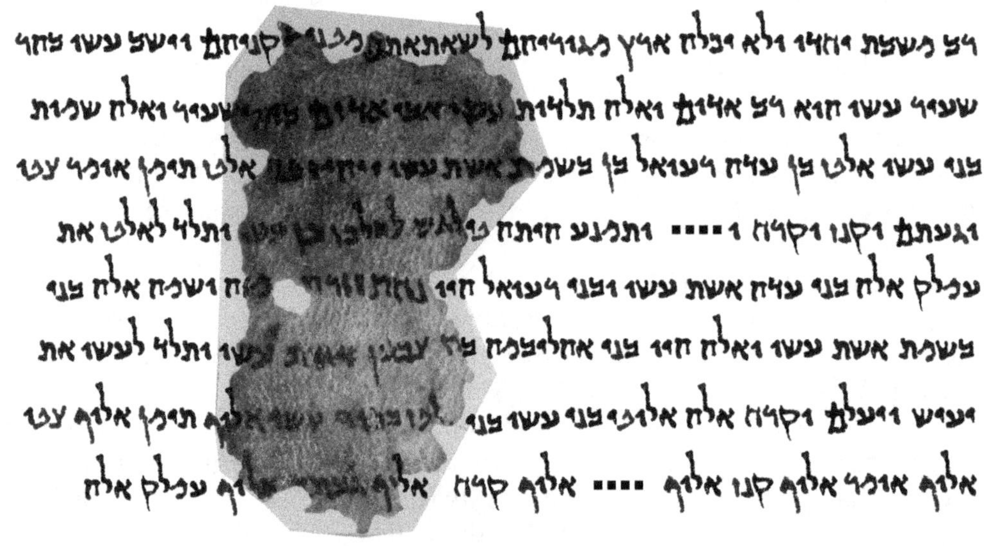

Figure 14.5. A reconstruction of 4Q(?)GenMiniature
(scale 2:1)

F. Textual Profile and Other Small-Sized Scrolls

In three cases the fragment exhibits a defective spelling where 𝔐 and 𝔴 have full spelling. Considerations of space suggest a shorter text in v. 10 than that of 𝔐, 𝔴, and 𝔊. In contrast, vv. 11, 13, and 15 either contained *vacats* or more probably a longer and different text.

The exceptionally small script-size of MS 4612/4 possibly indicates that this fragment survives from a small scroll (Tov 2004, 83–85).[7] J.T. Milik (1992, 363–64) suggested that such small-dimensioned scrolls were made for liturgical use. Emanuel Tov (1998a, 84–85; 2004, 90) notes that Milik's link between small scrolls and liturgical use explains only parts of the data now available.[8] Elgvin included 4QParaphrase of Genesis and Exodus (4Q422) as a small-sized scroll and suggested that some such scrolls were made for itinerant use by wandering teachers, *Yaḥad* officials, or travellers (Elgvin 2009, 231–32). However,

---

[7] But cf. for an unusual example of an average-sized scroll with very small script 4QM^a (4Q491). Letters measure a little under 2 mm on average, and lines are separated by 4–4.5 mm.

[8] Tov's list of small-sized scrolls contains a number of non-liturgical, community-related works: 4QS^b,d,f,j, 4QHalakha B, 4QList of False Prophets, 4QWords of the Maskil, 4QMMT^c-f, 4QCal Doc/Mish A. Also some parabiblical works were written on scrolls of small dimensions: 4QprEster^a,b,d ar, 4QDanSuz? ar, 4QapocrLam B, 4QapocrMos^a, 4QapocrDan ar, 4QApocryphal Psalm and Prayer, Masada apocryphon of Joshua (Mas 1l), MS 5095/7 (CommGen A), as were some excerpted biblical books (4QDeut^n,q [4Q41, 4Q44]; 4QExod^c [4Q14]; 4QPs^g).

Esther Eshel has rightly observed that the script in MS 4612/4 is so small as to render this text practically useless for public reading. Further, the genealogy of Esau does not immediately present itself as a good candidate for liturgical reading or preaching.

The small format of MS 4612/4 precludes its having survived from a complete book of Genesis.[9] As the fragment reflects a text considerably different from other textual witnesses, it is not self-evident that it should be classified as an excerpted *biblical* scroll.[10] More probably we are dealing with an anthology, a paraphrase or some kind of reworking of a small part of Genesis, or alternatively some kind of *testimonia*: a collection of different texts adapted from scripture.

Its small size and format more readily compare with phylacteries or amulets. Nevertheless, while the writing block for this text is extremely small, it is still on average slightly larger than what appears in phylacteries from Qumran.[11] Furthermore, virtually all copies of the Qumran phylacteries have been inscribed without word spaces (Tov 2005, 242). As illustrated in *Figure 14.4* above, the best, physically comparable Qumran scroll is 8QMez, which differs from other phylacteries at Qumran in content, its consistent word spacing, the uniform alignment of the text in a single column, and a much smaller sized script than the average (Tov 2005, 243). Another example of a similarly sized script is in 3QLam (3Q3). Letters in these small fragments range between 1.5–1.6 mm, but the reconstructed column measures closer to 9–10 cm wide (*DJD* 3:95, plate XVIII).[12]

The script-size and style in MS 4612/4 most closely resembles a copy of a mezuzah from Qumran. These features coupled by the extremely reduced legibility of the script size could suggest that this text served an imprecatory function. Perhaps it was used as a divinatory or cursing text, or possibly as an otherwise unattested reciprocal counterpart for more common *tefillin*, in which Esau/Edom and his descendants feature as objects of wrath. *Jubilees* may offer a relevant comparison: *Jub.* 25–27; 35; 37–38 portray Esau in a negative light as an antitype to Jacob, and destined to destruction (cf. in particular *Jub.* 26.34; 38.2, 10, see further below). MS 4612/4 might also be compared with 4QList of False Prophets ar (4Q339), also written in a small script and also containing only a list of names for a possible imprecatory function.

[9] Tov counts 57 excerpted and liturgical scrolls from Qumran. These scrolls should not be considered as regular biblical texts, but are included in his statistics for pragmatic reasons. They were published in *DJD* as biblical scrolls, and 'customary nomenclature for the Qumran scrolls [that] considers the liturgical and excerpted scrolls equally biblical as all other scrolls': Tov 2008, 149 (only in the reworked version of Tov 2002).

[10] 'All collections of excerpts (of biblical texts) are written in scrolls of small dimensions, and sometimes their limited scope is the main criterion for assuming the existence of an excerpted text' (Tov 2008, 29). 'The most striking feature of the excerpted and abbreviated texts is that ... none of the collections is close to MT. This indicates that these texts come from a certain milieu, one that differed from the circles fostering the tradition of the writing of Scripture texts ... fostered by rabbinic circles' (Tov 2008, 40).

[11] Cf. 1QPhyl (1Q13, Deut 5.23–27; 11.8–11), *DJD* 1:72–76; 4QPhyl A (4Q128, Deut 5.1–14, 27–6.3; 10.12–11.17 [recto] Deut 11.18–21; Exod 12.43–13.7 [verso]), *DJD* 6:48–51; 4QPhyl B (4Q129, Deut 5.1–6.2 [recto]; Exod 13.9–16 [verso]), *DJD* 6:51–53; 4QPhyl C (4Q130, Exod 13.1–16; Deut 6.4–9; 11.13–21, *DJD* 6:53–55; 4QPhyl D (4Q131, Deut 11.13, 16–17, 19, 21 [recto], Deut 11.14 [verso]), *DJD* 6:56; 4QPhyl E (4Q132, Exod 13.1–2, 5–9), *DJD* 6:56–57; 4QPhyl F (4Q133, Exod 13.11–18), *DJD* 6:57; 4QPhyl G (4Q134, Deut 5.1–21 [recto]; Exod 13.11–12 [verso]), *DJD* 6:58–60; 4QPhyl H (4Q135, Deut 5.22–6.5 [recto]; Exod 13.14–16 [verso]), *DJD* 6:60–62; 4QPhyl I (4Q136, Deut 11.13–21; Exod 12.43–13.10), *DJD* 6:62–63; 4QPhyl J (4Q137, Deut 5.1–24 [recto]; Deut 5.24–32; 6.2–3 [verso]), *DJD* 6:64–67; 4QPhyl K (4Q138, Deut 10.12–11.7 [recto]; Deut 11.7–12 [verso]), *DJD* 6:67–69; 4QPhyl L (4Q139, Deut 5.7–24), *DJD* 6:70; 4QPhyl M (4Q140, Exod 12.44–13.10 [recto]; Deut 5.33–6.5 [verso]), *DJD* 6:71–72; 4QPhyl N (4Q141, Deut 32.14–20, 32–33), *DJD* 6:74–75; 4QPhyl O (4Q142, Deut 5.1–16 [recto]; Deut 6.7–9 [verso]), *DJD* 6:74–75; 4QPhyl P (4Q143, Deut 10.22–11.13 [recto]; Deut 11.18–21 [verso]), *DJD* 6:75–76; 4QPhyl Q (4Q144, Deut 11.4–8 [recto]; Exod 13.4–9 [verso]), *DJD* 6:76; 4QPhyl R (4Q145, Exod 13.1–7 [recto]; Exod 13.7–10 [verso]), *DJD* 6:77–78; 4QPhyl S (4Q146, Deut 11.19–21), *DJD* 6:78; 4QPhyl T–4QPhyl U (4Q147–4Q148), *DJD* 6:79; 5QPhyl (5Q8, unrolled), *DJD* 3:178.

[12] Baillet's asserted letter height of 1 mm is incorrect. His identification of the few preserved letters of 3QLam frg. 1 with Lam 1.10–12 is questionable, and its assignment to the same scroll as 3QLam frg. 2 uncertain, based only on the same-sized miniature letters. Frg. 1 renders the tetragrammaton in palaeo-Hebrew letters.

G. MS 4612/4 and the Edomite Genealogy

A review of the nature and contents of the list of Esau's descendants may provide a background for better understanding the peculiar format and textual differences in MS 4612/4.

The genealogies of Esau in Genesis 36 present a somewhat complicated picture and produce a tension with other passages in Genesis, where mention is made of Esau's marriages (Gen 26.40; 28.9). Verses 2–5 mention Esau's three wives and five sons, introduced by the *toledot*-formula. Verses 9–14, introduced by the same formula, build up the family tree by adding six sons of Eliphaz and four sons of Reuel, but there is no offspring of the other three sons.[13] Verses 15–19 repeat the names of vv. 9–14 in a list of tribal chiefs, but add another son of Eliphaz, *viz.* Korah. A formula concluding the lists is found in vv. 5 and 19, but not in v. 14. Verses 40–42 contain yet another list of tribal chiefs, mostly different from those of the earlier one and sorted according to their place of settlement. According to Westermann, this latter list, which mixes personal, place, and regional names, may reflect a list drawn up for the Israelite administration of Edomite territory (Westermann 1995, 566). By inserting the term *'aluf*, the tribal list in vv. 15–19 shows the transition from clan to tribe. This suggests a point at which the sons of Esau acquire the function of political and military leaders (Westermann 1995, 564).

MS 4612/4 and ɯ probably reflect two contrasting ways of bringing the list of vv. 15–19 into compliance with that of vv. 9–14: ɯ omits the name Korah from the second list, while MS 4612/4 probably added Korah to the first one. On the other hand, considerations of space suggest that MS 4612/4 also added the name of another tribal chief in both v. 11 and v. 15. This figure was perhaps one of those mentioned in vv. 41–42 that do not occur in vv. 9–12. While the first move is easy to explain as a harmonization, the second is more difficult to understand. A polemical function of this text, perhaps in a divinatory role, might explain this second addition.

4QCommGen A (4Q252) IV 1–3 (frg. 5 1–3) connects Gen 36.12 to Saul's defeat of Amalek in 1 Sam 14.48, which was originally prophesied by Moses in Deut 25.19 (Brooke, *DJD* 22:203–4). The *pesher* in 4QCommGen A appears in a section of the text that elaborates on Jacob's blessing of his sons from Genesis 49, and situates these in an eschatological context. Shani Tzoref argues that the intersection of the three passages concerning Edom here 'serve[s] as prooftexts for the fulfilment of Isaac's pronouncement to Jacob and Esau', from Gen 27.39–40, but based on the adjusted formulation of this episode that appears in *Jub.* 26.33–34 (Tzoref 2011, 83). If Tzoref is right, then Israel's arch-enemy Amalek serves in 4QCommGen A as a representative of the whole line of Esau. Accordingly, Isaac's blessing in *Jubilees* 26 is connected to the birth of Amalek in Gen 36.12, Saul's destruction of Amalek in 1 Sam 15.1–9, and YHWH's promise of the annihilation of Amalek in Deut 25.19 in the last days.

According to John R. Bartlett (1989, 86–90), the lists of Genesis 36 to a large extent reflect a literary Judaean discourse on Edom as the typical arch-enemy of Israel. Post-exilic texts such as Jer 49.7–22; Ezek 32.29; Mal 1.2–5, and Isaiah 34 demonstrate that Edom acquired a symbolic status as a nation that deserved God's anger and would be punished (Bartlett 1989, 184–86).

The presence of the Edomite genealogy from Gen 36 in parallel with Jacob's blessing in 4QCommGen A may provide some contextual support for reading MS 4612/4 as a text with a divinatory function. Somewhat paradoxically, MS 4612/4 was copied around two generations after the Idumaeans were Judaized under John Hyrcan—Edom no longer existed as a distinct nation (Josephus, *Ant.* 13.257–

---

[13] Verses 9–10 contain a double introduction: The Priestly Source (P) added 'This is the line of Esau, the ancestor of the Edomites'. At the same time, P included an older genealogy which once stood independently and was headed by 'These are the names of Esau's sons' (Westermann 1995, 563).

58, cf. 13.397).[14] Thus, 'Edom' may have served as *typos* for enemies or antagonists such as threatening gentile nations.[15]

If MS 4612/4 was copied for or used by sectarian communities such as the *Yaḥad*, 'Edom' could be a sobriquet for other Israelite groups perceived as being in error. Here one may compare 1QS II 4–19, a covenant ceremony that included curses against the antagonists of the community. Based on material evidence and thematic parallels in other texts we suggest that MS 4612/4 may have been used in the *Yaḥad* as a mantic artefact; a divinatory text directed against outsiders.

[14] Hyrcan coins from 114 BC found in the destruction layer of Maresha show that the annexation of Idumaea happened shortly after this time.

[15] In later Jewish tradition 'Edom' became a type for a main antagonist, Christian Rome: the competing monotheist religion would be identified with the deviant brother of Jacob/Israel.

VIII

MS 5439/1. 4QRP^b (4Q364) frg. 8a (Gen 37.8)

Torleif Elgvin

DSS F.102, DSS F.RP1

This fragment was published by Émile Puech as 4QGen-Exod^a (4Q1; *DJD* 12:7–30) frg. 7a (Puech 2010).[1] A number of features suggest that it should rather be identified as belonging to 4QRP^b (4Q364). This would make it the oldest Judaean Desert fragment in The Schøyen Collection.

A. Physical Description and Identification

MS 5439/1 consists of two joined fragments (a, b) that together preserve 11.2 cm of the lower edge of a scroll with a margin of 2.3 cm. The larger inscribed fragment (a) measures 2.9 × 7.4 cm and is 0.3-0.35 mm thick. The second fragment (b) measures 2.1 × 4.6 cm, and is 0.9 mm thick at its lower edge, and 0.35 mm at the top.[2] The height of the letters is *c.* 3 mm. Three words and traces of a preceding letter are preserved. The finely prepared parchment has a reddish-brown colour on the *recto* side, and the *verso* is medium brown. The surface is smooth, but at the same time wavy due to shrinking.

A third piece of similar parchment and colour (MS 5439/2), originally thought to belong to the same fragment, is mounted on the plate.[3] Puech (2010) supposed that this was an uninscribed piece belonging to the lower margin. However, under infrared light one can see letters running vertically, indicating that this piece was not correctly mounted on the plate. A handful of physical differences make the assignment of MS 5439/1 and MS 5439/2 to the same scroll impossible: 1) The parchment of MS 5439/2 has a different surface, which is especially clear on the *verso*: the texture of the parchment and the orientation of the hair follicles differ from the two other pieces. 2) In MS 5439/2 the visible layer below is much lighter where the top layer of the parchment has disappeared. 3) FTIR spectra show the same presence of quartz, calcite, and aragonite in both pieces of MS 5439/1. In contrast, MS 5439/2 lacks aragonite, which suggests a different place of discovery (Rabin, unpublished report).[4] Further, the script of MS 5439/1 is substantially different from MS 5439/2.

---

[1] According to Puech, William Kando gave him the right of publication. When asked about this by Martin Schøyen, Kando said this was not the case.

[2] Reinhard Franke and Ira Rabin measured the thickness of most of the fragments with a Dino-Lite electronic microscope in October 2012.

[3] Puech published an infrared photograph of the main fragment, and a black-and-white one of the three fragments joined together. Fragment b and MS 5439/2 made their way separately from the vendor to The Schøyen Collection with the information that they belonged together with the larger inscribed fragment, and were subsequently mounted together with it on the plate.

[4] The analysis of MS 5439/1 showed substantial amounts of lead in the ink, but not in the parchment, indicating that the ink was made in another location than the parchment was.

Similarities in parchment texture and colour, in script, margin size, and orthography indicate that this fragment belongs to 4QRP[b]. Both in 4QRP[b] and our fragment the lower margin is 2.1–2.3 cm. 4QRP[b] was 'written on the smooth side of well-prepared leather which varies in color from a yellowish to a reddish brown' (*DJD* 13:197).[5] While the colour of our fragment is reddish-brown, the closest surrounding fragments in 4QRP[b] (frgs 7–9) are medium to dark brown.

The text of our fragment aligns with 4QRP[b] 8 ii 2; these two fragments preserve text from Gen 37.7–8. There are physical similarities between 4QRP[b] frg. 7 and MS 5439/1: damage to the lower edge in both fragments and a wormhole at the same distance from the lower edge could be explained as corresponding wear patterns in succeeding revolutions of the scroll. The same wavy surface can be observed in our fragment and in 4QRP[b] frgs 7–8. Fragment 8 is more wrinkled in the lower part, where we have located it closest to our fragment, henceforth designated 4QRP[b] frg. 8a.

Figure 15.3 shows frg. 8a aligned with 4QRP[b] frg. 8. *Figure 15.4* illustrates the probable location of the published frgs 7, 8, and 9ab relative to frg. 8a. Fragment 9ab preserves the lower right part of the column following frg. 8 cols i–ii and the beginning of a new sheet.

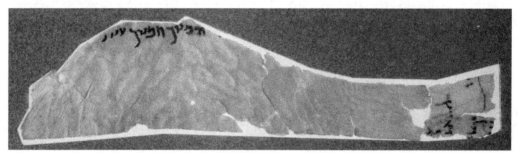

***Figure 15.1.** MS 5439/1 and MS 5439/2*

B. Palaeography

Langlois identifies the script as a Hasmonaean hand from the second century BC (see p. 81). Taking all the fragments of 4QRP[b] into account, he dates this scroll to the second half of the second century.[6] At the same time, a number of small differences distinguish the script from that of 4QGen-Exod[a], to which Puech ascribed this text.[7] The script of the third fragment, MS 5439/2, is late Herodian.

---

[5] Cf. James Sanders' suggestion for 11QPs[a] (1967, 6): 'The skin of the scroll is somewhat less than a millimetre thick, about .03 of an inch. It is the thickest of any in the scrollery, or so I am told, and it is not impossible that instead of being goatskin, as almost all the rest are, it may be calfskin ... the ink is carbon black and contrasts well with the deep yellow-to-brown of the skin itself.'

[6] In their *DJD* edition the editors Emanuel Tov and Sidney White Crawford dated 4QRP[b] between 4QSam[a] (4Q51) and 1QM, *i.e.* to *c.* 40–30 BC (*DJD* 13:201).

[7] The script of 4QGen-Exod[a] was dated by the editor James Davila to 125–100 BC, by Puech to the second half of the second century BC, while Frank M. Cross described the scroll (then designated 4QGen[a]) as early Hasmonaean (Cross 1961b, 169–72). Puech notes a difference with regard to *taw*, and states that the left leg is less curved than its counterpart in 4QGen-Exod[a], but finds *he* and ʿ*ayin* exactly the same. He has overlooked some differences: In general the letters of MS 5439/1 are slightly larger and drawn with a thicker culmus, while the strokes of 4QGen-Exod[a] vary in thickness. *He* in MS 5439/1 is more primitively drawn, with the crossbar protruding unusually far to the left. The left leg of *he* in 4QGen-Exod[a] is thinner at its lower end, different from MS 5439/1. The hook of *lamed* in MS 5439/1 is formed as a narrow semi-circle, in 4QGen-Exod[a] it is wider, with its upper part horizontally drawn. In one of two cases medial *mem* in MS 5439/1 has an exceptionally long horizontal baseline, a feature not found in 4QGen-Exod[a]. ʿ*Ayin* of MS 5439/1 is larger than in 4QGen-Exod[a]. In 4QGen-Exod[a] the foot of the left leg of *taw* extends markedly to the left, while *taw* in MS 5439/1 is more narrowly drawn. Further, the right leg of *taw* in 4QGen-Exod[a] is thinner at its lower end.

Figure 15.2. MS 5439/1

C. MS 5439/1

[ס המלוך תמלוך עלﬞינס]

]   *bottom margin*   [

Notes on Readings

The upper part of some letters has disappeared due to erosion of the upper layer of the parchment.

Line 1. המלוך ס[. There is trace neither of the word לו[that Puech reads in the beginning of the text, nor of the supralinear *waw* he suggests above this line (ending a supposed supralinear אחיﬞ]וֹ). The word space before המלוך is relatively large (3 mm compared with the next two wordspaces of *c.* 1 mm).

Line 1. The *nun* of עלﬞינס extends below the imagined baseline.

D. 4QRP^b frg. 8a (Gen 37.8)

וֹ[אחיﬞ לו ויואמרו]⁸   המלוך תמלוך עלﬞינוֹ] אם משול תמשול בנו

]   *bottom margin*   [

Translation

⁸ Hi[s brothers said to him,]   'Will you be king over us,[will you rule over us?'

Notes on Reconstruction and Comments

The column width is reconstructed to 12.3 cm.

Line 1 (37.8). [ויואמרו] = 𝔐 𝔰 (both: ויאמרו) ǀ ειπαν δε 𝔊.

Line 1 (37.8). וֹ[אחיﬞ = 𝔐 𝔰 ǀ οι αδελφοι 𝔊.

Line 1 (37.8). המלוך תמלוך = 𝔐 (המלך תמלך) 𝔰 (המלוך תמלוך). There is a space of 3 mm before המלוך. This is too short to indicate a section break,[8] which also would be somewhat irregular here even though it would directly precede the introduction of direct speech. The absolute infinitive of מלך is found twice

---

[8] See Tov (2004, 145) for a discussion of spaces corresponding to 2–7 letter spaces in the middle of a line. Cf. the space of 3.5 mm in 1QDan^b 1 6 (Dan 3.26), see p. 264.

in the Bible, here and in 1 Sam 24.21. In both cases 𝔐 uses a defective spelling (cf. the marginal note of the Masora). The full spelling of our fragment is characteristic for 4QRP^b.

E. The Schøyen Fragment and Its Implications for 4QRP^b

The *DJD* editors suggested that the columns of 4QRP[b] contained *c.* 39–41 lines (*DJD* 13:198). If the columns are reconstructed according to the Masoretic text, the column represented by 8 ii and our fragment would contain 49–50 lines. The preceding column (of frg. 8 i) would contain *c.* 68 lines and the subsequent column (of frg. 9ab) *c.* 59–75 lines.[9] Based on these estimations it is impossible to insert an 𝔐-like text into the surrounding columns. Our calculations demonstrate that these three columns of 4QRP[b] contained a substantially abridged text of Genesis 35–38 greatly at variance with 𝔐, a feature noted neither by the *DJD* editors nor by Molly Zahn in her recent monograph on the RP manuscripts.[10]

While the *DJD* editors, Emanuel Tov and Sidney White Crawford, ascribe five scrolls (4Q158, 4Q364–4Q367) to the same composition, 4QRP,[11] Zahn argues that these scrolls reflect scribes with somewhat different agendas in the way they rework the books of Moses (2011, 129–34, *passim*).

4QRP[b] preserves a number of fragments of Genesis, Exodus, and Deuteronomy, as well as two fragments of Numbers. This is a high-quality scroll: the parchment was finely prepared and the scribe was skilled. The copying of 4QRP[b] predates the Qumran settlement by one or two generations.

---

[9] Tov and White Crawford counted an average of 47 letter spaces for the lines of frg. 9ab (*DJD* 13:198). The reason for the discrepancy in calculating the column height for frg. 9ab has to do with some irregularities in the layout of this column as well as a text at variance with 𝔐 and 𝔪. Determining an average line length according to letter spaces is problematic because of the paucity of preserved text, the presence of a large word space in line 9, and several *vacats* at the beginning of lines, providing no clear idea where the text begins in lines 6–7. Some 58–59 letter spaces may be reconstructed in line 9, and 53 in line 10. However, if lines 2–3 are reconstructed according to their overlaps with Gen 38.14–16, this would produce line lengths of only 45 and 42 letter spaces. The text of this column is clearly so different from 𝔐 that it is impossible to provide a reasoned reconstruction.

[10] Zahn finds only small textual minuses in 4QRP[b] and argues that 𝔪 displays omissions of pentateuchal material on a scale not attested in the five RP manuscripts (2011, 112–13, 231). She further asserts that 4QRP[b] represents a less extensive reworking of the Pentateuch than 4QRP[a], its closest 'relative' among the RP scrolls (2011, 76–98). The evidence presented here supplements Zahn's analysis. With one exception, all cases of reworking in 4QRP[b] refer to haggadic parts of the Pentateuch, the patriarchal stories in Genesis, and elements of the Sinai and desert tradition. One may speculate that Genesis 38 contains material that easily would call for reworking.

[11] Tov has later suggested classifying it straightforwardly as a pentateuchal scroll, '4QPentateuch' (Tov 2010b). For similar judgements, see Ulrich 2000b, 56–57; Segal 2000. Michael Segal argues that 4QRP[b]/4QRP[c] and 4QRP[d]/4QRP[e] represent two different recensions of the Pentateuch. A common feature of these five RP texts is their dependence on the pre-Samaritan version of the Pentateuch. The harmonizing character of the RP texts is more extensive than what is true of their predecessor, the pre-Samaritan text.

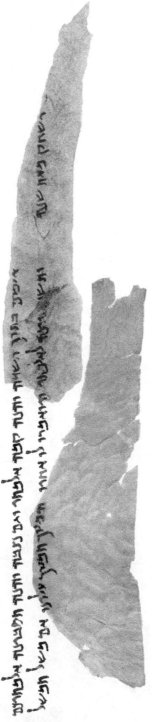

Figure 15.3. *A reconstruction of 4QRP[b] frgs 8 i–ii + 8a*
Image of frg. 8 courtesy IAA

Figure 15.4. 4QRP*b* frgs 7–9 (scale 1:2)
Images of frgs 7–9 courtesy IAA

IX

MS 4611. Mur/ḤevLev (Lev 26.3–9, 33–37)

Torleif Elgvin

DSS F.106, DSS F.Lev4[1]

A. Previous Publication, Physical Description

This fragment was published by Émile Puech in 2003, and as far as we can see, without proper authorisation (Puech 2003b).[2] Three joined fragments (a,b,c) preserve the upper part of two columns with margins: The larger frg. a covers most of the preserved part of col. i and the beginning of col. ii lines 3–5, including a top and right margin. Frg. b preserves the upper left part of col. i and the top of col. ii, and frg. c contains col. ii lines 3–8. When combined on the plate the fragments measure 8 × 21 cm. The line spacing is *c.* 5.5 mm.

Fragment a has decomposed along a wavy diagonal line in the middle and left part of col. i. This damage is partly caused by a crack and partly by a fold in the parchment. The lower left part of the fragment has shifted downwards (probably due to shrinking of the parchment), so that the ruling of lines 1–6 no longer matches. The fold accounts for the disappearance of parts of some letters, especially in lines 5–9, where the left piece has warped and curls under the right. The letters on both sides of the fold appear closer together on the photograph than in their original position, increasingly so from the top towards the bottom. The two parts of frg. a are still connected in lines 2–4. Small parts at the edges have been folded behind and thus traces of ink from letters on the *recto* are visible on the photograph of the *verso* (towards the end of line 2 and in line 9, see *Figure 16.2*).

Column i probably represents the beginning of the sheet, although no traces of sewing are preserved. The top margin varies between 19 and 35 mm, the opening right margin is 20–21 mm, the intercolumnar margin *c.* 18–21 mm, and the left margin of col. ii *c.* 25 mm. The columns are narrow; col. i has 35–43 letter spaces per line and col. ii 33–40. Column i is 7.5 cm wide and col. ii 7 cm.

The parchment is thick and brown in colour. Horizontal and vertical ruling lines are clearly visible. The skin structure can be discerned on both sides, more clearly on the *recto*. Large sections of the upper parchment layer have flaked off (especially along the diagonal damage line in col. i 1–7), exposing a

---

[1] Emanuel Tov (2010a, 24, 126) provisionally designated this scroll as both XLev^c and 4QLev^i [4Q26c].

[2] In the publication Puech stated that he had the owner's permission to publish the fragment. When asked about the matter in May 2007 he stated: 'I do not remember details. I have had so many photographs on my desk, and so many middlemen who have come to me with photographs since 1970. If I wrote that I had the owner's permission to publish, I surely had an oral permission, either from the owner or through the middleman who gave me the photograph. I do not recall if the owner was William Kando or another, or whether this photo was given to me by a middleman. I can neither say whether I got this photograph before or after 1995. Sometimes a photograph can be on my desk a long time before I get to study it and then possibly publish it. I never publish fragments without permission (as some people do with my Starcky material) but such permissions are always given orally.' The fragment was sold to The Schøyen Collection in 2001 with the vendor's information that Puech had been asked to provide a description of the text, but to refrain from publishing it.

light brown layer below. According to Ira Rabin's elemental analysis, this scroll was produced outside the Dead Sea region and shows the same features as XJudg: the tanned top layer of both texts is peeling off and the fragments have a similar ratio of Cl/Br, which are evenly distributed on the fragments. Traces of cave deposits can be identified, but the results are inconclusive (Rabin, unpublished report).

B. Palaeography

Puech (2003b) dated the script to the second half of the first century AD (referring to Cross 1961b, 139, Fig. 2, lines 8–9 [4QPs[b], c. AD 50, 5/6ḤevPs, c. AD 75–100]). Ada Yardeni characterizes the script as an elegant, developed late Herodian hand with few parallels, more easily dated after AD 70 than before. Michael Langlois describes it as a late Herodian formal script with some signs of transition from Herodian to post-Herodian scripts, concluding that the scroll was copied sometime during the second half of the first century AD (see p. 113).

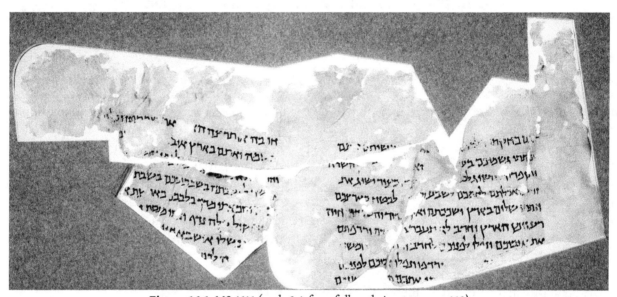

Figure 16.1. MS 4611 (scale 3:4; for a full-scale image, see p. 113)

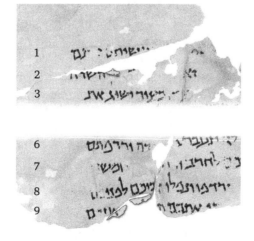

Figure 16.2. Placement of folds wrapped onto the verso in col. i

C. MS 4611 col. i

top margin

1 - אׄם בחקתי תׄלכׄו ואׄ[ ]◦◦[ ]◦ תׄ[ ]◦עׄשיתם אׄתם
2 ונתתי גשמיכם בע◦[ ]הׄא[ ]◦[ ]◦ץׄ השדׄה
3 יתן פריו ◦השיג לכׄםׄ[ ]צר ובציר ישיג את
4 זרעׄ ואכלתם לחמכם לׄשבע וי◦◦[ ]◦ לבטח בארצכם
5 ונתתי שלום בארץ ושכבתם ואיׄןׄ[ ]◦ריד והש◦דתׄ◦ חיה
6 רעה מן הארץ וחרב לא תעבר בׄ[ ]◦כׄם ורדפתם
7 את איביכם ונפׄלו לפניכם לחרב ו◦◦◦[ ]החׄמשׄה
8 [ ]◦◦ מׄכׄםׄ[ ]ירדפו ונפלו אׄ[ ]ביכם לפניכׄם
9 [ ]תׄי אתכם ו◦[ ]◦[ ]אתׄכׄם

Notes on Readings

Line 1. אׄם -. There is a section marker in the form of a short horizontal stroke in the margin, just to the right of *ʾalep*, positioned in the middle of the line (the surface has flaked off immediately above this stroke, so we cannot exclude the stroke's being part of a more composite sign).

Line 1. ואׄ[. The trace of the second letter fits the right leg of *ʾalep*.

Line 1.]◦◦[ ]◦ תׄ. At the right edge, following the lacuna, one can see a part of a slanting stroke that may fit *mem*, *ṣade*, or *ʿayin*. Then follow traces of what are seemingly two letters, possibly the lower part of *yod* or *waw* on top of the end of a baseline. Before the lacuna we see parts of two downstrokes connected by a crossbar, likely reflecting a *taw*.

Line 2. ◦[ ]◦ץׄ. Before the lacuna there is a slanting top line that would fit *reš*, *dalet*, or final *mem* (below this stroke the surface has flaked off). The descender of the final letter can only match a final *ṣade*. The top right corner of final *ṣade* and a trace of the preceding letter is preserved on the fold on the *verso* (see *Figure 16.2*). There is space for one letter (possibly two) in the lacuna.

Line 5. ואיׄןׄ. Tiny traces of *yod* and final *nun* can also be seen on the fold seen on the *verso* (see *Figure 16.2*).

Line 5. והש◦דתׄ◦. *Mem* is the most likely reading of the fourth letter. Parts of the surface have flaked off, and a hole in the leather ablates the upper part of the letter. *Taw* is irregularly shaped and has an exceptionally thick crossbar, perhaps due to a correction. The lower left trace of this letter matches the foot of *taw*. After this letter there may be traces of ink that would fit a narrow letter.

Line 7. ו◦◦◦. There are traces of three probable downstrokes after *waw*, the first of which could fit *reš*.

Line 8. מׄכׄםׄ[. The traces of the first letter fit nicely with *mem*. The remains of the last letter seem to represent the baseline and both lower corners of a final *mem*.

Line 8. אׄ[ ]ביכם. There is a *lacuna* between *ʾalep* and *bet* that is not clear on the photograph. The left part of the fragment has folded under the right.

Line 9. אתׄכׄם. Two folds under the rear side reveal ink traces. The first trace appears above the line and could represent a supralinear letter. The second trace belongs to the *ʾalep* (see *Figure 16.2*). Because of the fold going through this part of the column, the word restored in the lacuna would appear cramped. Possibly *bet* or *reš* could have been added supralinearly.

D. MS 4611 col. ii

top margin

∘∘ יׄ כֹל֯ ש֯∘תֹתיה אֹת] [הא֯ תרצה אז הרבה	1
]∘[בֹ֯] [∘איב בארץ ואתם השֹׁמה	2
]∘∘ [הֹשֹׁ ימי כל ∘שֹׁבֹֹתֹתֹיׄ אֹת ר֯∘]∘[וה	3
[בשבת בשבתתיכם שֹׁבתה ∘ לֹ שר]֯א	4
[א בארֹצת בלבבֹם מרך והבאתי ∘בֹ	5
∘[מנסת ונסֹו נדף עֹלה קול בֹ∘] [	6
[באחיו איש ∘וכשלו] [	7
[לבֹם ה∘] [	8

Notes on Readings

Line 1. ש֯ס֯תתיה. The second letter is either *bet* or *reš*.

Line 2. השֹׁמה. The traces of the first letter are only partially preserved, but they fit *he* rather precisely.

Line 3. Traces of this line are preserved on both frg. b and frg. c, but frg. c (the lower part) is clearly displaced. In order to create a straight right margin, the lower part of the fragment should be moved towards the left (see *Figure 16.3*). Fragment b preserves the top of the following underlined letters: <u>אֹת</u> <u>וה</u>ר֯[∘]∘ֹת <u>שֹׁבֹתֹתֹיׄ</u>, while frg. c preserves parts of the following: ∘[<u>הֹשֹׁ ימי כל</u> <u>שֹׁבֹתֹתֹיׄ</u> <u>אֹת</u> ∘תֹ∘]∘[הֹר֯וה. ∘[<u>הֹשֹׁ ימי כל</u>

Lines 3–4. On the larger photograph of frgs b and c, the letters of the first word in both line 3 and line 4 are divided and appear displaced both vertically and horizontally.

Line 3. וה∘[]תֹ. The third letter is more probably *reš* than *waw*. Before *taw* one can see the lower end of the preceding letter, the slanting stroke could fit the bottom stroke of several letters.

Line 3. שֹׁבֹתֹתֹיׄ∘. What is preserved of the last letter is the lower right corner on the lower piece, and the top left edge at the upper piece.

Line 6. בֹ∘[ ]. Only a handful of traces are preserved of the last letter, but final *mem* seems to be the only option.

Line 6. The last preserved letter of this line may be *he*, *ḥet*, or *dalet*.

E. Leviticus Scrolls from the Judaean Desert

Eighteen other Leviticus scrolls have been published, including two copies from Masada, one from Naḥal Arugot (Eshel, Baruchi, and Porat 2006), and two Greek copies from Cave 4. Three more will soon follow, bringing the total number up to 22. Azusa Pacific University has acquired a fragment of Lev 10.4–7, and Southwestern Baptist Theological Seminary another containing Lev 20.24 followed by Lev 18.28–30.[3] There is also a possible fragment of Leviticus in The Green Collection. Only ArugLev is known from

---

[3] Loveless 2012, 86. The sequence suggests we are dealing either with a harmonizing Leviticus scroll or an excerpted text (the column width is *c.* 9 cm, excerpted scrolls being often small-sized). Both passages deal with sexual offences that would lead to being exiled from the land. A single fragment does not constitute enough evidence to know if this scroll should be grouped with the harmonizing scrolls designated *Reworked Pentateuch* (cf. Crawford 2008, 19–57; Falk 2007, 107–19; Zahn 2011). A textual variant in 18.28 renders 'peoples' in the plural with 𝕲, 𝕾, 𝕿ᴼᴺ, while 𝔐, 𝔴, 𝔳 use the singular. Southwestern also acquired a previously published fragment of 11QpalaeoLevᵃ, covering Lev 21.7–12; 22.21–27 (Patterson 2012, 35–36).

the finds of the Bar Kokhba Revolt. ArugLev and MS 4611 are the two latest copies of Leviticus from the Judaean Desert, both copied in ornamental post-Herodian hands and formatted with narrow columns.

Leviticus 26.3–9 is not represented by any other Hebrew scroll. This makes MS 4611 the earliest Hebrew witness to these verses. 4QLXXLev[a] (4Q119) preserves Lev 26.2–16 (parallel to col. i of our fragment);[4] the early Hasmonaean 4QLev-Num[a] (4Q23) 21 i preserves Lev 26.26–33 and has one word of v. 33 (חרבה) in common with MS 4611 col. ii. As for Lev 26.34–38, MS 4611 is the earliest extant witness.

Figure 16.3. *Reconstruction of Mur/ḤevLev col. i*[5]

F. MS 4611 (Lev 26.3–9)

top margin

1 ‏3-אֹם בחקתי תלכֹו וֹאֹ[ת מ]צֹ[וֹ]תֹי תֹ[שמרו]וֹעֹשיתם אֹתם

2 ‏4וֹנתתי גשמיכם בעֹתֹ[ם ונתנה]הֹא[רץ יבול]הֹ ו]עֹץ השדֹה

3 ‏יתן פריו 5וֹהשיג לכֹם] דיש את בֹ[צר ובציר ישיג את

4 ‏זרֹע ואכלתם לחמכם לשבע ויֹשֹ[תֹ]תֹם לבטח בארצכם

5 ‏6ונתתי שלום בארץ ושכבתם ואֹיֹ]ן[מ]חֹריד והשמֹדֹתֹי חיה

6 ‏רעה מן הארץ וחרב לא תעבר בֹ[אר]צֹכֹם 7ורדפתם

7 ‏את איביכם ונפֹלו לפניכם לחרב 8ורֹדֹפֹ[ו מכם]חֹמשֹה

[4] This scroll is dated to the late second or more probably first century BC. It contains fifteen textual variants, seven of which are unique. According to the editor, this ms provides a more authentic witness to the Old Greek translation (*DJD* 9:10, 163, cf. Tov 2008, 350–54).

[5] On the plate the upper piece has shifted slightly to the left of its original location, as can be seen in *Figure 16.1*. In *Figures 16.3* and *16.4* the upper piece has been moved to the right to achieve a better alignment. Traces of ink preserved on small folds at the edges over to the verso have also been incorporated into the reconstruction.

8   [מאה ומ[אה מֿכֿבֿ] רבבה [ירדפו ונפלו אֿ[יֿ]ביכם לפניכם

9   [לחרב 9ופניתי אליכם והפרי[תֿי אתכם וה[ֿרביתי]אֿתֿכֿם

Translation

1.   If you walk according to my laws, and k[eep] my[commandme]nts and implement them,

2.   ⁴then I will grant your rains in [their]seas[on, so that]the e[arth shall yield]its [produce and the tre]es of the field

3.   their fruit. ⁵Your [threshing] shall overtake [the *vin]*tage, and the vintage shall overtake the

4.   sowing; you shall eat your fill of bread and dwell securely in your land.

5.   ⁶I will grant peace in the land, and you shall lie down untroubled [by]anyone; and I will *exterminate* vicious beasts

6.   from the land, and no sword shall cross your[la]nd. ⁷You shall give chase

7.   to your enemies, and they shall fall before you by the sword. ⁸Five[of you]shall give chas[e]

8.   [to a hundred, and a h]undred of you[shall give chase[to ten thousand;] your en[em]ies shall fall before you

9.   [by the sword. ⁹I will look with favour upon you, and ma]ke you[fer]tile and m[ultiply]you.

Notes on Reconstruction and Comments

A comparison with the biblical text indicates that MS 4611 col. i contained *c*. 37 lines from line 9 to the end of the column. Thus, the scroll had columns of about 46 lines with a text block *c*. 25 cm high and a total height for the scroll of at least 29 cm. Based on column size and upper margin, it would belong to Tov's category of *de luxe* editions (Tov 2004, 125–29), but it was published too late to be included in his list. On the basis of the size of cols i-ii, the length of this Leviticus scroll can be approximated to *c*. 3.1 m with 31 columns. A column width of 7–7.5 cm is remarkably narrow relative to the height of the columns, there is a 1:3.4 proportion between column width and height. As a post-Herodian biblical scroll with a careful scribal hand and columns that are at the same time high and narrow, MS 4611 can be grouped with MS 2713 (Josh), and probably also MS 4612/1 (Joel) and MS 2861 (Judg).

Line 1 (26.3). אם -. Parallels to the section marker preceding line 1 are found in 4QM^a (4Q491) frgs 1–3 lines 1, 4, 6, 14, 16, 18, 19.[6] Scribal signs in other scrolls have been connected by Tov with the so-called Qumran scribal practice (2004, 178–81). Tov suggests that these were usually inserted by a second scribe or reader. A new sense unit starts at this point (Lev 26.3), signalled by a closed section in 𝔐^L and an open one in 𝔐^A. We do not know if the last line of the preceding column of MS 4611 ended with a *vacat* as another sign of a sense division. The position of this section marker differs from the *paragraphos* stroke used in sectarian scrolls such as 1QIsa^a, where the marginal horizontal stroke is placed below the line in question.

Line 1 (26.3). בחקותי (בחקותי) ᛁᛁᛁ (בחקתי) 𝔐 = בחקתי.

Line 1 (26.3). מ[צֿ[וֿ]תֿי תֿ[שמרו = 𝔐 ᛁᛁᛁ. The reconstructed text (see *Figure 16.3*) is identical with that of 𝔐 and ᛁᛁᛁ. The word space is very small.

---

[6] Cp. especially the signs before lines 1 and 14, which represent the beginnings of sense units. I am indebted to Kipp Davis for this observation. We disagree with Jean Duhaime, who asserts that these strokes are 'vestiges of the scoring done in the preparation of the leather to mark the placement of the text' (Duhaime 1995, 143). A similar sign occurs in 1QpHab IV 12, but not before a new sense unit.

Lines 2-3. Due to the contraction of the parchment in the middle of the column the lines are 2–3 letter spaces longer than they appear on the photograph (*Figure 16.1*). In order to accommodate for what must have appeared in these lines one must imagine a greater separation between the two pieces of the fragment, even though they are still connected by small joins. In the reconstruction (*Figure 16.3*) an attempt is made to compensate for the discrepancy of space by separating the pieces.

Line 3 (26.5). ‎ב[צר וּבציר‎ = 𝔐 𝔴 (both ‎בציר ובציר‎). There is no space for a *yod* between *ṣade* and *reš* after the lacuna. ‎בציר‎ is spelled irregularly in the first instance.[7]

Line 4 (26.5). ‎זרֹע‎ = 𝔐 | ‎הזרע‎ 𝔴 𝔊 (τον σπορον) 4QLXXLevᵃ (τον σ]πορον). Both versions convey a meaningful text. 𝔊 and 𝔴 preserve a text that runs more smoothly, 'and the vintage shall reach unto *the* sowing (time)'. 𝔐 and MS 4611 render the four parallel nouns (threshing, vintage, vintage, sowing) without the determinative article. The usual 𝔊 rendering of ‎זרע‎ is σπερμα, while σπορος is used seven times, including in this verse.

Line 5 (26.6). ‎וא[יֹ]ן מ[חֹריד‎ = 𝔐 𝔴 | και ουκ εσται υμας ο εκφοβων 𝔊 | [και ουκ εσται ο]εκφοβων υμας 4QLXXLevᵃ. 𝔊 and 4QLXXLevᵃ add the object 'no one shall terrify *you*', probably for stylistic reasons.

Line 5 (26.6). ‎והשמׁדתֹיֹ‎ = 𝔊 (και απολω) 4QLXXLevᵃ (και α]πολω) | ‎והשבתי‎ 𝔐 𝔴. The reading ‎והשמׁדתֹיֹ‎ ‎חיה רעה מן הארץ‎ ('and I will *exterminate* vicious beasts from the land') most closely aligns with 𝔊 (και απολω θηρια πονηρα εκ της γης υμων, 'and I will exterminate vicious beasts from *your* land')[8] against 𝔐 and 𝔴 ‎והשבתי חיה רעה מן הארץ‎ ('and I will *remove* wild beasts from the land'). This reading probably reflects the *Vorlage* of 𝔊 and 4QLXXLevᵃ.[9]

Line 6 (26.6). ‎וחרב לא תעבר ב[אר]צֹכם‎ = 𝔐 𝔴 𝔊ᴬᴮ 4QLXXLevᵃ. In 𝔊ˢ this sentence is transposed to the beginning of v. 6.

Line 7 (26.7). ‎לחרב‎. While 𝔊 and 4QLXXLevᵃ at the end of v. 8 render ‎לחרב‎ with μαχαιραι (μαχαιρα is the regular 𝔊 equivalent of ‎חרב‎), both texts use φονωι ('by slaughter') for ‎לחרב‎ in v. 7 (φονωι reconstructed in 4QLXXLevᵃ), for which cf. φονος as translation of ‎חרב‎ in 𝔊Exod 5.3 and 𝔊Deut 28.22. Less probably φονωι may reflect ‎לטבח‎.

Line 8 (26.8). ‎רבבה [יֹרדפו‎ = 𝔐 𝔴 | διωξονται μυριαδας 𝔊 4QLXXLevᵃ ([διωξοντ]αι μυριαδας). The two Greek texts reverse the word sequence of the three Hebrew texts (Tov 2008, 350).

---

[7] Tov (2012, 217) comments on this same feature, occuring a number of times in 𝔐: 'In many pairs of identical words, the scribes seem to have purposely chosen a different orthography for each member of the pair.'

[8] In v. 6 𝔊 has 'your land' three times, while 𝔐, 𝔴, and our fragment has 'the land' twice, and then 'your land'.

[9] ‎שמד‎ *hipʿil* is translated by απολλυμι in Deut 2.21; 33.27; Josh 11.14; Isa 13.9; 23.11; 26.14; Esth 4.8. ‎שבת‎ *hipʿil* is translated by απολλυμι in Isaiah, Jeremiah, and Ezekiel, but elsewhere in the Pentateuch by καταπαυω (Tov 2008, 350).

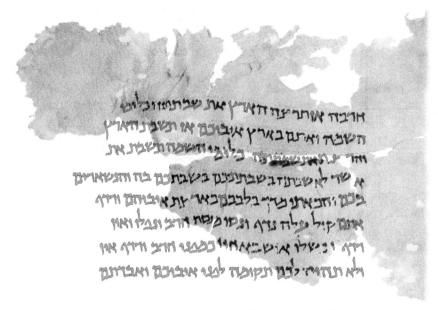

Figure 16.4. *Reconstruction of Mur/ḤevLev col. ii*

G. MS 4611 ii (Lev 26.33–38)

top margin

הרבה 34אז תרצה הא̇[רץ]א̇ת שב̇ת̇תיה כל יֹמ̇י	1
השמה ואתם בארץ איבי̇[כם אז ת̇]ש̇בֹ̇ת̇ [הֹ̇[ארץ]	2
והרֹ̇[]צֹ̇ת את שב̇ת̇תיֹ̇ה 35כל ימי הֹ̇ש̇[מה] תֹ̇ש̇[בת את	3
א̇[]שר לא̇ שבתה בשבתתיכם בשבת[כם בה 36והנשארים]	4
בֹכֹם והבאתי מרך בלבבם בא̇רצת א[יביהם ורדף]	5
[א]ֹתֹם קול עֹלה נדף ונֹסֹו מנסת ת̇[רב ונפלו ואין]	6
[רדף 37]וֹכשלו איש באחיו̇[כמפני חרב ורדף אין]	7
[ולא תה]ֹ̇יֹה לכֹ̇ם̇ תקומה לפני איביכם 38ואבדתם]	8

Translation

1. a desolation. ³⁴ Then shall the la[nd]make up for its sabbath years throughout all the days it is
2. desolate and you are in the land of[your] enemies;[then shall]the[land]res[t]
3. and make up for its sabbath years. ³⁵ Throughout all the days it is des[olate]it shall[observe the rest]
4. that it did not observe in your sabbath years while[you] were dwelling[*in it*. ³⁶ As for those who survive]
5. from among you I will cast a faintness into their hearts in the land of[their] en[emies. T]hey[shall flee]
6. at the sound of a driven leaf. Fleeing as though from the sw[ord, they shall fall though none]
7. [pursues. ³⁷ They shall stumble over one another[as before the sword but from no one pursuing.]
8. [So]yo[u sha]ll[not be able to stand your ground before your enemies, ³⁸ but shall perish]

Notes on Reconstruction and Comments

The left margin is preserved only in lines 1 and 2. A reconstruction of lines 4–8 based on 𝔐 makes these four lines (and in particular line 4) extend more to the left than lines 1–3. Since the preserved words and letters align with the text of 𝔐 and the beginnings of lines 4–6 are preserved, we tend to stay close to 𝔐 in the reconstruction of these lines.

    Lines 1–2 (26.34). ימי אשמה | (ܢܡܘܬܐ ܓܝ ܕܚܛܗܐ) S 𝔊 αυτης ερημωσεως της ημερας τας | 𝔐 = יְמֹיֹ הֹשֹמה .ﻡ. MS 4611 reads with 𝔐 ימי השמה 'days of desolation', 𝔊 has 'days of *its* desolation', while ﻡ reads ימי אשמה 'days of guilt', here and in v. 35. השמה and אשמה would be close to identical phonetically.

    Line 3 (26.34). וההֹ[רצֹת = וְהִרְצָת | 𝔐 וְהִרְצָתָה | ﻡ. 𝔐ᴸ has the archaic form וְהִרְצָת, ﻡ the more natural form וְהִרְצָתָה. *HALOT* 3:1282 presupposes the *hipʿil* form of רצה II here, *i.e.* 'bring for payment, have restored'.

    Line 3 (26.35). ימי אשמה | (ܢܡܘܬܐ ܓܝ ܕܚܛܗܐ) S 𝔊 αυτης ερημωσεως της ημερας τας | 𝔐 = [ימי הֹשֹ]מה. ﻡ, as in v. 34.

    Line 4 (26.35–36). בשבת[כם בה והנשארים. בשבתכם עליה והנשארים 𝔐 ﻡ. Line 4 would extend notably into the margin if it followed the text of 𝔐 (cf. *Figure 16.4*), something we would not expect from such a careful scribe. I therefore tentatively suggest that the scribe wrote בשבתכם בה for 𝔐 בשבתכם עליה, which would better align with the left margin.[10] Additionally, the scribe could have written והנותרים or והנותרם (for the latter short spelling, cf. Lev 10.16) for והנשארים, which would have further reduced the excessive line length.

H. Textual Character and Provenance

Puech (2003b) did not see any differences between this fragment and 𝔐 and characterized this scroll as thoroughly Masoretic. Based on this textual characterization and a dating to the second half of the first century AD, an origin outside of Qumran and a connection to one of the Jewish Revolts seemed probable to Puech. My readings differ from his in three instances: Col. i 3 contains a shorter spelling, ב[צר for 𝔐 בציר (26.5). Line 5 contains a hitherto unknown variant reading in 26.6, והשמֹדתֹיֹ, that may agree with 𝔊 and 4QLXXLevᵃ against 𝔐 and ﻡ. Finally, col. ii 4 probably contained a shorter text of Lev 26.35–36.

In Emanuel Tov's terminology, this Leviticus scroll should be classified as an 𝔐-like text.[11] We do not know where the scroll was discovered, but the late palaeographic dating and the peculiar format with high and narrow columns may suggest it was found in a cave from the Bar Kokhba Revolt.[12] This scroll shows more differences from 𝔐 than the Bar Kokhba texts hitherto published (with the possible exception of MurXII).[13]

---

[10] Such prepositions are frequently interchangable in texts from the Second Temple period. Further, when connected with ארץ, ישב ב- is more frequent than ישב על.

[11] On Tov's distinction between proto-Masoretic and 𝔐-like texts, see p. 56 note 20.

[12] See the chapter by Kipp Davis, p. 129.

[13] The same seems to be the case for MS 4612/1 (Joel) and to a larger degree, see p. 231.

X

MS 4612/5. 4Q(?)Num (Num 16.2–5)

Torleif Elgvin

DSS F.107, DSS F.Num1

A. Physical Description

The fragment, light brown in colour, measures 2.1 × 3.3 cm and preserves remnants of four lines. The parchment is thick with a coarse surface. The grain structure is visible under the sediments on the *recto*. The line spacing is *c.* 6 mm.

According to Ira Rabin's analysis the Cl/Br ratio indicates preparation of the skin outside the Dead Sea region. Cave sediments are recognized in the infrared spectrum, with large peaks of alumo-silicate and calcite, and a lower value of aragonite, tentatively suggesting the area of Qumran as place of discovery (Rabin, unpublished report).

B. Palaeography

According to Michael Langlois, this hesitant and inconsistent hand is difficult to date, especially given the limited size and degraded state of the fragment. On the basis of some Herodian features he concludes that the scroll was copied in the second half of the first century BC (see p. 92).

Figure 17.1. MS 4612/5

C. MS 4612/5

]∘א∘[	1
]∘בת וב כלם קדשים ∘∘∘[	2
]ל̇א̇ו̇ ח∘[ק]ל א וידבר∘[	3
] ריב[	4

Notes on Readings

Line 1.]○א○[. The first letter can be read as *he* or *waw* (cf. the *waw* in the last word of line 2). The oblique stroke preserved of the third letter likely belongs to an *ʿayin* or *šin*, less probably *mem* or *nun*. The trace does not show a more distinct elbow joining the right downstroke and the base line, which is characteristic for both *mem* and *nun* in formal scripts from the Herodian period.

Line 2.]○בֹתֹו. Both the baseline and crossbar of *bet* are equal in length and touch the right downstroke of *taw*.

Line 3. יֹדברֹ○[. The form of *reš* seems strange, as the foot turns left at the lower end like the corner of a *mem*. This is most easily explained as a scribal error or irregularity.

Line 3.]אֹלֹוֹ. The traces of the second letter make the identification as *ʾalep* likely; we see the upper part of the diagonal stroke with a *serif* at the top. Going by the width of the *ʾalep*, the preceding letter may be confidently identified as *waw*.

D. Identification

While working on the present edition Hanan Eshel suggested that this fragment could belong to 34Se-Num, the only published Numbers scroll with letters similar to MS 4612/5.[1] In connection with this suggestion, the following details should be remembered. In 1959, Israeli scholars heard rumours that Bedouin had found additional documents in Wadi Seiyal. This led Yohanan Aharoni to conduct an archaeological survey of the area in January 1960. He found three caves with relics from the Bar Kokhba Revolt (Aharoni 1961; *DJD* 38:209, plate XXXII). In Seiyal Cave 32, a large cave completely looted by the Bedouin, he found the bones of seven individuals but no remnants of scrolls. In Cave 34, a cave discovered by the archaeologists, Aharoni did not find signs of human habitation other than part of a phylactery and a fragment later identified as a fragment of Numbers, preserving a large top margin and four words from two columns (Num 18.21; 19.11, *DJD* 38:209). These fragments were found close to the nest of a vulture and it was suggested that they had been taken from Cave 32 to Cave 34 by this vulture.

34SeNum consists of two fragments. One of them preserves part of the scroll margin and no letters. The inscribed fragment measures 5.6 × 14 cm and preserves a large top margin of 5 cm, which places this scroll in Tov's group of *de luxe* editions (Tov 2004, 126). While *DJD* 38 published a photograph of 34SeNum, the present whereabouts of the fragments themselves are not known.

The script of our fragment is comparable to that of 34SeNum, but the few preserved letters are narrower and more carefully written in 34SeNum. The infrared photograph of 34SeNum shows the skin pattern, which is different from the *recto* of MS 4612/5, where the skin pattern is hardly recognizable under the layer of sediments. Thus, while Eshel's hypothesis was initially considered attractive, I conclude that we are dealing with two different Numbers scrolls.

E. Numbers Scrolls from the Judaean Desert

Thirteen copies of Numbers from the Judaean Desert are known. Seven copies were found in the Qumran caves, one in Cave 1, four in Cave 2, and two in Cave 4 (one of them is 4QLev-Numᵃ [4Q23]). Another

---

[1] Eshel lectured on this connection at the archaeological conference in Beersheba two weeks before his death on 7 April, 2010 (H. Eshel 2010a). I initially considered this identification, but later discarded this option.

four were found in the Bar Kokhba caves, one in Murabbaʿat, and three in Naḥal Ḥever and Wadi Seiyal (5/6ḤevNumᵃ [5/6Ḥev 1a],[2] XḤev/SeNumᵇ [XḤev/Se 2], 34SeNum [34Se 2]). Further, the Green Collection includes a copy of Num 8.4–5. The early Herodian 4QNumᵇ (c. 30–1 BC) covers the same passage as our fragment (*DJD* 12:220–22).

F. MS 4612/5 (Num 16.2–5)

[ישראל חמשים ומאתים נשיאי עדה קראי מועד]אַנֹ[שי שם ³ויקהלו על משה ועל]	1
[אהרן ויאמרו אליהם רב לכם כיא כול ה]עָדָֹה כלם קדשים ובתוֹ[כם יהוה ומדוע תתנשאו]	2
[על קהל יהוה ⁴וישמע משה ויפל על פניו ⁵]וַידברֹ אל קֹ[וֹ]רֹח וֹאֹל[כול עדתו לאמור בקר]	3
[וידע יהוה את אשר לו ואת הקדוש והק]ריב [אליו ואת אשר יבחר בו יקריב אליו]	4

Translation

1. [two hundred and fifty Israelites, chieftains of the community,]me[n of repute. ³They assembled against Moses and]

2. [Aaron and said to them, 'You have gone too far! For all the co]mmunity are holy, all of them, and[YHWH] is in [their] mid[st. Why then do you raise yourselves]

3. [above YHWH's congregation?' ⁴When Moses heard this, he fell on his face. ⁵]Then he spoke to K[o]rah and to [all his company, saying, 'Come morning,]

4. [YHWH will know who is His and who is holy, and will gr]ant [him access to Himself; he will grant access to the one he has chosen.']

Notes on Reconstruction and Comments

We have reconstructed the text with 62–72 letter spaces per line and a column width estimated to be about 11.5 cm.

Line 1 (16.2). אַנֹ[שי שם] = 4QNumᵇ 𝕲 (και ανδρες ονομαστοι) ¦ אנשי שם 𝔐 𝔪. The trace of the first letter is most likely *waw*, compatible with 𝕲 and 4QNumᵇ.[3]

Line 2 (16.3). [אליהם] = 𝔐 (אלהם) 𝔪 (אליהם) ¦ > 𝕲.

Line 2 (16.3). קדשים = 4QNumᵇ (קדושים) 𝔐 (קְדֹשִׁים) ¦ קדישים 𝔪.

Line 2 (16.3). עָדָֹה[. Only traces are preserved of this word, and these are consistent with the letters in 𝔐 𝔪.

Line 3 (16.5). קֹ[וֹ]רֹח = 4QNumᵇ 𝔐 (קרח) 𝔪 (קרח). The length of the lacuna shows that Korah was written here with full spelling, cp. *qop* followed by *dalet* in the word קדשים in the preceding line. Both 𝔐 (42 cases) and 𝔪 (23 cases) consistently use the defective spelling קרח. Both forms appear in Qumran texts.[4] Based on the reconstructed long spelling of קורח in line 3 we also suggest a *plene* spelling of the

---

[2] Fragments 1–2 and 4 were found by the Bedouin in 1951–52, while frg. 3 was found by Yadin in 1960/61. Yosi Baruchi assigns frg. 3 to a separate scroll (Baruchi 2009, 340–42).

[3] Cf. alternative formulations of v. 2 in 𝔗ᴶ, מאתן וחמשין אמרכלי כנישתא מערעי זמן למיטל ולמשרי מפרשין בשמהן, and in ട, ܐܠܦܝܢ ܘܚܡܫܝܢ ܓܒܪܐ ܘܢܫܐ ܘܐܬܟܢܫܘ ܥܠ ܡܘܫܐ ܘܥܠ ܐܗܪܘܢ.

[4] The full spelling is found in 4QNumᵇ (Num 16.5-6), 4QMᵃ (4Q491 1-3 1), 4QInstructionᵉ·ʰ (4Q418a 3 3; 4Q423 5 1), 4QPhyl A (4Q128, Deut 11.6); while the defective is used in 4QGen-Exodᵃ (4Q1, Gen 6.21), 4QPsᶜ (4Q85, Ps 49.1), 8QMez (8Q4, Deut 11.6).

words כול ,כיא, and לאמור in lines 2–3.[5] The reconstruction based on these spellings produces an alignment to both margins which strengthens our hypothesis that this text was written with a tendency towards full orthography.

Lines 3–4 (16.5). [ריב]והק ... וידע בקר] = 4QNum[b] ([...וידע בקר]) 𝕸 | יקריב ... ויודיע בקר | 𝔲 επεσκεπται και εγνω ... και προσηγαγετο 𝕲. The Hebrew text is difficult. 𝕸 vocalizes the first two words בֹקֶר וְיֹדַע. 𝔲 reads either בֹקֶר וַיוֹדִיעַ or בֹקֶר וְיֹדִיעַ. The 𝕲 translation probably corresponds to בֹקֶר וַיֵּדַע. The various vocalizations of בקר and the verbal forms of ידע and קרב reflect different understandings of v. 5: 'In the morning the Lord will know who are his, who are holy, whom he will bring near to himself' 𝕸; 'The Lord will visit(?) and show who are his, and those who are holy he will bring near to himself' 𝔲; 'God has examined and recognized the ones who are his and who are holy, and he brought them to himself' 𝕲. It is not possible to know with which of the versions our fragment agreed, since one can restore either ריב]והק or יק[ריב. The *BHK* editors suggest והקרוב 'and who are close'. MS 4612/5, which seems to read *yod* and not *waw*, could correspond to either 𝕸 or 𝔲, but not to the suggestion of the *BHK* apparatus.

Based on its predominant agreement with the text of 𝕸, MS 4612/5 is best characterized as an 𝕸-like text. Only the unusually long spelling ק[ו]רֹח departs from the 𝕸 tradition.

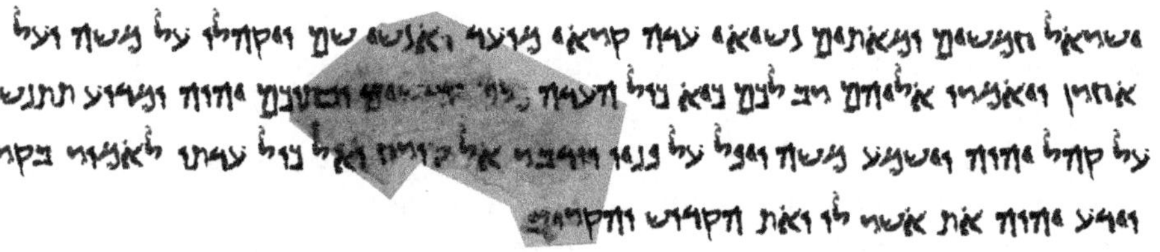

Figure 17.2. *A reconstruction of 4Q(?)Num*

---

[5] The defective spelling of קדשים in line 2 is consistent with a full spelling elsewhere in this text. קדשים is the ordinary biblical spelling of this word—only three times does 𝕸 use the spelling קדושים (Hos 11.12; 2 Chr 35.3; Ps 16.3). The same text is preserved in 4QNum[b] (4Q27) frgs 6–10 11-15, a manuscript that consistently uses *plene* spelling.

XI

MS 5214/1. 4Q(?)Deut1 (Deut 6.1–2)

Torleif Elgvin

DSS F.108, DSS F.Deut5

A. Physical Description

The fragment measures 1.5 × 3 cm. The parchment is dark brown, so dark that letters could only be discerned with the help of infrared photography. The surface of the *recto* is relatively smooth, while that of the *verso* is rougher. On both sides the skin can be seen under the sediments. The remains of three lines can be seen in the infrared photographs.

According to Ira Rabin's analysis the Cl/Br ratio indicates preparation of the skin outside the Dead Sea region (Rabin, unpublished report).

B. Palaeography

According to Ada Yardeni the scribe displays a personal style that is difficult to date within the early or middle Herodian periods. Michael Langlois characterizes the script as a somewhat developed Herodian semiformal hand, dating from the beginning of the first century AD (see p. 102).

Figure 18.1. *MS 5214/1*

C. MS 5214/1

‏[○ו] הֹמצוה והחוקים ו[	1
‏[ש○○] [‏בארֹ] ○עשות[	2
‏[לֹ]	3

D. Notes on Readings

Line 2. ‏[○עשות. The trace of the first letter is compatible with the hook of *lamed*. In such an irregular hand other options cannot be excluded.

Line 2.]שׁ◦[. The *šin* is much smaller and is shaped differently from the same letter earlier in this line. This letter and the ink trace to the right of it appear surprisingly high on the hypothetical dryline. The *šin* suspiciously follows the contours of the fragment, as if it has been 'squeezed' into the available space along the bottom edge.

E. Deuteronomy Scrolls from the Judaean Desert

Thirty five copies of Deuteronomy found in the Qumran caves have been published (Caves 1, 2, 4, 5, 6, and 11, see Tov 2010a, 116–17), one at Masada, one in Murabbaʿat, and one in Ḥever/Seiyal (XḤev/SeDeut). Emanuel Tov lists four unpublished copies as X15–X18 without any specifications (Tov 2010a, 127), and MS 5214/1 (Deut 6) and MS 5214/2 (Deut 32) may be among these. MS 5214/1 (Deut 6) and MS 5214/2 (Deut 32) raise the number of published copies of Deuteronomy from the Judaean Desert to 40. Fragments of two scrolls belonging to SWBTS contain text from Deut 9.25–10.1 and Deut 12.11–14.[1] The Azusa collection includes a fragment with Deut 8.2–4 and another with a variant text of Deut 27.4–6.[2] One more copy belongs to the Green Collection. At present, around 44 copies of Deuteronomy are known. Further, a tiny fragment with seven letters, perhaps preserving Deut 23.3–4, was exhibited in the US in 2005 (cf. Noah 2005).

The late Herodian 4QDeutʲ (4Q37) col. IV preserves Deut 5.29–6.3. Only the *he* in המצוֹ֔ה]תֹאֹ֯ז֯ו[from the beginning of Deut 6.1 on line 3 overlaps with our fragment. Col VI of the excerpted scroll 4QDeutⁿ (4Q41, dated to 30–1 BC) preserves Deut 5.28–6.1 (the top of an ʾalep is all that is preserved of 6.1). There is no overlap with our fragment.

F. MS 5214/1 (Deut 5.33–6.2)

[תירשון ¹וזאת]הֹמצוה והחוקים והֹ[משפטים אשר צוה יהוה אלוהיכם]	1
[ללמד אתכם]לֹ[ע]שות באר[ץ]אֹשׁ[ר אתם עברים שמה לרשתה ²למען תירא]	2
[את יהוה אלהיך]לֹ[שמור את כול חוקותיו ומצוותיו אשר אנוכי מצוכה]	3

Translation

1. [you are to inherit. ¹And this is]the instruction *and* the laws and the [rules that YHWH your God has commanded]

2. [to impart to you,]to be observed in the lan[d]tha[t you are about to cross into and inherit, ² so that you may revere]

3. [YHWH your God and]to[follow all his laws and commandments that I command you]

---

[1] For photographs of these, see Loveless 2012, 87–88. Both scrolls are provisionally dated to *c.* 50 BC–AD 50.

[2] The latter was published by James Charlesworth on the internet in 2008 and later on paper (Charlesworth 2009). This fragment, provisionally designated APU 4, reads *hargarizim* (for Mt. Ebal) and uses the long form כה- of the second person masculine suffix, a feature typical of the so-called Qumran scribal school. Similarly, ʿ*olot* is written in a full orthography. Further, the command in v. 4a seems to be written in the singular (to Moses), and not in the plural (to the people). On the different readings of Deut 27.4, see our discussion of MS 2713 (Josh) below.

Notes on Reconstruction and Comments

The fragment contains a textual variant in Deut 6.1 (a full spelling of והחוקים that includes the conjunctive) that aligns with 𝕲 and 4QPhyl H (4Q135) from Qumran, and is different from 𝔐.[3] Because of the plene spelling of this word and the space available in the lacunae we have tentatively restored the forms אלוהיכם (line 1) and ואנכי, ומצוותיו, חוקותיו, כול, לשמור, and אנוכי (line 3) in the reconstructed text (cf. Tov 2004, 261–73, 339–43). As there are no firm conventions within this scribal practice, considerations of space led us to reconstruct shorter forms in a few instances.

Line 1 (6.1). ת[וזא] | (וזאת]) המצ[וה] 4QPhyl H (וֹזֹאתֹ] המצוֹה[] 4QDeutʲ (וזאת המצוה) = 𝔐 | וזאות [הֹמצוה. ‏| צוא[מ]ה 8QPhyl | זאת המצוה 4QPhyl M XQPhyl 2 [XQ2] (זאת המצוה) | και αυται αι εντολαι 𝕲 | ܐܠܝ ܦܘܩܕܢܐ 𝖲.

Line 1 (6.1). והחוקים = 4QPhyl H[4] XQPhyl 2 (והחקים) 𝔐ᵐˢˢ 𝕲 (και τα δικαιωματα) 𝖲 (ܘܢܡܘܣܐ) | וחק[י]ם[8QPhyl | החוקים 4QPhyl M 𝔐 𝔰 (both החקים).[5]

Line 1 (6.1). והֹ]משפטים. > 8QPhyl.

Line 2 (6.1). לֹ]עשות בארץ כן.[| ל[עשות בארץ 4QPhyl M.

Line 2 (6.1). עברים = 4QPhyl H 𝔐 𝔰 | באים 4QPhyl B 4QPhyl M 8QPhyl XQPhyl 2.

Line 2 (6.2). [למען]. The *BHS*-apparatus, as well as a number of scholars (Christensen 1991, 132), mistakenly indicate that the Qumran witnesses do not include this word.

Lines 2-3 (6.2). [תירא את יהוה אלהיך] = 𝔐 | φοβηθε κυριον τον θεον υμων 𝕲.

Line 3 (6.2). [חוקותיו] = 𝔐 (חקתיו | חקיו 𝔰.

Line 3 (6.2). [מצוכה]. + היום 𝔐ᵐˢ 𝔰 𝕲 (σημερον).

Line 3 (6.2). [אנוכי] = 4QPhyl M (אנוכי) 4QPhyl H 8QPhyl XQPhyl 2 𝔐 𝔰 (all אנכי).

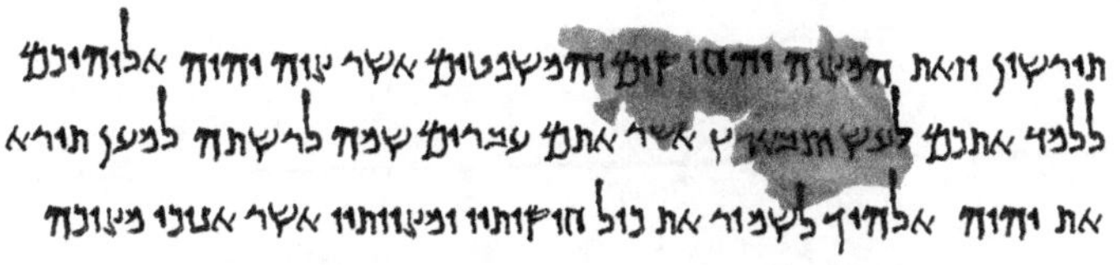

***Figure 18.2.** A reconstruction of 4Q(?)Deut1*

---

[3] Tov lists 4QPhyl H among the phylacteries written in the Qumran scribal practice, contrary to later rabbinic instructions (among other factors they include the Decalogue, see Tov 1997; 2004, 270–71).

[4] The second *waw* seems to be written sublinearly (cf. *DJD* 6:62, plate XVI).

[5] Somewhat surprisingly, the editor of 4QDeutʲ follows the 𝔐 reading החוקים in her reconstruction (*DJD* 14:9).

XII

MS 5214/2. 4Q(?)Deut2 (Deut 32.5–9)

Torleif Elgvin

DSS F.109, DSS F.Deut6

A. Physical Description

The fragment, medium brown in colour, measures 3.8 × 3.8 cm. Parts of the upper layer have flaked off. The skin structure is visible on the *verso*. Five lines are preserved with a right margin that measures 16 mm to the edge of the fragment, which may preserve the beginning of the sheet.[1] The line spacing is 6.5–7 mm.

According to Ira Rabin's analysis, the skin contains substantial amounts of lead. The Cl/Br spectrum indicates preparation of the skin outside the Dead Sea region (Rabin, unpublished report).

B. Palaeography

Ada Yardeni characterizes the script as a late Herodian formal hand, *c.* AD 30–100. Michael Langlois characterizes it as a skilled late Herodian or early post-Herodian formal hand, concluding that the scroll was copied sometime in the second half of the first century AD, perhaps in the third quarter (see p. 108).

Figure 19.1. *MS 5214/2*

---

[1] Tov remarks (personal communication) that a 16 mm margin is somewhat small to posit the beginning of a sheet. But cf. the 14 mm right margin in MS 4612/9 (Jer), where preserved traces of sewing indicates the edge of a sheet. Intercolumnar margins in the scrolls are usually 10–15 mm wide (Tov 2004, 103).

C. MS 5214/2

[ ]ווֹ קֹ○[	1
○[אֹבִיךָ קנאֹךָ	2
○[שאל אביך וֹ	3
בני אדם יצב גֹ[	4
תֹבל נחלֹתֹ ישֹׁ[	5

Notes on Readings

Line 1. קֹ○[. The second letter looks most like a *qop* (compare with קנאֹךָ in the following line). The head connected to the left of the long descender appears slightly out of place due to a crack in the leather.

Line 1.]ווֹ. The first downstroke is probably a *waw*. Then follows the lower part of a downstroke connected to a short baseline, compatible with *kap*, *nun*, or *pe*.

Line 2. אֹבִיךָ. The traces of the first letter precisely fit the two legs of ʾ*alep*; compare with ʾ*alep* in שאל in line 3. The traces match the chevron formed by the first stroke, which is in keeping with late Herodian scripts. The right foot of ʾ*alep* protrudes below the imagined base line.

Line 2.]○. The upper right corner of a letter is preserved, compatible with *he*, *ḥet*, or *dalet*.

Line 3.]○ו. After *waw* one sees the lower part of a downstroke.

Line 4. יצב. There is a vertical crack that bisects the crossbar and the baseline of *bet*. Inspection of the PTM of this fragment (SchoyenMS5412-2 OB Vp) reveals that there is possibly ink in the crack where the surface has worn, although this is inconclusive.

Line 5. תֹבל נחלֹתֹ ישֹׁ[. The first extant letter on the line appears most like a *taw*, which would result in reading תבל for the first word,[2] although חבל cannot be excluded. The space between the visible downstroke and the traces of the following *bet* suggest the presence of the foot of a *taw*. The reading נחלֹתֹ ישֹׁ[is clear. The right and centre arm of *šin* can be discerned.

D. MS 5214/2 (Deut 32.5–9)

[ ] דור [עֹקֹש וֹפֹ[תלתל 6הל יהוה תגמלו זאת עם נבל ולא חכם הלוא[	1
אֹבִיךָ קנאֹךָ הֹ[וא עשך ויכננך 7זכר ימות עולם בינו שנות דור ודור[	2
שאל אביך וֹ[גדך זקניך ויאמרו לך 8בהנח(י)ל עליון גוים בהפרידו[	3
בני אדם יצב גֹ[בלת עמים למספר בני אל(?) 9כי חלק יהוה עמו יעקב[	4
תֹבל נחלֹתֹ ישֹׁ[ראל 10ימצאהו בארץ מדבר ובתהו ילל ישמן יסבבנהו[	5

Translation

1. [... they are a]perverse and c[rooked generation. 6Do you thus requite YHWH, O dull and witless people? *Is not*]

2. your father who created you *the o[ne* who fashioned you and made you endure? 7Remember the days of old, consider the years of ages past.]

---

[2] First noted by Kipp Davis and Årstein Justnes.

3. Ask your father, he will[inform you, your elders, they will tell you: [8]When the Most High apportioned to the nations their heritage, when he set the divisions of]
4. mankind, he decided the bo[undaries of peoples according to the number of the sons of *God*. [9]Indeed,[3] the portion of YHWH is his people *Jacob*;]
5. *the world is Is[rael's] inheritance*. [He found him in a desert region, in an empty howling waste he engirded him]

Parallel Texts

Different from codices 𝔐[A] and 𝔐[L], where the 'Song of Moses' in Deut 32.1–43 is written stichometrically, this text was written in prose format. Four previously published Qumran scrolls preserve portions of the Song of Moses, three of them stichometrically:

Table 10. *The 'Song of Moses' in the Qumran Scrolls*

4QDeut[b] (4Q29 frgs 5–8)	vv. 1–3, stichometric (reconstructed)	*c.* 150–100 BC
4QDeut[j] col. xii (4Q37 frg. 34)	vv. 7–8, prosaic	*c.* AD 50
4QDeut[q] col. ii (4Q44 frgs 1–5)	vv. 9–10(?), 37–43, stichometric	*c.* 40 BC–AD 10
4QpalaeoDeut[r] (4Q45 frgs 38–40)	vv. 6–8, 10–11, 13–14, 33–35, stichometric	100–25 BC

4QpalaeoDeut[r] preserves four words from vv. 6–8 and 4QDeut[j] four words of vv. 7–8 without any overlap with MS 5214/2.[4]

Notes on Reconstruction and Comments

The text is tentatively reconstructed with 54–57 letter spaces per line. The column width is estimated at 9.5 cm. Based on the graphical reconstruction we suggest a previously unattested reading in the end of line 1, and a reading possibly in agreement with 𝔊 in line 4.

Line 1 (32.5).]   דור[עׄקׄשׁ. דור עקש 𝔐 ⅏ 𝔊 (γενεα σκολια). The reconstruction of the word דור would not fill the lacuna to the right margin, as there is room for three more letters or a two-letter word with a word space. There is not room for both דור and the word preceding it in 𝔐, מומם, or for the shorter מום in ⅏ = 𝔊 (μωμητα). A small *vacat* at the beginning of the line is not congruous with the prosaic arrangement of the text as a whole, and this suggests that MS 5214/2 probably contained a variant text here. Crawford calls the first clause of v. 5 'almost hopelessly corrupt' (Crawford, Joosten, and Ulrich 2008, 355).

Lines 1–2 (32.6). [הלוא] אׄביך קנאׄך הׄ[וא]. הלוא הוא אביך קנך הוא 𝔐 ⅏ 𝔊 (ουκ αυτος ουτος σου πατηρ εκτησατο σε). There are orthographic differences in קנאך between the manuscripts. Some ⅏[mss] share with our text the unusual spelling of קנה with *ʾalep*, 𝔐 ⅏ have the shorter spelling קנך, while 𝔐[mss], Bomberg ed., and a Genizah ms use קניך. Based on the graphical reconstruction it seems that our text contained a shorter text in the left part of line 1 compared to 𝔐 ⅏. Our scribe or his predecessor may have omitted הוא or less probably הלוא. An omission of הוא may be explained by *homoioteleuton* as both הלוא and הוא start with *he* and end with *ʾalep*. Alternatively an omission of הוא can be explained as

[3] כי should be understood as an emphatic, not causal particle: Craigie 1976, 378 note 18; McCarthy 2007, 141.

[4] According to Patrick Skehan 4QDeut[q] reads נח[לׄתו with 𝔐 (*DJD* 14:139), but Eugene Ulrich (2010, 240) rightly questions the identification of this fragment with Deut 32.9–10.

stylistic smoothening of the text. The text of 𝔐 has two hemistichs side by side ('Is not he your father who created you?—he fashioned you and made you endure!'), while our reconstructed text of MS 5214/2 would pull the two hemistichs together ('Is not] your father who created you the o[ne who fashioned you and made you endure?').

Line 3 (32.8). בהנחל 𝔐 ꟺ. | בהנחל 𝔐ᵐˢˢ ꟺᵐˢˢ 4QDeutʲ. [בהנח(י)/ל].

Line 4 (32.8). [בני אל(?)]. בני אלוהים 4QDeutʲ 𝔊 (αγγελων θεου) P.Fouad 848 Origenes VI 60 (υιων θεου) | בני ישראל 𝔐 ꟺ 𝔳 𝔖 𝔗ᴼᴺ. Considerations of space suggest a shorter text than 𝔐 ꟺ. I tentatively reconstruct בני אל, compatible with the readings of 4QDeutʲ, the Greek witnesses, and 𝔗ʲ.[5] However, it remains possible that the text read בני ישראל or בני אלוהים, with the variant occurring in another part of the line.[6] Both Greek versions are translations of either בני אל or בני אלהים.[7] Sidney White Crawford suggests that בני אל was the older reading in Deut 32.8.[8] The proto-Masoretic tradition may have censored this reading for theological reasons. It has been suggested that for some, a council of divine or semi-divine beings could contest the sovereignty of God.[9] The change to בני ישראל may have been inserted in 𝔐-like texts in the late third or early second century, after the 𝔊 translation of the Pentateuch and before the parting of the Samaritan textual tradition from its Jewish relatives some time in the second century.[10] The late Herodian manuscript 4QDeutʲ demonstrates that the reading בני אלוהים was still known in Judaea in the late Second Temple period.

Lines 4-5 (32.9). כי 𝔐[11] | כי חלק יהוה עמו יעקב חבל נחלתו. [כי חלק יהוה עמו יעקב] חבל נחלת יש[ראל]. ꟺ | חלק יהוה עמו יעקב חבל נחלתו ישראל | και εγενηθη μερις κυριου λαος αυτου Ιακωβ σχοινισμα κληρονομιας αυτου Ισραηλ 𝔊 | ארום חלקה דייי עמה בני ישראל יעקוב עדב אחסנתיה 𝔗ᴺ. 𝔊 begins v. 9 with και εγενηθη, equivalent to ויהי, while 𝔐 and ꟺ have כי. Both restorations are possible in our text. While the difference is fairly negligible, considerations of space slightly favour the shorter כי. 𝔐 and ꟺ/𝔊 differ on which half-verse the word 'Jacob' belongs to. In 𝔐 it belongs to the second stich ('Jacob is the lot of his inheritance'). In ꟺ/𝔊 it belongs to the first ('Indeed, the portion of YHWH is [𝔊: became] his people Jacob'). In my reconstruction, 'Jacob' belongs to the first stich. It is noteworthy that 𝔗ᴺ seems to have known both ways of reading this verse, since it includes the phrase 'Israel' (present in ꟺ/𝔊) in

---

[5] 𝔗ʲ knows both readings: באחסנות עילאה עלמא לעממייא די נפקו מבנוי דנח באפרשותיה מכתבין ולישׁנין לבני-נשׁא בדרא דפלוגתא בי היא זימנא רמא פיצתא עם שובעין מלאכיא רברבי עממין דאתגלי עימהון למחמי קרתא ובי היא זימנא אקים תחומי אומיא כסכום מניין שׁובעין נפשׁתא דישׁראל דנחתו למצרים 'When the Most High gave the world as an inheritance to the peoples who came from the sons of Noah, when he divided the writings and languages among mankind, in the generation of the division, at that time, he cast lots on *seventy angels*, the leaders of nations, with whom it was revealed to see the city; and at that time he established the borders of the nations according to the sum of the number of the *seventy souls of Israel* who went down to Egypt' (translation Clarke 1998, 90, cf. Barthélemy 1978, 104–5). This double interpretation may show that reading either בני אל or בני אלהים was remembered throughout the rabbinic period.

[6] An alternative would be the omission of יעקב, which would be without parallel in any other witness, whereas the suggested בני אל would run parallel to other witnesses.

[7] 1QHᵃ XXIV 33–34 seems to presuppose the reading בני אלהים or בני אל in Deut 32.8: כובדתה מבני אל שׁו[א] יצב ג[בֹלות עמים 'you are [ho]noured more than the sons of God who [... as he decided the bo]undaries of the peoples'.

[8] 'It is easy to suppose that the *Vorlage* of 𝔐 ꟺ, wishing to change a polytheistic text to monotheistic orthodoxy, inserted the consonants ישׁר before אל, thus creating the reading בני ישׂראל' (Crawford, Ulrich, and Joosten 2008, 357). Jan Joosten suggested בני שׁר אל 'the number of the sons of Bull El' as original text, later abbreviated into בני אל, and easily changed to the Masoretic בני ישׂראל (Joosten 2007).

[9] Barthélemy tentatively linked this and other corrections in the Bible that want to safeguard God's name against profanation (*e.g.* 1 Sam 3.13; 25.22; 2 Sam 12.14; Zech 2.12) to Sadducean scribes of the late Hasmonaean period (1978, 101–10). Against this Himbaza suggested that this change was introduced as late as the first century AD (2002, 527–29). Himbaza's view is difficult to uphold since the censored text is also found in ꟺ. This type of censorship may be compared with the editing of the Elohistic Psalter, where אלהים appears in place of the Tetragrammaton, an editorial process dated by Hartmut Gese to around 300 BC (1974, 159–67), and by Hossfeld and Zenger to the fifth century (2000, 30, cf. Ben-Dov 2011).

[10] Eshel and Eshel 2003, 237–40.

[11] The *BHS* editors suggested alternatively to read ישׂראל נ' ח' יעקב יהוה (וַיַחֲלֶק vel חלק וַיְהִי.

apposition to the first colon: 'for the portion of the Lord is his people, the children of Israel; Jacob the lot of his inheritance.'

The two possible readings for the beginning of line 5 are both problematic. On the one hand, תֵבל נחלת יש[ראל corrupts the parallel to the preceding stich and seems at odds with the statement about the division of the world between the nations in v. 8.[12] On the other hand, the alternative reading חֵבל נחלת יש[ראל hardly makes sense and would best be explained as a scribal error. With the presence of the word יש[ראל (cf. ⅏ 𝕲), MS 5214/2 attests to the currency of this version in the first century AD. The version of 𝔐 runs smoothly in chiastic style and a 3 + 3 metrum. The text of ⅏/𝕲 is more difficult; *yisrael* is usually seen as a secondary addition.[13] A possible line of textual development of v. 9 could be: 1) the text of 𝔐; 2) a shared *Vorlage* for ⅏ and 𝕲 supplements the older term 'Jacob' with the name 'Israel'; 3) in its transmission of this version, MS 5214/2 omits the suffix of נחלתו and writes תבל for חבל; 4) the reworking of the text in 𝕿[N], based on both main versions.

It would seem that this late copy of Deuteronomy preserves an independent text of Deut 32.5–9. This text exemplifies the somewhat fluid process of transmission of scriptural texts in the late Second Temple period. Its non-Masoretic character is compatible with a Qumran provenance, which would limit the date of the text to AD 30–68.

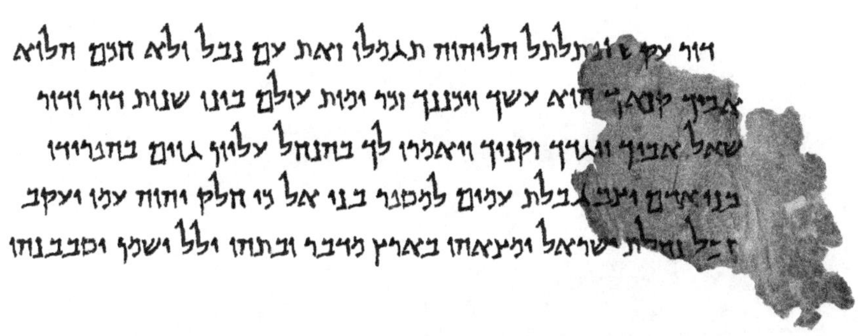

Figure 19.2. *A reconstruction of 4Q(?)Deut2*

---

[12] The notion that 'the world is Israel's inheritance' could be supported by Davidic texts such as Ps 2.8–9; 72.8–11; Zech 9.10.

[13] Most critical scholars prefer 𝔐 as the better text here, and regard ישראל in ⅏ and 𝕲 as a secondary addition that destroys the metrum and the chiasmus present in 𝔐 and moves the division of the cola (placing יעקב in the second half-verse). See Sanders 1996, 159–60; cf. also McCarthy 2007, 141: 'The longer text possibly reflects a tendency to supply the name "Israel" either as a replacement for, or as a supplement to the older term "Jacob".'

Part Three

—

Prophets (Nevi'im)

XIII

MS 2713. Mur/ḤevJosh (Josh 1.9–12; 2.3–5)

Torleif Elgvin

DSS F.110, DSS F.Josh1

This fragment was published by James Charlesworth as XJosh in *DJD* 38:231–39.

A. Physical Description

MS 2713 preserves the lower part of two columns of text that contain portions of chs 1 and 2 of Joshua. This large fragment measures 9.7 × 18.5 cm.[1] The margin preceding the first column is 5.8 cm. This uncharacteristically wide margin suggests that this is the beginning of the scroll. The scroll probably did not have a cover leaf as no traces of sewing are preserved. The width of col. i is 8 cm, with 30–36 letter spaces per line, and the intercolumnar margin *c.*18 mm. The line spacing is *c.* 7 mm, and faint remains of horizontal ruling lines can be observed. The lower margin is 4 cm, which would fit Tov's category of *de luxe*-editions (Tov 2004, 126 lists this scroll among these).

This fragment is among the few in The Schøyen Collection written on leather, not prepared parchment. The leather is thick and dark brown in colour. Large parts of the surface have worn off, exposing lighter-coloured spots of damage. The ink contains higher levels of iron than the parchment, which suggests that the skin and the ink were prepared in different locations (Rabin, unpublished report).

On the *verso*, specks of ink can be seen, both on the colour image and, more clearly, on the infrared photograph. This ink probably represents set-off of letters from the subsequent layer of the scroll. If the scroll were rolled the usual way, with the beginning on the outside, we would not expect set-off on the first 15–20 cm. This feature may suggest that the scroll had been rolled with the beginning on the inside when it was last deposited in the cave. This could in turn explain why only the beginning of the scroll is preserved, as the outer parts of scrolls tend to show higher levels of deterioration. Since only the lower part of the scroll has survived, this might suggest that the scroll was last deposited standing upside down on the cave floor or in a jar, perhaps causing the end touching the floor to erode more rapidly.

A small piece at the lower right edge was removed after the *DJD* photograph was taken. At that time it was attached by cello tape. This piece was in 1999 subjected to C-14 analysis by the NSF-Arizona AMS Facility, University of Arizona, Tucson, resulting in a 95% probability dating to the period 118 BC–AD 73 (*DJD* 38:234).[2]

---

[1] The height would be 10.1 cm if one includes a piece wrapped down at the upper left edge.

[2] Uncalibrated Radiocarbon Age: 2020±45 years BP. Calibrated Age Ranges: 86 BC–AD 49 (1s); 165 BC–AD 76 (2s). Probability distribution of 2s range: 160–129 BC (5%); 118 BC–AD 73 (95%).

B. Palaeography and C-14 Dating

The script is an elegant post-Herodian formal book hand.[3] According to Ada Yardeni the script should most probably be dated after AD 70. Yardeni notes the similarity between this script and documents from the Bar Kokhba caves (cf. Yardeni 2000, 113–17). According to Michael Langlois, this manuscript features one of the most developed and ornamental formal scripts among the Dead Sea Scrolls: although a date in the third quarter of the first century AD cannot be excluded, this hand best fits the post-Herodian period. Langlois concludes that the scroll was probably copied at the end of the first century AD or the beginning of the second (see p. 121).

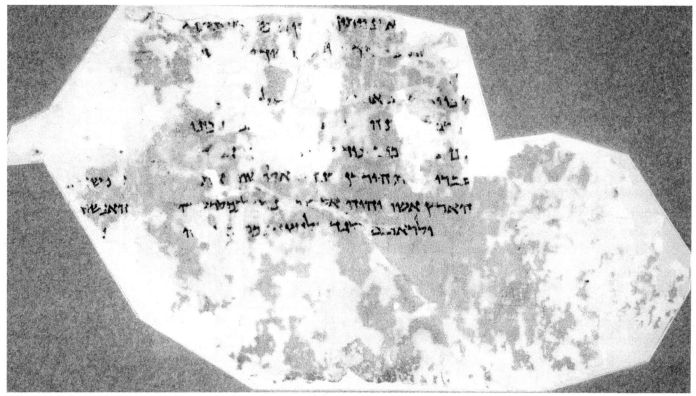

Figure 20.1. *MS 2713*

C. MS 2713 col. I

1   ‫א צויתיך[‬   ]קׄ וׄאׄמׄ‎ºלׄ תעׄרׄ‎ׄׄ‬

2   ‫שׄ[   ]ºליׄ‎דׄ בׄ‎[‬ º[]ºoº[]º עׄ‎מׄ‎דׄ ºº ‫ﬨº‎[‬

3   ‫ºº[‬   *vacat*

4   ‫סיצו יº[‬   ]שׄ‎עׄ אﬨׄ[‬ º ‫ºם לº[‬   ]ºº ‫ל‎[‬   ]º‬

5   ‫]º‎רׄ‎ב º[‬   ]נה [   ]ºi[   ]º[   ]º[   ]ºº [   ]כׄכׄבׄינו‬

6   ‫]º‎ם צׄ‎[   ]ºoº ‫כי בׄ‎עׄ‎וד‬ ‫]ººº ‫ºאׄ‎º o‬

7   ‫עׄ‎בריº ºﬨ הירדׄן הזׄה ººא לרשׄﬨ אﬨׄ‬

8   ‫הארץ אשׄ‎רׄ יהוה אלׄ‎הׄ‎יכׄ[ ] נﬨºׄ לׄ‎בׄ‎ם לרשºׄה‬

---

[3] According to Charlesworth, the scroll belongs to the period '40 BCE–68 CE, most likely near the end of the range' (*DJD* 38:234). Tov suggests AD 40–68 (2004, 126).

9   vac   ולראובני ○לגד [ ]○לחצי שבט ה○○ ה̇[

bottom margin

Notes on Readings

Line 1. ו̇אמ○. The lower part of the downstroke of *waw* is all that is preserved of the first letter. The second letter is clearly *ʾalep*. There are remains of the lower part of the oblique downstroke, as well as of the right arm.

    Line 2. ת̇○[. The short stroke of the first letter most probably represents the left leg of *ḥet*, less probably the downstroke of *waw*. There are also two dots of ink to the upper right that most likely belong to this letter. Only the lower part of the legs of *taw* are preserved.

    Line 2. ○○. The baseline of the first letter survives, and belongs either to a *bet* or a *kap*. Only a tiny speck of ink is preserved of the second letter.

    Line 2. עָמֹך. The scattered traces of the first letter fit perfectly with *ʿayin*. The top of both arms as well as the tip of the oblique stroke are preserved. The second letter is *mem*. Traces of the tip and the upper part of the oblique stroke with its *serif* can be seen. There are also faint traces of the baseline.

    Line 2. ○○ו○[]○. There are traces of ink belonging to one or two letters before the *waw*. After the *waw* follow traces of a downstroke compatible with *he* or *ḥet* as well as a trace of another letter.

    Line 2. ○ל○ד. A trace of another letter is visible at the lower right of the *lamed*. Most of the hook of the *lamed* is preserved as well as small parts of the arm.

    Line 2. בֹ[○. The right shoulder of *bet* is preserved. Only a tiny speck of ink is left of the second letter.

    Line 2. ○ש[. Remains of the upper part of a downstroke can be seen, belonging to the last letter.

    Line 3. ○○[. The last trace is probably a descender belonging to a final letter. This is followed by a *vacat* that extends to the end of the line.

    Line 4. שֹע[ ]○י. *Yod* is followed by what seems to be the middle part of a downstroke, compatible with *he, ḥet, dalet* and *reš*. Parts of the right and centre arms of the *šin* can be seen. The baseline and left arm of the *ʿayin* are preserved.

    Line 4. םֹ[. The upper left corner and the horn of final *mem* can be seen.

    Line 4. ל○○[. The thick dot of ink after the *lamed*, just below the ceiling line, seems to be compatible with the *serif* of *ʾalep*.

    Line 5. רֹ○ב[]. Just a small dot of ink, positioned slightly above the baseline, is left of the first letter. The second letter preserves the roof of *reš*.

    Line 5. נה○[ ]○. Only faint traces of ink, just below the ceiling line, are left of the first letter. *Nun* is preceded by scattered traces of what seem to be parts of a left downstroke.

    Line 5.]○[. The preserved stroke is compatible with the left leg of *ʾalep*.

    Line 5.] ○○[. Only a dot of ink belonging to the first letter is preserved above the baseline. The trace belonging to the second letter is the baseline of *mem, bet* or *kap*.

    Line 5. כבינו○. The upper part of a right downstroke, and scattered traces of a left downstroke are preserved from the first letter. *He, ḥet,* and *taw* seem possible readings.

    Line 6. ם○[ ]. The first preserved trace could fit the lower right corner of a letter. At the bottom right corner of the final *mem* is a small trace of the baseline of the preceding letter, compatible with *bet* or *kap*.

    Line 6. [ ]צֹ. The remains of this letter are only compatible with *ṣade*.

    Line 6. בֹעֹוד. At the beginning of this word the baseline and *serif* of a *bet* are preserved. Then follows the left arm and the oblique stroke of *ʿayin*.

Line 8. לרשׂה. The lower right arm of *šin* and parts of the two other strokes are preserved. The small triangle-shaped trace of the fourth letter is compatible with the top left corner of *he* or more probably *taw* (cf. *taw* in line 1).

Line 9. לחֹצִׁ׳○. A tiny triangle-shaped trace of ink, just below the ceiling line, precedes *lamed*. Only the upper halves of *ḥet*, *ṣade*, and *yod* are preserved.

Line 9. ה[ ]○הֹ. The first *he* is almost complete, although it is difficult to recognize because of the extensive damage on the surface. The dot of ink to the left of the second letter is compatible with the horn of *mem*.

D. MS 2713 col. II

]○   6

]○ ○שׂוֹתֹ ○   7

]האנשׂים   8

]○[   ]   9

bottom mar]gin

Notes on Readings

Line 7. ○תֹ. The two traces of ink of the first letter are compatible with the *serif* on top of the right arm of *ʾalep* and the tip of the oblique stroke.

Line 9. After a lacuna of about one or two letters we see the upper part of a downstroke with a hook. Below is a thick spot of ink that probably belongs to the same letter. Alternatively it could represent the foot or corner of the following letter. The preserved traces may fit *taw* or *šin*; *gimel* and *ʿayin* would also be possible.

E. Joshua Scrolls from the Judaean Desert

Two other Joshua scrolls have been published. 4QJosh[a] (4Q47) dates from around 100 BC; it consists of 22 fragments from five columns, and contains text from chs 6–10. 4QJosh[b] (4Q48) dates from the mid-first century BC; it consists of 6 fragments, and contains text from chs 2, 3, and 17. Since 4QJosh[b] preserves text from Josh 2.11 onwards, MS 2713 stands as the earliest textual witness to Josh 1.9–12; 2.3–5, even though it is the latest Joshua text from the Judaean Desert.

F. MS 2713 col. I (Josh 1.9–12)

According to the reconstruction in *DJD*, the columns had 27 lines. However, going by the biblical text and the width of col. I (8 cm), columns of *c.* 29 lines seem more probable.[4]

---

[4] There is a total of 919 letter spaces between the beginning of Josh 1.1 and המנשה, the last preserved word in col. I. There are 268 letters and spaces in the text preserved of Josh 1.9–12 in nine lines, but with a large *vacat* in line 23. The text in lines 24–29 contains 198 letters and spaces (including a three-letter spaced *vacat* in the final line), which would produce an average line length of 33 letter spaces. This in turn requires a space of about 19 2/3 lines to fill out the preceding 𝔐 text from Josh 1.1–9, and would make for a total column height of 29 lines.

[תשכיל 9הלו]א צוייתיْךָ חז[ק ואْמٰץ א̊ל תע̇רץֿ   21
[ואל ת]ח̇ת̇ כֿי עֿمֿךָ יְהוֹהּ○אֱلֹהֶיךָ בֿכֿ[ל א]ש̇ר̇   22
[ת]لֵֿךָ   vacat   23
10ו̇יְצו יְה̊[ו]שֻׁع̊ אֶת̊ ש̇[טרי הع̊]ם̇ לֵאֹמֹ̇ר 11ע̊[ברו]   24
[ב]קֶֿרֶב הֿ[מ]חֶנה [וצ]וֹ[ו אֶ[תֿ הֿ[ע]م̇] ל̊[אֹمֹ̇]ר [הֿכֿינו   25
[ל]כֶֿם צ̇[ידה] כי בֿעֿוד שֿלֹשֶׁ̊[ת ימי]ם̊ אֿתֶ̊ם   26
עֿברים אֿת הירדֿן הֿזֶה لֿבֿא לרשת אֿת   27
הארץ אשֿר יהוה אלהיכ[ם] נתֿן לﺑֿם לרשתה   28
12 vac. ו̇لראוֹבֿני וֿلﻮﻥﺪ[י] וֿلﺣﺼ̊י שבﻁ הﻣ̊[נש]ה   29

bottom margin

Translation

21. [shall you be successful. ⁹]'I charge you:[Be stro]ng and resolute; do not be terrified
22. [or dis]mayed, for YHWH your God is with you wher[ever]
23. [you] go.'   *vacat*
24. ¹⁰Josh[u]a then gave orders to the off[icials of the pe]ople, sayin[g: ¹¹]'D[isperse]
25. [th]rough the[c]amp [and ch]ar[ge]th[e peop]le[t]hu[s:]Prepare
26. [for] yourselves pr[ovisions,] for in thre[e day]s you
27. are to cross the Jordan, in order to enter and possess the
28. land that YHWH yo[ur]God is giving you as a possession.'
29. *vac.* ¹²Then unto the Reubenites, the Gadi[tes], and the half-tribe of Ma[nass]eh

Notes on Reconstruction and Comments

Line 22 (1.9). יֻהוֹהּ○אֱلֹהֶיךָ. The trace of the second letter appears at first glance to belong to the *yod*, but aligns better with the crossbar of *he*. There is a trace of ink that seems to be located between these two words. It belongs neither to the second *he* of יֻהוֹהּ nor to the *ʾalep*. I can find no reasonable explanation for this.

Line 23 (1.9). After the last word the remainder of this line is left open, which commonly indicates a section break (Tov 2004, 146). At this same point in the text there is an open paragraph in 𝔐ᴸ and 𝔐ᴬ.

Line 24 (1.10). שֿ[טרי. The traces are compatible with the top of the right arm of *šin* with its *serif*.

Line 25 (1.11). הֿ[מ]חֶנה] = 𝔐 ¦ + του λαου 𝕲.

Lines 25–26 (1.11). הֿכֿינו = [כ]לֿ]ם = 𝔐 ¦ ετοιμαζεσθε 𝕲. 𝕲 should not necessarily be considered a variant reading, as 'for yourself' is implicit in the use of the middle voice (cf. Butler 1981, 15).

Line 26 (1.11). אֿתֶם = 𝔐 ¦ και υμεις 𝕲. Butler (1981, 15) notes that the 𝕲 reading, with the conjunction following the temporal clause, is characteristic of Semitic grammar, not Greek. This might suggest that a Hebrew conjunction underlies the 𝕲 reading.

Line 27 (1.11). لֿבֿא = 𝔐 (לבוא). There is no space for a *waw*, suggesting a slight orthographic difference from 𝔐.

Line 28 (1.11). אלהיכ[ם]. = 𝔐 ¦ + των πατερων υμων 𝕲.

Line 28 (1.11). לרשתה = 𝔐 ¦ > 𝕲. This plus can be seen as a redundant addition in 𝔐, or could be explained as a stylistic abridgement by the 𝕲 translator.

Line 29 (1.12). Verse 12 opens with a short indentation; a signal to begin a new section unit. At this point in the text there is a closed paragraph in 𝕸[L] and an open one in 𝕸[A]. Qumran scrolls use this type of section division when the preceding line reaches the margin (Tov 2004, 145–49).

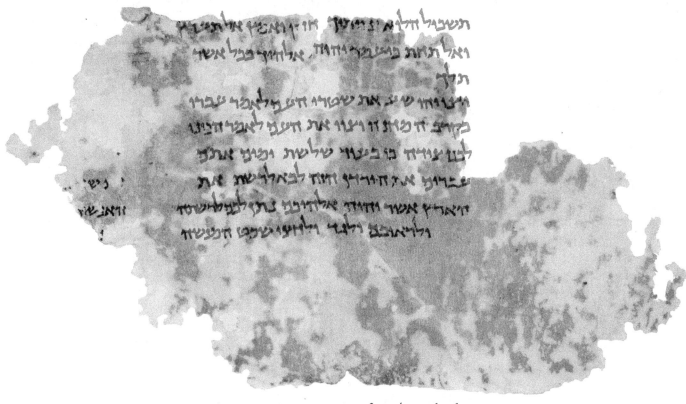

Figure 20.2. A reconstruction of Mur/ḤevJosh col. I

G. MS 2713 col. II (Josh 2.3–5)

26　　כ]י לחפר את כל הארץ באו 4ותקח האשה[
27　　אֹת שנֹ הֹ[אנשים ותצפנו ותאמר כן באו אלי[
28　　האנשיׂםֹ] ולא ידעתי מאין המה 5ויהי השער[
29　　[לס]גֹ[ור בחשך והאנשים יצאו לא ידעתי אנה[
　　　　　　　　　　　　　　　　　bottom mar]gin

Translation

26.　　f[or they have come to spy out the whole country. ⁴But the woman had taken]
27.　　the two [men and hidden them. 'It is true', she said, 'they did come to me,]
28.　　those men.[But I did not know from where they came. ⁵And when the gate was about]
29.　　[to be clo]se[d, when it was dark, then the men left, and I do not know where]

Notes on Reconstruction and Comments

The beginning of lines 27 and 28 is well preserved and these words can be identified with the biblical text. On the basis of the text of 𝔐 these lines can be reconstructed to a length of 8 cm and 35–37 letter spaces. Lines 26 and 29 are tentatively reconstructed on the basis of this line length. The preserved traces of these lines are so tiny that no words from the biblical text can be confidently identified.

The 𝔐 text of Josh 1.12–2.3 would fill out approximately 26 lines in col. II with the same line length as in col. I (8 cm). This reconstruction would also produce a column of 29 lines for col. II.

Line 26 (2.3). בֹּ[י]. I interpret the trace as the top of a *kap*, but this reading is tentative.

Line 27 (2.4). שֹנֹי = 𝔐 𝔊[B,Ocorr] (both δυο) 𝔖 𝔗 ¦ > 𝔊[SA] 𝔊[O*] 𝔙.

Line 27 (2.4). [ותאמר] = 𝔐 ¦ και ειπεν αυτοις λεγουσα (= ותאמר להם לאמור) 𝔊. The 𝔊 construction is a semitism, reflecting a Hebrew *Vorlage* longer than 𝔐.[5]

Line 28. [ולא ידעתי מאין המה] = 𝔐 ¦ > 𝔊. The text should be reconstructed with the 𝔐 plus at the end of 2.4.

Line 29. גֹ[ור]ֹ[לס]. This reconstructed reading, based on the 𝔐 text, is tentative.

Figure 20.3. A reconstruction of Mur/ḤevJosh col. II

H. Textual Character, Format, and Provenance

The surviving text from col. I seems to align with 𝔐 in its entirety. However, so many letters are poorly preserved that only knowledge of the 𝔐 text enables many of the restored readings. The alignment with 𝔐 is especially noteworthy in Josh 2.11: in lines 25 and 28 MS 2713 lacks pluses present in 𝔊. In line 26 MS 2713 reads אַתֶּם with 𝔐 while 𝔊 reads και υμεις, which seems to be a Hebraism (possibly

---

[5] On the relatively few pluses in the 𝔊 text, cf. Tov 1999, 388: 'It is noteworthy that the pluses of the LXX are Hebraistic in diction, and they can be retroverted easily into Hebrew.' Such additions can hardly be explained as the creative work of the 𝔊 translator, as asserted by van der Meer.

reflecting ואתם). In line 28 MS 2713 includes the 𝔐 plus לרשתה. It should also be noted that the section markers in lines 23 and 29 (before vv. 10 and 12) align with paragraphs in the later mediaeval codices 𝔐ᴬ and 𝔐ᴸ. The text of 𝔐 can be reconstructed in lines 27–28 of col. II, and a reconstruction based on the the text of 𝔐 suggests that both columns contained 29 lines.

In the case of Joshua 2 (partly preserved in MS 2713 col. II), where 𝔐 includes a handful of pluses compared with 𝔊, both MS 2713 and 4QJoshᵇ seem to follow the longer version of 𝔐. Since Samuel Holmes (1914), most scholars see the shorter 𝔊 text of Joshua as representing the earlier version. Tov (1999, 394–96) sees the 𝔐 text of Joshua as a harmonizing and expanded edition of the 𝔊 *Vorlage*. Tov's conclusion is contested by van der Meer 2004 with regard to Joshua 1, 5, 6, 8, and 18; and by van der Meer 2013 with regard to Joshua 2.[6]

If we assume columns of 29 lines,[7] the height of the writing block can be reconstructed to *c.* 19.5 cm, and the height of the full scroll perhaps to 26–27 cm (presuming a height for the top margin also of around 4 cm or slighly less). A column width of 8 cm is quite small relative to this projected column height,[8] but the line length seems to be the same in both columns. According to the size of cols I–II, and presuming that this scroll contained a complete copy of scriptural Joshua, the full scroll could be tentatively reconstructed with approximately 52–53 columns and a length of around 4.7 m.

A variety of textual traditions is preserved in the Joshua scrolls from the Judaean Desert: 4QJoshᵃ (4Q47), from around 100 BC, is a non-aligned text. 4QJoshᵇ (4Q48), from the mid-first century BC can be characterized as a semi-Masoretic text, closer to 𝔐 than to 𝔊.[9]

On the basis of C-14 examinations it may be suggested that MS 2713 was written before AD 70, while the late palaeographical features point to a post-70 date. Both the thoroughly Masoretic character of the text and the scroll format with high and narrow columns suggest that the fragment derived from a Bar Kokhba cave, perhaps Murabbaʿat or Naḥal Ḥever, sites discovered by the Bedouin close in time to their finding Cave 4.

---

[6] Michaël van der Meer kindly shared a pre-publication copy of his 2013 IOSCS paper with me. According to him, the textual variants in Joshua 2 are due to the creative work of the 𝔊 translator.

[7] The *DJD* edition of Charlesworth assumes 27 lines per column (*DJD* 38:234–35). Likewise Ulrich 2010, 247.

[8] On scrolls with such a format, especially prominent among Bar Kokhba texts, see the chapter by Kipp Davis, p. 129.

[9] Further, non-biblical Qumran writings show knowledge of Septuagintal readings of Joshua (García Martínez 2012, 150).

XIV

XJudg with MS 2861 (Judg 4.5–6)

Esther Eshel, Hanan Eshel, Årstein Justnes

DSS F.108, DSS F.Judg3

MS 2861, acquired by The Schøyen Collection in 1999, was published as XJudg by James Charlesworth in *DJD* 28 (*DJD* 28:231–33, plate LXIII). Six other fragments of the same scroll were later published (H. Eshel 2003b; Eshel, Eshel, and Broshi 2007; Puech 2003a; 2006). Four of these belong to the same column as col. i of the Schøyen fragment. In this chapter all the published fragments of XJudg will be presented.

A. Physical Description

MS 2861 measures 3.1 × 8.5 cm. The parchment is medium to dark brown with some sections in lighter brown where the surface has flaked off—especially on the upper sides. Text from two columns is preserved, as well as parts of a narrow intercolumnar margin. The ink traces from col. ii align with col. i lines 1–2.[1] The line spacing is *c.* 6 mm. The word spaces are relatively large, often between 1 and 2 mm.

According to Ira Rabin's mineral analysis this scroll was manufactured outside the Dead Sea region and shows the same features as MS 4611 (Lev): Parts of the top layer of these fragments have peeled off as a result of the tanning process, in which only the surface of the skin was tanned. The parchments of these two scrolls have a similar ratio of Cl/Br, evenly distributed on the fragments. Potassium detected in the upper layer probably derives from the tanning process. In both fragments, inhomogeneous distribution of calcium and iron indicates presence of cave deposits (Rabin, unpublished report).

A tiny fragment from the right edge without writing was subjected to C-14 analysis on 24 January 24, 2000, by D.J. Donahue and M. De Martino at the NSF-Arizona AMS Facility, University of Arizona, Tucson. The analysis gave the following results:

Uncalibrated Radiocarbon Age: 2050±50 years BP
Calibrated Age Ranges: 176–1 BC (1s); 338 BC–AD 54 (2s)

The date could be anywhere between the two extremes of the C-14 dating, and the middle should not be taken as indicating the most likely date (*DJD* 28:232).

---

[1] Contra *DJD* 28:231: 'there are no margins preserved'.

B. Palaeography

Émile Puech labels the script of this scroll as Herodian, dating it to the turn of the era or the first quarter of the first century AD.[2] According to Ada Yardeni the letters on the Schøyen fragment are too poorly preserved to allow a precise dating before or after AD 70. Michael Langlois characterizes the script as an elegant and consistent formal book hand with 'numerous features that appear in the latest Herodian scripts and become popular in post-Herodian hands.' He concludes that the scroll was copied in the second half of the first century AD (see p. 118).[3]

Figure 21. *MS 2861*

C. MS 2861

1. Col. i

‏°ית אל בה° °פרים °°°° °[‏	1
‏[°° °נֹי ישראל לֹמֹשפט ותשלֹח‏	2
‏[רֹק בן אבינעם מֹקדשֹ נפתֹלי‏	3
‏[לֹ] [אֹ צוה יהוה אל°י‏	4
‏[°°]‏	5

Notes on Readings

Line 1. ‏תֹי°‏ °°°° °[. We were able to detect more letters than noted in earlier editions of this fragment.

    Line 1. °°°°. The traces of the two last letters are compatible with *waw* and *final nun*.

    Line 1. ‏תֹי°‏. The traces of ink of the first letter are also compatible with the baseline of *kap, nun,* and *pe*.

    Line 1. ‏°פרים‏. The form of the somewhat fragmentary final *mem* is peculiar. The base seem to consist of two lines that do not meet, one above the other.

---

[2] Frg. 1: 'L'écriture est celle d'une main d'époque hérodienne, montrant des traits d'une écriture "Round semiformal" et quelques traces de la "developed formal" qu'on attribuerait au tournant ou au premier quart du premier siècle de notre ère, juste après 4QJuges^b' (Puech 2006, 184). See also Puech 2003a, 315: 'Ce fragment de manuscrit clairement en écriture hérodienne qui est seul à avoir préservé des restes de *Juges* 1:10-12, date du tournant de notre ère ou du premier quart du premier siècle après J.-C.'

[3] Such a late dating contrasts somewhat with the C-14 dating presented above. Langlois' analysis was based on the Schøyen fragment. Interestingly, there are some—not insignificant—differences in the handwriting between frg. 1 and MS 2861. Compare in particular final *nun* and *qop*.

Line 2. ישראל. There is an erased *lamed* in the area between *reš* and *ʾalep*, which might explain the rather considerable distance between these two letters. Perhaps the scribe mistakenly wrote *lamed* after *reš*, i.e. ישרל, and then erased *lamed* and corrected the word.

Line 3. אבינעם. There is some distance between the *yod* and the *nun* (ca. 0.8 mm).

Line 4. א[ ]ל֗[. Charlesworth (*DJD* 28:233) reads ה[לּ֗א and Puech (2003a, 317) ה[לא. There is a tiny speck of ink to the upper left of the *lamed*.

2. Col. ii

```
                                                    ]א֗[ ]     1
                                                    ]∘∘      2
```

Notes on Readings

The two preserved lines of col. ii are positioned slightly below those of col. i.

Line 1.]א֗[ ]. Eshel, Eshel and Broshi (2007, 355) read]א at the beginning of this line.

Line 2.]∘∘.[4] The first letter is easiest read as *yod* or *ʾalep*. Only four specks of ink are preserved of the second letter. In the intercolumnar margin two specks of ink and an ink stroke can be noted before line 2. The stroke is located 6.6 mm from the left column margin of col. i, and represents either a letter or a scribal marginal sign.

D. Judges Scrolls from the Judaean Desert

Until 2001 three copies of Judges were known from Qumran: 1QJudg (1Q6), found in Cave 1, was published in 1955 (*DJD* 1:62–64, plate XI), and in 1995 two manuscripts from Cave 4 were published, 4QJudg[a] (4Q49) and 4QJudg[b] (4Q50) (*DJD* 14:161–69, plate XXXVI).[5]

In 2001, the fragment from The Schøyen Collection (MS 2861) was published by Charlesworth under the label XJudg (*DJD* 28:231–33, plate LXIII.6). This fragment contains parts of Judg 4.5–6. Three unidentified parts consisting of five fragments, labelled as 'XUnidentified Text 1', 'XBiblical Text?', and 'XUnidentified Text 2', were published by Hagai Misgav on the same plate (*DJD* 28:227, plate LXIII.3–5).[6] Two years later Hanan Eshel was able to identify the three fragments of 'XBiblical Text?' as part of

---

[4] Eshel, Eshel, and Broshi (2007, 355) noted no letters in this line.

[5] Analyzing the other three manuscripts of Judges from the Judaean Desert, Julio Trebolle Barrera states that 4QJudg[a] 'represents a form of the text independent from any other known text-type, although it shares readings with the proto-Lucianic text' (*DJD* 14:162). This scroll is different from 𝔐 on the literary level, as it does not contain Judg 6.7–10, a late editorial note in deuteronomistic style. With regard to 4QJudg[b], the editor notes, 'The preserved readings of 4QJudg[b] are very close to 𝔐. The construction of its lines shows, however, that 4QJudg[b] possibly knew a variant shorter text or presented a text arrangement different from that of 𝔐.' He further says, 'The fragments of Judges from Cave 1 (1Q6) have similar problems in their relation to MT' (*DJD* 14:167).

For a short review of the Judges material from Qumran and XJudg with bibliographies, see Lange 2009, 203–9.

[6] These fragments were published provisionally by Misgav in *Michmanim* as early as 1994 (Misgav 1994).

XJudg (H. Eshel 2003b, 139–41).[7] The same year Puech added two more fragments to the same manuscript. The first, which contains Judg 1.10–12, is held in a private collection (Puech 2003a, 315). The second, containing Judg 3.22–24, was another fragment from the same plate as the above-mentioned fragments, published by Misgav under the label 'XUnidentified Text 2' (*DJD* 28:229, plate LXIII.5).[8] Puech suggested identifying all six fragments as part of one Judges scroll from Cave 4 and labelled it 4QJudg[c] (4Q50a; Puech 2003a, 315–19).[9]

In July 2005 Esther and Hanan Eshel were given access to another small fragment belonging to the same manuscript. This fragment, held in Israel in private hands, measures 4.5 × 2.9 cm. Only small remains of ink can be seen on it. However, with the aid of infrared photographs they were able to make out remains of more than 30 letters (Eshel, Eshel, and Broshi 2007, 357, Fig. 1). This fragment was identified as Judg 4.6–8, and positioned in lines 5–10 of the same column as the Schøyen fragment.[10]

E. Physical Features of the Scroll

The seven published fragments of this scroll contain parts of three rather narrow columns. The full height of the columns is not known. Fragment 1, which shows traces of six lines, may be located close to the bottom of the first column, preceded by approximately 20–21 lines.[11] Based on a count of 30 letter spaces per line there were approximately 25 lines of text between fragment 2 and fragments 3–7 (frgs 3–7 come from the same column). If this scroll had high columns, as is the case for MS 4611 (Lev) and MS 2713 (Josh), we may be dealing with two consecutive columns.

The column width in all three columns is 7.5–7.8 cm,[12] with 29–35 letter spaces per line. Fragments 3–7 (Judg 4.5–9) preserve twelve lines of a column. The margin between cols i and ii of our fragment is *c.* 12 mm. The length of the complete scroll cannot be established.

F. XJudg

In the following we present readings and a reconstruction of all seven published fragments of XJudg more comprehensively than in previous publications.[13]

---

[7] Eshel 2003b, 139: 'This fragment is composed of four small pieces that have been stuck together but not it [sic] the way they were written ... There are remains of letters on three pieces.' Eshel described the fragments as poorly preserved: 'In the course of time, the upper part of the parchment ... was peeled away, thus most letters are lost.'

[8] These fragments are housed in the Hecht Museum in Haifa.

[9] See also Puech 2006, 184.

[10] Another fragment of the same scroll is in private hands. This fragment measures 2.5 × 5 cm and contains parts of five lines, comprising Judg 8.3–6. Since the Schøyen fragment is one of eight fragments from the same scroll, we have chosen to retain the designation XJudg.

[11] Cf. Puech 2006, 184: 'Il est probable qu'on a affaire à un fragment de la première colonne du manuscrit, aux lignes 22 à 27 ou 23 à 28.'

[12] Puech (2003a, 316) estimates the column width at 7.5–7.7 cm.

[13] In Tigchelaar's system of designation, these fragments should be labeled DSS F.Judg1–DSS F.Judg7. Our reconstruction shows that previous editions by E. Eshel and Puech should be corrected at some points, cf. below. There are a number of typographical errors in Puech's edition (2003a, 315–16). For all the fragments we rely substantially on Ulrich 2010, 254. There are, however, also typos in his edition: frg. 2 line 2 (1.23): דלתאת (for דלתות), frg. 2. line 3 (1.23): נאו (for באו).

Table 11. *Inventory of XJudg fragments in publication*

XJudg	Text	Identified	First published
Frg. 1[14]	Judg 1.10–13a	Puech 2003a, 315–16 (picture in Puech 2006, 186a)	
Frg. 2	Judg 3.22–24	Puech 2003a, 316	Published by Misgav as 'XUnidentified Text 2' in *DJD* 28:229, plate LXIII.5.
Frg. 3/MS 2861	Judg 4.5–6	*DJD* 28:231–33, plate LXIII.6	
Frg. 4/MS H-1804	Judg 4.6–8	H. Eshel 2003b	Published by Misgav as 'XBiblical Text? frg. 2'[15] in *DJD* 28:227, plate LXIII.4.
Frg. 5/MS H-1804	Judg 4.8–9	H. Eshel 2003b	Published by Misgav as 'XBiblical Text? frg. 1' in *DJD* 28:227, plate LXIII.4, cf. also Misgav 1994, 41*.
Frg. 6/MS H-1804	Judg 4.9	H. Eshel 2003b	Published by Misgav as 'XBiblical Text?' in *DJD* 28, plate LXIII.4, but not transcribed. Cf. also Misgav 1994, 41*.
Frg. 7	Judg 4.6–8	Published by Eshel, Eshel and Broshi 2007	

1. Frg. 1 (Judg 1.10–13a)

1   [¹⁰וילך יהודה [א]ל הכנעני [ה]יושב בחברון]

2   [ושם ח]ברון לפנים קר[י]ת א[ר]ב[ע ויכו את]

3   [ש]שֿי וֿאֿת אחימֿן וֿאֿת תֿלֿמֿיֿ [¹¹ו]ֿילֿך [משם אל]

4   ישבי דביר ושֿם דביר לֿפֿנֿיֿם ק[רית ספר]

5   ¹²וֿיֿאמר כלב אשֿ[ר] יכה אֿת [קרית ספר ולכדה]

6   [ונתתי [לֿ]ֿו את עכסה בתי לאשה ¹³וילכדה]

Translation

1   [¹⁰ Judah marched]aga[inst the Canaanites]who[dwelt in Hebron,]

2   [and they defeated]

3   [She]shai, Ahiman, and Talmai. ([The name of He]bron was formerly Kir[ia]th-a[r]b[a.]). ¹¹ [From there] they marched [against]

4   the inhabitants of Debir (the name of Debir was formerly K[iriath-sepher)].

5   ¹² And Caleb announced, 'To the ma[n] who attacks[and captures Kiriath-sepher,]

6   [I will give]h[im my daughter Achsah in marriage.' ¹³ And he (*i.e.* Othniel) captured it,]

---

[14] Puech (2006, 184) gives a brief physical description of the fragment: 'Le fragment est un morceau de peau de couleur brun foncé avec des parties claires qui signalent une surface écaillée. Le dos est brun clair. Dimensions du fragment : largeur maximale 6,9 cm, hauteur 2,8 cm, épaisseur de la peau 0,3 mm. Les lignes sont tracées à la pointe sèche, et les interlignes varient entre 0,6 et 0,65 cm, mais la marge de droite est à peine visible.' Puech's article also contains a (poor) photograph of the fragment (Puech 2006, 186, plate II).

[15] See *DJD* 28:227: 'This is probably part of a biblical text of Judg 4:8 or Num 10:30 or, alternatively, a text of religious importance as indicated by the ornate scribal script. It possibly originates from Qumran. The script should probably be dated to the first century BCE.'

Notes on Readings

Since the quality of the photo published by Puech (2006, 186a) is so poor, we are following his description and readings of this fragment closely.

Line 1. The traces of the two letters are not visible on the photo. Puech (2006, 186) writes: 'De légères traces d'encre à gauche de la petite échancrure pourraient convenir au pied oblique du jambage droit de ʾaleph et au bas de l'axe de la lettre. Enfin, bas des deux jambages de *he*.'

Line 2. Cf. Puech (2006, 186): 'Base de *bet*, puis légères traces de *yod* et partie droite du *mem* final, ensuite hampe de *qoph* et partie gauche de *taw*, enfin trace de l'axe du ʾaleph avec la jonction du jambage droit, et haste et base de bet.' The traces of *yod* are not visible on the photo.

Line 3. שׂ[שׁ]יֹ וֹאֹת. Cf. Puech (2006, 186): 'Une écaille a enlevé le bas du premier *šin*, mais restes du suivant et du *yod* ainsi que du *waw*.'

Line 3. אחימֹןֹ וֹאֹת. Cf. Puech (2006, 186): 'Légère trace de la tête du *nun* final, et partielle de celle du *waw*.'

Line 3. תֹלֹמֹי. Cf. Puech (2006, 186): 'Jambage droit et pied gauche du *taw*, pied de *lamed*, base oblique du *mem* et bas du jambage du *yod*.' Only the traces of the first letter are clear on the photo.

Line 3. וֹ]יֹלֹך. Cf. Puech (2006, 186): 'Traces de la tête du *yod* et hampe du *lamed*.' The trace of the possible *yod* is barely visible on the photo.

Line 4. ושׁםֹ. Cf. Puech (2006, 186): 'Restes du jambage droit du *mem* final.' The small trace of ink that is preserved is also compatible with several other letters.

Notes on Reconstruction and Comments

Line 1 (1.10). [יהודה] = 𝔐. Both *BHK* and *BHS* conjecture כָּלֵב, cf. Josh 15.13–14.

Line 1 (1.10). [בחברון] = 𝔐 ¦ + και εξηλθεν Χεβρων (εξ εναντιας) 𝔊.[16]

Line 1 (1.10). [ה[יושב] = 𝔐. Or [ה[ישב], cf. the first word in line 4.

Line 2 (1.10). קר[י]ֹת אֹ[ר]בֹ[ע] = 𝔐 ¦ Καριαθαρβοκσεφερ 𝔊. 𝔊's transcription represents a conflation of קרית ספר and קרית ארבע (cf. vv. 11–12; Fernández Marcos, 2011, 41*).

Line 2 (1.10). ויכו. *BHK* and *BHS* propose ויד here on the basis of some Greek mss and 𝔳 (cf. Fernández Marcos 2011, 41*).

Line 3 (1.10). תֹלֹמֹי = 𝔐 ¦ + γεννηματα του Ενακ 𝔊^AB (cf. ילידי הענק Josh 15.14 𝔐). Fernández Marcos (2011, 41*) explains the addition as 'a gloss taken from Num 13.22'.

Line 3 (1.11). וֹ]יֹלֹך = 𝔐 𝔊^A (και επορευθησαν) 𝔊^Mss 𝔖 𝔳 ¦ και ανεβησαν 𝔊^B 𝔏 (*ascenderunt*) (cf. וַיַּעַל Josh 15.15 𝔐).

Line 4 (1.11). [יושבי] = 𝔐 ().

Line 4 (1.11). [ק[רית ספר] = 𝔐 𝔖 𝔳 ¦ Πολις γραμματων 𝔊 ¦ preceded by καριαθσωφαρ 𝔊^Mss ¦ קרית ארבי ('the City of Magistrates/of archives') 𝔗 (cf. Fernández Marcos 2011, 41*).

Line 5 (1.12). [קרית ספר] = 𝔐 𝔖 𝔳 ¦ την Πολιν των γραμματων 𝔊 ¦ קרית ארבי 𝔗.

2. Frg. 2 (Judg 3.22b–24a)

[ה[הֹמֹסֹדֹרֹוֹנֹ] ויצא אהוד²³[ויצא הפרשדנה]   1
[וֹהֹוֹאֹ²⁴ונעל [ויסגר דלתות העליה בעדו   2

---

[16] 𝔊^L 𝔏 omit και εξηλθεν Χεβρων.

יצא ועבדיו באו ויראו והנה ד[לֹתֹוֹת]   3

Translation

1. [²² and the filth came out. ²³ Stepping out into]the vestibul[e, Ehud]
2. [shut the doors of the upper chamber on him]and locked them. ²⁴ After he
3. [left, the courtiers returned. When they saw that the d]oors

Notes on Reconstruction and Comments

Line 1 (3.22). [ויצא הפרשדנה] = 𝔐 𝔙 𝔗 | > 𝔊. According to BHS 𝔐's ויצא הפרשדנה is probably a doublet of ויצא אהוד המסדרונה in the beginning of v. 23.
    Line 2 (3.23). ונעל = 𝔐 | εσφηνωσεν 𝔊 | ܢܥܠ 𝔖. BHS suggests reading וַיִּנְעֹל.

3. Frgs 3–7 i (Judg 4.5b–9a)[17]

[⁵בין הרמ]ה ֹוֹבֹיֹן בֵית אל בהֹר אֹפֹרים   1
[ויעלו אליה]בֹּנֹי ישראל למֹשפט ⁶ותשלֹח   2
[ותקרא לב]ֹרֹק בן אבינעם מֹקדש נפתלי   3
[ותאמר אליו ה]ֹלֹ[ו]ֹא צוה יהוֹה אלֹהֹי   4
[ישר]אֹל [ל]ֹך[ ]ֹ ומש[כֹתֹ] בהר תבור ו]לקחת   5
עֹמֹך עֹשֹרתֹ] אלפים איש מבנ]ֹי נפתלי   6
ומבני זבלון] ⁷ומשכתי אליך אל נח]ל קישון   7
את סיֹסרֹ]א שר צבא יבין ואת]רכבו   8
ואת המֹונו וֹנֹ[תתיהו בידך ⁸ויאמר] אליה   9
[ברק] אם תֹ]לכי עמי והלכתי ואם לא[10
[תלכי עמי]לֹא אלך ⁹וֹ]תאמר הלך אלֹ]ך עמך]   11
[אפס]כי לֹ]א תהיה] תפארתֹך] על הדרך]   12

Translation

1. [⁵ between Rama]h and Bethel in the hill country of Ephraim,
2. [and]the Israelites [would come to her] for decisions. ⁶ She
3. summ[oned Ba]rak son of Abinoam, of Kedesh in Naphtali,
4. [and said to him,]'YHWH, the God of
5. [Isra]el, has commanded: [G]o,[mar]ch[up to Mount Tabor, and]take
6. with you ten[thousand men] of Naphtali
7. and Zebulun.[⁷ And I will draw toward you up to Wad]i Kishon
8. Siser[a, Jabin's army commander, with]his chariots
9. and his troops, and [I will]d[eliver him into your hands.' ⁸ But]
10. [Bara]k said to her, 'If yo[u will go with me, I will go; if not,]

¹⁷ Frg. 3, lines 1–5; frg. 4, lines 6–10; frg. 5, lines 10–12; frg. 6, lines 11–12; frg. 7, lines 5–10.

11.   I will not go.' [9] Very well, I will g[o with you,'] she answered.
12.   ['Howev]er, [there will be] n[o] glory for you in[the course] (you are taking)

Notes on Reconstruction and Comments

Lines 1–5 (= frg. 3). The alignment of the right margin in these lines differs from the reconstruction in Eshel, Eshel and Broshi 2007, but corresponds with the arrangement in *DJD* 28:233, Puech (2003a, 317), and Ulrich (2010, 254). The first word in each of the lines 1–5 in the above transcription is placed by Eshel, Eshel, and Broshi at the end of the preceding line.[18]

    Line 4 (4.6). ‏א[ו]לֹ[ה‎ = 𝔐[L] (‏הֲלֹא‎).

    Line 5–10. Because of the low quality of the picture, it is difficult to make out ink from dark spots on frg. 7.[19] Ulrich's transcription does not include the letters from this fragment.

    Line 5 (4.6). ‏אֵל[ישר]י‎. Eshel, Eshel, and Broshi (2007, 356) read ‏ומ[שֹׁ]כת‎.

    Line 6–7 (4.6). In his reconstruction Puech (2003a, 317) places what we regard as the first word in each of these lines at the ends of the previous lines.

    Lines 7–11 (4.7–9). In his reconstruction of MS H-1804 from 2003, H. Eshel placed the left margin further to the right, and situated the two last words of each of our lines 7–11 at the beginnings of the following lines.

    Line 7 (4.7). ‏קישון נח[ל‎. Misgav (*DJD* 28:227) read ‏מ[לֹקוש‎.

    Line 8 (4.7). ‏[רכבו‎. Misgav (*DJD* 28:227) transcribed ‏עֹבל‎.

    Line 8 (4.7). ‏סֹיסֹרֹ[א‎. A tiny speck of ink is visible to the lower left of the second *samek*.

    Line 9 (4.8). ‏אליה‎ = 𝔐. So also Puech (2003a, 317) and Eshel, Eshel and Broshi (2007, 356, 358). Misgav (*DJD* 28:227) and H. Eshel (2003b, 140) read ‏אלה‎.

    Line 11–12 (4.8–9). Puech (2003a, 317) situates the first word in lines 11 and 12 respectively at the end of the previous lines.

    Line 11 (4.8). ‏אלך‎ = 𝔐 ¦ + οτι ουκ οιδα την ημεραν εν η ευοδοι κυριος τον αγγελον μετ εμου 𝔊.

    Line 12 (4.9). ‏[אפס]‎ = 𝔐 ¦ + γινωσκε [‏דע‎*] 𝔊. In line with the text of 𝔊, Puech (2003a, 317) reconstructs ‏אפס דע(ו)‎ here.

4. Frgs 3–7 ii

Too little is preserved of these two lines to be able to identify specific words in the continuation of Judges 4 to a reasonable degree of certainty.

G. Textual Character and Provenance

According to Charlesworth MS 2861 'probably derives from Qumran cave 1 or 4' (*DJD* 28:231). According to Puech the manuscript most probably comes from Cave 4 (2006, 184). Noting that the seven fragments of this scroll surfaced so late, Hanan Eshel suggested that they derive from a Bar Kokhba cave found by

---

[18] From the drawing in Eshel, Eshel, and Broshi (2007, 358), frgs 5 and 7 overlap each other.
[19] There seem to be several irregularities in this fragment that are difficult to account for.

the Bedouin in the 80s (cf. p. 48).[20] The fact that the scroll is Masoretic, without textual variants (there are some orthographic variants compared with 𝔐) and from a late date may point to Murabbaʿat or Naḥal Ḥever as place of discovery.[21]

---

[20] Concerning frg. 1 Puech (2006, 184) says: 'Ce fragment de rouleau du livre des *Juges* appartenant à une collection privée fut acheté le 16 août 1964 à l'antiquaire de Bethléem, Khalîl Iskandar Shahîn, alias Kando.' According to William Kando all fragments of this Judges scroll were held by his father in the '50s. This would point to Qumran, Murabbaʿat, or Naḥal Ḥever as possible places of discovery. Lange (2009, 203), following H. Eshel, says '[die] Handschrift dürfte aus einer der Fluchthöhlen des Zweiten Jüdischen Kriegs stammen.'

[21] Scrolls discovered at Masada or in Bar Kokhba caves are Masoretic in character, and tend to show orthographic differences only: ArugLev (two fragments found by the Bedouin in 2004) preserves a full spelling of the word בסכות (𝔐 בסכת) in Lev 23.43 (Eshel, Baruchi, and Porat 2006). MasLev[a] preserves a full spelling of ישפוך (𝔐 ישפך) in Lev 4.4 (Talmon 1999, 38), and MasDeut preserves a short spelling of שפני (𝔐 שפוני) in Deut 33.19. MasPs[a] reads אלהי אדום ('the gods of Edom') in Ps 83.7 for 𝔐 + Vss אהלי אדום ('the gates of Edom', Talmon 1999, 55, 80, 87). MurXII contains a number of minor variants, most of them orthographic ones (*DJD* 2:183–84).

XV

MS 5480. 4Q(?)Sam (1 Sam 5.10–11)

Torleif Elgvin

DSS F.113, DSS F.Sam2

A. Physical Description

The fragment, on dark brown parchment, measures 1.3 × 2.1 cm. The surface is smooth and has been completely preserved, with no points that have flaked away or been scraped off. The fragment contains remnants of two lines without margins. The lines converge slightly towards the left with a line spacing of 6–7 mm.[1]

Ira Rabin's analysis showed very high amounts of lead in the parchment, a feature that suggests that the skin was prepared outside Qumran (Rabin, unpublished report).

B. Palaeography

The manuscript displays a late Hasmonaean semi-formal hand, cautiously dated by Langlois to around 50 BC (see p. 86).

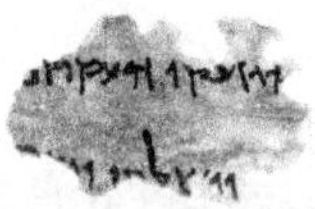

Figure 22.1. MS 5480

C. MS 5480

1   [[ויזעקו העקרונ]
2   [[וישלחו וי°°°]

---

[1] Langlois noted the possible presence of ink on the left edge of the fragment, leading him to question the authenticity of the fragment (if a forger wrote the text on a decomposed fragment, ink could have penetrated also onto the edge). However, a later infrared and ultra-violet microscopic examination of the fragment showed that these traces of blue ink actually derive from the text liner used to mark the carton frame. The same ink can be seen on the frame itself.

Notes on Readings

Line 1. וִיזעקו. A speck of ink can be seen touching the downstroke of the first *waw*. This is more probably a spill of ink than the remainder of a preceding letter without any word divider (cf. *ʿayin* in the same word, which ends at a position corresponding to this spot, in the middle between the top and bottom of the other letters).

D. MS 5480 (1 Sam 5.10–11)

ויהי כבוא ארון[	01
[האלהים עקרון] ויזעקו העקרונ[י]ם לאמור הסבו אלי את ארון אלהי ישראל[	1
[להמיתני ואת עמי] [11]וישלחו ויאס[פו את כול סרני פלשתים ויאמרו שלחו את[	2

Translation

01. [... when the ark]
1. [of God came to Ekron,] the Ekron[ites] cried out,['They have moved the Ark of the God of Israel]
2. [to us to slay us and our kindred.'] [11] They [too]sent word and assem[bled all the lords of the Philistines, and said, 'Send away the]

Parallel Text

4QSamᵃ col. VI frgs a–b preserve the same verses as MS 5480. Since MS 5480 probably is slightly older than 4QSamᵃ (dated to 50–25 BC), it likely represents the oldest textual witness to 1 Sam 5.10–11.

Notes on Reconstruction and Comments

The lines can be restored with *c.* 63 letter spaces per line and a column width of 9.5 cm.

Lines 01–1 (5.10). [ויהי כבוא ארון האלהים עקרון] = 𝔐 4QSamᵃ (reconstructed) ≈ 𝕲 (και εγενηθη ως εισηλθεν κιβωτος θεου εις Ασκαλωνα) ¦ > 𝕲ᴹˢˢ 𝕾ᴹˢˢ 𝕿 𝔙ᴹˢˢ. A number of witnesses have a shorter text in the first part of v. 10, as they omit the second of two similar sentences, 'they sent the ark of God to Ekron'/'But when the ark of God came to Ekron'. There is no way of knowing which version was followed by our text.

Line 1 (5.10). ויזעקו העקרונ[י]ם = עקרון = 𝔐 ¦ εις ασκαλωνα, και εβοησαν οι ασκαλωνιται 𝕲. The presence of העקרונ[י]ם suggests the restoration of עקרון in the lacuna (not אשקלון, for which cf. 𝕲). 𝔐 uses the shorter spelling העקרנים here, but the longer העקרוני in Josh 13.3. Drawing from the long spelling of this word the forms אלוהי, לאמור and כול are tentatively suggested in the reconstruction.

Line 1 (5.10). [הסבו] = 𝔐 𝕾 𝕿 𝔙 ¦ למה הסבותֿ[ם] 4QSamᵃ 𝕲 (τι απεστρεψατε). Cross notes that the interrogative particle למה of 4QSamᵃ 𝕲 makes more sense in the context, and may have fallen out of 𝔐 and its congeners after לאמור (*homoioarkton*) and before הסבותם, which begins with *he* (*DJD* 17:52).

Line 1 (5.10). [אלי] = 𝔐 ¦ 𝕲 (προς ημας) 𝕾 (حلى) 𝔙.

Line 2 (5.10). ‏[להמיתני ואת עמי‎] = 𝔐 4QSamᵃ ‏מ̇י[ע ת]א̇ו נ̇[להמית‎ | 𝔊 (θανατωσαι ημας και τον λαον ημων) 𝔖 (ܘܠܡܩܛܠ ܠܝ ܘܠܥܡܝ) 𝔙. We do not know if the fragment read these phrases in the singular with 𝔐 and 4QSamᵃ or in the plural with the versions.

The preserved text is too small to draw any conclusion on its textual character.

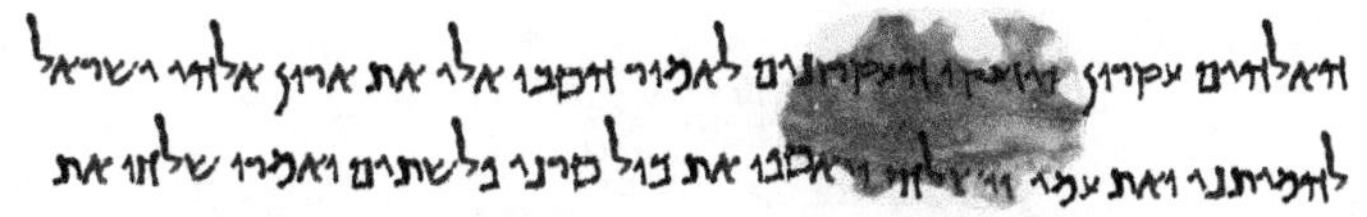

Figure 22.2. *A reconstruction of 4Q(?)Sam*

XVI

MS 5233/1. XQSam (2 Sam 20.22–24)

Torleif Elgvin

DSS F.114, DSS F.Sam3

A. Physical Description

The fragment measures 1.6 × 2.1 cm. The parchment is medium to dark brown. The grain structure can be discerned on the *recto*. The fragment is worn, but the remains of three lines can be seen.

According to Ira Rabin's analysis this fragment contained small amounts of lead. It did not exhibit mineral traces of water sources close to the Dead Sea, and must have been prepared outside the Dead Sea region. The infrared spectra show patterns of calcite and aragonite similar to those of marl. However, the presence of gypsum and salt crystals rather points towards a natural cave as find-place (Rabin, unpublished report).

B. Palaeography

According to Michael Langlois, the fragment is written in a late Hasmonaean or early Herodian semiformal hand, copied sometime in the second half of the first century BC, perhaps more precisely in the last third (see p. 96).

Figure 23.1. MS 5233/1

C. MS 5233/1

[וֹאבויתקע בֹּ] 1
[לֹד ויואב אל כול] 2
[ל המס ויהושׄ○] 3

Notes on Readings

Line 1. ‏ואבויתקע‏[. The ʿayin is very small in size, and somewhat unusual in form. There is no word space before ‏ויתקע‏.

Line 2. ‏לך‏[. Final *kap* appears like a large medial form, which extends below the imagined baseline.

Line 3. ‏ויהוש‏°[. The tops of all three strokes of *šin* are preserved along the bottom edge of the fragment. The centre arm seems to be highly situated relative to the left arm, and all three strokes appear slightly above the hypothetical dryline. However, the possibility that these are anomalies is difficult to determine without other examples of this letter for comparison. One can see only a tiny trace of the head of the last letter.

D. MS 5233/1 (2 Sam 20.22–25)

‏[בכרי וישלכו אל י‏[ואב ויתקע ב‏[שפר ויפצו מעל העיר איש לאהליו ויואב‏]   1

‏[שב ירושלם אל המ‏[לך ²³ויואב אל כול ‏[הצבא ובניה בן יהוידע על הכרתי‏]   2

‏[ועל הפלתי ²⁴ואדרם ע‏[ל המס ויהושפ‏[ט בן אחילוד המזכיר ²⁵ושיא ספר וצדוק‏]   3

Translation

1. [of Bichri and threw it down to J]oab. He then sounded the h[orn; every man dispersed from the city to his tents, and Joab]

2. [returned to the ki]ng [in Jerusalem.] ²³ Joab was commander of the whole [army; Benaiah son of Jehoiada was commander of the Cherethites]

3. [and the Pelethites; ²⁴ Adoram was i]n charge of forced labour; Jehoshaph[at son of Ahilud was recorder; ²⁵ Sheva was scribe, and Zadok]

Parallel Text

The same text is preserved in the contemporary or slightly earlier 4QSamᵃ (4Q51) frgs 147–148 5–7.

Notes on Reconstruction and Comments

Line 1 (20.22). ‏ויתקע ב‏[שפר = 𝔐 𝕲ᴮᴼ (και εσαλπισεν εν κερατινη)⁞ + יואב 𝕲ᴸ 𝕾 𝒱.

Line 2. There is no *vacat* corresponding to the closed paragraph before v. 23 in 𝔐ᴸ and the short indentation in 𝔐ᴬ.

Line 2 (20.23). ‏ויואב אל = 𝔐 𝕲ᴮᴼ ⁞ ויואב על 𝕲ᴸ 𝕮 𝕾 𝒱. 𝕲ᴸ 𝕮ᴶ 𝕾 𝒱 seem to presuppose the reading על ('Joab was *over* all Israel's army'). Cross makes mention of the frequent confusion between אל and על (*DJD* 17:176).

Line 2 (20.23). ‏כול = 𝔐 (כל). The full spelling would align with the so-called Qumran scribal practice, but we do not know if the text in general used a full spelling.

Line 2 (20.23). ‏הצבא‏] כול = 𝔐ᵐˢˢ 𝕲ᵐˢˢ (πασηι τηι δυναμει) cf. 2 Sam 8.16 ⁞ + ישראל 𝔐 𝕲 𝕾 𝒱. Only without the plus ישראל of 𝔐 𝕲 does the reconstructed text align with the left margin. Cross reconstructs the text of 4QSamᵃ without this plus (*DJD* 17:175).

Line 3 (20.24). ‎ט]וֹשֹׁפֹֿה‎‏ = 𝔐 𝕲^BO (Ιωσαφατ) ⦙ ‎ושפן‎ 𝕲^L.

E. Textual Character and Provenance

The preserved text is so fragmentary that it is not possible to draw firm conclusions about its textual character. The results of the mineral analysis are inconclusive, so we do not know if this fragment was found in a marl cave such as Cave 4, or a natural cave, such as Cave 6 or Cave 11. The fragment is therefore designated XQSam.

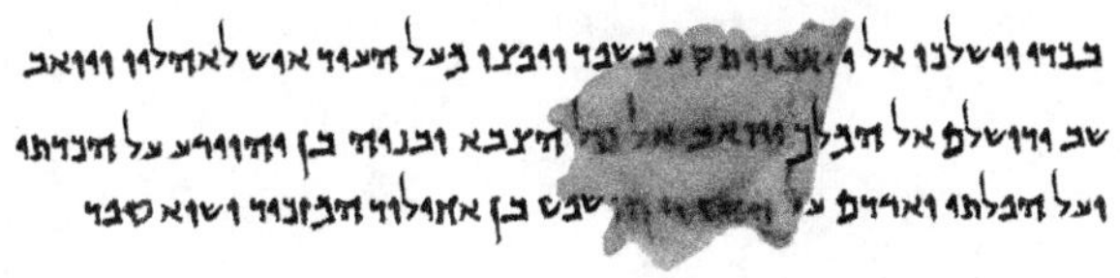

Figure 23.2. *A reconstruction of XQSam*

XVII

MS 5440. 4Q(?)Kgs (1 Kgs 16.23–26)

Kipp Davis, Torleif Elgvin

DSS F.115, DSS F.Kings1

A. Physical Description

The fragment measures 2.7 × 3.1 cm and has a thickness of 0.61±0.1 mm. The parchment is very dark brown. The lighter-coloured ink stands out from the darker skin. The surface of the *verso* is rough and that of the *recto* smoother. The grain structure can be discerned on the *recto*. Remnants of four lines are preserved, but the bottom line can only be read by infrared photography. The line spacing is 7 mm.

According to Ira Rabin's analysis the skin contains large amounts of lead. The ink and the parchment revealed the same trace elements, which suggest preparation in the same location.

B. Palaeography

According to Michael Langlois the fragment is written in a small and somewhat crude semiformal early Herodian hand from the end of the first century BC (see p. 100).

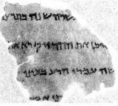

Figure 24.1. *MS 5440*

C. MS 5440

1	[◦שרה שנה בתרצ◦]
2	[◦יבן את ההר ויקרא את]
3	[שה עמרי הרע בעיני י]
4	[תו אשר]

Notes on Readings

Line 1. שרה○[. Only the left end of the baseline of the first letter has survived at the right edge of the fragment.

    Line 3. י[. There is a faint trace of ink at the left edge of the fragment which posits the presence of a letter. At high magnification, the residual ink visible on the fibres of the leather is in the shape of a *yod*, and cannot be construed as any other letter.

D. Scrolls of 1–2 Kings from the Judaean Desert

Fragments from four scrolls containing text from 1–2 Kings have been published: 4QKgs[a] (4Q54), 4QKgs[b] (4Q54a),[1] 5QKgs (5Q2), and 6QpapKgs (6Q4). 4QKgs[a] is palaeographically dated to the mid-first century BC (*DJD* 14:172). The other three scrolls are early Hasmonaean, palaeographically dated to 150–100 BC (*DJD* 3:107, 172; Puech 2012, 469). A fragment of 1 Kgs 13.20–22 belonging to the Kando family was exhibited at Forth Worth in 2012 (Loveless 2012, 101) bringing the total copies of 1–2 Kings up to six. Another writing related to the Book of Kings is 4QParaphrase of Kings (4Q382), which appears to recount the life of Elijah in an eschatological context (*DJD* 13:363–416).

    The Greek text of 1 Kings (3 Kingdoms) represents an edition substantially different from 𝔐. According to Emanuel Tov (2008, 285–92) the Greek is a translation of a Hebrew *Vorlage* that radically rewrites an earlier version represented by 𝔐.

    MS 5440 is the only preserved witness to 1 Kings 16.

E. MS 5440 (1 Kgs 16.23–26)

The column width is reconstructed to *c.* 10 cm with 59–60 letter spaces per line. Our reconstruction is provided below, based on the following image in *Figure 24.2*.

[מלך יהודה מלך עמרי על ישראל שתים ²⁴[עֿשרה שנה בתרצהֿ] מלך שש שנים ויקן את]   1

[ההר שמרון מאת שמר בככרים כסף]ויבן את ההר ויקרא את] שם העיר אשר בנה על]   2

[שם שמר אדני ההר שמרון *vac?* ²⁵ויע]שה עמרי הרע בעיני י]הוה וירע מכל המלכים אשר]   3

[היו לפניו ²⁶וילך בכל דרך ירבעם בן נבט ובחטא]תו אשר] החטיא את ישראל להכעיס]   4

Translation

1.   [king of Judah, Omri became king and reigned over Israel for twe]lve years; in Tirzah[he reigned for six years. ²⁴ Then he purchased the]

2.   [hill of Samaria from Shemer for two talents of silver;]and he fortified the hill, and called the[name of the city which he built, 'Samaria', after]

3.   [the name of Shemer, the owner of the hill. *vac?* ²⁵]Omri [d]id what was evil in the sight of Y[HWH, and did more evil *than all the kings who*]

[1] Emile Puech identified 4Q54a, a small fragment that preserves 1 Kgs 7.46–47, written in an early Hasmonaean hand (Puech 2012, 467–69). According to Puech there may be a fifth copy of Kings represented by a fragment that either preserves 2 Kgs 19.27–29 or Isa 37.28–30 (2012, 469–72). As this passage is extant in both Isaiah and Kings, the statistical precedence of Isaiah over Kings in Qumran makes it more reasonable to see this fragment as deriving from a scroll of Isaiah.

4.   [were before him. ²⁶ For he walked in all the ways of Jeroboam the son of Nebat, and in]his[sin]s,
which [he made Israel to sin, provoking]

Notes on Reconstruction and Comments

Line 1 (16.23). [מלך יהודה] = 𝔐 ¦ > 𝔊 ¦ 𝕿. מלך שבטא דבית יהודה.
  Line 1 (16.24). [ויקן] = 𝔐 𝔖 𝔙 ¦ + Αμβρι 𝔊.
  Line 2 (16.24). [ההר שמרון] = 𝔐 𝔊 𝔙 ¦ 𝕿. כרכא שמרון.
  Line 2 (16.24). [מאת שמר] = 𝔐 ¦ + του κυριου του ορους 𝔊.
  Line 2 (16.24). [העיר אשר בנה] = 𝔐 ¦ του ορους ου ωκοδομεσεν 𝔊.
  Line 3 (16.24-25). [שמרון ויע[שה *vac?*]. The alignment of the letters in *Figure 24.2* suggests that there
was possibly a small *vacat* separating v. 24 from v. 25. There are no section divisions at this point in any
of the witnesses.² A minor section break between vv. 24-25 would make sense in the literary context.
  Lines 3–4 (16.25). [מכל המלכים אשר היו לפניו] = 𝔖 (ܡܢ ܟܠܗܘܢ ܡܠܟܐ ܕܗܘܘ ܡܢ ܩܕܡܘܗܝ)¦ 𝔐 מכל אשר לפניו ¦
υπερ παντας τους γενομενους εμπροσθεν αυτου 𝔊. The available space in the lacuna suggests an
alternative text—possibly reflecting the *Vorlage* to the 𝔖. Cf. also Josephus' description of the reign of
Omri in *Ant.* 8.313 (διεφερε δ' ουδεν των προ αυτου βασιλευσαντων), which seems to indicate familiarity
with an alternate reading like what we have proposed here.
  Line 4 (16.26). [ובחטא[תו] = 𝔐ᵠ 𝔐ᴹˢˢ ¦ ובחטאתיו 𝔐ᴷ Vrs.

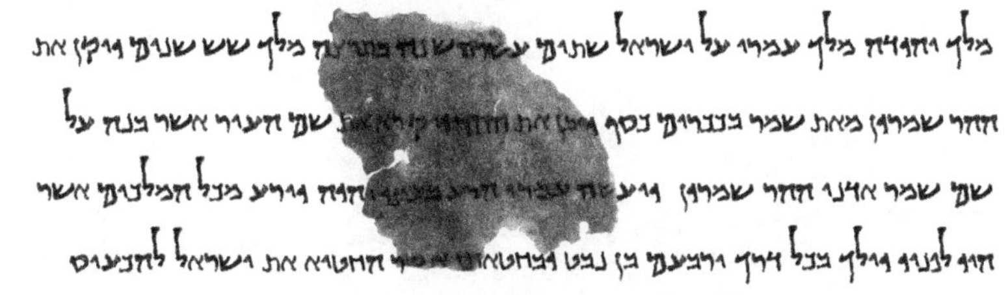

Figure 24.2. A reconstruction of 4Q(?)Kgs

The extant text of MS 5440 tends to correspond to the text of 𝔐 against 𝔊, although in one case it reads
with 𝔐ᵠ and 𝔐ᴹˢˢ, and in another one the available space cannot account for the text of 𝔐 in the lacuna.
A reconstruction of the text suggests that MS 5440 is better described as an independent text that
alternates between textual traditions preserved in 𝔐 and 𝔊 and with one reading possibly similar to 𝔖.

---

² However, there does appear to be a section marker of some sort in 𝔐ᴸ, folio 197 recto.

XVIII

MS 4612/9. 4Q(?)Jer (Jer 3.15–19)

Torleif Elgvin, Kipp Davis

DSS F.116, DSS F.Jer1

A. Physical Description

The fragment measures 5.3 × 6.2 cm. The leather varies in thickness between 0.43–0.8 mm, and is dark brown in colour. The skin strucure can be seen under the sediments. The top right part had broken off and has been reconnected with tape on the *verso*. A 14 mm right margin preserves the beginning of the sheet, and a thread from the sewing can be discerned on the *verso*. The shape of the top right corner may suggest that this is part of the upper edge of the scroll, but the evidence is not strong enough to support any firm conclusion. If this was the case, the top margin was 9 mm. The line spacing is 7.5–8 mm.

According to Ira Rabin the skin was prepared outside the Dead Sea region (Rabin, unpublished report).

B. Palaeography

Michael Langlois calls the script of MS 4612/9 quite irregular, and with some semicursive tendencies. He dates this text to the second half of the first century BC (cf. p. 87). Ada Yardeni characterizes the script as a late Hasmonaean or early Herodian hand from the period 100–40 BC.

Figure 25.1. MS 4612/9

C. MS 4612/9

1   אתכם רעה והש̇ש[

2   לא יאמרו ०וד ארון ברית̇[

3   ע̇שה עוד בעת ההיא ○○[

4   ]כלכו עוד אחרי שררות לבם ה○[

5   ]ת̇ ישראל ויבאו יחדו מארץ צפן[

6   ]○ אמרתי אמן יהו̇ה ○י כ̇[

Notes of Readings

Line 2. יאמרו. There are two wormholes that obscure this word where the *ʾalep* and *mem* occur. Both of these letters appear as though they were written around the edges of the holes.

Line 3. ע̇שה. On the infrared photograph of the *verso* one can see a speck of ink representing the lower left end of *ʿayin*, and another preserving the lower angle of *šin*.

Line 3. בעת ההיא. The two words are clearly visible in infrared light, but the first six letters are obscured on the colour plate and especially the PTM (SchoyenMS4612-9 OB Vp) by what seem to be vertical scratches. This feature might suggest that these words were erased. Microscopic inspection of the fragment failed to confirm any signs of scratching.

Line 3.]○○. A trace of the bottom part of the first letter of the word following ההיא is visible at the edge of the fragment, and a minute trace of a second letter can be seen on the microscopic infrared image in *Figure 25.2*.

Line 5. ת̇[. The left downstroke of the letter extends above the line, and trace of the right shoulder connecting the crossbar to the right downstroke is clearly visible, thus providing reasonable confidence that the letter is a *taw*.

Line 6. יהוה. One should more probably read יהוה than יהיה. Note the shape of the head of the third letter, which is narrower than the chevron that is characteristic of *yod* in this manuscript. This letter is also considerably longer than typical *yod*s from elsewhere on this fragment, and more clearly conforms to *waw*.

Line 6. ○י. Only the head of the first letter is visible.

Line 6. כ̇[. The last visible letter of this line is more probably *kap* than *bet*. Cf. the *kap* in line 1, the top of *bet* is wider, and more ornamental in this hand.

Figure 25.2. *MS 4612/9 line 3 microscopic infrared (scale 4:1)*

D. Jeremiah Scrolls from the Judaean Desert

Jer 3.15–19 is not contained in any of the other previously discovered Jeremiah scrolls from the Judaean Desert. Six Qumran copies of Jeremiah have been published: 2QJer (2Q13; *DJD* 3:62–69, plate XIII) and five copies from Cave 4 (*DJD* 15:142–207). 2QJer exhibits a beautiful Herodian formal hand from the first century AD (cf. *DJD* 3:62). It is the latest Qumran copy of Jeremiah, and contains a handful of verses from Jer 42; 44; 48. 4QJer[a] (4Q70) is palaeographically dated to 225–175 BC, and is one of the oldest scrolls from the Judaean Desert discoveries. It preserves text from Jer 7.2–22.16 in 35 fragments. 4QJer[c] is early Herodian, from the latter part of the first century BC. It is an extensive copy with portions of text from Jer 4.5–33.20 preserved in 55 fragments. 4QJer[b,d,e] are all single fragments that were first grouped together by the editors as part of the same manuscript. They were subsequently separated on the basis of a variety of distinguishing features. 4QJer[b] contains text from Jer 9.22–10.21, 4QJer[d] from Jer 43.2–10, and 4QJer[e] from Jer 50.4–6. Emanuel Tov dates both 4QJer[b,d] to 200–150 BC.[1] We suggest an early Hasmonaean dating of 4QJer[b], 150–125 BC. The Green Collection includes a copy of Jer 23.6–9. The dating of this fragment is unknown.

E. MS 4612/9 (Jer 3.15–19)

[*to]p margin?*

אתכם רעה והש[כיל 16והיה כי תרבו ופריתם בארץ בימים ההמה נאם יהוה] 1

לא יאמרו עֹוד ארון ברית[יהוה ולא יעלה על לב ולא יזכרו בו ולא יפקדו ולא] 2

עֹשה עוד (17)בעת ההיא 17וֹֹ[קֹ]ראו לירושלם כסא יהוה ונקוו אליה כל הגוים] 3

[ולא יֹ]כלכו עוד אחרי שררות לבם הרֹ[ע ... 18בימים ההמה ילכו בית יהודה] 4

[על בי]ֹת ישראל ויבאו יחדו מארץ צפן[ומכל הארצות על הארץ אשר הנחלתי את] 5

[אבותיהם 19ואנֹ[כֹי אמרתי אמן יהוה כֹי בֹ[נים אשיתך ואתן לך ארץ חמדה נחלת] 6

Translation

                   ... and in shepherding]

1. you[they will] *shepherd* with sk[ill. ¹⁶ And it will be, if you multiply and increase in the land, in those days, declares YHWH,]

2. they shall no longer say, 'The ark of the covenant of[YHWH', nor shall it come to mind. They shall not mention it, or miss it or]

3. make another at that time. ¹⁷ And[they]shall c[all Jerusalem 'Throne of YHWH', and all nations shall be gathered into her.]

4. [And they shall no longer w]alk after the notions of their ev[il]heart[. *vac* ¹⁸ In those days the house of Judah shall join]

5. [the ho]use of Israel; they shall come together from the land of the north[*and from all the lands* to the land I gave in heritage]

6. [to their fathers. ¹⁹ And I]said: '*Let it happen, O YHWH!*' *For like*[children I will set you, and I will give you a desirable land, a heritage]

---

[1] For the dating of the Jeremiah texts from Cave 4, see *DJD* 15:150, 182, 203.

Notes on Reconstruction and Comments[2]

With *c.* 60 letter spaces per line the column width is estimated at *c.* 10 cm (varying between 9.8 and 10.3 cm). The fragment probably preserves text from the first column on the second sheet of a Jeremiah scroll.

Line 1 (3.15). רעה = 𝔊 (ποιμαινοντες) | דעה 𝔐 𝔖. MS 4612/9 reads the absolute infinitive רְעֹה, close to 𝔊's ποιμαινοντες ('shepherding/tending'), against 𝔐 דעה ('knowledge'). Already the *BHK* apparatus retroverted 𝔊 to רְעֹה. From a grammatical viewpoint, 𝔐 represents a difficult, but possible text, 'and they will shepherd you (with) knowledge and skill'. The verse in 𝔐 ends with the difficult phrase דֵּעָה וְהַשְׂכֵּיל, a noun followed by an absolute infinitive.[3] The readings of MS 4612/9 and 𝔊 probably represent an older text. 𝔐 reflects a scribal error in which רעה was misconstrued as דעה. Thus Holladay (1986, 60), who points to a similar sequence with two absolute infinitives in a poetic passage in Jer 22.19, and a similar structure in 1 Sam 6.12 הלכו הלך וגעו.[4]

Line 2 (3.16). ארון ברית] יהוה = 𝔐 𝔖 | κιβωτος διαθηκης αγιου Ισραηλ 𝔊. We have reconstructed according to 𝔐. The longer 𝔊 reading would correspond to ארון ברית קדוש ישראל ('the covenant ark of the Holy One of Israel'). Considerations of space suggest that MS 4612/9 followed 𝔐 at this point.[5] The combined evidence of 𝔐 and MS 4612/9 suggests that the clause 'of the Holy One of Israel' in 𝔊 is a secondary expansion.

Line 2 (3.16). [יזכרו בו] = 𝔐 𝔊 | יזכרו בו עוד 𝔐[mss] | יזכרו עוד 𝔐[mss] | ܠܐ ܢܬܕܟܪܘܢ 𝔖.

Line 3 (3.16). יעשה 𝔐 𝔊 (ποιηθησεται) | ܠܐ ܬܬܥܒܕ ܬܘܒ 𝔖. The material evidence hardly allows for the reconstruction of a *yod* at the beginning of this line.

Line 3 (3.17). בעת ההיא יקראו. וְקֹ[ראו 𝔐 𝔖 | εν ταις ημεραις εκειναις και εν τω καιρω εκεινω καλεσουσιν 𝔊. The last clearly preserved letter of this line, opening a new word, cannot be identified with *qop* or *yod* of יקראו. The first vertical stroke is too short for the descender of a *qop*, and there is not enough space to reconstruct [י]קֹ[ראו] following ההיא. Conversely, this stroke is too long to be a *yod*, and is more probably a *waw*. The editors conducted a microscopic infrared inspection of the fragment in April 2013, and discovered a minute trace of a long descender in precisely the place we should expect a *qop*.

The text of 𝔊 would correspond to בימים ההמה ובעת ההיא יקראו, cf. the phrase בימים ההמה in the beginning of v. 18. Line 3 is problematic, and does not easily conform to the witnesses of either 𝔐 or 𝔊. Since the remaining space of this line after וְקֹ[ראו is not large enough for either of the witnesses in 𝔐 or 𝔊, we have suggested a reconstructed shorter text, without any apparent 'pluses' from either version. Our suggestion here holds most closely to the shorter text of 𝔐 at the beginning of the clause, followed by the text from 𝔊, and minus the appositional expansion לשם יהוה לירושלם in 𝔐. These three words of 𝔐 are a secondary explanatory gloss (Craigie, Kelley, and Drinkard 1991, 58–59).

[2] For a discussion of the textual character and readings of this fragment, see Popko 2013, 44–49, 175–86 (Lukasz Popko was given access to a photo of the fragment and permission to use this text in his Ecole Biblique Ph.D. dissertation).

[3] Cf. Job 34.35, where דעת is paralleled with the construct infinitive השכיל: לֹא־בְדַעַת יְדַבֵּר וּדְבָרָיו לֹא בְהַשְׂכֵּיל; and Dan 1.17 מדע והשכל, a noun followed by the absolute infinitive.

[4] Another, less likely altenative would see the original in 𝔐, which was misread by a scribe as ורעו אתכם רעה והשכיל =) MS 4612/9). This produced the verbal construct ורעו רְעֹה והשכיל, perfect followed by two absolute infinitives: 'and they shall pasture you, pasturing and being wise'. The *Vorlage* of 𝔊 would then represent an intended smoothing of this error: 'and in shepherding you they will shepherd with skill'.

[5] Another less likely possibility would be to see this as an unattested abbreviated text in the following clause, closely aligned to 𝔊, perhaps reconstructed as ארון ברית] קדוש ישראל ולא יעלה על לב ולא יזכרו בו ולא [עשה עוד, 'the covenant ark[of the Holy One of Israel, nor shall it come to mind. They shall not mention it or] make another'. In this alternative reconstruction we have omitted the second of the three consecutive verbal clauses, present both in 𝔐 (ולא יפקדו) and 𝔊 (ουδε επισκεφθησεται). The alignment in accordance with 𝔐 is preferable.

Line 3 (3.17). [כל הגוים] = 𝕲 (παντα τα εθνη) | + לשם יהוה לירושלם 𝔐 𝕮 | + ܠܐܡܗܐ ܣܓܝܐܐ S.

Line 4 (3.17). [יכלבו]י. ילכו 𝔐 𝕲 (πορευσονται). [יכלבו] is probably a scribal error in the form of an uncorrected transference. A similar phenomenon appears in 4QNum^b XV 10, in which the scribe began to write מלוך, following the *mem* with a *lamed*, but then recognized his mistake and went on to write a *he* to produce the correct reading מהלוך. Here too, the scribe probably started to write יכלו, but recognized his error before penning the *waw*.[6] There is no cancellation dot above or below the *kap*.

Line 4. The text from both 𝔐 and 𝕲 is too short to fill the available space to end the line. Both 𝔐^L and 𝔐^A have a closed paragraph before v. 18, and it is possible that MS 4612/9 included a similar section marker, a *vacat* of probably no more than 1 cm. The sense divider reconstructed in the figure below measures 6 mm. Alternatively MS 4612/9 contained a variant text.

Line 5 (3.18). צפן = 𝔐 (צפון).

Line 5 (3.18). [מארץ צפן] ומכל הארצות על הארץ] = 𝕲 (απο γης Βορρα και απο πασων των χωρων επι την γην) | מארץ צפן על הארץ 𝔐 (𝔐^mss אל הארץ) S. Considerations of space suggest that MS 4612/9 contained a text similar to 𝕲 here.

Line 6 (3.18). [אבותיהם] = 𝕲 S 𝕮^c.f.g | אבותיכם 𝔐. Holladay explains the change from אבותיכם to אבותיהם as a secondary accommodation to vv. 16–18a, a later expansion of the text (1986, 60). The restoration here aligns with the majority of the witnesses, but if MS 4612/9 preserves a witness to an earlier text—as suggested by the shorter text in v. 17 above—then אבותיכם must be considered as likely here.

Line 6 (3.19). ⁹[ואנ | ואנכי 𝔐. The allowable space between the right edge of the fragment and the right column margin suggests that the personal pronoun was most likely the shorter form ואני rather than the longer ואנכי in 𝔐. It is possibly of further interest to note that there is a higher frequency of the shorter form than the longer (54/37 in 91 occurrences) in scriptural Jeremiah.

Line 6 (3.19). ⁹[ואנ | אמרתי אמן יהוה = 𝕲 (και εγω ειπα γενοιτο κυριε) | ואנכי אמרתי 𝔐 S. MS 4612/9 closely corresponds to the longer text of 𝕲 where the prophet interrupts a divine oracle with a personal parenthetical statement: 'And I said, "Let it happen, YHWH!"'[7]

Line 6 (3.19). בי כ[בנים אשיתך. איך אשיתך בבנים 𝔐 𝕮 (איכדין אצלחינך בבניא) | 𝕲 οτι ταξω σε εις τεκνα | ܘܐܝܟܢܐ ܐܥܒܕܟ S. The last preserved letter is more likely *kap* than *bet*, but reading בנים[ב remains a possible alternative. 𝔐's use of איך here is awkward.[8] The *BHS* apparatus suggests as a solution that the 𝕲 *Vorlage* interpreted the word as an abbreviation for אמן יהוה כי (cf. Holladay 1986, 121–22). The sequence of verb and its modifier is inverted in 𝔐 and MS 4612/9. The former reads אשיתך בבנים, 'I will set you *among* the children', where the latter reads אשיתך בנים[כ, 'For *like*[children I will set you.'[9]

The interruption of the sequence of divine oracles in vv. 18–19 by ואנ(כ)י אמרתי and και εγω ειπα γενοιτο κυριε is awkward. Popko suggests that the 𝕲 *Vorlage* added אמן יהוה (= γενοιτο κυριε), and that the earliest text of v. 19 was identical with 𝔐 ואנכי אמרתי איך אשיתך בבנים, 'It was I who said: "How will I place you among the children?"' (2013, 181–83, 311–16).

---

[6] Lukasz Popko suggests moving ולא to the end of the preceding line and reconstructing an unattested, Aramacized verbal expression, יתל[כלבו], implying the translation 'they [will not be soi]led anymore after the stubbornness of their hearts' (Popko 2013, 47). He notes that the Boharic translation from the Old Greek here reads *fornicabuntur*, which would carry a similar meaning. We find his creative suggestion somewhat contrived, and the three letters he suggests would hardly fill the lacuna in the beginning of the line.

[7] For γενοιτο as a translation of אמן, cf. Num 5.22; Deut 27.15-26; 1 Kgs 1.36; Pss 40.14; 72.19; 89.53; 105.48; Isa 25.1; Jer 11.5; 15.11 (where 𝕲 reads אמן יהוה, not 𝔐's אמר יהוה).

[8] Lundbom (1999, 318) prefers 𝔐 to 𝕲 here, and refers to a parallel in Hos 11.8 as an explanation for this difficult construction.

[9] Another difficulty with 𝔐's reading here is the uncertainty about who the other children would be, among which restored Israel should be set.

We suggest that MS 4612/9 preserves a more original Hebrew text, כבנים אשיתך. The text of 𝕲, ταξω σε εις τεκνα, may render either כבנים אשיתך (the most probable text of MS 4612/9) or בנים אשיתך (the alternative reading of MS 4612/9), perhaps the option closest to 𝕲,[10] less probably 𝔐's בבנים אשיתך.[11]

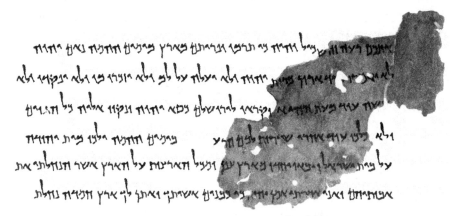

Figure 25.3. *A reconstruction of 4Q(?)Jer*

F. MS 4612/9 and the Different Recensions of Jeremiah

The Jeremiah scrolls from Qumran display a diachronically intriguing blend of textual plurality. 2QJer follows the 𝔐 recension, but represents an independent witness. Of its 27 textual variants compared with 𝔐, 7 follow 𝕲, 4 go with other versions, and 13 are unique to 2QJer. 4QJer[a] has been characterized by Tov as 'very close to the proto-Masoretic text' (*DJD* 15:151). Tov has depended heavily upon correspondences of paragraph divisions that appear in this manuscript and those among the major witnesses of 𝔐. However, the designation of 4QJer[a] as an 𝔐-like scroll requires further qualification.[12] 4QJer[c] is also closely related to 𝔐, but with a tendency towards shorter readings. Only one small fragment survives from 4QJer[e], and no conclusion can be drawn as to its textual character. After 4QJer[a], 4QJer[b,d] are the next oldest copies of Jeremiah. According to Tov, both texts are similar to 𝕲, while Armin Lange finds 4QJer[d] so poorly preserved that it cannot be classified typologically (Lange 2010, 55–56).

From the total of six texts, three of the Jeremiah scrolls, 4QJer[a,b,d], have been characterized as 'archaic' (*DJD* 39:372), and palaeographically assigned to the formative period of the *Yaḥad* Essene

---

[10] 𝕲[B] reads εθνη for τεκνα 'I will appoint you (to be) a *people*', cf. the reference to gentiles later in the same verse; we are indebted to Gunnar M. Eidsvåg in our understanding of line 6.

[11] 𝕲 uses the verb τασσω ('appoint/make'), which can render either שית (Jer 2.25) or שים (Jer 10.22; 11.13; 18.16; 19.8).

[12] While a closeness to the Masoretic text can be observed for the textual character and layout of 4QJer[a], this scroll contains a substantial correction/insertion, consisting of four verses. The first scribe made a long indentation before Jer 7.29 and a shorter one between 7.29 and the continuation of his text from Jer 8.4 onwards (in 𝔐[L] there is a major section break before 7.29, an indentation before 7.32, and another major break before 8.4; in 𝔐[A] there is a closed section before 7.29, an open section indicated by an empty line before 7.32, and a closed section before 8.4). A later hand inserted Jer 7.30–8.3 in smaller letters, written both horizontally between lines 5 and 7 of the column (= 4QJer[a] III 5, 7) and vertically between this and the following column. This insertion is the equivalent of 12 lines of text. Tov suggested that the original text was a result of parablepsis from one open space to the next in the scribe's *Vorlage* (*DJD* 15:156). However, it strains reason to imagine that the scribe's eye inadvertently skipped over nearly half a column of text in his transcription. As Jer 7.30–34 and Jer 8.1–3 are separate literary units, it would make more sense to suppose two different recensions, a shorter *Vorlage* without 7.30–8.3 and a longer recension that caused the later correction. For a further discussion of 4QJer[a] as an independent (not 𝔐-like) textual witness, see Davis 2014b, Davis 2015.

movement in the mid-second century BC or earlier. Two of the three witnesses aligned with the recension of 𝔐 (2QJer, 4QJer^c) have been dated to the late first century BC or early first century AD. In contrast, virtually all the 𝔊-type texts appear much earlier.

There are nine instances of textual variation in the short space of six lines of text in this fragment. The inventory of attested readings may be charted as follows, where the text of 4Q(?)Jer is indicated with an asterisk and in underline. All textual pluses appear in dotted underline:

Table 12. *Text critical synopsis of readings in 4Q(?)Jer*

	𝔐	𝔊	Independent
3.15	דעה	רעה * (ποιμαινοντες)	
3.16	* ארון בריתֿן] יהוה	κιβωτος διαθηκης αγιου Ισραηλ	
3.17	* בעת ההיא	pr. εν ταις ημεραις εκειναις και …	
3.17	יקראו	καλεσουσιν	* וֿקֿן]ראו
3.17	+ לשם יהוה לירושלם	[כל הגוים] * (παντα τα εθνη)	
3.18	>	[ומכל הארצות] * (και απο πασων των χωρων)	
3.19	ואנכי	και εγω	* ואנֿ]גֿ
3.19	איך	אמן יהוה כֿי * (γενοιτο κυριε οτι)	
3.19	בבנים אשיתך	ταξω σε εις τεκνα	* כֿ]בנים אשיתך

MS 4612/9 clearly aligns with 𝔊 in two cases (lines 1 and 6). The considerations of space prompt us to suggest that it aligns with the longer text of 𝔊 in line 5. The beginning of line 3 (Jer 3.17aα) preserves an independent reading that appears closest to 𝔐. In the same line (Jer 3.17aβ) the available space suggest that MS 4612/9 retained a shorter form of the text that conforms most closely to 𝔊. The reconstruction of the whole of v. 17 indicates an unattested shorter text that contained elements from both witnesses, but without the pluses present in either 𝔐 or 𝔊. כֿ]בנים אשיתך of line 6 is an independent reading, although slightly closer to 𝔊 than to 𝔐.

In one of these cases (Jer 3.17aβ) 𝔐 contains a plus, in three cases 𝔊 has a longer and different text. In one case (line 2), on the other hand, MS 4612/9 follows the shorter text of 𝔐 whereas 𝔊 contains a plus. Overall MS 4612/9 shows evidence of only one clear plus from either witness, and a general propensity for a more condensed text that probably is more original.

The evidence tentatively shows that MS 4612/9 may be grouped with 4QJer^{b,d} as a text related to the *Vorlage* of 𝔊, although preserving independent features that indicate a thus far unattested shorter text.[13] Both 2QJer and MS 4612/9 demonstrate that non-aligned or 𝔊-like texts of Jeremiah were transmitted until the first century AD.

With the Qumran provenance asserted for this fragment, three out of seven Qumran copies of Jeremiah represent apparently shorter versions mostly similar to 𝔊. Three of the remaining four copies are closer to the proto-𝔐 recension (4QJer^a, 4QJer^c, 2QJer), although both 2QJer and 4QJer^a also preserve features that are independent of 𝔐. 4QJer^d appears to align with 𝔐, but it is too small to make any firm judgement in regard to its textual character.

---

[13] Popko (2013, 48) notes that the text contains the shorter readings and lacks the expansions of both 𝔐 and 𝔊, and concludes that it probably represents a text that precedes both these versions. It bears some traces that are proper to the *Vorlage* of 𝔊, but cannot be identified with it.

XIX

MS 4612/1. Ḥev(?)Joel (Joel 4.1–5)

Torleif Elgvin

DSS F.117. DSS F.Joel1

A. Physical Description

The fragment measures 6.5 × 5.4 cm. The leather is remarkably thick, but varies in thickness (1.2±0.5 mm). A top margin of 3.5 cm and remnants of nine lines, with a line spacing of 7 mm, have been preserved. The leather has shrunk substantially, creating a wavy surface. Due to the shrinking the left parts of the lines slant downwards from line 3 onwards. Large sections of the surface have flaked off. These sections are thin and close to transparent when seen against a lamp. Where the original surface is preserved, the colour is dark brown, while the flaked-off sections are light brown. The grain structure is clearly visible on the *recto*. The *verso* has a smoother surface. With the naked eye one can see only traces of a few letters, but the infrared photo reveals several letters and ink traces where the surface is preserved. There is a deep, vertical fold in lines 6–9 below the hole between lines 5 and 6. This produces an illusion in which the letters on both sides of the fold appear closer together on the photograph than in their original position: 4–6 mm of the leather 'disappears' on the photograph.

1–2 mm of the right edge of the *recto* is folded over from line 1 and down to the bottom, and is visible on the photographs of the *verso*. The infrared photograph of the *verso* reveals two letters from this folded part in line 9 and traces of letters in lines 7 and 8. Microscopic images of the edge, taken from the side, reveal ink traces on the fold not seen on the infrared photos of the full fragment (see *Figures 26.1a–c*).

Figure 26.1a. MS 4612/1 recto microscopic infrared, line 1

Figure 26.1b. MS 4612/1 recto microscopic infrared, lines 1–2

Figure 26.1c. *MS 4612/1 recto microscopic infrared, lines 5-6*

According to Ira Rabin's analysis, the material is leather, not parchment. The chlorine/bromine ratio shows preparation of the leather outside the Dead Sea region. Where the surface has eroded one can detect magnesium—probably deriving from the stage of preparation. The calcium/strontium ratio is compatible with a place of discovery at Qumran. However, IR spectra do not show any presence of the aragonite to be expected at Qumran. Murabbaʿat is tentatively ruled out as a possible alternative place of discovery because of the absence of dolomite on the fragment (personal communication with Rabin).

B. Palaeography

According to Michael Langlois, the script represents a skilled formal book hand exhibiting developments that appear in the latest Herodian scripts. He concludes that the manuscript was copied in the second half of the first century AD, perhaps in the third quarter (see p. 110).

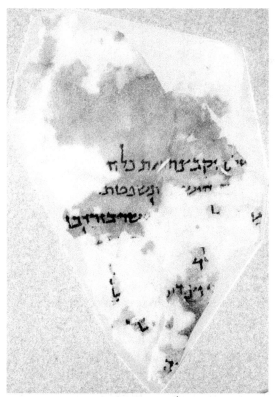

Figure 26.2*. MS 4612/1 recto*

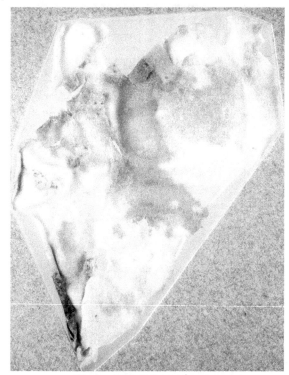

Figure 26.3*. MS 4612/1 verso*

C. MS 4612/1

]	*top margin* [	
[שלם וקבצת○אׄת כל ה]		1
]○ונשפטת[ ]○הוש○ קׄ[		2
[מׄיׄ]○[]ל[ ]לׄ [אׄשר בזרו בג]		3
]לׄ[ ]○○[ ]○○[		4
]○[ ]לׄד[		5
]לׄ○[ ]○○דׄיׄצׄ ור[		6
]○[ ]○ ם֯[ ]○○[ ]לׄמ[		7
]○○לׄ[ ]○אׄ[		8
]לׄקׄחׄ[		9

Notes on Readings

Line 1. אׄ○וקבצת. A downstroke is visible after the first *taw*, and a trace of the head of *yod* or *waw* appears above the crack. The *ʾalep* appears to be somewhat unusual, with a heavily shaded left downstroke, cf. the traces of the *ʾalep* in line 3 below.

    Lines 4–8. Only fragmentary parts of letters remain. The only clear readings are לׄד in line 5 and וצׄיׄד followed by traces of two letters in line 6.

    Line 6. וצׄיׄד○○[. The downstroke of a letter after the *dalet* is preserved. The last preserved downstroke curves downwards to the left. It could fit *nun*, final *mem*, or final *nun*.

    Lines 7–8. Only a few strokes of ink are preserved on the *recto*.

    Line 7.]לׄמ[. A trace of the top of the *lamed* is preserved on the *recto*. On the part of the front side of the fragment that has folded under, we see more of the head of the *lamed* followed by *mem*.

    Line 7.]○ ם֯[. The baseline and the left downstroke of the final *mem* are preserved. The warping of the skin has caused this letter to appear misaligned with the words above.

    Line 9.]לׄקׄחׄ[. On the fold wrapped around the edge one can see *lamed* and parts of the following letter; the head and a trace of the descender of a *qop*. On the photograph of the *recto* the upper left corner of the *qop* can be seen before a probable *ḥet*.

Figure 26.4. MS 4612/1 recto/verso joined

D. Judaean Desert Scrolls of the Twelve Minor Prophets

Ten or eleven other scrolls from the Judaean Desert containing fragments of the Twelve Prophets have been published.[1] Seven or eight of these were found in Cave 4, one in Cave 5, one in Murabbaʿat, and a Greek copy in Naḥal Ḥever. Two fragments of the Twelve were exhibited at Forth Worth in 2012:[2] a fragment of Amos 7.17–8.1 in mid-Herodian script with characteristics of the so-called Qumran scribal practice, and a small fragment of Joel 4.9–10 (=3.9–10 in most Bible translations). Three minor fragments of Amos 7.17–8.1 from the early first century AD, belonging to the Lanier collection, were published by Emanuel Tov (Tov 2014). The Green Collection has acquired a late Herodian copy of Jonah 4.2–5, bringing the total number of scrolls of the Twelve up to fifteen or sixteen.

Sirach 49.10 would suggest the Twelve were considered a collection around 190 BC.[3] This does not mean that the sequence of the individual books within a unified scroll was fixed, or that every scroll

[1] The preserved parts of 4QXII[a] contained Zech, Mal, Jonah; 4QXII[b] Zeph + Hag (actual physical overlap between individual prophets within a scroll is here indicated with '+'); 4QXII[c] Hos, Joel, Amos, Zeph; 4QXII[d] only Hos; 4QXII[e] Hag, Zech; 4QXII[f] only Jonah; 4QXII[g] Hos, Joel, Amos + Obad + Jonah, Mic, Nah, Zech (and perhaps Hab, Zeph); 8ḤevXIIgr Joel, Mic, Nah, Hab, Zeph, Zech; MurXII Joel, Amos, Obad, Jonah + Mic + Nah, Hab + Zeph + Hag + Zech. A fragment probably belonging to an additional ms. of XII (Mal 3.6–7?), with line spacing c. 8 mm and 33 letter spaces per line, is published *in DJD* 15:251 (plate XLVI) . According to Catherine Murphy PAM 41.964 shows the innermost part of 4QXII[g], which is still unrolled in the IAA collections, and rolled around the original scroll handle (personal communication).

[2] These fragments belong to the Kando family (Loveless 2012, 101).

[3] Guillaume 2007 notes that the number of individual prophets copied on a single scroll increases with time. He points out that there is no evidence from Judaea that all the Twelve were assembled in one scroll before the first century BC (8ḤevXIIgr, c. 50 BC; 4QXII[g] c. 25 BC). He suggests that the *collection* of the Twelve should be ascribed to Alexandrian Jewish scribes in the

with texts from the Minor Prophets contained all the Twelve (Brooke 2006, 34). 4QXIIᶠ (4Q81) preserves four fragments of Jonah, and may have contained this prophet only. 5QXII (5Q4) may have contained only Amos. 4QXIIᵃ (4Q76) from *c.* 150 BC has Jonah following Malachi, and this scroll probably ended with these two books. From the surviving fragments from Qumran it looks as if only parts of the Twelve were included together in the same scroll, with 4QXIIᵍ (4Q82) as the only copy that may have contained all the Twelve.

Most of the scrolls are from the pre-Christian era, while 5QXII is late Herodian and MurXII post-Herodian.⁴ Two other scrolls preserve the same passage as MS 4612/1. The well-preserved scroll MurXII contains Joel 2.26–4.16 and overlaps with most of the text preserved by MS 4612/1. The early Herodian 4QXIIᵍ preserves Joel 4.4–9, and overlaps with גלילות in MS 4612/1 line 6.

E. MS 4612/1 (Joel 4.1–5)

```
]                top margin                [
```

[וירו]שלם ²וקבצתי̊ את כל ה[גוים והורדתים]	1
[אל עמ]ק̊ יהושפ̊[ט]ונשפטתי̊ עמם שם על	2
[ע]מ̊[י]ו̊[נח]ל̊[תי ישרא[ל אשר בזרו בג[וים וארצי]	3
חלקו ³ואל אמי ידו גורר [ו̊י̊[תנ]ו̊ ה̊[י]ל̊[ד בזונה]	4
[ויזנו והי]ל[ד]ה מכרו ביין [ו̊]ישתו ⁴וגם מה	5
[אתם לי צ[ר וצידו̊ן[וכל גלי[לו̊]ת פלשת הגמול]	6
[אתם מש]למ[ים ע]ל̊י̊[ו̊א[ם̊ ג̊]מ[ל̊]ים אתם עלי]	7
[קל מהרה]אש̊[יב גמ[לכם̊ בראשכם ⁵אשר]	8
[כספי וזהבי]לק̊ח̊[תם ומחמדי הטבים]	9

Translation

1. [and Jeru]salem. ² I will gather all the [nations and bring them down]
2. [to the vall]ey of Jehoshaph[at.]I will contend[with them there, over]
3. my[peo]ple and[my her]it[age Israe]l, which they *scattered* among the na[tions. *And* my land]
4. [they divided among themselves, ³ and cast lots for my people;]and t[hey barter]ed a [b]o[y for a whore]
5. [*and whored*, and sold a g]ir[l for wine] th[at they drank. ⁴ So then, what]
6. [are you doing to me, O Ty]re, Sidon, [and all the dis]tri[cts of Philistia? Are]
7. [you requiting]me[for something I have done, o]r ar[e you]do[ing something for my benefit?]
8. [Quick as a flash, I will]p[ay] you[back. ⁵ For you]
9. [have] taken[my gold and my silver, and my precious treasures]

early second century BC. On the contents and character of the Twelve scrolls from the Judaean Desert, see Brooke 2006; Weissenberg 2012a; 2012b.

⁴ The palaeographical dates are: 4QXIIᵃ⁻ᵇ 150–125 BC, 4QXIIᶜ *c.*75 BC, 4QXIIᵈ late 1st century BC, 4QXIIᵉ 75–50 BC, 4QXIIᶠ *c.*50 BC, 4QXIIᵍ 35–1 BC. Milik dates 5QXII to the first century AD (*DJD* 3:173). The meagre remains of only a few words from Amos make a precise dating difficult. The form of final *nun* and *qop* suggests a date around AD 50, cf. Cross 1961b, Fig. 2, line 7. Milik dates MurXII to the early second century AD (*DJD* 2:72, 75, 183, cf. Cross 1961b, 177). The Greek ḤevXII, written by two hands, is dated to 50–1 BC (*DJD* 8:19–26).

Notes on Reconstruction and Comments

The reconstructed column is quite narrow, *c.* 7.5 cm wide, with 31–37 letter spaces per line.

Line 1. את וֹקבצתי. There is no word space between these words.

Line 3. פזרו בזרו 𝔐. בזרו is either a scribal error or more probably a phonetic variant. בזר (*qal* or *pi'el*) is probably an Aramaism with the same meaning 'scatter' as פזר (*pi'el*). בזר occurs elsewhere in the Hebrew Bible in Ps 68.31 and Dan 11.24 בזה ושלל ורכוש להם יבזור 'plunder, spoil, and goods he shall scatter among them'. The reading might have occurred from phonetic similarity, *i.e.* the labial consonantal shift between *bet* and *pe*.[5]

Lines 3–4. ואת ארצי חלקו 𝔐. [וארצי חלקו]. Most probably the *nota accusativi* in 𝔐 was added for syntactical clarification. Thus the shorter form reconstructed here may bear witness to an older text.

Line 4. ועל 𝔐 = [ואל] MurXII. The interchange of אל and על is common among biblical manuscripts.

Lines 4–5. ויתנו הילד בזונה 𝔐 | καὶ ἐδωκαν τα παιδαρια πορναις 𝕲. ו̇י̇.[תנ]ו ה̇.[י]̇ל[ד בזונה ויזנו]. Owing to considerations of space a longer text is reconstructed here. We suggest a textual plus at this point, *viz.* the verb ויזנו—a reconstructed variant without parallel in other witnesses. With the inclusion of this plus, the second tricolon of v. 3 would more precisely parallel the third, making ויזנו parallel to 𝔐's וישתו. *BHS* suggests that the word וישתו represents an addition, since it is without a counterpart in the preceding member. A possible textual development may be suggested: at an early stage, the text read ויתנו הילד בזונה והילדה מכרו ביין 'and they bartered a boy for a whore, and sold a girl for wine'. This was followed with the addition of וישתו 'that they drank' (the text of 𝔐) to the end of the stich. Finally, ויזנו was added to the version we have reconstructed in MS 4612/1 by a scribe in an effort to balance the parallels: 'and they bartered a boy for a whore *and whored*, and sold a girl for wine that they drank'.

Line 6. [וכל גלי]̇ל[ו]̇ת = 4QXII𝑔 (ו[כ]ל גלילת) MurXII 𝔐 (both וכל גלילות). The trace after *lamed* can be identified with either *waw* or *taw*, so that the reading גלילת with the shorter spelling of the *nomen regum* (= 4QXII𝑔) cannot be excluded.

Line 8. [קל מהרה] = 𝔐 | קל מהר 4QXII𝑔. 4QXII𝑔 has a shorter reading of the adverb. Our graphical reconstruction seems to give preference to the longer version of 𝔐.

Line 8. א̇ש̇[יב. Traces of ink on the fold are consistent with the left leg of ʾ*alep* followed by the upper right corner of *šin* with a hook to the left, enabling the reading א̇ש̇[יב.

Line 8. גמ[לכֶ̇ם]. Instead of *kap* and final *mem*, *šin* followed by another letter would be just as feasible.

---

[5] Such a shift can be found in the parallel text of 2 Sam 10.16 ושובך and 1 Chr 19.16 ושופך. Cf. the interchange between 𝔐 חרב and ܣ חרף (Gen 31.40); 𝔐 והמצפה and ܣ והמצבה (Gen 31.49); 𝔐 נשפת and ܣ נשבת (Exod 15.10).

Figure 26.5. *A reconstruction of Ḥev(?)Joel*

F. Textual Character, Format, and Provenance

Armin Lange classifies this text among those 'which cannot be classified text-typologically because of textual damage' (Lange 2010, 55–56). Our reconstruction may suggest that this scroll could be characterized as non-aligned, which would conform to what we see in other copies of the Twelve from the Judaean Desert. Most of the scrolls from Cave 4 show no clear alignment with either the 𝔐 or 𝔊 version (4QXII[a,c,d?,e,g], thus Brooke 2006, 21–27; cf. Weissenberg 2012a).[6] Lange differs somewhat in his understanding of 4QXII[g], which he sees as a semi-Masoretic text that is the result of stylistic, linguistic, and contextual harmonizations and improvements of its parent text (Lange 2013). Also 4QXII[c], which contains parts of Hosea, Joel, Amos, and Zephaniah, contains some harmonizing readings (Fuller 2013). The Greek ḤevXII from the second half of the first century BC represents a correction of the Old Greek towards a proto-Masoretic text. 4QXII[b], 4QXII[f], and probably 4QXII[d] too, can be classified as 𝔐-like scrolls (Brooke 2006, 32). The proto-Masoretic MurXII (Mur 88) is likely to have contained all the Twelve in a high quality scroll with a length of 4.9 m. MurXII displays a number of orthographic differences from 𝔐 as well as a few substantial variants (Nah 1.5; 2.13; 3.8; Hab 3.10 [where it adapts זרמו מים from Ps 77.18 for זרם מים 𝔐], cf. *DJD* 2:183–84; Brooke 2006, 27–28).

The script of MS 4612/1 is ornamental, written by a skilled scribe. The large top margin of 3.5 cm would fit Emanuel Tov's criteria for *de luxe* editions (Tov 2004, 125–29). However, it should be noted that the skin of this scroll was crudely prepared.

---

[6] 4QXII[c] and the text of Hosea represented by 4QpHos[a] seem to be related to the *Vorlage* of 𝔊 (Brooke 2006, 32). 4QXII[e] is characterized as non-aligned by Tov and Brooke, and as proto-Masoretic by Lange (Tov 2002, 156; Brooke 2006, 24; Lange 2009, 339).

The combination of a narrow column (7.5 cm) and a large top margin suggests that this scroll displayed the peculiar format with columns that are both high and narrow, evident in MS 4611 (Lev) and MS 2713 (Josh), scrolls that were also inscribed in the same ornamental late Herodian script type.[7] Taking the large top margin and late date into consideration it seems probable that this fragment survived from a large scroll that also contained several other books from the Twelve.

MS 4612/1 and MurXII display a striking resemblance in their scribal hands and the appearance of the leather.[8] The colour of MS 4612/1 is consistently more red where the surface has abraded, but, where the surface is preserved, both are very similar in their shades of dark brown. The surface of MurXII is light brown where it has abraded. The fragments for both scrolls have suffered significant warping, but this effect is more prominent in the much thicker fragment MS 4612/1. These resemblances could suggest a Murabbaʿat provenance for MS 4612/1. However, there were no multiple copies of any single composition recovered from this site.

The mineral analysis is not conclusive, but probably suggests a place of discovery other than either Qumran and Murabbaʿat. The elegant post-Herodian script points to a probable association with a Bar Kokhba cave, perhaps in Naḥal Ḥever.

With a line length of 7.5 cm one would need *c.* 26 additional lines to complete the book of Joel.

---

[7] See the chapter by Kipp Davis, p. 129.

[8] Torleif Elgvin and Kipp Davis examined MurXII and other scrolls from Murabbaʿat at the IAA scrollery 5–6 February, 2014.

Part Four

—

Writings (Ketuvim)

XX

MS 5233/2. 4Q(?)Ps (Ps 9.10, 12–13)

Torleif Elgvin

DSS F.118, DSS F.Ps2

A. Physical Description

The fragment is dark brown with some lighter spots, and measures 1.4 × 3.7 cm. The thickness is 0.67±0.1 mm. The skin can be seen under the sediments. The parchment has darkened and the text can now only be read in the infrared photographs. Two lines are clearly visible, with a spacing of 7.5 mm between them. Letters measure approximately 2.2–2.7 mm high, with word-spacing between 1.6–1.8 mm. There are minute traces of a possible top line, or supralinear addition, which is situated approximately 4 mm above the first extant line.

According to Ira Rabin the mineral analysis suggests preparation of the parchment outside the Dead Sea region. There are traces of cave deposits on the surface, some of which are visible on the colour photographs. The skin contains substantial amounts of lead (Rabin, unpublished report).

B. Palaeography

Michael Langlois notes some features that develop in the Herodian period and concludes that MS 5233/2 was copied in the second half (most likely third quarter) of the first century BC (see p. 90).

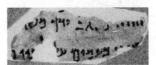

Figure 27.1. MS 5233/2

C. MS 5233/2

]○[ ]○[	1
[○משׁ לֹדך גב○○ oooo[	2
[כ תֹיו] [לֹ] [עלֹ בעמים oooo○הֹ]	3

Notes on Readings

Line 1. If the remnants of these two letters belonged to an ordinary line, there would be a line spacing of 4 mm between lines 1 and 2, and 7.5 mm between lines 2 and 3 of this fragment. A supralinear insertion would fit nicely between 7.5 mm of line spacing. Therefore it seems better to understand these letters as a supralinear addition of at least two words. We see the lower part of a descender and, to its left, the base line of another letter such as *bet* or *kap*. The tip of the descender is thin compared with the wider ductus elsewhere in the fragment. This first letter represents either *qop* or a final *kap, nun,* or *ṣade*.

　　Line 2. ○○○○[. We see the lower half of six downstrokes, which suggests the presence of some narrow letters.

　　Line 3. ○○○○הֿ[. The two traces that follow *he* either represent a single letter, such as *reš* or *dalet*, or two letters.

D. Scrolls of Psalms from the Judaean Desert

Around 40 scrolls that contain portions of the Psalms have been found in the Judaean Desert. Thirty-six of these were discovered at Qumran, two at Masada, and one in Naḥal Ḥever (*DJD* 39:173, 181). A fragment preserving Ps 22.3–12 is in the possession of SWBTS (Loveless 2012, 90) and another Psalms fragment is included in The Green Collection. Some of these scrolls may be collections of different kinds of psalms for liturgical use.

　　Psalms 9 is included in 11QPs^c, 11QPs^d (Ps 9.3–8; 9.3–6, *DJD* 23:49–76), and 5/6HevPs (Ps 9.12–22, *DJD* 38:141–66). All these scrolls follow the Masoretic order of the Psalms. There is no actual overlap between our fragment and 11QPs^c,d, while the last preserved letter of MS 5233/2 overlaps with 5/6HevPs. 11QPs^c is mid- or late Herodian, 11QPs^d late Herodian, and 5/6HevPs post-Herodian. Thus MS 5233/2 is the oldest extant witness of Psalm 9.

Table 13. Psalm 9 in Scrolls from the Judaean Desert

Psalm	Text and Publication	Date
Ps 9.3–6	11QPs^d (*DJD* 23:63–76)	mid 1st cent. AD
Ps 9.3–8	11QPs^c (*DJD* 23:49–61)	early-mid 1st cent. AD
Ps 9.10–13	MS 5233/2	mid-late 1st cent. BC
Ps 9.12–22	5/6HevPs (*DJD* 38:141–66)	mid 1st cent. AD

E. MS 5233/2 (Ps 9.9–10, 12–13)

1	[　　　　　　　　] ○[ ]○[　　　　　　　]
2	[במישרים ¹⁰ויהי] יְהֹוָהֿ מִֿשֹֿגב לדך משגֿ[ב לעתות בצרה ¹²זמרו]
3	[ליהוה ישב ציון]הֹגִֿיֹדֹוֹ בעמים על[י]ל[ו]תֿיו ¹³כ[י דרש דמים]

Translation

1.　　[　　]…[　　]…[

2.　　[with equity.] ¹⁰ YHWH[is]a haven for the oppressed, a have[n in times of trouble. ¹² Sing]

3.   [to YHWH who reigns in Zion;]declare his d[e]e[d]s among the peoples. [13] F[or he who requites bloodshed]

Notes on Reconstruction and Comments

The text is written in prose format, also found in 24 scrolls of the Psalms that do not display a sticho-metric layout (Tov 2004, 169).

No remains of margins are visible and the exact placement of the beginning and end of the lines is not certain. The preserved text corresponds with Ps 9.10, 12, and the beginning of v. 13. If the fragment preserved a complete running text from Ps 9.10–13 this would result in an unusual line-length of some 92 letter spaces measuring approximately 15–16.5 cm. Such a wide column is anomalous among the Psalms scrolls and can only be found in 4QPs^k (4Q92).[1] A text with such a small script in such a wide column would be unprecedented. It seems more likely that MS 5233/2 was structured in columns that were closer to a conventional width around 9 or 10 cm, if not smaller. By reconstructing only the extant vv. 10, 12, and the beginning of 13 we can position the text comfortably between right and left margins with a column width of approximately 7.5–8 cm (*c.* 47 letter spaces) as illustrated in *Figure 27.2a*.[2]

Line 2 (9.10). יֿהֿוֿהֿ. The lower parts of six downstrokes are compatible with the Tetragrammaton.

Line 3 (9.12). [הֿגִֿגֿידֿוֿ בעמים על[י]לֿ[ו]תֿיו. After the probable *he* one can see traces of the tops of three or four letters. These traces may be compatible with the word הגידו (= 𝔐), but *dalet* is highly uncertain as there is no trace of the top of the downstroke. The final *waw* lacks its characteristic hook. Judged by the appearance of the ink traces, it is not easy to come up with an alternative option to הֿגִֿגֿידֿוֿ. In 𝔐 הגידו is followed by the phrase בעמים עלילותיו. There are only three other occurrences of this construction in the Hebrew Bible (Isa 12.4; Ps 105.1; 1 Chr 16.8) and in these cases the phrase is preceded by the *hipᶜil* plural verb הודיעו. However, the extant traces belonging to the first word cannot be read as הודיעו, nor do they correspond to another conjugation of נגד.

It is suggested here that this text represents a free rendering of Ps 9. The supralinear addition above line 1 cannot be identified with any phrases or with any obvious errors in the reconstruction of v. 10. The free insertion of an additional stich, however, would make sense. Further, if this manuscript included v. 11, it would have been written in an inordinately long line. I tentatively suggest that v. 10 was followed directly by v. 12—possibly on the same line.

One option for the supralinear addition would be that the text of v. 11 was written above line 2. The reconstruction in *Figure 27.2b* shows how this may plausibly have occurred, with an alignment of the two small traces in this line corresponding to the final *kap* in שמך and the medial *kap* in כי. The full supralinear line would then read [ויבטחו בך יודעי שמ]ךֿ כֿ[י לא עזבת דרשיך יהוה]. This reading may find some support in the vertical alignment of the reconstruction, which would end fairly close to the transition between vv. 10 and 12. However, it should be noted that this remains a tentative suggestion.

One can minimally posit that v. 12 followed immediately after v. 10, but it is not known whether the absence of v. 11 represents an alternative version, an omission, or a scribal error. We do not know what kind of scroll MS 5233/2 represents—some kind of psalms scroll or a different kind of text quoting or

---

[1] In the reconstructed columns of this manuscript 'col. I contains *c.* 77–89 letter spaces per line, and col. II had *c.* 81–94' (*DJD* 16:123). 4QPs^k contains remains of two adjoining columns, preserved on one large fragment with a small piece attached. Col. i includes Ps 135.6–16, and col. ii Ps 99.1–5. Such an arrangement of these psalms is not known from other scrolls. One or more psalms would have been located between these two. Cp. also 4QPs^q, with a line length of 67–75 letter spaces in col. i, and 67–87 in col. ii (*DJD* 16:145).

[2] I am indebted to Kipp Davis, who first suggested this option.

alluding to Ps 9. A column width of 7.5–8 cm suggests that this fragment belonged to a small-sized or medium-sized scroll.

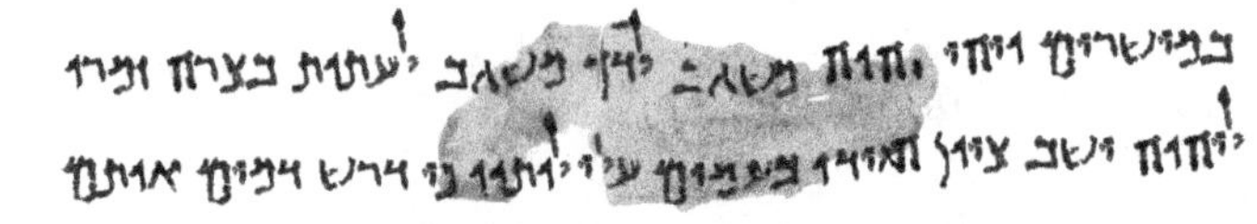

Figure 27.2a. A reconstruction of 4Q(?)Ps

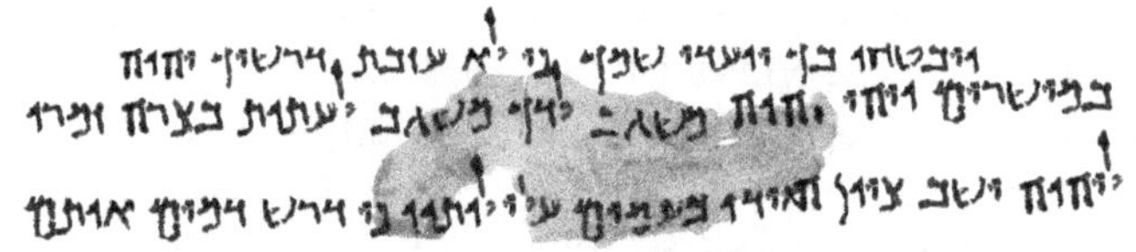

Figure 27.2b. 4Q(?)Ps: Ps 9.10, 12–13 with supralinear insertion of v. 11

XXI

MS 4612/11. 4Q(?)Prov (Prov 4.23–5.1)

Torleif Elgvin

DSS F.119, DSS F.Prov1

A. Physical Description

The fragment measures 2.4 × 4.7 cm and has a varying thickness of 0.2–0.5 mm. It preserves parts of three lines with a line spacing of 7 mm. The parchment is dark brown, with a lighter section at the left edge where the top layer has flaked off. The skin can be seen under the sediments. Minerals from cave sediments are equally distributed on the fragment (Rabin, unpublished report).

There are some suspicious features that possibly cast doubt on the authenticity of this text. First, in a few instances strokes of ink appear to follow the contours of damage. The second *mem* in line 1 forms an odd ligature with the preceding letter along the edge of the damaged part of the surface. The third *mem* in line 2 is oversized, and the pen strokes neatly surround an abrasion. Second, there are possibly two places in line 2 where there are small traces of ink on the underlayer where the surface has flaked off (cf. the *taw* and the *ḥet*). Finally, along the bottom edge there is a very well preserved trace of ink where the surface is obviously worn (the first *kap* on line 3). In spite of these observations, there is insufficient evidence to make any firm judgments about the authenticity of the text.

B. Palaeography

According to Ada Yardeni the script is a late Hasmonaean formal hand dating from *c.* 75–50 BC. Michael Langlois designates the script as a late Hasmonaean semiformal book hand copied around the middle of the first century BC (see p. 84).

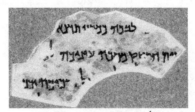

Figure 28.1. MS 4612/11

C. MS 4612/11

‏[○]‏[‏לבכה כממנֹו תוצא]‏	1
‏[‏○ים הרחק ממכה עיניכה ל○]‏	2
‏[‏לֹ]‏ [‏לֹ]‏ [‏○ל ○○כיכה יכנֹ]‏	3
‏[‏לֹ]‏	4

Notes on Readings

Line 2. ‏○ים[‏. The traces of the first letter are compatible with *ḥet* or *taw*.

Line 2. ‏[○ל‏. *Lamed* is followed by a baseline of one letter or, less probably, traces of two.

Line 3. ‏○○כיכה‏. We see part of a downstroke of the first letter. The traces of the following letter are compatible with *dalet*, *kap*, or *reš*.

D. Scrolls of Proverbs from the Judaean Desert

Four other manuscripts with text from Proverbs have been published. Only 4QProv[b] preserves a more substantial amount of text. Both 4QProv[a] and 4QProv[b] are dated around the turn of the era (*DJD* 16:183, 185). Émile Puech identified a third copy in early Herodian script (4QProv[c], 4Q103a), which preserves Prov 9.16; 10.30–32 (Puech 2001, 121–23). Hanan Eshel identified a fourth copy (6QpapProv, 6Q30), which preserves Prov 11.5–7, 10[1] in a late Herodian cursive script (Eshel 2003a). MS 4612/11 is the earliest witness to Proverbs.

Our text is written in prose format, different from 4QProv[a] (4Q102) and 4QProv[b] (4Q103), but similar to 4QProv[c]. 4QProv[a] and 4QProv[b] are written with short *vacats* between the stichs, more consistently in 4QProv[a] than 4QProv[b]. In 𝔐[L] and 𝔐[A] proverbs are written in stichometric form. Both 4QProv[a] and 4QProv[b] are textually close to 𝔐.

E. MS 4612/11 (Prov 4.22–5.1)

‏[‏ולכל בשרמה מרפא 23מכל משמר נ]‏צֹ[ר]‏ לבכה כממנֹו תוצא]‏ות חיים 24הסר]‏	1
‏[‏ממכה עקשות פה ולזות שפ]‏תים הרחק ממכה 25עיניכה לנֹ]‏כח יביטו]‏	2
‏[‏ועפעפיכה יישרו נגדכה 26פלס מעג]‏לֹ[‏ רג]‏לֹ[‏כה ו]‏כֹל דֹרֹכיכה יכנֹ]‏ 27אל תט]‏	3
‏[‏ימין ושמאול הסר רגלכה מרע 5.1בני לחכמתי הקשיבה]‏לֹ[‏תבונתי הט]‏	4

Translation

1.   [and healing to all *their* flesh. ²³ More than all that you guard, gu]ar[d] *your* heart, for from it [life] proce[eds. ²⁴ Put]
2.   [crooked speech away from you; keep de]vious talk far from you. ²⁵ Let *your* eyes[look]forwa[rd,]
3.   [your gaze be straight ahead. ²⁶ Survey the cours]e[you ta]ke[, and a]ll *your* ways will prosper.[²⁷ Do not swerve]

---

[1] The fragment probably omits Prov 11.8–10a, perhaps due to a scribal error.

4.   [to the right or the left; keep your feet from evil. ⁵·¹ My son, listen to my wisdom; incline] to[my insight]

Notes on Reconstruction and Comments

The lines are restored with 54–56 letter spaces, and the column width is estimated to 9 cm.

Line 1 (4.22). [ולכל בשרמה]. | ולכל בשרו 𝔐 | και παση σαρκι 𝕲 𝑆 (ܠܟܠ ܒܣܪܗܘܢ). The *BHS* apparatus suggests emending בשרו to בשרם. The reading of 𝔐 would be too short to align this line with the right margin. We prefer to reconstruct the text with the short spelling כל and the long plural suffix -מה (for בשרמה cf. 11QTᵃ XXXIV 9; XLVII 10). We base this on the consistent spelling of the second person singular suffix -כה as opposed to the short form כל in line 3.

Line 1 (4.23). [מכל משמר] = 𝔐 | πασηι (= בכל) φυλακηι 𝕲 𝑆 (ܒܟܠ ܘܗܡ).

Line 1 (4.23). (לבך) 𝔐 = לבבה.

Line 1 (4.23). (כי־ממנו) 𝔐 = כממנו. The conjunction כי is shortened and assimilated into the preposition. In five cases כי is connected to the following word without a word space, but not shortened as in this case (1QSa I 10; 4QGenᵍ 1 3, 12; 2 8; 4QJerᵃ VII 3, cf. Tov 2004, 133–34).

Line 2 (4.24). (ממך) 𝔐 = ממכה.

Line 2 (4.25). (עיניך) 𝔐 = עיניכה.

Line 3 (4.26). (רגלך וכל) = רג[ל]כה ו[כ̇]ל 𝔐 | σοις ποσιν και 𝕲. The available space between the two *lameds* hardly allows for the restoration of the *plene* form וכול.

Line 3 (4.26). (דרכיך) 𝔐 = דֿרֿכיכה.

Line 4. (4.27). [רגלכה] = (רגלך) 𝔐.

The text contains some specific orthographic features: the second person singular suffix is consistently spelled -כה, and the conjunction כי is assimilated to the subsequent preposition. These features are in line with the so-called Qumran scribal practice (Tov 2004, 261–73).[2]

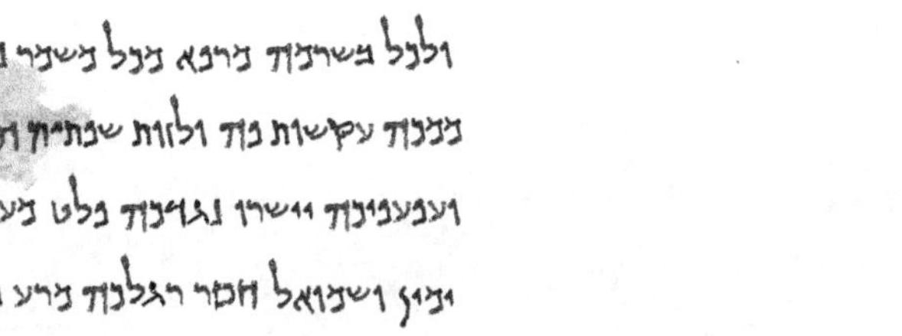

Figure 28.2. *A reconstruction of 4Q(?)Prov*

---

[2] If we exclude the liturgical scrolls 11QPsᵃ·ᵇ, Tov lists 23 biblical scrolls with these orthographic and morphological features (2004, 339–40). To this list one should now add MS 4612/11 (Prov), MS 5214/1 (Deut 6), perhaps also MS 5480 (1 Sam 5).

XXII

MS 5441. 4Q(?)Ruth (Ruth 2.1–2)

Torleif Elgvin

DSS F.120, DSS F.Ruth1

A. Physical Description

The fragment measures 5.7 × 4.1 cm and has a thickness of 0.58±0.08 mm. The skin can be seen under the sediments on both sides. Parts of three lines are visible, with a line spacing of 7 mm. The fragment preserves a bottom margin of 36 mm, compatible with Tov's main criterion for defining *de luxe* editions (Tov 2004, 125–29). The tanned upper layer of the parchment has flaked off immediately below the preserved part of line 3. However, high-resolution microscopic examination confirms that the surface is largely preserved in the lower part of the fragment, including where we would have expected to see traces of line 4. The parchment is dark brown in colour, lighter brown where the surface has flaked off. The preserved surface is quite smooth and clearly distinguished from the coarse damaged part of the fragment.

According to Ira Rabin's analysis, the Cl/Br ratio indicates preparation of the skin outside the Dead Sea region. Cave sediments can be observed, stronger on the *recto* (hair) side. FTIR spectra did not show calcite (Rabin, unpublished report).

B. Palaeography

According to Michael Langlois, this semiformal but hesitant script exhibits some late Herodian features that suggest it was copied around the middle of the first century AD (see p. 105).

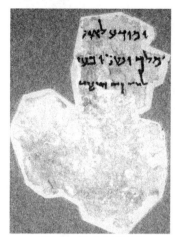

Figure 29.1. MS 5441

C. MS 5441

‬‬°י מודע לאיש[‬	1
‬°מלך ושמו בעז[‬	2
‬לכֹה נה השד[‬	3
‬bottom margin[‬	

Notes on Readings

Line 1. °י[. There is trace of an oblique stroke at the right edge of the fragment, compatible with ʿayin or *mem.*

Line 2. °מלך[. The final *kap* is heavily shaded.

Line 2. The line is not straight, even though the fragment does not show clear signs of shrinking. The second *mem* is set high on the imaginary dryline, and ʿayin is written lower than the neighbouring *bet.*

Line 3. לכֹה נה[. Only the upper part is preserved of both *he*s, as well as of the *kap.* Nevertheless, other readings are not possible. The vertical stroke of *nun* descends below the line. The foot of this letter would have extended below *he.*

D. Ruth Scrolls from the Judaean Desert

Four scrolls of Ruth have been published, two from Cave 2 and two from Cave 4. 4QRuth[a] and 2QRuth[b] are late Hasmonaean (*c.* 50 BC), 4QRuth[b] middle or late Herodian ('the end of the first century BCE or the first half of the first century CE' [*DJD* 16:192, plate XXIV]), and 2QRuth[a] late Herodian (*DJD* 3:72, 74, plates XIV–XIV). MS 5441 is the only witness to Ruth 2.1–2.

E. MS 5441 (Ruth 1.22–2.2)

[קצור שערים ¹ולנע]מֹּי מודע לאישׁ]ה איש גבור] 1
[חיל ממשפחת אל]ימֹלך ושמו בעז] ²ותאמר רות] 2
[המואביה אל נעמי א]לֹכֹה נֹה השד]ה ואלקטה] 3
]bottom margin[

Translation

1. [the barley harvest. ¹ Now Nao]mi had a kinsman on [her]husband's side[, a man of substance,]
2. [of the family of El]imelech, whose name was Boaz.[² Then said Ruth]
3. [the Moabite to Naomi, 'I]would *like to* go to the fie[ld and glean]

Notes on Reconstruction and Comments

The column is narrow with 36–40 letter spaces per line, the column width is estimated at 7 cm. The reconstruction suggests a placement of the fragment in the middle of the column. Other possible locations of the fragment closer to the right margin cannot be excluded.

Line 1 (2.1). מודע = 𝔐^Q 𝔐^Mss | מידע 𝔐^K.

Line 3 (2.2). נה = 𝔐 (נא). The regular spelling of the interjection is נא. It is spelled נה once in 4QParaphrase of Kings (4Q382) 9 6, contracted with the verb, שיבנה. In 1QIsaᵃ the word is commonly spelled נא, but נה appears in Isa 5.3; 7.13; 64.8,[1] as well as in 1QapGen XX 25. As ʾalep was not pronounced, the interchange of ʾalep and he as matres lectionis is easy to understand (Kutscher 1974, 57–60, 164).

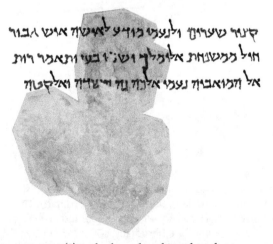

Figure 29.2. *4Q(?)Ruth aligned to the right columnar margin*

---

[1] 1QIsaᵃ IV 15; VI 27; LI 23. The first two cases were noted by Kutscher 1974, 164. In Isa 5.3; 64.8 the interjection is contracted with the verb—the scribes of 1QIsaᵃ often contracted נא with the verb, a feature that appears elsewhere only in 4QParaphrase of Kings 9 6.

F. Small-Sized Scrolls of Lamentations, Ruth, and Canticles

It is noteworthy that among the thirteen copies of Lamentations, Canticles, and Ruth from the Judaean desert, between eight and ten could be classified small-sized.[2] In contrast, both Qoheleth scrolls are closer in size to what we tend to see in the Qumran scrolls.

The dating and format of the scrolls of this group may reflect a diachronic line of development: two normal-sized scrolls are preserved from the mid-first century BC (2QRuth[b] and 4QRuth[a]). Most of the later scrolls of these books are small-sized. 4QLam is early Herodian; 4QRuth[b], 2QRuth[a], MS 5441 and 4Cant[a,b] are mid-Herodian; 3QLam[3] and 4QCant[c] are mid- or late Herodian; 6QCant and 5QLam[a,b] are late Herodian.[4]

Tov suggests that small copies of the five *megillot* were made for liturgical use (Tov 2004, 90; *DJD* 16:197–98).[5] Whether the small-sized scrolls of Ruth and Canticles indicate that these two books, too, were used in liturgical reading remains an open question.[6]

---

[2] Tov's definition of small-sized scrolls (4–14 lines per column) is 'impressionistic' (2004, 84). Two out of four copies of Lamentations are small-sized: 4QLam (early Herodian), 5QLam[a] (early Herodian). The same goes for three out of five copies of Ruth: 2QRuth[a] (late Herodian), 4QRuth[b] (mid-Herodian, *DJD* 16:191–92), and probably the fragment published here. Further, all four copies of Canticles are small-sized: 6QCant (late Herodian), 4QCant[a,b] (both mid-Herodian, my dating), 4QCant[c] (mid- or late Herodian), see Tov 2004, 84–86, 90; *DJD* 16:197–98.

[3] 3QLam is a special case. It is written in a middle or late Herodian script with a medium-sized column in stichometric form (two rows, together 9–10 cm wide), but with miniature letters, 1.5–1.6 mm high. See above, p. 149, especially note 12, on this scroll.

[4] 5QLam[b] is probably written in stichometric form (two rows, together 11 cm wide).

[5] One should be aware that the term 'the five *megillot*' is anachronistic when used about the Second Temple period.

[6] The older book of Lamentations could serve as an example of a small 'scriptural' scroll used in liturgical reading. According to Philip Alexander the small scrolls of Lamentations and 4QapocrLam A (4Q179) were used as mourning liturgies on the ninth of Ab, at least in sectarian circles such as the *Yaḥad* that regarded the present temple as polluted (Alexander 2013).

XXIII

1QDan^a (1Q71) with MS 1926/4a (Dan 2.4–5)

Torleif Elgvin, Årstein Justnes

DSS F.121, DSS F.Dan4

A. History of 1QDan^{a,b}

According to Athanasius Samuel a number of fragments were retrieved from Cave 1 by one of his men in 1948 (Trever 1965, 323; Trever 1977, 123). During a visit to the United States in February 1949 the archbishop handed John C. Trever a tin cigarette box containing some of these fragments, which Trever studied and photographed. He identified remnants of at least five scrolls. Among these were 1QDan^a (1Q71) and 1QDan^b (1Q72) (Trever 1965; Trever 1977, 121–30; cf. Wright 1949, 33).

Dominique Barthélemy published transcriptions of 1QDan^a and 1QDan^b in an appendix to *DJD* 1 without accompanying plates (*DJD* 1:150–52)[1] and suggested that two scribes could have copied different sections of the same Daniel scroll (1QDan^a preserves Dan 1.10–17; 2.2–6 in two columns; 1QDan^b frgs 1–2 preserves Dan 3.22–31 in one column).[2] In 1965 Trever published infrared photos of these fragments with a careful description of leather, letters, and readings, substantially improving on the first publication (Trever 1965). He drew attention to differences in leather, script, and column width between 1QDan^a and 1QDan^b, and concluded that the manuscripts most likely belonged to two separate scrolls. Trever precisely described how already-damaged remnants of these two scrolls together with a third text (1QLitPr^b [1Q34bis]), were stacked and folded together when they were deposited in the cave.[3] While most of the fragments stayed with Athanasius Samuel and were in a poor state of preservation when he published his autobiography in 1966,[4] some small ones including MS 1926/4 were kept by Trever. These were purchased by Martin Schøyen from the Trever family in 1994. Trever had mounted

---

[1] Cf. *DJD* 1:4: 'In the Appendix ... are published transcriptions of fragments of Daniel, etc., which are still with the Syrian Archbishop in America. These fragments came from the last illegal excavations, and are the property of the Jordan Department of Antiquities, with whose permission they are here published, as they are complementary to some fragments found in the excavation.'

[2] G. Ernest Wright (1949, 33) noted that the Daniel fragments were from two different scrolls.

[3] Trever suggested that the fragments had been violently damaged in antiquity, probably at the time of the Roman assault on Qumran in June 68, and that members of the community had then assembled the pieces and deposited them in Cave 1 (1965, 326–27; 1977, 129–30). Joan Taylor has suggested that Cave 1, Cave 4, and the graveyard at Qumran were used as temporary *genizot* or permanent burial places for worn-out Essene scrolls from Judaea (Taylor 2012, 284–306; Taylor 2013, 286–303). The state of these three scrolls could well fit Taylor's theory.

[4] These fragments are now the property of the Syrian Orthodox Church archdiocese, Teaneck, NJ, and were rephotographed in 2009 by Bruce Zuckerman and his team (Zuckerman 2010). The whereabouts of these fragments are not recorded in Tov's recent inventory, although 1QLitPr^b and 1QDan^a are annotated 'A. Samuel' (Tov 2010a, 15, 20).

them in a frame under a glass plate with the description 'Dead Sea Scroll Fragments from Qumran Cave I'.[5]

In March 1995 Bruce Zuckerman and Marilyn Lundberg produced a new series of photographs of these fragments. These bits were part of a group originally labelled by Trever as 'uninscribed fragments', believed to have only consisted of scraps, twine, and skin that had on various occasions broken off from 1QIsaᵃ, 1QS, and 1QapGen. The new photographs were made using visible-spectrum colour, visible-spectrum black-and-white and infrared black-and-white films. While photographs of most of the fragments registered no evidence of textual data, two wads (inseparable stacks of fragments) revealed readable letters when photographed in narrow-band infrared. One of the wads was identified as belonging to the upper margin of the *Genesis Apocryphon* (1Q20, see p. 283). Zuckerman and Lundberg suggested that the other wad (MS 1926/4), which measured 19 × 28 mm, preserved four layers. No letters could be identified on the first layer. On the second layer they were able to read five letters that could be ascribed to 1QDanᵇ. Preserving letters from two lines of Dan 3.26–27, this fragment forms a material join with 1QDanᵇ I 8–10. In the next chapter this piece is designated as 1QDanᵇ frg. 1b. On layer 3 they were able to read an ʾalep (Lundberg and Zuckerman 1996).

In January 2011 Zuckerman and his team rephotographed the two wads using a more advanced technology. On the wad with text from 1QDanᵇ one could now read more letters from layer 3. The lines assigned to layers 2 and 3 were found to be at crossing angles. The script of layer 3 was identified with that of 1QDanᵃ, and the letters were identified with Dan 2.4–5, forming a material joint with 1QDanᵃ 1 ii 5–7. This piece is here designated 1QDanᵃ frg. 2.

In the course of preparing our editions of 1QDanᵃ and 1QDanᵇ we consulted Barthélemy (*DJD* 1:150–52), Trever (1965), and Ulrich (2010, 755–56, 760).[6] We have further consulted the photographs taken by the Zuckerman team of the fragments belonging to the Syrian Orthodox Church archdiocese, Teaneck, New Jersey (see note 4 p. 247). These photographs, available on Inscriptifact, show that the fragments have badly deteriorated over the years. Despite this they reveal some notable details from 1QDanᵃ and 1QDanᵇ that as far as we know have not been previously published.

B. Physical Description

In *DJD* 1 Barthélemy gave the following short description of the physical features of 1QDanᵃ: 'Un seul fragment contenant deux demi-colonnes ... Lignes fines de ± 10 cm. de long. Colonnes de ± 15 lignes, soit ± 12 cm. de hauteur inscrite. Marges supérieures de 2 cm. Intercolonnement de 2 cm' (p. 150). Trever (1965, 325, 331) described the material as 'cream white' or 'cream-colored leather more like that of *1QS*'. The text is 'beautifully inscribed in perfectly preserved black ink', written on fine leather which was carefully ruled (Trever 1977, 129). The top margin of 1QDanᵃ (19 mm) is preserved only in col. i of the main fragment. The line spacing is *c.* 7 mm. The quality of parchment and script shows that this was a high quality scroll.

According to Trever, 1QLitPrᵃ (1Q34) is likewise from a beautifully inscribed scroll, but of very thin leather. The fragments of 1QDanᵃ,ᵇ consist of 'much thicker leather (about the thickness of *1QpHab*)' (1965, 325). Trever's description suggests that 1QLitPrᵃ and 1QDanᵃ were written on parchment, not

---

[5] On Trever's mounted plate there is a parchment piece without writing, measuring 9 × 22 mm, as well as a piece of linen cloth measuring 21 × 40 mm (excluding loose threads on both ends). The density of the weaving is 11 warp threads by 11 weft threads per cm. Attached to the top left of this piece of cloth is some dark material, which according to Trever's notes represents gelatinized leather from an unidentified scroll from Cave 1.

[6] Ulrich does not seem to engage with the readings in Trever 1965.

rough leather.[7] The visible surface of the 1QDan[b] part of the wad is smooth, which could indicate that this scroll also was made of well-prepared parchment.

The fragment that Trever published is a composite that consists of several pieces joined together. We have designated it frg. 1.[8] On Trever's plate VIIc there is a fragment ('frg. 4') 'originally found tucked inside the matted mass', which 'fell out during the removal of the second layer'. On the basis of its colour and texture (perhaps also the visible vertical and horizontal ruling lines), Trever associates this fragment with 1QDan[a] (1965, 326). The left edge of the fragment preserves sewing traces. The fragment measures 37 × 15 mm and preserves the upper left portion of a final letter from the end of a line. In our edition here we have designated it frg. 3. We have been unable to locate this fragment in any subsequent photographs.

Fragment 2, the Schøyen fragment, measures 19 × 18 mm, and is dark brown to black in colour. The fragment is a complex assemblage consisting of a number of layers of parchment bonded together. According to Ira Rabin and Reinhard Franke the wad consisted of three layers (not four), each c. 0.4 mm thick.[9] The right-side-thickness of the wad is 0.9 mm (two layers), and the left-side-thickness is 1.23 mm (three layers). Layer 3, the bottom layer, is 1QDan[a], with letters appearing in grey on the infrared photo. Layer 2 is 1QDan[b], with letters appearing more clearly in black. The uppermost layer to the left revealed traces of ink that we have not been able to identify.

C. Palaeography

Trever (1965, 333–34) described the handwriting of 1QDan[a] as follows:

> The scribe who executed this scroll of *Daniel* had no peers among the scribes of Qumrân, as far as this author can judge from the examples of script he has seen. The regularity of the letters and the attention to minute details to finish each letter artistically approach the quality of the finest Masoretic scribal calligraphy of the Middle Ages. The script impresses the author as the most advanced of any at Qumran, not far removed from the Wadi Murabba'at biblical fragments. The tendency toward the more regular heights of the letters, approaching the appearance of the printed page, is to be noted.

According to Trever (1970, 282; 1977, 134–35) the scribal hands in 1QDan[a] and MasShirShabb (Mas 1k) are very similar and possibly identical. This suggestion was noted neither in the *DJD* edition of Mas-ShirShabb nor in the publication by Newsom and Yadin in *Masada VI* (*DJD* 11:239–40; Talmon and Yadin 1999, 120). Ornamental late Herodian hands of this type are often dated after AD 70, but the discovery of 1QDan[a] and MasShirShabb at sites that we understand to have been abandoned at this time would suggest that these scrolls were written before the First Jewish Revolt. Trever dates the script of 1QDan[a]

---

[7] But cf. Wright 1949, 33: 'In the matted mass of leather fragments were three sections from Daniel in addition to several fragments from some other piece of Hebrew religious literature.' The cream-white colour may suggest that 1QDan[a] belongs to Rabin's carefully prepared 'Western type' of parchment together with 1QS, 1QSb, 1QIsa[a], and the 1QapGen repair sheet (see p. 64).

[8] Cf. Trever 1965, 325–26: 'Several small fragments with portions of letters were found to belong to the lower part of the larger fragment, with the result that the final photograph is composed from the several photographs which preserve every possible letter of the text ... This composite photograph became necessary, since the badly disintegrated lower right portion began to crumble toward the end of the process, and the earlier photographs preserved the text at that point more fully. But only small parts of a few letters were lost at this badly disintegrated point by the time the assembled fragments were finally mounted for preservation.'

[9] In October 2012 Rabin and Franke measured the thickness of the Daniel wad using a Dino-Lite digital microscope.

'perhaps as late as A.D. 60' (Trever 1965, 334). The late palaeographical features of 1QDan[a] would be more readily understood if this scroll belonged to a post-70 deposit.

D. Daniel Scrolls from the Judaean Desert

In addition to the two copies from Cave 1, we know of six other manuscripts with text from Cave 4 and 6 and four fragments of unknown origin:

Table 14. A synopsis of Judaean Desert scrolls containing text from the Book of Daniel

Scroll	Content	Date[10]
4QDan[a] (4Q112)	Dan 1.16–20; 2.9–11; 2.19–3.2; 4.29–30; 5.5–7, 12–14, 16–19; 7.5–7; 7.25–8.5; 10.16–20; 11.13–16; 12.27–28(?)	Late Hasmonaean or early Herodian (mid-first century BC)
4QDan[b] (4Q113)	Dan 5.10–12, 14–16, 19–22; 6.8–22; 6.27–7.6; 7.11(?); 7.26–8.8; 8.13–16	Herodian (AD 20–50)
4QDan[c] (4Q114)	Dan 10.5–9, 11–16, 21; 11.1–2, 13–17, 25–29	Early Hasmonaean (late second or beginning of the first century BC)
4QDan[d] (4Q115)	Dan 3.5–8, 23–25; 4.5–9, 12–16; 7.15–23	Early Herodian (25–1 BC)
4QDan[e] (4Q116)	Dan 9(?)	Early Hasmonaean (late second or beginning of the first century BC)
6QpapDan (6Q7)	Dan 8.16–17(?), 20–21(?); 10.8–16; 11.33–36, 38	Herodian[11]
DSS F.Dan2	Dan 6.22–24	
DSS F.Dan3[12]	Dan 7.18–19	
APU 5, DSS F.Dan1[13]	Dan 5.13–16	
DSS F.Dan6[14]	Dan 10.18–20	

The presence of as many as eight copies in the Qumran caves shows that 'the book of Daniel the prophet' (a citation formula used in 4QFlor [4Q174] II 3) was considered an important writing by the *Yaḥad* only two generations after the book was finalized. A number of Daniel-related writings were also retrieved from the Qumran caves. Among those are 4QPrNab ar (4Q242), 4QpsDan[a–c] ar (4Q243–4Q245), and 4QapocrDan ar (4Q246).[15] Some of these are dependent on the Aramaic *Vorlage* of 𝔊 (Segal 2013).[16]

    There is some overlap between our text and 4QDan[a]. The latter preserves Dan 1.16–20.

---

[10] On the dating of the 4QDaniel scrolls, see *DJD* 16:240–41, 256, 270, 279, 287.

[11] Baillet's dating of the scroll to *c.* 50 BC (*DJD* 3:114) is probably not correct. The forms of *bet*, *yod*, and *lamed* suggest a middle Herodian date, cf. the script of 4QDan[a], dated by Cross to AD 20–50 (Cross 1961b, Fig. 2, line 6). Ulrich (2001, 574) suggests the first half of the first century AD.

[12] These are papyri purchased by Southwestern Baptist Theological Seminary in January 2010 from the Kando family (Loveless 2012, 91; Patterson 2012, 33–34).

[13] This fragment belongs to Azusa Pacific University.

[14] This fragment belongs to The Green Collection.

[15] On the Daniel-related writings from Qumran and their relation to the 𝔐 and 𝔊 recensions of Daniel, see Hoegetorp 2010.

[16] The textual and literary tradition of Daniel seems quite fluid both in the second and first centuries BC. The Greek translation, probably made as early as 150–130 BC, provides evidence for a literary form different from 𝔐, in part reflecting a different Aramaic *Vorlage* (Rösel 2013).

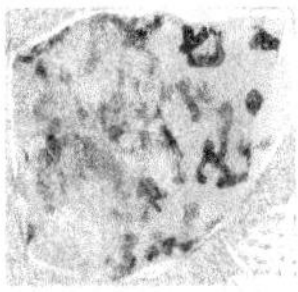

Figure 30/31. MS 1926/4

E. MS 1926/4a

○[1

[○○א ○[2

[נני ○ל○[3

Notes on Readings

Line 1. ○[. This letter can be *reš*, *dalet*, *waw*, or *yod*.

F. 1QDanᵃ frg. 1 i

top margin   [

[אׁשי למלך ויאמר דניאל אל   1

[הסריסים על דניאל חנניה   2

[את עבדיך ימים עשרה ויתׁ○○   3

[ׁמ נשתה ויראו לפניך מראינׁו   4

[○תבג המלך וכאשר תראה   5

[הׁם לדבׁר הזה וינסם ימים   6

[○אה מראׁיהם טוב ובריאי   7

[לך ויהי ○מלצר   8

[להםׁ] [זרעׁים   9

[מׁדעׁ]   10

Notes on Readings

Line 3. ויתׁ○○. The traces of the two last letters are only visible on Trever's photographs. Barthélemy (*DJD* 1:150) read ויתׁנׁוׁ.

Line 4. נשתה. Barthélemy and Ulrich read *waw* before this word. Already in 1965, however, Trever (1965, 330) noted that 'there is no *waw* at the beginning of the word NŠTH, but the final *mem* of the previous word, WMYM, is partially visible. It is perfectly clear on the color transparency, and an infrared photograph would probably bring out this detail.'[17]

Line 5. ○תבג[. Only the baseline of the first letter is preserved.

Line 6. הׁם[. The small trace preceding *mem* is compatible with the left part of the crossbar of *he*. Cf. the second word in the next line.

---

[17] Trever repeated this wish for infrared photographs in several places of his edition. The infrared photographs produced by WSR have in many regards fulfilled this wish.

Line 7. ‏‏°אה מראיהם‎[. Barthélemy (*DJD* 1:150) read only ‏א’יהם‎[while Ulrich reads ‏גר[‏‏א‏ֹ‏ה‏]‏ מר[‏א’יהם‎.
Trever (1965, 330) had already detected portions of the medial *mem*, 'and before them traces of the
ʾaleph and *he* of the previous word'.

Line 8. ‏°מלצר‎. Only two small traces of ink belonging to the first letter are preserved on either side
of a crack; one to the upper left of the *yod* in the preceding word, and one to the lower right of the *mem*.
The traces are compatible with the upper right part and tip of the left downstroke of *he* and *ḥet*.

G. 1QDanᵃ frg. 1 ii

‏כשדיים להגיד‎]	2
‏המלך ויאמ°‏ להם‎]°	3
‏לדעת את החלום וידבר‎‏ֹ‏°]	4
‏*vacat* מלכא לעלמין ח‎]	5
‏ופשרא נחוה ענא מלכא‎‏ֹ‏]	6
‏אזדא די הן לא תהוד‎°]	7
‏תתעבדון ובתיכ‎‏ו‏‏ן‏]	8
]° ‏נ‏‏ו‏‏ֹ‏‏נ‏°[	9

Notes on Readings

Line 4.]°‏וידבר‎‏ֹ‏. The downstroke of *reš* is preserved.
  Line 8. ‏ובתיכן‎‏ו‏. Traces of the final *nun* can be seen on Plate V in Trever (1965).

H. 1QDanᵃ frg. 3

Trever's plate VII.c depicts a small fragment, which he described as a 'fragment of cream-colored
leather (3,7 × 1,5 cm)' (1965, 336). This fragment preserves the left edge of a sheet with traces of sewing,
and one vertical and five horizontal ruling lines.

[	1
°[	2
[	3
[	4
[	5

Notes on Readings

According to Trever the fragment 'seems to have come from the left edge of Column II of *1 Q Danᵃ*' (1965,
331; cf. 336). He deduces from this that the first sheet of the scroll contained three columns of text.
  Line 2. Trever (1965, 326) understood the trace to belong to the top-left part of a final letter. The
shape would fit a final *nun*, less probably a final *kap*, *reš* or *dalet*. This letter could belong to [‏הדמין‎] of
line 7, in which case the fragment would preserve 1QDanᵃ frg. 1 col. ii l. 6–10.

I. 1QDanᵃ II 1–10 (frg. 1 i; Dan 1.10–17)

A comparison between cols i and ii of 1QDanᵃ frg. 1 suggests that the scroll probably had columns of 18 or 19 lines, which would produce a column height of *c.* 12.6–13.3 cm.[18] 1QDanᵃ 1 i–ii represent cols II–III in the original scroll.

top margin

1	[כגילכם וחיבתם את ר[אֹשי למלך ¹¹ויאמר דניאל אל
2	[המלצר אשר מנה שר] הסריסים על דניאל חנניה
3	[מישאל ועזריה ¹²נס נא]את עבדיך ימים עשרה ויתֹנֹוֹ
4	[לנו מן הזרעים ונאכלה ומי[ֹם נשתה ¹³ויראו לפניך מראינו
5	[ומראה הילדים האכלים את]פֹּתבג המלך וכאשר תראה
6	[עשה עם עבדיך ¹⁴וישמע ל]הֹם לדבֹר הזה וינסם ימים
7	[עשרה ¹⁵ומקצת ימים עשרה נ]רֹאֹה מראֹיהם טוב ובריאי
8	[בשר מן כל הילדים האכלים את פתבג המ]לך ¹⁶ויהי הֹמלצר
9	[נשא את פתבגם ויין משתיהם ונתן]להֹם זרעֹים
10	[¹⁷והילדים האלה ארבעתם נתן להם האלהים]מֹֹדֹעֹ[והשכל]

Translation

1. [¹⁰ of your age — and you will put]my [l]ife in jeopardy with the king.' ¹¹ Daniel replied to
2. [the guard whom the chief] officer [had put in charge]of Daniel, Hananiah,
3. [Mishael and Azariah, ¹² 'Please test]your servants for ten days, giving
4. [us legumes to eat and wat]er to drink. ¹³ Then compare our appearance
5. [with that of the youths who eat of]the king's food, and as you see fit, so you may freely
6. [do with your servants.' ¹⁴ He agreed t]o this plan of theirs, and tested them for [ten] days.
7. [¹⁵ When the ten days were over,]they looked better and healthier
8. [than all the youths who were eating of the k]ing's[food.] ¹⁶ So the guard
9. [kept on removing their food, and the wine they were supposed to drink, and gave]them *vegeta-bles.*
10. [¹⁷ God made all four of these young men]intelligent[and proficient]

Notes on Reconstruction and Comments

Line 1 (1.10). [כגילכם (אשר הילדים מן)] = 𝔐 θ´ (παρα τα παιδαρια τα συνηλικα υμων) ¦ παρα τους συντρεφομενους υμιν νεανιας των αλλογενων 𝔊. 𝔊 has an explanatory expansion here ('with the youths of the other nations who are brought up with you'; cf. Collins 1993, 128).

Line 1 (1.11). וחיבתם את ר[אֹשי למלך = 𝔐 θ´ (και καταδικασητε την κεφαλην μου τωι βασιλει) ¦ και κινδυνευσω τω ιδιωι τραχηλωι 𝔊.

[18] Cf. Wright (1949, 33): 'The ... fragment measures 5 1/2 by 3 in., and the columns were apparently less than 4 in. wide.' According to Trever (1965, 331–32), the columns were 10.5 cm wide, and contained about twenty lines. He suggested that the columns were about 14 cm high, and estimated a total height for the scroll of about 18 cm, including 2 cm top and bottom margins.

Line 2 (1.11). [המלצר] = 𝔐 (≈ Αμελσαδ θ′) | Αβιεσδρι 𝔊 (= אֲבִיעֶזֶר), cf 3a | לحمني ܟ (= מְשְׁנִיצַר) | ܠحܒܝ ܙ
ܝܐ (= מְנַצֵּר).

    Line 4 (1.12). [מי]ם נשתה = θ′ (και υδωρ πιομεθα) | 𝔐 ומים ונשתה | υδροποτειν 𝔊.

    Line 9 (1.16). [וייין] = 𝔐 | [יי]ןֹ וֹאֵֹת[4QDanᵃ.

    Line 9 (1.16). זרעֹים = σπερματα θ′ | זרעֹנים 𝔐 | απο των οσπριων 𝔊.

J. 1QDanᵃ III 2–9 (frg. 1 ii and frg. 2; Dan 2.2–6)

The preserved text on MS 1926/4a (underlined below) is from Dan 2.4–5.

2   [כשדיים להגיד] למלך חלמתיו ויבאו ויעמדו לפני[

3   המלך ³ויאמרֹ להם הֹ[מלך חלום חלמתי ותפעם רוחי[

4   לדעת את החלום ⁴וידברֹוֹ[הכשדיים למלך ארמית[

5   vacat   מלכא לעלמין חֹיֹי אמר חלמא לעבדיך[

6   ופשרא נחוה ⁵ענא מלכא וֹאֹמֹרֹ[לכשדיא מלתא מני[

7   אזדא די הן לא תהודעֹונני חֹלֹמֹ[א ופשרה הדמין[

8   תתעבדון ובתיכוֹן[נולי יתשמון ⁶והן חלמא ופשרה[

9   [תהחון מ]תֹנֹןֹ וֹ[נבזבה ויקר שגיא תקבלון מן קדמי[

Translation

2.   ² Chaldeans [to be summoned] in order to tell[the king what he had dreamed. They came and stood before]

3.   the king, ³ and the[king] said to them, ['I have had a dream and I am full of anxiety]

4.   to know what I have dreamed.' ⁴ [The Chaldeans] spoke[to the king in Aramaic,]

5.   *vacat* 'O king, liv[e] forever![Relate the dream to your servants,]

6.   and we will tell its meaning.' ⁵ The king said in reply[to the Chaldeans, 'I] hereby [decree:]

7.   If you will not make [the] dream[and its meaning] known to me, you shall be torn [limb from limb]

8.   and your houses[confiscated. ⁶ But if you tell the dream and its meaning,]

9.   [you shall receive from me g]ifts, [presents, and great honour']

Notes on Reconstruction and Comments

Line 2 (2.2). כשדיים. 𝔐 וְלַכַּשְׂדִּים θ′ (και τους Χαλδαιους) | και φαρμακους Χαλδαιων 𝔊.

    Line 3 (2.3). ויאמרֹ. Only a small trace of the corner of *reš* is preserved.

    Line 3 (2.3). הֹ[. A tiny trace of the right shoulder of *he* is preserved.

    Line 4 (2.4). The *vacat* coincides with the change from Hebrew to Aramaic in Dan 2.4.

    Line 6 (2.4). נחוה = 𝔐 (נחוא).

    Line 6 (2.5). ענא = 𝔐 (ענה).

    Line 6 (2.5). מלכא. Parts of the ʾalep are preserved both in 1QDanᵃ frg. 1 ii and MS 1926/4.

    Line 6 (2.5). לכשדיא = 𝔐ᴷ 𝐂 𝔊 θ′ (both: τοις Χαλδαιοις) | לכשדאי 𝔐ᵠ.

---

[19] Ulrich (2010, 754) has [המצלר] (*typo*).

Line 7 (2.5). די = θ′^{mss} ¦ > 𝔐 θ′.

K. Textual Character and Dimension of the Scroll

Our text follows 𝔐 quite closely, with a few minor exceptions:

Table 15. *Text critical synopsis of readings in 1QDanᵃ*

1QDanᵃ	𝔐	θ′	𝔊
נשתה (II 4)	ונשתה	= (πιομεθα)	υδροποτειν
זרעים (II 9)	זרענים	= (σπερματα)	απο των οσπριων
כשדיים (III 2)	ולכשדים	και τους Χαλδαιους	και φαρμακους Χαλδαιων
די (III 7)	>	> (= θ′^{mss})	

If the lower margin also measured 2 cm the height of the scroll would have been *c.* 17 cm. The high quality of the script and the parchment could suggest that this scroll contained the entire contents of the Book of Daniel, but there is not enough evidence from which to posit this with any certainty (see Davis, p. 270 below).

Figure 30.2. *1QDanᵃ + MS 1926/4, a partial reconstruction.*
Courtesy The Syriac Orthodox Church of Antioch, Archdiocese for the Eastern United States,
and West Semitic Research.

XXIV

1QDanᵇ (1Q72) with MS 1926/4b (Dan 3.26–27)

Kipp Davis, Torleif Elgvin

DSS F.121, DSS F.Dan5

A. Physical Description

MS 1926/4b measures 1.9 × 1.8 cm. Lundberg and Zuckerman 1996 identified it as a piece detached from lines 8–10 of 1QDanᵇ (1Q72) frg. 1a before the fragments were photographed by Trever. They were also able to identify letters of three to four words from Dan 3.26–27, with remnants of two letters (*lamed* and *kap*) preserved on both pieces. They even identified early photos by Trever, not used in his 1965 publication, showing the front and back of MS 1926/4. Barthélemy designated the two pieces published in *DJD* 1 as frgs 1 and 2, while Trever called them frgs a and b. We suggest designating the previously published two fragments frgs 1a, 1b, and the new fragment published here frg. 1c (MS 1926/4b). The following edition is based on Trever 1965 and the infrared photograph published there (plate VI), as well as WSR photos of frgs 1a and 1b, which are held by the Syrian Orthodox Archdiocese in New Jersey.[1]

The combined frgs 1a, 1b, 1c preserve parts of 17 lines of one column with no top or bottom margin. Fragment 1a measures 11.3 × 11.8 cm, and frg. 1b 5.9 × 6.8 cm. The right margin measuring 2.9 cm present in frg. 1a suggests that the combined fragments preserve the beginning of a sheet. Neatly inscribed horizontal dry lines are clearly visible in the right margin, as well as two vertical dry lines: one aligned with the right columnar margin, and another appearing 7.5 mm to the right of the text in the margin. The presence of this second dry line is difficult to account for.[2] Letters measure between 1.7–3.8 mm, and the average letter-size for this text is approximately 2.6 mm. The Schøyen fragment is 0.4 mm thick, has a smooth surface, and probably represents parchment, not roughly prepared leather (see the edition of 1QDanᵃ above). The line spacing is 7 mm, and our reconstruction of the text between the three fragments suggests a column width of ±16 cm.

---

[1] Available online through www.inscriptifact.com
[2] Tov (2004, 59–60) lists nine other Qumran scrolls with this same feature of double vertical ruling.

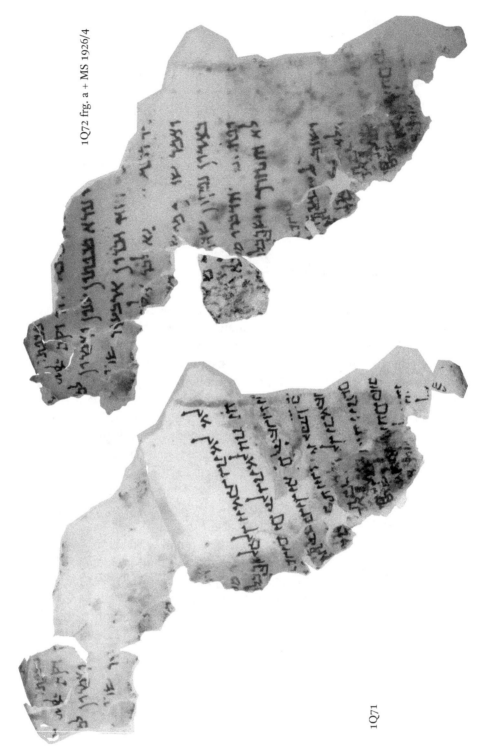

Figure 31.2. MS 1926/4 and reversed image of 1QDanᵃ, DSS SOC 1Q71A OBIR.
Courtesy The Syriac Orthodox Church of Antioch, Archdiocese for the Eastern United States,
and West Semitic Research.

B. Palaeography

Trever was strongly influenced by the Cave 1 provenance of the fragments and their close relation to 1QDan[a], which seems to have prompted him to date the text to the mid-first century AD (1965, 334). Peter Flint (1997, 42) and Eugene Ulrich (2000a, 171) have both characterized the script as Hasmonaean. There are some letters that are clearly early forms, *i.e.*, *'alep*, *he*, and medial *mem*. Other letters appear to be more decisively Herodian, such as medial *kap*, *taw*, and final *nun*. Especially significant to the dating of this text is the uniformity in letter height, which also suggests that the script is Herodian. Based on the combination of these features, we tend to set 1QDan[b] in the second half of the first century BC.

C. MS 1926/4b

[מ̇ישׁ̇ך̇]	1
[לכא ח̇ ∘∘ ל̇∘]	2
[∘i̇∘ ל̇∘]	3

Notes on Readings

Line 1. מ̇ישׁ̇. The right stroke of the *yod* touches the *mem*, and is mounted on top of it. We see traces of a final *kap*, with the top and lower end of the curved descender. Cf. *e.g.* other final *kaps* in התתרך in line 10, and ומשך in line 11 of the combined fragments.

Line 2. לכא[. Only a minute trace of ink is visible at the right edge of the fragment. It most probably conforms to the supralinear stroke of a *lamed*.

Line 2. ל̇∘ ∘∘ח̇. There is a handful of disconnected ink traces following the *'alep*, and space enough for three or four letters. In the first, one can see clear remnants of a crossbar connected to a rightward-descending stroke that extends above it, and would be compatible with a *het*. Following this are a series of ink-spots and 'smears' in a space of 5 mm in which it is possible to reconstruct two letters, or possibly three narrow letters. Just before the left edge of the fragment there is a faintly evident *lamed* minus the supralinear downstroke, which is possibly part of this text layer. This is then followed by a small ink trace at the left edge.

Line 3. ל̇∘]. There are traces of ink on the left edge of the fragment that fit the space of two letters. We suggest a *lamed* for the first letter because the trace is well above the line, and would precisely match the characteristic hook of *lamed* in this hand.

Figure 31.3. *1QDan^b, MS 1926/4 in alignment with frgs a–b.*
Combined from John Trever's Plate VI, and digital images published by Inscriptifact.³
Courtesy The Syriac Orthodox Church of Antioch, Archdiocese for the Eastern United States,
and West Semitic Research.

³ DSS SOC 1Q34bis Reverse Infrared; DSS SOC 1Q71A Obverse Infrared; DSS SOC 1Q72 Obverse 1Q71 Reverse Infrared.

D. Position of the Fragments and Reconstruction

The placement of this piece has been positively aligned with a partially preserved word at the end of 1QDan[b] frg. 1 9, read in *DJD* 1 as מל] and now restored in the context as מלכא. A close analysis shows that the match is virtually certain. The trace of the letter following the *lamed* on frg. 1 9 seems to fill out precisely the lower right corner of the *kap*, which is missing in frg. 1c. The situation of this piece is also confirmed by the alignment of MS 1926/4 line 1 with 1QDan[b] line 8. Our reconstruction below is in conversation with Trever's notes from his 1965 article, as well as the transcription of the same fragments published by Ulrich in his 2010 edition of the Qumran biblical scrolls.

E. 1QDan[b] frg. 1a,c (with frg. 1c underlined in lines 8–10)

	י נ֯ו֯[ס֯]	1
	[מכפתין]	2
∘∘∘[מ֯כא] [ס∘]ה וקם באת֯∘∘∘[		3
∘ו נורא מכפתין ענין ואמרין למ∘[		4
ס֯ה חזה גברין ארבעה שרין∘[∘∘∘]		5
די רביע֯∘∘[ ]מא לבר אלה∘∘∘ ב֯∘∘[		6
ואמר שד] [ד֯ מיש∘ ו֯ע֯∘]		7
באדין נפקין שדרך מיש֯ך֯		8
]ס[	ופחות֯א֯ והדברי מלכא֯ ח֯∘∘ ל֯∘]	9
]∘ בהון[	לא התחרך ושרבלי∘ו֯∘ ל֯∘]	10
]∘ ומשך ועבד [	*vacat* [ ]	11
]שניו ויהבו גשמ[	ושזב לעבדוהי ד֯[	12
]∘∘∘∘ אומ֯ עם כול די טעם ∘ימו[	ולא יס∘∘ון ל[	13
]∘ית֯ו ובית יתעבד הדמין גו[	ד֯י ס אמ֯]	14
הצלה כדנה באדין]∘[ל[	]∘∘שתו[	15
[*vacat*	] א∘א מלא	16
]די לשניא[		17

Notes on Readings

Line 1. י נ֯ו֯[ס֯]. The *yod*, *nun*, and *waw* are clearly visible on Trever's Plate VI, but have since disappeared (cf. *Figure 31.3*).

Line 2. [מכפתין֯. Barthélemy read [מ֯כפתין֯.[4] Ink from 1QDan[b] is impressed upon 1QDan[a] frg. 1. This impression clearly shows a *mem*.

Line 3. באת֯∘∘∘. Barthélemy read [באת]בהלה. There is a trace of ink following the *taw* on the edge of the fragment. A small piece that has broken off from the left edge preserves traces of two more letters. The last one is positioned high on the line.

Line 5. ה∘[ ]. Barthélemy read [חזה]. The distinct crossbar connected to the left downstroke of *he* is clearly visible in the ink impression from the 1QDan[a] layer, along with a trace of the foot of the first downstroke, and the left edge of what appears to be the baseline of another preceding letter. The

---

[4] For the readings of 1QDan[b] by Barthélemy, see *DJD* 1:151–52, cf. also Ulrich 2010, 760.

fragment preserves the right columnar margin in line six below, which is located 12.7 mm right of the trace belonging to the baseline for *nun* in אנה.

Line 5. שרי[ ]ooo[. Barthélemy read שרי[ן]. At high magnification traces of three or four letters can be seen on the left edge of the fragment. A trace of what is most likely a left-sloping oblique stroke belonging to *mem* is visible, with possibly the *serif* at the top.

Line 8. שדרך מישך [ ]. Barthélemy read שדרך. His reading has been confirmed by the join with MS 1926/4, which on its own contains the combination of letters]ך מישך[, visible on the new infrared image. The partial final *kap* at the right edge of the Schøyen fragment supplies the obvious ending to the reading שדר] of frg. 1a 8. The letters that follow are best read as *mem* ligatured to *yod* followed by a *šin*.

Line 9. מלכא ח֗ ooo ל֗ [o. Barthélemy read מל]כא. The lower portion of the *lamed* appears in frg. 1a, which aligns precisely with the 'bulbous' top-portion of the same letter in the Schøyen fragment to complete the word. Because frg. 1c contains three layers from three different texts, it is difficult to clearly make out several of the letters. The second layer overlaps with the first immediately after מלכא. There may be a trace of ink just beneath the second layer belonging to the *ḥet* that begins חזין, and a trace of what may be a *lamed* followed by another letter at the left edge.

Line 9.]o[. There is a minute trace at the top of frg. 1b belonging to the baseline of a letter (cf. *Figure 31.3*).

Line 12. לעבדוהי ד֗[. The reading is clearly visible on Trever's Plate VI, and he mentions a trace of the *dalet* at the left edge of frg. 1a. One can make out all the letters in the jumble of impressions from 1QDan[a] in the more recent Inscriptifact image, although the fragment has been damaged, resulting in a separation between the top and bottom portions of *he*, *yod*, and *dalet*. Notice also that the right downstroke of the *he*, clearly visible in Trever's photograph, has since been completely abraded.

Line 13. יס֗ooן. Barthélemy read ולא] at the right edge of the line, and Ulrich reads ולא יס֗ג֗דון. Traces of the top of the letters are more clearly visible on Trever's Plate VI than on the Inscriptifact photograph. The fragment has been damaged in subsequent years, and there is now only a very minute trace of *gimel*.

Lines 14–17. Neither Barthélemy nor Ulrich detects any traces at the beginning of the remaining lines. The recent Zuckerman photographs reveal layers of text, not visible to Trever, in which several letters may be detected.

Line 14.]ד֗י o אמ֗. The second and third layers on Trever's Plate VI badly obscure the underlying text on the bottom layer, even in infrared light. However, our reading here is confirmed by the Zuckerman photographs. At the right edge of the column, traces in horizontal alignment with this line are possible matches for *dalet* and *yod*. Trever originally reconstructed יאמר to begin line 14, but the clear appearance of the *ʾalep* approximately 11 mm to the left of the margin, and the surrounding traces, indicate that the line began with די. *ʾAlep* is clear. Following this letter, the right downstroke curving into the baseline of a probable *mem* is also visible.

Line 15.]שתוֹ֗oo. Zuckerman's infrared photograph reveals the beginning of line 15 beneath the top two layers. At the right edge of the column there is a vertical stroke that appears above the line, similar to the supralinear downstroke of a *lamed*. This, however, would position the *lamed* lower than expected.

Line 15. הצלה֗o[ ]ל֗o[. Barthélemy read ל[הצלה and Ulrich reads יכ[ל]ל֗ ל[הצלה. Trever's Plate VI reveals the ink trace on the right edge followed by the supralinear downstroke and hook of *lamed*. To the right of the clearly visible הצלה is another ink trace belonging to a previous letter.

Line 15. באדי֗ן. Ulrich reads באדי]ן, but the downstroke and baseline of medial *nun* are both clearly visible in the Trever Plate VI. There is possibly a trace belonging to another letter following *nun*, but this is far from certain.

Line 16. ‏מל‎ﻣﻠ‎°א[. Trever read ‏מל]כא‎. In the Inscriptifact photograph there is clear trace of *ʾalep*, as is illustrated in the reconstruction.

***Figure 31.4**. 1QDanᵇ frg. 1a through the layers*
Courtesy The Syriac Orthodox Church of Antioch, Archdiocese for the Eastern United States,
and West Semitic Research.

F. Frg. 1abc. Dan 3.22–31

[נגו קטל המון שביבא ד[י נור̇]א 23וגבריא אלך תלתהון שדרך מישך ועבד נגו נפלו[	1
לגוא אתון נורא יקדתא [מכפתין[vaca]t	2
24]אדין נבוכד[נצ̇צ̇ר̇ מל̇כא[ת[ו̇̇ה וקם באתב̇ה̇ל̇]ה ענה ואמר להדברוהי הלא גברין תלתא[	3
רמינא ל[ג̇וא נורא מכפתין ענין ואמרין למל[כא יציבא מלכא 25וענה נבוכדנצר ואמר להון[	4
הא א̇[נ̇ה חזה גברין ארבעה שרי[ן [מ̇ה̇ל̇]כין בגו נורא וחבל לא איתי בהון ורוה[	5
די רביע̇י̇א̇] ד[מא לבר אלה̇י̇ן 26בא̇ד̇]ין קרב מלכא לתרע אתון נורא יקדתא ענה[	6
ואמר שד[ר̇]ך מישך ע̇ב̇ד̇] נגו עבדוהי די אלה אלהא עליא פקו מן גוא נורא[	7
באדין נפקין שד̇ר̇ך מ̇י̇שך̇] ועבד נגו מן גוא נורא 27ומתכנשין אחשדרפניא סגניא[	8
ופחותא̇ והדברי מלכ̇א חז̇ז̇ן̇ ל̇ג̇]בריא אלך די לא של[ט̇] נורא בגשמהון ושער ראשהון[	9
לא התחרך ושרבליה̇ת̇ה̇ן̇ לא̇] שנו וריח נור לא עד[ה̇ בהון 28ענה נבוכדנצר ואמר[	10
vacat [בריך אלההון די שדר]ך ומשך ועבד [נגו די שלח מלאכה[	11
ושזב לעבדוהי ד̇]י התרחצו עלוהי ומלת מלכא [שניו ויהבו גשמ]יהון די לא יפלחון[	12
ולא יסגדו̇ן ל̇]כל אלה אחרן להן לאלההון 29וכען [שימו טעם די כל עם אומ̇ה̇ ולש̇ן[	13
ד̇י̇ י̇אמ̇]ר שלו על אלההון די שדרך משך ועבד נ[גו הדמין יתעבד וביתה̇] נולי[	14
∘∘שתו]ה vac? כול קבל די לא איתי אלה אחרן די י̇]כ̇ל[ ]להצלה כדנה 30באדין	15
מלכ̇א [הצלח לשדרך משך ועבד נגו במדינת בבל vacat [	16
] vacat 31נבוכדנצר מלכא לכל עממיא אמיא ו[לשניא די] דאר̇ין[	17

Translation

1. [a tongue of flame killed the men wh]o carried u[p Shadrach, Meshach, and Abed-Nego. 23 But those three men, Shadrach, Meshach, and Abed-Nego, dropped,]

2. bound,[into the burning fiery furnace.   vaca]t[   ]

3. 24[Then Nebuchadnezzar]the king was astonished and, rising in ha[ste, addressed his companions, saying, 'Did we not]

4. [throw three men,] bound, into the fire?' They answered and replied to the k[ing, 'Surely, O king.' 25 And Nebuchadnezzar responded and said to them,]

5. ['But]I see four men unbou[nd,]walk[ing and unharmed in the fire and the appearance]

6. of the fourth[is li]ke that of a divine being.' 26 The[n the king approached the hatch of the burning fiery furnace; he called out]

7. and said, 'Shad[ra]ch, Meshach, Abe[d-nego, servants of the Most High God of gods, come out from the blazing fire!']

8. So Shadrach, Meshach,[and Abed-nego]came out [of the blazing fire. 27 The satraps, the prefects,]

9. the governors, and the royal companions [gathered around]to l[ook at those men, on whose bodies the fire had had no ef]f[ect, the hair of whose heads]

10. had not been singed, whose tunics were not [changed, and not even the smell of fire cam]e from them.[28 Nebuchadnezzar spoke up and said,]

11. *vacat*   ['Blessed be the God of Shadra]ch, Meshach, and Abed-[nego, who sent His angel]

12. and has saved His servants wh[o, trusting in Him,]flouted[the king's decree] at the risk of[their] *lives*[rather than serve]

13. or worship a[ny *other* god but their own God. 29 Now] *issue* an order that any people, or nation or tong[ue]

14.   that blasp[hemes the God of Shadrach, *and* Meshach, and Abed-ne]go shall be torn limb from limb, and[his] house [will

15.   *become like* [a dunghill, for there is no other God who is ab]le[ ]to save in this way.' [30] Thereupon

16.   the king [promoted Shadrach, Meshach, and Abed-nego in the province of Babylon.]   *vacat*

17.   [*vacat*   [31] 'King Nebuchadnezzar to all people, nations and] tongues that[inhabit]

Notes on Reconstruction and Comments

Line 2. The restored text requires a *vacat* in line 2, before Dan 3.24, corresponding with an open paragraph in 𝔐^LA.

Line 3 (3.24). [נבוכד]נצֿר. There appears to be some impressions of ink from the 1QDan^a fragments that could be set-off of the final three letters *nun*, *ṣade* and *res*. Notice especially three traces of ink at the top edge of the fragment that quite plausibly fit this reconstruction, and correspond to the tops of the final three letters. The latter two impressions suggest links with darkened areas on Trever's Plate VI.

Line 3 (3.24). באתֿבֿהֿלֿ]ה. בהתבהלה 𝔐. This feminine noun is in 𝔐 spelled with *he*, in 1QDan^b with ʾalep.[5]

Line 4 (3.24). [רמינא ל]גֻֿו. רמינא לגוא 𝔐. Barthélemy read ל]גֻֿו at the beginning of line 4, but Ulrich's transcription (2010, 760) agrees with our reading. The reconstruction reveals that there is an appropriate amount of space to the right of the fragment to reconstruct רמינא. This helps to confirm a left margin for this column with the reconstruction of the previous line ending with תלתא.

Line 4 (3.25). [וענה נבוכדנצר ואמר להון]. ענה ואמר 𝔐 | > 𝔊 | και ειπεν ο βασιλευς θ′ | ܐܡܪ ܘ ܡܠܟܐ ܡܢܐ S 𝒱. עֿנֿה נֿבֿכֿדֿנֿצֿ]ר ואמר] להדברוהי 4QDan^d. Our reconstruction is prompted by the space available for restoring this line and the following line 5. The alternatives in 𝔐 and 𝔊 are deemed unlikely because they are too short. The reading from 4QDan^d (4Q115) provides some support for the expansion. Moreover, there is no section break at the end of Dan 3.24 in 𝔐. Dan 3.23–24 is the point in the narrative in 𝔊 where the Song of Azariah and the Three Young Men was inserted, and it presents itself as a logical place for a range of textual variation.

Line 5 (3.25). [הא א]נֿה] = 𝔐 𝔊 θ′ (Ιδου εγω). The average word-spacing of approximately 2 mm does not allow for enough space to include the introductory formula וענה ענה of 𝔐 (see previous note). On the other hand, adequate space does exist between where we would place the right margin and נֿה for reconstructing the two-letter word הא, a word space, and the first letter of אנה.

Line 5 (3.25). [בגו] = (בגוא). We reconstruct a defective spelling here based on the short form לגו of the same word with the inseparable preposition in line 4.

Line 6 (3.25). רביעֿ[אֿ] = 𝔐^K | רביעאה 𝔐^Q. Considerations of space suggest reading with *Ketib*.

Line 6 (3.25). ד[מא] = 𝔐 (דמה).

Line 6 (3.25–26). אלהיֿן[26] בֿא[דֿ]ין. Trever transcribes an unusually long word space after אלהיֿן, but this is unlikely (there is a closed paragraph in 𝔐^L before Dan 3.26, but no paragraph in 𝔐^A). More probably, the uninscribed area was caused by damage to the leather. The placement of these words is fairly certain, and produces an average-sized word separation. The damage has also affected the spacing for the second word. The crossbars of *bet* as well as *dalet* are visible, as well as a trace that might fit ʾalep.

Line 6 (3.26). [מלכא] = 𝔊 (ο βασιλευς) | נבוכדנצר 𝔐 | ܚܠܟܐ ܢܒܘܟܕܢܨܪ S. Ulrich's transcription agrees with 𝔐. The reconstruction clearly shows that there is not enough space for the full reading to align

---

with 𝔐. Drawing from 𝔊, καὶ προσελθὼν ὁ βασιλεὺς πρὸς τὴν θύραν τῆς καμίνου τῆς καιομένης τῶ πυρι, we reconstruct מלכא in place of נבוכדנצר.

Line 7 (3.26). [אלה אלהא עליא] = οʹ (του θεου των θεων του υψιστου) | 𝔐 אלהא עליא | ܐܠܗܐ ܥܠܝܐ 𝔖. Ulrich's transcription agrees with 𝔐. The reconstruction is suggested on the basis of the available space and also the translation in 𝔊, but a reconstruction on the basis of 𝔐 is also possible (see following note).

Line 7 (3.26). [פקו מן גוא נורא] ≈ 𝔊 (εξελθετε εκ του πυρος) | 𝔐 פקו ואתו | ܦܘܩܘ ܠܟܐ 𝔖. Our reconstruction differs from Ulrich, who follows 𝔐. Restoring the text to correspond to 𝔐 remains a possibility, which would result in an otherwise unattested open paragraph, measuring approximately 30 mm to the end of the line. A reconstruction closer to 𝔊, containing the independent preposition and the fuller spelling for גוא, results in an alignment close to the left columnar margin, and is thus deemed to be the more probable reading here.

Line 7 (3.27). [אחשדרפניא סגניא] = 𝔐. 𝔊 reads οι υπατοι τοπαρχαι και αρχιπατριωται και οι φιλοι του βασιλεως where 𝔐 has אֲחַשְׁדַּרְפְּנַיָּא סִגְנַיָּא וּפַחֲוָתָא וְהַדָּבְרֵי מַלְכָּא. Cf. also 𝔖 ܐܚܫܕܪܦܢܐ ܘܣܓܢܐ ܘܗܕܘܪܐ ܘܕܒܬܐ ܘܕܚܝܠܘܗܝ ܕܡܠܟܐ. As seen in the reconstruction, there might be a shortage of space to reconstruct according to 𝔐. But compare this with our proposed reading for the end of line 4 above, where we similarly suggest a reading that extends a little past the left margin. Alternatively, it is possible that the words used here for the first two groups from the list of officials were different, perhaps corresponding to others from the long roll-calls in Dan 3.2,3.

Line 9 (3.27). שׁל[ט]ט.The trace at the top of frg. 1b most likely corresponds to *ṭet* in שלט.

Line 10 (3.27). ושרבלי[הון] = 𝔐 (וסרבליהון). The interchange of *sin* and *samek* is also found in other scrolls, and may be due to contemporary pronunciation (cf. Kutscher 1974, 185).

Line 10 (3.27). עד[ה]. 𝔐 עדת. The masculine singular verb עדה agrees in gender with ריח against 𝔐, where the verb is feminine. The graphical similarity between *he* and *taw* may account for the difference.

Line 11 (3.28). There is a long *vacat* to begin the line, which is visible on Trever's Plate VI, but also clear in *Figure 31.3*. Going on our reconstruction of the line to the left of frg. 1b, the section divider was approximately 42 mm from the beginning of the column. There is no section division at this point in 𝔐^LA.

Line 11 (3.28). ומשׁך. 𝔐 מישׁך 𝔊 (Μισαχ). The scribe uses the spelling מישׁך in lines 7 and 8.

Line 12 (3.28). ושׁזב = 𝔐 (ושיזב).

Line 12 (3.28). גשׁמ[ה]יהון = 𝔐^K 𝔊 (τα σωματα αυτων) | 𝔐^Q גשׁמהון.

Line 13 (3.28). [אלה אחרן] = 𝔊 (θεω ετερω) | אלה 𝔐. Ulrich's transcription agrees with 𝔐. The space between frgs 1a–1b suggests a longer reading than in 𝔐, which is neatly filled by our suggestion following 𝔊. Compare this with Dan 3.29 (די לא איתי אלה אחרן, διοτι ουκ εστιν θεος ετερος), reconstructed below in line 15. Another alternative could be suggested by inserting a small section break of approximately 11 mm between Dan 3.28 and 29. There are no corresponding open or closed paragraphs in 𝔐^LA.

Line 13 (3.29). וכען [שׂימו]. 𝔐 | ומני שים κ. και νυν εγω κρινω 𝔊 𝔖 (ܘܡܢܢ ܦܩܕ ܐܢܐ). The extant verb is a *peʿal* plural imperative, and we have reconstructed the phrase to follow the syntax in Ezra 4.21 (כען שימו טעם). שים in 𝔐 is most likely a passive participle (*HALOT* 5:1986, cf. also Dan 4.3; 6.27; Ezra 4.19; 6.8, 11; 7.13, 21), 'in my presence a decree is given'.

Line 13 (3.29). כול = 𝔐 (כל). Based on the long spelling of this word we reconstruct כול and לכול in lines 13, 15, 17, where 𝔐 reads לכל/כל. 𝔐, 6QDan and 4QDan^a use the shorter spelling כל, while 4QDan^b and 4QDan^e use the longer כול (for 4QDan^e Ulrich restores כו[ל] in Dan 9.12 to fill the space to the reconstructed right margin, *DJD* 16:288).

Line 13 (3.29). אומה = 𝔐 (אמה).

Line 14 (3.29). [שלו ... משׁך] = 𝔐^Q שלה ... מישׁך = 𝔐^K. The reconstruction is suggested by the available space on the line between fragments 1a and 1b, and follows the Qere reading שלו over the Ketib שלה.

Line 14 (3.29). נ[גו = 𝔐 (נגוא).

Line 15 (3.29). ∘∘שתוה ישתוה.ה[תוֹשׁ 𝔐 | δημευθησεται 𝕲 | εις διαρπαγην θ´ | ܐܠܒܙ S. The reading at the beginning of line 15 is highly problematic because of what looks like a trace of a *lamed* that aligns with the right margin. This would suggest that the word cannot be the *itpaʿal* imperfect that appears in 𝔐, but a sensible alternative does not present itself. If the appearance of a *lamed* here is correct, the trace of the second letter could represent the left stroke of a *he*. This would suggest an infinitive construct with the inseparable preposition להשתוה (cp. Figure 31.4 p. 263), unattested in Aramaic.[6] However, this reading produces a grammatically awkward clause. It may otherwise be possible that the remnants of what looks like letters are actually carbon-based residue left on the leather that looks like ink under infrared light (cf. also MS 5439/2 [Ḥev(?)Unidentified Fragment], where something similar has occurred; see p. 299). This alternative would then prompt us to read שׄתוֹ[ה, which is in some ways more appealing, but also produces a strange space between the margin and the beginning of the first word on the line. Perhaps this may be further explained as a damaged spot on the original parchment that the scribe sought to avoid.

Lines 16–17 (3.30–31). The presence of the open paragraph at the end of line 16 is clearly visible in frg. 1b. We posit the presence of a long indentation at the beginning of line 17 based on the reconstruction that conforms to the visible word, לשניא[ו, on the same fragment.[7] The section marker in line 17 measures approximately 42 mm, and would correspond precisely with the comparable section break in line 11 above. The *vacats* are represented by open paragraphs in 𝔐^LA.

Line 17 (3.31). [דארין] = 𝔐^K | דירין 𝔐^Q.

---

[6] Compare with θ´ και οι οικοι αυτων εις διαρπαγην.

[7] Tov (2004, 148) notes similar major section divisions in 1QH^a VII 6, 26; 4QCant^b (4Q107) 2 ii 6–7; 4QTest (4Q175) 20–21; 4QBarkhi Nafshi^a (4Q434) 1 i 12.

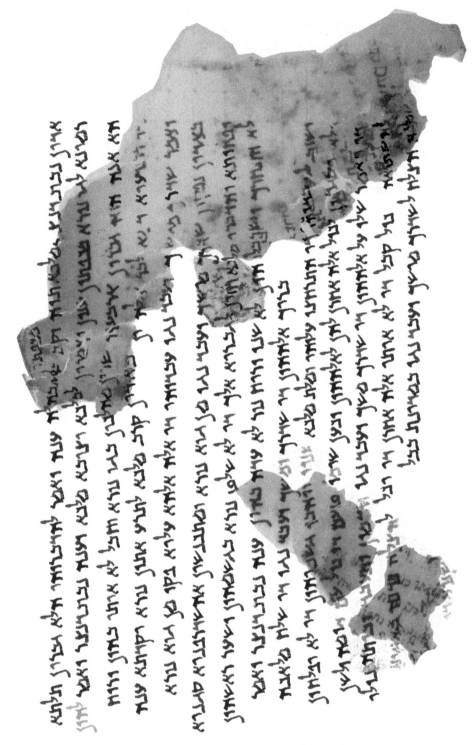

Figure 31.5. *A reconstruction of 1QDan^b frg. 1abc 3–16*

G. Textual Profile

1QDanᵇ is the earliest witness to Dan 3.26–31, while the early Herodian 4QDanᵈ contains Dan 3.23–25. The attested readings and reconstructions that deviate from 𝔐 may be charted as follows:

Table 16. *Text critical synopsis of readings in 1QDanᵇ*

	𝔊	Non-aligned	𝔐
l. 4 (3.25)	>	[וענה נבוכדנצר ואמר להון] (cf. 4QDanᵈ 2 ii 4–5)	ענה ואמר
l. 6 (3.26)	[מלכא] (ο βασιλευς)		נבוכדנצר
l. 7 (3.26)	[די אלה אלהא עליא] (του θεου των θεων του υψιστου)		די אלהא עליא (𝔐ᵠ עלאה)
l. 7 (3.26)	[פקו מן גוא נורא] (εξελθετε εκ του πυρος)		פקו ואתו
l. 10 (3.27)	ἦν	[עד]הֿ	עדת
l. 13 (3.28)	[אלה אחרן] (θεω ετερω)		אלה
l. 13 (3.29)	και νυν εγω κρινω	וכען [שׂימו	ומני שים
l. 15 (3.29)	δημευθησεται	°°שתו]ה	ישתוה

On the literary level 1QDanᵇ follows the 𝔐 recension of Daniel 3 (as does 4QDanᵈ), and does not include the Prayer of Azariah and the Song of the Three Young Men inserted in 𝔊 after Dan 3.23 (cf. Ulrich 2001, 582–83). However, there is an apparent difference from 𝔐 at the beginning of v. 25, which we read as a longer introduction to Nebuchadnezzar's response, וענה נבוכדנצר ואמר להון, that possibly attests to the 'parting of the ways' between the *Vorlage* of 𝔊 and 𝔐.

1QDanᵇ regularly uses section markers. These can be compared with what appears in the Masoretic system. There is an open paragraph before Dan 3.24 (= 𝔐ᴸᴬ), a 3.5 mm space before v. 26 where 𝔐ᴸ (but not 𝔐ᴬ) has a closed paragraph,[8] a closed paragraph in v. 28 without Masoretic parallel, and a closed paragraph before v. 31, corresponding to an open one in 𝔐ᴸᴬ.

Textually 1QDanᵇ is difficult to classify, since it corresponds inconsistently to a variety of readings from several of the witnesses. While the text does not support the elaborate revision in 𝔊 that prompted the inclusion of the Song of Azariah and the Three Young Men, the presence of seven or perhaps eight departures from 𝔐—four aligned with 𝔊, and three or four that are unattested—does not allow for a classification as an 𝔐-like text either.

The use of כול for 𝔐's כל (with 4QDanᵇ'ᵉ) suggests a tendency towards a full orthography, although this is far from conclusive. In four cases the manuscript differs from 𝔐 in the rendering of ʾalep or he.[9] The scribe is inconsistent with regard to spelling of the name מישך/משך, and seems to alternate between full and defective spelling for גוא/גו, reflecting the interchange between independent and inseparable prepositions. The spelling ושרבלי[הון for 𝔐's וסרבליהון (line 10) demonstrates an interchange of sin and samek also found in other scrolls. In addition, there is one case where the scribe uses primal/medial nun in a final position (line 15 באדין). It is impossible to know whether this was done in error, or if he did not always make use of this final form.

---

[8] See Tov 2004, 145, for a discussion of differently sized spaces in the middle of the line.

[9] Ulrich notes this feature in all the Daniel scrolls: 'the interchange of the letters א and ה is commonplace, with the correct letter sometimes preserved in a scroll, sometimes in the MT' (2001, 579).

It is important to note that two Daniel texts of very different character were deposited together in Cave 1 in a bundle with 1QLitPr[b]:[10] 1QDan[a] is an 𝔐-like text from the second half of the first century AD, written in an elegant hand on high quality light-coloured parchment, while 1QDan[b] is a non-aligned text, written in a much earlier hand from the second half of the first century BC. The first contains text from Daniel 1–2, the second from Daniel 3. 1QLitPr[b] (which according to Milik [*DJD* 1:136] likely belonged to same scroll as the single fragment of 1QLitPr[a] [1Q34]), comprises a collection of penitential and benedictory prayers in at least three columns, perhaps organized for recitation according to a festal calendar.

These three manuscripts were discovered in a state that suggests that they were not deposited like other scrolls. They were matted together, causing the ink to spread from one manuscript to the other in the form of set-off; the lines altogether appearing at crossing angles in a jumbled mess. Trever surmised that the condition of the scrolls upon their discovery indicated a violent end to their usage. He believed that they were destroyed by Roman invaders, but then the scraps of their remains were collected by pious Essenes who reverentially carried them for burial in Cave 1 (Trever 1965, 326–27). His highly entertaining and equally imaginative tale draws heavily from a historical narrative about the Qumran settlement, its residents, and their relationship to the Qumran caves that is no longer current in modern scholarship. He takes for granted a perspective of the *Yaḥad* Essenes and their texts that also fails to stand up to modern scrutiny.

There remain unanswered questions about the peculiar assemblage of these fragments. They belonged to manuscripts that were obviously collected or stored together at one time, but why? Were they victims of Roman maltreatment? Or were their owners not so careful when they deposited these parchments? It is perhaps worth considering that the grouping of these manuscripts which contained narratives from Daniel 1–3, and also a thematically related set of prayers, was not incidental. Were these three manuscripts, or parts of them, at one time in their history read together? In any event, Trever's anecdotal hypothesis ought not be accepted at face value without careful consideration of the possibilities for other connections between these texts.

---

[10] Trever identifies the elegant hand of 1QLitPr[b] as belonging to the scribe who inserted the correction in 1QIsa[a] col. XXVIII, and noted its close similarity to 1QH[a], which is dated to 30–1 BC (*DJD* 39:412). We prefer to date 1QLitPr[b] to the first half of the first century AD.

Part Five

—

Other Writings

XXV

MS 1909. 1QRule of Blessings (1Q28b) frg. 25a, 1QSb V 22–25

George J. Brooke[1]

DSS F.127. DSS F.1QSb

A. Discovery, Purchase, and Publication

This small fragment is part of the *Rule of Blessings*, one of the two appendices attached to the *Community Rule*. The fragments of 1QSa and 1QSb were sold to the Palestine Archaeological Museum in 1950 by Kando (*DJD* 1:4, 43, 107). The small fragment published here was not part of that lot, but instead came into the possession of Archbishop Athanasius Samuel. Possibly it was among the fragments recovered by members of St. Mark's Monastery,[2] all of which were supposed to be published as an Appendix in *DJD* 1 (pp. 150–55). In his autobiography Archbishop Samuel records that, at his request, George Ishaya Shamoun and Father Yusef visited Cave 1 in August 1947, and in addition to seeing a jar they 'reported seeing only shreds and scraps of scrolls such as we already had, and chips of wood and potsherds' (Samuel 1968, 150).[3] The precise details concerning the discovery and removal of many of the fragments from Cave 1 will never be known.

In August 1973, Professor William H. Brownlee received this fragment from Archbishop Samuel for identification. On 4 September, 1973 Brownlee wrote to the Archbishop saying that he considered it likely that the fragment belonged to 1QSb and that he would retain the fragment for a little longer to try to locate it suitably in the manuscript. In a letter dated 8 December, 1973, the Archbishop wrote: 'Concerning the scroll fragment that I sent you earlier, I wish to present this to you as a token of my friendship and respect for your labors on behalf of the Dead Sea Scrolls. Please do accept this small gift and feel free to display and use it as you feel will prove most beneficial.' Brownlee naturally acknowledged the gift with a warm letter of thanks.[4]

---

[1] Adapted from *DJD* 26:227–33. A more comprehensive account of the history and publication of this fragment appears in Brooke and Robinson 1995.

[2] G. Lankester Harding wrote that after the initial discovery in 1947, the Bedouin shepherds reported 'that during the next few months people from the monastery made frequent visits there, enlarging a lower entrance, and excavating it very thoroughly. In the course of this work they must have recovered all the rest of the known manuscripts and large fragments, some of which were eventually acquired by the Hebrew University' (*DJD* 1:5). John M. Allegro (1956, 18) also records that 'the Metropolitan organized his own expedition to the cave, which proceeded to ransack the place, making a large opening near the ground, and pulling out everything they could lay their hands on'.

[3] Weston Fields suggests that this visit probably occurred in August 1948 (Fields 2009, 85). If this was the case, the fragment featured here had possibly fallen off from the scroll bundle of 1QS, 1QSa, and 1QSb before the Bedouin had removed these from the cave. Another possibility is that this fragment was among other items from Cave 1 that arrived at St. Mark's Monastery from Kando's shop in Bethlehem, which were eventually sold by the Archbishop after placing his advertisement in the 1 June, 1954 issue of the *Wall Street Journal* (Brooke and Robinson 1995, 123).

[4] This correspondence between Brownlee and the Archbishop is quoted in Brooke and Robinson 1995, 120.

Brownlee never published the fragment, perhaps because he had not completed its identification to his own satisfaction. After some years, he asked John C. Trever to preserve it safely for him. On Brownlee's death in 1983, ownership of the fragment passed to his widow, for whom Trever continued to act as its custodian. In 1994 James Robinson asked George Brooke to identify the location of the fragment within 1QSb and publish it (Brooke and Robinson 1994/1995). The fragment was subsequently purchased by The Schøyen Collection in the summer of 1994.

B. Physical Description

The fragment has deteriorated since it first came into Brownlee's possession. Fortunately, some elements of his first readings have survived in note form together with a photograph of the fragment (*Figure 32.2*) so that the readings at the beginnings of lines 1 and 2 are certain.[5] As it is now (*Figure 32.1*), and as it was handed to Trever for safekeeping, the fragment is diamond-shaped, measuring 3.3 × 1.6 cm. As can be seen in *Figure 32.2*, the fragment originally had a small additional piece on its top right-hand corner which measured approximately 11 × 6 mm and preserved a few further letters.

To the *verso* of the fragment was attached a piece measuring 20 × 13 mm belonging to the next turn of the scroll. Two parts of this layer (9 × 7 mm and 5 mm²) have fallen off and are mounted on the plate with the main fragment (see *Figure 32.1*). The surface of these two pieces reveals no trace of writing. According to a recent examination by Torleif Elgvin of the main fragment, three small pieces from the layer below are still attached to the *verso*, measuring respectively 14 × 7 mm, 7 × 3 mm, and 7 × 1 mm (on this smallest piece one can notice ink at the edge).

The fragment published here is a uniform 0.26 mm thick, whereas the broken piece that was removed from the back of the fragment was 0.39 mm thick. The *recto* of the fragment is of a light, whitish hue and in this respect like the sheets of parchment used for 1QSa and 1QSb, as recorded in *DJD* 1 ('cuir blanchi').[6] The surface is smooth and shows a distinct grain which runs at an angle of approximately 60º from the horizontal. Where there is only one layer of parchment, the main fragment is transparent when seen against a lamp. This observation demonstrates that the scroll material was carefully prepared parchment.

The fragment preserves clear traces of having been ruled with a blunt instrument. These guide lines are visible, in particular, above line 2. Guide lines are also visible on 1QSb frg. 25, but not in the photograph of 1QSb V published in *DJD* 1 (Plate XXIX); however, the guide lines are visible on PAM 40.518 for 1QSb V 23 and on PAM 40.076 for 1QSb V 26.

The right-hand edge of the fragment is almost straight and vertical. This break aligns with the sharp, vertical left edge of both 1QSb frg. 26 and that which bisects 1QSb frg. 25. A similar vertical break can be observed on 1QSb col. I frg. 2 (located at the top of the scroll), and the right-edge of 1QSb frg. 18. The left-hand edge of the right section of 1QSb V 25 has a similarly straight undamaged edge. The line-spacing is somewhat uneven: 8.2 mm between lines 1 and 2, 8.5 mm between lines 2 and 3, and 7 mm between lines 3 and 4. These distances correspond precisely with those of 1QSb V 22–25.

When the fragment was scanned by Ira Rabin in 2012, the analysis showed exactly the same mineral composition as an uninscribed fragment from 1QS.[7] According to Rabin, these two pieces of parchment

---

[5] This image is based on a print of the fragment found by Brownlee's daughter, Martha, amongst her father's papers; she has confirmed that no negative for the image came to light as she was sorting through his materials.

[6] Brownlee noted that this fragment seemed to him even whiter than the rest of 1QS, 1QSa, and 1QSb. The composite image in *Fig. 32.3* (p. 280) would seem to confirm that.

[7] This fragment fell off from 1QS when John Trever photographed the scroll in 1948, and was purchased by The Schøyen Collection from the Trever family in 1994.

were prepared together in a process where calcium powder was applied to the surface while the skin was bound to a frame, and likely belonged to the same scroll (see p. 66). According to Milik, wear patterns from the end of 1QS can be followed in 1QSa and 1QSb (*DJD* 1:107, 119), but these patterns are not easily recognized in the more fragmentary 1QSb. Rabin's tests provide welcome confirmation that 1QSa and 1QSb were included with 1QS as parts of a composite scroll. Column V of 1QSb, to which this fragment is connected, is the last reconstructed column of the composite scroll, which was rolled with its beginning on the inside. The trace of ink observed on the small piece attached to the *verso* of the Schøyen fragment may suggest that yet another column followed col. V, since the turn of the scroll at the end of 1QSa is more than the width of a column (*DJD* 1:Plate XXIII-XXIV).

C. Palaeography

The few extant letters are of a formal Hasmonaean hand like that of 1QS, 1QSa, 1QSb, 1QIsa[a], and 4QDeut[c] (see Cross 1961b, 138, especially line 2), with some semiformal influence. *Dalet* is drawn with a downstroke angled slightly from left to right, and a narrow deep-cornered crossbar that forms the head. *He* is formed from three strokes; the initial downstroke has its head leaning slightly to the right, the left downstroke is straight, and the crossbar slopes down at its left side. *Waw* is gently curved with a marked head, the curve being characteristic of earlier Hasmonaean hands. *Yod* barely has the small shaded triangular head characteristic of the earlier formal hands. The right stroke continues as the downstroke of the letter which curves slightly to the left at the bottom, but not as markedly as in the *waw* with which it could sometimes be confused. One instance of *yod*, in line 4, has a head clearly closer to the inverted V-type, which Cross describes as belonging characteristically to early semiformal hands and is especially characteristic of semiformal elements that have influenced the formal Hasmonaean hand of 1QS, 4QTest (4Q175) and 4QSam[c] (4Q53).[8] *Taw* has a right downstroke as long as the left downstroke which is now given a left horizontal stroke that is a distinct part of the letter. The relative size of *taw*, being similar in dimensions to *he*, indicates a late second century development, earlier forms being characteristically larger. The hand found in this fragment is essentially formal but with the same characteristic semiformal influences as the hand of 1QS, 1QSa and 1QSb. It can be dated to 125–75 BC.[9]

D. Orthography

The fragment reflects the generally full orthography of 1QSb.

Line 2. קודש should probably be restored here (see Qimron 1986, 35–38). This spelling of the nominal form is especially common in Qumran Hebrew, with nearly fifty occurrences in 1QS, 1QSa and 1QSb; cf. Dan 11.30 על ברית קודש.

Line 3. ה[,ייתה[10] cf. 1QSb V 29.

---

[8] Cross 1961b, 158. On p. 196, note 97, Cross disagrees with Malachi Martin (1958, vol. I, 49–56): 'The same hand continues in 1QSa and 1QSb (*DJD* 1:Plates XXII-XXIX). Martin's analysis of the hands of the 1QSab complex is badly confused'.

[9] Elsewhere in the volume (p. 84) close analysis of the letter forms has resulted in a preference for a mid-first century BCE date, perhaps in the second quarter of the first century BCE.

[10] For the forms of the afformative in Qumran Hebrew, see Qimron 1986, 43; for הייתה in particular cf. היתה in Deut 28.26.

E. MS 1909

Photographs: *Figure 32.1* is the most recent photograph taken by Bruce Zuckerman in 2011. *Figure 32.2* is the photograph received from the Brownlee family, designated Institute for Antiquity and Christianity: BF 2.B = *MS 1909 Wm. Brownlee photograph*. *Figure 32.3* shows the Schøyen fragment (1QSb V 22–25) restored from *Figures 33.1* and *33.2*, and superimposed on the new IAA colour photograph, B–298313.[11] Cf. also Brooke, appendix *DJD* 26:227–33, Plates XXIV and XXIX.

Figure 32.1. 1QSb (1Q28b) col. V—MS 1909

Figure 32.2. MS 1909 Wm. Brownlee photograph

[שׁור ל]	1
[תו קודשׁ]	2
[ייתה כֹ]	3
[עֹ יתֹן]	4

[11] Part of the Leon Levy Digital Dead Sea Scrolls Library, Israel Antiquities Authority (http://www.deadseascrolls.org.il/explore-the-archive/image/B–298313; accessed 26 September, 2013).

Notes on Readings

Line 1. *Reš* and *lamed* are still clearly readable, the vertical stroke of the latter rising above the very faintly incised ruling, but the first two letters are no longer extant. The earlier photograph and Brownlee's original notes[12] record a reading for line 1 of ‏[שור ל‏].

Line 2. The remains of the first extant letter are the left downstroke of *taw*; the whole letter is clear on *Figure 32.2*. On the left edge, there is a very small trace of ink which is not incompatible with the right-hand downstroke of *šin*, as both Brownlee and Trever have proposed.

Line 3. Though *waw* and *yod* are commonly very similar, it is likely that the first two preserved letters of this line are both *yod*. For the restoration ‏ה[ייתה‏, cf. 1QSb V 29; 1QHᵃ XI 38; 4QCurses (4Q280) 1 3 (Milik 1972, 128); 4QApocryphon of Josephᶜ (4Q373) 1 i 5; 4QParaphrase of Kings (4Q382) 104 3; 4QInstructionᵈ (4Q418) 88 8; 103 ii 7; 127 3; 227 2. In light of 1QSb V 29 (‏והייתה כא]ריה‏),[13] the ink remains at the left-hand side of this line should most suitably be taken as a *kap*.

Line 4. The placing of this fragment in context in 1QSb V means that the ink traces at the start of line 4 belong to an ʿ*ayin*. These traces thus complete ‏רשע‏ of 1QSb V 25. The reading at the end of the line is less certain. The first letter of the word which continues beyond the left-hand edge of the fragment is *yod*, one with an inverted V-shaped head which is characteristic of semiformal influence on the hand of 1QSb. The next letter is *taw*, since the left downstroke is clear. All that remains of the third letter is traces of ink, well above the top of the *taw*; these could belong to several letters, *he*, *kap*, *ṣade*, or final *nun*.

The fragment is to be located in 1QSb V 22–25[14] as follows (see *Figure 32.3*).

1QSb V

22 ‏[ו[ל‏ הוכיח במישׁור ל]ע[נוי ארץ ולהתהלך לפניו תמים בכול דרכ]י‏ [‏

23 ‏ולהקים בריתו קודשׁ]   [צר לדורשיו]ו י]שׁ[אכ]ה‏ אדוני לרום עולם וכמגדל ע]ו[ז] בחומה‏

24 ‏נשגבה והייתה כ]   [בעז]פי[כה בשבׁטכה תחריב   ארץ וברוח שפתיכה‏

25 ‏תמית רשׁע יתן] לכה רוח עצ]ה וגבורת עולם רוח   דעת ויראת אל‏

Translation

22. [and] to reprove with equity the [hu]mble of the land and to walk before Him perfectly in all the ways of [

23. and to establish His covenant as holy[   ] distress to those seeking Him. May the Lord ra[ise y]ou to an everlasting height and like a stro[ng] tower on a high

24. wall. And you will be like[   ] by the power of your [mouth], by your sceptre you will destroy *vacat* the earth and by the breath of your lips

---

[12] Brownlee's notes now form part of the Dead Sea scroll archives of the John Rylands Library of the University of Manchester.

[13] 1QSb V 29 is restored by Milik (*DJD* 1:128–29) on the basis of the use of Gen 49.9; Milik also notes the lion imagery in Mic 5.7; 1 Macc 3.4; 2 Macc 11.11.

[14] Stegemann has reconsidered the height of the columns in 1QSb and has proposed that 1QSb V had 27 lines, not 29 as suggested by Milik. On Stegemann's calculations 1QSb V 22–25 should be renumbered V 20–23, see Stegemann 1996, 484. Milik's original numbering is preserved here for ease of reference.

25.   you will kill the wicked. May He give[you a spirit of coun]sel and everlasting might, a spirit of
        vacat knowledge and the fear of God.

Notes on Reconstruction and Comments

Line 22. Milik proposed for frg. 25 that at the start of line 22 במישור לעני should be restored. All this,
apart from the *'ayin* is now represented. The measurements are all thoroughly suitable. This restoration
was proposed on the basis of Isa 11.4 (והוכיח במישור לענוי ארץ).[15]

    Line 23. Milik proposed a restoration of ולהקים ברי]ת קודשו ב[צר לדורשיו from the start of the line.
The sense of the Hebrew in that restoration is a little awkward. Thus Jacob Licht proposed instead
ברי]תו לעמו ביום [צר (Licht 1965, 288). The extant remains now show that Licht was right to represent
ברית with the third person suffix; cf. Deut 8.18 למען הקים את בריתו.[16] However, the rest of the newly
placed fragment goes some way towards justifying Milik's original proposal. Since ברית has a pronomi-
nal suffix, the adjectival phrase can no longer be considered as a construct. If קודשו is restored, then
the result is an appositional use of one noun qualifying another ('his covenant, his holiness'). However,
it is probably preferable that קודש without a suffix should be restored, so that the noun is used as an
adverb of manner: cf. Lev 27.14 יקדש את ביתו קדש ליהוה.

    Line 24. The join is excellent and the whole of והייתה is easily legible. As in 1QSb V 29 it appears that,
after a phrase with God as subject, והייתה introduces a set of phrases addressed to the נשיא העדה directly
(V 20). This new fragment shows that there is indeed some repetition in the poetic structuring of this
blessing.

    Line 25. Again the join is thoroughly suitable. To the right of the new fragment, this results in the
restoration of the singular רשע, rather than the plural which Milik originally proposed. In light of the
singular in Isa 11.4 ימית רשע, Licht had restored רשע in 1QSb V 25. His insight is now vindicated.

    Isaiah 11 is also interpreted in a messianic way in 4QpIsa^a (4Q161) 7–10 iii 15–29 and 4QSM (4Q285)
5. Both 4QpIsa^a and 4QSM speak of the צמח דויד; 4QSM seems to identify this figure with the נשיא העדה,
a title also used in 1QSb V 20. 4QSM 5 4 contains the problematic phrase והמיתו נשיא העדה. In 1QSb V 25,
as now restored with this new fragment, it is clear that the נשיא העדה is blessed in his mission to 'kill
the wicked (singular)'. So it is most likely that the same figure is the subject of והמיתו in 4QSM 7 4: 'and
the Prince of the Congregation will put him to death'.[17]

    The word after רשע in 1QSb V 25 begins with ית; no proposed restoration is completely suitable.
Clearly, there is a break from the close correlation with Isa 11.4, as Isa 11.5 is only picked up again at
the very end of 1QSb V 25. It seems that Isa 11.2 is being followed, but not verbatim. In the light of Isa
11.2, the proposed restoration here is ית]ן לכה רוח עצ[ה. Similar phraseology can be seen at 1QSb III 5
שלו[ם ע]ו[לם יתן לכה ומלכות, and probably 1QSb V 18 י]תן לאחר וכבודכה לוא.[18]

    The proposed restoration of ית]ן reveals more of the structure of the blessing. The form יתן is the
middle element of a trio of similarly formed 3rd pers. sing. verbs (which open 1a, 2a and 3a below). It is

[15] This restoration was almost universally supported by other scholars, notably Licht 1965, 288; Carmignac 1963, 40–41;
Maier 1960, 178; Vermes 1997, 376. The restoration has also been followed by Charlesworth and Stuckenbruck 1994, 128–29
(cf. Brooke and Robinson 1995, 129).

[16] Cf. also 1QS V 21–22; CD III 13. Jean Carmignac (1961–1963, 2.40–41) also recognized the use of Deut 8.18 here, though
he left his translation without representation of the third person suffix on ברית: 'et pour établir une Allian[ce'.

[17] For the discussion of the matter that overlaps here with 4QpIsa^a and 4QSM (4Q285), cf. Eisenman and Wise 1992, 29;
Vermes and Alexander, *DJD* 36:240; Brooke and Robinson 1995, 133, esp. also n. 45.

[18] Cf. for יתנכה: 1QS II 5; 4QS^c 1 ii 2; 5QS 1 i 4; for יתן: 1QpHab V 4, X 3; 1QS II 17; 4Q487 8 1; 4Q511 144 2.

matched by the forms שׁ[אכ]ה י[in 1QSb V 23 which opens the blessing proper (1a), and by the subsequent ישם in 1QSb V 26 (3a). Thus, the new fragment assists in revealing the overall structure of the first part of the blessing. It is composed of three pairs of verses. In each pair, the first part has God as subject (1a, 2a, 3a), the second is addressed directly to the messianic prince (1b, 2b, 3b). This deliberate structuring technique may go some way towards explaining why the allusions to Isa 11.2–5 are not in scriptural order. In the first pair of verses, the second element (1b, addressed directly to the prince) is based on Isa 11.4; in the second pair of verses, the second element (2b, again addressed to the prince directly) is based on the next verse, Isa 11.5. In between comes a verse (2a) with God as the subject of the verb; this is based on Isa 11.2.

The other scriptural allusions in this blessing have been pointed out by various scholars and need not be repeated in detail here. The opening verse (1a) that matches scriptural phrases (Ps 61.4; Isa 30.13; Prov 18.10–11) used in 1QHᵃ XI 21; XV 11 is followed by a verse (1b) in which עז picks up on the earlier use of עוז. רוח is then the word which connects Isa 11.4 back to Isa 11.1. When Isa 11.5 is resumed, the references to parts of the body are followed through in the third pair of verses with an allusion to Mic 4.13 and the metaphor then applied in the last verse through Mic 7.10. B. Nitzan has noted in detail how, apart from the use of נשא at the very start of the blessing, there is no appeal to Num 6.24–26 in the blessing of the Prince of the Congregation, but rather a liturgical exegesis of prophecies concerning the royal messiah.[19]

1a.	[23]May the Lord ra[ise y]ou to an everlasting height and like a stro[ng] tower on a high [24]wall.	י[שׁ]אכ[ה אדוני לרום עולם וכמגדל עוֹ[ז] בחומה נשגבה
1b.	*And you will be like*[ ] by the power of your [mouth] by your sceptre you will destroy the earth and by the breath of your lips [25]you will kill the wicked.	והייתה כֹ[ ] בעז [פי]כה בשבטכה תחריב ארץ וברוח שפתיכה תמית רשע
2a.	*May He giv*[e you a spirit of coun]sel and everlasting might a spirit of knowledge and of the fear of God.	יתֹ[ן] לכה רוח עצ]ה וגבורת עולם רוח דעת ויראת אל
2b.	And righteousness shall be [26]the girdle of [your loins, and fait]h the girdle of your haunches.	והיה צדק אזור [מותניכה ואמונ]ה אזור חלצﬞיכﬞה
3a.	May He make your horns iron and your hooves bronze.	ישם קרניכה ברזל ופרסותיכה נחושה
3b.	[27]May you toss like a bu[ll many peoples and trample nat]ions like mud in the streets. For God...	תנגח כפֹ]ר עמים רבים ותרמוס גוי]ם כטיט חוצות כיא אל...

---

[19] Gen 49.8–11; Isa 11.2–5; Mic 4.13; 5.7–8. See Nitzan 1994, 164–67.

Figure 32.3. *1QSb (1Q28b) col. V reconstructed to include MS 1909 (scale 3:4)*

F. Appendix. 1QUnidentified Fragment (MS 1909)

DSS F.128. DSS F.1QUnidentifiedFragmentText2

On the Wm. Brownlee photograph there is another minor fragment included with 1QSb, which is different in colour and parchment texture. This fragment measures 9 × 7 mm and is darker than the 1QSb fragments in The Schøyen Collection. Remnants of two lines can be seen.

]◦שׁצ[1
]ל[2

Notes on Readings

Line 2. Only the head of a *lamed* is visible on the bottom edge of the fragment.

XXVI

MS 1926/2. 1QApocryphon of Genesis ar (1Q20) cols I, III, IV, V

Torleif Elgvin, Kipp Davis

DSS F.129. DSS F.1QapGen

A. History of Research

The wad presented here fell off from the main scroll while it was in John C. Trever's possession when he photographed the scrolls of Athanasius Samuel early in 1948 (Trever's notes date this to 21 February, 1948). It was kept by Trever and was bought by The Schøyen Collection from the Trever family in 1994, together with a wad containing 1QDan[a] and 1QDan[b]. Both wads were photographed in 1995 by Bruce Zuckerman and his team. Within the wad presented here they identified three layers, which they designated fragments c–e,[1] and were able to read at least three letters in lines 1–2 of the lower layer (layer 1). They suggested that the three layers represented fragments deriving from consecutive columns between col. 0 and col. III (Lundberg and Zuckerman 1996).[2] These fragments contain a handful of visible letters, but no single word has been preserved among them.

B. Physical Description

The Cave 1 *Genesis Apocryphon* has suffered a high degree of deterioration. Different from most Qumran scrolls, the ink contains copper, which suggests an origin in a scribal milieu different from that of the Qumran community. When exposed to UV light, the copper of the ink catalyzes the degradation of the parchment. At the altitude of the Dead Sea there is limited UV light. Since its discovery, the process of deterioration has accelerated with the dramatic increase of exposure to UV light in the course of the past sixty-years.[3] The wad from the scroll presented here does not show this peculiar pattern of destruction, since it had been kept in the dark or under glass that filters out UV radiation.

The two light-coloured fragments at the left side of *Figure 33.1* represent remnants of the separate protective sheet which covered the lower part of 1Q20 X–XV when the already worn scroll was packed away for storage in antiquity (Avigad and Yadin 1956, 14). The right piece measures 34.3 × 6.6 mm and

---

[1] Fragments a–b are two pieces of repair material assigned to 1QapGen, pictured to the left of the main fragment wad in *Figure 33.1*.

[2] 'Column 0' is comprised of fragments that were recovered from Cave 1 following the discovery of the first scrolls. These fragments originally published by J.T. Milik as '1Q20' in *DJD* 1 under the title 'Apocalypse de Lamech'. In 1991 the fragments were reconstructed by Bruce Zuckerman and Michael O. Wise and attached to the beginning of 1QapGen as cols 0–I. For transcriptions and translations cf. Wise and Abegg 2005, 91, and Machiela 2010, 31–32.

[3] Personal communication from Ira Rabin, cf. Avigad and Yadin 1956, 13–14.

the left piece 35.3 × 11.3 mm. The light-coloured parchment was not finally processed—high-resolution microscopic examination shows original hair still present on the grain side of the skin.

According to Ira Rabin's analysis, the protective sheet contained high amounts of lead, while the wad from the scroll contained no lead at all. The lead profile coincides with bromine on the hair side of the protective sheet, and with bromine, potassium, and chlorine on the flesh side. This indicates that the lead belongs to the stage of preparation of the skin, deriving from exposure to water containing lead. Further, the wad contained high amounts of salt and small amounts of sulfur, different from the protective sheet. Rabin concludes that the protective sheet and the main scroll reflect different modes of preparation, perhaps pointing to different milieus at the production stage and at the scroll's final deposit. Both the main scroll and the protective sheet were prepared outside the Dead Sea region, but in a location where the water did not contain lead (Rabin, unpublished report; see also p. 67).

The wad from 1QapGen probably contains material from the external layers of the scroll, which fell off before it was opened in 1956. The external layers represent the first columns of the book, since this text was rolled from end to beginning, with the beginning making up the outer layers (Stegemann 1992, 250–53). The top of this scroll is better preserved than its bottom. This could indicate that it was stored standing upright in a jar.[4]

The surface of this small wad is remarkably smooth, possibly indicating that the material may have been well-prepared parchment. The two lower layers are medium-to-dark brown in colour. The bottom layer (layer 1) measures 30 × 30 mm, and the second layer (layer 2) 24 × 26 mm. These are aligned to one another on the top edge. Layers 1–2 contain the top margin of the scroll, which measures 21 mm. On both layers there are traces of letters from the first line of the column(s). The physical shape of these two pieces may suggest a material join with another fragment, 1Q20 19, which also preserves a top margin and top line, and was assigned to col. 0 or col. I of the scroll (see further below).[5]

Layers 3–4 appear together as a single piece, located on top of layer 2. This piece is very dark brown in colour, measures 13 × 9 mm, and is situated in the centre of the wad, but on the right edge of the pile. This small piece has shifted off its horizontal axis, and contains traces of letters from two lines of text, positioned vertically relative to layers 1–2. Because this piece seems thicker than the two others, it probably represents a separate wad of two layers (3 and 4), of which we can only discern letters on the top layer, layer 4. Infrared microscope imaging of the right edge from the side shows traces of ink on both sides of this small group (see *Figure 33.3*), suggesting that it consists of two fragments that have been stuck together. Less probably the ink on the *verso* represents set-off from an adjoining layer. We do not know the relation between layers 3/4 and 1/2, but it is most reasonable to suppose that layers 3 and 4 also come from the top of the scroll.

The line spacing in layers 1 and 4 is 4.4 mm. The height of the only fully preserved letter in layer 1 (*he*) is 1.8 mm, which represents a relatively small script among the Qumran scrolls. Fragments from col. 0 appear in images by Inscriptifact, and these reveal letter heights between 1.8–2.6 mm from 1Q20 17–20. According to the images published by Daniel A. Machiela (2009, 152–75), letter-heights for the first six columns are as follows: 1Q20 I, 1.6–2.1 mm; 1Q20 II, 1.8–2.5 mm; 1Q20 III, 2.0–2.3 mm; 1Q20 IV, 1.8–2.0 mm; 1Q20 V, 2.0–2.6 mm; 1Q20 VI, 1.8–2.2 mm.

---

[4] On the other hand, Avigad and Yadin suggested the scroll had been lying on the cave floor, 'so that its lower part was constantly exposed to dampness, while its upper part was in a dry atmosphere' (1956, 12).

[5] Noted already by Lundberg and Zuckerman 1996, 4. Compare the image in Machiela 2009, 149.

C. Palaeography

There is not enough material preserved from which to analyze the palaeography of these fragments. For a discussion of the script of 1QapGen the reader is referred to the analysis published in the *editio princeps* (Avigad and Yadin 1956, 15, 38). The script is comparable with the hand of 1QM, which later was dated by Cross to 30–1 BC (Cross 1961b, Fig. 2, line 4).

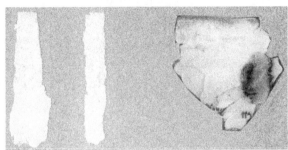

Figure 33.1. *MS 1926/2, a wad from 1QapGen with pieces from the protective sheet (left)*

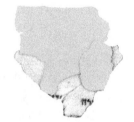

Figure 33.2a. *MS 1926/2 layer 1*

D. Layer 1 (bottom layer)

Examination of the *verso* shows that the fragment preserves a top margin of 21–22 mm.

]*top margin*[
]∘ד∘ *vacat* רה∘[1
]ל∘∘∘∘[2

Notes on Readings

Line 1. The length of the *vacat* is 4.6 mm.

   Line 1. Traces of the first letter after the *vacat* traces can be seen on both sides of the break; it is possibly *reš*, *kap*, or *he*. The second letter may be *kap*, but more probably *dalet*. A trace of a small curved stroke of the third letter is visible, perhaps the hook of a *lamed*.

   Line 2. The *lamed* is the only clearly identifiable letter. Traces of ink belonging to the second letter could match the top of the left stroke and of both arms of a *šin*. Between this letter and the *lamed* there is space for one or two letters.

E. Layer 2 (medial layer)

Figure 33.2b. MS 1926/2 layer 2

The fragment preserves a top margin of 21 mm, and remnants of the top of three letters in the first line of the column.

]*top margin*[

]○○ל[1

Notes on Readings

Line 1. Trace of the high-tip of the *lamed* is visible, followed by possibly two or three letters. Small specks that could perhaps be ink appear in the space of where we would expect a second letter. The third letter shows trace of a 'wedge' and could be either *yod*, *waw*, *reš*, or *he*. We see a long horizontal crossbar, possibly *he*, but more probably *taw* or a final *mem*.

F. Layer 4 (top layer)

The fragment preserves two lines of text, situated vertically relative to layers 1 and 2. It is affixed to an underlying layer that also shows minute traces of ink on its edge, but this piece, designated layer 3, is virtually unreadable.

Figure 33.2c. MS 1926/2 layer 3/4

]○ אֹ○○[1

]○שׁ○○[2

Notes on Readings

Line 1. The final *nun* is clearly visible, but the downstroke of the following letter appears so closely written as to suggest the absence of any word-space. However, compare with other places throughout 1QapGen in which the word-spacing is very small (*e.g.* באדין חשׁבֹת in 1QapGen II 1). The final letter appears most like a *waw*. The left downstroke and the oblique stroke of ʾ*alep* are both visible in microscopic infrared images.

    Line 2.]∘שׁ̇∘∘[. There are traces of three or four letters, and the *šin* is fairly prominent at high exposure. The preceding letter shows trace of a right-descending oblique stroke that is possibly characteristic of ʾ*alep*.

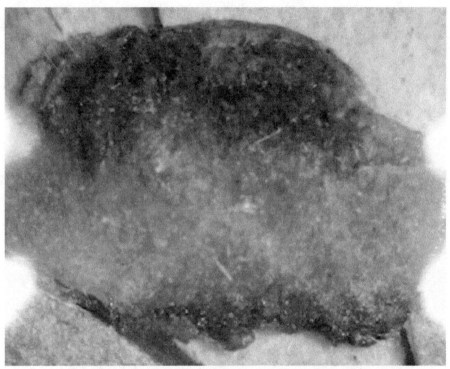

Figure 33.3. *MS 1926/2 Microscopic infrared, layers 3/4*
(scale 10:1)

Col. vi   Col. v   Col. iv

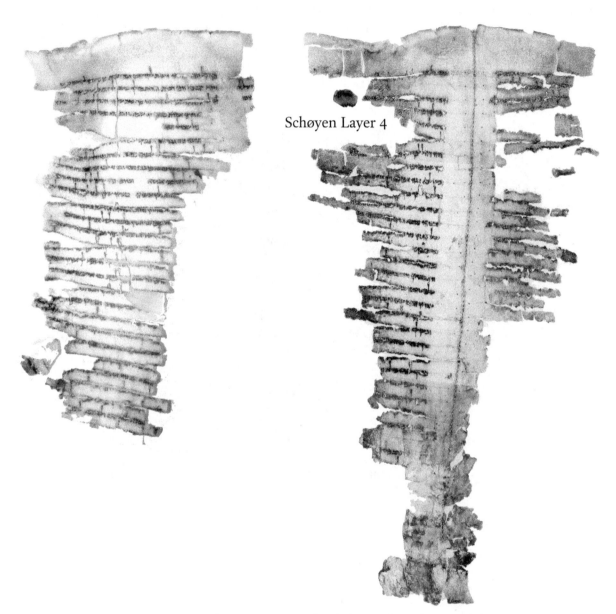

Schøyen Layer 4

Figure 33.4. *1QapGen cols I–V, reconstructed with the insertion of MS 1926/2 layers 1–4*
(scale 1:2 on double page; photograph © The Israel Museum, Jerusalem)

Col. iii   Col. ii   Col i

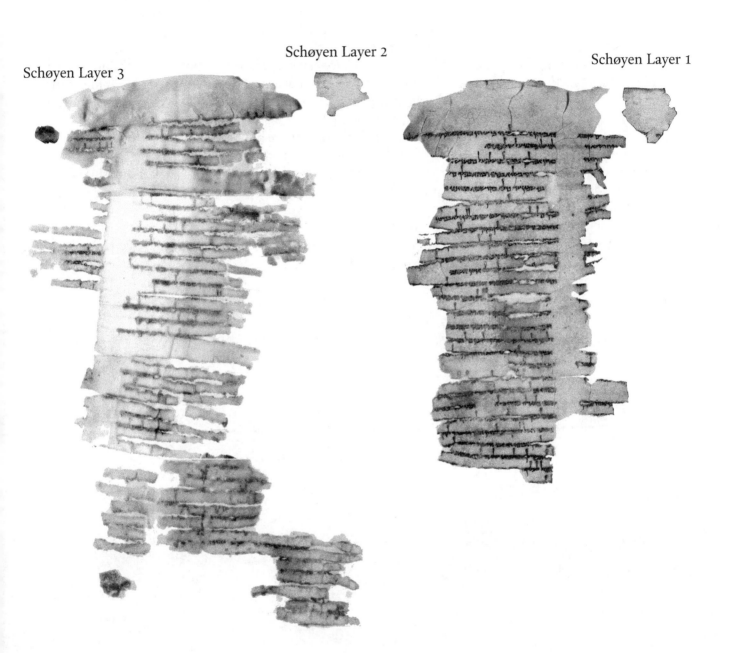

Schøyen Layer 2

Schøyen Layer 1

Schøyen Layer 3

G. Locating the Fragments from the Wad in the Scroll

The diameter of the scroll was not recorded by Avigad and Yadin before the scroll was opened. Based on the published photographs of the scroll while still rolled up, the diameter appears to be between 5–6 cm. This would imply that the circumference of the first turn of the scroll was between 15.7–18.8 cm. The column width varies substantially from one sheet to another, with an average of 12 cm.

Layer 1 appears very similar in height to 1QapGen frg. 19, which was assigned to col. 0, and also preserves the top margin and traces of the first line. However, the top margin of this piece measures 26 mm, and would be too big for a match with our first layer. Alternatively, layer 1 more likely belongs to col. I, whose top margin measures 22 mm. This would most likely also require placement of layer 2 in col. III. The top margin of layer 2 is exactly the same as that of col. III. When these two pieces are set among the remaining fragments containing cols I–III, we can suggest a more probable location of layer 1 in the third vertical quadrant of col. I, lines 1–2. Using an average measurement of 17.2 cm for the scroll's circumference, derived from the measurements of the photographed roll, would in turn suggest that layer 2 is best located near the beginning of col. III, line 1.

The remaining two layers can be hypothetically located on the basis of the placement of layers 1–2, and by estimating the circumference of each successive turn towards the end of the manuscript. Hartmut Stegemann observed that large scrolls like 1QapGen were always tightly rolled, and this would produce a decrease in the diameter of each turn of 1–2 mm (Stegemann 1992, 253). An approximate decreasing diameter of 1 mm would suggest locations for layers 3 and 4 in the first or second vertical quadrant of cols IV and V, line 1–2 respectively.

The situation of all four layers combined helps to confirm their individual respective placements within the spaces between the existing fragments that form cols I–V. Unfortunately, with no single preserved word among the new fragments, and in the absence of any material joins to the existing fragments of 1QapGen, we can say little about these fragments beyond their possible location.

XXVII

MS 5095/7. 4Q(?)Fragment with Text from *Commentary on Genesis A*

Torleif Elgvin

DSS F.130. DSS F.CommGen

A. Physical Description

MS 5095/6 and MS 5095/7 were acquired as pieces of a leather cord. After their arrival at The Schøyen Collection infrared photography revealed letters on three of these tiny pieces (see *Figure 34.1*). The assemblage was therefore separated into MS 5095/6 (a leather cord) and MS 5095/7—four tiny pieces of parchment, three of which contained writing (a, b, c). The cord may have been used for the specific scroll represented by these fragments.

Fragments a, b, and c measure 2.0 × 1.0, 0.7 × 1.5, and 0.5 × 1.5 cm respectively. Digital images of these three pieces have been set together to form a material join, and together they measure 2.5 × 2.3 cm, including a top margin of 13 mm. The line spacing is 7.5 mm and the height of the letters 2.5 mm. Fragment d, measuring 0.9 × 1.2 cm, probably preserves a piece from the top margin without writing. The text is written on well prepared and extremely thin parchment, grey in colour, probably belonging to the group that Ira Rabin identifies as 'Western type' parchments (see p. 64).

B. Palaeography

The script is a nicely formed early Herodian hand. Michael Langlois identifies scribal features common at the end of the Hasmonaean and the beginning of the Herodian period. He concludes that the scroll was copied in the second half (most likely the last quarter) of the first century BC (see p. 98).

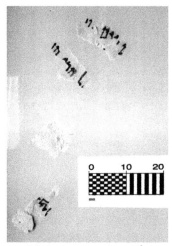

Figure 34.1. MS 5095/7

C. MS 5095/7

top] *margin* [

[○ה֫ יום םימ○]   1

[○ה הרי ל○]   2

Notes on Readings

Line 1.]○ה֫. One can see the lower part of a downstroke, followed by another downstroke topped by a hook, as well as a third one. The first two downstrokes are most easily read as a *he*.
    Line 2.]○ה. The preserved downstroke of the last letter can be interpreted as *waw, yod, nun,* or *reš*.

D. Identification

One of the pieces (frg. c) contains the letters]○ה הרי ל○[. This combination of letters does not align with any text from the Hebrew Bible, but was identified with a line in 4QCommGen A (4Q252) I 10, also from the same time period (50–1 BC). These words are part of the Noah story, a retelling of Gen 8.3–4: an account of the ark's landing 'on the mountains of Hu[rarat'. Thereafter the letters on frgs a and b were identified with words from the preceding line in 4QCommGen A. Fragments b and c represent a material joint (note the *lamed* that runs through frgs b and c, and the final *mem* of ימ֯ים preserved on frgs a and b), see *Figure 34.2*.

Figure 34.2. 4Q(?)*Fragment with Text from* Commentary on Genesis A

E. MS 5095/7 (= 4QCommGen A I 10)

] *top margin* [

[יום חסרו המים שני]יֹמים יום הרֹ[ביעי ויום החמישי]   1

[ויום הששי נחה התבה]עֹל הרי הוֹ[ררט   [2

Translation

1. [days the waters decreased for two]days, the fou[rth day and the fifth day,]
2. [and on the sixth day the ark came to rest]on the mountains of Hu[rarat;   ]

Notes on Reconstruction and Comments

The line length can be calculated as *c.* 7.5 cm with 44–45 letter spaces per line (4QCommGen A I has 49–57 letter spaces per line).

The parallel text of 4QCommGen A I 8-10 reads, 'And at the end of one hundred and fifty days the waters decreased for two days, the fou[rth day and the fifth day, and on the sixth day the ark came to rest on the mountains of Hurarat; i[t was] the seventeenth [da]y of the seventh month.'

Line 2. הוֹ[ררט = 4QCommGen A. The spelling הוררט, common for 4QCommGen A and our text, is shared by 1QIsaᵃ (Isa 37.38, ארץ הוררט). The name of the landing place is spelled in various ways, cf. *DJD* 22:197: אררט (𝔐 Gen 8.4; 2 Kgs 19.37; Isa 37.38; Jer 51.27; 4QpapTob [4Q196] to Tob 1.21), הררט (ᴍ Gen 8.4), האררט (1QapGen X 12), הוררט (4Q252 I 10; 1QIsaᵃ Isa 37.38).[1] Ararat or Hurarat is a kingdom in eastern Asia Minor, which flourished from the ninth century until 585 BC (cf. 2 Kgs 19.37; Isa 37.38; Jer 51.27). In Assyrian records it is usually called Urartu (*ABD* 1:351–52).[2]

Based on the physical evidence George Brooke argues that the first, almost complete column of 4QCommGen A represents the beginning of this scroll. He suggests that the six columns of 22 lines, written on a single sheet of leather about 60 cm long, represents the full length of the scroll (*DJD* 22:186–90).

With only six partially preserved words it is impossible to know much about the scroll represented by our fragments. If MS 5095/7 did preserve the same text as col. I of 4QCommGen A (4Q252), the top margin would suggest that this fragment survived from the second column of a scroll with columns of 10 lines. The full height of this scroll could then be reconstructed as *c.* 10 cm. Further, if Brooke is right about the length of the scroll of 4QCommGen A and our manuscript contained the full text of *Commentary on Genesis A*, the length of the scroll represented by our fragments could tentatively be calculated as *c.* 150 cm with 17 columns.

According to Brooke, the variety of material in *Commentary on Genesis A* suggests that this composition was compiled from different sources (*DJD* 22:187). Against Brooke, Shani Tzoref (2012) argues that 4QCommGen A is a unitary composition with patriarchal blessings and their fulfilment as the overarching theme. The covenants with Noah, Abraham, Isaac, and Jacob form a prelude to the coming Davidic messiah and his 'men of the community'. Puech (2013) similarly identifies patriarchal blessings

---

[1] 𝔊 transliterates this word as Αραρατ in Gen 8.4; 2 Kgs 19.37; Jer 28.27 (=51.27); Tob 1.21, but renders εις Αρμενιαν in Isa 37.38.

[2] The Schøyen Collection holds a royal inscription on bronze of King Minua of Urartu, *c.* 810–785 BC (MS 3185).

and election as the unifying thread of this sectarian text. The Schøyen text may be a second copy of *Commentary on Genesis A*, a literary source for this work, or a text quoting from it. The fragment is simply too small to conclude one way or the other. MS 5095/7 may be another example of a *pesher* or biblical commentary, produced in the *Yaḥad* and preserved in more than one copy.[3] Nearly all the Qumran *pesharim* were found in Cave 4,[4] and the same may be the case for MS 5095/7.

[3] Steudel 1994 suggested that 4QFlor (4Q174) and 4QCatena A (4Q177) represent different parts of the same eschatological midrash (4Q178, 4Q182, and 4Q183 may be copies of the same work). A *pesher* on Isaiah is preserved in five copies (4Q161–4Q165), while *pesharim* on Hosea and Psalms exist in two copies (4Q166; 4Q167; 4Q171, 4Q173).

[4] 1QpHab and 11QMelch are exceptions to this rule. The latter is a thematic commentary on various biblical texts influenced by priestly or Levitic tradition (on this background, see Elgvin 2010a and 2011a).

XXVIII

MS 4612/3. 11Q(?)Eschatological Fragment ar

Esther Eshel

DSS F.131. DSS F.Eschat

This text, with three fragmentary lines of an unknown Aramaic work, was published by Émile Puech in *DJD* 37:501–4, as 4QTestament[d] ar. Puech's publication is based on a black-and-white photograph from the early 1960s and a later colour image given to him by Kando. Our readings are based on better photographs and improve Puech's edition in *DJD* 37.

A. Physical Description

The fragment measures 2 × 2 cm and has a thickness of 0.33±0.05 mm. The parchment is thin, prepared on both sides, and shows a quality rare among the Schøyen fragments. The fragment is light to medium brown in colour; and the line spacing *c.* 6 mm, somewhat larger between lines 2–3 than between lines 1–2. Mineral deposits are visible as white spots, protruding from the surface. The deposits are more frequent on the uninscribed surface than on the letters, but at times they appear on top of the ink as grey spots on the infrared photograph. Similar deposits are even more visible on the *verso*, where they protrude more notably from the surface.

FTIR and XRF scanning as analyzed by Ira Rabin indicate that the white spots on both sides contain magnesium ammonium phosphate (struvite), a feature most easily explained as a product of the bat guano that permeated the atmosphere of Cave 11. No calcite or aragonite was detected on the fragment. High levels of chlorine and potassium are products of the process of manufacture. The parchment is of the 'Eastern' type, with potassium pointing to vegetable tanning. The chlorine/bromine ratio suggests preparation of the skin outside the Dead Sea region. The uneven distribution of chlorine might be caused by NaCl presence in sediments of a natural cave (Rabin, unpublished report).

B. Palaeography

Ada Yardeni classifies this hand as closer to early Herodian than late Hasmonaean script and suggests a date around 40–30 BC. Michael Langlois characterizes the script as a smooth and beautiful Herodian book hand that integrates some of the new Herodian techniques. He concludes that the scroll was copied towards the end of the first century BC (see p. 99).

Figure 35*. MS 4612/3*

C. MS 4612/3

[ברי]מ יד°[	1
[זדי ימכון °[	2
[ט שין[ ]ל̇[	3

Notes on Readings

Line 1. [○יד . Puech read א[]ד̇ח̇יד. On the 2007 photos, a thick speck of ink can be seen at the lower right end of the *yod*, which at first glance could resemble the baseline of a *nun*. A careful study of the photographs suggests that this actually belongs to a tiny piece of parchment with ink upon it, dislodged from the edge of the main fragment.

Before *yod* one sees the upper part of a vertical stroke. A tiny speck of ink touches this stroke. These traces represent one or two letters (in the rest of the fragment consecutive letters do not touch each other). If it is one letter, *ṭet* would be an attractive option. *Nun* preceded by another letter is possible, but less likely.

Line 1. מרי○[. Puech read מריא̇[. The trace of the last letter is compatible with *ʾalep*, *zayin*, *reš*, or *dalet*.

Line 2. זדי. Puech read this word as ז̇די. With the new photograph our reading is clear.

Line 3.]ל̇[. We see a trace of ink above the line, which should be identified as the top of a *lamed*.

D. Identification and Provenance

Puech suggested identifying the scribal hand in this fragment with the hand in XQOffering ar (*DJD* 36:490–91), and published both together as frgs 1 and 2 of 4QTestament[d] ar (4Q587). We disagree with this identification. *Šin*, *waw*, and final *nun* are the same in these two fragments. *Kap* is similar, but the top stroke is drawn a little longer to the left in XQOffering. *Yod* in MS 4612/3 has a thicker head, and *reš* is different. In XQOffering the head of *reš* ascends slightly towards the right (see in particular *reš* in line 3), but not so in MS 4612/3. More decisively, *mem* is drawn differently in these two fragments: MS 4612/3 uses two separate strokes, adding the left descender at the end (cf. the linear nature of the opening ascending line). XQOffering draws the full letter in one stroke, breaking the initial line to make the left.

One should further note that the topic is different in these two fragments. It is difficult to make a connection between the humiliation of the arrogant (line 2 below) and the sacrifices of XQOffering. We were unable to identify the fragmentary remains of the text with any known composition. The probable mention of the Lord and 'arrogant ones' who 'will be brought low' tentatively suggests that the fragment be classified as an eschatological or prophetic text, similar to a number of texts from Qumran, many of which were unclassified.

Ira Rabin's analysis suggests that the fragment was found in a natural cave in the cliffs, not in a cave in the marl terrace. The identification of the white mineral spots as struvite points to a possible Cave 11 provenance, and the text has been designated 11Q(?)Eschatological Fragment ar.

E. MS 4612/3

1   [°יד מריֿאֿ]
2   [ימכון זדי]°
3   [ט שין] [ ]לֿל[

Translation

1.   ]your [...] the Lord of [...]
2.   ] the arrogant ones of [...] will be brought low [
3.   ].[ ]...[

Comments

Line 1. °יד[. We interpret the combination of *yod* and final *kap* as the 2nd person masculine suffix. In the absence of any details about the context other options cannot be excluded.

Line 1. מריֿאֿ[. On the basis of the verbal clause in line 2 we tend to interpret the trace of the last letter as *ʾalep*, reading מריא, meaning 'the Lord' or 'the master', referring either to a human dignitary (cf. 1QapGen 2 9; 22 18) or to God (cf. 1QapGen 20 15). The personal name Miriam is also possible (cf. 4QVisions of Amram[g]? ar [4Q549] 2 8 מריאם). Another option would be to posit the last letter as *reš*, leading to the reading מריֿרֿ['bitter'.

Line 2. ימכון. This word is from the Aramaic root מכך 'make low, humiliate' (Sokoloff 2002, 307), here used either in the active (*paʿel*) 'they defiled' or the passive (*hopʿal*) 'they were defiled'.[1] In Aramaic texts from Qumran we find the verb in 11QtgJob (11Q10) 2 6 רוח המכת לאנתתי 'I humble my spirit to my wife', (translating Job 19.17 רוחי זרה לאשתי 'My odour is repulsive to my wife'); and 4QpapVision[b] ar (4Q558) 67 6 י[אֿמֿכֿון ויאמֿ]רון 'they will go down and sa[y'. The verb appears with the same meaning in the Hebrew text 4QInstruction[d] (4Q418) 87 14 [אתה לוא תמוֿךֿ]°[']you will not be humbled['.

Line 2. זדי. This is probably the noun זד, used in the plural construct. This usage is not attested elsewhere and is unexpected in an Aramaic text.[2] The corresponding Hebrew noun is used in the plural in Isa 13.11, perhaps with a meaning similar to our text: והשבתי גאון זדים וגאות עריצים אשפיל 'I will put an end to the pride of the arrogant and humble the haughtiness of tyrants.' In Qumran texts the plural זדים is used twice for arrogant or wicked persons, 11QPs[a] (11Q5) 18 13 (= S Ps 154.10); 1QH[a] XIV 38. The *Hodayot* text refers to the end-time judgement of evil forces, where God will put an end to מלחמות זדֿים (cf. Sollamo 2011).

We may translate line 2 as passive, 'the arrogant ones of [...] will be brought low', or as active '... they brought down, the arrogant ones of ['.

---

[1] The Hebrew equivalent of this verb is used in Ps 106.43, Job 24.24, and Eccl 10.18.

[2] Both Biblical and Qumran Hebrew use זד (adjective or noun, 'insolent, arrogant'), זדון ('pride, arrogance') and the verb זיד.

In Biblical Aramaic the verb זוד occurs in Dan 5.20 וכדי רם לבבה ורוחה תקפת להזדה 'But when he grew haughty and willfully presumptuous', where the *apᶜel* form means 'behave maliciously' or 'act presumptuously' (see 𝕿° to Exod 21.14; 𝕿ᴶ Josh 9.4, 12).

The Targum to Isa 13.11 uses the root in a verbal form: ואסער על דדירין בתבל בישא ועל רשיעיא חוביהון ואבטיל רבות רשיעין ותקוף תקיפין אמאיך 'And I will punish those who reside in the world for [their] evil and the wicked for their sins, and I will put an end to the pride of the wicked and *humble* the strength of the strong ones'—אמאיך is from the root מכך.

A parallel may be found in the early synagogal prayer *Ten Pahdeka* (used at Rosh Hashanah and Yom Kippur), which according to David Flusser has origins in the Second Temple period and was later integrated into *birkat haminim*: 'falsehood shall shut its mouth, all wickedness shall cease like smoke, when you remove the arrogant kingdom from the earth' (כי תעביר ממשלת זדון מן הארץ, Flusser 1994).[3]

Line 3. ‏[שין ט. The only combination of these letters in early Aramaic texts appears in 𝕿ᴶ to 1 Sam 15.22, הא קבלא למימריה מנכסת קדשין טב לאצתא למלי נביוהי מתרב פטימין, 'Indeed! Obedience to the Lord is better than holy sacrifices. Better to heed the words of my prophets than the fat of fatlings.' The noun ending with ‏[שין could be reconstructed as ‏[שין‏]קד (as in the targum) or ‏[שין‏]נ, but other reconstructions could also be imagined. Possible reconstructions could be ‏[שין ט‏]מאו‏[נ ('[wo]men were de[filed'), possibly referring to the myth of the Watchers in *1 En.* 6–11, or ‏[שין ט‏]מאו‏[קד ('the [ho]ly ones de[filed...'), with the Watchers as a possible subject (for which cf. *1 En.* 9.8).

---

[3] As reason for his early dating of this section (or source) of the *Ten Pahdeka* prayer Flusser pointed to close parallels with 1QMyst (1Q27) 1 i 5–7 'Wickedness will disappear before justice as darkness disappears before light — as smoke vanishes and i[s no] more — so shall wickedness vanish forever. And justice will be revealed like the sun that regulates the world. And all those who support "wonderful mysteries" will be no more. Knowledge shall fill the world, and folly shall nevermore be there.'

XXIX

MS 5439/2. Ḥev(?)Unidentified Fragment

Torleif Elgvin

DSS F.132. DSS F.Unident

A. Physical Description

At the time of the acquisition, this fragment, measuring 2.0 × 1.7 cm, was described as an uninscribed piece deriving from the lower margin of the same scroll as the Schøyen fragments assigned to 4QRP[b] (MS 5439/1). However, subsequent infrared photographs revealed remnants of four lines of text. The top layer of the fragment has flaked off in places, and the layer below is much lighter in colour. The skin is thicker than the parchment of the Schøyen 4QRP[b] fragment.

There are short *vacats* in at least three of the four lines (at least 11 mm in line 1; 8 mm in line 2; at least 5 mm in line 3), a feature that could suggest this is a stichometrically structured text.[1] The line spacing varies somewhat, with an average of 5 mm. Unlike the 4QRP[b] fragment, the letters on this fragment can only be seen on the infrared photographs. The parchment is red-brown in colour, similar to the Schøyen 4QRP[b] fragment. A more detailed account of the identification of this fragment and its separation from the 4QRP[b] fragments appears in the physical description of MS 5439/1 above.

There is a horizontal crack or fold between lines 1–2 that in the infrared photographs appears like a stray line of ink. However, a close physical examination reveals that what looks like ink in the IR spectrum is actually some kind of residue that has seeped into the fold. There may be faint traces of ink on the *verso*. If so, they would represent set-off from the next revolution of the scroll.

FTIR spectra show the presence of quartz and calcite, but not aragonite. Conversely, all these three minerals were also found in the two fragments of 4QRP[b]. This fragment also exhibits a different concentration of chlorine from that in the 4QRP[b] fragments. These results indicate that MS 5439/2 might not derive from Cave 4 (Rabin, unpublished report). Since aragonite has been invariably found on the fragments from Qumran, the absence of aragonite suggests a place of discovery other than Qumran. Furthermore, the absence of dolomite eliminates the possibility that the fragment came from Murabbaʿat. We tentatively designate the fragment Ḥev(?)Unidentified Fragment.

B. Palaeography

Michael Langlois characterizes the script as a skilled formal hand from the late Herodian period. He cautiously concludes that the text was copied around the middle of the first century AD (see p. 104).

---

[1] A similar layout is found in 5/6ḤevPs (*DJD* 38:Plate XXV–XXVII).

Figure 36. MS 5439/2

]*vacat* ○○[	1
]○י *vac* ילו○[	2
]הָארץ *vac*[	3
] ○ל[	4

Notes on Readings

Line 1. One can see the lower part of three vertical strokes, representing two or three letters.

Line 2. ילו○[. Infrared capture of the fragment upon its removal from the frame (in October 2012) showed more traces of ink than previous photos. Parts of the surface are eroded where the first letter was written. With the help of an infrared digital microscope one can see a vertical stroke slanting slightly upwards to the left, possibly with a tiny projection sticking out to the left, as well as some ink further up to the right. The best material options for this letter are *šin* or *samek*. The second letter is *yod* with a notably triangular head, and the last letter of this word is *waw*.

Line 2.]○י or]○ן. A small trace of an elbow belonging to the second letter has survived.

Line 3.]הָארץ[. The only clear reading in this text, 'the land'. A speck of ink can be seen in the *vacat*.

Line 4.] ○ל[. The letter following *lamed* is most likely *waw*, less so *reš* or final *mem*. There is probably a word space or *vacat* after the last letter.

Comments

Before the latest infrared capture of the fragment we pondered over tentative identifications with the biblical texts Ezek 48.13–15, 2 Kgs 3.18–21, and Hos 8.7–9. However, these parallels were discarded in the light of our inability to convincingly arrange the text into a plausible column structure. The possible stichometric layout may point to a poetic text.

Line 2. ילו○[. Based on the options for the first letter suggested above, what remains as the most likely reading is שִׁילו[.

One could restore a verbal form of משל 'rule', or 'be like', such as המשילו 'he set him to rule', or 'they set [someone] to rule', 'they compared' (*hipʿil* perfect of משל third sing. with suffix or plur.). *Hipʿil* forms of other verbs ending with *sin/šin* and *lamed* such as כשל (cause to) 'stumble', or בשל 'cook' could be alternative options. Another option would be to identify the term שִׁילה from Gen 49.10, with the spelling שילו as in the *Qere*. The text from Gen 49.10b עד כי יבא שילה cannot be aligned with the text of lines 3–4, but a reuse of this Davidic promise cannot be excluded.

Based on the late Herodian script both a Qumran and a Bar Kokhba provenance could be possible, but the mineral analysis points to a Bar Kokhba cave as place of discovery.

XXX

MS 5095/1, MS 5095/4. Wads from 11QTᵃ, Unidentified Fragments from Cave 11

Torleif Elgvin, Kipp Davis

DSS F.133.

A. Wads from 11QTᵃ

1. Physical Description

There remain many petrified wads of scroll fragments and other materials from Cave 11 in the IAA collections, most of which have never been photographed. Some items from the cluster presented here are similar to these, and are asserted also to have derived from Cave 11. MS 5095/1 includes 16 minor fragments or wads and one piece of textile. MS 5095/4 includes seven pieces of leather or parchment, plus a number of pieces of textile (cf. *Figures 37.1* and *37.3*). Kando asserted that both groups derived from the outside layers of the *Temple Scroll*, which had broken off before it was unrolled.[1]

In a number of the MS 5095/1 pieces parchment and linen cloth are fused together. Where the cloth is well enough preserved to be measured, the e.p.c. density of the weave is 15–16 threads per cm, and the p.p.c. density is 12–13 threads per cm.[2] Ira Rabin's analysis of one of the wads fused with textile demonstrated that the textile piece had the mineral features characteristic of Cave 11 also found in the *Temple Scroll* wrapper (MS 5095/2, see the contributions by Rabin and Sukenik, pp. 327 and 339). Rabin's 2012 on-site analysis of some fragments did not yield any further information about mineral composition. However, she was able to determine the thickness of one fragment as 0.58±0.04 mm (Rabin, unpublished report).

Yigael Yadin described how 'wad Y' of 11QTᵃ with four layers (1983, 3:plate 4.2) had been wrapped in cellophane together with the main scroll. He later identified these layers as cols II–V. Since there was set-off of letters also on the *verso* of col. II, Yadin concluded that this column had been preceded by at least one column. Columns II–V were written by a different scribe, and in a later script. According to Yadin, these columns were part of a repair sheet that had replaced the once damaged beginning of the scroll (1983, 1:5, 11–12). As the upper part of the scroll is more damaged than the lower part, the scroll must have been standing upside-down in the jar.[3] Accordingly, wad Y would also appear to come from the lower part of the scroll (= the upper part when standing in the jar). Some of the Schøyen wads and

---

[1] 11QTᵃ was published in Yadin 1977 (the English translation appeared in Yadin 1983), and 11QTᵇ in *DJD* 23. 11Q21, consisting of two halakhic fragments, is designated 11QTᶜ?, and was also published in *DJD* 23.

[2] 'Ends per centimetre (e.p.c.) density' counts the number of warp threads per centimetre woven into the fabric, and 'picks per centimetre (p.p.c.) density' is the weft thread count.

[3] For photos of this jar with its lid, see Mébarki and Puech 2002, 31; Patterson 2012, 25.

fragments may have been closely connected with Yadin's wad Y. If so, they preserve at least one more layer, consisting of fragments still attached to pieces of the wrapper.

Five of the MS 5095/1 wads of textile and parchment are rather thick (3–5 mm), and constitute petrified wads with two, three, or more layers from the external part of the scroll. The parchment in these wads has shrunk, and they appear rather wavy. On two of the wads one can see remnants of letters, and these are designated as wads Z and ZZ.[4] Wad Z is the largest of the wads, measuring 60 × 35 mm. It consists of a bundle of three layers of parchment attached to a piece of textile. A handful of letters are visible on the parchment layers. Wad ZZ, situated on the second row from the top, second item from the right, measures 17 × 11 mm. It is pictured turned counter-clockwise 90º. No textile was attached to this second wad. Traces of letters from two or three layers are visible, but they appear as crowded lines of text in the IR photograph. The distinction between the layers can be seen in the colour image.

In MS 5095/4, remnants of letters are visible on four of the parchment pieces, only on three can we identify letters with some confidence. These three pieces are here designated frgs b, c, and d. Fragment b measures 9 × 7 mm; frg. c, 12 × 15 mm; and frg. d, 11 × 18 mm. Fragment c is attached to a piece of woven textile similar to other pieces of the wrapper, which suggests that it belonged to the outer layer of a scroll. The impression is created that frgs c and d belong together, as they always appear together on the same photograph. However, the three fully preserved letters of frg. d, which read באר, seem different from the script of the other fragments on these two plates. Fragment d is also darker and substantially thicker than frg. c.

Based on Kando's statements about the provenance of these wads, we have attempted to identify their inscribed portions with the script in cols II–V of 11QT[a]. However, we have had little success in this endeavour. There are simply not enough letter samples to make any positive identification, but for at least two of the fragments the script clearly does not match. The script in wad ZZ is different from 11QT[a], and while the line spacing cannot be determined, it is probably smaller than in 11QT[a]. The line spacing in frg. c cannot be determined, but we can see that it is smaller than what appears in the first columns of 11QT[a]. The few visible letters in frg. d are clearly different from all the other fragments in the lot, and are not a match with 11QT[a]. While we cannot determine how many of these wads and pieces actually derive from 11QT[a], some of them certainly do not. This may further suggest that there were more scrolls in Cave 11 than previously recognized.

Nevertheless, an identification with 11QT[a] for some of the fragments may be suggested from the presence of several wads fused with textile, with a similar density of weave as the *Temple Scroll* wrapper. Such is the case especially for wad Z. Further, the line spacing of the upper layer of this fragment is 8.5–9 mm; the same as in 11QT[a] cols II–V (Yadin 1983, 1:13). If this fragment indeed represents the beginning of 11QT[a], we may have remains of three columns. This is suggested by the circumference of the first few turns of 11QT[a], which was close to the width of a single column.[5] If this identification holds, it cannot be ascertained if wad Z contains remnants of cols I–III, or if col. II was preceded by more than one column.[6]

---

[4] Yadin's introduction lists wads X and Y (1983, 1:5–6). Vol. 3, Further, Supplementary Plates, Plate 40, lists 15 fragments not attributed to specific columns.

[5] Yadin suggested that cols I–V were on one sheet that measured *c.* 60 cm. With the exception of the shorter last sheet, the other sheets of the scroll measured between 37 and 61 cm (1983, 1:10–11).

[6] Based on the contents of col. II, Yadin suggested that only one column (plus an extra blank column at the beginning of the scroll) was lost before col. II (1983, 1:10).

2. 11QTᵃ Wad Z

11QTᵃ wad Z is a wad of three inseparable layers from the external turns of a scroll. We have tentatively identified it with the first few columns of 11QTᵃ. The wad is attached to textile from the wrapper and measures 60 × 35 mm. There is some variation in the direction of the lines. Some letters can be discerned, but no complete words can be confidently restored.

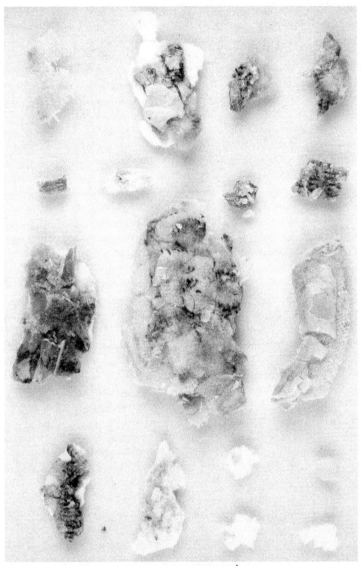

Figure 37.1. MS 5095/1

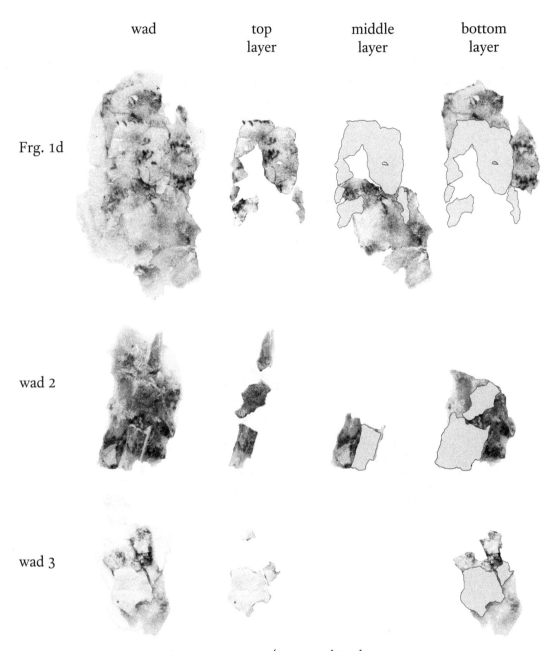

Figure 37.2. MS 5095/1 *separated into layers*

3. Wad Za. Top Layer (col. III?)

```
           ]○○○○        1
          ]      y      2a
        ]○[ ]○○ש        2
       ]y○[    ]ה̇        3
```

Notes on Readings

This layer probably preserves the beginning of a column. The line spacing between lines 1 and 2 is 9.5 mm, and between lines 2 and 3, 8.9 mm. The distance from the beginning of the line to the right edge of the fragment is 4.8 mm in line 2, and 3.2 mm in line 3.

Line 2a. ʿAyin is supralinear.

Line 2. The šin is clear, but it seems to be situated underneath more sharply inscribed ink that belongs most likely to an ʾalep. The shape of the šin may be comparable to those in cols II–V of 11QTᵃ. The ʾalep does not appear to be part of the text in this line, and its presence is difficult to account for (see also discussion of the bottom layer below). The šin is followed by a trace of a downstroke, and there also appears to be a trace of the top of another letter after the lacuna, immediately preceding the last visible letter. Only the baseline of the last letter is visible, followed by a word space. There appears to be a trace of a downstroke attached at the right side, and this most closely resembles a ṣade.

Line 3. A small piece of the top layer has broken away from the rest. It is situated on a down-sloping angle in alignment with line 3 and contains two letters. The first letter is badly worn. The second letter is clearly an ʿayin, which is visible in both natural and IR light.

4. Wad Zb. Middle Layer (col. II?)

]ר∘∘[

Notes on Readings

The reš is fairly clear, but the preceding letters are not. Ṣade for the second letter is possible, but far from certain. The first letter possibly resembles a šin (cf. the šin in line 2 of the top layer), or an ʾalep followed by a ḥet.

5. Wad Zc. Bottom Layer (col. I?)

	]∘∘∘[	1
]∘[	]∘∘∘∘[	2
	]∘בח̊[	3

Notes on Readings

Line 1. There are possibly traces of ink belonging to the first line, but these are difficult to distinguish.

Line 3. There appears to be a faintly visible mem that overlaps with the left edge of the bet. We cannot explain the presence of what appear to be three or four letters: a possible yod, and a mem situated between two unreadable letters, that are not part of this line of the text, but also seem to be written on the parchment at this layer.

6. Bottom Layer Set-Off (?)

]ooo[1
]o֯מ֯יֹo[2

Notes on Readings

Beneath lines 2–3 of the bottom layer some letters are visible on the IR image. The text of the top line is too badly obscured by what is superimposed on it. The second line contains four letters: the first and the last are not clear; the second letter is narrow, and is most likely a *yod* or a *waw*; the third is a fairly clear *mem*, and only a trace of the right edge of the final letter is visible.

Figure 37.3. MS 5095/4

B. Unidentified Fragments from Cave 11

Since the identification of many of the pieces on these two plates with 11QT^a is uncertain, we prefer to designate them here as 11QUnidentified fragments a–z, aa, and wads ZZ and W.

1. Wad ZZ

This wad measures 17 × 11 mm. Letters and ink traces from two or three layers of text are visible, but these appear as closely crowded lines on the IR photograph. The top layer (a) appears as the bottom line, the intermediate layer (b) the second line, and the bottom layer (c) the first line—it is difficult to discern which layer was the upper one and which the lower. What appear to be ink traces belonging to layer c may possibly be part of layer b.

Layer a

]ooo[

Layer b

]oשני o[

Layer c

]oo[

Notes on Readings

Layer a. There are several bits of ink belonging to two or three letters. The final letter appears as an oblique stroke with an arm attached, and is possibly a *ṣade* or perhaps an *ʾalep*.

Layer c. It is difficult to determine if the dark portions in the IR photograph belong to ink traces, or if they are merely shadows or something else in the wad. The darkened portions on the IR photograph that appear to be ink closely follow the contours of the fragmented bits of lighter coloured parchment that are situated on top of this piece.

2. Frg. b

]oה[

Notes on Readings

Above the *he* one can see ink impressions from another layer.

3. Frg. c

]oo[ ]oo[
]oרֿאֿש[

Notes on Readings

Line 2. The reading]שׂרֹאֹלׄ[י is hardly possible, as no head of *lamed* is visible on the preserved parchment. Another suggestion for this word does not present itself, but cf. Dan 2.22 where there appears an Aramaic verb based on the root שרא, meaning 'to loosen'. Due to the attachment to the cloth, the fragment has been stretched so that line 1 slants downwards to the left. The density of the weave of the textile is 12 weft threads per cm.

4. Frg. d

The script of this fragment may be middle or late Herodian, and the height of the letters is 2 mm.

[בֹּארץ]

Notes on Readings

A speck of ink below the crossbar of *bet* is located too high to represent the base stroke. *Bet* is nevertheless the only meaningful option, as]הארץ[is not possible. The scribe left a stroke at the top of the left arm of *ʾalep*. *Reš* ends in a hook. The left arm of final *ṣade* bends upwards to the left.

XXXI

MS 1926/1, MS 1926/3. Uninscribed Fragments from 1QIsa[a] and 1QS

Torleif Elgvin

DSS F.134. DSS F.1QIsa[a]
DSS F.135. DSS F.1QS

A. Minor Fragments and Repair Material from 1QIsa[a]

According to John C. Trever's typed notes, these pieces fell off the Isaiah scroll while he was photographing it in February 1948, and he held on to them.[1] They were acquired by The Schøyen Collection from the Trever family in 1994 (see *Figure 38*).

1. Physical Description

Several small pieces of parchment and repair material from 1QIsa[a] are included along with bits of cord from the repair made in 1QIsa[a] XII, and another collection of small pieces that are lighter in colour. These lighter-coloured pieces probably represent the cover sheet.

The several small items in the photograph can be described as follows: there are nine pieces of repair material, measuring between 28.5 × 9.5 mm and 2 × 2 mm. Each of the three larger ones contains more than a square centimetre of material, but do not preserve any traces of text.

In addition, there are ten fragments measuring between 14.5 × 10.5 mm and 3 × 1 mm. The three largest pieces contain minute traces of ink. Microscopic infrared inspection of all the fragments was conducted in April 2013. While this produced a handful of sharp images, it was not possible to reconstruct individual letters from the ink traces.

An intact piece of the braided cord from the repair in 1QIsa[a] XII, measuring 30 mm in length, is sewn into a parchment fragment measuring 20 × 4 mm. In addition, there are several smaller frayed bits and pieces that appear in the figure. These are probably parts of the same thread, based on their similarly 'coiled' appearance.[2]

---

[1] Trever's notes, which were mounted on the frame, read as follows: 'Received by John C. Trever in Jerusalem, February 21, 1948 / Repair material — sewing repair from col. XII — leather pieces lower edge — bits of linen thread — fragments of "cover"? / DEAD SEA SCROLL FRAGMENTS FROM QUMRAN CAVE I: Repair material 1QApocGen — Upper edge of 1QApocGen — Linen cloth adhering to gelatinized leather from unidentified scroll — Piece of 1QS.' The Schøyen fragments are mentioned in *DJD* 32.1:xvii and in 32.2:19–20.

[2] Probably not from the textile wrapper, *pace DJD* 32.1:xvii (cf. also www.schoyencollection.com/dsscrolls.html#12.1, accessed 20 April, 2013).

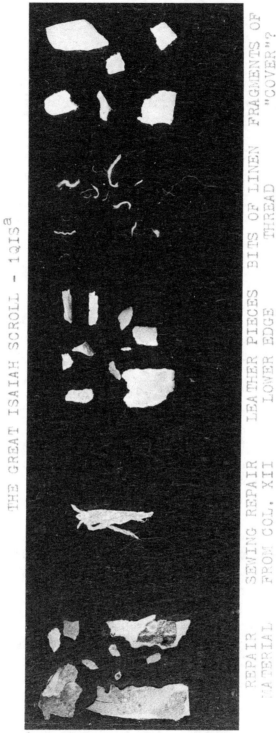

Figure 38. 1QIsaᵃ (uninscribed minor fragments and repair material)—MS 1926/1

Six pieces are probably remnants of the cover sheet that at one time was attached to the scroll.[3] These pieces measure between 17.3 × 8.5 mm and 4 × 6 mm. To our knowledge, these are the only parts of the cover sheet that have been preserved.

[3] According to Athanasius Samuel, a cover sheet was still attached when he purchased it (*DJD* 32.2:3, 7–8).

The thickness of the two larger pieces of repair material is 0.34±0.02 mm and 0.53±0.05 mm respectively, of the largest piece from the lower edge 0.53±0.04 mm, and of the largest piece of 'cover?' 0.49±0.05 mm (Rabin, unpublished report). According to Ira Rabin's analysis the FTIR and XRF spectra show a fundamental difference between the repair material and the two other pieces (the repair piece had chlorine as its main mineral element followed by calcium—while the two others had sulphur as their main component). It also showed some minor differences between the piece from the lower edge and that from the cover sheet, indicating that while these two pieces were produced with the same technique in the same workshop, they do not belong to the same sheet. These two reflect a different and more advanced production process and represent the 'Western' type of light-coloured parchment (see p. 64).

2. The Repair of 1QIsa[a]

Trever's photographs of the scroll show a tear almost from top-to-bottom near the end of 1QIsa[a] XII, measuring 23.5 cm. The scroll had been sewn back together to fix the tear, and repair material was added to the bottom where the original parchment had broken off. The surface has abraded where the tear widens at the three lower lines of the column (Trever 1972, 38–39).

I recently examined the first 22 columns of the scroll together with Adolfo Roitman and Hasya Rimon to investigate the repairs made in antiquity.[4] We were not able to see the *verso*, which was reinforced with paper during the process of modern conservation. However, we were able to see the edges of the scroll with repair pieces in profile from the side.

Pieces of dark coloured repair parchment are firmly attached to the underside of the original parchment, and visible at the top and bottom edges of some parts of the scroll. There are a handful of places where the repair material is sewn together with the original parchment, but with only a few stitches, unlike the large repair in 1QIsa[a] XII. Sewing can be seen in 1QIsa[a] IV (four stitches, cf. *DJD* 32.2:99) and in 1QIsa[a] XVIII–XIX (one stitch only, just above the beginning of col. XIX). The repair patch used in 1QIsa[a] XVIII–XIX is at least 4 cm wide, but it is thinner than that used in col. XII and in the beginning of the scroll.

The repair piece at the bottom of col. XII is 11.5 cm wide and reaches 1.5 cm into col. XIII. In cols XII–XIII both the original parchment and the repair piece are quite thick (roughly estimated as *c.* 0.6–0.7 mm each).

In 1QIsa[a] I–V a long repair band can be seen underneath the top edge from the beginning (stretching down to line 9), and continuing to 4 cm into col. V. It measures 9 cm where it is visible on the vertical edge, and approximately 54.5 cm along the horizontal edge. Close to the top edge of col. IV four stitches have been added in antiquity for reinforcement. The parchment of the first sheet, 1QIsa[a] I–III, is relatively thin, while the repair band below the upper part is more than twice as thick (approximated to *c.* 0.3 and 0.7 mm, respectively). Remnants of another repair band can also be detected at one point close to the bottom edge of the scroll, now visible only in the intercolumnar margin between cols III and IV. It is not known how long this lower repair band was originally, although it may have covered also cols I and II. The nine pieces of repair material represented in MS 1926/1 may derive from any of the repair bands or pieces described above.

---

[4] The investigation was done 23 September, 2014. Flint and Ulrich only state briefly, 'The manuscript was also damaged in antiquity, requiring repair; see especially col. XII' (*DJD* 32.2:61).

The edges of the scroll above and below the first four columns were probably more badly worn than the scroll in general (a normal feature with regular usage of a scroll that was rolled with the beginning on the outside). This part of the scroll was therefore reinforced by supportive bands at the top and bottom, in an effort to extend its time of use.[5] The thickness of the repair pieces may have been a hindrance for smooth rolling, and probably contributed to further deterioration of the scroll, including the fragmentation of the cover sheet. The repairs to 1QIsa^a altogether were probably made after long time usage of this scroll that was highly esteemed in the *Yaḥad*. They were made perhaps at Qumran some time before the scroll was deposited in Cave 1.

B. Piece of the Community Rule

1. Physical Description

According to Trever's notes, MS 1926/3 is an uninscribed piece of the *Community Rule* scroll ('Piece of 1QS'). The material is fine, leight beige parchment. It measures 13 × 5 mm and has a thickness of 0.31±0.08 mm.

Ira Rabin's analysis shows exactly the same mineral composition for this piece and the Schøyen fragment of 1QSb (MS 1909). She concludes that these skins were processed in the same preparation batch and therefore likely belonged to the same scroll. Further, the two fragments she tested from 1QIsa^a—one from the lower edge of the scroll and the other regarded as deriving from the cover sheet—had the same characteristics as the 1QS/1QSb fragments. She concludes that the skins of the large Isaiah scroll and those of 1QS/1QSb originated from the same workshop. The exceptional quality of these scrolls suggests that they were prepared by highly skilled craftsmen, who were likely accustomed to using high quality materials (see p. 66).[6]

---

[5] Large margins in mediaeval codices were probably intended to protect the text from damage or smudging. Indeed, there are several surviving ancient codices where the text has been badly obscured by fingerprints on the edges (cf. Rudy 2010). Kipp Davis suggests that since scrolls were handled only on the *verso*, large margins were likely intended to offer protection from environmental damage. Davis argues that 'If scrolls were stored upright in jars as they were discovered in Qumran Cave 1, and spent most of their time resting on their bottom edge, then the bottoms of the manuscripts were also especially prone to early deterioration. Whether this storage model was common or not, it seems reasonable to posit that margins on scrolls were intended for similar protective purposes, and by extension: the larger the margins, the higher the concern to ensure that the surrounded text is preserved' (Davis 2014b, 14).

[6] If Michael Langlois is right in his dating of the script of 1QSb to 75–50 BC (see p. 83), 1QS was copied slightly later than often asserted (100–75 BC, *DJD* 26:20). This assumption carries implications for 1QIsa^a (dated by Cross to 125–100 BC, *DJD* 32.2:61–64), which must also have been copied relatively close in time to the production of 1QS and 1QSb, that is, within a single generation.

XXXII

MS 4612/7. Fragments of Wadi ed-Daliyeh Documentary Texts[1]

Jan Dušek

DSS F.136. DSS F.Scraps

It is possible that the fragments on plate MS 4612/7 belong to the corpus of Samaria papyri from Wadi ed-Daliyeh, written in the fourth century, before 332 BC (Dušek 2007). Their script is identical to the script of the Wadi ed-Daliyeh manuscripts and some fragments seem even to contain some of the proper names attested in the corpus.

   The fragments are presented on plate MS 4612/7 in six groups and we follow this grouping in our description.

A. First Group: Fragments 1–3

Fragments 1–3 possibly belonged to one papyrus, but that is not certain. We are unable to confirm it, having worked only the photograph.

1. Frg. 1

$$]\mathring{\text{בֿ}}\backslash\mathring{\text{גֿ}}\mathring{\text{ה}}[\qquad\qquad [\qquad 1$$
$$] \qquad\qquad \mathring{\text{ﭏ}}\mathring{\text{ﭏ}}\mathring{\text{ﭏ}}[\qquad 2$$

The three small curves on the right side may have belonged to three numbers 20, but this reading is very uncertain. The three letters on the right appear to be on the inferior level, compared to the three signs on the left. The three numbers 20 possibly concerned some payment, as it is in the other contracts from Wadi ed-Daliyeh.

2. Frg. 2

$$]\mathring{\text{ﬡ}}\mathring{\text{א}}[$$

]brother[

---

[1] This study is the result of a research undertaking, which is part of the grant project GAČR 401/07/P454 'Critical analysis of the new epigraphic evidence related to the history of the province of Samaria from the 4th century BCE to the 1st century CE'.

3. Frg. 3

1   ]הֹגֹ\יֹ ∘∘[

2   ]∘   [

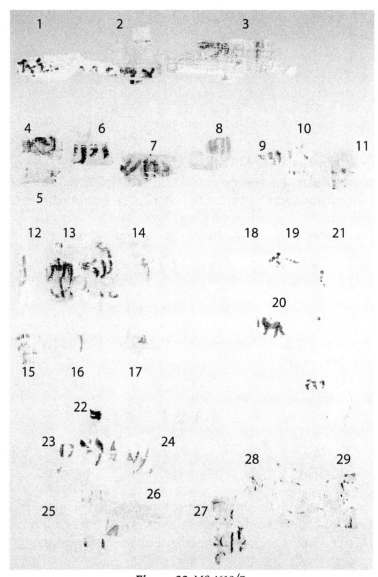

Figure 39. MS 4612/7

B. Second Group: Fragments 4–11

The colour of frgs 4–12 is similar, as is the script on the fragments numbering 4, 6 and 7.

1. Frg. 4

] בֹרֹיֹ [

This fragment appears to contain the beginning of a dating formula with the number 10 and two vertical bars indicating the number 12. The vertical bars could be followed by seven more bars. Thus, the dating formula would refer to the day of month between the 12th and 19th; cf. for example WDSP 6,1.[2]

In the Wadi ed-Daliyeh manuscripts, the dating formula was either at the beginning of the document or at the end. The letter ב seems to be preceded by a possible mark in ink. If it is actually a mark in ink, the dating formula would be at the end of the document, as for example, in WDSP 3,11.

2. Frg. 5

]○   [1
]   i○[2

3. Frg. 6

]○נזז[

The word might have been connected to זון 'food' attested in the manuscript concerning the loan of silver *TAD* B3.1, lines 10 and 17, from Elephantine (Porten and Yardeni 1989, 54–57). The form of *waw* is similar to the form attested in WDSP 28 *recto*, frg. 1, line 2.

4. Frg. 7

]ת\ח̊○[שׁ]

The reading of the first letter on the right as well as the interpretation of the whole word is uncertain. The middle letter seems to be a *taw*, but the reading of a *ḥet* is also possible.

It is possible to propose the reconstruction of the name Artaxerxes: [אר̊ת̊ח̊שׁ[סש].

5. Frg. 8

א̊[נ̊ח̊נ̊]ה

It is possible to reconstruct אנחנה 'we'.

6. Frg. 9

This fragment seems to bear traces of two or three illegible letters.

---

[2] WDSP = 'Wadi Daliyeh Samaria Papyrus'.

7. Frg. 10

$$\text{]}\mathring{\text{א}}\mathring{\text{ו}}\backslash\mathring{\text{ף}}\text{[} \qquad 1$$
$$\text{]}\circ\circ\text{[} \qquad 2$$

The word on line 1 could be אוֹ 'or' or אַף 'also'.

8. Frg. 11

$$\text{]}\mathring{\text{ת}}\mathring{\text{נ}}\text{[}$$

These letters could belong to some word with the root נתן 'to give', which appears in the legal formulae of the Samaria papyri from Wadi ed-Daliyeh (see the glossary in Dušek 2007, 614).

C. Third Group: Fragments 12–17

1. Frg. 12

$$\text{]}\circ\text{ל}\text{ [}$$

This is probably the preposition ל. This form of *lamed* is not often used, but is attested in several manuscripts (for example, in WDSP 10 and WDSP 18).

2. Frg. 13

$$\text{] } \circ \text{]כֹּ\נֹּ\פֹּ[ ] } \circ\text{[} \qquad 1$$
$$\text{]ננֹא\ה מסֹ[} \qquad 2$$
$$\text{]אֹשֹלֹםֹ[} \circ\circ\text{[} \qquad 3$$

A part of this text seems to have been corrected and overwritten. The remains of some erased letters are visible. The remains between the two words on line 2, slightly under the level of the line, look like a half-erased *mem*. Traces of some letter are visible as well in the upper-right part of the *mem* in]מסֹ on line 2.

The left part of line 3 seems to contain the word אשלם 'I will pay' which appears in the Wadi ed-Daliyeh manuscripts in the contravention clause, in the formula compelling the seller to pay a penalty to the buyer in case of violation of the contract by the seller who acted in bad faith (Dušek 2007, 85–88; Dušek 2011, 864–65).

3. Frg. 14

$$\text{]}\text{ו}\text{ [}$$

4. Frg. 15

]○ [1
]לֹנֹנֹ[2

This fragment, turned 90° to the left, seems to contain three letters]לֹנֹנֹ[on line 2.

5. Frg. 16

] וֹ\פֹ [

The leg on the fragment can belong to *waw* or to *pe*.

6. Frg. 17

]בֹדֹ\רֹ [

These letters could belong to עבד 'slave' or בר 'son', both well attested in the Wadi ed-Daliyeh manuscripts.

D. Fourth Group: Fragments 18–21

The papyrus of the four fragments, numbers 18–21, is similar. The script is not well preserved.

1. Frg. 18

]שֹ[

Turned 90° to the left, it might be perhaps a *šin*.

2. Frg. 19

]וֹ\פֹ[

Turned 90° to the left, it might be a leg of *pe* or *waw*.

3. Frg. 20

י]הוֹפֹ]דֹ(י)נִי

It is possible to reconstruct the proper name Yehopada(y)ni. This name is spelled יהופדיני in WDSP 3, WDSP 11, WDSP 27 and יהופדני in WDSP 5, WDSP 9, and WDSP 17. It is possible that the fragment belonged to one of the contracts from the archive of Yehopada(y)ni (Dušek 2007, 474–75).

4. Frg. 21

לׄ]	1
יׄ]	2
וׄח\הׄ]	3
○]	4

This fragment probably belonged to the right margin of the manuscript. It contains the beginnings of four lines.

The letter on the first line can be interpreted as the right part of a *lamed*.

The mark of ink on the second line perhaps belonged to the number 10.

The reading of the second letter on the third line is uncertain. If it is *ḥet*, the line may have begun with a proper noun like חגי, חלפן, חני, חנן, or חניה with a conjunction ו. These names are attested in other manuscripts in the corpus (Dušek 2007, 616).

E. Fifth Group: Fragments 22–26

Although frgs 22–26 are grouped together on the plate, these joints do not seem to be correct. For this reason we analyze each fragment separately.

1. Frg. 22

ל] [	1
נט[יׄרׄאׄ]	2

On line 2 it is possible to reconstruct the name of Neṭiraʾ. This is the name attested in WDSP 5, WDSP 8, WDSP 9, WDSP 17 and in WDSP 33, frg. 75r. These manuscripts constitute an 'archive of Neṭira', son of Yehopada(y)ni' (Dušek 2007, 476–77).

2. Frg. 23

מ ו\פ○] [	1
○] [	2

3. Frg. 24

○ ש[	1
] ○[	2

4. Frg. 25

]∘∘∘∘∘[	1
vacat	
] ∘[ ]∘[	2

5. Frg. 26

]∘[

F. Sixth Group: Fragments 27–29c

Fragments 28 and 29 are stuck together on the reverse with a strip of adhesive tape. This placement appears to be correct.

The text on the three fragments 27–29 is erased and illegible.

Part Six

—

Artefacts

XXXIII

Leather Cord from Qumran, Shoe Remains. MS 5095/6, MS 1655/5

Torleif Elgvin

A. Leather Cord

The item designated MS 5095/6 consists of eight pieces of a leather cord, including two pieces tied together in a knot. The leather is relatively thin. The width of the pieces is *c.* 6–7 mm. The longest piece, pictured in the upper left quadrant of the plate, is 74 mm, and the piece directly beneath it measures 70 mm. Two small pieces are pictured in the top right quadrant, amidst three fragments belonging to 4QFragment with Text from Commentary on Genesis A. They measure 9 mm and 16 mm. Two pieces situated directly beneath these measure 28 mm and 26 mm. The final piece pictured in the bottom right quadrant consists of two ends of the cord tied together in a knot; one measures 33 mm and the other 13 mm. The total cumulative length of the pieces is *c.* 27 cm.

A large number of leather cords and tabs were found in the Qumran caves. A linen cord was used to tie the wrapper around the *Temple Scroll* (see Sukenik's article, p. 339). Forty-two tabs were found in Cave 4, while Cave 8 contained 68 tabs but no scrolls—the scrolls had probably disintegrated (*DJD* 3:31). Two scrolls from Cave 4 (4QDᵃ [4Q266] and 4QApocryphal Psalm and Prayer) had tabs still attached,[1] showing that cords were used to tie these scrolls (*DJD* 6:23–28).

The cord pieces of MS 5095/6 came to The Schøyen Collection together with three pieces that later revealed text known from *Commentary of Genesis A* (frgs a–c of MS 5095/7). At this stage these pieces were thought to be parts of the cord, but infrared photographs later revealed that they contained text. Since *Commentary of Genesis A* is a sectarian composition we are probably dealing with a leather cord from Qumran, and possibly the cord that was used to fasten this same scroll.

---

[1] An untanned leather tab measuring 2.9 × 2.9 cm is folded over the right edge of 4QApocryphal Psalm and Prayer (4Q448): http://www.loc.gov/exhibits/scrolls/libr.html (accessed 26 February, 2015); cf. also Tov 2004, Plate 11. The tab on the outside of 4QDᵃ (4Q266) is visible in *DJD* 18:Plate I.

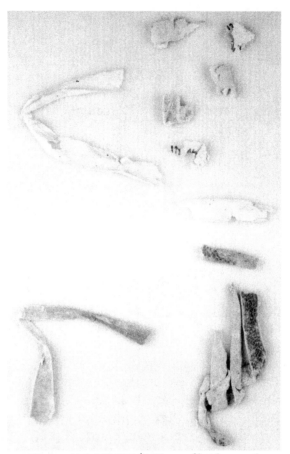

Figure 40.1. MS 5095/6: Pieces of leather cord

B. Shoe Remains

MS 1655/5 includes seven pieces of leather shoe remains, sold by the Bedouin to Kando as finds from Qumran. It is impossible to say whether these pieces were found in a Qumran cave, in Murabbaʿat or Naḥal Ḥever. The colour is medium to dark brown, and the total weight of the pieces is *c.* 5 g. The largest piece (a) is part of a shoe sole, 50 × 34 × 1 mm, with 7 sewing holes. The second largest piece (b) measures 21 × 35 × 2 mm, with 28 mm of a thread preserved. The thread is hardened and almost fused together with the leather; it is only visible to the naked eye, and not on the photograph. Two thin pieces (c, d, directly to the right of a) measure 11 × 3 × 1 mm and 9 × 5 × 2 mm. In three thick pieces (e, f, g, pictured on the left side) the leather has fused together into lumps. These pieces measure from top to bottom 24 × 15 × 5 mm, 16 × 9 × 4 mm (with a hole penetrating the entire lump), and 13 × 10 × 4 mm.

The IAA collections include some shoe remains from the Qumran caves. Item 461517 (15 × 8 cm) consists of four layers of soles stitched together (a common practice in the Roman period), and is presently exhibited in the Shrine of the Book. 351270 preserves three layers of soles (22 × 7 cm) stitched together. 351271 preserves two layers of soles (21 × 8.5 cm) with remains of stitching. 464295 from Cave 4 preserves a piece of leather (8 × 5 cm) with stitching. 477613 from Cave 2 comprises two leather strips and some pieces of soles, one of which consists of six sole layers stitched together. In their 1995–96 excavations at Qumran, Magen Broshi and Hanan Eshel found sixty iron nails that had dropped from sandals along a path leading north from the community center (Eshel and Broshi 1999, 337, 339–40,

Leather Cord from Qumran, Shoe Remains. MS 5095/6, MS 1655/5

325

343). Sixteen iron nails, between 5 and 20 mm in length, are on display in the Shrine of the Book (IMJ no 97.18[153]).[2]

Figure 40.2. *MS 1655/5: Shoe remains*
(from top left and clockwise: e, a, c, d, b, g, f)

[2] I am indebted to Hasia Rimon (Shrine of the Book) and Na'ama Sukenik (IAA) for providing me with this information.

XXXIV

The *Temple Scroll*: Wrapper and Fragment. MS 5095/2, MS 5095/4

Ira Rabin

A. Experimental Methods

The following specification of experimental methods refers to tests performed in 2009–10 on vellum, textile, ink, pottery, leather, and palm-fibre tool, as described in the chapter written by me and Roman Schütz.[1]

Optical microscopy was performed with an Askania SM4 stereo microscope to determine the regions of interest.

SEM micrographs and EDX spectra were produced with an FEI Quanta 200 FEG and an EDAX Genesis 4000 with Si(Li) detector, type Sapphire. The measurements were carried out at accelerating voltage of 20kV, pressure of 1.1kPa in H_2O vapour, secondary electron (SE) mode plus backscattered electrons.

X-ray Fluorescence (XRF) profile scans were carried out with the mobile energy-dispersive micro-X-ray spectrometer ArtTAX® (Bruker AXS Microanalysis GmbH, formerly Röntec-GmbH, Berlin, Germany), which consists of an air-cooled low-power X-ray tube, poly-capillary X-ray optics (measuring spot size 70 μm diameter), an electro-thermally cooled Xflash detector, and a CCD camera for sample positioning. The unit is equipped with open helium purging in the excitation and detection paths. All measurements were performed using a 30W low-power Mo tube, operated at 50 kV and 600 μA, and with an acquisition time of 70 s (live time). The quantification of the XRF-results is based on the fundamental parameter method.

Raman measurements were performed with a confocal Raman microscope (model: CRM200, WITec, Ulm, Germany) equipped with a piezo-scanner. For excitation a diode-pumped 785 nm near-infrared (NIR) laser was used in combination with a 20× (Nikon, NA=0,4) or a 100× (Olympus MPlan IR, NA=0,95) microscope objective. The slit width of 100 μm was defined by the fibre between the microscope and the spectrograph. The spectra were obtained using an air-cooled CCD (DU401A-DR-DD, Andor, Belfast, Northern Ireland) behind a grating (300 g/mm) spectrograph (Acton, Princeton Instruments Inc., Trenton, NJ, USA) with a spectral resolution of 6 cm^{-1}.

For better statistics, from 10 to 20 spots on each sample were investigated. The measurements were carried out with 1 sec of integration time, 30 sec hardware and 10 sec software accumulation time.

Alternatively we used a Bruker FT-Raman spectrophotometer RFS 100/S equipped with Ge Diode detector cooled to liquid nitrogen temperature (77K) and a near-infrared [YAG:Nd] laser operating at

[1] The author would like to thank Kerstin Meissner for the digital optical microscopy mapping; Roman Schütz, Emanuel Kindzorra, Ulrich Schade, Maren Stämmler and Peter Lasch for their contribution of the FTIR and Raman investigation; Timo Wolff and Oliver Hahn for conducting the micro-XRF analysis and Gisela Weinberg for performing scanning electron microscopy studies. My special thanks go to Juan Manuel Madariaga and Maite Maguregui Hernando for their help in identifying nitrate compounds, Reinhard Franke for his technical support and Marcello Binetti for discussions and proofreading of the manuscripts. The funding by Stiftung Preussischer Kulturbesitz is gratefully acknowledged.

1064 nm with 500mW output power. Measurements were carried out in the spectral range 200–3600 cm^{-1} with spectral resolution of 4 cm^{-1}. Since the 5 mm interaction spot of the FT-Raman spectrometer offers good statistics, samples were characterized in triplicates with 250 scans co-added per spectrum.

ATR-FTIR measurements were performed at room temperature with a resolution of 8 cm^{-1} in the 4000–650 cm^{-1} range with a Nexus Nicolet Fourier transform infrared (FTIR) spectrometer, equipped with a ZnSe cell and a liquid nitrogen cooled MCT/A detector. For each spectrum a total of 400 scans were averaged.

To obtain *transmission FTIR spectra*, micro samples were prepared in a Diamond micro compression cell and measured at room temperature with a Continuum microscope (Nicolet) equipped with a liquid nitrogen cooled MCT detector. The measurements were performed using infrared synchrotron radiation from the BESSY II storage ring on the IRIS beamline. A 32× Cassegrain objective was used to focus the beam onto the sample. The area of investigation was 50 μm × 50 μm and a total of 256 scans were co-added per sample spectrum in the wavenumber range between 4,000 and 800 cm^{-1}.

B. *Temple Scroll* Fragment, MS 5095/4

When comparing two fragments of antique parchment or leather, the effects of production and those related to use, storage and post-discovery activities must be considered separately.

The act of production leaves certain fingerprints that affect the composition of both the main and the trace elements as well as the carbon-oxygen-nitrogen-hydrogen of the collagen matrix. The main elements can be correlated with the salt additives used in the hide de-hairing and finishing (Reed 1972, 47–85). Trace elements corresponding to impurities of the water source are usually present in very small concentrations.

The second class of process to consider is the change in the leather/parchment during the years of use, storage and post-discovery activities. On one hand, fragments accumulated new substances in the course of their existence; on the other hand, they underwent substantial degradation after they were produced. In addition, one has to consider that manufacture was a manual process, not an industrialized one. Therefore, quantitative variations in the additives found on fragments derived from different skins are possible. The degree of variance can be determined through analysis of a considerable number of different sheets from one and the same scroll. The study of the variance across a specific fragment allows us to estimate the influence of degradation on the composition of the skin.

To sum up, although we expect the same pattern for the additives to the skins produced for one scroll, we do not necessarily expect them in exactly the same amounts from one sheet to another. The long sojourn in a particular cave would suggest that accumulated substances would be the same for different scrolls or fragments. Post-discovery activities would have similar effects on fragments prepared in the same way and stored in the same cave.

In our previous work we studied 19 fragments from the *Temple Scroll* (11QTª): two of them were taken from the repair sheet of col. V, thirteen belonged to col. LII,[2] one to col. XXXVIII, while three uninscribed pieces had no column identification (Rabin et al. 2010). Characterization of the fragments was performed with the techniques described above under 'Experimental Methods'.

From this study it was clear that the main part of the scroll was tawed with potash alum, followed by the application of a gypsum paste. The repair sheet did not display clear evidence of the use of alum. Its finishing was done with a paste consisting mainly of calcite. Furthermore, ammonium and calcium

---

[2] Recently Eibert Tigchelaar assigned some of the col. LII fragments to other columns. The new assignment doesn't affect the results of the analysis nor their interpretation.

nitrate impurities were found on the fragments belonging to the repair sheet. Ammonium nitrate was also found on the uninscribed pieces that probably belonged to the scroll edge. No such impurities could be detected in the inner part of the scroll. We attributed the appearance of the nitrate compounds to the reaction of the scroll with ammonia gas, whose presence in Qumran cave 11 (the so-called 'bat-cave') is attested by its characteristic odour (Mcfarlane et al. 1995). Post-discovery activities, such as high humidification and freezing of the scroll, application of different glues for consolidation etc. resulted in the appearance of different organic and inorganic compounds on the scroll surface. The main effect of the degradation can be roughly described as an inhomogeneous wearing-off of the mineral surface layer, accompanied by the gelatinization of the underlying collagen.

For our comparative analysis of small vellum fragments found attached to the *Temple Scroll* wrapper (MS 5095) we obtained a triangular piece of 3 mm in length and 1.5 mm in width. The results are presented below.

Figure 41. Optical micrograph of sample MS 5095/4, magnification 200, scale bar 100 μm

1. Optical Microscopy

The layered structure characteristic of the *Temple Scroll* is observed in the high resolution micrograph of the edge of the fragment (*Figure 41*). Furthermore, a rough and inhomogeneous surface consisting of a continuous mineral layer has so far only been found on the parchment of the major part of 11QT^a. The thickness of the fragment, varying from 150 to 200 µm, is consistent with that measured on the TS. It is noteworthy that the usual thickness of the Dead Sea Scrolls is more than 300 µm.

2. Electron Microscopy and Elemental Analysis

Scanning electron microscopy confirmed our observation of a continuous layer on the fragment surface (*Figure 42* [top]). In addition, we observed islands of different minerals. Their elemental composition obtained from the spots marked on the micrograph is presented below in series of the EDX spectra (*Figure 42* [bottom]). In the top spectrum (curve d) of the surface, the elements carbon (C) and oxygen (O) predominate. The pattern of relative abundances for I_C:I_N:I_O reflects the elemental composition of the collagen matrix underlying the surface layer. This layer contains aluminium (Al) and sulphur (S) as predominant elements while silicon (Si) and calcium (Ca) are present in lesser amounts. Compared with the high intensity of the collagen elements, the lower intensity of the surface elements indicates the thinness of this layer. Such an elemental distribution has so far been found only on the surface of the *Temple Scroll*. Other Dead Sea Scroll fragments usually have calcium as the most abundant element, closely followed by silicon and aluminium for the fragments found on the floor of the caves. The elemental composition of islands (a-c) corresponds to that of common salt (NaCl), sulphates of potassium, and gypsum respectively. Islands of common salt are often found on the Dead Sea Scrolls and have been attributed to the recrystallization of the salt contained in the parchment matrix consequent upon changes in its environmental conditions. Gypsum, one of the sediments of the caves, is sometimes detected as an impurity. The presence of potassium together with a high intensity of aluminium and sulphur on the surface are a strong indication of the use of alum for the tawing of this leather fragment, as in the case of the *Temple Scroll*. It should be mentioned, however, that the shape of the crystals (*Figure 42* [bottom]) points to a potassium bisulphate, a common impurity of potash alum (Dana et al. 1951, vol. 2, 395–97). No such crystals could be detected on the *Temple Scroll* fragments. Complementary analysis by a quantitative micro-x-ray fluorescence technique reveals a similarity in the average Cl/Br ratio between MS 5095/4 and fragments from the major part of the *Temple Scroll*,[3] but quite different relative intensities of the surface elements sulphur, potassium and calcium. This could be due to the post-discovery treatment of the *Temple Scroll*: humidification and consolidation with water-based glue may have partially washed off its surface layer. Since the surface layer consisted of different compounds, partial removal of the layer might result in different relative intensities of the residue.

---

[3] Columns I–VI of the *Temple Scroll* belong to a repair sheet from antiquity.

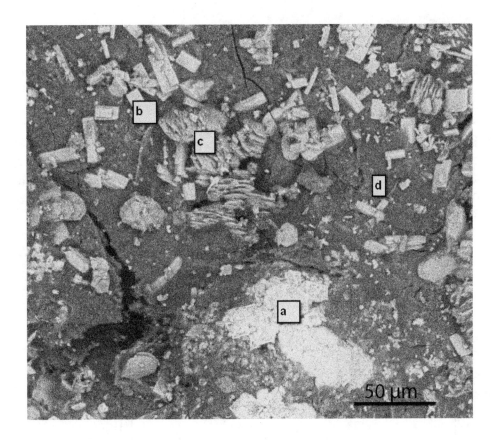

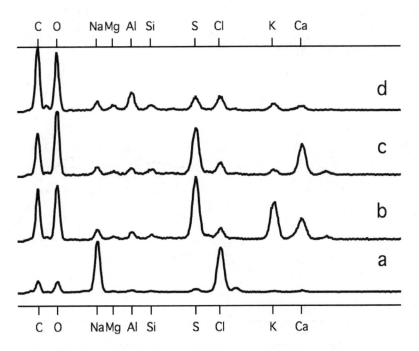

Figure 42. *SEM micrograph of sample MS 5095/4, magnification 550, scale bar 50 μm, environmental conditions: pressure 130 Pa (top); EDX spectra of the areas marked in the top image (bottom).*

3. Vibrational Spectroscopy

The strongest indication of the similarity between fragment MS 5095/4 and the *Temple Scroll* comes from the results of FTIR and Raman spectroscopy. In *Figure 43*, micro-FTIR spectra of three fragments practically coincide. The micro samples for the measurements in a diamond cell with a synchrotron radiation source were extracted from the top layer of a fragment that has shown a lesser degree of degradation, from MS 5095/4 and from the 'mirror' layer, *i.e.* a layer of the back side of the scroll that contained a set-off of text from the *verso* (writing side) of the neighbouring column. The spectrum corresponds to pure collagen despite the fact that it was taken from the top layer. This means that gypsum was applied in the form of a paste with parchment glue as a main constituent. It should be noted that a FTIR-ATR spectrum of the surface displays both ingredients of the paste.

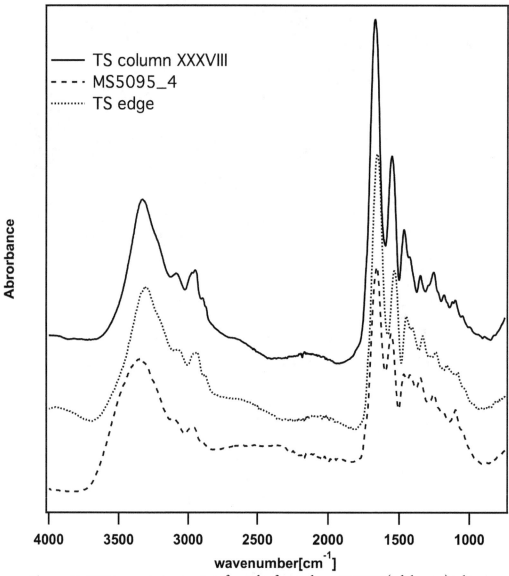

Figure 43. *FTIR transmission spectra of samples from column XXXVIII (solid curve), edge fragment (dotted curve), MS 5095/4 (broken curve)*

The relevant portions of the Raman spectra of four different fragments from the *Temple Scroll* are plotted together with the spectrum of MS 5095/4 and the spectra of standards in *Figure 44*. Spectra a and c were collected from different points of the same edge fragment of the *Temple Scroll*. The bands at 1005 and 986 cm^{-1}, corresponding to gypsum and alum respectively, are clearly detected on all the fragments with the exception of the fragment from the repair sheet (d). Here one can speculate on the attribution of the peak at 986 cm^{-1} to alum, whereas the broadening of the band at 1005 cm^{-1} suggests the presence of yet another compound not observed on the other fragments. Furthermore, the repair sheet is the only one to contain calcite, as witnessed by the band at 1086 cm^{-1}. It is noteworthy that the relative intensities of the alum and gypsum bands are not constant, supporting the hypothesis that the original treatment of the hide consisted of alum tawing followed by the application of gypsum-glue paste. In the course of time, different areas on the parchment underwent different degradation processes and this resulted in a quantitative, inhomogeneous change of the initial composition (cf. a and c). However, the most interesting band is found at 1045 cm^{-1} (c, d, f). From the panel presenting the standards it can be seen that this band might correspond to a mixture of nitrates of ammonia and calcium. This band, never identified on the fragments of the inner part of the scroll (col. LII) that we have studied, only appears on some points of the fragments from the edges (cf. a and c) and repair sheet (cf. d). The presence of bicarbonates of ammonium and sodium, which also have strong absorption bands in this area, could be ruled out since none of the strong lines characteristic of these salts could be detected in the far infrared region (Degen and Newman 1993). Nitrates of ammonium and calcium found in the sediments of Cave 11 correlate strongly with ammonium gas present in this particular cave. Since no fragments from Qumran Caves 1 and 4 and/or Murabbaʿat were found to display such a band we suggested that the band at 1045 cm^{-1} could be used as a fingerprint of Cave 11. Summarizing, the spectrum of fragment MS 5095/4 (cf. e) displays all the features corresponding to the fragments of the major part of the *Temple Scroll*, including the fingerprint of Qumran Cave 11. In the past, some scholars have expressed doubt that the *Temple Scroll* indeed came from Cave 11.[4] Our analysis has clearly shown that the scroll bears the stamp of the 'bat cave', Cave 11.

4. Conclusion

The majority of the tests conducted on MS 5095/4 indicate its similarity to fragments from different parts of the *Temple Scroll*. However, quantitative elemental analysis has shown large discrepancies between it and the *Temple Scroll* fragments. But since in-homogeneous degradation of the surface layer might be responsible for considerable changes in the initial elemental distribution, we conclude that the probability of MS 5095/4 belonging to the *Temple Scroll* is very high.

---

[4] William Kando has reported that his father had acquired the *Temple Scroll* years before 1956 (oral information from Weston Fields).

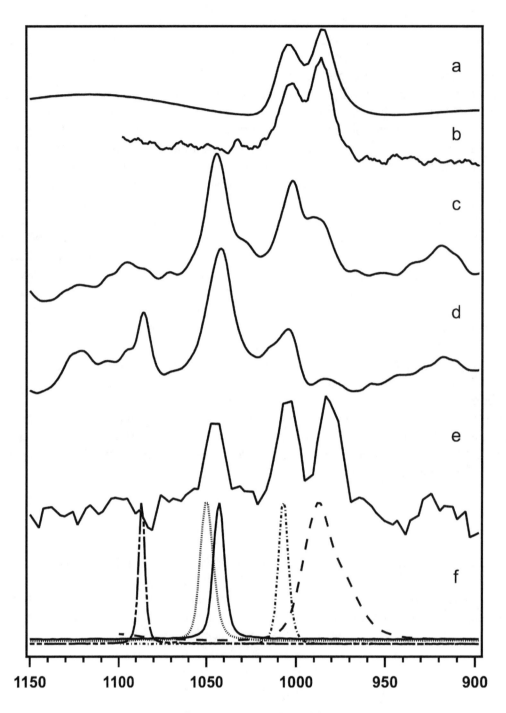

Figure 44. *Portions of Raman spectra collected from the samples.*
Edge samples from an unidentified column (a, c), from column LII in the main scroll (b), sample from the repair sheet in column V (d), sample MS 5095/4 (e).
Standards from right to left (f): potash alum[5], gypsum[5], ammonium nitrate[6], calcium nitrate[6], calcite[5]

[5] Database of Raman spectroscopy, X-ray diffraction and chemistry of minerals, http://rruff.info.
[6] Juan Manuel Madariaga, Maite Maguregui Hernando, private communication.

C. **Textile from the *Temple Scroll* Wrapper, MS 5095/2**

To study the samples from textile MS 5095/2 we have used optical and scanning electron microscopy (SEM), energy-dispersed X-ray analysis (EDX), Fourier Transform infrared and Raman investigation. Combining the results from the scanning micrographs (*Figure 45*) and FTIR and FT-Raman spectra (*Figure 47*), we could positively identify the fibres as linen.

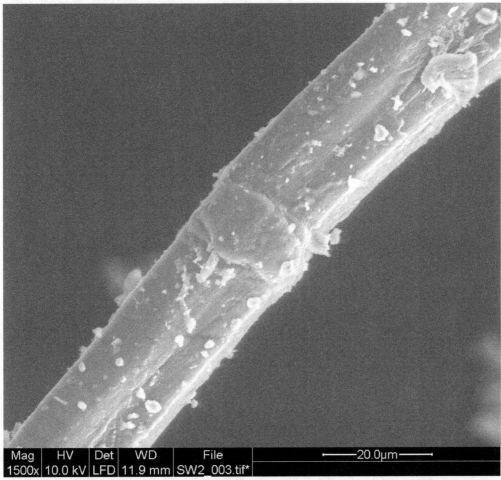

Mag	HV	Det	WD	File	———20.0μm———
1500x	10.0 kV	LFD	11.9 mm	SW2_003.tif*	

***Figure 45.** SEM micrograph of sample SW 2, magnification 1550, scale bar 20 μm, fibre diameter ~17 μm, preliminary identification as flax fibre confirmed by FTIR/Raman*

The fibres in *Figure 45* are clearly of plant origin, with a typical fibrillated surface and cross-markings characteristic of bast fibres. Their width (5–20 μm) and cross-section (not in the picture) closely match the description of flax.[7]

---

[7] cf. Latzke and Hesse 1988.

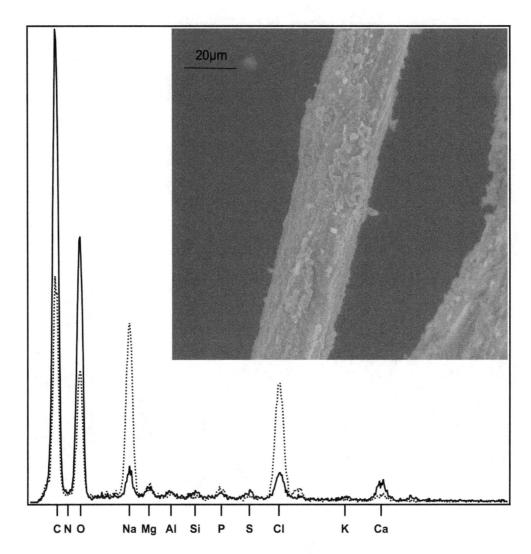

Figure 46. *EDX spectra of sample MS 5095 at HV=10kV.*
Solid line corresponds to entire fibre; broken line — to the crystals on the surface. The insert shows the SEM micrograph of the sample.

The elemental composition of the deposits observed on the fibres is presented in *Figure 46*. The most abundant foreign substance found is clearly identified as common salt (NaCl). Great quantities of salt crystallites are often found on Dead Sea Scrolls parchment fragments that were exposed to high humidity or substantial changes in the surrounding temperature. Since the salt was not distributed throughout all samples but was largely concentrated on one sample we believe that it was transferred from the parchment rather than that it emerged from the fibre itself. Similarly, only a small number of spots contain a sizable amount of sulphur, and this correlates with a high concentration of calcium.

Usually parchment and textile found on the floor of the caves contain a certain amount of mineral deposit corresponding to the sediments from the caves, namely calcite, aragonite, dolomite, clays and gypsum. This is reflected in a stable background of the elements corresponding to these sediments, with a predominance of Al, Si, S and Ca. The negligibly small amount of sediments traces found throughout textile MS 5095/2 indicates that it had little or no contact with the cave floor.

FTIR transmission spectra of all the samples investigated were identified as coming from flax with a certainty of 95%, or from ramie with a certainty of 92%, with the help of the IRUG spectral database (www.irug.org).

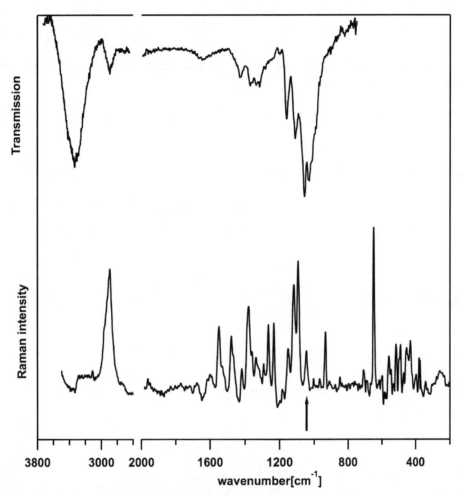

Figure 47. FTIR (upper curve) and FT-Raman of sample MS 5095

In *Figure 47*, both the FTIR spectrum (upper curve) and the FT-Raman spectrum (lower curve) of sample MS 5095/2 are presented. The high fluorescence exhibited by all samples hindered the use of confocal Raman spectroscopy with an interaction window of several microns. The 5 mm investigation spot of the FT-Raman spectrometer offers better statistics but demands a larger sample. Therefore, we could only apply this technique to a single sample (MS 5095/2).

FT-Raman and FTIR spectra in *Figure 47* show well preserved flax fibre, manifested by the characteristically shaped pattern of ν(COC) glycosidic link stretching modes at around 1100 cm^{-1}. The information in the FT-Raman spectrum allows differentiation between natural fibres that display practically identical features in their IR spectra. According to Edwards[8] only flax exhibited a ν (C=C) scattering at about 1570 cm^{-1}, typical of an aromatic ring.

---

[8] H. G. M. Edwards, E. Ellis, D. W. Farwell, R. C. Janaway, Preliminary study of the application of Fourier transform Raman spectroscopy to the analysis of degraded archaeological linen textiles, *Journal of Raman spectroscopy*, 27(1996): 663-69; H. G. M.

In addition to the characteristic vibrations of the natural fibres, we observe sharp peaks at 1265, 1233, 1047, 935 and 649 cm^{-1} respectively. The peak at 649 cm^{-1} is caused by the glue used to attach the fibre to the holder and is of no importance here. The peak at 1047 cm^{-1} corresponds to a mixture of ammonia and calcium nitrate and is a link to Cave 11 in Qumran, known as a 'bat cave'. These nitrates are of organic origin and their presence reflects the fact that bats have inhabited the cave for a long time. Nitrate of ammonia and of calcium have been detected in the sediments of the cave and also on the surface of the *Temple Scroll*.

For a positive assignment of the peaks at 1265, 1233 and 935 cm^{-1} respectively, further analysis involving extraction techniques is needed.

Conclusion

MS 5095/2 has been identified as linen and presents a positive correlation with Qumran Cave 11. The textile had not been in extensive contact with the floor of the cave. This observation fits Kando's information that the *Temple Scroll* was found in a closed jar, a jar still in the family's possession, and supports his assertion that the linen wrapping indeed covered this scroll.

Edwards, D. W. Farwell, D. Webster, FT-Raman microscopy of untreated natural plant fibres, *Spectrochimica Acta Part A* 53 (1997): 2383-92.

XXXV

The *Temple Scroll* Wrapper from Cave 11. MS 5095/2, MS 5095/4, MS 5095/1

Naʿama Sukenik

A. Introduction*

Qumran scholarship usually focuses on the hundreds of scrolls that were found at Qumran from 1947 onwards. At the same time the issue of textiles has been pushed to the periphery of research and has received little attention among researchers. The Qumran Caves are the first site in Israel where textiles were found. Unfortunately, most of the textiles were discarded by the Bedouin who first discovered the scrolls since they did not recognize their importance.[1] The first textiles from Qumran that were analyzed scientifically were taken for examination prior to the organized excavations of Roland de Vaux in the 1950s. These textiles were collected from Cave 1 in 1949 by de Vaux and Gerald Lankester Harding and published by Grace Mary Crowfoot in 1955. Apart from Crowfoot's report at that time no further research was conducted on the textiles for about fifty years. Only in 2003 were further reports about Qumran textiles published (Bélis 2003, Müller et al. 2003).[2]

More than sixty years have passed since the discovery of the scrolls, yet there is still a great deal of research to be conducted in this field. Textiles from Qumran were taken by researchers and collectors to various locations around the world. Today these textiles can be found in Israel Antiquities Authority, in Jordan, in England, and in private collections (Bélis 2003, 223, 228; Taylor et al. 2005, 164). The publication of any research about these textiles is of great importance and contributes to the enhancement of our knowledge of the textiles from Qumran.

This article examines one specific piece of textile believed to have been found in Cave 11 and currently located in The Schøyen Collection. This piece of textile has not been studied, although a photo of its main part was published in 2002 (Mébarki and Puech 2002, 31). The wrapper was obtained from Khalil Iskander Shahin ('Kando'), a shoemaker and antique dealer from Bethlehem who bought scrolls from the Bedouin. According to Kando this textile (MS 5095/2) was originally used as the wrapper for the *Temple Scroll* that was found in Cave 11 in 1956. Kando maintains that the following items were found in the same jar as this scroll, two groups of threads (SW2 and SW3), a linen cord (SW4); small pieces of

* I would like to thank Martin Schøyen and Torleif Elgvin who made it possible for me to examine the textile in The Schøyen Collection. I would also like to thank Ira Rabin for permission to use the results of her research, and professor Zohar Amar for his important comments.

[1] According to Eliezer Sukenik the Bedouin who arrived first at the caves threw out a number of textiles because of the strong smell that emanated from them (Crowfoot 1955, 18–19).

[2] The textiles were examined by Mireille Bélis before cleaning. As a historian she emphasized issues such as the material relationship between the manuscripts and the textiles rather than technical details.

textile (MS 5095/4), and pieces of textile to which strips of parchment were adhering (MS 5095/1). It looks as if all these items can be connected to the same scroll wrapper.[3]

Like the scrolls found at Qumran, these textile pieces were preserved due to the dry climate in this region. Unfortunately, and like the fate of the *Temple Scroll*, the textiles have been damaged through the ages.[4] This article examines for the first time the textile that appears to have been used as a wrapper for the *Temple Scroll*.

B. Textile MS 5095/2—The *Temple Scroll* Wrapper

The textile comprises three pieces: MS 5095/2a, which is the largest piece, was acquired by The Schøyen Collection from a Swiss collection in 1995,[5] and two additional pieces, the upper right corner (MS 5095/2b) and the lower part (MS 5095/2c), obtained later by The Schøyen Collection. This textile, believed to have been the wrapper of the *Temple Scroll*, is incomplete.

Its current size is 53 × 65 cm (20 × 26 inches), and the bottom section appears to be missing. A number of dark stains are visible on the textile. In addition to these, there are at least six tears that appear to have been caused by a sharp instrument. These tears were probably made by the Bedouin who found the scroll with its wrapping. Textiles with similar tears have been found among other textiles from Qumran Cave 1, for example, No. 30 (*DJD* I:Plate VII; Bélis 2003).

According to the Scanning Electron Microscopy (SEM) and Energy Dispersed X–ray Analysis (EDX) conducted by Ira Rabin, the textile is made of linen. The woven threads are not coloured and they are spun in S–Spun, a spinning technique characteristic of other linen textiles that have been found in Israel generally and in Qumran in particular (Wild 1970, 38; Shamir 2006a, 79; Crowfoot 1955, 19; Shamir and Sukenik 2011). The thickness of the threads is not uniform which is consistent with reports from Crowfoot regarding other textiles (Crowfoot 1955, 19). The threads were woven by a simple weaving technique called tabby.[6] The weave is medium with a density of 15 warp threads by 12 weft threads per cm. In the area between the decorations the weave is denser and stands at 16 warp by 13 weft.

The textile is decorated at the bottom with the self-band technique. In this technique several weft threads are passed in a single warp a group of weft strands in a single shed (Sheffer and Granger-Taylor 1994, 164; Bender Jørgensen 2008). This decoration is also characteristic of linen cloth found at other sites such as the decoration on a child's tunic from the Cave of Letters (nos 7.62–65, Yadin 1963, 257–58; Shamir 2010, 120–21), on the Masada textiles (Sheffer and Granger-Taylor 1994, 163–64), on the Murabbaʿat textiles (nos 78, 80, 83, 84–89; Crowfoot and Crowfoot 1961, 59-60) and at Wadi ed-Daliyeh (nos 13, 29, 30; Crowfoot 1974, 69–72). Because of the difficulty of dying linen any colour other than blue (Wild 1970, 80; Yadin 1963, 259), linen textiles decorated with coloured woollen threads were common in the Roman world as in Palmyra (Pfister 1934, 13) and in the textiles from Dura Europos (Pfister and

---

[3] According to Kando, a stylus was also found in the jar, http://www.schoyencollection.com/dsscrolls.html#12.4; and Rabin's article on the palm fibre tool, p. 357.

[4] Yigael Yadin believed that the textiles were damaged mostly during the years they were stored in Kando's home (Yadin 1985, 41). However, it may alternatively be assumed that the scroll with the wrapper was damaged at its bottom end (that touched the bottom of the jar) during the many centuries the jar remained in Cave 11 due to changing conditions of humidity and temperature (personal communication from Kando to Martin Schøyen).

[5] The larger piece was in Kando's possession until 1961, when he gave it to a Swiss customer who died in 1980. The Schøyen Collection bought it from the heirs of the latter in 1995.

[6] This is the simplest and most common type of weave. It is a basic binding system or weave based on a unit of two ends (warp) and two picks (weft), in which each end passes over one pick and under the other pick (Shamir 2006a, 39).

Bellinger 1945, 25, no. 256). However this practice is almost completely absent among Jewish populations because of *sha'atnez*, the religious prohibition of combining linen and wool.[7]

Through the self-band technique decoration was possible using only linen threads without any colour. This technique, used by Jewish people in the making of linen textiles, enabled the artist to create *clavi,* the bands of colour that were characteristic of clothing from the Roman period (Yadin 1963, 207, 209), without using dyed wool and thus violating the prohibition against *sha'atnez.*

In the textile that is the focus of this research the self-band created the appearance of having two parallel bands at a distance of 2 cm from each other in the lower third of the textile. Each band consists of two thin strips of self-band, each of which consists of three weft threads that pass together. Afterwards one weft thread is woven in a regular weave and after that another three weft threads are passed together. After a gap of 2 cm the decoration is repeated in exactly the same way—three wefts together, a space of one weft, and then three wefts together (see *Figure 48*). The use of self-band is uncommon amongst the textiles from Qumran (Shamir 2006a, 80) and has been identified in only two other fabrics (nos 7, 58; Crowfoot 1955).

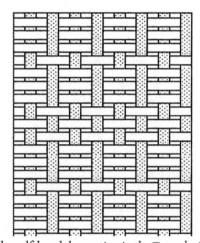

Figure 48. *The self-band decoration in the* Temple Scroll *wrapper*

Three edges of the textile remain. The upper right hand edge is well preserved; the left edge is partly preserved. From inspection of the textile it is apparent that all the edges were rolled up and sewn (as in *Figure 49*). The sewing thread was also made of linen, and is composed of two threads that were not plied. The stitches are positioned at equal intervals of 0.5–0.8 cm; they are of equal length and seem to

---

[7] *Sha'atnez* is a prohibition that forbids the combination of linen and wool in a single fabric as written in Lev 19.19 and Deut 22.11. For the most part, textiles found in Israel do not violate the *sha'atnez* prohibition. There are a few exceptions to this, three textiles from Kuntillet 'Ajrud (800–750 BC, Sheffer and Tidhar 1991, 1–2; Sheffer and Tidhar 2012, 307); three textiles from Wadi ed-Daliyeh (Samaritan, fourth century BC, Crowfoot 1974, 63); a number of textiles from Mezad Tamar (first century BC–eighth century AD, Shamir 2003, 23; Shamir 2006b, 191); and one textile from Masada was published (1043-2189/1, Granger-Taylor 2006, 128, footnote 65). Sheffer and Tidhar suggest that the priestly character of the site of Kuntillet 'Ajrud could explain the presence of a *sha'atnez* textile beautifully ornamented in red and blue since a priestly vestment can be coloured only if the linen is interwoven with wool (2012, 301, 307–8; cf. Exod 28.4–8, 39), see Shamir 2014 (the occupation of Kuntillet 'Ajrud is earlier than the common dating of the pentateuchal sources).

have been carefully sewn.[8] This technique was identified in many other textiles found in Cave 1 including, inter alia, nos 4, 33, 51, 54, and 56. In some cases, the edges were sewn using blue thread (Crowfoot 1955, 19).

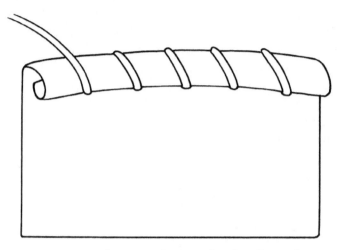

Figure 49. *Whipping and sewing the edge of a textile*
(Sheffer and Granger-Taylor 1994, 171, Fig. 21, © Israel Exploration Society)

The textile underwent a bleaching process. This is especially apparent with parts MS 5095/2b and MS 5095/2c, which appear to have been preserved in a better manner and were not exposed to the sun. Bleaching is a long process that takes place after the textile has been woven and includes immersing the textile in various chemical materials in order to whiten the linen, which is naturally cream or beige in colour (Forbes 1956, 81). The process of bleaching was quite common in Egypt, where there was specialization in the linen textile industry, most of the produce of which was made for clothing (Forbes 1956, 27–30; Hall 1986, 9).

Bleached textiles have been found at a number of sites in Israel. These include En Rahel on the Spice Route (Shamir 1999, 96) and the El Masaia Cave in Naḥal Deragot (Shamir 2006a, 160).[9] A number of other textiles that underwent a bleaching process similar to that of this textile were also found in Qumran. These include nos 30, 15 and 36 from Cave 1, and most of the textiles from Cave 11 that are in the IAA collections.[10] Although there is no reference to the bleaching process in Crowfoot's report, it is noted that nos 7 and 8 stand out for their white colour. It is likely that these textiles also underwent a bleaching process (Crowfoot 1955, 30; see also Shamir 2003, 79).[11] Another element that attests to the

---

[8] In other textiles found at Qumran, only linen thread was found in the stitching; textile 464131 is an example. This contrasts with textiles from Masada, for example, where linen threads were found in woollen textiles (Sheffer and Granger-Taylor 1994, 160). The same is the case for Textile 2.12 from the Cave of Letters, made of wool. Yadin did not notice the linen thread (1963, 241–44), while Sheffer recognized stitches of linen thread on the wool (1993, 70). According to Sheffer this textile could be a scroll wrapper. Indeed, the majority ruling of the Mishnah exempts scroll wrappers from the *shaʿatnez* prohibition, 'Handkerchiefs, wrappers for scrolls, and bath towels do not come under the law of diverse kinds. But R. Eliezer forbids them' (*m. Kil.* 9.3; see also *m. Meg.* 3.1). One could speculate that the Qumran community had the same strict ruling as R. Eliezer ben Horkanos of the late first century.

[9] The textiles were not imported from Egypt because they do not have the same number of threads as Egyptian textiles. Bleached linen textiles were probably not rare, but they are rarely mentioned in research.

[10] We can assume that 47 textiles from Cave 11 underwent a bleaching process.

[11] For the white dress of people from Qumran, see Tigchelaar 2003.

high level of craftsmanship that went into making the *Temple Scroll* wrapper is that there are no signs of weaving mistakes. This indicates a highly skilled artist.

C. Groups of Threads—SW2 and SW3

The Schøyen Collection includes two related textile items, two tassel skeins comprising several threads (SW3 and SW2). On the main photograph these threads are placed in the lower right corner, just above the smaller piece c of the textile, but I suggest they belonged to the missing bottom section, and represent decorative fringes from the edge. According to Kando these threads were found inside the same jar as the wrapper. When compared with similar items found in Qumran, these threads may represent elements of decoration in parts of the textiles that did not survive. There seems to have been a fringe made with the warp threads in the border decoration of the textile, similar to what has been found in other textiles from Qumran (for example, nos 2, 3, 4, 19, 37; Crowfoot 1955, see plates V.7; V.8; V.14).

D. The Cord—SW4

A cord (SW4) that appears to have been used for tying the wrapper around the scroll was found alongside the scroll wrapper. This cord is also made of linen. It is 85 cm long and consists of three unbleached threads, each of which is spun in the S–Spun technique. The threads are Z-plied (see *Figure 50*).

The cord found in Cave 11 is unique and of great importance, since it belongs to the wrapping of the *Temple Scroll*. Although it is likely that other scroll wrappers were tied with similar cords, this is the only textile cord from Qumran that has survived.

Figure 50. *The cord consisting of three S-spun threads, Z-plied (3SZ)*

E. Parts of Textile, MS 5095/4 and MS 5095/1

In addition to the large textile, 40 small fragments of textile (MS 5095/4) were found in the same jar. All these pieces are made from S–Spun linen and woven in the same tabby weave as the larger textile. The largest of these pieces is 2.8 × 3 cm, and the density is 16 warp threads by 12 weft threads. This is as it is in the decorated area of the wrapper. Some of the pieces look as if they underwent a bleaching process (while others have many dirt stains) and it is likely that these pieces were part of the large fabric.

An additional 14 fragments (MS 5095/1, MS 5095/4) were also found. Some of these are pieces of leather with linen adhering to them, which indicates that the linen was used to wrap the scroll. Hebrew letters in the same script as the first part of the *Temple Scroll* can be deciphered on some of the pieces.

Rabin has analyzed one of the fragments designated MS 5095/4 and concluded that it belongs to the *Temple Scroll*.[12]

F. Discussion and Conclusions

The *Temple Scroll* is the longest scroll found in Qumran. Its length when found was 8.148 m; Yadin believed its original length was 8.75 m (1985, 57), slightly longer than the great Isaiah scroll. The height of the scroll was approximately 24–26 cm (Yadin 1985, 59). It can be assumed that when the scroll was rolled, its diameter was approximately 5–7 cm.[13] Since the cord used to fasten the wrapper is approximately 85 cm long, it could be brought several times around the scroll for a secure hold. It appears, therefore, that the scroll had a double layer of protection. First, it was wrapped in a scroll wrapper; afterwards, it was buried in a jar for increased protection (Yaniv 2006, 410; Taylor 2012, 281). The mineral test conducted by Rabin support Kando's report that the wrapper was found inside a jar: deposits on the surface of the textile did not include materials from the floor of the cave, as did other textiles found in Qumran (Crowfoot 1955, 18, note 2). Hence it is likely that this textile had minimal contact with the cave floor.[14]

The use of wrappers to protect scrolls was known at this time. The common way of protecting scrolls in the first centuries after the turn of the millennium was to wrap them or put them in cases, or sometimes both, and then to put the wrapped or encased scrolls in a cupboard. This is still done today, when wrapping biblical scrolls in synagogues (Yaniv 2006). In talmudic literature and the Mishnah, scroll wrappers are called *Mitpehoth Hasepharim* (cf. *m. Kil.* 9.3 [see note 8]; see also *m. Meg.* 3.1).

In Mishnaic times scroll wrappers were regarded as holy items. They were not discarded after they had been worn out; instead, and as was customary with sacred objects such as holy books, they were stored in a repository for sacred objects known as a *genizah*. This is shown in the following example from the Gemara quoting Mar Zotra, 'Wrappings of scrolls which are worn out may be used for making shrouds for a *Meth Mitzvah*; and this act constitutes their "stowing away"' (*b. Meg.* 26b).

The materials used for scroll wrappers in the ancient world appear to have varied. In classical times leather is mentioned, no doubt as a good protective wrapper for papyrus scrolls. Books written on skins were strong enough to need only a light wrapper (Crowfoot 1955, 24). This is consistent with the findings of the *Temple Scroll*. Some scroll wrappers were decorated, as mentioned in *Kil'ayim*,

> Scroll wrappers, whether or not figures are portrayed on them, are susceptible to uncleanness. So says the School of Shammai, and the School of Hillel says, If figures are portrayed on them they are not susceptible to uncleanness; if figures are not portrayed on them they are susceptible. Rabban Gamaliel says, In either case they are not susceptible to uncleanness (*m. Kil.* 28.4).

---

[12] See the text edition by Elgvin and Davis (p. 301), and Rabin's analysis of the textiles (p. 335).

[13] According to David Shenhav who opened the scroll (personal communication).

[14] Textiles that were found on the floor of the cave contain large quantities of sediments that are found on cave floors, such as calcite, aragonite, dolomite, clays and gypsum. According to tests by Rabin the quantity of aluminium, silicon, sulphur, and calcium on Textile MS 5095/2 (the textile under examination in this research) is negligible.

Figure 51. *Wrapper from Masada reconstructed by Bracha Sadovski*
(Sheffer and Granger-Taylor 1994, 224, © Israel Exploration Society)

According to Crowfoot's report on the textiles from Cave 1, remnants of wrappers that protected the scrolls were found in Qumran (Crowfoot 1955; Taylor et al. 2005, 163). According to photographs in the report, a wrapper can be seen wrapped around one of the scrolls (Crowfoot 1955, Plate I. 8–10; Bélis 2003, 209, 229–41). Unfortunately when study of these scrolls began more than 50 years ago, the textiles were placed in cardboard boxes, sometimes without any precise record of their origin (Bélis 2003, 207). The original location of most of the textiles discussed in Crowfoot's report is not known.[15] Today it is not clear which of the scrolls were found wrapped.[16]

From the various wrappers that Crowfoot examined, two primary types were identified, wrappers decorated with lines of blue decoration,[17] and wrappers that were not decorated with colour, but were decorated with fringes that appear to have been used to wrap the scrolls, or as packing pads to protect the sides of the scroll. A third group of textiles was identified by Crowfoot. These were coarsely woven textile pieces that appear to have been used as jar covers (Crowfoot 1955, 19).

All the scroll wrappers from Qumran were woven from linen and only some of them were decorated in blue. By contrast, two scroll wrappers dating to the Roman period and found in excavations were made of wool and decorated in assorted colours. In Masada, a scroll wrapper made of wool with yellow and red embroidery in the borders was found (textile no. 4 [AA] 8–206, Sheffer and Granger-Taylor 1994, 223–26); in the Cave of Letters a textile was found which Yadin believed was used to wrap a scroll (nos 2.12–49, Yadin 1963, 241–44). This textile was decorated in shades of red, yellow, blue and green, and had tassels on both sides of the fabric.[18]

Linen is a plant fibre derived from the stalks of the flax plant *Linum usitatissimum* which is characterized by a strong flexible fibre that reaches a length of over 35 cm. Linen thread has been used since the Neolithic Age and became a popular raw material in the textile industry throughout Israel and around the world (Forbes 1956, 27; Zohary and Hopf 1994, 119–20). The first evidence of the use of linen in the Land of Israel dates back 10,000 years in the findings of a comb held together by linen threads at Wadi Murabbaʿat (Schick 1995). The production of linen takes place in several stages including harvesting the flax plant, sun-drying it, soaking or retting the flax fibres in water in order to separate the stalks from the inner fibres, re-drying the flax stalks, crushing and winnowing them to separate the fibres, spinning the fibres into yarn, and weaving the yarn into cloth (Herschberg 1924, 58–90; Forbes 1956,

---

[15] During the conference 'The History of the Caves of Qumran' in Lugano 20–21 February, 2014, Mireille Bélis announced that there are many textiles from Qumran in the Amman archaeological museum, textiles that have not been studied. Furthermore, another scroll wrapper from Cave 11 was recently discovered in the École Biblique collections. It will soon be published together with other artefacts and small fragments from this cave (personal communication by Marcello Fidanzio to Torleif Elgvin).

[16] Bélis raised the hypothesis that the textile designated Textile 1 by Crowfoot wrapped the Hodayot scroll (Bélis 2003, 234–36).

[17] According to Crowfoot, 22 pieces of textile with lines of blue found in Cave 1 seem to have belonged to 16 different wrappers (Crowfoot 1955, 20).

[18] In addition to this wrapper, Yadin believed that other textiles in the Cave of Letters had also been used to wrap scrolls, for example, Textile no. 2.40–17 (Yadin 1963, 244).

27–32). The use of linen for weaving spread during the Hellenistic–Roman periods and is mentioned in Graeco-Roman literature such as Pliny (*Historia Naturalis*, XIX, 2), Strabo (*The Geography of Strabo*, XI, 2, 17), and Josephus who mention that the population near Jericho and Ein Gedi wore linen clothing because of the hot climate (*War*, IV, 473). It is also mentioned frequently in Jewish sources such as the Talmud and the Mishnah (see *e.g. m. B. Qam.* 10.9; *m. Kil.* 9.9; *m. Šabb.* 6.1).

However, the fact that scroll wrappers as well as other textile artefacts found at Qumran were made only from linen is unusual, considering the rich quantity of wool found in other excavations in the area. In most of the sites from this period, with the exception of cemeteries, where linen burial shrouds were found (Shamir 2006a, 79), the use of linen is less than 35 percent. In Qumran, 100 percent of the textiles found were made of linen (Shamir and Sukenik 2011). As it is unlikely that this choice was unintentional, this probably demonstrates an ideological perception among the residents here (Shamir and Sukenik 2011). A similar preference for using linen over wool is mentioned in *The Life of Apollonius*, written by Philostratus in the second century AD. Philostratus presented a religious worldview in accordance with which people refrained from wearing woollen garments while praying or bringing sacrifices because the source of the material was taken from living creatures and by this God's creation would be demeaned (Philostratus, *The Life of Apollonius*, VII, 5, 7).

Besides the similarity of the textile materials, there are other parallels between the *Temple Scroll* wrapper and the textiles found in Cave 1. All the threads were spun in S-Spun and woven in tabby weave. According to Crowfoot's report the textiles with the blue decoration were of higher quality than those without coloured decoration (Crowfoot 1955, 19) since the former had a larger number of threads per cm. In the first group the number of threads is as follows, no. 1, 18 × 12; no. 25, 12 × 16; no. 28, 13 × 16; no. 42, 12 × 16 (Crowfoot 1955, 27–38). In the second group, the number of threads is lower, no. 7, 13 × 13; no. 58, 12 × 14; no. 35, 12 × 12 (Crowfoot 1955, 27–38).

The density of the weave is another common factor between the *Temple Scroll* wrapper (which stands at 12 × 15 and 13 × 16 per cm) and the decorated blue textiles that belong to the higher quality textiles from Cave 1. However the blue decoration does not appear on the textile we are discussing. The unique example of decoration that appears in a number of textiles (see especially no. 1, Crowfoot 1955, Plate IV, 1–2) is a model which produced three blue rectangles, one inside the other. This example is unique, difficult to make, and created by a special method. The blue weft threads turn 90 degrees and become warp threads. The blue lines, formatted in a rectangular pattern, were discussed by Crowfoot. She saw religious significance in them and found it hard to believe that people would take so much trouble over a rather uninteresting design unless it had some meaning for them. She suggested that the rectangles represented the ground plan of some religious building (Crowfoot 1955, 25). Yadin noted that this design corresponds with the plan of the Temple as described in the *Temple Scroll* (1985, 162–63). Following this suggestion, one might expect to find this decoration on the *Temple Scroll* Wrapper. However this textile lacks any vestige of blue thread.

When attempting to determine whether this textile was initially made as a cover for the scroll, similar to other textiles decorated in blue, or whether its use as a wrapper was secondary and it was cut from worn-out clothing, as with some of the other textiles from Cave 1,[19] the functional role of the textiles must be examined. In my opinion, and even though the textile is not identical to the more delicate textiles that are decorated in blue, it can be assumed that the textile is not in secondary use as a decorated wrapper. In other words, and like other scroll wrappers, the textile we are discussing was intended for this purpose from the outset, and was found in its primary use.

---

[19] For example, the third group which, according to Crowfoot, was used to cover jars. Most of these textiles were cut from worn out textiles and used for this purpose. See Shamir and Sukenik 2011 on textiles from Qumran and the garments of its inhabitants.

There is no evidence that this textile was cut from another textile. The sewing of the borders was done precisely, the stitches were evenly spaced and of even length, and were not done haphazardly, as often appears in textiles found in a secondary use (Shamir 2006a, 288).[20] Moreover, in most cases of secondary use, the textiles are relatively small squares of fabric that were cut from a larger textile that was worn out and no longer suitable for use. An instructive example of this is a blanket from the Moʾa site along the Spice Route, made from many small squares that were cut from various fabrics (nos 179–209; Shamir 2005, 113). By contrast, the textile under discussion is a single large piece. In addition the density of the weaving, the bleaching process, the high quality of weaving craftsmanship (evident in the absence of mistakes), and the decorative tassels that appear to have adorned the textile, all suggest that great effort was invested in its preparation.[21]

A comparison of this scroll wrapper with other textiles that were found in Qumran[22] reveals the following similarities: the method of spinning, the manner of weaving, the decorations, the method of making the borders, the varying thickness of the thread, and even the similarity in the simplicity of the textiles, from which the colourful decorations characteristic of the Roman period are absent. All these features suggest that the textiles were made in the same workshop.

This textile does not appear to have been made locally by Qumran residents, since its high quality of craftsmanship would not be typical of such a settlement. Although the findings from de Vaux's excavations were not published in a final report, his published field notes include lists of the objects found in each locus (Humbert and Chambon 1994). From these lists, we know that only two spindle whorls, indications of spinning, were found in Qumran.[23] These findings are not enough to prove local production of textiles. Although a few objects described as clay balls were found here, there are no illustrations of these objects. In the absence of a final report about them (Humbert and Chambon 1994, for example nos 140, 407, 422, and others), it is impossible to determine whether they were used as loom weights (Magness 2004, 145). These clay balls could also have been used for other purposes (Shamir 1996, 142–43). Furthermore, in recent excavations, Yizhak Magen and Yuval Peleg did not find such items (Magen and Peleg 2007). At the same time it is unlikely that this textile came from another country. Although Egypt had a highly developed linen industry (Amar 1998b, 114), textiles originating in Egypt were characterized by thinner thread and a higher weaving density than the textiles at Qumran. It is logical, therefore, to accept Crowfoot's conclusion that this fabric, like other fabrics over which care appears to have been taken to obey the shaʿatnez prohibition, were acquired from the Jewish population in Israel (Crowfoot 1955, 22).

---

[20] An example is the belt found in the Cave of Letters (no. 97–7.90, Yadin 1963, 267).

[21] According to Zohar Amar's hypothesis, wrappers of holy books were considered sacred objects. For example, in the Gemara it is said that when wrappers of holy books cease to be used, they are not thrown away, rather they are used as shrouds for the dead (b. Meg. 26a). It seems, therefore, that just as the ritual fringes on a prayer shawl are made from the beginning with the intention of fulfilling a biblical commandment (beshem mitswah), this was also the case with scroll wrappers. In other words, while they were being woven it was known that they would be used to wrap a scroll. This issue, however, should be examined further.

[22] Primarily for the textiles that Crowfoot attributed to the first two groups used to protect scrolls, first, cloths with decoration of blue lines; second, plain cloths, some with fringes.

[23] One of these spindle whorls is not associated with the sectarian settlement at Qumran (Magness 2004, 123).

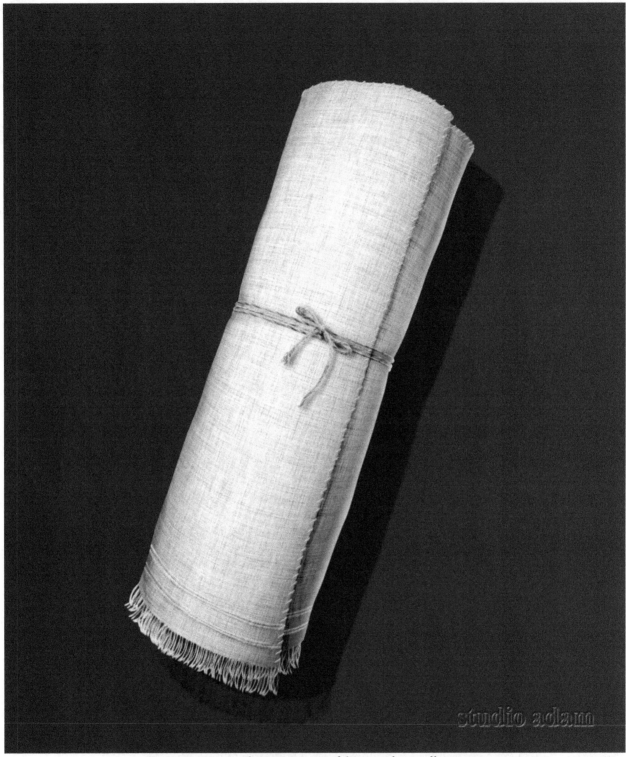

Figure 52*. Suggested reconstruction of the Temple Scroll wrapper.*
The textile is decorated at the bottom with the self-band technique and fringes. Drawing by
Dror Adam; scale unknown. A cord that appears to have been used for tying the wrapper
around the scroll is pictured alongside the scroll wrapper; see Figure 53 p. 350.

G. Reconstruction of the Wrapping Technique

To go by archaeological finds at Masada and in the Cave of Letters, it can be assumed that there were two main techniques of wrapping scrolls. In one method the scroll was wrapped and put inside a scroll wrapper that served as a type of satchel or 'bag' (Yaniv 2009, 8). An example of this technique is found in a fabric from the Cave of Letters where signs of sewing are seen between the two sides of the fabric that made up the bag (nos 20.49–2.12; Yadin 1963, 241–44).

By contrast it can be seen from a scroll wrapper found at Masada that the fabric was wrapped around the scroll and then tied (no. 4 (AA) 8–206, Sheffer and Granger-Taylor 1994, 223–26—see *Figure 51*). It appears that this was the method of binding used in the wrappings described in the Tosefta, 'They wrap a Torah with Torah wrappings', (*t. Meg.* 3.20). An examination of the *Temple Scroll* wrapper makes it clear that there are no signs of sewing that would indicate that the textile was made of two pieces of fabric that were connected at the edges and functioned as a 'bag'.

It can be assumed that this textile was used like the textile found at Masada. It appears that the scroll was first closed with a leather closure (cf. Carswell, *DJD* 6:23–28), then wrapped in fabric that was tied (see *Figure 52*), and finally placed in a vessel or cupboard that was intended for this purpose. In this case, there seems to be a close connection between the cylindrical jar used for this purpose, the linen, and a particular scroll (cf. Taylor 2012, 274–82; Taylor 2013, 277–81).

H. Summary

When the scrolls were first found at Qumran by the Bedouin, many of the textiles were discarded and not preserved. Unfortunately, most archaeologists did not find much of interest in them. Crowfoot was the exception. Her research on the textiles from Cave 1, conducted more than 50 years ago, provides an accurate and important picture. The publication of the current research on the *Temple Scroll* wrapper contributes significantly to research on textiles from Qumran in general, and scroll wrappers in particular.

A comparison with the textiles found in Cave 1 suggests that we are indeed dealing with a scroll wrapper. The method of spinning and the weaving technique indicate that this wrapper, along with other artefacts from Cave 1 and other textiles examined by Bélis and the IAA from Cave 8 and Cave 11, were all made at the same weaving centres. We can assume that with these artefacts we actually have the scroll wrapper and the cord that was used to tie the wrapper. Furthermore, and for the first time ever, these items can be connected to the specific scroll they were used to protect. For this reason this textile and this research are unique and of great importance.

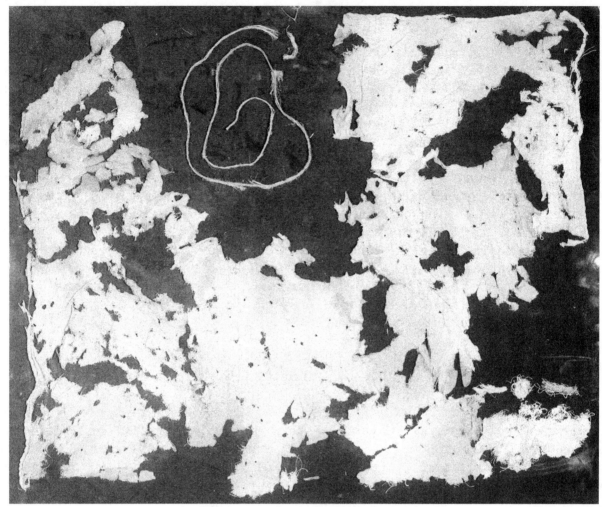

Figure 53. Temple Scroll *wrapper (scale 1:4)*

XXXVI

Radiocarbon Dating of the *Temple Scroll* Wrapper and Cave 11Q

Joan E. Taylor, Johannes van der Plicht

A key question concerning the Qumran caves is the dating of the deposits within them. The 'quick hiding scenario', whereby all the scrolls were placed in the caves ahead of the Roman advance in AD 68, has been the most popular theory to account for the presence of manuscripts within the caves. The view that there were several deposits at different times remains an alternative proposition. However, the deposits are configured in terms of different rationales, time periods and relationship with the site of Qumran (see Taylor 2011; 2012, 272–302; Magness 2002, 89; Stökl Ben Ezra 2007). In this context the dating of objects from the caves is of great interest.

The *Temple Scroll* and its wrapper come from Qumran Cave 11Q. This cave was already found by the Bedouin before the arrival of the archaeological team (de Vaux 1956, 573–77; 1973, 51; Fields 2009, 299), but further material uncovered in the cave, including broken pottery and manuscript fragments such as a scroll of Ezekiel, proved interesting. Compared to other Qumran caves the repertoire of Cave 11Q is richer: it had a wider range of objects than identified in other Qumran caves. The items are listed as follows: Gr 11Q-1: a lid; Gr 11Q-2: a fragment of an iron blade; Gr 11Q-3: a copper buckle; Gr 11Q-4: iron chisel; Gr 11Q-5: a lamp; Gr 11Q-6: an iron pick; Gr 11Q-7: juglet Gr 11Q-8: lamp; Gr 11Q-9a and b: two hide (skin) items; Gr 11Q-10: an iron rod; Gr 11Q-11: an iron key; Gr 11Q-12: a glass bead; Gr 11Q-13: part of a (Chalcolithic) small jar, along with fragments of jars from the Iron Age as well as two lamps from this time (de Vaux 1956, 574; 1973, 51; Humbert and Chambon 1994, 265–66, 344). Two jar lids found here are defined as 'upturned bowls' (de Vaux 1956, 574). There were also textiles, basketry and cord strings, now in the Organic Material Storage Unit of the Israel Antiquities Authority. The archaeological team identified three distinguishable periods of occupation—Chalcolithic, Iron Age II and Roman.

Before the arrival of the archaeologists a number of items were removed from the cave: numerous manuscript pieces (Fitzmyer 2008, 110–16) and at least two scroll jars, one containing the *Temple Scroll* (11Q19) in a linen wrapper, that passed to the well-known antiquities dealer Khalil Iskander Shahin, or Kando, and thereafter to private collections (these jars are shown with Kando in a picture in Fields 2009, 98, cf. 301, and Puech 1989, Pl. 3). The manuscripts excavated by the Bedouin were offered to the Palestine Archaeological Museum by Kando, while the *Temple Scroll* itself was requisitioned by Yigael Yadin upon the capture of Bethlehem in 1967 (Yadin 1985; Fields 2009, 300; Fitzmyer 2008, 110–16).

Kando reported that in the same jar with the *Temple Scroll* there were: the *Temple Scroll* wrapper (MS 5095/2), two groups of threads (SW2 and SW3), a linen cord (SW4), a small piece of textile (MS 5095/4), pieces of textile upon which strips of parchment were stuck (MS 5095/1) and what has been designated as a palm leaf stylus (MS 5095/3), cf. Sukenik, p. 339. The distinction between the linen wrapper (MS 5095/2) and the pieces of linen (MS 5095/1) is not significant. The larger fragments were put in the large display case together with the string (cf. *Figure 53*). When acquired by The Schøyen Collection, the smaller fragments were also first put there, but shifted place when there was handling of the large frame, so they were then mounted in a small frame, where they are more stable (personal communication from Martin Schøyen; see *Figure 54*). They are designated MS 5095/4.

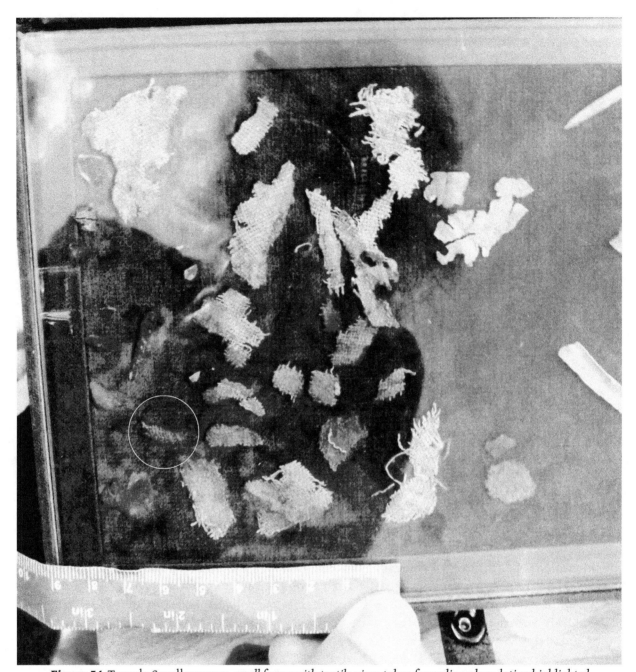

Figure 54. Temple Scroll *wrapper, small frame with textile piece taken for radiocarbon dating highlighted*

The fragments of the *Temple Scroll* wrapper are particularly useful for radiocarbon dating because, unlike many textile fragments from the Qumran caves, they have never been cleaned or treated, so that there are no modern contaminating residues that would influence radiocarbon dating results. They appear to have been bleached in antiquity (cf. Sukenik, p. 342). Since these small fragments were already separated from the larger piece they proved to be ideal for radiocarbon dating, as no cutting is required. Martin Schøyen kindly permitted one of the present authors, Joan Taylor, to take a piece for dating by the Centre for Isotope Research, Groningen, and this was sent to the laboratory on 17 December, 2014 (*Figure 54* shows the piece chosen).

A. Preparation and Testing of the Sample

Successful dating depends on the samples being cleaned thoroughly since they may contain foreign carbon with a different ^{14}C content, such as carbonate, humic substances and/or plant remains, and preservatives. These must be removed in order to obtain the correct radiocarbon age of the sample itself. Standard procedures for the chemical pre-treatment of samples have been developed (*e.g.* Mook and Streurman 1983).

The standard treatment of samples consists of the following steps: (i) Acid (HCl) in order to remove soil carbonate and possibly infiltrated humic acids; (ii) Alkali (NaOH) to remove *e.g.* soil humates; (iii) Acid (HCl) to remove any CO_2 absorbed during step (ii). This treatment is referred to as the 'AAA' (Acid-Alkali-Acid) treatment.

The scroll wrapper was an 18.6 mg sample of linen textile, yielding 6.0 mg of extracted Carbon after the AAA treatment. The prepared and purified sample fraction is combusted into CO_2 gas using an Elemental Analyser coupled to an Isotope Ratio Mass Spectrometer (IsoCube/IsoPrime). This EA/IRMS provides the stable isotope ratio $^{13}C/^{12}C$.

For ^{14}C analysis, part of the CO_2 is routed to a cryogenic trap to collect the samples for further processing. The CO_2 is transferred into graphite powder by the reaction $CO_2 + 2H_2 \rightarrow 2H_2O + C$ at a temperature of 600°C and using Fe powder as catalyst (Aerts et al. 2001). Next, the graphite is pressed into target holders for the ion source of the AMS (Accelerator Mass Spectrometer). The AMS is based on a 2.5 MV particle accelerator built by High Voltage Engineering Europa. The AMS measures the $^{14}C/^{12}C$ and $^{13}C/^{12}C$ isotope ratios of the graphite (van der Plicht et al. 2000). From these numbers the conventional ^{14}C age is determined.

This conventional ^{14}C age is based on the Libby half-life value, oxalic acid as a reference material and correction for isotopic fractionation using $^{13}C/^{12}C$ (Mook and van der Plicht 1999). These ages are reported in BP, 'Before Present'. For absolute dates, the conventional ^{14}C ages need to be calibrated into calendar ages. This is done by the recommended calibration curve IntCal13 (Reimer et al. 2013). The calibrated ages are reported in calBC or calAD.

For the *Temple Scroll* wrapper, the conventional ^{14}C age is determined as 1900±30 BP. The laboratory code is GrA-62331, and the $^{13}C/^{12}C$ ratio (expressed in the ^{13}C value) is -25.12‰. Both the ^{13}C value and the organic Carbon content (the most important quality parameters for sample integrity) are well within acceptable range for linen textile.

The calibration is shown in the figure (*Figure 55*). The radiocarbon date is plotted in red along the vertical axis, the calibrated date in black along the horizontal axis. The relevant part of the calibration curve IntCal13 is shown in blue. The calibrated age range is 70–130 calAD. Both the ^{14}C age in BP, and the calibrated age range in calAD are reported at 1-sigma (68.2%) confidence level, with numbers rounded to the nearest significant 5. At 2-sigma (95.4%), the calibrated age range is 30–215 calAD (numbers rounded and combined).

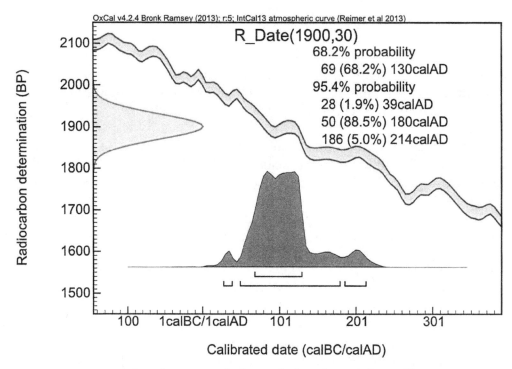

Figure 55. *Radiocarbon test results for textile from the* Temple Scroll *wrapper*

B. Other Datings from Cave 11Q

The calibrated date range of the linen sample from the *Temple Scroll* wrapper is particularly interesting given the later than usual parameters. Within the 2-sigma range (95.4%) probability, 88.5% confidence attaches to a date between 50 and 180 AD. The relatively late date range of the results needs to be contextualized within other dates that have been obtained from Cave 11Q.

Gelatinized and ungelatinized samples of the *Temple Scroll* were radiocarbon dated in the ETH Zurich laboratory in 1990 and provided a result of 2024±49 (gelatinised) and 2066±78 (ungelatinized) years BP, at 1 sigma (68% probability), giving it an averaged result of 2030±40 years BP, or calibrated date range of 97 BC–1 AD (Bonani 1992, 845), and the 2-sigma calibration of Gregory Doudna (1998) has yielded a range of 166 BC–67 AD. Tests done in 2004 (Rasmussen et al 2005, 151–52) included six samples from Cave 11Q. Of these, a cotton textile yielded a result of 860–1020 AD at 2-sigma, a dating result matched by two wood samples, indicating an employment of the cave in the Abbasid to Fatimid periods, not identified by the archaeologists. In addition, there were two linen samples that provided dates of 190 BC–30 AD, and 100 BC–70 AD at 2-sigma, while a piece of wood was dated 1880–1610 BC, in the Middle Bronze Age. The linen samples clearly cohere with the occupation period of the Qumran settlement and deposit of scrolls in jars in the Qumran caves.

The current test of the *Temple Scroll* wrapper would be consistent with a date of hiding around the time of the First Revolt, but it would also keep open the question of whether this scroll was deposited later than AD 68, at a time corresponding to occupation Period III in de Vaux's system, or even the Bar Kokhba period, and only further tests would enable greater precision in this regard. It should also be remembered that the radiocarbon date relates to the cutting of the flax to make the linen, and not the date of the deposit, which would have been any time after this linen was made. The dating range of the linen is also significantly later than the dating range of the manuscript at 1-sigma, with overlapping dates only in the 2-sigma range. This may indicate that the *Temple Scroll* was an older manuscript that was covered in a relatively fresh wrapper prior to its deposit. Yadin has suggested that textiles tended to be used for a relatively short time, perhaps fifteen years (1963, 171). It should also be borne in mind that the scripts of Cave 11Q are often of a later date than those of other caves. In agreement with Stökl Ben Ezra (2007; 2010), García Martínez (2010, 205) states, 'That Cave 11 is a "young" cave seems certain, since Herodian and late-Herodian manuscripts make up the majority of its holdings.'

XXXVII

Palm Fibre Tool from Cave 11Q. MS 5095/3

Ira Rabin

The Schøyen Collection includes a palm fibre object claimed to have come from Cave 11. According to Kando, it was found by the Bedouin together with the *Temple Scroll*, the *Temple Scroll* wrapper and minor fragments from 11QTᵃ (MS 5095/1) in the scroll jar that is still the property of William Kando.[1]

1. Physical Description

The object was sold to The Schøyen Collection by the Kando family with the information that this was a pen from Cave 11. The object has a long groove and its tip is stained black. It is 8.6 cm long with a thickness of 9 × 5 mm. The tip shows indications of wear, probably from usage.

2. Examination

Initially, a C14 test was planned. However, the fragility of the object and its light weight (0.7501 g ± 0.0001) prevented successful sampling. Furthermore, the discovery of a remarkably similar artefact unearthed in a controlled excavation[2] has sufficiently substantiated its authenticity and obviated the need for C14 dating. However, its purpose remained obscure.

[1] Kando sold it to a private collection in Switzerland in 1961. Through the mediation of William Kando it was bought by The Schøyen Collection in 1996. For a picture of the *Temple Scroll* jar with its bowl lid, see Mébarki and Puech 2002, 30.

[2] It is designated 'pointe de bois' (wood tip), *DJD* 3:9; Plate 7, Fig. 15–4. This artefact comes from Cave 15, one of the northern caves that contained artefacts, but not scroll jars or scroll fragments. It has not been possible to locate this artefact in the IAA collections. With its 12.5 cm it is longer than the Schøyen artefact. In 2009 Southwestern Baptist Theological Seminary claimed to have acquired a pen from Qumran from the Kando family. Patterson (2012, 33) includes a small photograph of this artefact, which appears nearly identical to the Schøyen artefact. The length of the Southwestern Baptist Theological Seminary artefact is not known.

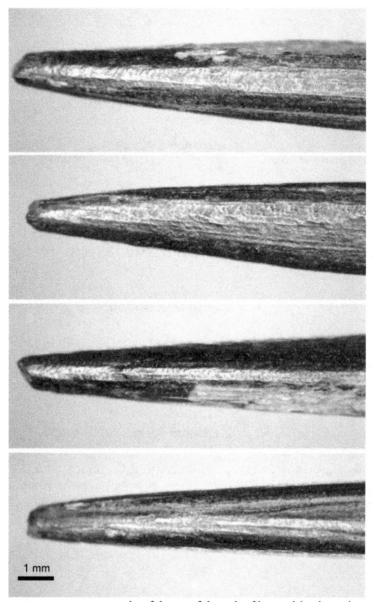

Figure 56. *Micrographs of the tip of the palm fibre tool (scale 10:1).*
The bottom image shows the natural groove that appears only on one side.
It is not uniformly deep and ends short of the tip.

Microscopic study reveals that a natural groove found on one side of the artefact does not extend to the tip. Strong fluorescence prevented us from using Raman spectroscopy to study the black staining. Therefore we could not by an exclusively non-destructive technique unequivocally establish the nature of the black staining. However, it was possible to ascribe it to soot ink on the basis of IR photography and IR spectroscopy. The latter indicated the presence of gum Arabic, which we attribute to the ink binder. Furthermore, IR spectroscopy also revealed the presence of gypsum in the groove, and gypsum is not expected to be a constituent of carbon ink. In contrast to ink, gypsum does not form a continuous layer but unevenly distributed speckles. No sediments such as calcite or aragonite could be detected on this artefact.

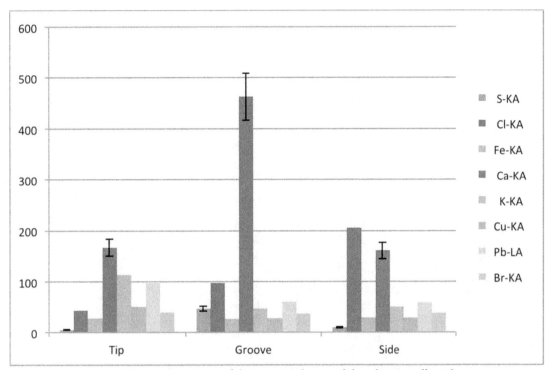

Figure 57. *Comparison of the average elemental distribution collected*
from the tip, groove and flat side of the palm fibre tool.
Error bars (10%) are indicated only for the most and least abundant elements.

Analysis of the elemental distributions shows that the tip is richer in potassium (K), copper (Cu), and lead (Pb). Enhanced amounts of these elements are compatible with the presence of gum Arabic and, curiously enough, with some traces of bronze. On the other hand the groove shows high intensity of calcium (Ca) and sulphur (S) that corresponds to the main components of gypsum ($CaSO_4 \times 2H_2O$), in agreement with IR spectroscopy. The reduction of the intensity of chlorine on the tip and the groove is explained through the absorption of its signal by overlying ink (tip) and gypsum (groove). The elements iron (Fe) and bromine (Br) have constant intensity on all three spots measured.

3. Conclusion

Since the natural groove does not extend toward the tip, this artefact was likely not used as a pen. Presence of soot ink together with traces of bronze and gypsum might indicate that it was used for mixing various substances.

XXXVIII

The Jar that Came from the South. MS 1655/1

Jan Gunneweg, in cooperation with Marta Balla

A. Introduction

To our present knowledge only a few complete 'scroll jars' have come from the *caves* of Qumran. According to the Bedouin there were eight complete jars in Cave 1 when the cave was discovered in 1946 or 1947; only one of them contained scrolls, one large scroll and two smaller ones. Two of these scrolls were wrapped in linen.[1] Another complete jar was found in Cave 4 (*DJD* 6:17). Only four of these jars, plus another from Cave 11, are known and located today. Most of these passed through the hands of Kando, the Bethlehem antique dealer through whose hands most of the Dead Sea scrolls have passed. Two or three fragmented jars from Cave 1, reassembled by de Vaux's team, ended up in North America in the early 50s.[2] Many jars of the same type were found in excavations at Khirbet Qumran, and sherds of 'sort of' similar ones in Jericho and Masada.

Two complete scroll jars from Cave 1 were bought by Eliezer Sukenik on behalf of The Hebrew University, and are now on permanent display in the Shrine of the Book in Jerusalem. They have been analyzed for their provenance. One (QUM199, Shrine no 5584), was manufactured from *motsa* clay from Bet ʾUmmar (Gunneweg and Balla 2003, 18), while the second one (QUM198, Shrine object no 5582), which is less cylindrical in shape, was brought from Jericho, where it was made.[3] QUM199 has no handles, while QUM198, the jar from Jericho, has three small horizontal loop handles, somewhat different from other scroll jars. Out of a total of 320 pottery samples found at Qumran and tested for their provenance 66 are storage jars and, of these, 34 are cylindrical 'scroll jars'. Of the scroll jars only QUM198 came from Jericho. The others match the chemical fingerprints of either Qumran or the *motsa* clay from Bet ʾUmmar near Hebron. A substantial part of the pottery in general, around 19%, was made in Jericho (Gunneweg and Balla 2003, 18–19).

The Kando family still has a jar with a bowl lid, now located in its shop in Bethlehem. This, according to Kando, was the jar in which the *Temple Scroll* was found in Cave 11.[4] The scroll was subsequently

---

[1] *DJD* 1:5, confirmed orally by Muhammad ed-Dhib to Weston Fields and Martin Schøyen in 1993. De Vaux asserts that the large scroll was 1QIsaᵃ, the two smaller ones probably the Community Rule and the Habakkuk pesher. However, Anton Kiraz quotes the sworn testimony of Muhammad edh-Dhib and Juma Muhammad in 1961 to having found only three jars in Cave 1, one containing scrolls and two empty ones (Kiraz 2005, 91–93).

[2] Kraeling 1952, with photograph on p. 1. This jar from Cave 1, bought from the Jordanian Government by the Oriental Institute of the University of Chicago, is 71.7 cm high. Fresh breaks indicated that the jar was smashed by the Bedouin when they searched the cave. It was reassembled from more than a hundred fragments at the Palestine Archaeological Museum. Kraeling refers to two additional reassembled jars from Cave 1 (p. 5 n. 1).

[3] Gunneweg and Balla 2003, 13–14, 18–19; Gunneweg and Balla 2006, 105. For a picture of these two jars, see Schofield 2009, 235.

[4] For a picture of the *Temple Scroll* jar with its bowl lid, see Mébarki and Puech 2002, 30.

packed in paper and hidden under a tiled floor in Kando's Bethlehem home from 1956 to the Six Day War.

John Marco Allegro, then a fresh member of the publication team, bought two scroll jars in separate transactions from Kando in 1953. One of them is still the property of his daughter. This jar has not been subjected to neutron activation analysis. Allegro's first jar passed through various hands between 1963 and 1993, when it was acquired by The Schøyen Collection.

B. Physical Description, Sampling, Comparison with Other Jars

In 1998, when I started to trace pottery found in Qumran to the various locations where pottery was produced in antiquity, Emanuel Tov, a colleague at the Hebrew University, mentioned that Schøyen had a jar. I wrote Mr. Schøyen a letter asking him to allow me to sample the jar. At that time Martin Schøyen was reluctant to have his jar sampled. He knew where the jar came from (Cave 1) and no analytical technique was needed to prove it.

Nine years later, however, when all the Qumran-related items of The Schøyen Collection were processed for publication, Schøyen generously sponsored my travelling to Oslo to sample the jar. In September 2008 I sampled this jar for analysis by means of instrumental neutron activation analysis (henceforth INAA). In my table below 'Schøyen 6' is a sample from the Schøyen jar (MS 1655/1). The sample was taken out with an electric drill fitted with a sapphire drill bit. At the same time I sampled a fragment of the bottom of a wide bowl (MS 1655/3c), one of four ceramic sherds numbered MS 1655/3.

The Schøyen jar is 43 cm in height, c. 21 cm in diameter, and weighs 3660 g. It flattens sharply at top and bottom to a 15 cm-wide collared neck above, and a ring base with a diameter of 11.5 cm below. It has three pierced ledge handles on the shoulder, through which a string could be passed to retain the lid in position. The lid is now missing.[5]

The two samples were subjected to instrumental neutron activation analysis (INAA) at the nuclear reactor of the University of Technology and Economics at Budapest by Marta Balla. INAA is a nuclear technique used in ceramic analysis. Every clay source on earth has its specific chemical composition that may serve as its fingerprint. When the chemical fingerprint of a jar provides a statistical match with pottery from a specific clay source, one may assume that the pottery can be traced to that specific site. Since 1968 INAA analysis of pottery has never identified clay from different sites as having the same chemical fingerprint.

When he excavated En Gedi Village in 1985, Gideon Hadas found a house from the first century AD with pottery and ovens at the foot of a small hill (Hadas 2008). Among the pottery finds was a small jar with a height of 20.6 cm that to the naked eye looked similar in shape to the previously analysed and published KhQ 1465 (QUM162) from Locus 80 at Qumran (Gunneweg and Balla 2003, 11/2).

[5] For further specifications, see chapter XLII by Torleif Elgvin, p. 427.

Figure 58. QUM162, the small En Gedi jar, and MS 1655/1

The Schøyen jar and KhQ 1465 (QUM162) are of the same size, while the En Gedi jar is substantially smaller, as indicated above. The Schøyen jar and the one from En Gedi have three horizontal pierced handles, while QUM162 has two handles. All three have a high upstanding rim with a wide mouth, and a ring base bottom. QUM162 has a more rounded body than the En Gedi jar. The similarities between the two jars prompted Hadas to ask: is it possible that Qumran provided En Gedi with pottery, of which this jar was the most important representative?

C. Results

The Qumran jar bore a chemical fingerprint similar to that of locally-made Qumran pottery such as fired clay balls with a diameter of 1.5–2 cm, funnel shaped vessels of which we have analysed about a third of the sixty at our disposal, a Bedouin *tabun* of the nineteenth century, inner linings of a kiln, and a handmade inkwell I made myself from the upper layer of a dried up rain puddle, and finally a kiln waster; all of these analysed the same and thus were all made at Qumran (Gunneweg and Balla 2010, 50). If the En Gedi jar and the Schøyen jar were made at Qumran, they had to demonstrate the same chemical composition as the Qumran pottery made locally.

The INAA test of the En Gedi jar did not match any data we have on three databases (Gunneweg and Balla 2010, 54–55). The first database is the small one at Budapest, with all relevant data of pottery and clay pertaining to the Qumran project, based on samples of pottery from Qumran, Jerusalem, Masada, the Cave of Letters, Bet ꜥUmmar and Dead Sea mud. Then, there is a larger database of what had previously been called the Archaeometry Unit at the Archaeological Institute of the Hebrew University of Jerusalem, based on samples of pottery from all over Israel, Jordan, Turkey, Greece, Egypt, Cyprus and other locations. Finally, we have the INAA data set from Berkeley.[6] Since the Berkeley set includes pottery data from Greece, Cyprus and Israel, as well as from Arabic countries such as Egypt, Iraq, Jordan and Saudi Arabia and Iran, the Middle East is pretty well covered. The Berkeley data set will become

[6] I received this database as a loan from Iz Perlman and Frank Asaro in 1989 when I was on sabbatical leave at the Ernesto Lawrence National Laboratory of the UC in Berkeley, California.

open to scientists through the good offices of the Nuclear Reactor INAA Website of Missouri University. As far as the authors know, there is no match for the scroll jar of The Schøyen Collection, either with Qumran or other known sites (Gunneweg and Balla 2010, 39–61).

The chemical fingerprint of the Schøyen jar showed no match with any of the three main groups of pottery earlier established among the finds at Khirbet Qumran, *i.e.* locally made Qumran pottery, the Jericho type, and Hebron-made pottery. I suggest the two latter types were brought to Qumran and not manufactured there. The Schøyen jar, however, matched two cooking pots found by de Vaux in Qumran (QUM169, QUM196). Further, these pots matched pottery that originated in Beer Sheba as well as some pottery we had analysed from Horvath Qitmit, with a distribution in the triangle of Beer Sheba, Horvath Qitmit, and Arad in the eastern Negev desert. A cooking pot found at En Gedi matched the Schøyen jar with a Chi-Square dissimilarity of 0.6 while the Euclidean Distance provided 0.41, both far below the required 1.0. Again, the En Gedi cooking pot matched the two Qumran cooking pots that came from Beer Sheba (Gunneweg and Balla 2010, 55).

Our second test case from The Schøyen Collection, the bottom sherd from the wide bowl (MS 1655/3c), proved to have been made locally in Qumran. It matched a clay ball (QUM130), the funnel jar (QUM127), an ostracon (QUM375), and a scroll jar from Khirbet Qumran (QUM163). All these have been shown to belong to Chemical Group I, with the local chemical fingerprint of Qumran. The sherd tested belongs to a group of four sherds designated MS 1655/3, found by Dr. William Brownlee at the surface of the Khirbet Qumran ruins in the period 1948–1951. Kept in his personal collection, they were bought by The Schøyen Collection from Louise Brownlee in July 1994.

Table 17. *List of 12 elements in five pottery samples[7]*

	Schøyen DS # 257	BrSh 100 DS 280	BrSh 101 DS 279	Halutza 3 DS 288	En Gedi 2 DS 245
Ca %	14.9	15.0	15.0	9.3	6.2
Ce	71.0	60.0	71.0	59.0	66.0
Co	15.3	16.4	23.0	15.8	14.8
Cr	109.0	108.0	123.0	104.0	111.0
Fe %	4.2	3.9	4.9	3.6	4.44
Hf	9.4	9.4	10.7	10.8	8.96
La	32.6	35.0	34.0	28.5	30.6
Lu	0.44	x	x	0.37	0.35
Na	0.57	x	x	1.0	0.65
Sc	13.2	12.4	16.8	12.5	13.5
Sm	7.0	7.42	8.40	4.9	6.1
Th	7.7	5.6	6.5	7.35	8.24

[7] Values in ppm if not otherwise stated. Schøyen DS # 257 is the jar from The Schøyen Collection. BrSh stands for pottery analyzed from biblical Beer Sheba. Similarities in chemical composition are obvious for these 12 elements. The sign X means that the abundance is unavailable. DS # stands for the sample number on our Budapest Dead Sea database. Ca in the first three samples is 2.5 times that of the last two samples at the right.

Table 18. Elements from the Schøyen scroll jar and bowl sherd (M6 and M7)

	M6	M7
As	6.3±0.3	7.0±0.3
Ba	350±40	
Ca%	14.9±2.3	7.38±0.52
Ce	71.2±2.3	58.2±2.1
Co	15.3±0.7	11.7±0.5
Cr	109±5	97±4
Cs	2.0±0.3	5.20.3
Eu	1.5±0.1	1.20.1
Fe%	4.2±0.1	4.48±0.14
Hf	9.4±0.4	5.6±0.3
K%	1.4±0.1	2.43±0.12
La	32.6±0.9	26.4±0.7
Lu	0.44±0.02	0.39±0.08
Na%	0.57±0.02	0.39±0.08
Rb	50±7	87±9
Sb	0.7±0.03	0.39±0.08
Sc	13.2±0.3	17.5±0.4
Sm	7.0±0.2	6.4±0.01
Ta	1.2±0.1	0.9±0.1
Tb		0.7±0.1
Th	7.7±0.3	7.0±0.3
U	3.8±0.2	3.2±0.2
Yb	3.4±0.1	3.1±0.1
Zn	230±16	175±15
Br	16.0±0.5	21.2±0.7

D. Conclusions

At this point two possible conclusions can be drawn regarding the Schøyen scroll jar. The first, that Kando acquired the jar from a Bedouin who came from the Negev, where he had found one or two jars, and that Kando subsequently sold them to Allegro as 'Qumran jars' to get a better price. Given the extreme rarity of cylindrical storage jars and their distribution in the Dead Sea region only, the chance that a Bedouin from the south had got his hands on one or two of these at an illegal excavation in the Negev is slim. The second possibility is that the jar was indeed found in one of the Qumran caves and brought by the Taamire Bedouin to Kando. This latter option is preferable since the two cooking pots mentioned above (QUM169, QUM196), excavated by de Vaux at Qumran, chemically match the Schøyen jar. This jar was probably produced in the south and brought to Qumran, perhaps by people related to the Qumran community.

The presence in ancient Qumran of two cooking pots and this scroll jar made from clay from the Beer Sheba district demonstrates the community's commercial links to various parts of Judaea. Pottery in general was brought to this centre mainly from Hebron and neighbouring Jericho, but also from Negev and Edom.[8]

Elements with blank spaces have not been measured. Elements are in parts-per-million if not stated otherwise. The analyses were performed in 2008 at the Nuclear Reactor of the University of Technology and Economics at Budapest by Marta Balla.

---

[8] Nine tested pottery samples from Qumran and one from En Feshka originated in Edom. Among these were two ovoid jars. Further, two juglets unearthed at ʿAin ez-Zara on the Eastern shore of the Dead Sea were made at Qumran (Gunneweg and Balla 2003, 19–20). Only two ceramic samples found in Qumran and tested for provenance came from Jerusalem: The first is a bag-shaped jar (jar-35, QUM359) with two handles and covered by a bowl-lid, unearthed at Qumran's southern plateau in 2004, among cooking installations from Qumran period II. This jar matched the *motsa* clay from Jerusalem and it contained remains of wine: Gunneweg and Balla 2006, 104–7; Buti et al. 2006. The contents of this jar were C14-dated to the period 90 BC–AD 18: Rasmussen et al. 2010, 142. The second sample consisted of remnants of a pot: a sherd with a handle scratched with some letters in Hebrew (Gunneweg and Balla 2010, 50–51).

XXXIX

Compositional Analysis of Two Ceramic Specimens

Matthew T. Boulanger, Michael D. Glascock

A. Introduction

This report details the compositional analysis by neutron activation analysis (NAA) of two ceramic specimens (QUM001 and QUM002) submitted to the University of Missouri Research Reactor (MURR) Archaeometry Laboratory by Torleif Elgvin. Both specimens were reportedly found in the Dead Sea Valley, specifically from the area surrounding Khirbet Qumran, and both are presently curated in The Schøyen Collection (*Table 19*). Here we describe sample preparation and analytical techniques used at MURR, and we compare the compositional data of the two ceramic specimens to compositional databases maintained by the MURR laboratory.

Table 19. *Descriptions and identifications of ceramic specimens analysed in this report*

ANID	Alternate ID	Archaeological Context	Description
QUM001	MS 1655/1	Cave 1?, Dead Sea Valley	Cylindrical jar
QUM002	MS 1655/3c	Khirbet Qumran	Jar base

B. Sample Preparation

Specimen QUM001 comprises ceramic powder extracted by Elgvin from the base of an intact jar using a tungsten-carbide (WC) drill bit. Elgvin reported that powder from the drilled holes was collected on aluminium foil and immediately transferred into a clean vial for transport to the laboratory.

Unlike QUM001, specimen QUM002 arrived as an intact fragment of a pottery sherd. This specimen was prepared for NAA using procedures established at the Archaeometry Laboratory (Glascock 1992, Glascock and Neff 2003). The fragment was abraded using a silicon carbide burr in order to remove surface treatments (*e.g.*, glaze, slip, paint) and adhering soil, thereby reducing the risk of measuring contamination. The specimen was then washed in deionized water and allowed to dry. Once dry, the specimen was ground to powder and homogenized in an agate mortar.

Powders from both specimens were transferred to glass vials capped with filter-pulp paper and allowed to dry for more than 24 hours in an oven at 105 °C. Once dry, two analytical samples were prepared from each specimen. Portions of approximately 150 mg of powder were weighed into high-density polyethylene vials used for short irradiations at MURR. At the same time, 200 mg aliquots from each sample were weighed into high-purity quartz vials used for long irradiations. Individual sample weights were recorded to the nearest 0.01 mg using an analytical balance. Both vials were sealed prior to irradiation, with the quartz vials being sealed under vacuum. Along with the unknown samples, standards made from National Institute of Standards and Technology (NIST) certified standard reference materials of SRM-1633b (coal fly ash) and SRM-688 (basalt rock) were similarly prepared, as were quality control samples (*e.g.*, standards treated as unknowns) of SRM-278 (obsidian rock) and Ohio Red Clay (a standard developed for in-house applications).

C. Irradiation and Gamma-Ray Spectroscopy

Procedures used for the irradiation and gamma-ray spectroscopy follow established MURR Archaeometry Laboratory protocol (Glascock 1992; Glascock and Neff 2003; Neff 2000). Neutron activation analysis of ceramics at MURR, which consists of two irradiations and a total of three gamma counts, constitutes a superset of the procedures used at most other NAA laboratories (Glascock 1992; Glascock and Neff 2003; Neff 2000). As discussed in detail by Glascock (1992), a short irradiation is carried out through the pneumatic tube irradiation system. Specimens in the polyvials are sequentially irradiated, two at a time, for five seconds by a neutron flux of 8×10^{13} n cm^{-2} s^{-1}. The 720-second count yields gamma spectra containing peaks for nine short-lived elements aluminum (Al), barium (Ba), calcium (Ca), dysprosium (Dy), potassium (K), manganese (Mn), sodium (Na), titanium (Ti), and vanadium (V). The specimens are encapsulated in quartz vials and are subjected to a 24-hour irradiation at a neutron flux of 5×10^{13} n cm^{-2} s^{-1}. This long irradiation is analogous to the single irradiation utilized at most other laboratories. After the long irradiation, specimens decay for seven days, and then are counted for 1800 seconds (the 'middle count') on a high-resolution germanium detector coupled to an automatic sample changer. The middle count yields determinations of seven medium half-life elements, namely arsenic (As), lanthanum (La), lutetium (Lu), neodymium (Nd), samarium (Sm), uranium (U), and ytterbium (Yb). After an additional three- or four-week decay, a final count of 8500 seconds is carried out on each specimen. The latter measurement yields the following 17 long half-life elements: cerium (Ce), cobalt (Co), chromium (Cr), cesium (Cs), europium (Eu), iron (Fe), hafnium (Hf), nickel (Ni), rubidium (Rb), antimony (Sb), scandium (Sc), strontium (Sr), tantalum (Ta), terbium (Tb), thorium (Th), zinc (Zn), and zirconium (Zr).

D. Interpreting Chemical Data

The element concentration data from the three measurements were tabulated in parts per million using Microsoft® Office Excel. Descriptive and contextual information for the specimen were appended to the spreadsheet of elemental abundances. These data are provided as an appendix to this report and as an accompanying digital file. Additional copies of these data are available upon request to the MURR Archaeometry Laboratory. Following our Data Management and Sharing Plan (Boulanger and Stoner 2012), these data can be made publicly via our data-sharing portal within a period of not less than two years from the issuance of this report.

Analyses at MURR typically produce elemental concentration values for 33–34 elements. Some elements are present at or below the detection limits for neutron activation using our current procedures. If greater than 50% of specimens are missing values for a particular element, this element is removed from consideration in the analysis. Statistical analyses are carried out on base-10 logarithms of elemental concentrations. Use of log concentrations rather than raw data compensates for differences in magnitude between the major elements, such as Na, and trace elements, such as the rare earth or lanthanide elements (REEs). Transformation to base-10 logarithms also yields a more normal distribution for many trace elements.

The interpretation of compositional data obtained from the analysis of archaeological materials is discussed in detail elsewhere (*e.g.*, Baxter and Buck 2000; Bieber et al. 1976; Bishop and Neff 1989; Glascock 1992; Harbottle 1976; Neff 2000) and will only be summarized here. The main goal of data analysis is to identify distinct homogeneous groups within the analytical database. Based on the provenance postulate of Weigand et al. (1977), different chemical groups may be assumed to represent geographically restricted sources. For lithic materials such as obsidian, basalt, and cryptocrystalline silicates (*e.g.*, chert, flint, or jasper), raw material samples are frequently collected from known outcrops or secondary deposits and the compositional data obtained on the samples is used to define the source localities or boundaries. The locations of sources can also be inferred by comparing unknown specimens (*i.e.*, ceramic artefacts) to knowns (*i.e.*, clay samples) or by indirect methods such as the 'criterion of abundance' (Bishop et al. 1982) or by arguments based on geological and sedimentological characteristics (*e.g.*, Steponaitis et al. 1996). The ubiquity of ceramic raw materials usually makes it impossible to sample all potential 'sources' intensively enough to create groups of knowns to which unknowns can be compared. Lithic sources tend to be more localized and compositionally homogeneous in the case of obsidian or compositionally heterogeneous as is the case for most cherts.

Compositional groups can be viewed as 'centres of mass' in the compositional hyperspace described by the measured elemental data. Groups are characterized by the locations of their centroids and the unique relationships (*i.e.*, correlations) between the elements. Decisions about whether to assign a specimen to a particular compositional group are based on the overall probability that the measured concentrations for the specimen could have been obtained from that group.

Initial hypotheses about source-related subgroups in the compositional data can be derived from non-compositional information (*e.g.*, archaeological context, decorative attributes) or from application of various pattern-recognition techniques to multivariate chemical data. Some pattern recognition techniques used to investigate archaeological datasets are cluster analysis (CA), principal components analysis (PCA), and discriminant analysis (DA). Each of the techniques has its own advantages and disadvantages which may depend upon the types and quantity of data available for interpretation.

The variables (measured elements) in archaeological and geological datasets are often correlated and frequently large in number. This makes handling and interpreting patterns within the data difficult. Therefore, it is often useful to transform the original variables into a smaller set of uncorrelated variables in order to make data interpretation easier. Of the above-mentioned pattern recognition techniques, PCA is a technique that transforms from the data from the original correlated variables into uncorrelated variables most easily.

Principal components analysis creates a new set of reference axes arranged in decreasing order of variance subsumed. The individual PCs are linear combinations of the original variables. The data can be displayed on combinations of the new axes, just as they can be displayed on the original elemental concentration axes. PCA can be used in a pure pattern-recognition mode, *e.g.*, to search for subgroups in an undifferentiated data set, or in a more evaluative mode, *e.g.*, to assess the coherence of hypothetical groups suggested by other criteria. Generally, compositional differences between specimens can be expected to be larger for specimens in different groups than for specimens in the same group, and this implies that groups should be detectable as distinct areas of high point density on plots of the first few components.

Principal components analysis of chemical data is scale dependent, and analyses tend to be dominated by those elements or isotopes for which the concentrations are relatively large. As a result, standardization methods are common to most statistical packages. A common approach is to transform the data into logarithms (*e.g.*, base 10). As an initial step in the PCA of most chemical data at MURR, the data are transformed into log concentrations to equalize the differences in variance between the major elements such as Al, Ca and Fe, on one hand and trace elements, such as the rare-earth elements (REEs), on the other hand. An additional advantage of the transformation is that it appears to produce more nearly normal distributions for the trace elements.

One frequently exploited strength of PCA, discussed by Baxter (1992), Baxter and Buck (2000), and Neff (1994; 2002), is that it can be applied as a simultaneous R- and Q-mode technique, with both variables (elements) and objects (individual analysed samples) displayed on the same set of principal component reference axes. A plot using the first two principal components as axes is usually the best possible two-dimensional representation of the correlation or variance-covariance structure within the data set. Small angles between the vectors from the origin to variable coordinates indicate strong positive correlation; angles at 90 degrees indicate no correlation; and angles close to 180 degrees indicate strong negative correlation. Likewise, a plot of sample coordinates on these same axes will be the best two-dimensional representation of Euclidean relations among the samples in log-concentration space (if the PCA was based on the variance-covariance matrix) or standardized log-concentration space (if the PCA was based on the correlation matrix). Displaying both objects and variables on the same plot makes it possible to observe the contributions of specific elements to group separation and to the distinctive shapes of the various groups. Such a plot is commonly referred to as a *biplot* in reference to the simultaneous plotting of objects and variables. The variable inter-relationships inferred from a biplot can be verified directly by inspecting bivariate elemental concentration plots.

Whether a group can be discriminated easily from other groups can be evaluated visually in two dimensions or statistically in multiple dimensions. A metric known as the Mahalanobis distance (or generalized distance) makes it possible to describe the separation between groups or between individual samples and groups on multiple dimensions. The Mahalanobis distance of a specimen from a group centroid (Bieber et al. 1976; Bishop and Neff 1989) is defined by:

$$D^2_{y,x} = [y - \bar{X}]^t \, I_x \, [y - \bar{X}]$$

where y is the $1 \times m$ array of logged elemental concentrations for the specimen of interest, x is the $n \times m$ data matrix of logged concentrations for the group to which the point is being compared with $\bar{X}$ being it $1 \times m$ centroid, and I_x is the inverse of the $m \times m$ variance–covariance matrix of group x. Because Mahalanobis distance takes into account variances and covariances in the multivariate group it is analogous to expressing distance from a univariate mean in standard deviation units. Like standard deviation units, Mahalanobis distances can be converted into probabilities of group membership for individual specimens. For relatively small sample sizes, it is appropriate to base probabilities on Hotelling's T^2, which is the multivariate extension of the univariate Student's t.

When group sizes are small, Mahalanobis distance-based probabilities can fluctuate dramatically depending upon whether or not each specimen is assumed to be a member of the group to which it is being compared. Harbottle (1976) calls this phenomenon *stretchability* in reference to the tendency of an included specimen to stretch the group in the direction of its own location in elemental concentration space. This problem can be circumvented by cross-validation, that is, by removing each specimen from its presumed group before calculating its own probability of membership (Baxter 1994; Leese and Main 1994). This is a conservative approach to group evaluation that may sometimes exclude true group members.

Small sample and group sizes place further constraints on the use of Mahalanobis distance: with more elements than samples, the group variance-covariance matrix is singular thus rendering calculation of I_x (and D^2 itself) impossible. Therefore, the dimensionality of the groups must somehow be reduced. One approach would be to eliminate elements considered irrelevant or redundant. The problem with this approach is that the investigator's preconceptions about which elements should be discriminate may not be valid. It also squanders the main advantage of multielement analysis, namely the capability to measure a large number of elements. An alternative approach is to calculate Mahalanobis distances with the scores on principal components extracted from the variance-covariance or correlation matrix for the complete data set. This approach entails only the assumption, entirely reasonable in light of the above discussion of PCA, that most group-separating differences should be visible on the first several PCs. Unless a data set is extremely complex, containing numerous distinct groups, using enough components to subsume at least 90% of the total variance in the data can be generally assumed to yield Mahalanobis distances that approximate Mahalanobis distances in full elemental concentration space.

Lastly, Mahalanobis distance calculations are also quite useful for handling missing data (Sayre 1975). When many specimens are analysed for a large number of elements, it is almost certain that a few element concentrations will be missed for some of the specimens. This occurs most frequently when the concentration for an element is near the detection limit. Rather than eliminate the specimen or the element from consideration, it is possible to substitute a missing value by replacing it with a value that minimizes the Mahalanobis distance for the specimen from the group centroid. Thus, those few specimens which are missing a single concentration value can still be used in group calculations.

E. Comparative Databases

Comparative data used in this study come from the ceramic databases of the MURR Archaeometry Laboratory and the current version of the Lawrence Berkeley National Laboratory (LBNL) archaeometry program digitized and publicly distributed through the MURR laboratory[1] (Asaro and Adan-Bayewitz 2007; Boulanger 2012, 2013). Comparison against the LBNL database was made after adjusting the data by linear regression formulae calculated for 25 ceramic and SRM specimens analysed at both MURR and LBNL (*Table 20*). Importantly, neither the MURR nor the LBNL database contains specimens representative of on-site ceramic production at Khirbet Qumran or other localities adjacent to the Dead Sea[2]. Thus, regardless of the results of this analysis, there remains the possibility that one or both specimens represents localized ceramic production. In short, a comparative analysis such as this can only determine what specimens already present in a database are most similar to newly analysed pieces.

Table 20. *Slope (m), intercept (b), and coefficient of determination (R^2) for 32 elements*[3]

	m	b	R2
Al	1.0037	0.0415	0.9831
As	0.9228	4.0423	0.9464
Ba	0.9992	53.836	0.9958
Ca	0.9442	0.0638	0.9805
Ce	0.999	0.6541	0.9977
Co	0.9906	0.3973	0.994

[1] The current database contains chemical data for roughly 80% of all archaeological materials analysed at LBNL between 1968 and 1988.

[2] Balla (2005) reports the analysis of a large sample of ceramic objects from Khirbet Qumran conducted at Budapest University of Technology and Economics. To the best of our knowledge, no attempts have yet been made to cross-calibrate data from this laboratory and our own.

[3] Calculated for linear regressions of elemental abundances determined for the same specimens (n = 25) by neutron activation at Lawrence Berkeley National Laboratory and at the MURR Archaeometry Laboratory. Regression formulae are used for converting MURR data to compare with Berkeley data.

Cr	1.0007	5.2595	0.9905
Cs	0.9563	0.415	0.9917
Dy	1.0746	0.3989	0.9581
Eu	1.0199	0.0307	0.9833
Fe	1.0088	0.0405	0.995
Hf	1.0034	0.0541	0.9681
K	0.9633	0.1273	0.6715
La	1.001	0.216	0.9962
Lu	0.9151	0.0138	0.938
Mn	0.9412	11.567	0.9927
Na	1.0092	0.0195	0.9963
Nd	1.0471	-0.8891	0.9872
Ni	1.1673	5.9414	0.7784
Rb	1.1169	0.4888	0.9606
Sb	1.0071	0.0337	0.9969
Sc	1.0537	0.103	0.9904
Sm	0.9658	-0.3348	0.9955
Sr	0.8791	122.88	0.8852
Ta	0.9047	0.0178	0.9924
Tb	1.0165	-0.0465	0.9427
Th	1.0771	-0.1399	0.9967
Ti	0.7675	0.0356	0.8364
U	1.0179	-0.3468	0.9801
V	0.9253	49.139	0.7243
Yb	1.0333	0.0368	0.9839
Zn	1.537	-47.936	0.7887

F. Results and Discussion

Both the MURR and LBNL databases were queried to obtain the 10 specimens in each database with the lowest squared mean Euclidean distance, across all elemental abundances, relative to each of the newly analysed specimens. Results of this search are presented in *Tables 21* and *22*. In interpreting these results, a critical value of 0.02 is arbitrarily selected. As a further test, we include the two newly analysed specimens in a cluster analysis of all Levantine ceramics in the LBNL database. We discuss the results and significance of each of these results in turn.

1. QUM001 (MS 1655/1)

Table 21. *'Best match' specimens to QUM001 (MS 1655/1), a Second Temple Period cylindrical jar assigned to Cave 1, Dead Sea Valley[4]*

ID	Distance	Site	Comment
ASH0478	*0.0124*	*Tel Ashdod, Stratum XXI, N13*	*G2358i*
PMG562	0.0131	Ashkelon	Middle Bronze IIA, amphora
PMG029	0.0134	Tell el-Fukhar, Jordan	Late Bronze IIB, cooking pot
BRSH0003	*0.0135*	*Beersheba, Locus 229*	*Iron Age II, red-burnished ware bowl*
BRSH0017	*0.0142*	*Beersheba, Locus 97*	*Iron Age II, red-burnished ware*
ARAD0055	*0.0145*	*Tell Arad, Locus 700*	*Iron Age II, red-burnished ware*
SHUR0008	*0.0147*	*Shurafa, Egypt*	*Buff-on-red bowl, Reisner Collection 6-9355*
ARAD0056	*0.0149*	*Tell Arad, Locus 967*	*Iron Age II, red-burnished ware bowl*
PMG561	0.0153	Ashkelon	Middle Bronze IIA, amphora
PMG328	0.0153	Thebes, Valley of the Kings	Late 18th-19th Dynasties, amphora
JCIT0007	*0.0156*	*Jerusalem Citadel*	*No description, Rockefeller Museum P.1227*
ASK0101	*0.0156*	*Ashkelon*	*No description, catalog no. A-699-12*
PMG338	0.0159	Thebes, Palace of Amenhotep III (Malkata)	No context, amphora
FUST0032	*0.016*	*Fustat, Egypt*	*Medieval*
ASK0031	*0.016*	*Ashkelon, Stratum II*	*Philistine Ware*
PMG274	0.0161	Thebes, Palace of Amenhotep III (Malkata)	Rubbish piles, amphora
PMG272	0.0165	Thebes, Palace of Amenhotep III (Malkata)	Middle palace, amphora
PMG252	0.0172	Thebes, Palace of Amenhotep III (Malkata)	Palace, amphora
PMG317	0.0173	Tell el-Dabʿa	Middle Bronze IIB, amphora
PMG265	0.0174	Thebes, Palace of Amenhotep III (Malkata)	No context, amphora

The results of the Euclidean-distance search routine (*Table 21*) suggest that QUM001 is most similar to a number of amphora recovered from sites on the coast of Israel (Ashdod, Ashkelon) and in Egypt (Thebes). All of the amphora from Egypt in these results were analysed as part of McGovern's (2000) study, and likely do not represent valid 'matches' except in the very general sense that they are the closest specimens present in the MURR database.[5] The specimens indicated as presumably locally produced bowls and jars from sites in the northern Negev (Beʾer Sheva/Beersheba and Tel Arad) seem more appropriate from the perspective of likely provenance. Cluster analysis of the QUM001 with Levantine ceramics in the LBNL database further supports a provenance of the northern Negev for this specimen. QUM001 is located within a cluster comprised almost exclusively of specimens from Beʾer Sheva and Tel Arad (*Figure 59*). Viewed from this perspective, the single specimen from Tel Ashdod likely represents an imported vessel rather than a locally made piece.

[4] Matches based on squared mean Euclidean distance among logged elemental concentrations. MURR specimens in Roman, LBNL specimens in italics.

[5] Note: the MURR ceramic database is somewhat deficient in material from southern Israel and the Negev.

2. QUM002 (MS 1655/3c)

Table 22. 'Best match' specimens to QUM002 (MS 1655/3c), a Second Temple Period jar base
from Khirbet Qumran[6]

ID	Distance	Site	Comment
AVD0004	*0.0168*	*Avdat*	*Fine decorated ware*
PET0009	*0.0175*	*Petra*	*Nabataean Fine Decorated*
AVD0015	*0.0175*	*Avdat*	*Fine decorated ware*
TAW0010	*0.0179*	*Tawilan*	*Midianite or Edomite*
FRN0008	*0.018*	*Tell Firan, Egypt*	*Nabataean Fine Decorated*
AVD0008	*0.0182*	*Avdat*	*Fine decorated ware*
AVD0043	*0.0186*	*Avdat*	*Fine decorated ware*
AVD0014	*0.0187*	*Avdat*	*Fine decorated ware*
NTZ0005	*0.019*	*Nitzana*	*Nabataean Fine Decorated*
AVD0007	*0.0192*	*Avdat*	*Fine decorated ware*
PMG460	0.0173	Tell Nimrin	Iron Age IIB, red-burnished bowl
PMG139	0.0178	Tell Abu al-Kharaz	Chocolate-on-White jar
PMG416	0.018	Abydos, Tomb U-j	Syro-Palestinian type Storage Jar
PMG217	0.0188	Beth Shan	Iron Age IA, chocolate-on-White jar
SHR091	0.0195	Stiri, Greece	Early Bronze, painted jar

The ten closest specimens to QUM002 all derive from the LBNL database, and all are classified as Nabataean fine decorated pottery (*Table 22*). All except one of these (FRN0008) derive from sites in the southern Negev and adjacent southern Jordan (*e.g.*, Avdat, Petra, and Tawilan). Results of the cluster analysis are nearly identical, suggesting a strong affinity of QUM002 with fine decorated wares (esp. Nabataean fine wares) from the southern Negev and environs of Petra (*Figure 59*).

Comparison of these data to the, presumably local to Petra, NAB-II compositional group defined by Gunneweg et al. (1988) indicates that QUM002 differs only in major-element chemistry (Fe, Na, and Ti) and two transition metals (Co and Cr). The sample of Gunneweg et al. (1998) was analysed at the Hebrew University Archaeomety Department (HU), but also contained some specimens analysed at LBNL. Though both laboratories used the same internal standard reference material in their analyses, in the early 1980s LBNL revised their reference value for Cr in Standard Pottery downward, and HU did not (Asaro and Adan-Bayewitz 2007, 209). The observed differences in Cr between QUM002 and NAB-II may therefore reflect differences in laboratory protocol rather than real-world chemical differences.

G. Conclusions[7]

Comparison of the compositional data for QUM001 and QUM002 to the LBNL and MURR databases provides some indication of provenance for these specimens. Of those specimens most similar to QUM001, those that are presumably recovered from the sites at which they were made (*i.e.*, those whose compositions may be used to infer provenance) derive from sites in the northern Negev desert, specifically

---

[6] Matches based on squared mean Euclidean distance among logged elemental concentrations. MURR specimens in Roman, LBNL specimens in italics.

[7] We are indebted to Cody Roush and Erica Murren who were responsible for preparation and irradiation of project specimens. This project was supported in part by NSF grant BCS-1110793 to the Archaeometry Laboratory of the Research Reactor, University of Missouri.

Be'er Sheva and Tel Arad. QUM002 is chemically most similar to Nabataean decorated finewares from the southern Negev and the environs of Petra and Tawilan in Jordan.

As stated above, other specimens from Khirbet Qumran are not present in either the MURR or the LBNL database. Thus, there remains open the possibility that one or the other specimen may represent a compositional profile of local ceramic production at Khirbet Qumran or other localities adjacent to the Dead Sea. Given the similarities of QUM001 to specimens that most likely represent localized production at Be'er Sheva (and environs), we feel comfortable proposing this as the *most likely* source for QUM001 given our current knowledge. Because QUM002 is most similar to decorated fine wares from the southern Negev, a possible connection with this region should be explored from an archaeological standpoint and perhaps by additional archaeometric investigations. Yet, because there are differences in major-element chemistry (*i.e.*, Fe, Na, and Ti) between QUM002 and the NAB-II compositional group assumed to be local to the area surrounding Petra and Tawilan. Thus, there remains the possibility that the chemical profile of QUM002 represents on-site ceramic production at Khirbet Qumran using raw materials that differ only slightly in their chemistries with those used near Petra.

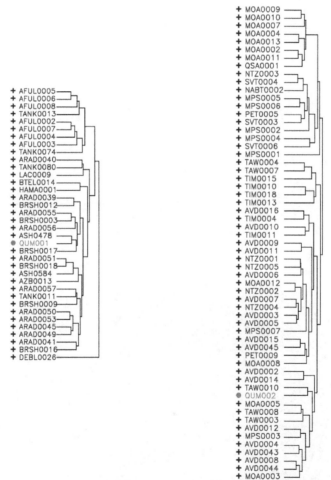

Figure 59. Two portions of a dendrogram showing the results of a hierarchical cluster analysis based on mean Euclidean distance and average-linkage algorithm.
Left: QUM001 is most similar to specimens from Beer Sheba (BRSH) and Arad (ARAD). Right: QUM002 is most similar to specimens from Tawilan (TAW), Avdat (AVD), and Moyat Awad (MOA), all of which are classified as Nabataean decorated finewares. Note the additional similarity of specimens from Petra (PET), Nitzana (NTZ), and Timna (TIM), also all classified as Nabataean fineware.

XL

Samples from the Cylindrical Jar MS 1655/1

Ira Rabin, Roman Schütz[1]

The aim of our work was to check whether the assumption that the jar was discovered in Qumran can be substantiated. In order to establish the archaeological provenance of the jar we conducted a series of analytical tests on samples of material collected from the jar in April and June 2009. The samples were either found loose within the jar, these being probably constituted by remnants of its original contents, or were clay detached from the inner and outer surface of the jar. In addition, a portion of sand deposit coating the inside of the jar handles was analysed.

A. General Description of the Samples

Besides dust and plaster, the loose content of the jar included two pieces of organic matter denominated sample 1a and 1b.

Inorganic material made up the clay samples from the inner walls of the jar, taken from different spots and denominated sample 3 and 6. The slip was sampled both at the side exposed to the environment (samples 9, 8i) and at the side protected from it (sample 8a). Also sampled were the deposits of white material that formed craters on the inner wall of the jar. The black deposits on the outer walls of the jar were sampled (samples 10 and 12), sample 12 being part of the deposit found close to the fracture. Finally, a portion of the sand encrusted on the jar handle holders was also sampled.

To establish their elemental composition and identify relevant trace elements the samples were investigated with X-ray fluorescence analysis by different excitation methods (x-rays, electrons and protons). To identify chemical species we used sy-FTIR and Raman spectroscopy. Mineral composition of the sand was determined by XRD. In addition, all the samples were studied by scanning electron microscopy and optical microscopy.

[1] We would like to thank Marcello Binetti for his help in preparing the manuscript, Emanuel Kindzorra and Ulli Schade for their contribution to the FTIR measurements, Peter Lasch and Maren Stämmler from the Robert Koch Institute and Anka Kohl from the BAM for conducting the measurements with an FT-Raman spectrometer, Franziska Emmerling from the BAM for providing x-ray diffraction results, Timo Wolff for quantification of the elemental distributions from the XRF measurements. Our special thanks go to Gisela Weinberg from the Fritz Haber Institute for her patience in conducting innumerable SEM/EDX measurements and Reinhard Franke for helping with the literature search. We would like to thank Martin Schøyen for his generous cooperation, allowing us to sample the jar thoroughly.

B. Organic Material

Two pieces of fibrous tissue impregnated with dark material were found loose inside the jar (*Figure 60*): they were neither fixed nor glued to a surface. The pieces, designated sample 1a and sample 1b, underwent a set of identical non-destructive analyses. Sample 1a closely resembles degraded leather-like writing material from the Dead Sea Scrolls collections, and may well represent ancient parchment. This observation was corroborated by optical and electron scanning microscopy (cf. Rabin and Franzka 2006). Sample 1b is of a different nature: it consists of a stone covered with a black tar-like mass containing small quantities of degraded collagen, *i.e.* gelatin and fibres probably of plant nature, tentatively identified by infrared spectroscopy as flax or ramie.

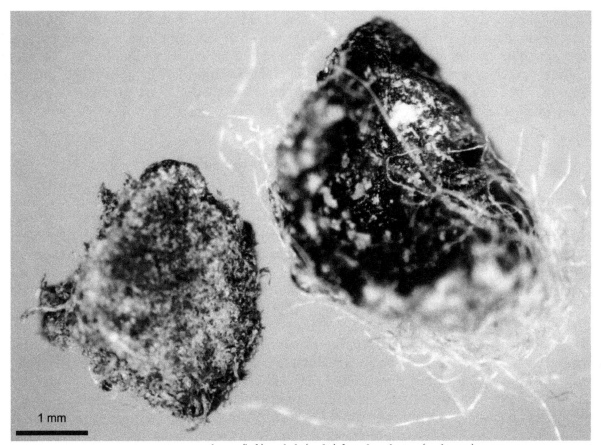

Figure 60. Samples 1a (left) and 1b (right) found in the jar (scale 20:1)

In accordance with electron scanning microscopy results, μ-FTIR analysis of sample 1a attested for the presence of collagen in an inhomogeneous state of preservation (*Figure 61d*). With the exception of the element lead, the elemental composition obtained by micro X-ray fluorescence (*Figure 62*) in combination with the EDX study (*Figure 61c*) shows the presence of the same mineral contaminants also frequently found in Dead Sea Scrolls fragments. The two most interesting features of the relative intensity pattern of these elements are the high concentrations of Cl and the absence of halite crystals: these features have never before been observed on leather/parchment fragments found in the vicinity of the Dead Sea (cf. *Figures 61c* and *d* respectively). By contrast, the relative intensities of the elements present in sample 1b display the usual 'Dead Sea picture' of chlorine and sodium accompanied by halite crystals clearly visible in the scanning electron micrograph (*Figures 61a* and *b* respectively).

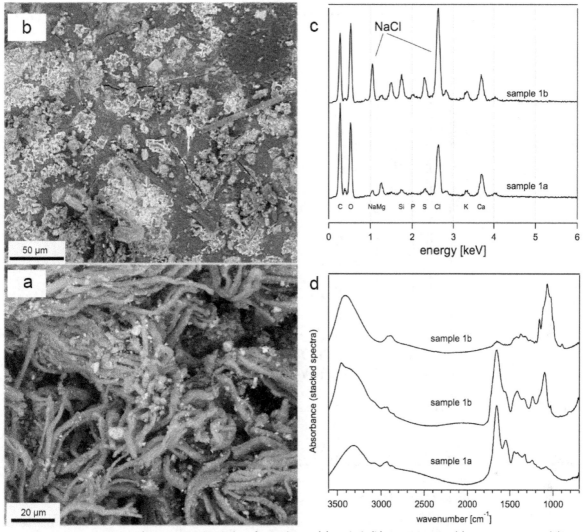

Figure 61. *Scanning electron micrographs of samples 1a (a) and 1b (b); EDX spectra (c); μ-FTIR spectra (d)[2]*

In this study lead was detected only in samples 1a and 1b. The presence of lead is noteworthy since it is not characteristic of parchments found in the caves of Qumran. It was detected, however, in the 'repair' sheet of the *Genesis Apocryphon* and in a number of the Schøyen fragments in 2012 (see p. 66). Furthermore, the ratio of the Cl and Br elements (~260) points to a place of production other than the Dead Sea region. The combination of high [Cl]/[Br] numbers with the presence of lead has so far been observed only in some Murabbaʿat and Naḥal Ḥever documents. A purely non-destructive analysis of the tar-like mass of sample 1b did not permit separation of the components and an unambiguous identification of the non-gelatinous fraction.

[2] Elemental composition of samples 1a and 1b determined by EDX; μ-FTIR spectrum from sample 1a shows identifying amide peaks at 1650 cm^{-1} and 1540 cm^{-1}; amide peaks are recognizable in the middle curve (sample 1b) but disappear in the top one. In the middle curve the peak at 1097cm^{-1} shows the presence of rutile, whereas in the upper curve the group at 1165 cm^{-1} indicates the presence of plant fibres.

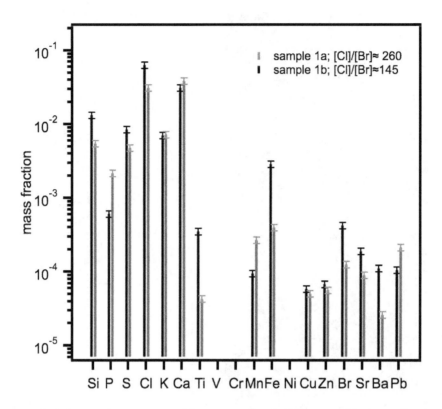

Figure 62. *Quantified elemental composition of fragments 1a and 1b determined by x-ray fluorescence analysis*

c. Body of the Jar

Table 23. *List of samples extracted from the body of the cylindrical jar*

3, 6	Clay	Inner wall, upper part
4, 5	White deposits	Inner wall
8i, 8a	Slip	Outer wall
9	Slip	Outside, bottom
10	Black mass from the repair spot	Outside, close to bottom
11	Clay from the repair spot	Outside
12	Black mass from large spot	Outside
Sand	Sand residues	Inside handles

1. Sand and a Sample from the Jar Body

Figure 63 shows the results of electron dispersive x-ray spectrometry (EDX) for a sample of the jar body and the sand encrustations from the handles. Both of them present a similar pattern of main elements, with a significant presence of calcium in addition to silicon and aluminium, but no striking difference attributable to environmental influence.

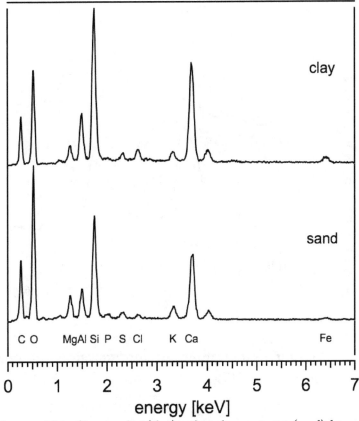

Figure 63. *Elemental composition of jar sample 6 (clay) and sand encrustation (sand) determined by EDX*

In Qumran, aragonite is the main polymorph of the calcium carbonate present in the natural caves. Together with calcite it is also a major component of the marl sediment characteristic of the man-made caves. So its presence on an artefact can be taken as an indicator of a find-place in the Qumran region.

Typical μ-FTIR spectra of Qumran sediments are shown in the lower part of *Figure 64*, where the characteristic aragonite absorption peaks at 854 cm^{-1}, 711 cm^{-1} and 705 cm^{-1} are visible, together with the 871 cm^{-1} peak that corresponds to calcite.

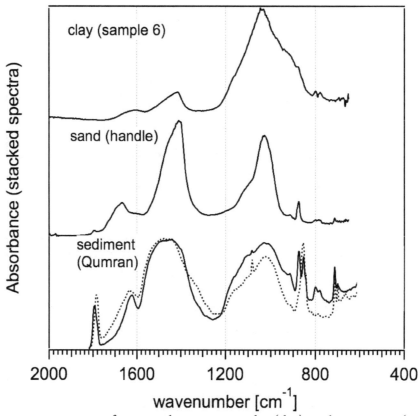

Figure 64. *μ-FTIR spectra: from top to bottom: jar sample 6 (clay); sand encrustation (sand); limestone Qumran (dotted line), Qumran marl (solid line)*

In the Raman spectrum of *Figure 65*, the difference between the calcium carbonate polymorphs manifests itself in the low frequency region, with peaks at 205 cm^{-1} and 281 cm^{-1} for aragonite and calcite respectively. XRD analysis showed that the material from the handle consisted of quartz, calcite and dolomite, but not aragonite. The corresponding micro-FTIR spectra (middle portion of *Figure 64*) indicate the presence of quartz (doublet at about 779 and 798 cm^{-1} respectively) and of a considerable amount of carbonates (broad peak at ~ 1410 cm^{-1}). Here, the calcite peak at 871 cm^{-1} has a shoulder at 878 cm^{-1} that corresponds to the absorption of dolomite. Furthermore, the micro-FTIR spectrum shows a broad peak in the region 950–1200 cm^{-1} that appears to correspond to a mixture of calcareous and quartzitic sands. In this case, unfortunately, the Raman spectra (middle portion of *Figure 65*) reveal no additional information as to the presence of calcite polymorph of the carbonates.

In summary, the most relevant result of the XRD, μ-FTIR and Raman study of the samples is the absence of the aragonite peaks characteristic of Qumran limestone.

At the upper part of *Figure 65*, spectra from two samples are shown: sample 6, taken from the inner wall of the jar, and sample 9, taken from the underside of the jar bottom. Calcite could only be detected in the spectrum of sample 9 whereas sample 6 bears no traces of mineral carbonate. Furthermore, sediments along the west shore of the Dead Sea are known to contain sizeable amounts of gypsum and halite, as attested by their x-ray diffraction spectra. The absence of any of the species usually ascribed to Qumran sites, both in the sample from the bottom of the jar and in the sand from the handles, makes the Qumran caves an unlikely place for a prolonged storage of the jar.

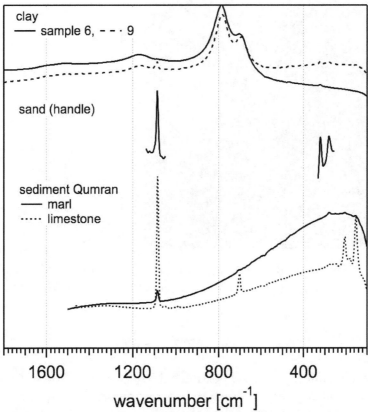

Figure 65. *FT-Raman spectra: from top to bottom: jar sample 6 (solid line), sample 9 (broken line); sand encrustation (sand); limestone Qumran (dotted line), Qumran marl (solid line). Excitation wavelength used is 1064 nm.*

Our study of the sand from inside the handles did not allow a definitive determination of its origin. Our results from XRD, EDX, μ-FTIR analysis show elements common to many sands, namely quartz and elements of limestone. Sand of such composition would fit well with the loess of the Northern Negev (Gilead and Goren 1989), cf. the contribution by Jan Gunneweg in the present volume (p. 361). However, the FTIR spectra of the sand and the fired clay also agree well with those measured for smectitic clays from northern Israel fired at 700 C (Shoval 2003; Shoval and Beck 2005). Therefore, although Raman (Pinzaru et al. 2008) and FTIR spectroscopy (Shoval and Beck 2005) are extensively used for the characterization of ancient ceramics and establishing the provenance of the raw clay material, we think that no reliable results can be obtained on the basis of these point analyses only and without the support of petrographic data.

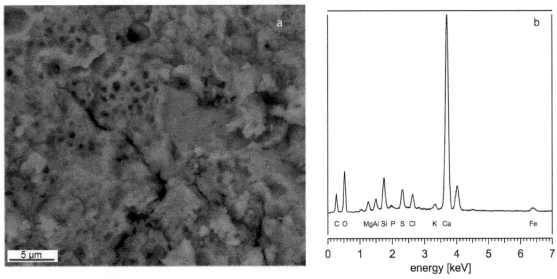

Figure 66. *(a) Scanning electron micrograph of a portion of jar sample 6;*
(b) corresponding elemental composition determined by EDX

2. Samples 4 and 5

In the scanning electron micrograph of a portion of the jar sample (*Figure 66a*) we see the typical porosity pattern of calcareous clay. And indeed, the corresponding EDX spectrum (*Figure 66b*) indicates a massive presence of calcium. One could therefore expect a sizeable presence of calcite. The absence of calcite features in the corresponding FTIR and Raman spectra of this sample indicates that the firing temperature was above 700ºC, in the region of calcite to calcium oxide transformation ($CaCO_3 \rightarrow CaO + CO_2\uparrow$): Cultrone et al. 2004. When macroscopic (> 0.5 mm) calcium carbonate inclusions lie close to the surface, the resulting calcium oxide may react with humidity to form calcium hydroxide ($CaO + H_2O \rightarrow Ca(OH)_2$) and an explosive growth of the corpuscular volume occurs. The effect is generally known as 'calcium carbonate inclusion effect' or 'lime blowing', and it leads to flaking off of the clay layer and exposure of the inclusion (Manfredini and Schianchi). The resulting spots have a yellowish-white colour due to the presence of the clay material. We believe that the white deposits constituting samples 4 and 5 originated from such an effect (*Figure 67*) and, thus, belong to the original material of the jar. Their chemical compositions were determined with μ-FTIR and μ-Raman spectroscopy (*Figures 68* and *69* respectively): sample 4 consists mainly of calcite, whereas sample 5 has a considerable fraction of gypsum (dotted curve) and clay (solid curve) in addition to calcite, as exemplified by the spectra in the lower part of *Figure 68*. The gypsum may result from the reaction of the exposed calcite with atmospheric sulphur (Edwards and Farwell 2008; Martinez-Ramirez et al. 2003). Its non-uniform distribution within the calcite sample is the result of the sampling process [cf. 3]. It is not astonishing that these samples are rich in calcite: since the thermal decomposition reaction starts at the boundaries of the inclusion, it does not have to lead to its complete transformation. Notably, the presence of calcium hydroxide on the jar samples can be observed in the FT-Raman spectra at 790 cm^{-1} (cf. *Figure 65*, top spectra). The broad double peak at 790/695 cm^{-1} has been observed in the study of limestone mortars and attributed to the slaked lime. This feature can only be observed with FT-Raman at an excitation wavelength of 1064 nm Edwards and Farwell 2008).

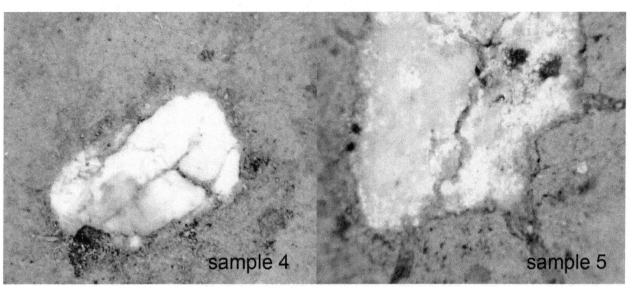

Figure 67. Whitish inclusions on the inner wall of the jar

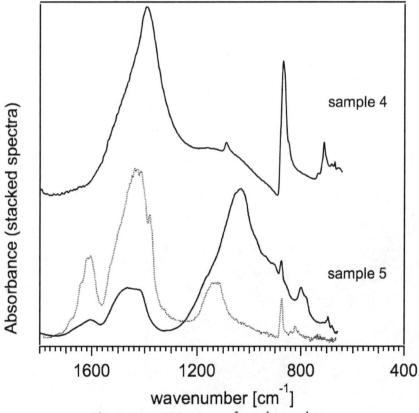

Figure 68. *μ-FTIR spectra of samples 4 and 5.*
In the lower part spectra from two spots are shown.

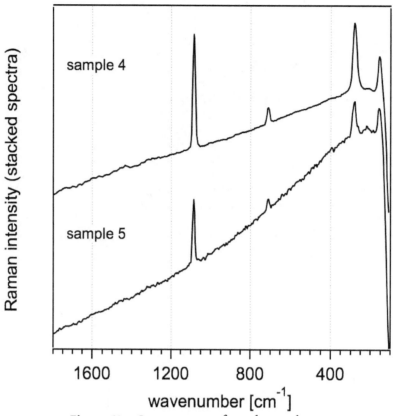

Figure 69. *μ-Raman spectra of samples 4 and 5.*
Excitation wavelength used is 785 nm.

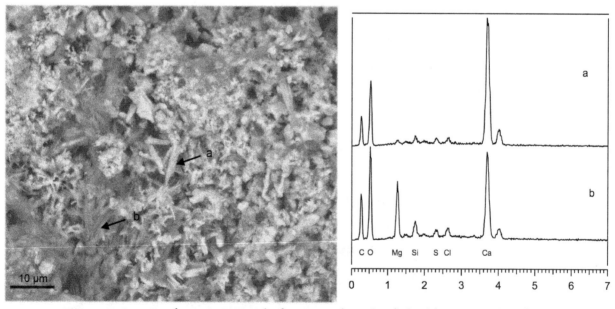

Figure 70. *Scanning electron micrograph of a portion of sample 4 (left side); corresponding elemental composition of spots designated a and b determined by EDX (right side).*

A representative portion of sample 4 is shown on the scanning electron micrograph (*Figure 70*, left side). The EDX spectrum of the region indicated by arrow *a* corresponds to the composition of $CaCO_3$, whereas area *b* is rich in magnesium (*Figure 70*, right side). Since dolomite decomposition occurs at temperatures below 700ºC, we expect to find no dolomite in this region, consistently with the corresponding μ-FTIR and μ-Raman spectra presented in *Figures 68* and *69* respectively. The differences between the two inclusions observed in our spectra correspond to the amount of silicates and gypsum (prominent peaks at 1033 cm^{-1} and 1100 cm^{-1} respectively in the μ-FTIR spectrum from sample 5). Morphologically, needle crystals from region a of *Figure 70* could be assigned to the aragonite polymorphic form. Furthermore, structures were found in sample 5 (SE-micrographs in *Figures 71a* and *71b*) that are reminiscent of brucite and periclase respectively, known as transformation phases of dolomite decomposition coexisting at temperatures close to 650ºC. The elemental composition of the structures in *Figure 72* (main component Mg) corroborates this conclusion. However, the dimensions of what we interpret as periclase are larger than is reported in the literature (Trindade et al. 2009). Morphologically it is also strongly reminiscent of vaterite, another polymorph of calcium carbonate usually produced by biological (organic) activity, probably by some kind of fungi or lichens. Since no indication of its presence could be found by Raman and IR spectroscopy, the question of unambiguous identification remains open. Similarly, no direct confirmation of the presence of aragonite in the inclusions could be obtained by micro-FTIR or Raman spectroscopy (*Figures 68* and *69*). However, quantitative analysis of the ratios of the calcite peaks at 281 cm^{-1} and 711 cm^{-1} in micro-Raman spectra indicates that the samples might contain more than one polymorph of calcium carbonate (Martinez-Ramirez et al. 2003).

Figure 71. *Scanning electron micrographs of two portions of sample 5: (a) might correspond to periclase; (b) might correspond to brucite*

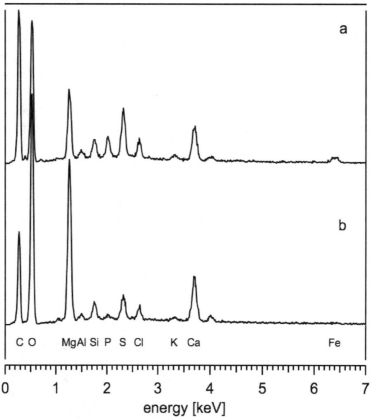

Figure 72. Elemental composition of the areas of Figures 71a and 71b respectively determined by EDX

3. Slip Samples

Two samples of slip were taken from the external wall of the jar: sample 8i corresponds to the inner part of the slip, *i.e.* protected from environmental influences whereas sample 8a was exposed to them. The results of EDX analysis presented in *Figures 73 a* and *b* respectively show that the environmental influence is limited to an increase in the sulphur content on the exposed surface. The reaction leading to gypsum formation when calcite or slaked lime is exposed to a sulphur-rich (SO$_x$) atmosphere has been well attested in the studies of Roman mortars (Edwards and Farwell 2008) and frescoes in Pompei (Maguregui et al. 2010). Strictly speaking, gypsum could have accumulated on the jar had it been kept in a gypsum rich environment. In such a case, however, the sand in the handle should also have shown a detectable gypsum amount. Since we have already seen that this is not the case, we conclude that the gypsum appears to be a result of the known transformation from calcite.

Furthermore, on the rough surface of the exposed sample (second micrograph in *Figure 73*) two new types of crystals can be seen: large and small ones. The large ones (marked with a white arrow) have the elemental composition Na, S, Cl, Ca, (bottom curve of *Figure 73c*), which corresponds well to that of crude Dead Sea salt (NaCl + CaSO$_4$ × 2H$_2$0). The small crystals that appear in large quantities on the surface are presented additionally in a separate se-micrograph in the lower left corner of *Figure 73*. Their form and elemental composition (K, Cl) correspond to sylvite, KCl. This is a remarkable finding, since sylvite neither constitutes an impurity of the rock salt at the Dead Sea nor is known to naturally precipitate from Dead Sea water. However, sizable amounts of sylvite can be found at evaporating ponds of the potash production sites (Garret 1996; Yechieli and Ronen 1997), or, generally, at the southern basin of the Dead Sea.[3]

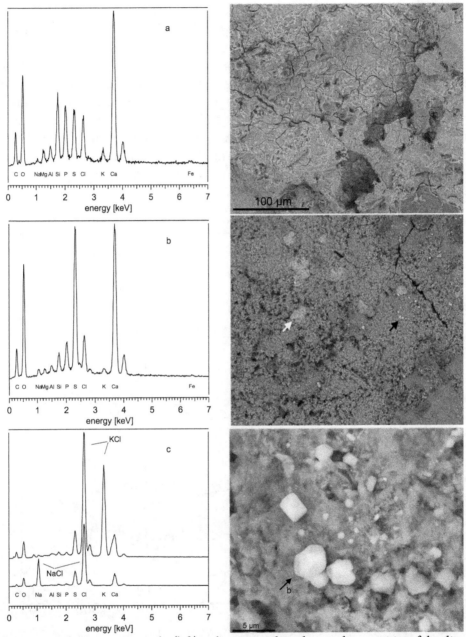

Figure 73. *Scanning electron micrographs (left) and corresponding elemental composition of the slip samples (right) 8i and 8a.*
Representative area of the sample not exposed to the environment (upper row); representative area of sample from the sample exposed to the environment (middle row); sylvite crystals (lower left corner); elemental composition of crystals (lower right corner).

[3] In 2014 we detected a small amount of the KCl crystals in the sediment on a piece of a rope excavated in the Caves of Letters.

4. Black Mass: Samples 10 and 12

Samples 10 and 12 were taken from the black mass on the outside of the jar, sample 10 coming from a repair spot. Both samples were identified by µ-FTIR spectroscopy as natural bitumen, in all probability from the Dead Sea (see *Figure 74*). Bitumen consists mainly of hydrocarbons with weight percentage close to 90. Sulphur is the most abundant heteroatom in bitumen, close to 10 wt%. Of the metals, vanadium and nickel are always present and have even been referred to as markers of Dead Sea bitumen (Ilan et al. 1984).[4] In our samples carbon and sulphur were determined as the main light elements of the matrix by EDX, whereas the elements V and Ni were observed with µ-XRF technique (*Figure 75*). The difference between the elemental compositions of the samples is attributed to different amounts of contaminants, *i.e.* quartz and kaolinite, found on one of the spots. No synthetic or other modern materials were discovered in the samples. In general terms, the use of bitumen to waterproof jars has been known since the early days of human history (Connan 1999). It would be interesting to check whether other jars repaired with bitumen have been discovered in Qumran.

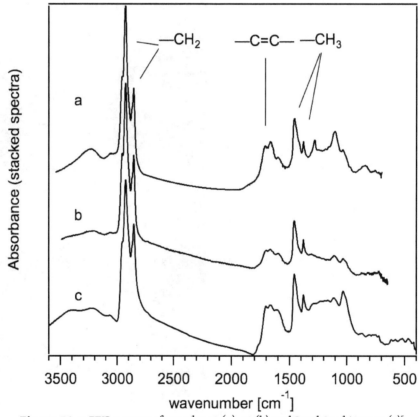

***Figure 74.** µ-FTIR spectra of samples 10 (a), 12 (b) and Dead Sea bitumen (c)[5]*

---

[4] Dead Sea Bitumen from the IRUG database (file INR00077).

[5] The band assignments are given for bands that function as identifying peaks, since they describe collective modes. In the region between 1000 and 1300 cm^{-1} there are no group frequency modes, hence the shape and the position of the bands are not constant.

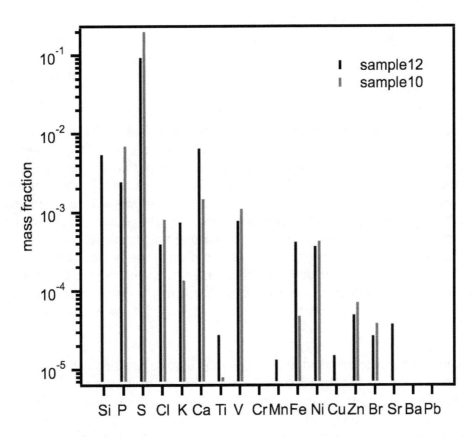

Figure 75. *Quantified elemental composition of samples 10 and 12 determined by x-ray fluorescence analysis*

D. Conclusions

As is often the case with archaeological artefacts, the material is not homogeneous and the sampling may influence the results. The use of point analysis on the samples does not make the problem any easier. Therefore conclusions based on such measurements are tentative in nature. In this section we summarize the results of the analyses and conclude with a plausible picture taking all of them into account:

A degraded piece of leather or parchment found in the jar resembles ancient parchment similar to that of the Dead Sea scrolls. If the plant fibres found together with the parchment represent remnants of a wrapper the finds could support the assumption that we are dealing with an archive jar.

No element traces recalling those found on artefacts that have been a long time in Qumran could be detected in this study.

Should the sand extracted from the handles of the jar have originated in the discovery place, the similarity between its characteristics and that of the jar clay would lead to the tentative conclusion that the jar was found at the production site or in its vicinity. On this assumption, we can infer a probable finding site in the Northern or Northeastern Negev, which would correspond to INAA analyses by Gunneweg and Boulanger suggesting the jar was made of clay from this region.

The white inclusions originated in the clay. The scarcity of the crystals tentatively identified as aragonite indicates that they did not originate in the storage area.

The black mass on the jar could be identified as asphalt, often used in antiquity to make repaired pottery waterproof. Though Ni/V ratios could be taken as indication that the asphalt originated in the Dead Sea we would like to stress that point analysis is not an appropriate method to provenance asphalts. It would be interesting to know whether other artefacts connected with Qumran or the Dead Sea region have similar traces.

Traces of large halite crystals and sylvite crystals were found on the sample taken from the slip on the outside of the jar, from the surface known to have been exposed to the environment. The large halite crystals correspond well to crude Dead Sea salt. The presence of sylvite probably indicates that the jar spent some time in the area of the southern Dead Sea basin, perhaps close to potash works. Since neither halite nor sylvite could be found in the sand in the handles we are inclined to attribute this stay to the post-discovery time. Alternatively, remembering that the jar passed through various hands between its discovery and its purchase by The Schøyen Collection in 1993, the salts detected could have come from any household since the use of KCl as an additive to NaCl (table salt) is common.

Evidence of calcite $\rightarrow$ gypsum conversion was detected on a number of samples. Such transformation occurs in a sulphate rich atmosphere and could indicate a proximity to the Dead Sea (Levin et al. 2005). However it could also occur in conditions of pollution in any place in the industrialized world.

Some indications of biological activity were found. However, a detailed study and possible identifications lay outside the realm of point analysis.

The analysis of samples from the jar failed to establish a decisive connection between the jar and Qumran, thus producing a so-called 'negative result'. Such a negative result does not prove that the jar was not found in Qumran. The Bedouin who discovered the jar could have kept it in his possession for some time and even used it, unintentionally removing traces of a Qumran background. One should remember that the value of artefacts from Qumran had not been anticipated from the very beginning.

XLI

The Allegro and Schøyen Jars Among the Qumran Jars

Joan E. Taylor

In this chapter I explore whether the Allegro and Schøyen jars would fit the context of Cave 1 (1Q) or another cave in the area. I am examine as many as possible of the published broken and whole vessels uncovered in cave 1Q, some of which are dispersed in collections worldwide (see de Vaux 1949; *DJD* 1: 8–17; Table 1), as part of on-going research into the artefact repertoire and typology, but some preliminary findings are presented here.

A. The Cave 1Q Jars

Late in 1946 or early in 1947, the Taamire herder Muhammad ed-Dhib found jars with ancient scrolls wrapped in linen in the cave later designated 1Q. According to John C. Trever, Muhammad found about ten jars standing in the cave, some of them with small handles, some covered with lids. On the floor of the cave one could see much broken pottery, and a pile of rocks that had fallen from the ceiling. Muhammad also noticed a wooden pole in the cave, about three inches in diameter. All but two of the jars were empty. From the other, a jar with a lid, Muhammad pulled two bundles wrapped in cloth (*Pesher Habakkuk*, 1QpHab, and *Community Rule*, 1QS), which he described as 'greenish' in appearance. A larger scroll was without wrapping (the Isaiah scroll, 1QIsaᵃ).[1] Muhammad later returned to the cave with his relatives Juma and Khalil and helped them remove two large jars.

According to Allegro, who liaised a great deal with the Bedouin, there were seven or eight jars, and some had large, bowl-like lids (Allegro 1956, 17; also *DJD* 1:5; Milik 1959, 12). According to Cross (1961a, 7), Muhammad 'found decaying rolls of leather in one of a number of strange elongated jars embedded in the floor of the cave'.

Mohammad and his cousin Juma opened a jar and found it full of red earth (Trever 1977, 192; cf. Brownlee 1957, 263). Presumably, in this case the lid was quite firmly attached to the top of the jar. The nature of the red earth has not been discussed anywhere, but it is not consistent with the colour of decomposed scrolls, which turn black. Clay is used for jar stoppers, and some clay used for jars is quite red. Perhaps, then, they viewed a decomposed stopper, typical of this era (cf. Fields 2009, 25, who notes that some jars were sealed on top with clay), and assumed the whole jar was full of this material.

---

[1] Trever 1977, 99, 192. Trever's is the most accurate and detailed of all early accounts, cf. Fields 2009, 521. The suggestion that some manuscripts came from another cave (Fields 2009, 110–13) is both late and unsupported.

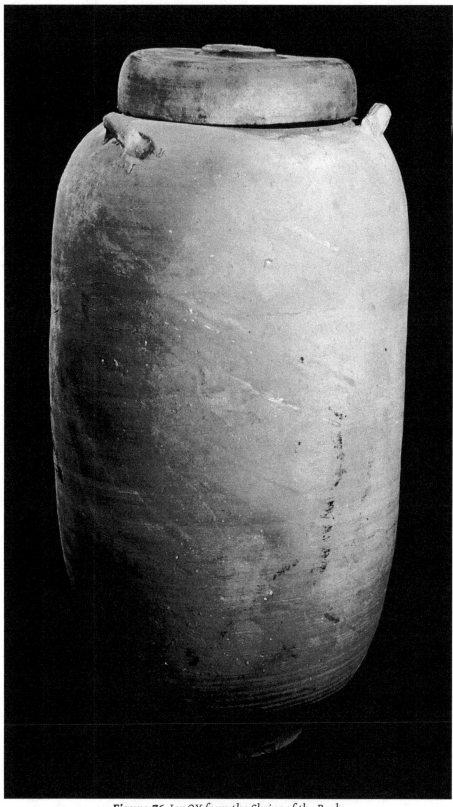

Figure 76. *Jar QX from the Shrine of the Book*
(Shrine of the Book Photo © The Israel Museum, Jerusalem)

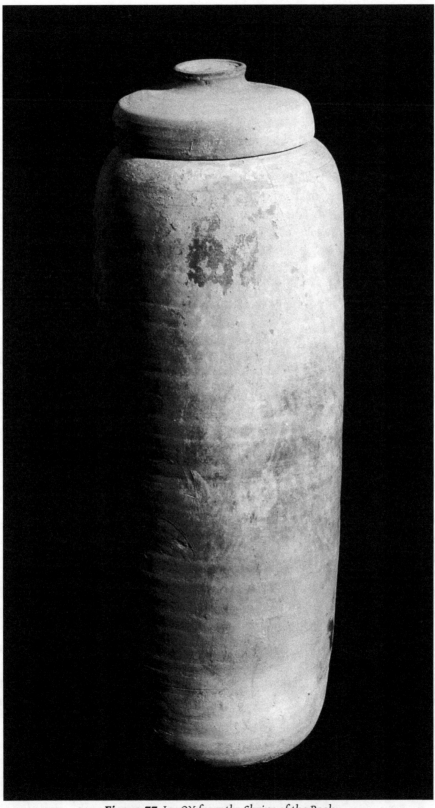

Figure 77. *Jar QY from the Shrine of the Book*
(Shrine of the Book Photo © The Israel Museum, Jerusalem)

According to Trever '[t]hey removed two complete jars with covers from the cave. Each jar and each cover had three handles.' These jars were left standing outside the entrance to the cave until Juma took them away with the scrolls to the Taamire camp south-east of Bethlehem. In March 1947 he and his relative Khalil Musa took the manuscripts and jars to Bethlehem: the scrolls (1QIsaᵃ, 1QS, and 1QpHab) and jars were left in the shop of Judah Ibrahim ʿIjha for about a month (Trever 1977, 100, 192).

Since ʿIjha thought there was no market, Juma left the jars with him but took the scrolls away. He consulted with his friend George Ishaya and others, including Khalil Iskander Shahin (Kando), who helped Juma sell the three scrolls to the Syriac Christians of St. Mark's Monastery, at that time headed by Metropolitan Athanasius Samuel.

George Ishaya, Juma, and Khalil Musa returned to the cave. Then or a little later they secured four more scrolls that they sold to the antiquities dealer Faidi Salahi, who also bought two jars (Trever 1977, 101–2, 193). The original two jars and lids taken from the cave are both described as having three handles (Trever 1977, 192). One of the jars later in the possession of Salahi does not match this description, and none of the extant lids do. However, the Bedouin visited the cave at various points and brought material to Bethlehem on at least three occasions (Trever 1977, 228). This complicates matters in terms of the jars, because jars would have been removed from the cave at different times during the course of these visits. When the second batch of manuscripts came out of the cave, a second pair of jars may also have been removed.

Trever states that Salahi 'secured the two jars for twenty piasters each (about 80 cents)', assuming these were the first two jars. In late November 1947 Eliezer Sukenik came to Bethlehem and met Salahi (Trever 1977, 100, 197; Fields 2009, 522, n. 21). He noted in his diary, on 25 November, 1947: 'A Hebrew book has been discovered in a jar. He [Salahi] showed me a fragment written on parchment. *Genizah!*' (Sukenik 1955, 17). Soon after he bought three scrolls and two jars for the Hebrew University (Trever 102, 108, 198). These two jars are now exhibited in the Shrine of the Book, loaned from the Hebrew University (see *Figures 76* and *77*). Following Trever, it is often assumed that the two jars bought by Sukenik were the first two jars brought to Bethlehem (*e.g.* Fields 2009, 526, n. 92), but these two jars are actually associated with the second batch of manuscript discoveries, not the first one. This second batch comprises the *Hodayot* (1QHᵃ), the *War Scroll* (1QM), a fragmentary copy of Isaiah (1QIsaᵇ), all bought by Sukenik, and the *Genesis Apocryphon* (1QapGen), bought by Metropolitan Samuel.

There is an anomaly in the accounts: early in 1948 Butros Sowmy told Trever that the original two jars were 'being used as water jars' (Trever 1977, 70). Trever had told the Syriac priests of the monastery that the jars were important for dating the scrolls (Trever 1977, 33), and Sowmy reported that 'they had been trying to obtain the jars' but had failed to get them. In other words, the original jars were elsewhere than in the hands of Sukenik.

Sowmy told Trever that Father Yusif, one of the priests of St. Mark's Monastery, had been to the cave and 'seen one of the jars in which the scrolls had been found, and many fragments of broken ones. Also, there was a pile of small fragments and cloth wrappings which the Bedouins had tossed aside as worthless' (Trever 1977, 69). This visit had taken place in August 1947 (Trever 1977, 197). This means that only one of the scroll jars remained in the cave at this point. Millar Burrows reported the testimony of the Syrians as follows:

> At the suggestion of the archbishop, George Isaiah persuaded the Bedouins to take him to the cave, where he saw one jar and fragments of others, a mysterious piece of wood lying on a stone, and many fragments of manuscripts, as well as bits of cloth in which the scrolls had been wrapped. In August the archbishop sent one of his priests, Father Yusef, to examine the cave again. The idea of removing the whole jar still in the cave was considered but abandoned, because the jar was too heavy to carry in the intense summer heat of the region (Burrows 1955, 7).

What happened to this piece of wood, which matches the description of the wooden pole recorded by Trever, is not known, and no one knows what happened to this jar.

Summing up, there is Bedouin testimony to about eight whole jars originally in 1Q. Some of these were brought to Bethlehem for selling, with the two first jars being used for water. These first two jars, and possibly their lids too, had three handles each. Only one of the jars bought by Sukenik and now displayed in the Shrine of the Book has three handles (see *Figures 76* and *77*). In 1953, Allegro bought a jar from Kando, sourced from the Taamire Bedouin who stated that it came from 1Q (Allegro 1956, 77). Allegro was in no doubt that the jar with handles that he purchased in 1953 came from 1Q; it is this jar that is now in The Schøyen Collection. It matches the description of an original jar taken from the cave in having three handles. Its small size may be a factor here, since the Bedouin who went to the cave with Father Yusif were loath to carry a large, heavy jar in the heat of summer; the Schøyen jar is the smallest of all alleged scroll jars. It would have made sense to the Bedouin to take the smaller jars first rather than the larger ones. However, its exact provenance is open to question.

Since the Taamire Bedouin who dealt with the dealers in Bethlehem only operated in this region, it seems obvious to assume that the Schøyen jar came from this vicinity. This type of jar was unknown from any other area (Allegro 1956, 78), and the Bedouin had testified to there being a number of whole jars in 1Q, jars they removed in stages. Once two jars were sold to Sukenik, the Bedouin would have realized the other jars had a market value and would have brought them to dealers in Bethlehem.

From 1947 to the start of 1949 1Q was a cave only known by the Bedouin. But in January 1949, Captain Akkash el-Zebn of the Arab legion identified it. Gerald Lankester Harding, chief inspector of the Department of Antiquities of Jordan, invited the Palestine Archaeological Museum and Roland de Vaux of the École biblique et archéologique française de Jérusalem to undertake a proper excavation of this cave with him, and the Bedouin were hired as workers. Excavations took place between 15 February and 5 March, 1949 (Trever 1977, 148).

Harding and de Vaux affirmed that the cave had been looted, but there was still a large number of manuscript fragments in the cave debris. The Bedouin's observation of past cave collapse was confirmed: there was around 50 cm of fill and rocky debris. The original floor was covered by a layer of dung, in places some 15 cm thick, including 'several large lumps of coagulated animal droppings' (*DJD* 1:6). Linen was found beneath this layer, which indicates the antiquity of the jar breakage and the exposure of scrolls, after which dung built up from feeding animals (Harding 1949, 113). Grace Crowfoot, who cleaned the textiles, identified the dung as from rodents: '[t]he textile fragments were full of a thick dark brown dust mixed with rat and mouse droppings' (*DJD* 1:18). Damage to the scrolls indicated that both rats and white ants had fed on the leather (Harding 1949, 114). The ancient damage had led to some scrolls compacting (Harding 1949, 114–15). In 1Q there were also many jars that had had been smashed and their contents spilt, with only small fragments surviving. Initial excavations determined that in the half metre of earth and dung built up in the cave there were six hundred fragments from different Hebrew manuscripts, phylactery cases, as well as approximately fifty broken cylindrical jars and lids, some other pottery, and many pieces of linen scroll wrappers and packing. There were some 51 identifiable manuscripts originally placed in jars in 1Q (Fitzmyer 2008, 14–24). One part of a decomposed scroll still lay inside its linen wrapper, stuck to the broken neck of a jar (*DJD* 1:12, Plate I:8–10); this is still preserved in the holdings of the IAA, classified as 990e,[2] and it is the most important archaeological evidence that links scrolls, linen wrappers and jars.

---

[2] I am grateful to Pnina Shor for allowing me to inspect it during a research visit in July 2014.

B. Other Caves of the Qumran Region

In 1951 the Bedouin discovered the caves of Murabbaʿat and de Vaux and Harding left Qumran to concentrate on excavations there (Harding 1952). They did not find scroll jars or lids, but a large number of fragmentary manuscripts and papyri that had been lying decomposing in the caves for a long time.

In February 1952, the Bedouin, who were continuing to search in the Qumran area, found another manuscript cave, 100 m south of the first cave: Cave 2 (2Q). Following this discovery the archaeologists managed to retrieve manuscript fragments, two cylindrical jars, pieces from six such jars, a lid and three bowls (*DJD* 3:9, 14–15).

Given the Bedouin discoveries, in March 1952 the American School of Oriental Research in Jerusalem, the École biblique and the Palestine Archaeological Museum together undertook a search of around 300 caves, from two kilometres north of 1Q to the region between Qumran and Ein Feshkha in the south (Reed 1954; de Vaux 1953a; *DJD* 3:3–13). In this survey Cave 3 (3Q) was discovered, which provided fragments of parchment and papyrus, a large quantity of broken jars and lids (5 catalogued and 30 uncatalogued jars, 21 catalogued and at least 5 uncatalogued lids), two jugs and a lamp, as well as the Copper Scroll. Forty of these caves contained pottery and other objects, and 26 of these had pottery corresponding to the distinctive type and repertoire found in 1Q: jars, lids, bowls, occasional small storage pots and lamps (de Vaux 1973, 51). As the survey was done with the help of the Bedouin, one cannot exclude that some of these jars may have found their way to the antiquities market.

A different system of numeration was adopted for the cave survey: cave 8 (GQ8 = grotte de Qumrân 8) is manuscript Cave 3 (3Q); cave 14 (GQ14) is manuscript Cave 1 (1Q); cave 19 (GQ19) is manuscript Cave 2 (2Q), cave 26 (GQ26) is manuscript Cave 6 (6Q—see *DJD* 3:6; de Vaux 1973, Plate XL; Fidanzio 2015). In de Vaux's inventory list a jar labelled '8-11' (*DJD* 3:Fig. 2: type 1) therefore derives from GQ8 = manuscript Cave 3Q, not Cave 8Q. Usefully, for the artefacts found in Cave 1Q, de Vaux applied a running list of items designated Q1, Q2, Q3 etc. (see Humbert and Chambon 1994, 343).

At any rate, ahead of the archaeologists, the Bedouin had by 1953 uncovered caves 1Q and 2Q as well as the Murabbaʿat caves, and they had worked alongside archaeologists on a large-scale cave survey in which many cylindrical jars and lids were found. They also managed to discover the manuscript Caves 4Qa and 4Qb before the archaeologists, but subsequently, in September 1952, the Department of Antiquities of Jordan, the École biblique and the Palestine Archaeological Museum jointly excavated there. They found in Cave 4Qa four almost complete ovoid (slightly bulging) jars, rims of a further four, three small pots, three lids, five bowls, three carinated bowls, three jugs and one lamp (*DJD* 6:9–20). There were no distinctive cylindrical jars with lids, but there were scroll tags and ties, phylactery cases and wood. After his initial investigation of Cave 4Qa Cross noted:

> I was struck with the fact that the relatively small quantity of fragments from the deepest levels of the cave nevertheless represented a fair cross section of the whole deposit in the cave, which suggests, among other things, that deterioration of the manuscripts must have begun even before time sealed the manuscripts in the stratified soil, and that the manuscripts may have been in great disorder when originally abandoned in the cave. The paucity of sherds in the cave certainly indicates that the scrolls of Cave IV were not left stored away in jars (Cross 1961a, 28).

Further, analysis of fragments of 4QSam[a] showed crystals of old urine from animals, yet they were found covered with nearly a metre of debris and bat dung (*DJD* 17:5; Fields 2009, 197).

Another small marl cave, 5Q, not found by the Bedouin, was excavated in September 1952. It contained some manuscript fragments but no pottery. In 1955 de Vaux searched for further collapsed marl caves and discovered Caves 7–10 (7Q–10Q). Close to Wadi Qumran the Bedouin discovered Cave 6 (6Q =

GQ26). Here the archaeologists found manuscript fragments, a bowl, and a somewhat bulging jar, 52 cm high, with a rounded bottom and two pierced ledge handles (*DJD* 3:10, 20–21, 26, Fig. 3.9). So here we have another example of a scroll cave containing a jar with pierced ledge handles, like the Schøyen jar.

In *DJD* 3 de Vaux synthesized the information on jars and lids and defined a basic typology, a work he had begun in *DJD* 1 with the pottery from 1Q (*DJD* 1:14–17; *DJD* 3:3–31—the last publication includes a useful description of the caves). In this survey he distinguished 13 key types of jars and 23 types of lids (not including Cave 1Q=GQ14 in the cave survey), with a total of the surprisingly high number of 74 indeterminate jars, and 14 indeterminate lids. Of these, 30 jars he could not classify were in 3Q alone (=GQ8). The reasons for not classifying them were partly their fragmentary state, but this adds to the complex picture of the jar types in the caves. Finally, in 1977, de Vaux presented the pottery typology of Caves 4Qa and b (*DJD* 6:16–20), which also enabled him to establish links between caves based on jar typology. De Vaux also identified some jars in 1Q as 'cousins' of types 9 and 10 (*DJD* 1:Fig. 2:10, 2:12). This raises questions about where the Schøyen jar might fit.

C. Cylindrical Jars in and around the Qumran Buildings

Jars similar to those in the caves were also found in the excavations of Khirbet Qumran. Such a jar was found early on, sunk into the floor of Locus 2 and covered with a limestone slab (Harding 1952; de Vaux 1953b, 94). Other jars and lids were found in various locations of the site, often sunk into floors or in niches. De Vaux noted that all the types of jars in the caves, apart from type 11, are attested at Khirbet Qumran, with the same clays and the same firing.[3] However, not all the jars found at Qumran and designated as 'cylindrical' are necessarily similar to those in the caves (*e.g.* KhQ1401 is more bulging). Possible cylindrical jars and lids were found in sixteen different locations (loci 1, 2, 10A, 13 [3 jars], 17, 28, 34, 41, 45a, 61, 80 [3 jars], 81, 84, 100, 124, as well as in the South trench, and Trench B).

There was a concentration of three cylindrical jars in a niche in Locus 13, and another close by in Locus 2, on either side of a bench room (Locus 4). There was also a concentration in Locus 80, close to the kiln, and in Locus 81.

The dating of the jars at the site is debated and tricky, since some were sunk into later floors or in niches (Magness 2004, 157–58). According to de Vaux, the jars range from his Periods Ib (*c.* 100–31 BC) through to II (4–1 BC to AD 68; de Vaux 1973, 54), with jars most clearly indicated in Period Ib (Magness 2004, 158). Gregory Doudna has argued that they are more clearly associated with Period Ib than Period II (Doudna 2006), though often these seem to continue in use through Period II, as in Locus 2.

In terms of clays, samples from the 'scroll jars' found at the site of Qumran and the caves were subjected to Neutron Activation Analysis (INAA), along with a range of other pottery, and reported in the doctoral dissertation of Marta Balla (2005), as well as in Gunneweg and Balla (2003). In their numbering system, the jars and lids designated QUM 120, 132, 139, 154, 156, 161, 162, 163, 182, 186, 187, 231, 240 were found to be made of local Qumran clay (Type I). A second group (QUM 115, 116, 117, 118, 119, 122, 123, 124, 125, 138, 153, 164, 165, 166, 199, 238, 245, 250, 255, 257) were made of a type of Motza (Beit ᵓUmmar) clay, named from a locality between Bethlehem and Hebron (Type II), and two (QUM 198, 256) were made of clay from Jericho (Type III: Balla 2005, 90, Table 20). Matching these types to the actual provenance of the clays of the jars and lids of the cave survey, as far as these can be distinguished, yields the following results:

[3] De Vaux 1953b, 96–97, Fig. 2:4 (KhQ27), found in Locus 2, and plates vi and vii; de Vaux 1954, 225, Fig. 5:4 and 7 (KhQ768 and KhQ939, and see plates XIb and XIIa; de Vaux 1956, 560–61, Fig. 5:15, KhQ1107). For a full list of these jars found at the site, see Doudna 2006, 155–57; Gunneweg and Balla 2003, 12, Plan 1; Magness 2004, 157–58.

GQ8 (= 3Q): QUM 115, 116, 122, 123, 124, 125, 164, 249 from Motza (Beit ʾUmmar) clay, but also of Qumran clay (QUM 132, 154, 186);[4]

GQ3: QUM 248 from Motza (Beit ʾUmmar) clay, QUM 256 from Jericho clay;[5]

GQ6: QUM 231 from Qumran clay;

GQ7: QUM 137, 138, 246, from Motza (Beit ʾUmmar) clay;[6]

GQ12: QUM 247 from Motza (Beit ʾUmmar) clay;

GQ28: QUM 250 from Motza (Beit ʾUmmar) clay;

GQ29: QUM 153, 245, 255 from Motza (Beit ʾUmmar) clay, QUM 159 is not indicated as determined;

GQ 39: QUM139 and 163 from Qumran; QUM 166 from Motza (Beit ʾUmmar) clay;

'Cave XI' (probably 11Q)[7] 'scroll jar (green dot)' from Qumran clay.

Of designated 'scroll jars' and lids from the site of Qumran, they found five with Motza (Beit ʾUmmar) clay (QUM 117–119, 238, 279), and six with clay from Qumran (QUM 120, 161–2, 156, 182, 187, 279).

The type of clays found in jars in the caves parallel the types used for the jars found at Khirbet Qumran, except that no Jericho clay is used in the existing jars or lids found at the site of Qumran. However, the prevalence of Motza (Beit ʾUmmar) clay was far more indicated in the cave jars and lids than any Qumran or Jericho clay. Jericho clay is found in many bowls, jugs and cups from the site of Qumran, far more than Motza (Beit ʾUmmar) or local Qumran clay (see Balla 2005, 90, Table 20; Gunneweg and Balla 2003, Appendix 1). However, regular storage jars from the site were regularly made of all three main types of clay. Given the differences in jars and clays the most natural assumption would be that various clays were used for manufacture, and/or that some pottery arrived at Qumran from Jericho or further afield. It should also be noted that two jar stoppers found in the tower were made of Jericho clay (Gunneweg and Balla 2003, 19).

INAA analysis has still not identified all clay provenance, and several items could not be determined: these include QUM140, a waster, which means that at least some pottery made at Qumran used clay from elsewhere. However, QUM148 (KhQ2622) had clay similar to pottery in the Arad-Beer Sheva area. QUM 232, a jar from 4Q (no. 3) was probably also made of clay from this Beer Sheva zone (Gunneweg and Balla 2003, 24). This is also important in terms of the analysis of the Schøyen jar.

A note of caution, however, may be rung from the results of the petrographic studies of clay by Michniewicz and Krzysko (2003, cf. Michniewicz 2009), who analyzed clays from 50 jars and some other pottery, mainly from the caves but also from the site of Qumran. As noted by Michniewicz (2009, 25): 'It must be emphasised that the conclusions formulated … were entirely different' from the INAA results of Gunneweg and Balla (2003). As noted in the first study, '[m]ost vessels have a white, carbonate slip on their surface' (Michniewicz and Krzysko 2003, 67). There was a diversity of clays in all the jars sampled (Michniewicz and Krzysko 2003, 75)—and therefore this warns against simple INAA testing alone for the establishment of provenance. For comparison, they noted that a potter working in present day Jericho made clay vessels with clay from the region of el-Jib, leaned with sand from the Mediterranean coast (Michniewicz and Krzysko 2003, 75). However, they state that, 'Qumran jars, compared with the ceramics made presently in Jericho, are more diversified both macro- and microscopically, they are

[4] Unfortunately, Gunneweg and Balla (2003, 13) have confused 'Grotte 8' in the Qumran store records (GQ8) with manuscript cave 8Q. No cylindrical jars were found in 8Q. It is unclear whether some of the lids listed in the table actually come from 8Q. Also the inventory of Humbert and Chambon (1994, 343) is confused here.

[5] Gunneweg and Balla (2003, 18) incorrectly assume that 'GQ3' indicates Cave 3, 'the same cave wherein the Copper Scroll was found'. The label given by Balla 2005, as '3-1' for QUM256 correlates with the jar illustrated as 3-1 in *DJD* 3:18–19, Fig. 2, as coming from cave GQ3, not Cave 3 (3Q).

[6] One jar and lid were found in cave GQ7 and the items here match this rather than manuscript cave 7Q.

[7] 'Cave XI' should refer to manuscript cave 11Q, discovered by the Bedouin in 1956, rather than cave GQ11 from the 1952 survey, where no Qumran-type pottery was found (*DJD* 3:8). These two caves are located quite close to each other.

different in respect to colour, content of fragments of limestone rocks and content of fine clayey silts.' According to Michniewicz and Krzysko (2003, 75) the jars were not made from Qumran clay, but rather from Motza clay, but such clay does not derive from one and the same location (Michniewicz and Krzysko 2003, 76), and Motza clay can be found in pockets as close to Qumran as the Wadi Zarqa Main region (Michniewicz 2009, 137–38).

The Qumran jars were formed with this non-silty clay with an admixture of quartz sand (10%), but while the technique was the same the raw materials were not. In other words, one may more correctly refer to Motza *clays* rather than Motza clay specific to one site only; these clays were widely used in Judaea, and pottery from such clays was found nearby at Jericho, Khirbet Mazin as well as ez-Zara/Callirrhoe (Michniewicz 2009, 136). The shale particles also differed in the jars, and 'the petrographic differences in the ceramics found are an indication that the clays were not obtained from the same location at the same time' (Michniewicz and Krzysko 2003, 76). The clays did not come from Qumran (see also Michniewicz 2009, 26–27, Table 16 on pp. 85–86, 139, 141), but may have come from the eastern side of the Dead Sea (Michniewicz 2009, 137–38).

Thus, aside from the broad categorizations that INAA provides, the petrographic studies indicate a great deal of variety in the core make up of clay mixture in the jars.

D. Morphology of Cylindrical Jars and Lids from the Qumran Caves

The cylindrical jars found in the caves and at the site of Qumran are very similar to each other in morphology, and they are distinguished from common storage jars of the Second Temple period by not usually bulging out in their body, in a bag-shaped form (Bar-Nathan 2006, 277, note 77). Allegro provided an initial description as follows:

> [...] the jars were practically unique in shape and size. Generally between 21 in. and 27 in. long, they were cylindrical in shape, flattening sharply at top and bottom to a wide collared neck and ring base respectively. Marks of turning are clearly visible on the sides, and the deep firing has given the pottery a hard, almost metallic quality, with a characteristic rose pink or grey colouring (Allegro 1956, 77).

The wide, collared neck seems to have been designed to fit a distinctive type of lid that could be positioned snugly over the mouth of the jar. They do not usually have a round lip, though this does occur on the smaller jar in the Shrine of the Book (QX), and in Type 6, found in GQ28 and 29 (*DJD* 3:18, Fig. 2:6, Plate VI). The jar mouths are wide in relation to the overall width of the jars, gaping as if to allow the maximum width possible while still allowing the jar to be lidded. The high collar suggests the jars were designed to be covered with a lid with correspondingly long sides. The bases can be variable, but are generally ring or disk in form, though one type has a rounded bottom.

The jars are made with clays that have a reddish to peachy coloration, often a bit gritty with limestone particles, with clear signs of a high firing temperature evidenced in a thin grey ashy layer. They are slipped with creamy-coloured clay and sometimes covered with whitish wash, a finishing applied after the jars were fired. De Vaux defined the hue of the slip quite precisely. While this type of finishing is known in Judaea in the Herodian and early Roman period, it is more common in Jericho, and quite distinctive of Qumran pottery (personal observation). The jars are not finely made but are coarse ware in that there is little finishing, use of quite rough clay, and sloppiness evident in much of their manufacture.

The pottery of the Qumran caves is strongly linked with the pottery repertoire of the site of the Qumran buildings. Rachel Bar-Nathan has shown that Khirbet Qumran pottery is very similar to that of

Jericho, with various types being identical (Bar-Nathan 2002, 2006). In Jericho, of the houseware forms '[o]nly a few are decorated or slipped, and these were made in the regional workshops from near the Dead Sea and the plain of Jericho, such as at Qumran and Jericho' (Bar-Nathan 2006, 264). Bar-Nathan defines the 'scroll jar' type as 'cylindrical or ovoid' (Bar-Nathan 2006, 275); there are clearly markedly ovoid (bulging body) types of jars in Jericho, dating from the early Hasmonaean period (Jericho group 1: Bar-Nathan 2006, Fig. 271), but straight-up cylindrical jar types only begin in the Herodian period post 31 BC (Jericho group 2, cf. KhQ group 2; Bar-Nathan 2006, Fig. 15.6). As Bar-Nathan (2006, 275) notes, the 'scroll jars' found at the site of the buildings of Qumran were identified as coming from Period Ib and II, which in the revised chronology of Humbert (1994, 211) would date them post 90 BC through to the latter part of the first century AD.

Some cylindrically-shaped jars, generally with handles, were also found in Masada (Bar-Nathan 2006, 276), which leads Bar-Nathan to narrow the date of all the cylindrical jars found in caves at Qumran to just before the First Revolt in AD 66. However, this runs contrary to her observation of these forms at the site of Qumran where they span a much longer period. Similar forms of cylindrical hole-mouthed jars/vases have appeared at Jericho, Masada and En Gedi,[8] in contexts dating from the reign of Herod the Great to the late 1st century AD (*DJD* 3:12–13), but there are questions about how exact the parallels are (Magness 2006, 662–63; Mizzi 2009, 120–24). More work needs to be done to classify the morphology of Qumran jar types to determine what types have parallels elsewhere. At the time of writing there are no exact parallels for the large-sized, elongated cylindrical jar of the Qumran caves, the type often considered to be the 'classic' scroll jar. This jar is the majority type in 1Q.

E. Variation among the Qumran Cave Jars

As Gunneweg has observed (2012, 1), there is an overarching similarity in morphology of jars from the Qumran caves, but at the same time distinctive differences between jars. On closer inspection even similar-looking cylindrical jars and lids show a number of variables. They are by no means entirely uniform, and de Vaux himself distinguished a variety of types of jars and lids discovered in the 1952 cave survey. Whole or fragmentary jars were found in 22 caves in the natural hills west of Qumran. De Vaux seems to have been principally interested in defining a ceramic repertoire of Qumran Periods Ib and II, which he saw evidenced in the pottery he recovered during the cave survey (*DJD* 3:13–25), though we do not possess a count of potsherds from the caves.

Variables were noted by Allegro, who wrote:

> Some of the jars vary somewhat from this general pattern, being smaller and with rather more bulging sides, whilst one has a rounded bottom. Another characteristic of the smaller jars are the handles on the shoulders, sometimes small and vertical like those of a cup, but other times nothing more than horizontal lugs, pierced with holes through which string could be passed to retain the lid in position (Allegro 1956, 77).

There are also some anomalies in terms of how jars are matched with lids. All the 23 types of lids of cave jars, as defined by de Vaux, despite being variable in form, have a central knob, often slightly everted (*DJD* 3:Fig. 4). The knob allows a string to be tied around the lid, wound around it, but there are usually no corresponding ledge handles for the lid to be tied on to the jar, even though some cave jar types do

---

[8] Jericho and Masada (J-SJC-D and M-SJ18-19). A cylindrical jar very like the Qumran type was found in the 2006 En Gedi excavations under the direction of Gideon Hadas, and is illustrated at https://sites.google.com/site/eingediexcavations/home/the-second-temple-period-village/season-4 (accessed 19 December, 2014).

have ledge handles, namely types 9, 10 and 11. In the marl caves 7Q and 8Q the same kinds of lids were discovered (*DJD* 3:Fig. 6:1, 2, 9, 10, 11), but in 7Q the extant lid (7Q4) does not fit the top of the two surviving jars, which are somewhat ovoid and have ledge handles (7Q5 and 7Q6, *DJD* 3: Fig. 6:12 and 6:5 respectively, with the latter having the letters רומא). Similar lids have also been found at the site of Qumran, but not clearly connected with extant jars. As with jars that match the forms of the cave jars, the lids can be ascribed to Period Ib (see de Vaux 1954, 221, Fig 3:14; Locus 10A, KhQ383) and Period II.[9] Some lids have everted button-shaped knobs (*e.g. DJD* 3:Fig. 4:10, from cave GQ29:13; Fig. 4:13 from cave GQ8:18; Fig. 4:15 from cave GQ29:5; and KhQ1024, de Vaux 1956, Fig. 5.2), but most knobs are a straight-up or an everted disk. Jar types 12 and 13 from the cave survey have handles and narrow necks, which would make scroll placement within them almost impossible, but de Vaux noted that these types are only evidenced by two incomplete examples and two potsherds.

The more one studies the jars and lids, the more variation becomes apparent. Even putting aside the handled forms of jars and the varieties of lids, the jars are different in terms of the overall body shape, the size of the mouth, the base, the hue of the slip and (where evident) wash, the type of clay, and the size. This variation is particularly surprising given that they are associated with one key location only: Qumran. Even in 1Q alone there are variations in the forms of cylindrical jars (*DJD* 1:14–17, Figs 2 and 3), but there is also a cluster that appears to be quite similar, jars that have the cylindrical form. This clustering of types is also apparent in the 1952 cave survey: de Vaux's types were found only in one or two examples across the caves, but with only types 2 and 4 being found in seven and six cases respectively. Type 2 is a cylindrical jar similar to a type found in 1Q, Q46 (*DJD* 1:Fig. 3:10), but type 4 is squatter and more ovoid in shape. De Vaux states that nearly all the indeterminate pieces appear to belong to types 1–8 (*DJD* 3:13). Still, eight recognizable types are significant, given that the forms range from highly cylindrical to more ovoid. In order to narrow down the clusters by a close scrutiny of clay, shape and so on one would need to re-examine the collection in its entirety.

The chronological development from ovoid to cylindrical forms distinguished by Bar-Nathan in Jericho is a key factor. The pottery was clearly not made in a single batch to furnish the jars found in all the caves. Archaeologists base relative chronologies on uniformity of types across different places at a certain time, and therefore the variations within this type of jar must be taken into account. The variety itself could indicate different times of the manufacture of jars, by different potters, using different clays, even if they are all made at Qumran. Given that the associated pottery that de Vaux identified belongs to Periods Ib and II—not just to the end of Period II—this suggests a longer time span and not a 'quick hiding scenario' or manufacture in AD 68 alone.

Regional parallels to the cylindrical jars of the Qumran caves are hard to define, since the Qumran repertoire is distinguished by a range of different forms. We should be alert to correspondences of key features of single jars in order to become more precise about the typology of the cylindrical jar forms.

Lamps found in the excavations may give us clues for dating both the jars and the deposit in the caves. The pottery associated with the jars sometimes included lamps, and these have now been carefully analyzed by Jolanta Mlynarczyk. Of the lamps from the cave survey, Mlynarczyk (2013, 125) notes two examples from the period AD 1–60/68 (GQ29-1 and GQ9-1, of types 036.3 and 036.4, *DJD* 3:24–25, Figs 5:2; Plate V and VII 1; *DJD* 3:Fig. 5:5; Plate VII). In contrast, lamps Q43 and Q44 from 1Q, classified as type 033.1 and 033.2, should be dated before the middle of the 1st century BC (*DJD* 3:16–17, Fig. 3:4, 5; Mlynarczyk 2013, 105–6). Mlynarczyk herself places types 032–035 in the range of 104–63/56 BC (Humbert's Level 2, Phase A).

---

[9] De Vaux 1954, 223, Fig 4.1; Locus 36 KhQ525; de Vaux 1956, 561, Fig 5:1 and 2; 5:1, KhQ112 found in Locus 61 and 5:2 KhQ1024 found in Locus 56.

Another wheel-made 'Herodian' lamp (in two pieces) from 1Q (Q56) is defined by Mlynarczyk as being unclassifiable, though this lamp could be somewhat later, through the 1st century AD. It is paralleled by a second fragment from 1Q (Q57) and a lamp from the site, KhQ5068 (Mlynarczyk 2013, 117, note 83). However, as Mlynarczyk informed me in an email of 16 April, 2014:

> [Q56] pertains to Qumran type 036.3 ... [and] the 'Herodian' lamps with strap handles, like those of 036.3 and 036.7, may in fact belong to the second half of the 1st century BC. However, the shape (and the 'decoration': a groove across the nozzle top) of the nozzle do suggest that the lamp pertains to the advanced(?) 1st century AD. It may be decades (and probably is) apart from the two lamps pertaining to the 'Qumran family', the latter dated to 50-30 BC(?).

This, along with the variety of jar forms, would suggest that there was more than one deposit of scrolls in jars in 1Q: one dated to the middle of the first century BC, and another later on. As Mlynarczyk stated in her email: 'I am very much inclined to think that there were two different chronological episodes in Gr 1Q.'

Interestingly, Allegro notes that on the basis of these lamps (1956, 78):

> At first this was interpreted by the archaeologists as pointing to a Hellenistic date for the deposit with a later Roman entry. However, after excavations had been made on the ruined Settlement itself, where more jars were found and where coins gave an exact final dating for the main periods of occupation to A.D. 68, it was conceded that the early dating of the cave was probably wrong, and the deposit there would have to brought down to Roman times. The earlier types of the lamps must then be attributed to later copying.

It is now clear that there was no such later copying of Hellenistic/Hasmonaean lamps. The conclusion reached on the basis of the end of the Essene occupation of Khirbet Qumran in AD 68 was used to interpret 1Q. However, the pottery repertoire of the cave alone, taken on its own terms, points in a different direction. Both the original archaeological conclusion and the current analysis of the lamps concur. This is important for the jars because we may have a corresponding situation of deposits of jars at different times.

F. Jars and Lids from Cave 1Q

The jars from 1Q have been widely dispersed. After the excavation of 1Q and the publication of the materials from the cave de Vaux and Harding sought funds for excavations in Qumran, and de Vaux's team (who were in charge of publishing the pottery) restored a number of broken jars discovered in the cave to sell them to museums worldwide.[10] There has been to date no comprehensive list of all catalogued pottery items in 1Q, though there is now one in preparation by Marcello Fidanzio and Jean-Baptiste Humbert, on the basis of a detailed hand card index recorded by de Vaux and his team.[11] It must be noted, however, that the catalogued items do not list all the items found in the cave, which included fragments from about 50 jars and lids (de Vaux 1949, DJD 1:8).

---

[10] Some jars and lids are described and illustrated in de Vaux 1949, 587; DJD 1:8–17, Plates II–III; Humbert and Chambon 1994, 343.

[11] I am grateful to Marcello Fidanzio for discussing his work with me. The following table is only a preliminary presentation on the basis of available data, and does not use the hand card data or observations of jars held in the Rockefeller stores.

Table 24. *Items from Cave 1Q = GQ14 from de Vaux's Excavations*

No.	Object	RB 56 (1949)	DJD 1	Published elsewhere or on web	Comments (DV = de Vaux ; JT = observations by author)	Dimensions in cm	Balla and Gunneweg INAA results	Location (other than Rockefeller Museum, Jer.)
Q1	bowl	Fig. 2.1	Fig. 2.1		DV: curving edge, small ring base; fine clay, rose, grey in section, well fired.	7.8 h.; 14.2 w.	Balla: Qum 271 local Qumran	
Q2	bowl							
Q3	bowl		Fig. 2.3		DV: curving sides, lips slightly flared; disk base with a slight circular groove. Fine clay, grey with some grits of limestone, well fired. Rose surface, with a light off-white slip on the exterior.	6.6 h.; 17.5 w.		
Q4	plate lid		Fig. 2.2; Pl. II.2		DV: jar cover in the form of a plate with oblique lip. A bit fine, red, w/ grey in section, very well fired. White-cream slip on upper face.	2.2 h.; 17.5 w.; base 5 w.	Poss. Balla Qum 269 if their 'L.1' is mistakenly Cave 1? INAA Jordan connection.	
Q5	lid		Fig. 3.6		DV: knob a thickened and expanded disk, concave face. rose clay, medium fired; off white slip	7.5 h; 18.7 w.; knob 7 w.		
Q6	lid	Fig. 2.7	Fig. 2.4		DV: button knob, w/ ribs under button, off-white slip on exterior;	7.1 h; 17.7 w.; knob 4.2 w.		
Q7	lid	Fig. 2.2	Fig. 2.5		DV: knob a thin disk carved with a circular groove, fine clay with fine limestone grits, rose, grey in section, tan slip	5.5 h.; 17.1 w.; knob 6.8 w.	Balla QUM 154 local to Qumran	
Q8	lid							
Q9	lid	Fig.2.5	Fig. 3.8		DV: knob a thickened and expanded disk, flat face; fine clay with some big bits of limestone, rose, well fired; slip rose-tan in the interior and exterior	7.5 h.; 18.5 w.; knob 7 w.		
Q10	lid	Fig.2.3	Fig. 2.6		DV: knob a disk not expanded, concave face; rose clay, medium firing; slip rose-tan	6.9 h.; 17.8 w.; knob 6.8 w.		
Q11	lid		Fig. 2.7		DV: knob an expanded disk, flat face; fine clay with some grit; rose and grey in section; white cream slip on exterior	7.5 h.; 17.8 w.; knob 7 w.		
Q12	lid	Fig. 2.4						
Q13	lid		Fig. 2.9	http://cartelfr.louvre.fr/cartelfr/visite?srv=car_not_frame&idNotice=37415; Długosz 2005	DV: knob a very enlarged disk, flat face; rose clay, grey in section; rose slip JT: lid medium high w/ knob that has a lip	DV: 7.5 h.; 18 w.; knob 7 w. Długosz: 7 h.; 18 w.		Louvre Museum A020148
Q14	lid	Fig. 2.8						

No.	Object	RB 56 (1949)	DJD 1	Published elsewhere or on web	Comments (DV = de Vaux ; JT = observations by author)	Dimensions in cm	Balla and Gunneweg INAA results	Location (other than Rockefeller Museum, Jer.)
Q15	lid							
Q16	lid				JT: medium high shaping w/ knob, same as Q18	JT: 7.7 h.; 18.2 w.; inner 16.7; knob 8.4 w.		British Museum, London ANE 131444
Q17	lid				JT: medium high, protruding top (with thanks to Chris Hamilton and Pablo Torijano)	JT: 8 h.; 18.5 w.; inner 17.3 w.; knob 6.7 w.		University of Madrid, Dean's Office display
Q18	lid		Fig. 3.7	Kraeling 1952	DV: knob and enlarged disk w/ almost flat face; fine rose clay limestone grits, well-fired; rose-to-white slip JT: medium high shaping with protruding knob	DV 7.7 h.; 18 w.; knob 7.8 w. Kraeling: 6.4 h.; 18.7 w.; top knob being like a flat inverted base 7.5 w.		Chicago Oriental Institute; Reg: A 29304 A; Accession Number: 3120
Q19	lid							
Q20	lid (broken)			http://art.the walters.org/detail/29930	JT: on basis of web image; squat like Q5 w/knob; reddish clay; thin whitish slip	dimensions not given on website, but maybe like Q5		Walters Art Museum, Baltimore 48.2058
Q21	lid	Fig. 2.6	Fig. 2.8		DV: button knob, oblique lip enlarged towards interior; fine rose clay with very few grits; medium firing; white slip on exterior	DV: 6.9 h.; 7.5 w.; knob 4.7 w.		
Q22	lid							
Q23	lid							
Q24	lid							
Q25	lid							
Q26	lid							
Q27	lid							
Q28	lid							
Q29	lid							
Q30	lid							
Q31	lid							
Q32	lid							
Q33	lid							
Q34	lid							
Q35	lid							
Q36	lid							
Q37	lid							
Q38	lid							
Q39	lid							

No.	Object	RB 56 (1949)	DJD 1	Published elsewhere or on web	Comments (DV = de Vaux ; JT = observations by author)	Dimensions in cm	Balla and Gunneweg INAA results	Location (other than Rockefeller Museum, Jer.)
Q40	jar (broken)		Fig. 2.10	http://images.met-museum.org/CRDImages/an/original/hb64_26a_b.jpg	DV: cylindrical jar, large mouth, collar slightly flared, flattened lip, 2 circular lines in relief at the beginning of the collar; shoulder well marked; 4 small handles vertically attached on shoulder; rounded bottom; ochre clay, fine with fine limestone grits; medium fired. JT: jar has accompanying lid with brown substance on it; 4 loop handles originally but only 2 reconstructed; rounded bottom and missing base(?), sharply cut turning marks in lower part; red clay, very little remains of white wash; bulging shaping, defined shoulders.	64.5 h.; 27 w.; mouth 14.5 w.; Met.: 62 h.		Metropolitan Museum of Art, New York. Gift of Hashemite Kingdom of Jordan, 1964 Accession Number: 64.26a, b
Q41	jar (broken)	Fig.1; Pl. XV	Fig. 2.11		DV: cylindrical jar, large opening, straight up collar, straight shoulder, without handles, base a thin disk, concave with turning marks; fine clay with limestone grits, red and grey in section, well fired, off yellow slip or grey with whitish streaks;	DV: 64 h; 26 w.; mouth 16 w.; base 11.5 w.		
Q42	jar (broken)		Fig. 2.12 Pl. II.6		DV: cylindrical jar, large opening, collar slightly everted, a circular line in relief on shoulder, 4 little handles vertical on shoulder, disk base; ochre clay without grits, medium firing, rose slip, turning to white in parts, chipped	DV: 58.5 h x 27 w.; mouth 13.5 w.; base 12 w. JT: 57.5 h.; 28 w.; 2.5 h. mouth ext 13.5 w.; base 12 w.		
Q43	lamp	Pl. XVI.b	Fig. 3.4; Pl. 3.b.3	Mlynarczyk 2013	DV: turned lamp, body circular and flattened; base a bit rounded. Long spout, rounded nose. Mlynarczyk determines early-mid 1st cent. BCE - Hellenistic/Hasmonaean -	4.2 h.; 14.2 l.; 9 w.	Balla Qum 286 - Jericho	
Q44	lamp	Pl. XVI.b	Fig. 3.5; Pl. 3.b.1	Mlynarczyk 2013	DV: turned lamp, body circular and flat plate; base a bit rounded. Long spout, rounded nose. Mlynarczyk determines early-mid 1st cent. BCE – Hellenistic/Hasmonaean	4.1 h.; 14.3 l.; 9 w.		
Q45	jar (broken)			Kraeling 1952	JT: cylindrical jar, tube-like form, particularly high but consistent width; turning marks and creamy coloured slip; displayed with lid Q18	Kraeling: 71.7 h. × 24.7 w.; base 13.1 w., mouth 16.5 w.		Oriental Institute, University of Chicago, Reg: A 29304 A; Accession Number: 3120

No.	Object	RB 56 (1949)	DJD 1	Published elsewhere or on web	Comments (DV = de Vaux ; JT = observations by author)	Dimensions in cm	Balla and Gunneweg INAA results	Location (other than Rockefeller Museum, Jer.)
Q46	jar (broken)		Fig. 3.10	http://cartelfr.louvre.fr/cartelfr/visite?srv=car_not_frame&idNotice=37415; Długosz 2005	DV: cylindrical jar, type of Q41; fine clay with fine limestone grits; rose and grey in section, well fired, rose white slip and mauve on exterior; JT: displayed with lid Q13; tube-like cylindrical jar, with rounded shoulder and bottom, looks more like ochre clay and cream slip, turning marks visible	DV: 61.4 h.; 25 w.; mouth 14.8 w.; base 12.4 w. Louvre: 63 h.; 25.6 w.; mouth 14.6 w.		Louvre Museum A020147
Q47	jar (broken)				JT: cylindrical jar, no base reconstruction; reddish clay with off-white slip that has worn off in patches, rounded shoulder and bottom tube-like jar form	JT: 61.5 h.; 25 w., interior mouth 14.4 w.; exterior mouth 16 w.		Ashmolean Museum, Oxford AN1951.477
Q48	jar (broken)			http://art.thewalters.org/detail/29930	JT: ochre clay with grey and creamy slip worn off in patches, turning marks, appears very like Q52 in body, neck taller than base; displayed with lid Q20	72 h. × 24.4 w.		Walters Art Museum 48.2058
Q49	jar (broken)		Fig. 3.11		DV: cylindrical jar, type of Q46, same clay, same slip (red-grey clay; rose-mauve slip).	DV: 54.7 h.; 25 w.; mouth 14.8 w.; base 11.7 w.		
Q50	jar (broken)		Fig. 3.9		DV: type of Q41, fine clay with fine limestone grits, rose and grey in section, well fired. JT: cylindrical jar, tube-like, rounded shoulder and bottom, slightly wider at top that bottom, with turning marks, slightly concave disk base but with slight ring, reddish clay and creamy coloured slip, including streaks from brush	DV: 55.7 h.; 25 w.; mouth 15 w.; base 13.5 w. JT: 54.5 h.; 23.5 w. (not max?); 15.2 w. mouth ext.; mouth interior 13.7 w.		British Museum, London ANE 131444
Q51	jar (broken)							
Q52	jar (broken)				JT: cylindrical, rounded shoulder and bottom, tube-like, symmetrical, whitish slip on ochre clay with grey; slightly irregular shaping; slightly concave disk base (with thanks to Chris Hamilton and Pablo Torijano)	JT: 62 h.; 24 w.; mouth ext. 15.5 w.; mouth int. 13.9; base 11.3 w.		University of Madrid, Dean's Office
Q53	jar (broken)							
Q54	cooking pot		Fig. 3.2; Pl. III.a.2		DV: low collar w/ oblique lip, two handles, body slightly corrugated, rounded base slightly tapering to a point, red clay, fine, well-fired.	19.5 h.; max 23 w.; opening 9.4 w.		

No.	Object	RB 56 (1949)	DJD 1	Published elsewhere or on web	Comments (DV = de Vaux ; JT = observations by author)	Dimensions in cm	Balla and Gunneweg INAA results	Location (other than Rockefeller Museum, Jer.)
Q55	juglet		Fig. 3.3; Pl. III.b.2		DV: spherical body, straight neck and enlarged lip, a flat handle a little twisted from the lip to the shoulder; sides very marked. Rose clay, fine, well-fired.	12.5 h.; max 8.5 w.; opening 2 w.		
Q56	lamp (broken)		Fig. 3.1	Mlynarczyk 2013	DV: two fragments of a lamp with arced spout and a ribbed handle. Grey clay, fine and well fired. Mlynarczyk says type lasted to end of 1st cent. CE	11, in length, when reconstructed		
Q57	lamp (fragment)			Humbert and Chambon 1994: 343 note lamp fragment 'Herodienne'	very similar to Q56			
QX	jar (whole) and lid			'Shrine 2' drawing in Pfann 2002	JT: reddish clay. Quite sharp contour of shoulder. 3 loop handles and lip at top of collar. Red clay with hardly any slip or white wash adhering though streaks diagonal below shoulder. Black streaks (of bitumen?) in vertical lines. Slightly similar to Q42 but shorter.	47.5 h.; 26.5 w.	Balla 15582? Qum 198 Jericho 'rounded'	Israel Museum The Hebrew University of Jerusalem 96.46/236
QX	lid				JT: Flat and squat lid like Q7.			
QY	jar (whole)			'Shrine 1' drawing in Pfann 2002	JT: cylindrical jar, rounded shoulder and bottom, elongated and tube-like, symmetrical, reddish clay with creamy slip and brown stains on side	65.7 h.; 25 w.	Balla 15584? Qum 199 'long, narrow'; Hebron type Motza	Israel Museum 96.46/235
QY	lid				Prominent knob and medium lid like Q9			

Table 24 shows that there are two main clusters of jars in 1Q: a cluster that is largely cylindrical, elongated, tube-like, symmetrical, without handles, with a straight-up collar and disk base, rounded shoulder and lower side, exhibiting some turning marks and a light to medium-heavy white-cream slip. This is what people often consider the 'classic' scroll jar, and it is illustrated by the example from the Israel Museum (QY, *Figure 77*). This cluster of jars is represented by Q41, Q45, Q46, Q47, Q48, Q49, Q50, Q51, Q52, and QY. While they vary in height, they are remarkably the same in width, with widths recorded as being in the range 24.4–25.5 cm. This consistency of width is particularly striking.

However, there is also a second small cluster that I call the 'outliers'. This cluster in 1Q is represented by QX, Q40, and Q42.

While there is uniformity in the classic 'scroll jar' type, with the key variable being height, the three outliers are slightly more bulging than the classic tube-like jars. They all have handles.

QX (*Figure 76*) is 47.5 cm high and 26.5 wide, shorter and wider than the jars of the main cluster. There is a lip at the top of the straight-up collared neck, which may suggest that it was designed to have a plate or slab on top of the neck rather than a lid with sides; this was tied down using the three horizontal loop handles. A plate used as a lid was in fact found in 1Q (number Q4).

Q40[12] has four loop handles and a rounded base, with a fairly sharp shoulder and flared collar, with a more bulging form, 64.5 cm high and 27 cm wide (see *DJD* 1:12–14, Fig. 2:10).

Q42[13] has a sharper shoulder than the common type, with narrower neck and base in relation to its width, a slightly everted and high collar, and four small loop handles on the shoulder. The jar is 58.5 cm high and 27 cm wide (*DJD* 1:14–15, Fig. 2:12). Both Q40 and Q42 have vertical loop handles and are more similar to each other than to QX.

QX (*Figure 76*) is the jar often assumed to have contained the first three scrolls, one large and two small, and is identified by Pfann as 'Shrine 2'. In the neutron activation study by Balla (2005) it was labelled QUM198; the clay of this jar was identified as coming from Jericho, similar to a Hasmonaean lamp found in the cave (Q43, Balla 2005, 90).

The other jar exhibited in the Shrine of the Book (QY; Balla's QUM199, *Figure 77*), an example of the 'classic' type, was made of Motza (Beit ʾUmmar) clay (Balla 2005, 93; Gunneweg and Balla 2003, 18).

The link between the 'outlier' jar QX and the Hasmonaean lamp is important, since it may indicate not only a different manufacture but also an earlier time of deposit. A jar from cave GQ3 (3-1, QUM 256) is a type 3 jar which is squatter than the 'main cluster' type, with a slightly everted rim and a more bulging body, somewhat like QX, though about 57 cm high. Also this one was made of clay from Jericho.

A. The Allegro Jar and Lid

In his book *The Dead Sea Scrolls*, Allegro mentioned a jar he owned, bought from Kando in 1953 (Allegro 1956, 77), which had a hole in the body sealed with bitumen. This is clearly a reference to the Schøyen jar. The time of purchase demonstrates that this jar derives from clandestine excavations prior to 1953. However, Kando continued to receive materials from the Qumran caves, both artefacts and scrolls, and released them in a paced operation. Allegro bought another jar as well as a lid in the early 1960s. Both jars and the lid were kept in Allegro's home and photographed on certain occasions, until the first jar was sold back to Kando's son Sami. This jar passed through five owners until it was acquired for The Schøyen Collection. The accompanying jar and the lid remained in the possession of Allegro and, after his death, passed to his daughter Judith Brown. In 2010 Jan Gunneweg visited Judith Brown, noted some features of the jar and took a sample of the jar for INAA analysis (Gunneweg 2012).

Gunneweg (2012) reports that in a letter of 13 September, 1983, Allegro states that he bought the second jar from Kando in 1962. He notes it has a small hole in one side but is otherwise intact, and that he bought a lid at the same time, still containing 'bat's dung'. The cave from which this jar and lid came was not identified, but at this time Kando had in his possession a number of smaller, but not identical, 'scroll jars', and Allegro surmised that these were released because the Bedouin's operations had only recently been discovered. In a letter written to Sotheby's, dated 16 September, 1983, he notes that he took a photograph of the jar and the lid in Cave 4 'about the time that I purchased the jar from Kando' (Allegro's letters, in Gunneweg 2012).

---

[12] This jar is now in the Metropolitan Museum of Art http://images.metmuseum.org/CRDImages/an/original/ hb64_26a_b.jpg [accessed 17 January, 2015]. I was able to make this connection thanks to seeing materials in the Harding archive at the Institute of Archaeology, University College London (February 2015), with thanks to the curator Rachael Sparks, and Katie Turner in New York.

[13] I am grateful to Father Jean-Baptiste Humbert for permitting me to view this and other jars in the Rockefeller Qumran stores in July 2014 and respect his wish that I do not report here any of my findings or publish my photographs or technical details as a result of this visit. A full inventory and re-examination of the jars, with additional information, will soon be provided by Fr. Humbert and Marcello Fidanzio.

Figure 78. *Allegro jar in the glass fronted window recess*
(Photo: Joan Taylor)

I visited Allegro's daughter Judith Brown and her husband David on 3 September, 2014, to study the Allegro jar and lid.[14] For 19 years the jar has been stored in a blocked-up window recess with a glass front (see *Figure 78*). Judith and David commented that they were worried about the possibility of recent dampness in the atmosphere. I inspected the jar by turning it around to view all sides, without gloves. When I removed my hands I noticed that the white wash coating the jars had come off as a fine powder and that I had left marks on the jar itself. In retrospect, in the handling of such objects plastic gloves would be advisable, though this is not general practice in excavations or necessarily in viewing objects in collections, and especially not in the case of private collections. I tried to turn the jar using a cloth but the white wash powder also shed onto this, and I then felt quite nervous about touching the object directly, though I did lie it on its side to view the interior and base properly.

1. Jar

The jar is of the cylindrical type (as described in Allegro 1956, 77) with a slightly narrowing width towards the base. There is a collared rim, with the rim standing straight up. The collar slightly dips on one side, creating an imperfection. There is a slightly concave ring base that has an obvious central protrusion from the wheel centre. It was covered with a slip, though it is quite rough, and there are a couple of encrustations. This slip seems to have a slightly creamy colour tending to yellow hue, including over the base but not in the interior. As noted there is in addition a whitish wash. In the interior, and in a crack in the rim, the underlying reddish clay is clearly seen, which tends to a peachy colour, and no grey layer of high firing was discernible. The clay is not particularly fine and has white and grey grit. There are two large cracks on either side of the jar running down from the rim, showing clear evidence of attempts at modern maintenance, since the exterior of one of the cracks shows traces of strips of cellotape glue, and the corresponding interior is obviously stained with glue. The residue of the cellotape corresponds with the conservation techniques used in the jars elsewhere, but the glue is more roughly done.

There is a small hole at the end of one of the cracks. This would be most easily explained as being due to a breakage when the jar—originally standing upright on its base—fell over, since above the hole there is an area where the white wash has been rubbed off and become stained from contact with the cave floor (see *Figure 79*). This feature explains why the white wash (turning to chalk powder) is now unstable on the jar as a whole: the white wash is vulnerable to damp, which makes it powdery, after which it rubs off. It was observed that the wash around the base has also slightly rubbed off, showing that the very bottom of the jar was also in contact with earth for some time, indicating its original upright position. The ring rim originally touched flat ground, and the base interior, being slightly concave, was lifted away from it. Some soil built up around the edges of the base over time, and then the jar fell over. As noted, this brownish hue and wash degradation is clearly seen more deeply on the jar at the upper side associated with the hole, and shows how it fell over to lie on its shoulder with its base protruding into the air at some point (perhaps because of an earthquake). However, it was clearly preserved in a very clean environment, since its exterior and interior are almost without any damage or staining, and encrustations appear only slightly. There is no sign of rat droppings.

---

[14] I am deeply indebted to Judith and David Brown as well as George Brooke, who connected me with the Browns.

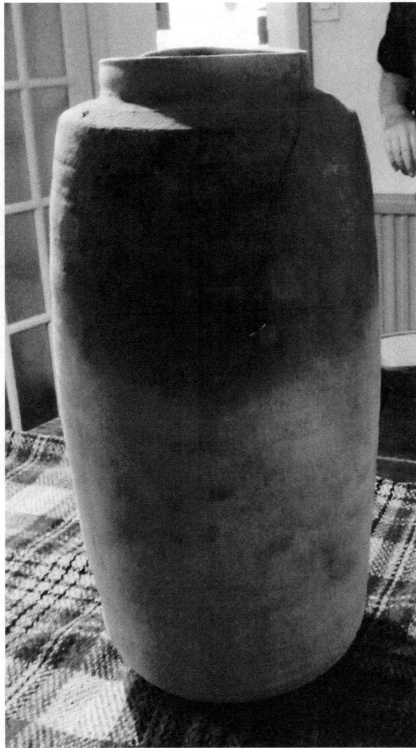

Figure 79. *Allegro jar: staining above the hole*
(Photo: Joan Taylor)

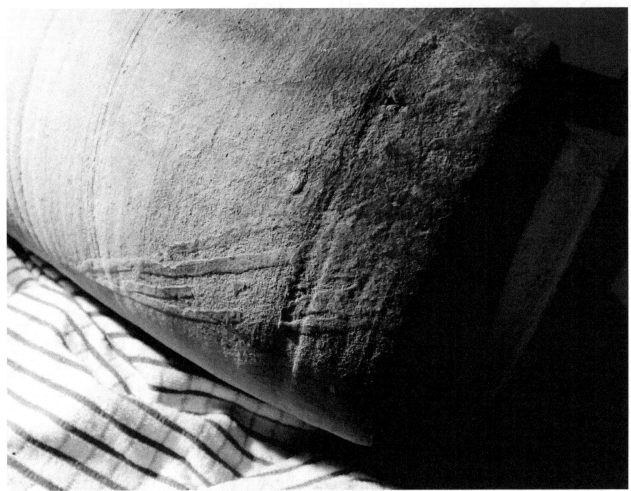

Figure 80*. Allegro jar: striations of clay*
(Photo: Joan Taylor)

There are raised diagonal striations caused by wet clay being applied prior to the removal of the jar from the wheel, running down from the shoulder to midway along the jar body. This creates a slightly rough look to the exterior (see *Figure 80*). At the lower part of the jar the ribs are quite clear, without showing a noticeable attempt at smoothing. The fact that the collar dips and has not been reshaped adds to the impression of a jar that is functional rather than decorative.

Overall the jar has a clean appearance, both on the exterior and the interior. In the interior there is no marking around the neck and no defined water mark, but there is a white staining around the lower part near the base and some mottled brown staining on the bottom. The white staining would be consistent with there being a substance at the bottom of the jar only, which could be crystalline salts from water.

The dimensions of the jar may roughly be estimated as follows: the straight-up collared neck rim is 2 cm high. It has an internal diameter of minimum 13.3 cm and an external diameter of maximum 14.5 cm. The slightly concave ring base has a diameter of 11 cm and slightly worn edges. The total height is 50.1 cm. At its maximum the width is 26 cm, narrowing to 23 cm at the bottom. The curve from rim to sharp shoulder measures 3 cm.

This type of jar is typical of Qumran cylindrical jars in having a creamy slip and white wash on reddish-peachy clay, basic cylindrical design with some narrowing towards the base, and a wide, collared neck. It resembles the 1Q jar QX (Israel Museum 96.46/236) and the Schøyen jar in having smaller dimensions than most Qumran cylindrical jars and in having an angled, sharp (rather than rounded) shoulder, but it lacks the handles of the Israel Museum jar and the Schøyen jar. QX is 47.5 cm high, slightly smaller than the Allegro jar; the Schøyen jar is approximately 43 cm high. In size and form the Allegro jar closely resembles the jar shown in Fig. 3 of the 1952 expedition report (*DJD* 3:21, Plate V), defined as type 8, from 3Q (= GQ8), artefact number 9, which was recovered broken. The only difference is that the Allegro jar tapers slightly more at the bottom; otherwise it appears virtually identical. This type of jar was identified by de Vaux as being found in caves 2Q and 3Q (GQ19, GQ8), both being scroll caves.

In the interior of the jar there was some dust and debris. Since there was no way of knowing whether this was ancient or modern (though one may suspect the latter) two samples were taken for a mineral analysis.

Figure 81. *Allegro lid*
(Photo: Joan Taylor)

2. Jar Lid

There is no reason to assume that this lid was originally on the Allegro jar, or even from the same cave. As with the cylindrical jars, these lids are only found in the region of the Dead Sea close to Qumran. Its importance lies in the fact that it is partially filled with material from the cave where it was found. The lid is stained on its upper surface, corresponding exactly to where it lay top down on the cave floor, at an angle, with the material filling its interior horizontally, corresponding to the cave floor fill. It was therefore partially buried in the floor of the cave (*Figures 81-82*). It is unknown which Qumran cave this lid came from, but it matches most closely types 13 and 14 of lids documented by de Vaux from the cave survey of 1952, found in 3Q (= GQ8; 8–3 and 8–18; *DJD* 3:23, Fig. 4). These types of lid are quite high, with a small but pronounced protruding knob. While such knobs are typical of 3Q (GQ8), a somewhat similar form was found in GQ29 (type 15). This contrasts with lids found in 1Q, which are squatter and have flatter and wider knobs. The lid is remarkably high in comparison with the published lids from 1Q, which vary from squat shaping to moderately tall, with a height ranging from 5.5 cm to 7.1 cm. Most of the white wash has rubbed off, but there are traces of it in mottled patches. The destruction of the wash is not surprising given its position upside down on the cave floor.

Figure 82. *Allegro lid, interior full of animal dung, probably rat*
(Photo: Joan Taylor)

The material filling the lid appears solid. To sample the material I dug a small hole into the material with a sterilized (by flame) knife. The material crumbled into fine brown powder as I did so. It appears to me to be dried animal droppings, possibly rat, given its brown rather than grey (bat) colouration. The surface of the material may be contaminated with modern dust etc. but the inner part into which I dug should be clear of contaminants.

The lid has the following dimensions: lid base exterior 17.6–18.2 cm, lid base interior 17 cm ± 2 mm, lid knob 4 cm wide, height of lid: 9 cm to the top of the knob. It should be noted that the width of this lid is too wide for a snug fit with the Allegro jar neck.

The Manchester University Museum holds an important collection of photographs from Allegro, published in a microfiche edition (Brooke, with Bond, 1996). Among these photographs are several that depict both the Allegro jar and the Schøyen jar. The set includes the photographs of the jar taken in 4Q that Allegro referred to: a Bedouin man is positioned with the jar and lid in Cave 4Q in fiche 10, photos B2–10. It appears that Allegro bought the jar and lid in Bethlehem, and subsequently brought them to Qumran to take photographs, before exporting the items to the UK.

The jar is associated with other photographs taken in 1962–63, when Allegro was engaged in a search for further caves, a search described in his book *Search in the Desert* (1965). In this book, Allegro is largely interested in the Christmas Cave, where a number of items had been excavated and brought to dealers in Bethlehem. However, he was also shown two caves he calls 'Ibrahim's Caves', located just south of 11Q, in the same ridge that 3Q was located. In the second cave '[t]here were signs of intensive working all around. Every nook and cranny had been searched and newly turned dust and rockfall covered the floor of the cave' (Allegro 1965, 159). Allegro was shown here part of a Roman cooking pot, a cave deeper in, and a lower storey to the cave complex. In fact, he left the excavation with Ibrahim and his men still continuing here and further in this region. Ibrahim himself died in June 1963 (Allegro 1965, 164), taking information about his digging to the grave. Given the intense activity of Ibrahim in this area prior to Allegro's visit, it would match with the arrival of jars and lids in Kando's shop in Bethlehem that have a strong similarity to 3Q pottery.

B. The Schøyen Jar (MS 1655/1)

This jar was originally purchased by Allegro in 1953. He states in his book *The Dead Sea Scrolls*:

> By this time [1949] all the intact jars had been taken away or broken. Professor Sukenik had purchased two from Kando [sic], and I myself bought another from him which was quite intact, apart from a small hole near the bottom sealed with pitch, and which had probably been used all this time by the Bedouin in their camp as a storage vessel (Allegro 1956, 77).

I had the privilege of studying the jar on 9 September, 2014.[15] The Schøyen jar was originally Allegro's first jar, bought in 1953. It was sold back to the Kando family and passed through five different owners before it was acquired for The Schøyen Collection.

The jar is smaller than all other cylindrical jars said to come from 1Q.[16] However, in other ways it matches the morphology of a cylindrical jar. It has an obvious ring at the base, and therefore not the disk base of the 'classic' set of 1Q jars, but this is like the Allegro jar. The clay seemed to be peachy

---

[15] I am indebted to Martin Schøyen for his permission and for his enthusiasm about understanding the object.

[16] It is also illustrated in the Allegro photograph collection (Brooke, with Bond 1996) in Fiche 10 (B10–C10), and slide pictures of the jar have been made available to me by Judith Brown.

coloured, without the obvious grey burning from high firing, but such grey coloration is most obvious in broken pieces or cracks, and the jar does not have these available for observation.

Figure 83. *Picture of the Schøyen jar taken by Allegro in the 1960s.*
The pencil marking now located below the handle to the left may have been
added after this earlier photograph was taken (Courtesy of Judith Brown).

Figure 84a. *Schøyen jar showing pencil markings below the handle, spelling the word SORTIE, with two uprights drawn for the T*
(Photo: Joan Taylor).

Figure 84b*. Schøyen jar showing pencil markings below the handle, spelling the
word SORTIE, with two uprights drawn for the T
(Photo: Joan Taylor).*

The ring base is slightly more concave than the Allegro jar, and also has a small protruding central button, but otherwise the form of this ring base is extremely similar and it measures about the same in diameter. It has a sharp shoulder, rather than a rounded contour, which defines it as different from most of the common cluster of 1Q jars, though there is an exception in the sharp shoulder of Q51), but this is consistent with Q40, one of the outliers. In addition it has three ledge handles. The slip tends to be creamy coloured and also looks similar to the Allegro jar. There are turning marks/ribs more pronounced at the lower part of the jar, and the overall appearance of the vessel is rough, in common with other types of coarseware of this period. It has not been smoothed over to create a polished piece. This roughness is also apparent in the collared neck, which ranges from straight up to slightly everted, as if the collar has not been applied in a careful way.

On the side of the jar, someone has written with a pencil the French word SORTIE in capital letters. This pencil marked word is not visible on the Allegro photograph, as supplied to me by Judith Brown (*Figure 83*, cf. *Figure 84*), and is clearly written after the time of Allegro.

For the dimensions of the jar, see the discussion by Elgvin in this volume (p. 427). In summary, it is 43 cm high, has a diameter of 21 cm and a 15.3 cm wide collared neck. As with other jars and lids there

are variations based on the site of the measurement spots, and these should be understood as being ±
2–4 mm in this case.

The most striking feature of the jar is its dirty deposits: splattered brown encrustations are found
on the lower part and there are brown marks on the base. This brown splattering adheres on top of the
wash and is therefore post-manufacture. It appears very similar in coloration to the deposit inside the
Allegro lid. In coloration and texture it in no way appears like the rocky earth of any cave or from the
Qumran site, and would appear organic in nature, as with the Allegro lid deposit. Two samples were
taken from this brown deposit, and it was noted that it crumbled into brown dust. Given the attested
rodent droppings within 1Q that required cleaning of much of the linen (Harding 1949, 113; *DJD* 1:6, 18),
the deposit seems consistent with dung. Alternatively, it may be mud, but only analysis could define its
nature. If it is mud it does not, however, have the coloration of Qumran mud, which is greyer.

Above the largest area of this deposit on one side of the jar are two areas of water damage that has
rubbed the wash off almost completely: one large area covering most of the jar and a smaller one within
it. On the other side of the jar, in the area towards the shoulder the wash has rubbed off in the more
typical way as a result of damp earth contact, similar to the Allegro jar. This suggests that this part of
the jar lay on the ground. But the exposed side was damaged by water on at least two occasions. This
initial water damage may have been quite heavy, resulting in the brown splattering in the lower part
of the jar that has been deposited as a kind of ricochet, since the brown splattering covers part of the
water damage. Alternatively the brown encrustations may derive from another event.

By comparing photographs of the present state of the jar with the photographs of the jar when it
was in the possession of Allegro, it is possible to determine that the second, smaller water marking was
the result of modern damage. As with the word SORTIE, this water marking is not visible on the Allegro
photographs, while other markings are clearly visible. Also some other brown marking now found on
the jar was not there at the time it was with Allegro (*Figure 85*, compared with *Figure 86* p. 428).

The state of the jar may be consistent with a vessel that has lain partly on its side in a closed environment that was nevertheless subject to the intrusion of water. Water damage is observable on some
key texts of the Dead Sea Scrolls, particularly the *Temple Scroll*, where column 1 is missing and there is
significant damage to the upper and outer parts as a result of water infiltration (see Werrett 2007, 107–
8).

Figure 85. *Picture of the Schøyen jar taken by Allegro in the 1960s*
(Courtesy of Judith Brown)

The late Herodian *kap* (*Figure 87* p. 429) written on the interior of the jar appears to provide a weight measurement, suggesting that this jar indeed had a utilitarian use at some point. The meaning of the letter *kap* could relate to the unit of measure of a *kikkar* or talent, used for precious metals. The *kikkar* was slightly of different weights/volumes at different times, but in the Hebrew Bible it was about 75 lbs or 35 kg (Holladay 1971, 156).[17] One *kikkar* was 60 *minas* and a *mina* was 571.2 g, or 50 *shekels*, thus there were 3000 *shekels* to a talent/*kikkar* (cf. Exod 38.25–26; Ezek 45.12), though Josephus states of Crassus' plunder of the Temple that 'a *mina* weighed two *litra* and a half' (*Ant.* 14: 106). Given that a *litra* (= *libra*, Roman pound) was 326.4 g, for Josephus a *mina* was 816 g. Perhaps this is because the smaller weight of a *shekel* in biblical times had changed by the first century BC, since Tyrian silver didrachmas, used for the Temple tax *shekel*, or *sela*, weighed about 14 g; thus a *kikkar* measure holding 3000 of such silver coins would be even weightier, up to 42 kg.[18] However, it may be better to consider whether 3000 coins could even fit in the jar rather than be too scrupulous about the weight, given the variables.

One may note also, as the *Jewish Encyclopedia* (1906) states (cf. the *qab* in 2 Kgs 6.25): 'With regard to the names of the units, it must be noted that the hollow vessels used as measures also served as ordinary utensils; and the name of the vessel likewise designated the measure.'

The original scroll jars taken from 1Q were apparently used by the Bedouin as water containers (Trever 1977, 70). As with the Allegro jar, there is a noticeable white powdery adhesion in the interior. This goes up to and surpasses the Hebrew letter *kap* written on the interior of the jar. It is possible that this white deposit is the residue of white micro-crystalline gypsum and salt grains characteristic of quite saline waters.

There are also some white encrustations on the exterior, as well as the bituminous sealing of an ancient crack in the side. There are two deposits of a black bituminous substance: a large one that runs from the turn of the lower bottom side to the base and another smaller one to the left of this, closer to the brown encrustations below the word SORTIE. Both are applied on top of the wash. Some small black bits on the surface of the jar exterior and interior can also be observed. Access to bitumen may suggest a location close to the Dead Sea.

The samples taken for INAA on the base also included the slip. Gunneweg's sample from the base seemed to include a large amount of the slip, but the other (drilled by Elgvin and analysed by Boulanger) contained a little bit of the peachy coloured clay of the fabric of the vessel. The first sampling largely removed the slip and only a small amount of the fabric clay itself, which would have created a melange in terms of the analysis. The slip is often particularly thick on the bases of jars.

As noted, the jar is smaller in size than the common cluster of 1Q jars. These were defined by a rounded shoulder, elongated, generally cylindrical shape, symmetrical appearance, close similarity of moulding top and bottom, no handles, disk base, very similar clay (defined as Motza through INAA tests), and firing. However, the Schøyen jar has similarities to the group of outliers within 1Q. It should be remembered that the Bedouin who spoke to Trever told him that the first two jars they removed from Cave 1Q both had three handles. This is true for only one of the jars now in the Shrine of the Book (QX), but it matches the Schøyen jar. QX also matches the Schøyen jar in having a sharper shoulder, and its size is similar, although somewhat larger (47.5 cm in height). Nevertheless, it does not otherwise resemble the outliers since it is not bulging and the clay not so red. They also have loop handles, not ledge handles.

---

[17] Milik notes this kind of measurement on a storage jar found by the Taamire in September 1952 in a cave in Wadi Qumran. It bears an inscription in charcoal, indicating its capacity, '2 seah and 7 log'. From the volume of the jar, the value of the seah can be established at *c.* 15.5 litres: Milik 1959, 151; *DJD* 3:37–41; this is the jar called 6Q1, shown in Lemaire 2003, 374.

[18] Interestingly, in Herodotus, *Hist.* 3.89–97 the tribute to Darius was in the form of liquid gold and silver poured into ceramic jars of talent weight and then the ceramic was chipped off. For biblical weights and measure values see http://www.oxfordbiblicalstudies.com/resource/WeightsAndMeasures.xhtml.

Could the Schøyen jar come from 2Q? This cave was also found by the Bedouin. De Vaux defined eight types of cylindrical jars in his 1952 cave survey. In 2Q (= GQ19) there was one jar of type 2 and one of type 8, plus undetermined sherds of six more cylindrical jars (*DJD* 3:9, 13–14, 18–21). Type 8 is very similar to the Schøyen jar in form (cf. *DJD* 3:21; Fig. 3, Plate V, jar GQ8–9). There is the same sharp shoulder, a slightly everted rim, a concave base, and a very similar shape, with large neck in relation to its width. The difference is that the published example from 3Q (= GQ8) does not have handles, but the shape and proportions are very close. De Vaux does not give the dimensions in his list, but using his scale it can be determined that the GQ8-9 jar is about 50 cm high and about 25 cm wide, slightly larger than the Schøyen jar. De Vaux was interested in shapes rather than sizes or handles, and he indicates that this shape of jar was *only* found in 2Q and 3Q (GQ19, GQ8).

The wide neck (the largest neck in relation to its width I have seen) might suit a plate lid that could be tied on with string running through the ledge handle holes. The only lid found in 2Q belongs to types that are quite high and have a protruding knob (*DJD* 3:Fig. 4, no. 9).

The sand found in the inside of the holes of the handles is perplexing. In regard to the results published in this volume by Ira Rabin and Roman Schütz (p. 377), I would interpret them differently, as indicators of a cave environment. Two pieces of fibrous tissue—one likely parchment with another piece indicating flax or ramie—surely represent tiny parts of the scroll wrapper or packing material and scroll. The linen (flax) does also have the Dead Sea picture of chlorine and sodium. Given the organic appearance of the 'sediment' identified, the sample from the external side of the jar bottom may not actually be earth. It is noted that it does contain calcite, but not enough aragonite to fit the environment of natural caves in the cliffs. The question is whether it might be dung splattered on the jar in the cave environment. However, the increased amount of sulphur, the relation calcite/gypsum, halite and sylvite salts on the surface of the jar all correspond very well to storage in a Dead Sea environment, even with a jar being washed by Dead Sea water. Mention of potash/potassium work may be connected with Zohar Amar's identification of the nearby Cave of the Column as a potassium plant, since here it was an industrial zone where they were burning potassium rich plants for the making of soap (Amar 1998a). This is close to the caves 1Q, 2Q, and 3Q. But the key indicator is that the salts are distinctive of the Dead Sea. This kind of evidence seems to me far more important than an encrustation at the exterior bottom of the jar, which may be dung.

The tentative conclusion of Rabin and Schütz, that the jar was found somewhere in modern times in the Negev and then taken to Kando, seems unlikely. The Taamire Bedouin have nothing to do with the Negev and there is no site there that could have produced this jar. Jars like this are only attested from the area of Qumran. The exterior surface salts indicate storage in a Dead Sea environment. It is not clear when the sand in the jar handles was deposited. If it was ancient, it is something that arrived post-manufacture as the result of early storage. This was not the final storage because the remainder of the vessel is completely clear of this sand, even though there are dark deposits on the side and base which should have picked up sand traces if the sand was subsequent. We would not have a jar with this kind of exterior damage and residue found buried in sand without sand adhering to it. Rather, the jar was stored in an open environment in which there was damage by water and a brown residue was splattered on the sides and base.

The issue is to arrive at a scenario which makes sense of all the scientific information. The jar might well have been manufactured in the Negev, initially stored in a sandy environment (hence sand inside the handles), taken to Qumran and been buried in a cave, where it fell over at some point (dampness) and got the brown residue splattered on it. That is a correlating scenario only, and there may be several alternate correlating scenarios that can make sense of archaeological evidence. Even when clay and place of manufacture do match, trade and other factors permitted the distribution of jars in antiquity, so that an appropriately-shaped jar from Negev may well have arrived in Qumran, just as in the case of jar no. 3 from 4Q (Gunneweg and Balla 2003, 24: QUM 232), with clay that may come from the Qitmit/Beersheva region.

C. Conclusions

Examinations of 1Q jars and lids have led to the conclusion that there is here a clear common set of jars with defined features: cylindrical, elongated, symmetrical top and bottom, tube-like, with straight up collars, rounded shoulders and bottoms and disk bases. These have a fabric of reddish to ochre clay and a slip that can be creamy coloured or tending to white-grey. There are turning marks but not tightly defined ribs. This was noted by de Vaux in his presentation of the jars in *DJD* 1, and they are often seen as the 'classic' scroll jars. Their different proportions do not distinguish them as different jar types, and they are extremely similar in width, about 25 cm wide. The fact that they are made in different heights, presumably on purpose, might have made them more recognizable by size. One would even have been able to stand them neatly in a line of different heights.

But if we consider the Schøyen jar as part of the 1Q repertoire, it would be one of the alternative group I call 'outliers'. However, typologically it seems closest to a form found in cave 2Q and 3Q. The problem is that we do not have enough detailed analysis from the Qumran caves as a whole that would define typologies more exactly, and until this is completed the most likely provenance of the jar will remain conjectural.

XLII

Archive Jars and Storage Jars in Context. MS 1655/1, MS 1655/3abcd

Torleif Elgvin

A. Physical Description[1]

The Schøyen jar (MS 1655/1) weighs 3660g, has a height of 43 cm, a maximum diameter of 21.6 cm, and a volume of *c.* 11 litres. It has a cylindrical shape, and curves sharply at the top and bottom to a *c.* 15 cm wide collared neck above and a ring base with a diameter of 11.5 cm below. The mouth has an external diameter of 15.4–15.8 cm and an internal diameter of 14–14.4 cm, narrowing inside to 13.4–13.8 cm before it widens to the shoulder. At the mouth the thickness is 8–9 mm, in the main body it is 10–11 mm. The internal diameter of the body varies between 19.1 and 19.6 cm.[2] The internal height of the jar is 42.6 cm—and 41.4 cm at the centre, since the central part is raised *c.* 12 mm from the bottom. The hollow base leaves 14 mm of air space above the floor.

The jar has three pierced ledge handles on the shoulder. The handles are 65 mm wide at their base, and protrude 15 mm outwards from the jar body. The dimension of the holes is 2 × 2, 4 × 2, and 4 × 3 mm respectively. One of the pierced holes was filled with soil that was removed for sampling in June 2009.

The circular layers of clay from the potter's hand (the ribs) are visible at the lower part, creating a pattern of 22 circles on the lower 18 cm of the jar. The outer surface is smooth, the jar seems to have received some kind of glazing ('white wash' or 'slip'). Close to the base there is a bulge from the time of manufacture, created by the thumb of the potter carrying the jar to its place of drying in the sun before firing.

There are large cracks in the bottom, which were strengthened by pitch from the outside and some glue added on the inside. The glue seems modern. The repair was done before the jar reached Allegro, who reported: 'It was quite intact, apart from a small hole near the bottom sealed with pitch' (Allegro 1964, 86). There are deposits on the outside, caused by wet dung or mud splattering onto the jar (see Taylor's article, p. 393). The jar is similar in form to de Vaux's type 8 (GQ8–9, found in Caves 2 and 3; *DJD* 3:Plate V; cf. jar no. 42 from Cave 1, *DJD* 1:14–15, Fig. 12).

During examination in 2009 Roman Schütz noted a letter written in ink on the inside, 12 cm below the top of the jar. This letter has been identified as a late Herodian *kap*, is 14 mm high and positioned upright. Such a letter written on the inside of a Qumran jar is without parallel.

---

[1] I am indebted to Jodi Magness and Joan Taylor for useful responses on this chapter.

[2] At 10 cm from the top of the jar, the external diameter is 21.6 cm and the internal one 19.4–19.6 cm. 20 cm from the top, the external diameter is 21.6 and the internal one 19.4–19.6 cm. 27 cm from the top, at the most narrow part of the body, the external diameter is 20.7 cm and the internal one 19.1–19.8 cm.

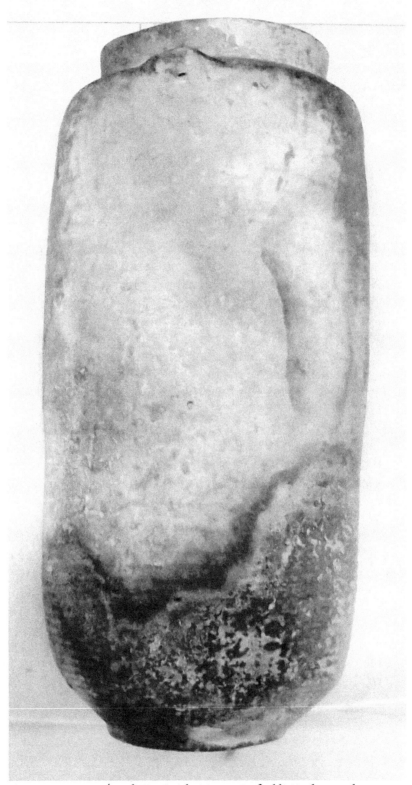

Figure 86. *MS 1655/1. Schøyen jar showing area of additional water damage not on the jar when it was in the hands of Allegro*
(Photo: Joan Taylor)

Figure 87. Schøyen jar interior inscribed with letter kap
(Photo: Roman Schütz)

B. Possible Provenance

The place of finding and odyssey of this jar before Kando sold it to John Allegro in 1953 remains uncertain.[3] When questioned by Martin Schøyen in 1993 about the provenance of the two Allegro jars, Kando reported that both these and the two sold to Eliezer Sukenik by Feidi Salahi came from the cave later designated Cave 1.

According to Jan Gunneweg, INAA analysis of a sample from the Schøyen jar identified clay from the Beer Sheba region. The more recent analysis of Matthew Boulanger found a match with pottery from the northern Negev, from sites such as Beer Sheba and Arad.[4] Seen together, the analyses by Gunneweg, Boulanger, and Ira Rabin suggest that this jar was made in the northern Negev and at a certain time was brought to the Dead Sea region. Rabin's analysis of sand still present in one of the pierced handles did not match sands of the Dead Sea region, whereas it would fit the loess of the northern Negev. However, the results could also match other regions such as northern Israel. Rabin tends towards the option that the jar was found in the Negev sometime in the twentieth century, afterwards brought to the Dead Sea region where it remained for at least some years (cf. minerals from the southern Dead Sea atmosphere on the exterior surface), and then passed through the hands of the Bedouin and Kando, to be sold to Allegro as a 'Cave 1 jar'. Based on a comparison with other Qumran jars, Joan Taylor argues that we are possibly dealing with a scroll jar from Cave 1 or Cave 2. Cave 2 was cave discovered by the Bedouin early in 1952—a year before Kando sold this jar and its companion to Allegro as 'Cave 1 jars'.

[3] Allegro sold it through Sotheby's in London 11 November, 1963 (lot 72) to H.M. Serota, Chicago, who again sold it to the Los Angeles dealer Fayez Barakat in 1987. It is mentioned in the 1989 catalogue of *Masterpieces in the Barakat Collection* as PF 1123. The jar then passed through the hands of Leonard Berman, Los Angeles (1991–92) and David Goldstein, Los Angeles (1992–93). Through the mediation of Fayez Barakat it was bought by The Schøyen Collection in March 1993. The jar is mentioned in Allegro 1956, 77, and illustrated in Brooke 1996, frames 10 (B10–C10), AQ, pots 9–19.

[4] The distance from Arad to Qumran is relatively short—58 km as the crow flies, and probably three times that distance on foot, which would equal 4–6 days walk. There was a direct trade route from Arad to the Dead Sea, protected by a series of fortresses.

Because of the 1948 wars and the subsequent political borders between Israel and the Jordanian-held West Bank, the chances that a jar could have been moved from the Negev into Kando's hands in Bethlehem during the period 1948–1953 are slim (and Kando was not active as an antiquities dealer before 1948). If indeed discovered in the South in modern times, the jar must have been found substantially earlier in the South and brought to the Dead Sea region before 1948. Rabin does not exclude the option that the jar was brought to Qumran in antiquity with sand staying in the pierced handles from the place of manufacture. The cylindrical shape of this jar suggests links of some sort to Qumran in the first century. With two or three exceptions such cylindrical jars have only been found in the Dead Sea region.[5] This is also Gunneweg's preferred opinion.

In the following I survey scholarship on cylindrical jars to place the Schøyen jar in context.[6]

C. Cylindrical Jars

Similar jars with wide openings and bowl-formed lids were found in excavations at Khirbet Qumran and Jericho. They have been designated 'archive jars', 'cylindrical storage jars', or given the more neutral label 'cylindrical jars' (Roland de Vaux used 'jarre' or 'jarre cylindrique', *DJD* 3:13). During de Vaux's 1949 excavations of Cave 1 he recovered sherds representing at least fifty cylindrical jars and the bowl-shaped lids that covered them (de Vaux 1949, 591). During the excavations of Khirbet Qumran in 1951 and 1953–56 many examples of cylindrical jars were unearthed. Some of these were sunk into the floors and were covered with round stone slabs or plaques.[7]

Cylindrical jars were found in a number of caves, including caves without scroll remains, such as Cave 29 (personal communication from Dennis Mizzi). Of the more than 150 cylindrical jars estimated by de Vaux as having derived from the caves or Khirbet Qumran, only 47 have been registered and 25 of these are complete (most are kept in the collections of the Rockefeller Museum). Humbert and Gunneweg count around 100 restored jars together with bottoms of unrestored jars (Gunneweg and Balla 2003, 28). According to Stephen J. Pfann (2002, 170), these jars vary from 46.5 to 75.5 cm in internal height. With its height of 43 cm the Schøyen jar belongs on the lower edge of this spectrum. According to Pfann (2002, 170–73) the larger cylindrical jars were too high to store scrolls and would have been designed to store foodstuffs or liquids. Taylor, however, argues that small scrolls well packed in their wrappers could be stacked on top of each other in such a jar (personal communication). In contemporary Jericho somewhat similar jars either have a height of *c.* 55 cm or are, measuring 23–28 cm high (Bar-Nathan 2002, 23).

Following de Vaux, Rachel Bar-Nathan differentiates between cylindrical jars and ovoid storage jars; the bodies of the latter are more curved and bag-shaped. Ovoid storage jars are common in Hasmonaean Jericho and contemporary Qumran (de Vaux's stratum 1b), suggesting commercial or other links between these two communities (Bar-Nathan 2002, 27).[8] According to Bar-Nathan, the cylindrical jar with a rounded shoulder is found at Herodian Jericho, but is more typical of Qumran. It appears from the

---

[5] One or two cylindrical jars were found in Qalandiya, stemming from a late Second Temple agricultural settlement (Magen 2004, 85, Plate 3.7, noted in Bar-Nathan 2006b, 275 and Magness 2006, 662–63). Another cylindrical jar (without specifications) was found in a second century AD tomb in Quailba (ancient Abila) in Jordan (Magness 2006, 662).

[6] For another recent survey, see Schofield 2009, 229–36.

[7] *DJD* 1:figs 2; 3:6–11; *DJD* 3:figs 2-4; 6:1, 2, 5, 7, 9–12; *DJD* 6:figs 5:2–3; 6:12, 15–17; Humbert and Chambon 1994, *passim*. For a good survey, see Magness 2004, 151–3.

[8] For further links between Qumran and Jericho, cf. the ostracon found at Qumran in 1995, documenting a deed from the district of Jericho from 'Year 2' (probably year 2 of the First Jewish Revolt, *i.e.* AD 67). See *DJD* 36:497–507; Yardeni 1997. An ovoid jar without handles found in the Jericho excavations, JER 102, was made of clay from Qumran (Gunneweg and Balla 2006, 106).

end of the first century BC and stays in use until the destruction of Qumran and Masada (cf. Magness 2004, 154–55). Bar-Nathan asserts that the primary purpose of the larger cylindrical jars was storage of written documents. For this theory to be proven the inner contents of more jars would need to be analyzed, provided they have not been cleansed. Bar-Nathan thinks the precise locations where such jars were found point to use as archive jars: corners of rooms (Qumran and the twin palaces at Jericho) or wall niches (the industrial area at Jericho). From potsherds found in the Zealot occupational strata at Masada, Bar-Nathan reconstructs both ovoid and cylindrical jars (Bar-Nathan 2006, 67–71).

The Jericho 'cylindrical jars' are in fact less cylindrical than those found at Qumran. They are more curved downwards toward the base and closer to the earlier ovoid type (see illustrations in Bar-Nathan 2002, 25–26). Furthermore most of the Jericho jars have handles. Gunneweg questions Bar-Nathan's view that cylindrical jars similar to the Qumran type have been found in Jericho or Masada. Only one sherd with a loop handle from Jericho is adduced as example; it does not necessarily reflect a cylindrical jar (Gunneweg and Balla 2006, 105–6, with photo of this sherd).

Allegro remarks that the Qumran cylindrical jars were practically unique in shape and size, generally between 53 and 69 cm high. He expands, 'For Palestinian ceramics these jars were unique', and 'Marks of turning are clearly visible on the sides, and the deep firing has given the pottery a hard, almost metallic quality, with a characteristic rose-pink or grey colouring' (Allegro 1964, 86–87).

With the finds at Qumran, Jericho, Masada, and the jar from En Gedi discussed by Gunneweg, the distribution of ovoid and cylindrical storage jars with large openings in Judaea is limited to the Dead Sea region, and genuinely cylindrical jars to Qumran only (Gunneweg, personal communication). These jars may have two, three or no handles. The two jars from Qalandiya are the only exception to this rule.

Referring to Michniewicz 2009, Jodi Magness recently concluded that all the cylindrical jars and most other pottery found at Khirbet Qumran and the caves were made locally in Qumran from clay collected from different sources in the region (Magness 2014).

D. Storing Scrolls in Jars

The practice of storing scrolls in jars may go back to biblical times, cf. Jer 32.14, 'Take these documents, both the sealed and unsealed copies of the deed of purchase, and put them in a clay jar so they will last a long time.' According to the *Testament of Moses* (first century AD) Moses should store the writings revealed to him in earthenware jars, so that they could be preserved until the end-times (*T. Mos.* 1.16–18).

This tradition was not unique to Israel, and is documented in Egypt. Two jars containing a family archive from the second century BC were unearthed at Deir el-Medineh in 1905. These jars were 39 cm high with a diameter of 23–24.5 cm. The lids were attached to the jars' three handles with straps, tied with the concave side of the lids facing upwards. The papyrus scrolls of this portable family archive, written in Greek and Demotic, were dated between 188 and 101 BC (Milik 1950; Pfann 2002, 168; Lönnqvist and Lönnqvist 2011, 476–79). The Deir el-Medineh jars are even more cylindrical than their Qumran counterparts but lack a ring base. In another location at Deir el-Medineh, a family archive containing 32 Demotic papyri from 317–217 BC was unearthed in two jars in 1922 (Lönnqvist and Lönnqvist 2011, 479). Ovoid jars containing Aramaic documents and Greek family archives from the fourth-third centuries BC were unearthed in Elephantine (Rubenson 1907, 4, 5, 34). Aramaic texts from the sixth century BC have been found at Saqqara and Hermopolis (Lönnqvist and Lönnqvist 2011, 480). Lönnqvist and Lönnqvist suggest that the Qumran community learned the practice of using jars as document archives from Ptolemaic Egypt (2011, 483–87). With the late dating of the cylindrical jars at Qumran such a line of influence seems unlikely.

The fourth century AD Nag Hammadi codices were hidden away in a jar (see Robinson 1979). This jar was smashed by the finder, but the dish-formed lid remains preserved in The Schøyen Collection.[9] When it was found the jar was sealed with tar with the concave (dished) side of the lid facing upward, different from Qumran practice.

The Chester Beatty papyri were found in 1928–1930 in three jars buried in the sand, probably close to Afroditopolis in Egypt, the location of the earliest monastery of the desert fathers (Horton 2004, 157–58; Sagrusten 2014, 84–85). The Bodmer papyri were found in a jar close by in 1952 (Robinson 2011, 72; Sagrusten 2014, 103–20). Origen's report about Hebrew and Greek scrolls found in a jar in a cave close to Jericho may relate to the same 'collection' we know as the scrolls from Qumran. In contrast, patriarch Timotheos' report from AD 795 of scrolls in Hebrew script found in a cave close to Jericho does not mention jars (Braun 1901, 305–6). Also the Talmud (*b. Meg.* 26b) mentions the custom of hiding worn-out biblical scrolls in clay jars with reference to Jer 32.14.

E. Storage Jars and *Yaḥad* Purity

Large jars used for storing food would usually have two handles to enable pouring, tipping out, and carrying (by one or two men). Jars with three pierced handles (such as the Schøyen jar) are exceptional. They were made for a specific purpose, to enable the lid to be fixed with straps. According to Gunneweg (personal communication), cylindrical jars from Qumran usually lack handles with the exception of a few (with either two or three handles) that also have a more bulging body. If a jar such as one of these without handles (or with three handles) contained scrolls, one man could easily carry it alone. The tallest of the Qumran scrolls, the *Hodayot* scroll, was *c.* 36 cm high. This would well fit the height of the Schøyen jar of 43 cm and other relatively small jars from Qumran. Gunneweg tends to designate only the cylindrical jars without handles as real 'scroll jars' (Gunneweg and Balla 2006, 105), while Pfann and Eshel (personal communication) include jars with three pierced handles as archive jars, cf. the two archive jars with three handles from Deir el-Medineh. Allegro notes as a characteristic of the smaller jars that their handles were 'pierced with holes through which string could be passed to retain the lid in position' (1964, 87). According to the 1961 testimony of the Bedouin about Cave 1, they found 'about ten jars ... some of which had covers on top and some without covers'. They removed two empty jars with covers, 'each jar and each cover had three handles' (Trever 1977, 192; Kiraz 2005, 91).

Pfann (2002) argues that most of these jars, and certainly the larger ones, were intended for tithing agricultural produce. The letter *ṭet* incised before firing into jar no 10 from Cave 3 (3Q10, Humbert and Gunneweg 2004, 376–77) probably designated the contents as טבל, produce from which the priestly and levitical dues had not yet been set aside.[10] To ensure the purity of a jar and its contents for priestly consumption according to Qumran *halakha*, special jars had to be manufactured for priestly tithes. These jars were designed to contain either one, two, or three *seahs* of produce (15, 30, or 45 litres; cf. *DJD* 3:37–41; Pfann 2002, 175–76). The volume of the Schøyen jar is 11 litres, less than one *seah*. Since jars produced to contain priestly tithes were halakhically pure they could subsequently be used to store sacred scrolls. The meaning of the *kap* written in ink in late Herodian script inside the Schøyen jar is uncertain. *Kap*'s numerical value of 20 may provide a clue. Joan Taylor suggests (p. 423) that this *kap*

---

[9] MS 1804/7. For photographs, see www.schoyencollection.com, collection 15.1.

[10] Cf. *m. Maʿaś.* 4.11 'If a vessel was found on which was written a *qof*, it is *Qorban* ... if a *ṭet*, it is *tevel*, if *taw*, it is *terumah*' (priestly tithe from produce); *b. Ber.* 35b 'the *tevel* is not subject to tithes, until it is brought home'. The *ṭet* may alternatively signify טוב 'good', *i.e.* high quality wine, or טהור 'pure' (Lemaire 2003, 376–77). A storage jar from Cave 6 bears an inscription in charcoal, '2 *seah* and 7 *log*' (ibid. 374).

could refer to the unit of weight talent or *kikkar* (כבר). The heavy silver talent contained 43.6 kg, the light one 21.8 kg, while the Mishnaic *kikkar* contained 20.4 kg.[11] One may compare the late Herodian *ʾalep* written in black charcoal on the shoulder of a bag-shaped jar found by Joseph Patrich in a cave just north of Cave 11 in 1984–1985 (Patrich 1994, 90).[12]

Jodi Magness asserts that ovoid and cylindrical jars may originally have been designed for storing documents and that the sectarians extended their use to storage of food and liquids for purity reasons (for the following, see Magness 2004, 151–68). The opposite line of development seems more logical to this writer.

The usual Judaean storage jar of the Roman and Byzantine period is bag-shaped with a tall vertical neck, often with a slightly everted rim, a relative narrow mouth, and ring handles on the shoulders. These jars were used for both foodstuffs and liquids. The high neck prevented spillage (when tipping or pouring), and the mouth could easily be corked or sealed.

The ovoid or cylindrical type from the Dead Sea region differs fundamentally in shape. Instead of a rounded base, they have a disc or ring base. Unlike bag-shaped jars, the ovoid jars are wider at the top than at the bottom. Their most distinctive feature is a short neck and wide mouth. The bowl-shaped lid was designed to cover the wide mouth of these jars. The ring or disc base enabled these jars to stand solidly on their own. Their short necks and wide mouths would not have prevented spillage and could not have been easily sealed.

Magness suggests that the peculiar form of these jars could be explained by the purity regulations of the *Yaḥad*. CD XI 9 prescribes 'he should not open a plastered vessel on the Sabbath'. Jars were usually sealed with a cork of clay that dried and formed a seal. To open the jar, the clay seal had to be broken. The features of the ovoid and cylindrical jars enabled them to be opened on the Sabbath according to sectarian *halakha*. Furthermore, according to sectarian *halakha*, a cork of wet clay that dried would contaminate pure foodstuff in the jar below, cf. 11QT^a XLIX 5–10: food that was moistened by liquids would be susceptible to impurity. The peculiar bowl-shaped lid would also draw any moisture (dew, rain, bird and bat droppings) that fell on such a jar down the outer sides of the jar.

Furthermore, with the Sadducees (and against Pharisaic and rabbinic *halakha*) the sectarians ruled that impurity could follow a liquid stream upwards if one poured liquids from a ritually pure jar into a defiled one (4QMMT B 55-58; *m. Yad.* 4.7, cf. *DJD* 10:161–62, 188). For the purity-obsessed sectarians, bag-shaped jars could easily be rendered impure when tipping or pouring their contents. However, the short neck and wide mouth of ovoid and cylindrical jars allowed the contents to be scooped out using a cup, bowl or dipper. In this way the risk of contaminating the contents were minimized. Moreover, the wide mouth allowed their contents to be easily inspected.

Pure food was important in the *Yaḥad*. Only after one year of probation was a new member allowed to partake of the pure food and drink of the Community (1QS VI 16–21). Magness suggests that the jars with their peculiar shape served as markers to those who were allowed or denied contact with them. The sinking of cylindrical jars into the floors at Khirbet Qumran is unique to this purity-oriented milieu. If such jars had been generally regarded as suitable for the storage of food and drink, we should expect to find them in large numbers at other sites—but we do not. For Magness the high number of sherds of cylindrical jars found in the caves demonstrates that the Community stored quantities of pure food and drink there.

Bar-Nathan and Magness agree that the discovery of similar jars at Herodian Jericho attests to sectarian presence there, or at least that of a group with similar purity concerns. Magness further asserts

---

[11] www.jewishencyclopedia.com/articles/9316-kikkar (accessed 3 June, 2014). The weight of the contents of the jar would be dependent on what substance it contained.

[12] This cave contained pottery from the late first century AD and was probably occupied by Jewish refugees during the First Revolt.

that remnants of cylindrical and ovoid jars in Zealot contexts at Masada might support Yadin's hypothesis that some Qumranites joined the Zealots at Masada when their own settlement was taken by the Romans in AD 68 (1966, 173–74). Gunneweg disagrees and points to a substantial difference between the ovoid jars from Jericho and Masada and the more cylindrical ones found in Qumran. Only one cylindrical jar found at Qumran was made of clay from Jericho and it is less cylindrical in shape than other jars from Qumran.

Ovoid and cylindrical storage jars with large mouths have so far been found only in the Dead Sea region. *Pace* Magness, it seems likely that these jars originally were designed for foodstuffs and liquids and that archival use represents a secondary development. The peculiarly cylindrical jars are so far found only at Qumran and should primarily be ascribed to *Yaḥad* contexts in Qumran and elsewhere.

The cylindrical jars appear at Qumran only from the end of the first century BC onwards. The site was settled by *Yaḥad* members from some time in the first century BC.[13] This type of jar may have been developed within the *Yaḥad* during their stay at Qumran in the process of refining their purity customs. The pattern of existing ovoid and close-to-cylindrical jars from the Jericho region was refined to fulfil the purity needs of the sectarians.

Magness suggests that the cylindrical design served to set apart the clean food and drink for *Yaḥad* members. This appealing idea would explain the peculiar habit of sinking large jars into the floors of the settlement. Further, many large cylindrical jars were found in caves without scrolls. *Yaḥad* members could have produced their jars in Hebron and Jericho and brought them as ritually pure to Qumran—this would be a condition for full members of the *Yaḥad* to receive foodstuffs for consumption. Vessels made by non-*Yaḥad* members would be suspected of impurity according to *Yaḥad halakha*. And earthen vessels that had been rendered impure could not be purified but would be smashed and discarded.

F. Concluding Remarks

Agricultural products such as wine and oil must have been brought to Qumran from outside. This factor could explain the presence in Qumran of pottery from Jericho and Hebron and some items from Jerusalem, Edom and the Negev. The pottery originating elsewhere supports the view that the *Yaḥad* should not be confined to Qumran. The *Yaḥad* predated the settlement by at least two generations and probably continued to have members in other locations (cf. Elgvin 2005; Schofield 2009, 42–67, 266–81).

The analysis of the exterior surface of the Schøyen jar shows that this jar was made far from the Dead Sea (cf. the low values of bromine and potassium on the original surface), but that it had spent time in storage in the Dead Sea region (cf. the high values of bromine and potassium on the surface). If the Schøyen jar should indeed be connected to the *Yaḥad,* these results suggest that, in some cases at least, *Yaḥad* members brought ready-made pottery to their centre at Qumran instead of bringing raw clay for making it there. Gunneweg suggests this was the rule. According to Magness, only fine wares (such as *terra sigillata*) and amphoras containing imported wine would be transported. In most cases it was more cost-effective to transport clay than fired vessels. Such jars would have to be transported to Qumran by pack animal down paths along steep cliffs—an expensive alternative that would have caused much breakage along the way.

---

[13] Coins found in the tower suggest that the tower was in use from the time of Jannaeus (103–76) onwards. Pfann has identified a cooking pot from the second century BC among those found by de Vaux (personal communication from Pfann, this dating has been accepted by Eshel and Magness). However, one pot from the second century does not prove a second century settlement at the site. While Magness (2002, 63–66) suggests a sectarian settlement from early in the first century BC, Taylor (2012, 93–94, 99, 239–42, 251–61) argues that a fortified settlement from the time of Jannaeus was converted to a sectarian settlement only under Herod, around 34 BC.

The presence in Qumran of two cooking pots made of clay from the Negev, and possibly a cylindrical jar with the same place of origin, suggests the *Yaḥad* had members from this region also, cf. Philo's assertion that the Essenes live scattered around cities and villages in Judaea (*Apology of the Jews* 1 in *Hypothetica*; *Good Person* 76). The evidence from the pottery suggests clusters of *Yaḥad* members in Jericho and the highlands between Jerusalem and Hebron, and perhaps a small group close to Beersheba.

The provenance of the Schøyen jar cannot be proven. The connection asserted with Cave 1 has not been confirmed by the analyses performed by Gunneweg, Boulanger, and Rabin. A production place in the south seems most probable. Whether surface traces of a Dead Sea environment represent a stay there in antiquity or only in modern times is an unsettled issue. The 'Qumranic' cylindrical shape would make this jar a unique sample from the Negev. Magness notes that transporting clay was easier and more cost effective than transporting ready-made pottery on rough tracks. But to transport clay all the way from the Negev to a *Yaḥad* centre at Qumran would be difficult to explain. Ceramic items made from Negev clay and found at Qumran were more likely produced in the south and brought to Qumran. Taylor's suggestion that the jar Kando sold to Allegro in 1953 (the Schøyen jar) was possibly found by the Bedouin in Cave 1 or Cave 2 seems best to concur with the 'map' of the ceramic assemblage found in the Qumran caves as well as the deposits identified on the jar.

G. Appendix. Four Potsherds, MS 1655/3abcd

The Schøyen Collection holds four potsherds, which were collected from the soil at Khirbet Qumran by William Brownlee around 1950, before de Vaux started his excavations in 1951. All four are covered by 'white wash' of varying colour shades, a final polish typical of pottery from Khirbet Qumran and the Qumran caves.

MS 1655/3a, 11.2 × 9.4 cm, is slightly curved and probably preserves part of a dish. MS 1655/3b, 6.6 × 5.3 cm, preserves a section of a bowl, with decorated circular lines on both sides: there are seven partly preserved circles on the inner side, six on the outer, which is painted in a beige-grey colour. MS 1655/3c, 10.3 × 5.8 cm, preserves the base and the lower part of the body of a dish or wide bowl. One half of the circular base, with a diameter of 6.3 cm, is extant. The moderate curvature of the body points to a relatively flat dish. MS 1655/3d, 8.0 × 4.2 cm, preserves part of the rim of a jar. The rim extends over the shoulder of the jar, creating a profiled edge 'overhanging' the shoulder.

Clay samples from MS 1655/3c have been subjected to INAA testing by Jan Gunneweg and Marta Balla as well as Matthew Boulanger. Gunneweg concludes that this bowl or dish was made locally in Qumran. It matched four ceramic pieces that he had tested and allocated to his Chemical Group I, with the local chemical fingerprint of Qumran. According to Boulanger's more recent analysis, this sherd is chemically most similar to Nabataean decorated fine wares from the southern Negev (*e.g.* Avdat) and the environs of Petra and Tawilan in Jordan, but local production in Qumran from clay similar to that of Petra cannot be excluded. Joan Taylor characterized the vessel as more crudely made than Nabataean fine ware.

Figure 88.1. Potsherd MS 1655/3a.
Photo Torleif Elgvin (scale unknown)

Figure 88.2. Potsherd MS 1655/3b.
Photo Bruce Zuckerman

Figure 88.3. *Potsherd MS 1655/3c.*
Photo Torleif Elgvin (scale unknown)

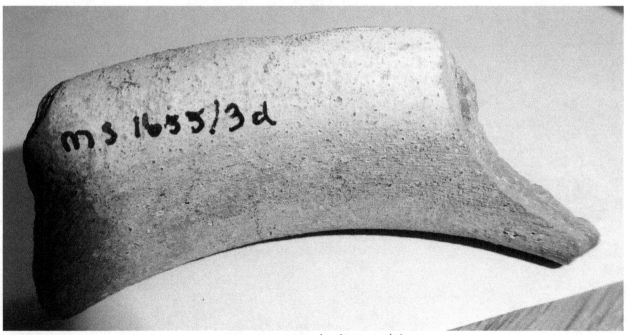

Figure 88.4a. *Potsherd MS 1655/3d.*
Photo Torleif Elgvin (scale unknown)

Figure 88.4b. Potsherd MS 1655/3d.
Photo Torleif Elgvin (scale unknown)

XLIII

Incense Altar from Naḥal Ḥever? MS 1655/4[1]

Torleif Elgvin

A. Introduction

In the early 1990s Stephen Goranson published the larger bronze inkwell from The Schøyen Collection (Goranson 1992; 1994, cf. p. 451). Goranson did not mention that the inkwell was reported found together with a bronze incense altar. According to Khalil Iskander Shahin (Kando), these two items were found together by the Bedouin at Khirbet Qumran some time before Roland de Vaux and G. Lankester Harding started their preliminary excavations in November 1951. Kando sold these two artefacts to John Allegro in 1953.[2] Both pieces have been the property of The Schøyen Collection since 1994.

The incense altar and further details on the inkwell were presented in a joint publication by the author and Stephen J. Pfann (Elgvin and Pfann 2002). At that time we were open to the possibility that these items could indeed be surface finds from Qumran. If so, they should probably be dated to Period III. *Pace* de Vaux, we suggested that the remains of Period III reflected an agricultural settlement from the period between the two Jewish Revolts. I now offer another option as more probable—that these two bronze artefacts were found by the Bedouin in Naḥal Ḥever in 1952, and further that they represent Nabataean workmanship. Elaborate bronze vessels were found by the archaeologists in the Cave of the Letters in Naḥal Ḥever during the 1960–1961 expeditions (Yadin 1963, 42–63). The fine artistry represented by the inkwell and the altar in The Schøyen Collection seems to fit the context of Naḥal Ḥever better than that of Qumran Period III. Kando's report of a surface find at Khirbet Qumran around 1950 is also questionable, since these fairly exquisite artefacts almost certainly would have been spotted and removed before 1951 were they in open view on the ground. Furthermore, Khirbet Qumran was not connected to the finds in the caves, neither by Bedouin nor archaeologists, before de Vaux started his excavations there in December 1951.

[1] Thanks are due to Seymour Gitin, Hanan Eshel (ל″ז), Shimon Dar, Dennis Mizzi, and Stephen J. Pfann for their helpful response, to Alegre Savariego (IAA), David Mevurach and Yael Israeli (Israel Museum), and to Avshalom Zemer (Haifa Museum) for their kind assistance.

[2] John Allegro sold these two items to an anonymous private collector in 1963. Subsequent owners were Fayez Barakat, Los Angeles, 1975; Mathias Komor, New York, 1975; an anonymous collector until 1992; David Goldstein, Los Angeles, 1992. In 1993 Kando confirmed that the inkwell and the altar were found by the Bedouin at Qumran around 1950 and that these two items were subsequently sold to Allegro (personal communication to Martin Schøyen).

B. Physical Description

The incense altar and the inkwell are both beautiful pieces of bronze casting with green patina. Both items were chemically tested in November 1996. The composition of the bronze in both of them is close to identical.[3] Neither of them shows patterns of deterioration, although the altar has corroded more than the inkwell.

The squarely constructed altar is 67 mm high, with a weight of 110 g. It has four horns—one on each corner, with four small stepped ornamental elevations between the horns. The distance between the horns varies from 39 to 44 mm. The upper part is wider than the base, which measures 36 × 37 mm. At its narrowest, the slim middle section is 16–17 mm wide. Nine circular recesses decorate the middle part, six of them form three bands. The horns and elevations are *c.* 3 mm thick, and somewhat thinner at the tip. Relatively large quantities of residue of burned incense are preserved on the platform (a layer of 1–3 mm).

C. Incense Altars from the Ancient Near East

In the Ancient Near East 'the four-horned incense altar had an intrinsic quality of sanctity, an attribute symbolically transmitted to the physical space it occupied, even when that space was not already defined as a sacred area by conventional standards' (Gitin 2002, 96). Iron Age excavations in the Levant unearthed large, horned incense altars of stone (Stern 1982, 182–95, 234–35). A different type is found in Mesopotamia of the late Assyrian, Babylonian and Persian periods (from the late seventh to the fourth century): these altars are made of terracotta, decorated and formed as small chests standing on four legs.[4] Altars from Judaea from the Persian period show developments from the Mesopotamian type (Lachish alone revealed more than 200), but are made of limestone.[5] Ephraim Stern assumes Phoenician manufacture for all these,[6] and suggests that the decoration reflects a local school. The decorated altars cover the period from the late sixth to the fourth century, while undecorated altars extend from the late Iron Age to the Hellenistic period. Miniature stone altars are also known from South Arabia, dated from the fourth to the first centuries BC.[7]

Excavations at North Saqqara in Egypt unearthed two hammered, horned bronze altars from the fourth to the second centuries BC, the first 78 cm high, the second 15 cm.[8] A tiny bronze altar with a height of 25 mm was unearthed in the Sepphoris excavations. This altar was found in a cistern together with a bronze bowl and remnants of a bronze bull figurine. The cistern was abandoned in the mid-

[3] Inkwell: 55–68% copper, 23–39% lead, 5–8% tin. Altar: 58–62% copper, 35–40% lead, 1–2% tin. Thanks to Helge Semb at The Norwegian Technical University, Trondheim, who performed these tests 11 November, 1996. For a physical description of this inkwell, see p. 451.

[4] Some of these altars preserve remnants of horns that have deteriorated. Stern pictures one Mesopotamian altar with four two-stepped horns, similar to the elevations of the altar discussed here (Stern 1982, 195, Fig. 313, no. 21).

[5] Gitin 1992, 46. A single example from Megiddo is of basalt. A Lachish altar dated to the fifth or fourth century carried the word לבונה 'incense' (Gitin 1992, 46). Scholars disagree on the provenance of this altar: Jewish, Arab, Edomite, and Phoenician have been proposed.

[6] He excludes a Jewish provenance due to 'what is known of the nature of the Jewish ritual in that period' (Stern 1982, 194). Jacob Milgrom would differ on this issue (see below).

[7] See *ANET*, items 579 and 581: two south-Arabian altars dated between the third and the first centuries BCE, 90 and 80 mm high respectively. Both are square troughs on four legs.

[8] Green 1987, 27–29, items 52 and 53. I am indebted to Seymour Gitin for this reference.

fourth century AD. James F. Strange asserts that these items were used in Seraphis worship. The Sepphoris altar is different in style from the one featured for discussion here.[9]

D. Miniature Bronze Altars

The Schøyen altar belongs to a particular subgroup of oriental incense altars. Six such miniature bronze altars are known, remarkably similar in style, found in the Levant and dating to Roman or early Byzantine periods. Three of these altars were found in excavations. The first was found in 1964 at Givᶜat Katzenelson near Nahariyah, a site with graves from the Roman and Byzantine periods (height 63 mm, width at the top 43 mm, base 34–37 mm, weight 97 g).[10] This altar is hollow. Four holes below the elevations were used to carry a platform (which is not preserved), two horns have been broken. The second altar comes from an Ituraean temple at Har Senaim (Mount Hermon, excavated 1983–89; height 68 mm, width at the top 45 mm, weight 127 g), probably dated between the first and third centuries AD.[11] The third was found close to a hoard of iron tools in a dwelling close to the synagogue of the Jewish village Sumaqa on Mount Carmel, a site excavated 1983–95 (height 63 mm, width at the top 45–50 mm, base 40 mm, weight 115 g).[12] A fourth altar was found in the sea outside the Carmel (height 58 mm, width at the top 37.5–39 mm, base 39–41 mm, weight 111 g).[13] A fifth, of unknown provenance, was acquired by the Palestine Archaeological Museum (now the Rockefeller Museum) around 1930 (height 68–70 mm, width at the top 41–47 mm, base 38–39 mm, weight 141 g).[14]

Shimon Dar, the excavator of Har Senaim and Sumaqa, dates all these altars to the first and second centuries AD. This date receives some support from a ceramic altar of similar style from Jerash from the early second century[15] and a limestone altar from Mount Carmel dated to the second or third century.[16] The finds from Sumaqa, Senaim and Givᶜat Katzenelson reflect use of such altars up to the fourth and perhaps fifth century.

---

[9] It has four short legs that form an arch on each side. Above each arch is a round opening. The flat top is slightly larger than the base (Watkins 1996, 173; Strange 1996, 345).

[10] Israel Museum no. 66–604. Excavated by Yael Israeli and Miriam Mann. As far as Israeli recalls, it derives from a grave from the Byzantine period.

[11] Dar 1993, 63–64, 267; Dar 1994, 123–30. The altar consists of two castings, attached to one another with a nail. Its small receptacle contained signs of soot and shared organic matter. The altar was found on a paved courtyard outside the lower temple. Senaim was a cult centre from the second century BC to the fifth century AD that flourished in the Roman period, from the first to the third century (Dar 1993, 82–86). A small circular incense burner of basalt (170 × 100 mm) was found not far from the altar.

[12] In the same house, built in the third century and destroyed in the early fifth century, was found an oil lamp decorated with a seven-branched menorah (Sumaqa was founded in the second century and flourished in the fourth).

[13] Now in the Haifa Museum (pictured in Dar 1994, 129). This museum also exhibits a limestone incense altar from the Carmel with a certain resemblance to the bronze altars discussed here. The limestone altar is approximately double the size of the bronze altars. It has four horns and four elevations, and a zigzag decoration around the body. It is dated to the second or third century (Yeivin and Finkelstein 1999, 32).

[14] Rockefeller Museum no. I 10734. See Iliffe 1945, 18 and plate VI.

[15] Iliffe saw the Rockefeller bronze altar as the model for the ceramic altar with eight horns (one damaged and one missing), deriving from a potter's workshop in Jerash from the early second century AD, excavated in 1933–34. The base of this altar is missing. The height of the preserved part is 80 mm. The horns were cut with a knife, and the upper part of the altar was painted black.

[16] Dar 1999, 65. According to Dar altars of this type were common in the Ancient Roman East. My suggestion that the Schøyen altar was found in Naḥal Ḥever would support Dar's dating of the three others to the first and second centuries. A similar altar from Egypt (more simple in style and 10.2 cm high) with a flat base and a high lid (11 cm) was offered for sale January 11, 2016, at an electronic auction of Classical Numismatic Group.

All six altars have (or had) four horns tipped with knobs and four somewhat lower elevations between the horns. The Sumaqa altar is the exception, with its four horns and two elevations. The altars are decorated with incised circles. The Rockefeller altar and the Ituraean one are of exactly the same design, and probably come from the same workshop. The hollow altar from Nahariyah is of a somewhat different design from the others. The Schøyen altar is the most beautiful one, carefully made and well preserved. It is the only one with a stepped design.

E. Incense Altars in Israelite Cult

Were incense altars used by Jewish inhabitants in places such as Qumran, En Gedi, or Mahoza (such as Babatha, whose archive was found in the Cave of the Letters)? Seymour Gitin and Jacob Milgrom have argued convincingly (*pace* Menahem Haran) that incense altars were used outside the Jerusalem temple.[17] According to Gitin, 46 horned limestone altars from the tenth to the seventh centuries have been found in the land of Israel, half of them at Israelite sites. Incense altars were found at Beersheba from the eighth and the sixth centuries BC (Gitin 2002). There was an incense altar in the Israelite sanctuary in Arad—according to the excavator Yohanan Aharoni this temple was established in the ninth century and dismantled in Hezekiah's time, these dates have been contested by other archaeologists. Jer 44.23 refers to ordinary Israelites, not just temple priests, burning incense. After the fall of the first temple, there are reports that Israelites continued to burn incense at the Temple Mount (Jer 41.5).

According to Milgrom, there was a continuous tradition in Israel of ritual incense burning throughout the Second Temple period.[18] This custom continued after the destruction of Herod's temple and at least to the ninth century. The references in *T. Levi* 3.5 and Rev 5.8 to incense burning in the heavenly temple probably reflect an earthly reality, and Revelation dates from after the fall of the temple. Rabbinic sources indicate that ritual incense burning was an accepted custom in Talmudic times that the sages, in spite of their scepticism to offering incense outside the temple precincts, did not dare to forbid.[19] In addition to the Talmudic evidence, there are also carvings and mosaics from early synagogues showing incense shovels.[20] To this archaeological evidence from Jewish sites one may now add the miniature bronze altar found in the Jewish village of Sumaqa. This extensive evidence suggests that, also in the period between the two Revolts, Jewish settlers in the Dead Sea region could have continued to observe a widespread Jewish custom and accompanied their prayers with incense.

F. Nabataean and Phoenician Design

The crow-step ornamentation of the Schøyen altar is reminiscent of Assyrian and Nabataean design. The stair motif belongs to Assyrian and Achaemenid architecture from the eighth to the fifth centuries, and was subsequently adopted by the Nabataeans. Crow-step ornamentation is particularly common in

---

[17] In Israel, according to Haran, incense was only burned in the Jerusalem temple (Haran 1960; Haran 1978, 235–41; Haran 1993). Cf. Gitin 1989; Gitin 1992; Milgrom 1979. On the incense altar and burning of incense in the temple, see *e.g.* Exod 30.1–10; 37.25–28; 1 Kgs 6.20–22; 7.48; 2 Chr 26.16.

[18] Milgrom 1979, 333–34. So also Finkelstein 1966, 654–60.

[19] Milgrom 1979, 334. Milgrom refers to *m. Zebaḥ.* 13.6; *t. Zebaḥ.* 12.4–5; *b. Ber.* 53a (which states that daughters of Israel use incense for magical purposes); *y. Meg.* 1.11; *y. ʿAbod. Zar.* 4.4; *Tanḥ. Aḥare Mot* 14 (ed. Buber, *Aḥare Mot* 9).

[20] See Shanks 1979: mosaics from Jerash (p. 41), Hamat Tiberias (p. 114), Bet Alpha (p. 113), Bet Shean (p. 129), a column capital from Capernaum (p. 66, this synagogue probably was built around AD 400). These images may reflect temple symbolism as well as contemporary customs.

the tomb facades of the first century AD at Petra (MacKenzie 1990, plates 5–19; Weber and Wenning 1997, 87–88; Browning 1980, 79–88).

A small step-designed ornamental piece of bronze was found in recent excavations of a Hellenistic temple-site from around the turn of the era at Omrit close to Banias (the place of the Augusteum built by Herod, *Ant.* 4.363), The artefact is hammered flat and measures 28 × 46 mm.[21] This Omrit parallel in cast bronze may support a first century date for our altar.

This ornamental style was also known in Phoenicia.[22] Renan asserts that this ancient design was preserved in Phoenicia until the beginning of the Byzantine period. The Assyrian crow-step ornamentation imitates the style of the Mesopotamian ziggurat, which symbolizes the (ascent to the) mountain of God. Altars with stepped elevations may preserve the memory of this ancient symbolism.[23] A horned altar with stepped elevations uses a plurality of iconic symbols in creating a sacred space for the worshippers.

The miniature incense altars discussed above preserve ancient Assyrian and Near Eastern design, kept alive in Phoenicia and northern Israel and among the Nabataeans. Five of these miniature bronze altars have simple triangular elevations between the horns. Their design may represent a simplification of the form of earlier stone altars. Alternatively, the crow-stepped Schøyen altar may preserve more details of the ancient model—similar in this regard to Nabataean architecture of the first century. This could suggest a find-place somewhere in the Dead Sea region or Jordan of today. The knobs at the end of the horns of the bronze altars have no parallel in earlier stone altars. Such knobs are easier to make in metal than in stone.

G. Function, Setting, and Provenance

Small-sized altars like those discussed here were probably made for domestic use or intended as votive gifts to a temple (as was probably the case with the one found at the Ituraean temple). One might be inclined to ascribe such customs exclusively to a gentile setting (as in the Ituraean temple of Hermon) and not to a Jewish context. However, one of these altars was found in a Jewish village. And as argued above, incense burning was not uncommon among Jews in the late Second Temple or early rabbinic periods.

The provenance of the altar and the inkwell (see p. 451) should be discussed together, although we have no evidence that both items derive from the same location or were made at the same workshop. Magen Broshi found these items too beautiful in style to come from Qumran, and suggested that they more likely belonged to a larger Hellenistic site on the East Bank such as Jerash.[24] Of the six inkwells found by archaeologists at Qumran and ʿAin Feshka, only one is made of bronze, and the others are pottery; all are simple in style—different from the Schøyen inkwell that was reported found together

---

[21] The site housed three temples that were built in the same location, one atop the ruins of the former. The temples date to the period 50 BC–AD 80. Based on Assyrian parallels, the excavator Daniel Schowalter suggests that this piece could represent decoration of a crown (2013).

[22] A stone base found in the nineteenth century in the debris outside the walls of ancient Byblos may be relevant to this discussion. The base, which is only partially preserved, was probably made to carry a statuette. It portrays an altar with four horns and four elevations of four steps—with horns and elevations of the same height (Renan 1864/1998, 162–63, 208). As analogy to the stone base, Renan points to a stone relief from the Koyoundjik palace of ancient Nineveh, with crow-step ornamentation and an image of an altar similar to those discussed here (see chart of illustrations). An altar of the same type appears on a relief from Ashurbanipal's palace in Niniveh (see illustration in Stager 2000, 46).

[23] I am indebted to the late prof. K. Arvid Tångberg for pointing out this connection.

[24] Nir-El and Broshi 1996, 158; as well as personal communication.

with the altar. The discussion between Pauline Donceel-Voute and Jodi Magness on the character of the Qumran settlement demonstrated that both elegant and everyday glassware and pottery were used there (Donceel-Voute 1994; Magness 1994). One should therefore not *a priori* separate the inkwell and the altar from Qumran because of their ornamental style.

In our 2002 publication Pfann and I focused our attention to Period III at Qumran, when only one third of the site was in active use. De Vaux asserted that the site was occupied and maintained between 68 and 132 only as a Roman military post until the fall of Masada (1973, 41–44, similarly Magness 2002, 62–63). This has been contested by Pfann and Joan Taylor. They suggest that the Roman garrison was soon followed by civil occupation.[25] Pfann suggested (Elgvin and Pfann 2002) that the site was used as a farmstead for a substantial period following the fall of Masada. The new inhabitants did not share the purity concerns of the previous occupants: 'Community life at Qumran no longer exists' (de Vaux 1973, 43). When Pfann compared the overall plan of Qumran with the locations where glassware and pottery of elegant design were found, he noticed that these finds came only from those parts of the site that were occupied during Period III.[26] He therefore concluded that these occupants (probably not Roman soldiers) brought with them more elaborately decorated housewares than their purity-oriented predecessors.

Decorated strainer jugs from Period III reflect Nabataean style (Clamer 1997, 73–79), and relatively large quantities of Nabataean cream ware, probably coming from Period III at Khirbet Qumran, have been recovered.[27] If the inkwell and incense altar were indeed found by the Bedouin at Khirbet Qumran, as surface finds they would likely represent the last period of occupation.[28] The style of the altar could be compared to Nabataean-style pottery from Period III. When Jerusalem and the surrounding region were laid waste by the Romans (cf. Geva 1997), the natural trade contacts from the Dead Sea region seem to have turned eastward.[29] New settlers at Khirbet Qumran could have been Jewish refugees from the ravaged Jerusalem region or Jericho (which was destroyed in AD 68), or Nabataeans. If the inkwell was found at Khirbet Qumran, it could have belonged to these settlers. Alternatively, Roman soldiers, who had obtained the altar somewhere in the Levant, could have left it there during the brief Roman occupation of the site.

By 1953 Kando was trading pieces together from Qumran, Murabbaʿat, and Naḥal Ḥever, and there were a number of items from the latter two sites that he sold as 'Qumran finds', probably because he perceived that they would fetch a higher price.

[25] Taylor (2006; 2012, 242–43, 261–62, 269) argues for the presence of an agricultural settlement in the period AD 73–115, ending with the large earthquake of 115. The Buqeia plains above Qumran were resettled in this period by refugees from Judaea and cultivated again (Cross and Milik 1956, Cross 1993). Jodi Magness disagrees with Pfann, Taylor, and Dennis Mizzi on the features of Period III, and does not see any civil presence after the Roman garrison (personal communication).

[26] Dennis Mizzi notes (personal communication) that a substantial part of the glassware seems to come from Period II.

[27] Magness notes that some potsherds described by de Vaux as 'Islamic', rather represent Nabataean cream ware (2002, 63). Some nicely cut architectural elements from Period Ib were reused in Period III (Magness 2002, 69) — this feature could also point to a more permanent type of occupation than a short-lived military post. Dennis Mizzi (personal communication) notes a number of pieces of Nabataean cream ware from Period III, still in the collections of École Biblique. From de Vaux's excavation dumps Magen and Peleg recovered 'many fragments of Nabataean vessels' (Magen and Peleg 2006, 68). Eshel and Broshi published a piece of a Nabataean cream ware jug (Broshi and Eshel 2004, 326–27, frgs 6:1, 7:2). The clay of one of the ceramic pieces picked up by William Brownlee at Khirbet Qumran around 1950 is now identified by Matthew Boulanger as similar to decorated fine Nabataean wares from Petra or the Negev (see p. 374).

[28] According to Ira Rabin's analysis of ink from the inkwell, the ink is different from ink used for writing scrolls found in the Qumran caves (see p. 463). The inkwell should therefore be separated from Qumran Period II, but Period III cannot be ruled out.

[29] At least fifteen Nabataean legal documents dating to Qumran Period III were found in the Judaean Desert caves, especially Naḥal Ḥever 5/6 and Wadi Murabbaʿat. This reflects increased Nabataean influence or presence in Judaea in the period between the two Jewish Revolts (Levine 2000, Schiffman 2012).

In the Cave of the Letters in Nahal Hever a number of bronze items were found, among them mirrors, jugs, bowls, incense shovels, and *patera*. Also found was glassware of elaborate design, as well as wooden boxes for jewellery and cosmetics (Yadin 1963, 42–83, 101–10, 123–24). The high standard of workmanship evidenced in these artefacts, brought to the cave by refugees from En Gedi and Mahoza (a village at the southern end of the Dead Sea with a mixed population), is similar in quality to the Schøyen inkwell and incense altar. Both the bronze vessels from the Cave of the Letters and the altar and inkwell discussed here are remarkably well preserved, and do not show patterns of deterioration.

Four of the incense shovels are today on display in the Israel museum. These shovels served as firepans that held hot charcoal, upon which the incense was placed. The incense shovels are so large (with pans from 80 × 110 mm up to 130 × 170 mm) that they cannot have been used together with miniature altars. Yadin suggested that the incense shovels and *patera* were carried by Roman soldiers or auxiliaries for ritual purposes, and subsequently were captured by Bar Kokhba warriors. They could also have come into Jewish hands in more peaceful ways, originating from a Roman military unit that was stationed in En Gedi in AD 124 (Yadin 1963, 45). Graeco-Roman decorative images on these artefacts had been defaced after coming into Jewish hands. Yadin asserts that most of these Roman ritual vessels were made in southern Italy (1963, 45). The size of the altar discussed here points more to domestic than community use. Its style points to the Levant, not to Roman Italy as place of origin. However, an origin in the Levant does not necessarily exclude use in private cult by Roman auxiliaries before these vessels could have ended up in Jewish hands.

H. Conclusion

It seems most likely that the altar and the inkwell were found by the Bedouin in a Nahal Hever cave, perhaps the Cave of the Letters, in 1952, before the first archaeological survey of these caves in 1953. The altar could have been used by Jewish inhabitants of Mahoza or En Gedi in private cult, to accompany their prayers after the devastation of their temple in Jerusalem. Alternatively, the altar could represent a liturgical vessel that a Roman soldier or auxiliary had acquired in the Levant — a vessel that subsequently came into Jewish hands, perhaps as the war booty of Bar Kokhba soldiers.

Figure 89. MS 1655/4
(scale unknown)

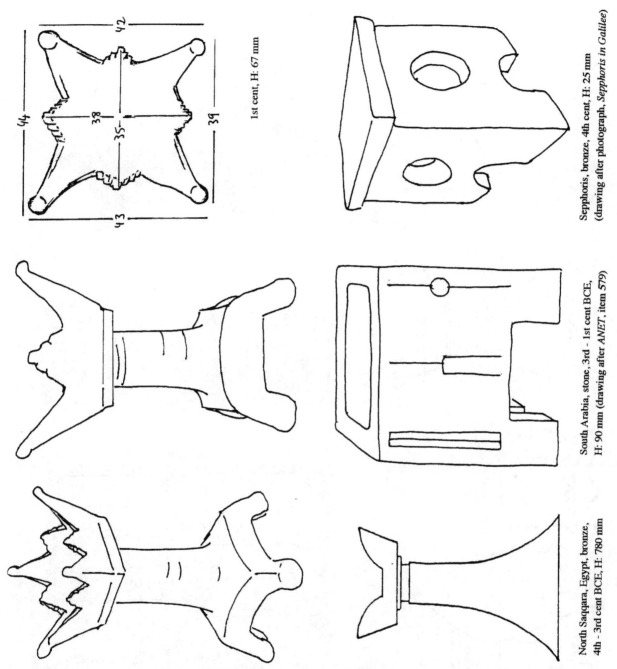

Figure 90. *Drawing of the Schøyen altar (top row) compared with altars from North Saqqara, South Arabia,*
and Sepphoris (bottom row).
Drawings by Grete Kvinnsland (top row) and Torleif Elgvin (bottom row)

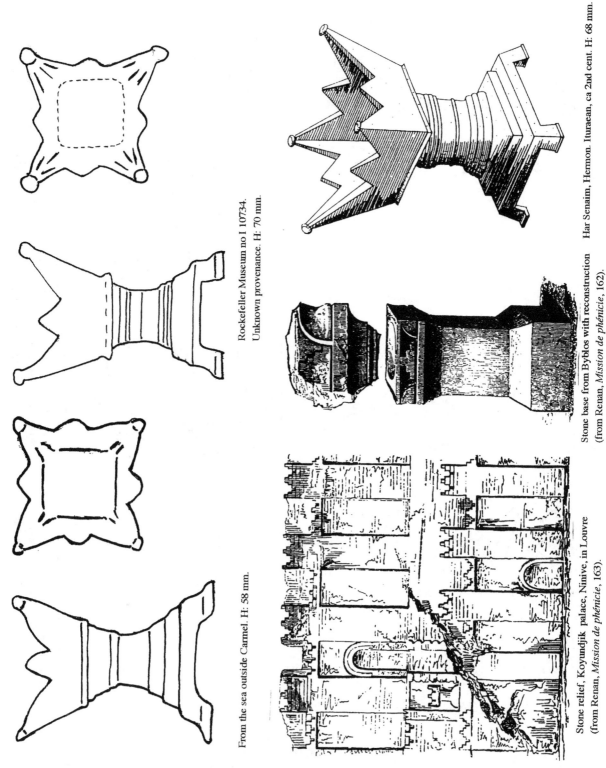

Rockefeller Museum no I 10734. Unknown provenance. H: 70 mm.

From the sea outside Carmel. H: 58 mm.

Har Senaim, Hermon. Ituraean, ca 2nd cent. H: 68 mm.

Stone base from Byblos with reconstruction (from Renan, *Mission de phénicie*, 162).

Stone relief, Koyundjik palace, Ninive, in Louvre (from Renan, *Mission de phénicie*, 163).

Figure 91a. *Top line, drawings of altars from the sea outside Carmel and Rockefeller altar no. I 10734 by Torleif Elgvin. Bottom line, stone relief from Nineveh and base from Byblos (from Renan 1864), and stylized drawing of Har Senaim altar (from Dar 1993).*

Sumaqa, Carmel, third–fourth century; height: 63 mm. (drawing after photograph in Dar, 191)

Ceramic altar, Jerash, early second century CE; base missing; height: 80 mm (drawing after Iliffe, "Imperial Art in Transjordan," pl. VI).

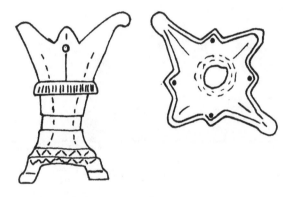

Giv'at Katzenelson, ca 4th cent. H: 63 mm. (Israel Museum no 66–604)

Figure 91b. *Bronze altars from 3rd-4th century, ceramic altar from 2nd century. Drawings by Torleif Elgvin.*

XLIV

Bronze Inkwells from Naḥal Ḥever(?) and Nabataea. MS 1655/2 and MS 1987/15

Torleif Elgvin

A. Three Bronze Inkwells from Antiquity

Three elaborately decorated bronze inkwells from the same workshop are presented here, made to exactly the same design, and differing only in size (height of body 66 mm, 53 mm, and 49 mm respectively). Two of these belong to The Schøyen Collection, while the third was published by Nabil I. Khairy in 1980.

The largest inkwell (MS 1655/2) was sold by Kando to John Allegro in 1953 as a surface find at Khirbet Qumran around 1950, together with the miniature bronze incense altar presented in the previous chapter. It was first published by Stephen Goranson (1992; 1994). The second inkwell (MS 1987/15) surfaced in Jordan, northeast of the Dead Sea, in 1961. It was purchased in London by The Schøyen Collection in 2001. The smallest one, of unknown provenance, was bought in 1970 from a Bedouin in the West Bank by E. Krüger of the German Evangelical Institute of the Holy Land, Amman (Khairy 1980; Goranson 1994).

These cast bronze inkwells demonstrate a remarkably high level of workmanship. Especially noteworthy is the circular tube around the dipping hole, to prevent spillage of ink if the inkwell is overturned. The smaller inkwell is somewhat worn on the surface, but those belonging to The Schøyen Collection are still in excellent shape.

B. Physical Description

1. MS 1655/2

All three inkwells consist of four basic parts, not including affixed hinges and handles: (1) the base, (2) the receptacle, (3) the top cover, and (4) the circular tube. The base of the largest inkwell is 8 mm high and has a diameter of 50–51 mm. The base is hollow, with an 8 mm airspace above the floor. The diameter is 22 mm at the point where the base joins the receptacle. The receptacle has a diameter (at the top) of 78 mm. 8 mm down from the top of the inkwell is a prominent groove, which creates a separation between the rim and the rest of the receptacle. The height of the inkwell from the base to the top of the receptacle is 65–66 mm. The total height of the inkwell including the hinges varies slightly (78 and 80 mm—the hinges are *c.* 13 mm high and 17 mm wide). The shape of the top cover is concave: from a 4 mm wide brim it slopes down to a flat circular disc (10 mm lower than the brim), designed to collect spilled ink. This disc has a diameter of 48 mm. The dipping hole has a diameter of 12 mm. The distance from the top cover to the bottom of the inkwell is 45 mm. The dipping hole forms an opening in the cover to a 17 mm long circular tube. This feature was designed to prevent the spillage of ink even if the inkwell were overturned. The weight is 395 g (compare with the 110 g of the altar presented in the previous chapter).

The inkwell is decorated with circular bands: one recessed into the cover surrounding the dipping hole; one on the base; three bands on the rim above the groove, another closing the main part of the receptacle just below the groove; and two recessed circles underneath the base.

The inkwell has two basket-type handles that can be elevated for carrying. These two moveable handles attached to the hinges are 79 mm in diameter, and form a circle when resting on the top of the receptacle. When the handles are raised to their full height at a 90° terminus, the total height of the inkwell is 104 mm. The handles are 2–3 mm thick and 8 mm wide. The thickness of the hinges is 3 mm. As the thickness of the hollow base is 2.5–3.5 mm, I suggest that the thickness of the main body is likely also c. 3 mm, which fits well with the distance from cover to bottom of the ink receptacle. There is a bulge at the middle of the body, similar to the impression of a thumb, that was perhaps incidentally produced at the time of manufacture.

The four components of all three inkwells were likely fashioned separately and then fused together. First, a wax model of the bowl-shaped receptacle was encased in clay, and then fired, causing the fluid wax to pour away. Then molten bronze was poured carefully into the ceramic form. The clay was subsequently chiselled away. The curved base was probably made in the same fashion, also from a ceramic form. The cylindrical tube was made as a separate piece and subsequently attached to the top cover, which again may have been made from a ceramic form. The hinges and handles were attached in the final stage, after the larger pieces had been fused together. The thumb-shaped bulge in the body probably derives from the wax model stage.

A sample of the bronze showed the following composition: 55–68% copper, 23–39% lead, 5–8% tin.[1] Some traces of ink from the larger inkwell were chemically tested in November 1996, although the remains were too meagre to enable a full analysis. One could, however, confirm that the ink was black and manufactured from lamp-soot, as was the ink used in Qumran.[2] Ira Rabin later performed further tests on tiny quantities of ink from this inkwell, and she concludes that the ink is different from that used on the Qumran scrolls (see p. 463).

---

[1] Test performed by Helge Semb at The Norwegian Technical University, Trondheim, 11 November, 1996.

[2] Cf. Nir-El and Broshi 1996. The 1996 analysis of the ink in Trondheim, Norway, showed basically carbon, with some contamination by copper and lead. The analysis of ink from the larger inkwell by a team led by Jan Gunneweg and Kaare Rasmussen appeared in a controversial, unauthorized publication in 2012 (Rasmussen et al. 2012), see Rabin 2014. While substantial amounts of ink were retrieved, two tests to provide a C-14 date for the ink failed. Another test of ink from the Schøyen inkwells will be undertaken.

Figure 92. *MS 1655/2*
(scale unknown)

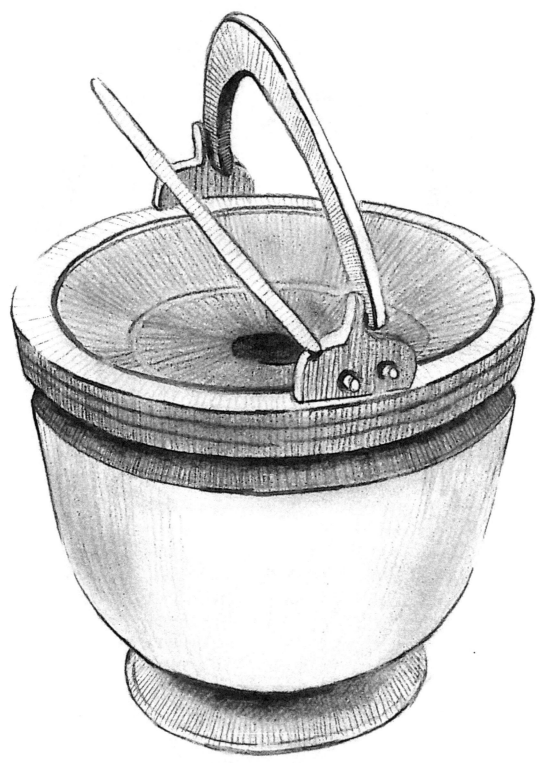

Figure 93. *MS 1655/2. Drawing*
by Trine Filtvedt Elgvin (scale unknown)

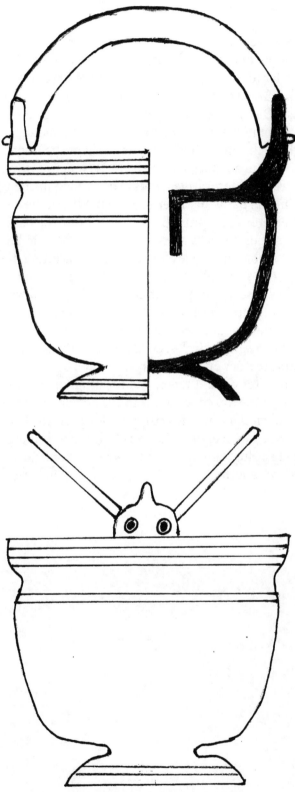

Figure 94. *MS 1655/2 graphical sketches*
(scale 1:1)

2. MS 1987/15

The second inkwell of The Schøyen Collection, which here is presented for the first time, displays exactly the same shape as the larger one. The only difference is that the radius of the handle of the smaller one is disproportionally smaller (only one of the handles is preserved).

The height of the inkwell is 52–53 mm, and 61 and 63 mm with the hinges included. The diameter at the top is 60 mm, at the base 43 mm. The diameter of the surviving half-circle handle is 65 mm; in its lower position it extends 2.5 mm from the receptacle. With the handle raised, the full height of the inkwell is 83 mm. The weight of this inkwell is 200 g; half that of the larger one.

The base is hollow, with a 5 mm airspace above the floor. It curves up to a flat disc with a diameter of 12 mm. Under the base are four decorative bands. The groove in the upper part of the receptacle appears 10 mm below the rim and has a diameter of 53 mm. Where the base joins the receptacle (5–10 mm above the floor), the diameter is 25 mm. The concave top cover has a 4 mm wide brim (identical with the larger inkwell) and slopes down to a flat circular disc (12 mm lower than the brim). This circular disc has a diameter of 33 mm. The hinges for the handles are 15 mm wide and rise 10 and 11 mm respectively above the body. The surviving handle is 2 mm thick and 6 mm broad. The thickness both of the hinges and of the hollow base is 3 mm, identical to the larger inkwell.

The inkwell is decorated with three recessed circles on the upper section of the receptacle and one circle just below the groove, creating four decorative bands. The disc of the top cover is incised with a decorative band made of two concentric circles. On the side of the main body there is a thumb-shaped bulge, very similar to the same feature on the larger inkwell.

The dipping hole has a diameter of 12–13 mm, and forms an opening in the cover to a 14 mm long circular tube. The distance from the top cover down to the bottom of the receptacle is 35 mm.

This inkwell has a beautiful circular lid with stopper, designed to close the dipping hole. The lid is 17 mm in diameter and decorated with eight coloured circles surrounding a larger circle, much like an eight-petalled flower. The petals alternate in colour between red or brown and white. The lid is 2–3 mm thick, and the stopper protrudes another 6 mm. Thick residues of ink are still attached to the stopper.

***Figure 95**. MS 1987/15*
© Kipp Davis, used with permission (scale unknown)

Figure 96.1. *Inkwell stopper (profile)*
© *Kipp Davis, used with permission (scale unknown)*

3. The Smaller Inkwell from the West Bank

The inkwell published by Khairy is 49 mm high. It has a maximum diameter of 54 mm, a 9 mm wide dipping hole, and a body thickness approximating to 2–3 mm. Its weight is not specified, and it is somewhat worn on the surface. Khairy (1980, 159) describes it as follows:

> Cup-like ink-well with vertical walls, concave top, low pedestal base, up-standing thickened rim, flattened on top, three horizontal incised lines on rim and a large groove below rim outside, filling hole, two flattened semi-circular handles are fixed by rivets opposite each other on both sides of the upper part of the rim, one could bend them up to carry the ink-well like a basket and lay them down on top of the flattened rim while the ink-well was in use, consequently, they form a complete circle of the same size of the rim diameter.

Figure 96.2. MS 1987/15 Inkwell stopper
© *Kipp Davis, used with permission (scale unknown)*

C. Inkwells from Qumran

Six inkwells were found by archaeologists at Khirbet Qumran and one at ʿAin Feshkha — a remarkable number when one takes the size of the Qumran site into account, which furthermore suggests a scribal milieu (de Vaux 1954, 212, 229; Gunneweg and Balla 2003, 32; H. Eshel 2009a, 61). In his 1951 excavations of Khirbet Qumran Roland de Vaux found three cylindrical inkwells. One clay and one bronze inkwell were asserted to derive from the collapsed second floor 'scriptorium', and a third clay inkwell was found in the adjacent locus 31. Each of the three survived with a small piece of a handle still attached to the body. A complete ceramic inkwell containing dried ink was found by Solomon Steckoll in his 1966–67 excavations of Khirbet Qumran, but the exact locus is unknown (Steckoll 1969).[3] This fourth inkwell was made in the form of a slightly rounded cup with a circular handle and measuring 55 × 39 mm. Gunneweg

---

[3] This inkwell is property of the Hecht Museum in Haifa. An inkwell of exactly the same type was found by the Jordanian Department of Antiquities in Queilbeh, Jordan, in 1959 (Khairy 1980, 159, 4c).

reports the discovery of part of a clay inkwell found in locus 129 (QUM 221). Another clay inkwell was discovered at ʿAin Feshkha (QUM 193), and appears to have been manufactured locally from clay at Qumran (Gunneweg and Balla 2003, 13).[4] In their 1993–2004 excavations at Qumran Yitzhak Magen and Yuval Peleg found a ceramic inkwell in the eastern dump.[5]

Two further inkwells that passed through the hands of Kando have been attributed to Khirbet Qumran: the larger one in The Schøyen Collection and a clay inkwell in the collection of the University of Southern California. The latter was acquired from Kando in 1967 (Fine 1987; Goranson 1991). This inkwell is in the shape of a cup with a circular handle, similar to the one found by Steckoll. It is 53 mm high, with approximately the same diameter, and it is made with a vertical shaft.[6]

The inkwells from Qumran and ʿAin Feshkha are simpler in style than the two bronze inkwells in The Schøyen Collection and the third one published by Khairy.

D. Comparison with Other Bronze Inkwells

Ceramic inkwells were far more common in the Levant than bronze ones, while inkwells of stone are also known.[7] The bronze inkwell from de Vaux's 'scriptorium' is cylindrical and cast from four individual pieces: a circular tube and cover, each made from a rectangular bronze sheet, as well as a bottom and lid. It is 52 mm high, has a diameter of 30 mm and a 12 mm wide dipping hole, the thickness of the body approximates to 1.5 mm (de Vaux 1954, 212, 229). This inkwell is similar in style to others from Graeco-Roman contexts of the first and second centuries AD. The cylindrical form continues to be in use until the fourth century (Khairy 1980, 161).

Khairy published a second bronze inkwell of unknown provenance, also the property of E. Krüger. This one is bowl-shaped: a 'squat bronze ink-well in a fragmentary state and fragile, almost a third of the body is missing, slightly concave top with rounded base, filling hole, two basketry handles' (Khairy 1980, 159–60). Its height is 38 mm, the body diameter 61 mm, the dipping hole is 9 mm wide, the thickness of the body is approximately 0.75–1 mm. The style of this inkwell is simpler than the three inkwells presented above.

---

[4] According to Michniewicz (2009, 117–18, 134–42) caution is needed with regard to petrographic and chemical analysis of Qumran pottery. He identifies the same clay in pottery from Qumran, Jericho, Khirbet Mazin, and ez-Zara (Callirhoe), and suggests that all the pottery was manufactured locally in Qumran with clay collected from different sources in the region.

[5] Magen and Peleg 2007, 20-21, Plate 5.5. The main body is 50 mm high, the protruding neck is broken. This inkwell has no vertical shaft.

[6] A similar clay inkwell (50 mm high, 38 mm in diameter) was given to Eric Meyers in 1976 by an East Jerusalem antiquities dealer (Nagy et al. 1996, 202, artefact 68). According to James Charlesworth (personal communication), he possesses two similar clay inkwells, acquired by an American collector in the 1950s. All these three are asserted to come from Qumran.

[7] Khairy also published one of alabaster from Petra (1980, 157–58). The excavations at Dura-Europos unearthed two pens and a terracotta inkwell (no 1938.4758, found in block 63, L 1), dated between the first and the mid-third century. The inkwell is exhibited at Yale University Art Gallery and measures 7 × 4.6 cm. The dipping hole is 2 cm wide, the top cover has four decorative circles (Dyson 1968, 43, no. 277, Fig. 10; http://ecatalogue.art.yale.edu/detail.htm?objectId=24811, accessed 11 June, 2014). Further, five ceramic inkwells were found in the same locus in the 2003 salvage excavations at Shuafat north of Jerusalem, a large settlement with a well-to-do Jewish population from the period between the two Jewish Revolts (Sklar-Parnes, Rapuano, and Bar-Nathan 2004, I am indebted to Dennis Mizzi for this reference).

Khairy pointed to possible Graeco-Roman parallels to Krüger's inkwell from the West Bank:[8] Jacobi (1897) pictures a cylindrical bronze inkwell with a diameter of 54 mm from the Roman fortress in Saalburg at Homburg, Germany (first century BC–third century AD).[9] The circular rotating lid is decorated with circular bands. Comstock and Vermeule (1971) present two cylindrical inkwells decorated by circular bands from Macedonia of the Hellenistic period, 46 mm high and 39 and 40 mm respectively in diameter; as well as a worn circular inkwell with lid from a Graeco-Roman sarcophagus from Assos, with a height of 48 mm and a diameter of 27 mm. The latter is of a simple type, made of a rectangular strip of bronze, and was found with an ivory stylus inside. A wall fresco from Pompeii shows a double metal inkwell: two cylinders attached to each other (one of them with the lid opened), with a handle and a reed pen leaning against the top of the inkwell.[10] From the same region but deriving from a later period comes a scribe's case of bronze found in En Gedi.[11]

E. Nabataean Provenance

In the previous chapter I suggested that the altar and the larger inkwell were brought by refugees to Naḥal Ḥever during the Bar Kokhba Revolt, where they were found by the Bedouin in 1952.

The presence of the mineral monohydrocalcite in the ink of the larger inkwell suggests a physical link to Sinai, the only location in the region where this mineral has been found (Rabin 2014, 126; cf. Rasmussen et al. 2012, 2965–67). This circumstantial evidence lends weight to some kind of Nabataean provenance for this inkwell, since Nabataean traders regularly passed through Sinai.

There are a number of reasons to suggest that both the altar and the three inkwells described above derive from a Nabataean workshop in the first or early second century AD.[12] The smaller Schøyen inkwell was found east of the Dead Sea, the ancient territory of the Nabataeans. As the inkwell published by Khairy was bought from a Bedouin in the West Bank, a find-place in the Judaean Desert seems probable. The incense altar and the larger inkwell were in Kando's hands in 1953, when they were sold to Allegro. At that time Kando traded Bedouin finds from Murabbaʿat, Naḥal Ḥever, and Cave 4. As other bronze artefacts were found in Naḥal Ḥever, a provenance from one of these caves seems more likely than an incidental surface find from Khirbet Qumran.

Those who fled from Mahoza at the southern shore of the Dead Sea (such as Babatha) and En Gedi to Naḥal Ḥever had close contacts with the Nabataeans. The Babatha archive and other documents found in the Bar Kokhba caves demonstrate that, between the two Jewish Revolts, Jews in the Dead Sea region lived in a mixed cultural environment. The Nabataean kingdom centred in Petra was annexed to the Roman empire by AD 109. Mahoza had a mixed population of people from Nabataean, Jewish, and Graeco-Roman backgrounds. A letter from the Judaean Desert shows that by AD 124 Roman soldiers

[8] Vermeule 1960, 109–10, Fig. 22; Comstock and Vermeule 1971, 324, 345, figs 454, 455, 485; Jacobi 1897, 451–52, Plates LXX.1 and LXX.1a.

[9] At this site 127 slate pencils were found (Jacobi 1897, 449).

[10] http://www.vroma.org/images/mcmanus_images/writing_fresco.jpg, housed at http://www2.cnr.edu/home/araia/learning.html (accessed 7 February, 2014).

[11] This scribe's case, consisting of a cylindrical ink-case with lid attached to a long, tubular stylus-holder, was unearthed in En Gedi in 2003 (Porat, Eshel, and Frumkin 2007b). The ink-case contained a mixture of dry ingredients used in the preparation of black ink, not the remains of actual liquid ink. Adjacent to this scribe's case was found a glass jug from the Ottoman period, which gives a clue to the dating of the ink-case. Five similar scribes' cases are known, found in Egypt or the land of Israel. The excavators dated this type to the end of the Byzantine and the early Islamic periods, the sixth-eight centuries, substantively later than the inkwells discussed here.

[12] For this dating, cf. also the early second century ceramic altar from Jerash in northern Jordan, similar in style to the altar in The Schøyen Collection (see n. 15 p. 441).

stationed in En Gedi had close relations with their Jewish neighbours (Yadin 1963, 45). The Jews lived peacefully, and maintained close cultural and financial ties to their neighbours. Towards the end of the Second Revolt Jews such as Babatha must have felt that life in the Roman province of Arabia was fraught with danger.[13] From En Gedi they set out to find refuge in the caves of Naḥal Ḥever, probably out of fear of Roman reprisals (Schiffman 2012).

The three inkwells discussed above are distinguished from other inkwells of the Roman period by their extraordinary artistic quality. The survival of these artefacts represents a remarkable testimony to Nabataean workmanship in the first or early second century, and probably to interaction between Nabataeans and Jews in the period between the two Jewish Revolts.

---

[13] The Babatha documents date from between AD 94 and 132. Beneath the pouch with the Babatha archive were papyri from Eliezer bar Shmuel's archive, the latest of which was dated to November 134. Therefore the refugees arrived at this cave late in 134 or early in 135. As Babatha's second husband was from En Gedi, Babatha and her family would have fled from Mahoza to En Gedi before moving on to the caves of Naḥal Ḥever.

XLV

Ink Sample from Inkwell MS 1655/2

Ira Rabin

We have obtained a minute amount of dry ink scratched from the bronze inkwell MS 1655/2. The powder was stored between two glass slides to minimize contamination. For micro analysis by FTIR a sample of the ink powder was transferred into a diamond cell while for confocal Raman spectroscopy a micro sample was placed onto sticky tape. The same portion of the sample was also investigated by scanning electron microscopy, where the elements distribution was determined by EDX.

Raman micro spectroscopy provides a good basis for identification of the carbon inks. It should be kept in mind, however, that excitation line and fitting parameter do not allow simple comparison with reference materials. The spectra presented in this work were obtained at the same excitation line (785 nm) and were fitted using the same routine.

All Raman spectra in *Figure 97* show that the inks investigated were pure carbon black ink. They present the two characteristic peaks at about 1310 cm^{-1} and 1585 cm^{-1} that correspond to disordered (D)'s and graphite (G)'s respective contributions to soot (Sadezky et al. 2005). The D-peak position and relative intensity (area) ratios I_D/A_G correlate well with the spectra of soot produced from vegetable oils.[1] As can be seen from the comparison with modern Chinese ink (dotted curve) and an ancient ink of the *Temple Scroll* (broken curve), the main features are independent of age.

With the help of FTIR spectroscopy we determined the binder used to make the ink from the soot. In *Figure 98* the top curve corresponds to the ink sample from inkwell MS 1655/2. Its spectrum combines contributions from different compounds. Proteinous gelatin, the binder used in this case, dominates the spectrum (cf. *Figure 97*, broken curve). The amide I and II bands at 1650 cm^{-1} and 1540 cm^{-1} respectively, as well as the shoulder at 3056 cm^{-1}, constitute an easily recognizable pattern of a protein-based glue. Impurities such as kaolinite, iron oxide, and quartz-containing earths are probably responsible for the broad band at about 1050 cm^{-1} and OH stretching frequencies at 3620 and 3700 cm^{-1}, as can be seen from the comparison with the spectrum of a mixture of those materials (cf. *Figure 98*, dotted curve). A considerable amount of calcite is manifested by a sharp absorption at 876 cm^{-1} and a broad band at 1400 cm^{-1} that appears blended with the C-N stretch of the amide III band in gelatin. It is noteworthy that the aragonite usually accompanying or even dominating calcite in the sediments of the Qumran caves is not detected here (Arkin 1985).

In the SEM micrograph the sample powder appears strongly contaminated by large-sized particles. The element distribution in the EDX spectra in the bottom picture allows the identification of the main contaminants as copper (Cu), silicon (Si), sulphur (S), calcium (Ca), aluminium (Al), iron (Fe) and lead (Pb). Copper and lead impurities correspond to the bronze of the inkwell whereas the rest of the elements points to sediments from an unspecified location. The elements sodium (Na), magnesium (Mg) and potassium (K), are usually detected in considerable quantities on the artefacts found in Qumran or its vicinity, were not detected in this case.

---

[1] Ira Rabin, unpublished results.

A. Conclusion

The ink from MS 1655/2 is carbon black ink with a proteinous binder. Proteinous binders have so far not been found in the inks of the Dead Sea Scrolls. Impurities present in the ink have no specific features that would point to Qumran or its vicinity as archaeological provenance. Our analysis hangs a question mark over Kando's information that the inkwell was found by the Bedouin at Khirbet Qumran some time before the archaeological investigation of the site.

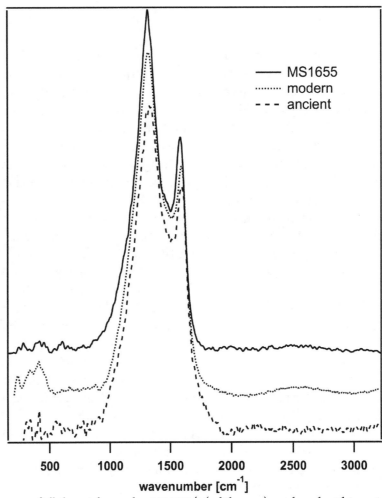

Figure 97. *Raman spectra of all three ink samples: MS 1655/2 (solid curve), modern dry Chinese ink (dotted curve), ink from the Temple Scroll col. LII (broken curve)*

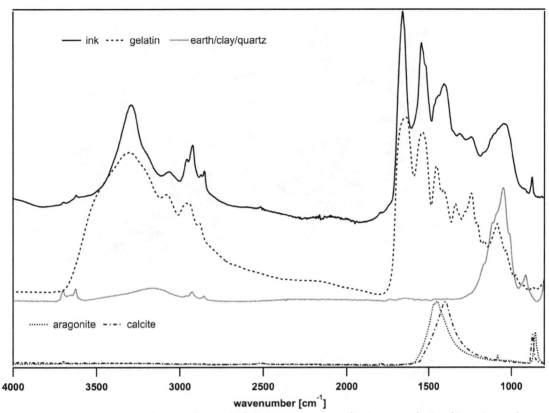

Figure 98. FTIR transmission spectra: ink sample (solid curve), gelatin (broken curve), clay (dotted curve). For comparison the standard spectra of aragonite (dotted curve) and calcite (broken curve) are displayed in the lower panel.[2]

[2] IRUG spectral database, http://www.irug.org/default.asp; RRUF spectral database for minerals, http://rruff.info/.

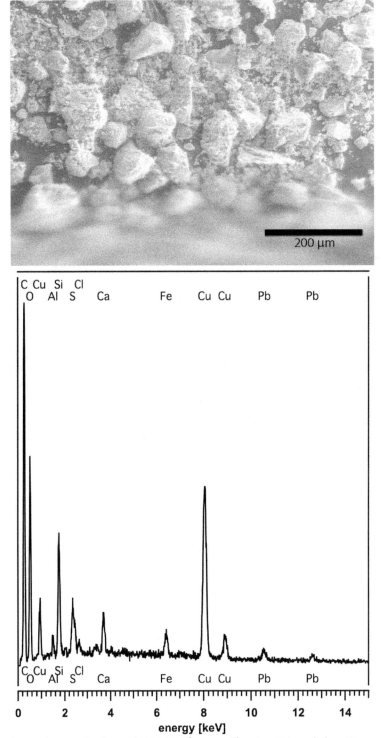

Figure 99. Top: SEM micrograph of sample MS 1655/2, magnification 200, scale bar 200 μm, environmental conditions: pressure 100 Pa; bottom: EDX spectrum was obtained at 30kV

Appendices

Bibliography

Abegg, Martin G. 1997. Exile and the Dead Sea Scrolls. Pages 111–26 in *Exile: Old Testament, Jewish, and Christian Conceptions*. Edited by J.M. Scott. Journal for the Study of Judaism Supplement Series 56. Leiden: Brill.

Aerts, A.T., J. van der Plicht, and H.A.J. Meijer. 2001. Automatic AMS Sample Combustion and CO2 Collection. *Radiocarbon* 43:293–98.

Aharoni, Yohanan. 1961a. Expedition B. *Israel Exploration Journal* 11:11–24.

_____. 1961b. The Caves of Naḥal Ḥever. *Atiqot* 3:148–62.

Alexander, Philip S. 2006. *Mystical Texts*. London: T&T Clark.

_____. 2013. Was the Ninth of Av Observed in the Second Temple Period? Reflections on the Concept of Continuing Exile in Early Judaism. Pages 23–38 in *Envisioning Juidaism: Studies in Honor of Peter Schäfer on the Occasion of his Seventieth Birthday*. Edited by R.S. Boustan, K. Herrmann, R. Leicht, A.Y. Reed, and G. Veltri, with the collaboration of Alex Ramos. Tübingen: Mohr Siebeck.

Allegro, John M. 1956. *The Dead Sea Scrolls*. Harmondsworth: Penguin.

_____. 1964a. *The Dead Sea Scrolls: A Reappraisal*. Harmondsworth: Penguin.

_____. 1964b. *Search in the Desert*. London: W.H. Allen.

_____. 1965. *Search in the Desert*. Edinburgh: Smith and Ritchie.

Amar, Zohar. 1998a. The Ash and the Red Material from Qumran. *Dead Sea Discoveries* 5:1–15.

_____. 1998b. Written Sources Regarding the Jaziret Fara'un (Coral Island) Textiles. *Atiqot* 36:114–19.

Amit, David, and Hanan Eshel. 1995/96. The Bar Kokhba Revolt in the Southern Hebron Mountains. *Eretz-Israel* 25:463–70 (Hebrew), 106 (English).

Arkin, Yakov. 1985. Deformation of Laminated Sediments of the Dead Sea. *Geological Survey of Israel Current Research* 5:57–65.

Asaro, Frank and David Adan-Bayewitz. 2007. The History of the Lawrence Berkeley National Laboratory Instrumental Neutron Activation Analysis Programme for Archaeological and Geological Materials. *Archaeometry* 49:201–14.

Avigad, Nahman, and Yigael Yadin. 1956. *A Genesis Apocryphon: A Scroll From the Wilderness of Judaea: Description and Contents of the Scroll: Facsimiles, Transcription and Translation of columns II, XIX - XXII*. Jerusalem: Magnes Press and Heikhal ha-Sefer.

Baillet, Maurice. 1963. Un livret magique en christo-palestinien à L'Université de Louvain. *Le Muséon* 76:375–401.

Balla, Marta. 2005. Provenance Study of Qumran Pottery by Neutron Activation Analysis. Ph.D. diss., Budapest.

Bar-Asher, Moshe. 2009. On the Language of the Vision of Gabriel. *Revue de Qumran* 23:494–524.

Bar-Nathan, Rachel. 2002. *The Pottery*. Vol. 3 of *Hasmonean and Herodian Palaces at Jericho: Final Reports of the 1973-1987 Excavations*. Jerusalem: Israel Exploration Society.

_____. 2006a. *Masada VII: The Yigael Yadin Excavations 1963-1965: Final Reports: The Pottery of Masada*. Jerusalem: Israel Exploration Society.

_____. 2006b. Qumran and the Hasmoneaen and Herodian Winter Palaces of Jericho: The Implication of the Pottery Finds for the Interpretation of the Settlement at Qumran. Pages 263–77 in *Qumran: The Site of the Dead Sea Scrolls: Archaeological Interpretations and Debates. Proceedings of a Conference held at Brown Univeristy, November 17-19, 2002*. Edited by K. Galor, J.-B. Humbert, and J. Zangenberg. Leiden: Brill.

Bartlett, John R. 1989. *Edom and the Edomites*. Supplements to Journal for the Study of the Old Testament 77. Sheffield: JSOT Press.

Baruchi, Yosi. 2005. Fragmentary Biblical Scrolls from Bar Kokhba Revolt Refuge Caves. *Meghillot* 3:177–90 (Hebrew); XV–XVI (English).

Baruchi, Yosi. 2009. The Biblical Scrolls from the Bar Kokhba Refuge Caves. Pages 339–53 in vol. 2 of *Refuge Caves of the Bar Kokhba Revolt*. Edited by H. Eshel and R. Porat. Jerusalem: Israel Exploration Society (Hebrew).

Baruchi, Yosi, and Hanan Eshel. 2006. Another Fragment of Sdeir Genesis. *Journal of Jewish Studies* 57:136–38.

Baxter, Michael J. 1992. Archaeological Uses of the Biplot—A Neglected Technique? Pages 141–48 in *Computer Applications and Quantitative Methods in Archaeology, 1991*. Edited by G. Lock and J. Moffett. BAR International Series 577. Oxford: Tempvs Reparatvm.

_____. 1994. *Exploratory Multivariate Analysis in Archaeology*. Edinburgh: Edinburgh University Press.

Baxter, Michael J., and Caitlin E. Buck. 2000. Data Handling and Statistical Analysis. Pages 681–746 in *Modern Analytical Methods in Art and Archaeology*. Edited by E. Ciliberto and G. Spoto. New York: John Wiley and Sons.

Beentjes, Pancratius C. 1997. *The Book of Ben Sira in Hebrew: A Text Edition of All Extant Hebrew Manuscrips and a Synopsis of All Parallell Hebrew Ben Sira Texts*. Supplements to Vetus Testamentum 68. Leiden: Brill.

Bélis, Mireille. 2003. Des textiles, catalogues et commentaires. Pages 207–76 in *Khirbet Qumrân et 'Aïn Feshkha II: Études d'anthropologie, de physique et de chimie*. Edited by J.-B. Humbert and J. Gunneweg. Novum Testamentum et Orbis Antiquus, Series Archaeologica 3. Fribourg: Academic Press.

Ben-Dov, Jonathan. 2011. The Elohistic Psalter and the Writing of Divine Names at Qumran. Pages 79–104 in *The Dead Sea Scrolls and Contemporary Culture: Proceedings of the International Conference Held at the Israel Museum, Jerusalem (July 6–8, 2008)*. Edited by A.D. Roitman et al. Studies on the Texts of the Desert of Judah 93. Leiden: Brill.

Bender Jørgensen, Lise. 2008. Self-Band and other subtle patterns in Roman textiles. Pages 135–41 in *Purpureae Vestes II: Vestidos, textiles y tintes: Estudios sobre la producción de bienes de consumo en la Antigüedad*. Edited by C. Alfaro and L. Karali. Valencia: Universitat de València.

Bentor, Yaacov. 1961. Some Geochemical Aspects of the Dead Sea and the Question of Its Age. *Geochim Cosmochim Acta* 25, no. 4:239–40.

Beyer, Klaus. 1984. *Die aramäischen Texte vom Toten Meer samt den Inschriften aus Palästina, dem Testament Levis aus der Kairoer Genisa, der Fastenrolle und den alten talmudischen Zitaten. Aramaistische Einleitung, Text, Übersetzung, Deutung, Grammatik/Wörterbuch, Deutsch-aramäische Wortliste, Register*. Vol. 1 of *Die aramäischen Texte vom Toten Meer samt den Inschriften aus Palästina, dem Testament Levis aus der Kairoer Genisa, der Fastenrolle und den alten talmudischen Zitaten*. Göttingen: Vandenhoeck & Ruprecht.

_____. 1994. *Die aramäischen Texte vom Toten Meer samt den Inschriften aus Palästina, dem Testament Levis aus der Kairoer Genisa, der Fastenrolle und den alten talmudischen Zitaten*. Ergänzungsband. Göttingen: Vandenhoeck & Ruprecht.

Biblia Hebraica Stuttgartensia. 1976/77. Stuttgart: Deutsche Bibelstiftung.

Bieber, A.M., D.W. Brooks, G. Harbottle, and E.V. Sayre. 1976. Application of Multivariate Techniques to Analytical Data on Aegean Ceramics. *Archaeometry* 18:59–74.

Biondi, Lee. 2003. *From the Dead Sea Scrolls to the Forbidden Book: A Brief History of the Bible Told through Ancient Manuscripts & Early Printed Bibles*. Dallas: HisStory.

_____. 2004. *From The Dead Sea Scrolls to the Bible in America*. Chicago: Bible League.

Bishop, Ronald L. and Hector Neff. 1989. Compositional Data Analysis in Archaeology. Pages 576–86 in *Archaeological Chemistry IV*. Edited by R.O. Allen. Advances in Chemistry 220. Washington, D.C.: American Chemical Society.

Bishop, Ronald L., Robert L. Rands and George R. Holley. 1982. Ceramic Compositional Analysis in Archaeological Perspective. *Advances in Archaeological Method and Theory* 5:275–330.

Bonani, G., S. Ivy, W. Wölfli, M. Broshi, I. Carmi, and J. Strugnell. 1992. Radiocarbon Dating of Fourteen Dead Sea Scrolls. *Radiocarbon* 34:843–49.

Boulanger, Matthew T. 2012. Lawrence Berkeley National Laboratory (LBNL) Nuclear Archaeology Program Archives. Version 1.0. Hosted on the Digital Archaeological Record (tDAR). Online: http://core.tdar.org/collection/7901.

_____. 2013. Salvage archaeometry; lessons learned from the Lawrence Berkeley Laboratory archaeometric archives. *The SAA Archaeological Record* 13:14–19.

Boulanger, Matthew T. and Wesley D. Stoner. 2012. Data Management and Sharing Plan (v. 1). Online: http://archaeometry.missouri.edu/data_management_policy.html. Accessed 28 December, 2012.

Braun, Oskar. 1901. Ein Brief des Katholikos Timotheos I über biblische Studien des 9 Jahrhunderts. *Oriens Christianus* 1:299–313.

Brizemeure, Daniel, Noël Lacoudre, and Émile Puech. 2006. *Le Rouleau de cuivre de la grotte 3 de Qumran (3Q15)*. Studies on the Texts of the Desert of Judah 55. Leiden: Brill.

Browning, Iain. 1980. *Petra*. London: Chatto & Windus.

Brooke, George J., ed. 1996. *The Allegro Qumran Collection: Supplement to the Dead Sea Scrolls on Microfiche*. Leiden: Brill.

_____. 2001. 4Q158: Reworked Pentateuch[a] or Reworked Pentateuch A? *Dead Sea Discoveries* 8:219–41.

_____. 2002. The Rewritten Law, Prophets and Psalms: Issues for Understanding the Text of the Bible. Pages 31–40 in *The Bible as Book: The Hebrew Bible and the Judaean Desert Discoveries*. Edited by E.D. Herbert and E. Tov. London: British Library.

_____. 2006. The Twelve Minor Prophets and the Dead Sea Scrolls. Pages 19–43 in *Congress Volume, Leiden 2004*. Edited by A. Lemaire. Supplements to Vetus Testamentum 109. Leiden: Brill.

_____. 2013. *Reading the Dead Sea Scrolls: Essays in Method*. Early Judaism and Its Literature 39. Atlanta: Society of Biblical Literature.

Brooke, George J., and James M. Robinson. 1994. A Further Fragment of 1QSb: The Schøyen Collection MS 1909. Page 30 in *Institute for Antiquity and Christianity Occasional Papers* 30. Claremont, CA: Institute for Antiquity and Christianity [= *Journal of Jewish Studies* 46 (1995): 120–133, Plates 1–4].

Broshi, Magen, and Elisha Qimron. 1986. A House Sale Deed from Kefar Baru from the Time of Bar Kokhba. *Israel Exploration Journal* 36:201–14.

_____. 1994. A Hebrew I.O.U. Note from the Second Year of the Bar Kokhba Revolt. *Journal of Jewish Studies* 45:286–94.

Broshi, Magen, and Hanan Eshel. 1999. Residential Caves at Qumran. *Dead Sea Discoveries* 6:328–48.

_____. 2004. Three Seasons of Excavations at Qumran. *Journal of Roman Archaeology* 17:321–331.

Brown, Judith. 2005. *John Allegro: Maverick of the Dead Sea Scrolls.* Grand Rapids: Eerdmans.

Brownlee, William W. 1957. Muhammed ed-Deeb's Own Story of His Scroll Discovery. *Journal of Near Eastern Studies* 16:236–38.

Bülow-Jacobsen, Adam. 2009. Writing Materials in the Ancient World. Pages 3–29 in *The Oxford Handbook of Papyrology.* Edited by R.S. Bagnall. Oxford: Oxford University Press.

Burnham, Dorothy K. 1980. *Warp and Weft: A Textile Terminology.* Toronto: Royal Ontario Museum.

Burrows, Millar. 1955. *The Dead Sea Scrolls.* New York: Viking.

Butí, S., N. Salvadó, L. Nuria, E. Papiol, E. Heras, and J. Gunneweg. 2006. Determination of Wine Residues in Qumran Amphora-35. Pages 71–80 in *Bio- and Material Cultures at Qumran. Papers from a COST Action G8 working group meeting held at the Hebrew University of Jerusalem, Israel on 22-23 May 2005.* Edited by J. Gunneweg, C. Greenblatt, and A. Adriaens. Stuttgart: Fraunhofer IRB Verlag.

Butler, Trent C. 1981. *Joshua.* Word Biblical Commentary 7. Waco, Texas: Word Books.

Cargill, Robert R. 2009. *Qumran through (Real) Time: A Virtual Reconstruction of Qumran and the Dead Sea Scrolls.* Piscataway, NJ: Gorgias.

Carmignac, Jean. 1961, 1963. *Les textes de Qumran traduits et annotés.* 2 vols. Paris: Letouzey et Ané.

Carswell, J. 1977. Fastenings on the Qumrân Manuscripts. Pages 23–28 in *DJD* 6.

Charlesworth, James H., ed. 1985. *The Old Testament Pseudepigrapha.* 2 vols. New York: Doubleday.

_____. 2009. What is a Variant? Announcing a Dead Sea Scrolls Fragment of Deuteronomy. *Maarav* 16:201–12.

Charlesworth, James H., and Loren T. Stuckenbruck. 1994. Blessings. Pages 119–31 in *Rule of the Community and Related Documents.* Vol. 1 of *The Dead Sea Scrolls: Hebrew, Aramaic, and Greek Texts with English Translations.* Edited by J.H. Charlesworth. Tübingen: J.B.C. Mohr.

Christensen, Duane L. 1991. *Deuteronomy 1-11.* Word Biblical Commentary 6A. Dallas, Texas: Word.

Clamer, Christa. 1997. *Fouilles archéologiques des 'Ain ez-Zara/Callirhoé villégiature hérodienne.* IFAPO Bibliothèque Archéologique et Historique 147. Beirut: Institut Français d'Archéologie du Proche-Orient.

Collins, John J. 2010. *Beyond the Qumran Community: The Sectarian Movement on the Dead Sea Scrolls.* Grand Rapids: Eerdmans.

Connan, Jacques. 1999. Use and Trade of Bitumen in Antiquity and Prehistory: Molecular Archaeology Reveals Secrets of Past Civilizations. *Philosophical Transactions of the Royal Society London* 354:33–50.

Cotton, Hannah M. 1995. The Archive of Salome Komaise Daughter of Levi: Another Archive from the Cave of Letters. *Zeitschrift für Papyrologie und Epigraphik* 105:171–208.

_____. 2002. Women and Law in the Documents from the Judaean Desert. Pages 123–47 in *Le rôle et le statut de la femme en Egypte Hellénistique Romaine et Byzantine.* Edited by H. Melaerts and L. Mooren. Leuven: Peeters.

Cotton, Hanna M., and Joseph Geiger. 1989. *Masada II: Yigael Yadin Excavations 1963-1965, Final Report.* Jerusalem: Israel Exploration Society.

Crane, Eve. 1999. *The World History of Bee-Keeping and Honey Hunting.* London: Routledge.

Crawford, Sidnie White. 2008. *Rewriting Scripture in Second Temple Times.* Grand Rapids: Eerdmans.

_____. 2012. Understanding the Textual History of the Hebrew Bible: A New Proposal. Pages 60–69 in *The Hebrew Bible in Light of the Dead Sea Scrolls.* Forschungen zur Religion und Literatur des Alten und Neuen Testaments 239. Edited by N. David. Göttingen: Vandenhoeck & Ruprecht.

Crawford, Sidney W., Jan Joosten, and Eugene Ulrich. 2008. Sample Editions of the Oxford Hebrew Bible: Deuteronomy 32:1-9, 1 King 11:1-8, and Jeremiah 27:1-10 (34 G). *Vetus Testamentum* 58:352–66.

Cross, Frank Moore. 1961a. *The Ancient Library of Qumran.* Revised edition. New York: Doubleday/Anchor.

_____. 1961b. The Development of the Jewish Scripts. Pages 133–202 in *The Bible and the Ancient Near East: Essays in Honor of William Foxwell Albright.* Edited by G.E. Wright. New York: Doubleday.

_____. 1993. El-Buqei'a. Pages 267–69 in *New Encyclopedia of Archaeological Excavations in the Holy Land.* Jerusalem: Israel Exploration Society.

_____. 1998. Paleography and the Dead Sea Scrolls. Pages 379–402 in vol. 1 of *The Dead Sea Scrolls After Fifty Years: A Comprehensive Assessment.* 2 vols. Edited by P.W. Flint and J.C. VanderKam. Leiden: Brill.

Cross, Frank Moore, and Esther Eshel. 1997. Ostraca from Khirbet Qumrân. *Israel Exploration Journal* 47:17–28.

Cross, Frank Moore, and Josef T. Milik. 1956. Explorations in the Judaean Buqei'a. *Bulletin of the American Schools of Oriental Research* 141:3–17.

Crowfoot, Elisabeth. 1974. Textiles. Pages 60–77 in *Discoveries in the Wâdi ed-Dâliyeh.* Edited by P.W. Lapp and N.L. Lapp. Annual of the American Schools of Oriental Research 41. Cambridge, Mass.: American Schools of Oriental Research.

Crowfoot, Grace Mary. 1955. The Linen Textiles. Pages 18–38 in *DJD* 1.

Crowfoot, Grace Mary, and Elizabeth Crowfoot. 1961. The Textile and Basketry. Pages 51–63 in *DJD* 2.

Cultrone, Giuseppe, Eduardo Sebastian, Kerstin Elert, Maria Jose de la Torre, Olga Cazalla, and Carlos Rodriguez-Navarro. 2004. Influence of Mineralogy and Firing Temperature on the Porosity of Bricks. *Journal of the European Ceramic Society* 24:547–64.

Dana, James Dwight, Edward Salisbury Dana, Charles Palache, Harry Berman, and Clifford Frondel. 1951. *The System of Mineralogy of James Dwight Dana and Edward Salisbury Dana.* New York: Wiley.

Dar, Shimon. 1993. *Settlements and Cult Sites on Mount Hermon, Israel: Ituraean Culture in the Hellenistic and Roman Periods.* BAR International Series 589. Oxford: Archaeopress.

_____. 1994. *The History of Hermon: Settlements and Temples of the Itureans.* Tel Aviv: Hakibbutz Hameuhad (Hebrew).

_____. 1999. *Sumaqa. A Roman and Byzantine Jewish village on Mount Carmel, Israel.* BAR International Series 815. Oxford: Arcaeopress.

Davis, Kipp. 2014a. 4QJer^a (4Q70): From Anthology to Scripture in the Oldest Known Copy of Jeremiah. Paper presented at the SBL Annual Meeting. San Diego, November 22–25.

_____. 2014b. Margins as Media: The Long Insertion in 4QJer^a (4Q70). Paper presented at the Conference 'Bible as Notepad'. Oslo, 12 December.

_____. 2014c. *The Cave 4 Apocryphon of Jeremiah and the Qumran Jeremianic Traditions: Prophetic Persona and the Construction of Community Identity.* Studies on the Texts of the Deserts of Judah 111. Leiden: Brill.

_____. 2016. The Social Milieu of 4QJer^a (4Q70) in a Second Temple Jewish Manuscript Culture: Fragments, Manuscripts, Variance, and Meaning. *Proceedings of the 2013 IOQS papers*, forthcoming.

Degen, I.A., and G.A. Newman. 1993. Raman Spectra of Inorganic Ions. *Spectrochimica Acta Part A: Molecular Spectroscopy* 49:859–887.

Discoveries in the Judaean Desert. Vols I–XL. Oxford: Clarendon, 1955–2010.

Dimant, Devorah. 2011. The Vocabulary of the Qumran Sectarian Texts. Pages 347–95 in *Qumran und die Archäologie. Texte und Kontexte.* Edited by J. Frey, C. Claussen, and N. Kessler. Wissenschaftliche Untersuchungen zum Neuen Testament I 278. Tübingen: Mohr Siebeck.

Długosz, Dariusz. 2005. Qumrân au Musée du Louvre. *Revue de Qumrân* 22:121–29.

Donceel-Voute, Pauline. 1994. The Archaeology of Khirbet Qumran in Light of Its Pottery. Pages 1–38 in *Methods of Investigation of the Dead Sea Scrolls and the Khirbet Qumran Site: Present Realities and Future Prospects.* Edited by M.O. Wise, N. Golb, J.J. Collins, and D.G. Pardee. New York: The New York Academy of Sciences.

Doudna, Gregory L. 1998. Dating the Scrolls on the Basis of Radiocarbon Analysis. Pages 430–71 in Vol. 1 of *The Dead Sea Scrolls after Fifty Years: A Comprehensive Assessment.* Edited by P.W. Flint, and J.C. VanderKam. 2 vols. Leiden: Brill.

_____. 2006. The Legacy of an Error in Archaeological Interpretation: The Dating of the Qumran Cave Scroll Deposits. Pages 147–57 in *Qumran: The Site of the Dead Sea Scrolls: Archaeological Interpretations and Debates: Proceedings of a Conference Held at Brown Univeristy, November 17–19, 2002.* Edited by K. Galor, J.-B. Humbert, and J. Zangenberg. Leiden: Brill.

Driver, Godfrey R. 1954. *Aramaic Documents of the Fifth Century B. C.* Oxford: University Press.

Duhaime, Jean. 1995. War Scroll (1Q, 1Q33). Pages 80–203 in *Damascus Document, War Scroll, and Related Documents.* Vol. 2 of *The Dead Sea Scrolls: Hebrew, Aramaic, and Greek Texts with English Translation.* Edited by J.H. Charlesworth. Tübingen: Mohr Siebeck.

Duncan, Julia A. 1997. Excerpted Texts of Deuteronomy at Qumran. *Revue de Qumran* 18:43–62.

Dušek, Jan. 2007. *Les manuscrits araméens du Wadi Daliyeh et la Samarie vers 450-332 av. J.-C.* Culture & History of the Ancient Near East 30. Leiden: Brill.

_____. 2011. Protection of Ownership in the Deeds of Sale: Deeds of Sale from the Judean Desert in Context. Pages 857–79 in vol. 1 of *The Dead Sea Scrolls in Context: Integrating the Dead Sea Scrolls in the Study of Ancient Texts, Languages, and Cultures.* Edited by A. Lange, E. Tov, and M. Weigold. Supplements to Vetus Testamentum 140.2. Leiden: Brill.

Dyson, Stephen L. 1968. *The Commonware Pottery; the Brittle Ware. The Excavations at Dura-Europos, Final Report iv, Part i, fasc. 3.* New Haven: Dura-Europos Publications.

Edwards, H.G.M., E. Ellis, D.W. Farwell, and R.C. Janaway. 1996. Preliminary Study of the Application of Fourier Transform Raman Spectroscopy to the Analysis of Degraded Archaeological Linen Textiles. *Journal of Raman Spectroscopy* 27:663–69.

Edwards, Howell G.M., and Dennis W. Farwell. 2008. The Conservational Heritage of Wall Paintings and Buildings: An FT-Raman Spectroscopic Study of Prehistoric, Roman, Mediaeval and Renaissance Lime Substrates and Mortars. *Journal of Raman Spectroscopy* 39:985–92.

Edwards, H.G.M., D.W. Farwell, and D. Webster. 1997. FT-Raman Microscopy of Untreated Natural Plant Fibres. *Spectrochimica Acta Part A* 53:2383–92.

Eisenman, Robert H., and Michael Wise. 1992. *The Dead Sea Scrolls Uncovered: The First Complete Translation and Interpretation of 50 Key Documents Withheld for over 35 Years.* Shaftesbury, UK: Element.

Elgvin, Torleif. 2005. The Yahad Is More Than Qumran. Pages 273–79 in *Enoch and Qumran Origins: New Light on a Forgotten Connection*. Edited by G. Boccaccini. Grand Rapids: Eerdmans.

_____. 2009. How to Reconstruct a Fragmented Scroll: the Puzzle of 4Q422. Pages 223–36 in *Northern Light on the Dead Sea Scrolls*. Studies on the Texts of the Desert of Judah 80. Edited by A. Klostergaard Petersen, T. Elgvin, C. Wassen, H. von Weissenberg, M. Winninge, and assistant editor Martin Ehrensvärd. Leiden: Brill.

_____. 2010. Temple Mysticism and the Temple of Men. Pages 227–42 in *The Dead Sea Scrolls: Text and Context*. Edited by C. Hempel. Studies on the Texts of the Desert of Judah 90. Leiden: Brill.

_____. 2011. From the Earthly to the Heavenly Temple: Lines from the Bible and Qumran to Hebrews and Revelation. Pages 23–36 in *The Dead Sea Scrolls and Early Christianity: Questions of Origins and Relationships*. Edited by C.A. Evans. Peabody, Mass.: Hendrickson.

_____. 2014. Eschatology and Messianism in the *Gabriel Inscription*. *Journal of the Jesus Movement in Its Jewish Setting* 1:5–25.

Elgvin, Torleif, with Stephen J. Pfann. 2002. An Incense Altar from Qumran. *Dead Sea Discoveries* 9:20–33.

Eshel, Ester, and Hanan Eshel. 2003. Dating the Samaritan Pentateuch's Compilation in Light of the Dead Sea Scrolls. Pages 215–40 in *Emanuel. Studies in Hebrew Bible, Septuagint, and Dead Sea Scrolls in Honor of Emanuel Tov*. Supplements to Vetus Testamentum 94. Edited by Shalom Paul *et al*. Leiden: Brill.

_____. 2005. New Fragments from Qumran: 4QGen^f, 4QIsa^b, 4Q226, 8QGen, and XpapEnoch. *Dead Sea Discoveries* 12:134–57.

_____. 2007. A Preliminary Report on Seven New Fragments from Qumran. *Meghillot* 5-6:271–78 (Hebrew).

Eshel, Esther, Hanan Eshel, and Magen Broshi. 2007. A New Fragment of XJudges. *Dead Sea Discoveries* 14:354–58.

Eshel, Esther, Hanan Eshel, and Gregor Geiger. 2008. Mur 174: A Hebrew I.O.U. Document from Wadi Murabba'at. *Liber Annuus* 58:9–27.

Eshel, Esther, Hanan Eshel, and Ada Yardeni. 2009. A Deed from 'Year Four After the Destruction of the House of Israel'. *Cathedra* 132:6–24 (Hebrew), 199 (English summary).

_____. 2011. A Document from 'Year 4 of the Destruction of the House of Israel'. *Dead Sea Discoveries* 18:1–28.

Eshel, Hanan. 1991. The Prayer of Joseph, a Papyrus from Masada and the Samaritan Temple on ΑΡΓΑΡΙΖΙΝ. *Zion* 56:125–36 (Hebrew), xii (English).

_____. 1996. Wâdi Dâliyeh Papyrus 14 and the Samaritan Temple. *Zion* 61:359–65 (Hebrew), xxvi (English).

_____. 1997. The Contribution of Documents and Other Remains Found in the Judean Desert Between 1979 and 1993 to the Understanding of the Bar Kokhba Revolt. *Bulletin of Anglo-Israel Archaeological Society* 15:108–10

_____. 1998. The History of the Research and Survey of the Finds. Pages 52–54 in *Refuge Caves of the Bar Kokhba Revolt*. Edited by H. Eshel and D. Amit. Tel Aviv: Eretz (Hebrew).

_____. 2001a. A Three Shekel Weight (?) from Qumran. *Judea and Samaria Research Studies* 10:33–34 (Hebrew); xi (English).

_____. 2001b. Three New Fragments from Qumran Cave 11. *Dead Sea Discoveries* 8:1–8.

_____. 2002a. Documents of the First Jewish Revolt from the Judean Desert. Pages 157–63 in *The First Jewish Revolt: Archaeology, History and Ideology*. Edited by A.M. Berlin and J.A. Overman. London: Routledge.

_____. 2002b. Another Document from the Archive of Salome Komise Daughter of Levi. *Scripta Classica Israelica* 21:169–71.

_____. 2003a. 6Q30, a cursive 'sîn', and Proverbs 11. *Journal of Biblical Literature* 122:544–46.

_____. 2003b. A Second Fragment of XJudges. *Journal of Jewish Studies* 54:139–41.

_____. 2003c. The Dates Used During the Bar Kokhba Revolt. Pages 93–105 in *The Bar Kokhba War Reconsidered*. Edited by P. Schäfer. Tübingen: Mohr Siebeck.

_____. 2007. The Governors of Samaria in the Fifth and Fourth Centuries B.C.E. Pages 223–34 in *Judah and the Judeans in the Fourth Century B.C.E.* Edited by O. Lipschits, G.N. Knoppers, and R. Albertz. Winona Lake: Eisenbrauns.

_____. 2009a. *Qumran*. Jerusalem: Carta.

_____. 2009b. *Masada*. Jerusalem: Carta.

_____. 2010a. The Culprit—the Vulture. *Haaretz* 9.4 (Hebrew).

_____. 2010b. Gleaning of Scrolls from the Judean Desert. Pages 49–87 in *The Dead Sea Scrolls: Texts and Context*. Edited by C. Hempel. Studies on the Texts of the Desert of Judah 90. Leiden: Brill.

Eshel, Hanan, Yosi Baruchi, and Roi Porat. 2006. Fragments of a Leviticus Scroll (ArugLev) Found in the Judean Desert in 2004. *Dead Sea Discoveries* 13:55–60.

Eshel, Hanan, and Magen Broshi. 2003. Excavations at Qumran, Summer of 2001. *Israel Exploration Journal* 53:61–73.

Eshel, Hanan, Boaz Zissu, and Amos Frumkin. 1998. Two Refuge Caves in Naḥal Mikhmas (Wadi Suweinit). Pages 103–7 in *Refuge Caves of the Bar Kokhba Revolt*. Edited by H. Eshel and D. Amit. Tel Aviv: Eretz (Hebrew).

Falk, Daniel K. 2007. *The Parabiblical Texts: Strategies for Extending the Scriptures in the Dead Sea Scrolls*. Library of Second Temple Studies 63. London: T&T Clark.

Fernández Marcos, Natalio. 2011. *Judges*. Biblia Hebraica Quinta 7. Stuttgart: Deutsche Bibelgesellschaft.

Fidanzio, Marcello 2015. Which Cave Does This Pottery Come from? The Information Written on the Pottery Found in the Qumran Caves (R. de Vaux Excavations 1949-1956). *Revue Biblique* 122:128–31.

Fields, Weston W. 2006. *The Dead Sea Scrolls: A Short History*. Leiden: Brill.

_____. 2009. *The Dead Sea Scrolls: A Full History*. Leiden: Brill.

Fine, Stephen. 1987. *University of Southern California Archaeological Research Collection*. Los Angeles: University of Southern California.

Finkelstein, Louis. 1966. *The Pharisees*. 2d ed. Philadelphia: Jewish Publication Society.

Fitzmyer, Joseph T. 1971. *The Genesis Apocryphon of Qumran Cave 1*. Rome: Biblical Institute Press.

_____. 1995. The Aramaic and Hebrew Fragments of Tobit from Qumran Cave 4. *Catholic Biblical Quarterly* 57:655–75.

_____. 2008. *A Guide to the Dead Sea Scrolls*. Grand Rapids: Eerdmans.

Flint, Peter W. 1997. The Daniel Tradition at Qumran. Pages 41–59 in *Eschatology, Messianism, and the Dead Sea Scrolls*. Edited by C.A. Evans and P.W. Flint. Studies in the Dead Sea Scrolls and Related Literature. Grand Rapids: Eerdmans.

Flusser, David. 1994. 'The Book of Mysteries' and a Synagogal Prayer. Pages 3–20 in *Knesset Ezra: Literature and Life in the Synagogue: Studies Presented to Ezra Fleischer*. Edited by S. Elizur, M.D. Herr, G. Shaked, and A. Shinan. Jerusalem: Ben Zvi (Hebrew).

Forbes, Robert James. 1956. *Studies in Ancient Technology*. Vol. 4 of *Studies in Ancient Technology*. Leiden: Brill.

Freedman, David N., and Jack R. Lundbom. 1999. Haplography in Jeremiah 1–20. *Eretz-Israel* 26:28*–38*.

Freedman, David N., and Kenneth A. Mathews. 1985. *The Paleo-Leviticus Scroll*. Winona Lake: American School of Oriental Research.

Fuller, Russel E. 2013. Harmonizing Readings in 4QXII^c and in the Masoretic Text. Paper presented at SBL Annual Meeting. Baltimore, 24 November.

Garret, Donald E. 1996. *Potash: Deposits, Processing, Properties and Uses*. London: Chapman & Hall.

García Martínez, Florentino. 1994. Les Manuscrits du Désert de Juda et la Deutéronome. Pages 63–82 in *Studies in Deuteronomy: In Honour of C.J. Labuschagne on the Occasion of His 65th Birthday*. Edited by F. García Martínez, A. Hilhorst, J.T.A.G.M. van Ruiten, and A.S. van der Woude. Supplements to Vetus Testamentum 53. Leiden: Brill.

_____. 2010. Cave 11 in Context. Pages 199–209 in *The Dead Sea Scrolls: Texts and Contexts*. Edited by Charlotte Hempel. Leiden: Brill.

_____. 2012. Light on the Joshua Books from the Dead Sea Scrolls. Pages 145–59 in *After Qumran: Old and Modern Editions of the Biblical Texts - the Historical Books*. Edited by H. Ausloos, B. Lemmelijn, and J. Trebolle Barrera. Bibliotheca Ephemeridum Theologicarum Lovaniensium 246. Leuven: Peeters.

Gese, Hartmut. 1974. Die Entstehung der Büchereinteilung des Psalters. Pages 159–67 in *Vom Sinai zum Zion: Alttestamentliche Beiträge zur biblischen Theologie*. München: Kaiser.

Geva, Hillel. 1997. Searching for Roman Jerusalem. *Biblical Archaeology Review* 23, no. 6:35–45, 72–73.

Gilead, Isaak, and Yuval Goren. 1989. Petrographic Analyses of Fourth Millennium BC Pottery and Stone Vessels from the Northern Negev, Israel. *Bulletin of the American Schools of Oriental Research* 275:5–14.

Gitin, Seymour. 1989. Incense Altars from Ekron, Israel and Judah: Context and Typology. *Eretz Israel* 20:52–67.

_____. 1992. New Incense Altars from Ekron: Context, Typology and Function. *Eretz Israel* 23:43–49.

_____. 2002. The Four-Horned Altar and Sacred Space: An Archaeological Perspective. Pages 95–123 in *Sacred Time, Sacred Place Archaeology and the Religion of Israel*. Edited by B.M. Gittlen. Winona Lake: Eisenbrauns.

Glascock, Michael D. 1992. Characterization of Archaeological Ceramics at MURR by Neutron Activation Analysis and Multivariate Statistics. Pages 11–26 in *Chemical Characterization of Ceramic Pastes in Archaeology*. Edited by H. Neff. Madison, WI: Prehistory Press.

Glascock, Michael D., and Hector Neff. 2003. Neutron Activation Analysis and Provenance Research in Archaeology. *Measurement Science and Technology* 14:1516–26.

Goranson, Stephen. 1991. Further Qumran Archaeology Publications in Progress. *Biblical Archaeologist* 54, no. 2:110–11.

_____. 1992. An Inkwell from Qumran. *Michmanim* 6:37–40.

_____. 1994. Qumran. A Hub of Scribal Activity? *Biblical Archaeology Review* 20, no. 5:37–39.

Granger-Taylor, Hero. 2006. Textiles from Khirbet Qazone and the Cave of Letters, Two Burial Sites Near the Dead Sea: Similarities and Differences in Find Spots and Textile Types. Pages 113–34 in *Textiles in Situ: Their Find Spots in Egypt and Neighbouring Countries in the First Millennium CE*. Edited by S. Schrenk. Riggisberger Berichte 13. Riggisberg, Switzerland: Abegg-Stiftung.

Green, Christine Insley. 1987. *The Temple Furniture from the Sacred Animal Necropolis at North Saqqara 1964-1976*. London: Egypt Exploration Society.

Greenfield, Jonas C., Michael E. Stone, and Esther Eshel. 2004. *The Aramaic Levi Document: Edition, Translation, Commentary*. Leiden: Brill.

Gross, Netty C. 1999. The Mystery of the Angel Scroll. *Jerusalem Report* 27 September.

Guillaume, Philippe. 2007. A Reconsideration of Manuscripts Classified as Scrolls of the Twelve Minor Prophets (XII). *Journal of Hebrew Scriptures* 7, art. 16:2–12.

Gunneweg, Jan. 2012. Four Similar Looking Dead Sea Jars that All Have a Different Provenience: Appearances Provide Sometimes the Wrong Information. Chapter 7 in *Outdoor Qumran and the Dead Sea: Its Impact on Indoor Bio- and Material Cultures at Qumran and the Judaean Manuscripts: Proceedings of the Joint Hebrew University and COST Action D-42 Cultural Heritage Workshop Held at the Hebrew University of Jerusalem in May 25-26, 2010.* Edited by J. Gunneweg and C. Greenblatt. Hebrew University of Jerusalem. E-book: http://micro5.mscc.huji.ac.il/~msjan/qumranproceedings2010.html, specific article at http://micro5.mscc.huji.ac.il/~msjan/aeqsj.pdf.

Gunneweg, Jan, and Marta Balla. 2003. Neutron Activation Analysis: Scroll Jars and Common Ware. Pages 3–53 in *Khirbet Qumrân et ʿAïn Feshkha II: Études d'anthropologie, de physique et de chimie.* Edited by J-B. Humbert and J. Gunneweg. Novum Testamentum et Orbis Antiquus, Series Archaeologica 3. Fribourg: Academic Press.

_____. 2006. The Provenance of Qumran Pottery by Instrumental Neutron Activation Analysis. Pages 99–108 in *Bio- and Material Cultures at Qumran: Papers from a COST Action G8 Working Group Meeting Held at the Hebrew University of Jerusalem, Israel on May 22-23-2005.* Edited by J. Gunneweg, A. Adriaens, and C. Greenblatt. Stuttgart: Fraunhofer IRB Verlag.

_____. 2010. Was the Qumran Settlement a Mere Pottery Production Center? What Instrumental Neutron Activation Revealed. Pages 39–66 in *Holistic Qumran: Trans-disciplinary Research of Qumran and the Dead Sea Scrolls.* Edited by J. Gunneweg, A. Adriaens, and J. Dik. Studies on the Texts of the Desert of Judah 87. Leiden: Brill.

Gunneweg, Jan, Isadore Perlman, and Frank Asaro. 1988. The Origin, Classification and Chronology of Nabataean Painted Fine Ware. *Jahrbuch des Romisch-Germanischen Zentralmuseums Mainz* 35:315–45.

Hadas, Gideon. 2008. Ein Gedi, Where They Grow the Best Dates and the Opobalsamum (balsam). Pages 87–103 in *Melakh Haaretz (Salt of the Earth).* Edited by O. Navon. Vol 3 of *Melakh Haaretz (Salt of the Earth).* A Series for Dead Sea Studies. Jerusalem: Magnes (Hebrew).

Hahn, Oliver, Timo Wolff, Birgit Kanngiesser, Wolfgang Malzer, and Ioanna Mantouvalou. 2007. Non-Destructive Investigation of the Scroll Material: '4QComposition Concerning Divine Providence' (4Q413). *Dead Sea Discoveries* 14:359–64.

Haensch, R. 2001. Zum Verständnis von P.Jericho 16 gr. *Scripta Classica Israelica* 20:155–67.

Haran, Menahem. 1960. The Uses of Incense in the Ancient Israelite Ritual. *Vetus Testamentum* 10:113–29.

_____. 1978. *Temples and Temple Service in Ancient Israel: An Inquiry into the Character of Cult Phenomena and the Historical Setting of the Priestly School.* Oxford: Clarendon.

_____. 1992. Technological Heritage in the Preparation of Skins for Biblical Texts in Medieval Oriental Jewry. Pages 35–43 in *Pergament: Geschichte, Struktur, Restaurierung und Herstellung.* Edited by P. Rück. Sigmaringen: Jan Thorbecke Verlag.

_____. 1993. 'Incense Altars'—Are They? Pages 237–47 in *Biblical Archaeology Today: Proceedings of the Second International Congress on Biblical Archaeology, Jerusalem, June-July 1990.* Jerusalem: Israel Exploration Society.

Harbottle, Garman. 1976. Activation Analysis in Archaeology. *Radiochemistry* 3:33–72.

Harding, Gerald Lankester. 1949. The Dead Sea Scrolls. *Palestine Exploration Quarterly* 81:112–16.

_____. 1952. Khirbet Qumran and Wady Murabbaʿat: Fresh Light on the Dead Sea Scrolls and the New Manuscript Discoveries in Jordan. *Palestine Exploration Quarterly* 84: 104–9.

Henze, Matthias, ed. 2011. *Hazon Gabriel: New Readings of the Gabriel Revelation.* Atlanta: Society of Biblical Literature.

Herschberg, Avraham Shmuel. 1924. *Textiles and the Textile Industry.* Warsaw (Hebrew).

Hogeterp, Albert L.A. 2010. Daniel and the Qumran Daniel Cycle: Observations on 4QKingdoms[a-b] (4Q552–553). Pages 173–91 in *Authoritative Scriptures in Ancient Judaism.* Edited by M. Popovic. Journal for the Study of Judaism Supplement Series 141. Leiden: Brill.

Holladay, William L. 1971. *A Concise Hebrew and Aramaic Lexicon of the Old Testament.* Grand Rapids: Eerdmans.

_____. 1986. *Jeremiah 1: A Commentary on the Book of the Prophet Jeremiah: Chapters 1-25.* Hermeneia: A Critical and Historical Commentary on the Bible. Philadelphia: Fortress.

Horton, Charles. 2004. The Chester Beatty Biblical Papyri: A Find of the Greatest Importance. Pages 149–60 in *The Earliest Gospels: The Origins and Transmission of the Earliest Christian Gospels: The Contribution of the Chester Beatty Gospel Codex P[45].* Edited by C. Horton. The Library of New Testament Studies. London: T&T Clark.

Hossfeld, Frank-Lothar, and Erich Zenger. 2000. *Psalmen 51-100.* Herders Theologischer Kommentar zum Alten Testament. Freiburg: Herder.

Humbert, Jean-Baptiste. 1994. L'espace sacré à Qumrân. Propositions pour l'archéologie (Planches I-III). *Revue Biblique* 101:161–211.

Humbert, Jean-Baptiste and Alain Chambon. 1994. *Fouilles de Khirbet Qumrân et de ʿAïn Feshkha I: Album de photographies, répertoire du fonds photographique, synthèse des notes de chantier du Père Roland de Vaux.* Novum Testamentum et Orbis Antiquus, Series Archaeologica 1. Fribourg: Éditions Universitaires.

Humbert, Jean-Baptiste, Alain Chambon, and Stephen J. Pfann. 2003. *The Excavations of Khirbet Qumran and Ain Feshkha: Synthesis of Roland de Vaux's Field Notes.* Novum Testamentum et Orbis Antiquus, Series archaeologica 1B. Fribourg: Department of Biblical Studies.

Humbert, Jean-Baptiste, and Jan Gunneweg, eds 2003. *Khirbet Qumrân et ʿAïn Feshkha II: Études d'anthropologie, de physique et de chimie.* Novum Testamentum et Orbis Antiquus, Series Archaeologica 3. Fribourg: Academic Press.

Iliffe, J.H. 1945. Imperial Art in Transjordan. *The Quarterly of the Department of Antiquities in Palestine* 11:1–26 + plates I-X.

Ilan, O., R. Amiran, A. Serban, and A. Nissenbaum. 1984. Dead Sea Asphalt From the Excavations in Tel Arad and Small Tel Malhata. *Paléorientalia* 10:157–61.

Jerusalem Crown: The Bible of the Hebrew University of Jerusalem. 2000. Jerusalem: The Hebrew University of Jerusalem.

Joosten, Jan. 2007. A Note on the Text of Deuteronomy xxxii 8. *Vetus Testamentum* 57:548–55.

Khairy, Nabil I. 1980. Inkwells of the Roman Period from Jordan. *Levant* 12:155–62.

Kiraz, George A. 2005. *Anton Kiraz's Archive on the Dead Sea Scrolls.* Piscataway: Gorgias.

Kislev, Mordechai E., and Mina Marmorstein. 2003. Cereals and Fruits from a Collapsed Cave South of Khirbet Qumran. *Israel Exploration Journal* 53:74–77.

Kister, Menahem. 2008. Liturgical Formulae in the Light of Fragments from the Judaean Desert. *Tarbiz* 77:331–55 (Hebrew).

Koehler, Ludwig, and Walter Baumgartner. 1996–2000. *The Hebrew and Aramaic Lexicon of the Old Testament.* Leiden: Brill.

Kraeling, Carl H. 1952. A Dead Sea Scroll Jar at the Oriental Institute. *Bulletin of the American Schools of Oriental Research* 125:1, 5–7.

Kratz, Reinhard G. 2001. The Visions of Daniel. Pages 91–113 in *The Book of Daniel: Composition and Reception.* Edited by J.J. Collins and P.W. Flint. Supplements to Vetus Testamentum 83.1. Leiden: Brill.

Kutscher, Eduard Y. 1974. *The Language and Linguistic Background of the Isaiah Scroll (I Q Isaᵃ).* Studies on the Texts of the Desert of Judah 6. Leiden: Brill.

Lange, Armin. 2009. *Handbuch der Textfunde vom Toten Meer.* Vol. 1 of *Die Handschriften biblischer Bücher von Qumran und den anderen Fundorten.* Tübingen: Mohr Siebeck.

_____. 2010. The Textual Plurality of Jewish Scriptures in the Second Temple in Light of the Dead Sea Scrolls. Pages 43–96 in *Qumran and the Bible: Studying the Jewish and Christian Scriptures in Light of the Dead Sea Scrolls.* Edited by N. David and A. Lange. Contributions to Biblical Exegesis and Theology 57. Leuven: Peeters.

_____. 2013. Textual Revision of the Minor Prophets in Light of 4QXIIᵍ. Paper presented at SBL Annual Meeting. Baltimore. 24 November.

Langlois, Michael. 2011. *Le texte de Josué 10. Approche philologique, épigraphique et diachronique.* Orbis Biblicus et Orientalis 252. Fribourg: Academic Press / Göttingen: Vandenhoeck & Ruprecht.

Latzke, Peter and Rolf Hesse. 1988. *Textile Fasern.* Frankfurt/Main: Dt. Fachverlag.

Leese, M.N., and P.L. Main. 1994. The Efficient Computation of Unbiased Mahalanobis Distances and their Interpretation in Archaeometry. *Archaeometry* 36:307–16.

Lemaire, André. 1996. Nouveaux fragments du Rouleau du Temple de Qumran. *Revue de Qumran* 17:271–74.

_____. 1997. Un fragment araméen inédit de Qumran. *Revue de Qumran* 18:331–33.

_____. 2003. Inscriptions du khirbeh, des grottes et de ʿAin Feshka. Pages 341–88 in *Khirbet Qumrân et ʿAïn Feshkha II: Études d'anthropologie, de physique et de chimie.* Novum Testamentum et Orbis Antiquus, Series Archaeologica 3. Edited by J-B. Humbert and J. Gunneweg. Fribourg: Academic Press.

_____. 2006. New Aramaic Ostraca from Idumea and Their Historical Interpretation. Pages 413–56 in *Judah and the Judeans in the Persian Period.* Edited by O. Lipschits and M. Oeming. Winona Lake: Eisenbrauns.

Levin, Zev, Hezi Gershon, and Eliezer Ganor. 2005. Vertical Distribution of Physical and Chemical Properties of Haze Particles in the Dead Sea Valley. *Atmospheric Environment* 39: 4937–45.

Levine, Baruch A. 2000. The Various Working of the Aramaic Legal Tradition: Jews and Nabateans in the Naḥal Ḥever Archive. Pages 836–51 in *The Dead Sea Scrolls Fifty Years After their Discovery: Proceedings of the Jerusalem Congress, July 20-25, 1997.* Edited by L.H. Schiffman, E. Tov, J.C. VanderKam, and G. Marquis. Jerusalem: Israel Exploration Society.

Lewis, Naphtali. 1989. *The Documents from the Bar Kokhba Period in the Cave of Letters: Greek Papyri.* Jerusalem: Israel Exploration Society.

Lifshitz, Baruch. 1961. The Greek Documents from Naḥal Seelim and Naḥal Mishmar. *Israel Exploration Journal* 11:53–62.

Licht, Jacob. 1965. *The Rule Scroll: A Scroll From the Wilderness of Judaea: 1QS, 1QSa, 1QSb.* Jerusalem: Bialik Institute (Hebrew).

Lisker, Sorin, Roi Porat, and Amos Frumkin. 2010. Late Neogene Rift Valley Fill Sediments Preserved in Caves of the Dead Sea Fault Escarpment (Israel): Palaeogeographic and Morphotectonic Implications. *Sedimentology* 57:429–45.

Lönnqvist, Minna and Kenneth. 2011. Parallels to Be Seen: Manuscripts in Jars from Qumran and Egypt. Pages 471–87 in *The Dead Sea Scrolls in Context: Integrating the Dead Sea Scrolls in the Study of Ancient Texts, Languages, and Cultures.* Edited by A. Lange et al. Supplements to Vetus Testamentum 140. Leiden: Brill.

Loveless, Gary and Stephanie. 2012. *Dead Sea Scrolls & the Bible: Ancient Artifacts, Timeless Treasures.* Forth Worth: Southwestern Baptist Theological Seminary.

Lundberg, Marilyn, and Bruce Zuckerman. 1996. New Aramaic Fragments from Qumran Cave One. *Comprehensive Aramaic Lexicon Newsletter* 12:1–5.

Lundbom, Jack R. 1999. *Jeremiah 1-20: A New Translation with Introduction and Commentary.* AB 21A. New York: Doubleday.

Magen, Yitzhak. 2004. Qalandiya – A Second Temple-Period Viticulture and Wine-Manufacturing Agricultural Settlement. Pages 29–144 in *The Land of Benjamin.* Edited by Y. Magen et al. Jerusalem: Israel Antiquities Authority.

Magen, Yitzhak, and Yuval Peleg. 2006. Back to Qumran: Ten Years of Excavation and Research. Pages 55–113 in *Qumran: The Site of the Dead Sea Scrolls: Archaeological Interpretations and Debates: Proceedings of a Conference held at Brown Univeristy, November 17-19, 2002.* Edited by K. Galor et al. Leiden: Brill.

_____. 2007. *The Qumran Excavations 1993–2004: Preliminary Report.* Judea & Samaria Publication 6. Jerusalem: Israel Antiquities Authority.

Magness, Jodi. 1994. The Community at Qumran in Light of Its Pottery. Pages 39–48 in *Methods of Investigation of the Dead Sea Scrolls and the Khirbet Qumran Site: Present Realities and Future Prospects.* Edited by M.O. Wise, N. Golb, J.J. Collins, and D.G. Pardee. New York: The New York Academy of Sciences.

_____. 2002. *The Archaeology of Qumran and the Dead Sea Scrolls.* Grand Rapids: Eerdmans.

_____. 2004. *Debating Qumran: Collected Essays on Its Archaeology.* Leuven: Peeters.

_____. 2006. Qumran: The Site of The Dead Sea Scrolls: A Review Article. *Revue de Qumran* 22:641–64.

_____. 2014. The Site of Qumran and the Scroll Caves in Light of the Ceramic Evidence. Paper presented at the University of Lugano Conference on 'The History of the Caves of Qumran'. 21 February.

Maguregui, Maite, Ulla Knuutinen, Kepa Castro, and Juan Maunel Madariaga. 2010. Raman Spectroscopy as a Tool to Diagnose the Impact and Conservation State of Pompeian Second and Fourth Style Wall Paintings Exposed to Diverse Environments (House of Marcus Lucretius). *Journal of Raman Spectroscopy* 41:1110–19.

Maier, Johann. 1960. *Die Texte vom Totem Meer: I Übersetzung.* München: Ernst Reinhardt.

Manfredini and Schianchi. Srl. Calcium Carbonate Inclusions In Mixtures For Extruded Products: Behaviour, Problems & Solutions. http://www.manfredinieschianchi.com

Maranz, Felice. 1991. The Case of the Missing Scrolls. *Jerusalem Report* 26 December.

Martin, Malachi. 1958. *The Scribal Character of the Dead Sea Scrolls.* Bibliotheque du Museon 44. Louvain: Institut Orientaliste, Unversité de Louvain.

Martinez-Ramirez, S., S. Sanchez-Cortes, J.V. Garcia-Ramos, C. Domingo, and M.T. Blanco-Varela. 2003. Micro-Raman Spectroscopy Applied to Depth Profiles of Carbonates Formed in Lime Mortar. *Cement and Concrete Research* 33:2063–68.

Mcfarlane, Donald A., Raymond C. Keeler, and Hiroshi Mizutani. 1995. Ammonia Volatilization in a Mexican Bat Cave Ecosystem. *Biogeochemistry* 30:1–8.

McKenzie, Judith. 1990. *The Architecture of Petra.* Oxford: Oxford University Press. Plates 5–19.

McGovern, Patrick E. 2000. *The Foreign Relations of the "Hyksos": A Neutron Activation Study of Middle Bronze Age Pottery from the Eastern Mediterranean.* BAR International Series 888. Oxford: Archaeopress.

Mébarki, Farah, and Émile Puech. 2002. *Les Manuscrits de la mer Morte.* Paris: Éditions du Rouerge.

Meer, Michael N. van der. 2004. *Formation and Reformulation: the Redaction of the Book of Joshua in the Light of the Oldest Textual Witnesses.* Leiden: Brill.

Michniewicz, Jacek. 2009. *Qumran and Jericho Pottery: A Petrographic and Chemical Provenance Study.* Posnan: Wydawnictwo Naukowe UAM.

Milgrom, Jacob. 1979. The Burning of Incense in the Time of the Second Temple. Pages 330–34 in *Studies in Bible and the History of Israel.* Jerusalem: Kiryat-Sepher (Hebrew).

Milik, Josef T. 1950. Le giarre dei manoscritti della grotta del Mar Morto e dell'Egitto Tolemaic. *Biblica* 31:304–8.

_____. 1959. *Ten Years of Discovery in the Wilderness of Judaea.* London: SCM Press.

_____. 1972. *Milkî-ṣedeq et Milkî-reša'* dans les anciens écrits juifs et chrétiens. *Journal of Jewish Studies* 23:95–144.

_____. 1992. Les modèles araméens du livre d'Esther dans la grotte 4 de Qumrân. *Revue de Qumran* 15:321–99.

Misgav, Hagai. 1994. Four Segments of Inscribed Parchments from the Judean Desert. *Michmanim* 7:37–43 (Hebrew); 40*–41* (English summary).

Mlynarczyk, Jolanta. 2013. Terracotta Oil Lamps from Qumran: The Typology. *Revue Biblique* 120:99-133.

Mook, W.G., and H.J. Streurman. 1983. Physical and Chemical Aspects of Radiocarbon Dating. Pages 31–55 in *Proceedings of the First International Symposium on ^{14}C and Archaeology, Groningen.* Edited by W.G. Mook and H.T. Waterbolk. PACT 8. Strasbourg: Council of Europe.

Mook, W.G., and J. van der Plicht. 1999. Reporting 14C Activities and Concentrations. *Radiocarbon* 41:227–39.

Morgenstern, Matthew. 1997. Language and Literature in the Second Temple Period. *Journal of Jewish Studies* 48:130–45.

_____. 2007. The Apostrophe to Zion–A Philological and Structural Analysis. *Dead Sea Discoveries* 14:178–98.

Müller, Martin, Miroslav Z. Papiz, David T. Clarke, Mark A. Roberts, Bridget M. Murphy, Manfred Burghammer, Christian Riekel, Emmanuel Pontoz, and Jan Gunneweg. 2003. Identification of the Textiles Using Microscopy and Synchrotron Radiation X-RAY Fiber Diffraction. Pages 277–86 in *Khirbet Qumrân et 'Aïn Feshkha II: Études d'anthropologie, de physique et de chimie.* Edited by J.B. Humbert & J. Gunneweg. Novum Testamentum et Orbis Antiquus, Series Archaeologica 3. Fribourg: Academic Press.

Nagy, Rebecca M., Carol L. Meyers, Eric M. Meyers, and Zeev Weiss, eds. 1996. *Sepphoris in Galilee: Crosscurrents of Culture.* Winona Lake, Ind.: Eisenbrauns.

Nebe, Wilhelm G. 1989. Die Masada-Psalmen-Handschrift M1039-160 nach einem jüngst veröffentlichten Photo mit Text von *Psalm* 81,2-85,6. *Revue de Qumran* 14:89–98.

_____. 1999. Qumranica IV: Die jüngst in Khirbet Qumran gefundene hebräische Schenkungsurkunde auf einer Tonscherbe. *Zeitschrift für Althebraistik* 12:96–103.

Neff, Hector. 1994. RQ-Mode Principal Component Analysis of Ceramic Compositional Data. *Archaeometry* 36:115–30.

_____. 2000. Neutron Activation Analysis for Provenance Determination in Archaeology. Pages 81–134 in *Modern Analytical Methods in Art and Archaeology*. Edited by E. Ciliberto and G. Spoto. New York: John Wiley and Sons.

_____. 2002. Quantitative Techniques for Analyzing Ceramic Compositional Data. Pages 15–36 in *Ceramic Source Determination in the Greater Southwest*. Edited by D.M. Glowacki and H. Neff. Monograph 44. Los Angeles: Cotsen Institute of Archaeology.

Neff, Hector, Ronald L. Bishop, and Edward V. Sayre. 1988. A Simulation Approach to the Problem of Tempering in Compositional Studies of Archaeological Ceramics. *Journal of Archaeological Science* 15:159–72.

_____. 1989. More Observations on the Problem of Tempering in Compositional Studies of Archaeological Ceramics. *Journal of Archaeological Science* 16:57–69.

Nir-El, Yoram, and Magen Broshi. 1996. The Black Ink of the Qumran Scrolls. *Dead Sea Discoveries* 3:157–67.

Nissenbaum, Arie. 1975. The Microbiology and Biogeochemistry of the Dead Sea. *Microbial Ecology* 2:139–61.

Nitzan, Bilha. 1994. *Qumran Prayer and Religious Poetry*. Studies on the Texts of the Desert of Judah 12. Leiden: Brill.

Noah, William H. 2005. *Ink & Blood: From the Dead Sea Scrolls to the English Bible*. Murfreesboro: Aco.

Patrich, Joseph. 1985. Inscriptions Araméennes Juives dans les grottes d'El -'Aleiliyât. *Revue Biblique* 92:265–73.

_____. 1994. Khirbet Qumran in Light of New Archaeological Explorations in the Qumran Caves. Pages 73–95 in *Methods of Investigation of the Dead Sea Scrolls and the Khirbet Qumran Site: Present Realities and Future Prospects*. Edited by M.O. Wise, N. Golb, J.J. Collins, and D.G. Pardee. New York: The New York Academy of Sciences

Patterson, Armour. 2012. *Much Clean Paper for Little Dirty Paper: The Dead Sea Scrolls and the Texas Musawama*. Collierville, TN: Innovo Publishing.

Paul, Shalom. 2012. *Isaiah 40-66: Translation and Commentary*. Grand Rapids: Eerdmans.

Pfann, Stephen J. 2002. *Kelei Dema': Tithe Jars, Scroll Jars and Cookie Jars*. Pages 163–79 in *Copper Scroll Studies*. Supplements to Journal for the Study of the Pseudepigrapha 40. Edited by G.J. Brooke and P.R. Davies. Sheffield: Sheffield Academic Press.

Pfister, Rodolphe. 1934. *Textiles de Palmyre*. Paris: Art et Histoire.

Pfister, Rodolphe, and Louisa Bellinger. 1945. *Excavations at Dura Europos* IV, 2: *The Textiles*. New Haven: Yale University Press.

Pînzaru, Simona Cîntă, Dana Pop, and Loredana Nemeth. 2008. FT-Raman and FT-Infrared Investigations of Archaeological Artifacts from Foeni Neolithic Site (Banat, Romania). Studia Universitatis Babeş-Bolyai. *Geologia* 53:31–37.

Plicht, J. van der, S. Wijma, A.T. Aerts, M.H. Pertuisot, and H.A.J. Meijer. 2000. The Groningen AMS Facility: Status Report. *Nuclear Instruments and Methods* B172:58–65.

Ploeg, Johannes P.M. van der, and Adam S. van der Woude. 1971. *Le Targum de Job de la Grotte XI de Qumran*. Leiden: Brill.

Politis, Konstantin D. 2006. The Discovery and Excavation of the Khirbet Qazone Cemetery and Its Significance Relative to Qumran. Pages 213–19 in *Qumran: The Site of the Dead Sea Scrolls: Archaeological Interpretations and Debates: Proceedings of a Conference held at Brown Univeristy, November 17-19, 2002*. Edited by K. Galor et al. Leiden: Brill.

Poole, John, and Ronald Reed. 1962. The Preparation of Leather and Parchment by the Dead Sea Scrolls Community. *Technology & Culture* 3:1–36.

Popko, Lukasz. 2013. *Marriage Metaphor in Jer 2:1-4:2: A Diachronic Study Based on the MT and LXX*. Ph.D. diss. Jerusalem: École Biblique et Archéologique Française de Jérusalem.

Porat, Roi, Hanan Eshel, and Amos Frumkin. 2006. Two Groups of Coins from the Bar Kokhba War from Ein-Gedi. *Israel Numismatic Journal* 15:79–86.

_____. 2007a. Finds from the Bar Kokhba Revolt from Two Caves at En-Gedi. *Palestine Excavations Quarterly* 139:35–53.

_____. 2007b. A Bronze Scribe's Case from En Gedi. *Israel Museum Studies in Archaeology* 6:3–12.

Porten, Bezalel, and Ada Yardeni. 1989. *Contracts*. Vol. 2 of *Textbook of Aramaic Documents from Ancient Egypt*. Jerusalem: The Hebrew University.

Puech, Émile. 1980. Fragment d'un rouleau de la Genèse provenant de Désert de Juda. *Revue de Qumran* 10:163–66.

_____. 1989. Notes en marge de 11QPaléoLévitique: le fragment L, des fragments inédits et une jarre de la Grotte 11. *Revue Biblique* 96:161–89.

_____. 2001. Identification de nouveaux manuscrits bibliques: Deutéronome et Proverbes dans les débris de la Grotte 4. *Revue de Qumran* 20:121–27.

_____. 2003a. Notes sur le manuscrit des Juges 4Q50a. *Revue de Qumran* 21:315–19.

_____. 2003b. Un autre manuscrit du Lévitique. *Revue de Qumran* 21:311–13.

_____. 2006. Les Manuscrits 4QJuges^c (=4Q50^a) et 1QJuges (=1Q6). Pages 184–202 in *Studies in the Hebrew Bible, Qumran and the Septuagint: Essays presented to Eugene Ulrich on the Occasion of his Sixty-Fifth Birthday*. Edited by P.W. Flint, E. Tov, and J.C. VanderKam. Supplements to Vetus Testamentum 101. Leiden: Brill.

_____. 2010. Un nouveau fragment 7a de 4QGn-Ex^a = 4QGn-Ex 1 et quelques nouvelles lectures et identifications du manuscrit 4Q1. *Revue de Qumran* 25:103–11.

_____. 2012. Nouvelles identifications de manuscrits bibliques dans la grotte 4: 4QRois^a (4Q54^a) et 4QRois^b-4Q54^b(?) ou 4QIs^s-4Q69^c(?). *Revue de Qumran* 25:467–72.

_____. 2013. 4Q252: 'Commentaire de la Genèse A' ou 'Bénedictions partiarchales'? *Revue de Qumran* 26:227–51.

Puech, Émile, and Annette Steudel. 2000. Un nouveau fragment du manuscrit 4QInstruction (XQ7 = 4Q417 ou 418). *Revue de Qumran* 19:623–27.

Qimron, Elisha. 1986. *The Hebrew of the Dead Sea Scrolls.* Harvard Semitic Studies 29. Atlanta: Scholars Press.

_____. 2003. Improving the Editions of the Dead Sea Scrolls. *Meghillot* 1:144–45 (Hebrew), vi (English).

_____. 2006. Improving the Editions of the Dead Sea Scrolls: Benedictions. *Meghillot* 4:195–200 (Hebrew), xv (English).

Rabid, Liora. 1999. The Special Terminology of the Heavenly Tablets in the Book of Jubilees. *Tarbiz* 68:463–71 (Hebrew), v (English).

Rabin, Ira. 2013. Archaeometry of the Dead Sea Scrolls. *Dead Sea Discoveries* 20:124–42.

_____. 2014. From Analysis to Interpretation. A Comment on the Paper by Rasmussen et al. (2012). *Journal of Archaeological Science* 43:124–26.

Rabin, Ira, and Steffen Franzka. 2006. Microscopy and Parchment Degradation: A Comparative Study. Pages 269–76 in *Bio- and Material Cultures at Qumran: Papers from a COST Action G8 Working Group Meeting Held at the Hebrew University of Jerusalem, Israel on May 22-23-2005.* Edited by J. Gunneweg, A. Adriaens, and C. Greenblatt. Stuttgart: Fraunhofer IRB Verlag.

Rabin, Ira, and Oliver Hahn. 2013. Characterization of the Dead Sea Scrolls by Advanced Analytical Techniques. *Analytical Methods* 5:4648–54.

Rabin, Ira, Roman Schütz, Emanuel Kindzorra, Ulrich Schade, Oliver Hahn, Gisela Weinberg, and Peter Lasch. 2010. Analysis and Preservation of an Antique Alum Tawed Parchment. ICOM-CC Interim Meeting, Working group 'Leather and related materials'. Rome, 23–26 March.

Rasmussen, K.L., J. Gunneweg, G. Doudna, J.E. Taylor, M. Bélis, J. van der Plicht, J.B Humbert, and H. Egsgaard. 2005. Cleaning and Radiocarbon Dating of Material from Khirbet Qumran. Pages 139–64 in *Bio- and Material Cultures at Qumran: Proceedings of Cost Action G8 Working Group 7.* Edited by J. Gunneweg, C. Greenblatt, and A. Adriaens. Stuttgart: Fraunhofer IRB Verlag.

Rasmussen, Kaare L, Jan Gunneweg, Johannes van der Plicht, and Marta Balla. 2010. On the Age of Jar-35. Pages 135–43 in *Holistic Qumran: Trans-disciplinary Research of Qumran and the Dead Sea Scrolls.* Edited by J. Gunneweg, A. Adriaens, and J. Dik. Studies on the Texts of the Desert of Judah 87. Leiden: Brill.

Rasmussen, Kaare L. et al. 2013. The Constituents of the Ink from a Qumran Inkwell: New Prospects for Provenancing the Ink on the Dead Sea Scrolls. *Journal of Archaeological Science* 39:2956–68.

Rasmussen, Kaare L. et al. 2014. Reply to Ira Rabin's Comment on Our Paper Rasmussen et al. (2012). *Journal of Archaeological Science* 43:155–58.

Redfield, Robert. 1961. *The Little Community.* Chicago: University of Chicago Press.

Reed, Ronald. 1972. *Ancient Skins, Parchments and Leathers.* New York: Seminar Press.

Reed, Ronald, and John Poole. 1964. A Study of Some Dead Sea Scroll and Leather Fragments from Cave 4 at Qumran: Chemical Examination. *Proceedings of the Leeds Philosophical and Literary Society* 9:171–82.

Reed, Stephen A. 1991. Survey of the Dead Sea Scrolls Fragments and Photographs at the Rockefeller Museum. *Biblical Archaeologist* 54, no. 1:44–51.

_____. 1994. *The Dead Sea Scrolls Catalogue.* Atlanta: Scholars Press.

Reed, William L. 1954. The Qumran Caves Expedition of March, 1952. *BASOR* 135:8–13.

Reimer, P. J., E. Bard, A. Bayliss, J.W. Beck, P.G. Blackwell., C. Bronk Ramsey, C.E. Buck, R.L. Edwards, M. Friedrich, P.M. Grootes, T.P. Guilderson, H. Haflidason, I. Hajdas, C. Hatté, T.J. Heaton, D.L. Hoffmann, A.G. Hogg, K.A. Hughen, K.F. Kaiser, B. Kromer, S.W. Manning, M. Niu, R.W. Reimer, D.A. Richards, E.M. Scott, J.R. Southon, R.A. Staff, C.S.M. Turney, and J. van der Plicht. 2013. IntCal13 and Marine13 Radiocarbon Age Calibration curves 0-50,000 years cal BP. *Radiocarbon* 55:1869–87.

Renan, M. Ernest. 1864. *Mission de phénicie.* Paris: Imprimerie Imperial. Repr. Academie Francaise, 1998.

Rice, Prudence M. 1987. *Pottery Analysis: A Sourcebook.* Chicago: University of Chicago Press.

Robinson, James M. 1979. The Discovery of the Nag Hammadi Library and Its Archaeological Context. *Biblical Archaeologist* 42:206–24.

_____. 2011. *The Story of the Bodmer Papyr: From the First Monastery's Library in Upper Egypt to Geneva and Dublin.* Eugene, Or.: Wipf & Stock.

Rubensohn, Otto. 1907. *Elephantine-Papyri.* Berlin: Weidmannsche Buchhandlung.

Rösel, Martin. 2013. Daniel Reloaded: The Greek Edition of the Book of Daniel. Paper presented at SBL Annual Meeting. Baltimore, 26 November.

Rudy, Kathryn M. 2010. Dirty books: Quantifying Patterns of Use in Medieval Manuscripts Using a Densitometer. *Journal of Historians of Netherlandish Art* 4/1–2. Available online at http://www.jhna.org/index.php/past-issues/volume-2-issue-1-2/129-dirty-books.

Sadezky, A., H. Muckenhuber, H. Grothe, R. Niessner, and U. Pöschl. 2005. Raman Microspectroscopy of Soot and Related Carbonaceous Materials: Spectral Analysis and Structural Information. *Carbon* 43:1731–42.

Sagrusten, Hans Johan. 2014. *Det store puslespillet. Jakten på de tidligste manuskriptene til Bibelen.* Oslo: Verbum.

Samuel, Athanasius Yeshue. 1968. *Treasure of Qumran: My Story of the Dead Sea Scrolls.* London: Hodder and Stoughton (Philadelphia: Westminster, 1966).

Sanders, James A. 1967. *The Dead Sea Psalms Scroll.* Ithaca: Cornell University Press.

_____. 2002. The Modern History of the Qumran Psalms Scroll and Its Relation to Canon Criticism. Pages 393–411 in *Emanuel: Studies in Hebrew Bible, Septuagint, and Dead Sea Scrolls in Honor of Emanuel Tov.* Edited by S.M. Paul, R. Kraft, and L.H. Schiffman. Leiden: Brill.

Sanders, Paul. 1996. *The Provenance of Deuteronomy 32.* OS 37. Leiden: E.J. Brill

Sayre, Edward V. 1975. Brookhaven Procedures for Statistical Analyses of Multivariate Archaeometric Data. Brookhaven National Laboratory Report BNL-23128.

Schick, Tamar. 1995. A 10,000 Year Old Comb from Wadi Murabbaʿat in the Judean Desert. *Atiqot* 27:199–202.

Schiffman, Lawrence H. 2012. On the Edge of the Diaspora: Jews in the Dead Sea Region in the First Two Centuries C.E. Pages 175–95 in *'Go Out and Study the Land' (Judges 18:2): Archaeological, Historical and Textual Studies in Honor of Hanan Eshel.* Edited by A.M. Meir, J. Magness, and L.H. Schiffman. Journal for the Study of Judaism Supplement Series 148. Leiden: Brill.

Schofield, Alison. 2009. *From Qumran to the* Yaḥad: *A New Paradigm of Textual Development for* The Community Rule. Studies on the Texts of the Desert of Judah 77. Leiden: Brill.

Schowalter, Daniel. 2013. Building on the Border: The Early Shrine Complex at Omrit. Paper delivered at ASOR Annual Meeting. Baltimore, 21 November.

Segal, Michael. 2000. 4QReworked Pentateuch or 4QPentateuch? Pages 391–99 in *The Dead Sea Scrolls Fifty Years After their Discovery: Proceedings of the Jerusalem Congress, July 20-25, 1997.* Edited by L.H. Schiffman, E. Tov, J. C. VanderKam, and G. Marquis. Jerusalem: Israel Exploration Society.

_____. 2013. The Masoretic and Old Greek Versions of Daniel 4: A Reevaluation of the Textual Evidence. Paper presented at the IOSCS Congress. München, 8 August.

Seters, John van. 2009. *The Biblical Saga of King David.* Winona Lake: Eisenbrauns.

Septuaginta. 1979. Ed. Alfred Rahlfs. Stuttgart: Deutsche Bibelgesellschaft.

Shamir, Orit. 1996. Loom Weights and Whorls. Pages 135–70 in *Excavations at the City of David 1978-85, Directed by Yigal Shiloh IV: Various Reports.* Edited by D.T. Ariel. Qedem 35. Jerusalem: The Hebrew University of Jerusalem.

_____. 1999. Textiles, Basketry and Cordage from ʿEn Rahel. *Atiqot* 38:91–124.

_____. 2003. Textiles, Basketry and Cordage from Nabatean Sites along the Spice Route between Petra and Gaza. Pages 35*–38* in *The Nabateans in the Negev.* Edited by R. Rosental-Heginbottom. Haifa (Hebrew).

_____. 2005. Textiles, Basketry, Cordage and Whorls from Moʿa (Moje Awad). *Atiqot* 50:99–152.

_____. 2006a. *Textile in the Land of Israel from the Roman Period till the Early Islamic Period in the Light of the Archaeological Find.* Thesis Submitted for the Degree Doctor of Philosophy, Jerusalem.

_____. 2006b. Textiles, Basketry, Cordage and Fruits from ʿEn Tamar, Preliminary Report. Pages 191–94 in *Crossing the Rift Resources, Routes, Settlement Patterns and Interaction in the Wadi Arabah.* Edited by P. Bienkowski and K. Galor. Oxford: Oxbow.

_____. 2008. Organic Materials. Pages 116–34 in *The Dead Sea Scrolls.* Edited by D.T. Ariel, H. Katz, S. Sadeh, and M. Segal. Jerusalem: Istral Antiquities Authority.

_____. 2010. Textiles with 'Sacs', from the Cave of Letters. Pages 120–21 in *Angels and Demons: Jewish Magic through the Ages.* Edited by in F. Vukosavovic. Jerusalem: Bible Lands Museum Jerusalem.

_____. 2014. Two Special Traditions in Jewish Garments and the Rarity of Mixed Wool and Linen Threads at the Same Textile in the Land of Israel. Pages 298–308 in *Prehistoric, Ancient Near Eastern and Aegean Textiles and Dress: an Interdisciplinary Anthology.* Edited by Marie Louise Nosch and Mary Harlow. Series 18. Oxford: Oxbow.

Shamir, Orit, and Naʿama Sukenik. 2011. Qumran Textiles and the Garments of Qumran's Inhabitants. *Dead Sea Discoveries* 18:206–25.

Shanks, Hershel. 1979. *Judaism in Stone: The Archaeology of Ancient Synagogues.* Jerusalem: Steimatzky.

Sheffer, Avigail. 1993. Ancient Textiles Decorated with Color from the Land of Israel. Pages 66–75 in *Colors from Nature - Natural Colors in Ancient Times.* Edited by C. Sorek and E. Ayalon. Tel Aviv: Eretz Israel Museum (Hebrew).

_____. 2000. Textiles. Pages 938–43 in vol. 2 of *Encyclopedia of the Dead Sea Scrolls*. Edited by L.H. Schiffman and J.C. Vanderkam. 2 vols. Oxford: Oxford University Press.

Sheffer, Avigail and Hero Granger-Taylor. 1994. Textiles from Masada: A Preliminary Selection. Pages 153–256 in *Masada* IV. Edited by Y. Aviram, G. Foerster, and E. Netzer. Jerusalem: Israel Exploration Society.

Sheffer, Avigail and Amalia Tidhar. 1991. Textiles and Basketry at Kuntillat ʿAjrud. *Atiqot* 20:1–26.

_____. 2012. Textiles and Basketry. Pages 289–311 in *Kuntillet ʿAjrud (Horvat Teman): An Iron Age II Religious Site on the Judah-Sinai Border*. Edited Ze'ev Meshel. Jerusalem: Israel Exploration Society.

Shoval, Shlomo. 2003. Using FTIR spectroscopy for study of calcareous ancient ceramics. *Optical Materials* 24:117–22.

Shoval, Shlomo, and P. Beck. 2005. Thermo-FTIR Spectroscopy Analysis as a Method of Characterizing Ancient Ceramic Technology. *Journal of Thermal Analysis and Calorimetry* 82:609–16.

Sklar-Parnes, Deborah A., Yehudah Rapuano, and Rachel Bar-Nathan. 2004. Excavations in Northeast Jerusalem — a Jewish Site in between the Revolts. *New Studies on Jerusalem* 10:35*–41*.

Sokoloff, Michael. 1974. *The Targum of Job from Qumran Cave XI*. Ramat Gan: Bar Ilan University Press.

_____. 2002. *A Dictionary of Jewish Palestinian Aramaic of the Byzantine Period*. 2nd ed. Ramat Gan: Bar Ilan University Press.

Sollamo, Raija. 2011. זדון *zadon*. Pages 827–29 of vol 1 of *Theologisches Wörterbuch zu den Qumrantexten*. Edited by H.-J. Fabry and U. Dahmen. 2 vols. Kohlhamar, 2011, 2013.

Stager, Lawrence E. 2000. Jerusalem as Eden. *Biblical Archaeology Review* 26, no. 3:36–47, 66.

Steckoll, Solomon H. 1969. Marginal Notes on the Qumran Excavations. *Revue de Qumran* 7:33–40.

Stegemann, Hartmut. 1992. How to Connect Dead Sea Scrolls Fragments. Pages 245–55 in *Understanding the Dead Sea Scrolls: A Reader from the Biblical Archaeology Review*. Edited by Hershel Shanks. New York: Random House.

_____. 1996. Some Remarks to 1QSa, to 1QSb, and to Qumran Messianism. *Revue de Qumran* 65–68:478–505.

Steponaitis, Vincas, Michael J. Blackman, and Hector Neff. 1996. Large-scale Compositional Patterns in the Chemical Composition of Mississippian Pottery. *American Antiquity* 61:555–72.

Stern, Ephraim. 1982. *Material Culture of the Land of the Bible in the Persian Period 538-332 B.C.* Warminster, Wiltshire: Aris & Phillips.

Steudel, Annette. 1994. *Der Midrasch zur Eschatologie aus der Qumrangemeinde (4QmidrEschat^a,b)*. Studies on the Texts of the Desert of Judah 13. Leiden: Brill.

Stökl ben Ezra, Daniel. 2007. Old Caves and Young Caves. *Dead Sea Discoveries* 14: 313–33.

_____. 2010. Further Reflections on Caves 1 and 11: A Response to Florentino García Martínez. Pages 211–24 in *The Dead Sea Scrolls: Texts and Contexts*. Edited by C. Hempel. Studies on Texts from the Desert of Judah 90. Leiden: Brill.

_____. 2011. Wie viele Bibliotheken gab es in Qumran? Pages 327–46 in *Qumran und die Archäologie: Texte und Kontexte*. Edited by J. Frey, C. Claussen, and N. Kessler. Tübingen: Mohr Siebeck.

Strange, James F. 1992. Six Campaigns at Sepphoris. Pages 339–55 in *The Galilee in Late Antiquity*. Edited by L.I. Levine. New York: The Jewish Theological Seminary of America.

_____. 2006. The 1996 Excavations at Qumran and the Context of the New Hebrew Ostracon. Pages 41–54 in *Qumran, the Site of the Dead Sea Scrolls: Archaeological Interpretations and Debates*. Edited by K. Galor et al. Studies on the Texts of the Desert of Judah 57. Leiden: Brill.

Sulman, E. van Staalduine. 2002. *The Targum of Samuel*. Leiden: Brill.

Süssenbach, Claudia. 2005. *Der elohistische Psalter*. Tübingen: Mohr Siebeck.

Talmon, Shemaryahu, and Yigael Yadin. 1999. *Masada VI: Yigael Yadin Excavations 1963-1965, Final Report*. Jerusalem: Israel Exploration Society and The Hebrew University of Jerusalem.

Taylor, Joan E. 2006. Khirbet Qumran in Period III. Pages 133–46 in *Qumran: The Site of the Dead Sea Scrolls: Archaeological Interpretations and Debates: Proceedings of a Conference Held at Brown University, November 17-19, 2002*. Edited by K. Galor et al. Leiden: Brill.

_____. 2011. Buried Manuscripts and Empty Tombs: The *Genizah* Hypothesis Reconsidered. Pages 269–316 in *'Go Out and Study the Land' (Judges 18:2). Archaeological, Historical and Textual Studies in Honor of Hanan Eshel*. Edited by A.M. Meir, J. Magness, and L.H. Schiffman. Supplements of the Journal for the Study of Judaism 148. Leiden: Brill.

_____. 2012. *The Essenes, the Scrolls, and the Dead Sea*. Oxford: Oxford University Press.

Taylor, Joan E., Kaare L. Rasmussen, Gregory Doudna, Johannes van der Plicht, and Helge Egsgaard. 2005. Qumran Textiles in the Palestine Exploration Fund, London: Radiocarbon Dating Result. *Palestine Exploration Quarterly* 137, no. 2:159-67.

Terrien, Samuel. 2003. *The Psalms: Strophic Structure and Theological Commentary*. Grand Rapids: Eerdmans.

Testuz, Michel. 1955. Deux fragments inédits des manuscrits de la mer Morte. *Semitica* 5:37–38.

The Schøyen Collection: Checklist of Western Manuscripts 1-1914. 1994. 12th ed. Oslo and London: Martin Schøyen.

Tigchelaar, Eibert J.C. 2001. *To Increase Learning for the Understanding Ones*. Studies on the Texts of the Desert of Judah 44. Leiden: Brill.

_____. 2003. The White Dress of the Essenes and the Pythagoreans. Pages 301–21 in *Jerusalem, Alexandria, Roma: Studies in Ancient Cultural Interaction in Honour of A. Hilhorst*. Edited by F. García Martinez and G.P. Luttikhuizen. Leiden: Brill.

_____. 2005. Notes on the Ezekiel Scroll from Masada (MasEzek). *Revue de Qumran* 86:269–75.

_____. 2012. Notes on Three Qumran-Type Yadin Fragments Leading to a Discussion of Identification, Attribution, Provenance, and Names. *Dead Sea Discoveries* 19:198–214.

Tov, Emanuel. 1997. *Tefillin* of Different Origin from Qumran? Pages 44*–54* in *A Light for Jacob: Studies in the Bible and the Dead Sea Scrolls*. Edited by Y. Hoffman and F.H. Polak. Jerusalem and Tel Aviv: Bialik Institute and Tel Aviv University.

_____. 1998. The Rewritten Book of Joshua as Found at Qumran and Masada. Pages 232–56 in *Biblical Perspectives: Early Use and Interpretation of the Bible in Light of the Dead Sea Scrolls*. Studies on the Texts of the Desert of Judah 28. Edited by M.E. Stone and E. Chazon. Leiden: Brill.

_____. 1999. *Collected Papers. The Greek and Hebrew Bible. Collected Essays on the Septuagint*. Leiden: Brill.

_____. 2002. The Biblical Texts from the Judaean Desert – An Overview and Analysis of the Published Texts. Pages 152–57 in *The Bible as Book: The Hebrew Bible and the Judaean Desert Discoveries*. Edited by E.D. Herbert and E. Tov. London: The British Library and Oak Knoll Press.

_____. 2004. *Scribal Practices and Approaches Reflected in the Texts Found in the Judean Desert*. Studies on the Texts of the Desert of Judah 54. Leiden: Brill.

_____. 2008. *Hebrew Bible, Greek Bible, and Qumran. Collected Essays*. Tübingen: Mohr Siebeck.

_____. 2010a. *Revised List of the Texts from the Judaean Desert*. Leiden: Brill.

_____. 2010b. From 4QReworked Pentateuch to 4QPentateuch (?). Pages 73–91 in *Authoritative Scriptures in Ancient Judaism*. Edited by M. Popovic. Journal for the Study of Judaism Supplement Series 141. Leiden: Brill.

_____. 2012. *Textual Criticism of the Hebrew Bible*. 3rd edition. Minneapolis: Fortress.

_____. 2014. New Fragments of Amos. *Dead Sea Discoveries* 21:3–13.

_____. 2015. *Textual Criticism of the Hebrew Bible, Qumran, Septuagint. Collected Essays, Volume 3*. Supplements to Vetus Testamentum 17. Leiden: Brill.

Tov, Emanuel, with Stephen J. Pfann. 1993. *The Dead Sea Scrolls on Microfiche: Companion Volume*. Leiden: Brill.

Trebolle Barerra, Julio. 1989. Textual Variants in 4QJudgᵃ and the Textual and Editorial History of the Book of Judges. *Revue de Qumran* 54:229–45.

_____. 2006. Samuel/Kings and Chronicles. Book Divisions and Textual Composition. Pages 96–108 in *Studies in the Hebrew Bible, Qumran, and the Septuagint. Presented to Eugene Ulrich*. Edited by P. W. Flint et al. Supplements to Vetus Testamentum 101. Leiden: Brill.

Trever, John C. 1948. Preliminary Observations on the Jerusalem Scrolls. *Bulletin of the American Schools of Oriental Research* 111:3–16.

_____. 1965. Completion of the Publication of Some Fragments From Qumran Cave I. *Revue de Qumran* 5:323–44.

_____. 1970. I Q Danᵃ: The Latest of the Qumran Manuscripts. *Revue de Qumran* 7:277–86.

_____. 1972. *Scrolls From Qumran Cave I: The Great Isaiah Scroll, The Order of the Community, The Pesher to Habakkuk: From Photographs by John C. Trever*. Jerusalem: Albright Institute and Shrine of the Book.

_____. 1977. *The Dead Sea Scrolls. A Personal Account*. Grand Rapids: Eerdmans. Reprint 2003. Piscataway, NJ: Gorgias.

Trindade, M. J., M. I. Dias, J. Coroado, and F. Rocha. 2009. Mineralogical Transformations of Calcareous Rich Clays With Firing: A Comparative Study Between Calcite and Dolomite Rich Clays from Algarve, Portugal. *Applied Clay Science* 42:345–55.

Tzoref, Shani. 2011. Covenantal Election in 4Q252 and *Jubilees*' Heavenly Tablets. *Dead Sea Discoveries* 18:74–89.

_____. 2012. 4Q252: Listenwissenschaft and Covenantal Patriarchal Blessings. Pages 335–57 in *'Go Out and Study the Land' (Judges 18:2). Archaeological, Historical and Textual Studies in Honor of Hanan Eshel*. Edited by A.M. Meir, J. Magness, L.H. Schiffman. Journal for the Study of Judaism Supplement Series 148. Leiden: Brill.

Ulrich, Eugene. 1998. The Dead Sea Scrolls and the Biblical Text. Pages 79–100 in *The Dead Sea Scrolls after Fifty Years: A Comprehensive Assessment*, vol. 1. Supplements to Vetus Testamentum 134. Edited by P.W. Flint, and J.C. VanderKam. Leiden: Brill.

_____. 2000a. Daniel, Book of. Pages 170–74 in *Encyclopedia of the Dead Sea Scrolls*, vol. 1. Edited by L.H. Schiffman, and J.C. VanderKam. Oxford: Oxford University Press.

_____. 2000b. The Qumran Scrolls and the Biblical Text. Pages 51–59 in *The Dead Sea Scrolls Fifty Years After their Discovery. Proceedings of the Jerusalem Congress, July 20-25, 1997*. Edited by L.H. Schiffman, E. Tov, J.C. VanderKam, and G. Marquis. Jerusalem: Israel Exploration Society.

_____. 2001. The Text of Daniel in the Qumran Scrolls. Pages 573–85 in *The Book of Daniel. Composition and Reception*, vol. 2. Edited by J.J. Collins and P.W. Flint. Supplements to Vetus Testamentum 88.2. Leiden: Brill.

_____. 2010. *The Biblical Qumran Scrolls: Transcriptions and Textual Variants*. Supplements to Vetus Testamentum 134. Leiden: Brill.

Vaux, Roland de. 1949. La grotte des manuscrit hébreux. *Revue Biblique* 56:586–609.

_____. 1954. Fouilles au Khirbet Qumran: Rapport preliminaire sur la deuxieme campagne. *Revue Biblique* 61:206–32.

_____. 1956. Fouilles de Khirbet Qumrân. *Revue Biblique* 63:533–77.

_____. 1973. *Archaeology and the Dead Sea Scrolls*. London: Oxford University Press.

Verhelst, Stéphane. 2003. Les Fragments du Castellion (Kh. Mird) des évangiles de marc et de Jean (P⁸⁴). *Le Muséon* 116:15–44.

Vermes, Geza. 1997. *The Complete Dead Sea Scrolls in English.* 5th ed. London: Penguin.

Vermeule, Cornelius. 1966. Small Sculptures in the Museum of Fine Arts, Boston. *The Classical Journal* 62:97–113.

Wallert, Arie. 1996a. Deliquescence and Recrystallization of Salts in the Dead Sea Scrolls. Pages 198–201 in *Archaeological Conservation and Its Consequences.* Edited by A. Roy and P. Smith. Preprints of the Contributions to the Copenhagen Congress, 26–30 August 1996.

_____. 1996b. Tannins of the Parchment of the Dead Sea Scrolls. Pages 560–64 in Vol. 2 of ICOM Committee for Conservation, 11th Triennial Meeting in Edinburgh, Scotland, 1–6 September 1996: Preprints. London: James & James (Science Publishers) Ltd.

Weber, T., and R. Wenning. 1997. *Petra. Antike Felsstadt zwischen Arabischer Tradition und Griechischer Norm.* Mainz: Philipp von Zabern.

Weigand, Phil C., Garman Harbottle, and Edward V. Sayre. 1977. Turquoise Sources and Source Analysis: Mesoamerica and the Southwestern U.S.A. Pages 15–34 in *Exchange Systems in Prehistory.* Edited by T.K. Earle and J.E. Ericson. New York: Academic Press.

Weissenberg, Hanne von. 2012a. 'Aligned' or 'Non-Aligned'? The Textual Status of the Qumran Cave 4 Manuscripts of the Minor Prophets. Pages 381–96 in *Perspectives on the Formation of the Book of the Twelve.* BZAW 433. Edited by R. Albertz et al. Berlin: De Gruyter.

_____. 2012b. The Twelve Minor Prophets at Qumran and the Canonical Process: Amos as a 'Case Study'. Pages 357–76 in *The Hebrew Bible in Light of the Dead Sea Scrolls.* Edited by Nóra Dávid et al. Forschungen zur Religion und Literatur des Alten und Neuen Testaments 239. Göttingen: Vandenhoeck & Ruprecht.

Werrett, Ian C. 2007. Ritual Purity and the Dead Sea Scrolls. Studies on Text of Desert of Judah 72. Leiden: Brill.

Westermann, Claus. 1964. Zur Sammlung des Psalters. Pages 336–43 in *Forschung am Alten Testament. Gesammelte Studien.* München: Chr. Kaiser.

Wild, John Peter. 1970. *Textile Manufacture in the Northern Roman Provinces.* Cambridge: University Press.

Wolff, Timo, Ira Rabin, Ioanna Mantouvalou, Birgit Kanngiesser, Wofgang Malzer, Emanuel Kindzorra, and Oliver Hahn. 2012. Provenance Studies on Dead Sea Scrolls Parchment by Means of Quantitative Micro-XRF. *Analytical and Bioanalytical Chemistry* 402:1493–1503.

Wright, G. Ernest. 1949. Archaeological News and Views. *The Biblical Archaeologist* 12, no. 2 (May):32–36.

Wright, Jacob L. 2007. A New Model for the Composition of Ezra-Nehemiah. Pages 333–48 in *Judah and the Judeans in the Fourth Century B.C.E.* Edited by O. Lipschits et al. Winona Lake: Eisenbrauns.

Yadin, Yigael. 1963. *The Finds from the Bar Kokhba Period in the Cave of Letters.* Jerusalem: Israel Exploration Society.

_____. 1965. *The Ben Sira Scroll from Masada.* Jerusalem: Israel Exploration Society and Shrine of the Book.

_____. 1966. *Masada. Herod's Fortress and the Zealots' Last Stand.* New York: Random House.

_____. 1967. The *Temple Scroll. The Biblical Archaeologist* 30:135–39.

_____. 1969. *Tefillin from Qumran (XQPhyl 1–4).* Jerusalem: Israel Exploration Society.

_____. 1971. *Bar-Kokhba.* London: Weidenfeld and Nicholson.

_____. 1977. *The Temple Scroll.* Vols I–III. Jerusalem: Israel Exploration Society.

_____. 1983. *The Temple Scroll.* Jerusalem: Israel Exploration Society.

_____. 1985. *The Temple Scroll: the Hidden Law of the Dead Sea Sect.* London: Weidenfeld and Nicolson.

Yadin, Yigael, and Joseph Naveh. 1989. The Aramaic and Hebrew Ostraca and Jar Inscription. Pages 1–68 in *Masada I: The Yigael Yadin Excavations 1963-1965, Final Report.* Jerusalem: Israel Exploration Society.

Yadin, Yigael et al. 2002. *The Documents from the Bar Kokhba Period in the Cave of Letters.* Jerusalem: Israel Exploration Society.

Yaniv, Bracha. 2006. From the Spain to the Balkans Textile Torah Scroll Accessories in the Sephardi Communities of the Balkans. *Sefarad* 66/2:407–42.

_____. 2009. *Maʿase Rokem: Textile Ceremonial Object in the Ashkenazi, Sephardi and Italian Synagogue.* Jerusalem: Ben-Zvi Institute (Hebrew).

Yardeni, Ada. 1991. *The Book of Hebrew Script.* Jerusalem: Cartha (Hebrew).

_____. 1997. A Draft of a Deed on an Ostracon from Khirbet Qumrân. *Israel Exploration Journal* 47:233–37.

_____. 2000. *Textbook of Aramaic, Hebrew and Nabatean Documents and Texts from the Judean Desert and Related Material: A. Documents.* Jerusalem: Ben Zion Dinur Center (Hebrew).

_____. 2001. The Decipherment and Restoration of Legal Texts from The Judaean Desert: A Reexamination of Papyrus Starcky (P. Yadin 36). *Scripta Classica Israelica* 20:121–37.

_____. 2002. *The Book of Hebrew Script: History, Palaeography, Script styles, Calligraphy and Design.* London and New Castle, Del.: British Library and Oak Knoll Press.

_____. 2007. A Note On a Qumran Scribe. Pages 287–98 in *New Seals and Inscriptions, Hebrew, Idumean and Cuneiform.* Edited by M. Lubetski. Sheffield: Sheffield Phoenix.

Yechieli, Yoseph, and Daniel Ronen. 1997. Early Diagenesis of Highly Saline Lake Sediments After Exposure. *Chemical Geology* 138:93–106.

Yeivin, Zeev, and G. Finkelstein. 1999. *Castra, at the Foot of Mount Carmel. The City and its Secrets*. Haifa: Haifa Museum/National Maritime Museum (Spring Catalogue).

Yellin, Joseph, Magen Broshi, and Hanan Eshel. 2001. Pottery of Qumran and Ein Ghuweir: The First Chemical Exploration of Provenience. *Bulletin of the American Schools of Oriental Research* 321:65–78.

Yellin, Joseph, and Jan Gunneweg. 1989. Instrumental neutron activation analysis and the origin of Iron Age I collared-rim jars and Pithoi from Tel Dan. Pages 133–41 in *Recent Excavations in Israel: Studies in Iron Age Archaeology*. Annual of the American Schools of Oriental Research, Vol. 49. Edited by S. Gitin and W.G. Dever.

Zahn, Molly M. 2008. The Problem of Characterizing the 4QReworked Penteteuch Mansucripts: Bible, Rewritten Bible, or None of the Above? *Dead Sea Discoveries* 15:315–39.

_____. 2011. *Rethinking Rewritten Scripture: Composition and Exegesis in the 4QReworked Pentateuch Manuscripts*. Studies on the Texts of the Desert of Judah 95. Leiden: Brill.

Zerdoun Bat-Yehouda, Monique. 1983. *Les encres noires au Moyen Âge*. Paris: CNRS.

Ziegler, Joseph, ed. 1957. *Jeremias. Baruch. Threni. Epistulae Jeremiae*. Göttingen: Vandenhoeck & Ruprecht.

Zohary, Daniel and Maria Hopf. 1994. *Domestication of Plants in the Old World*. Oxford: Clarendon.

Zuckerman, Bruce. 2010. The Dynamics of Change in the Computer Imaging of the Dead Sea Scrolls and other Ancient Inscriptions. Pages 69–88 in *Rediscovering the Dead Sea Scrolls: An Assessment of Old and New Approaches and Methods*. Edited by M.L. Grossmann. Grand Rapids: Eerdmans.

Zuckerman, Bruce, and S.A. Reed. 1993. A Fragment of an Unstudied Column of 11QtgJob: A Preliminary Report. *Comprehensive Aramaic Lexicon Newsletter* 10:1–7.

Index of Biblical and Apocryphal Books

Index of Ancient Artefacts and Literature

Index of Modern Authors

Manuscripts in The Schøyen Collection Series

MSC 1. *Buddhist Manuscripts I*. Eds. Jens Braarvig, Jens-Uwe Hartmann, Kazunobu Matsuda, Lore Sander. Oslo: Hermes Publishing, 2000.

MSC 2. *Coptic Papyri I. Das Matthäus- Evangelium im mittelägyptishen Dialekt des Koptischen (Codex Schøyen)*. Hans-Martin Schenke. Oslo: Hermes Publishing, 2001.

MSC 3. *Buddhist Manuscripts II*. Eds. Jens Braarvig, Paul Harrison, Jens-Uwe Hartmann, Kazunobu Matsuda, Lore Sander. Oslo: Hermes Publishing, 2002.

MSC 4. *Medieval Seal Matrices in The Schøyen Collection*. Richard Linenthal and William Noel. Oslo: Hermes Publishing, 2004.

MSC 5. *Papyri Graecae (Schøyen I)*. Rosario Pintaudi. Papyrologica Florentina XXXV. Firenze: Edizioni Gonnelli, 2005.

MSC 6. *A Remarkable Collection of Babylonian Mathematical Texts*. Jöran Friberg. In: Sources and Studies in the History of Mathematics and Physical Sciences. Berlin: Springer, 2007. (Cuneiform Texts I)

MSC 7. *The Crosby-Schøyen Codex MS 193 in The Schøyen Collection (Coptic papyri II)*. Ed. James E. Goehring. Corpus Scriptorum Christianorum Orientalium 521, Subsidia Tomus 85. Louvain: Peeters, 1990.

MSC 8. *Codex Sinaiticus Zosimi rescriptus*. Alain Desreumaux. Histoire du texte Biblique 3. Lausanne: Éditions du Zèbre, 1997.

MSC 9. *Das Liesborner Evangeliar, The Schøyen Collection, Oslo/London, MS 40*. Eef Overgaauw and Bennie Priddy. Warendorf: Museum Abtei Liesborn, 2003.

MSC 10. *L'Évangile selon Matthieu d'après le papyrus copte de la Collection Schøyen, analyse litteraire*. M.-É. Boismard, O.P. In: Cahiers de la Revue Biblique. Paris: Gabalda, 2003. (Coptic papyri III)

MSC 11. *Sumerian Proverbs in The Schøyen Collection*. Bendt Alster. Cornell University Studies in Assyriology and Sumerology (CUSAS) 2. Bethesda, MD: CDL Press, 2007. (Cuneiform texts II)

MSC 12. *Buddhist Manuscripts III*. Ed. Jens Braarvig. Oslo: Hermes Publishing, 2006.

MSC 13. *Babylonian Tablets from the First Sealand Dynasty in The Schøyen Collection*. Stephanie Dalley. Cornell University Studies in Assyriology and Sumerology (CUSAS) 9. Bethesda, MD: CDL Press, 2009.

MSC 14. *Babylonian Literary Texts in The Schøyen Collection.* Andrew R. George. Cornell University Studies in Assyriology and Sumerology (CUSAS) 10: Bethesda, MD: CDL Press, 2009.

MSC 15. *Papyri Graecae (Schøyen II).* Diletta Minutoli and Rosario Pintaudi. Papyrologica Florentina XL. Firenze: Edizioni Gonnelli, 2010.

MSC 16. *The Lexical Texts in the Schøyen Collection.* Miguel Civil. Cornell University Studies in Assyriology and Sumerology (CUSAS) 12. Bethesda, MD: CDL Press, 2010. (Cuneiform texts V)

MSC 17. *Traces of Gandharan Buddhism: An Exhibition of Ancient Buddhist Manuscripts in The Schøyen Collection.* Jens Braarvig and Fredrik Liland. Hermes Publishing, Oslo, in collaboration with Amarin Printing and Publishing Co. Ltd., Bangkok, 2010.

MSC 18. *Cuneiform Royal Inscriptions and Related Texts in The Schøyen Collection.* A. R. George, with contributions by M. Civil, G. Frame, P. Steinkeller, F. Vallat, K. Volk, M. Weeden and C. Wilcke. Cornell University Studies in Assyriology and Sumerology (CUSAS) 17. Bethesda, MD: CDL Press, 20011.

MSC 19. *Codex Schoyen 2650: Discerning a Coptic Manuscript's Witness to the Early Text of Matthew's Gospel.* James M. Leonard. Ph.D. diss, Faculty of Divinity, University of Cambridge, 2011.

MSC 20. *Aramaic Bowl Spells. Jewish Babylonian Aramaic Bowls, volume 1.* Shaul Shaked, James Nathan Ford, and Siam Bhayro. Leiden: Brill, 2013.

MSC 21. *Babylonian Divinatory Texts Chiefly in The Schøyen Collection.* Andrew R. George. Manuscripts in The Schøyen Collection Cuneiform Texts VII. Cornell University Studies in Assyriology and Sumerology (CUSAS) 18. Bethesda, MD: CDL Press, 2013.

CPSIA information can be obtained
at www.ICGtesting.com
Printed in the USA
LVHW061627220219
608478LV00016B/195/P